AGING FOR THE
TWENTY-FIRST CENTURY

READINGS IN
SOCIAL GERONTOLOGY

Jill Quadagno
Debra Street
Florida State University

St. Martin's Press
New York

Editor: Sabra Scribner
Managing editor: Patricia Mansfield Phelan
Project editors: Melissa Holcombe, Jennifer Valentine
Production supervisor: Dennis J. Para
Art director: Lucy Krikorian
Cover design: Lucy Krikorian
Cover art: Fiona King Illustration

Library of Congress Catalog Card Number: 94–74760

Manufactured in the United States of America.

0 9 8 7 6
f e d c b a

For information, write:
St. Martin's Press, Inc.
175 Fifth Avenue
New York, NY 10010

ISBN: 0–312–09496–5

Acknowledgments

PREFACE

In 1900 life expectancy in the United States was only 47 years; by 1994, however, life expectancy had increased to nearly 80 years. Initially, much of the improvement was due to a reduction in infant mortality; more recently, advances in medicine have increased life expectancy among the old. Indeed, the fastest growing segment of the American population is people over 85.

One result of an increased life expectancy has been an overall aging of the population. In 1994 more than 12 percent of the population in the United States was over 65. By the year 2020, this figure is expected to exceed 17 percent. Nearly one out of every five people will be over 65.

Do these numbers matter? Many of our political leaders seem to think so. They are disturbed by warnings that Medicare, the program of health insurance for people over 65, will soon have trouble paying its bills, and they fear that when the baby boom generation begins to retire in 2010, the taxes coming in will be insufficient to meet present commitments for Social Security benefits.

In coming years, Americans will have to make important decisions regarding the consequences of population aging. It will take an informed citizenry to do so. Thus, in *Aging for the Twenty-First Century,* we have assembled this collection of readings to provide students, our future decision makers, with a broad introduction to key issues in social gerontology.

We have organized the readings into twelve sections. The first three sections introduce students to the study of aging from the perspectives of gerontological theory, history, and anthropology. We next include a series of readings that elucidate aspects of the aging process as they affect individual lives. These include stereotypes and ageism, life course transitions, living arrangements, generational and family relationships, and the transition from work to retirement. Finally, we turn to issues with policy implications. Here we provide material on politics, economics, health care, and death and dying. We believe that these selections provide students with a broad foundation for making personal decisions about their own aging and for making the crucial policy decisions facing our nation in the not-so-distant future.

In selecting the readings and organizing the sections in this text, we were fortunate to have the wise counsel of several prominent social gerontologists chosen by St. Martin's Press as reviewers for our book. We thank Toni Antonucchi, University of Michigan; Toni Calasanti, Virginia Polytechnic Institute; J. Kevin Eckert, University of Maryland–Baltimore County; Debra Gold, Duke University Medical Center; Jon Hendricks, Oregon State University; and Dale Jaffe, University of Wisconsin–Milwaukee. We are also grateful to our editor at St. Martin's Press, Sabra Scribner, and her assistant, Elizabeth Bast, for their thoughtful comments and wise advice.

Jill Quadagno
Debra Street

CONTENTS

INTRODUCTION

Eleanor Miller, a 69-year-old widow, lives with her six cats in a small trailer on the edge of a southern city. She worked for nearly thirty years as a dietician for a state hospital in Michigan but earned no pension. Now her Social Security check is her only source of income. A widow for fourteen years, Miller receives a small check, of $440 a month. To supplement this meager income, she works as a hostess at Burger King, clearing tables, mopping floors, and doing other odd jobs. Eleanor is part of an expanding number of older workers in what is called the "contingent" workforce.

Nate and Selma Fiske are snowbirds. They spend the winter in their condominium in Fort Lauderdale, Florida, and their summers in Boston. Nate is a retired accountant, and Selma is a retired bookkeeper. They live comfortably on his pension, their investments, and their Social Security benefits. Neither Nate nor Selma has to work, and they spend their time playing golf, having dinner with friends, going to the theater, and occasionally babysitting for their grandchildren.

These vignettes of real people indicate how poorly a term like "the elderly" describes the older population today. People over age 65 are no more alike in terms of race, gender, geographic distribution, marital status, or living arrangements than Generation X or Thirty-Somethings. Some struggle to make ends meet; others are able to enjoy a comfortable life-style; a very few are wealthy.

PATTERNS OF DEMOGRAPHIC CHANGE

Understanding population trends means taking account of large-scale patterns, like the aging of the baby boom generation, while recognizing that diversity exists among the aged. Deciding how to adequately prepare for the baby boomers' retirement means considering the effect of changes in social, political, or economic arrangements on men and women, racial and ethnic minorities, the old-old and the young-old, and widows and married couples.

Gender Composition

The ratio of males to females among the aged clearly illustrates the dramatic changes that have taken place among the aging population in this century. In 1930 the number of older males and older females was nearly equal. By 1985 there were only sixty-eight males for every one hundred females. These ratios reflect trends in life expectancy. From 1930 to 1990, life expectancy for men increased from 58 to 71.1, but for women it increased from 61.3 to 78.8 (U.S. House of Representatives, 1994). What caused this remarkable transformation? And what implications does it have for public policy?

In part, life expectancy has improved more for women than for men because of medical advances. Death during childbirth, which once threatened all women of child-bearing age, has almost been eliminated. Less progress has been made in reducing death from heart disease, emphysema, and cancer, leading causes of death among men. The higher mortality of men during wartime, the higher risk occupations of men, and differential patterns of immigration also increase the proportion of women in later life (Siegel, 1993).

Marital Arrangements

The high ratio of women to men in old age has consequences for other life-style factors. For both sexes, the probability of becoming widowed increases with age, but women are at greater risk than men. In 1993, a total of 79 percent of men aged 65 to 74 were married and living with their wives compared to only 53 percent of women. Among those over 75, a total of 70.2 percent of men were still married but only 25.6 percent of women (U.S. House of Representatives, 1994).

Several factors account for this difference, the most obvious being that women live longer. Also important, however, is that men who become widowed are three times more likely than women to remarry. Older men are more likely to find a new partner than older women because the sex ratio favors them. In addition, societal norms encourage men to marry younger women, thus giving men a larger pool of marriageable women to choose from. Few are disturbed when a 65-year-old man takes a 30-year-old bride, but imagine the reaction if the bride were 65 and the groom 30. Given that women, on average, live longer than men, it would make more sense for women to marry younger men. Then there would be fewer widows living alone. But deeply ingrained practices override what seems like common sense.

Life expectancy trends mean that the cost of fiscal decisions about social programs will be borne disproportionately by women, many of them widows living alone. Despite improvements in income security that have reduced poverty rates among the aged as a whole, the poverty rate among widowed women remains high. At 21 percent, their risk of poverty is nearly as high as that of young, single mothers.

Racial Composition

Although African Americans represent approximately 10 percent of the U.S. population, they make up only 8.1 percent of the elderly, and the disparity has been steadily widening. African Americans have higher mortality rates over the life course; fewer blacks than whites survive to age 65.

One reason for this difference is that many African Americans receive poorer health care than do whites. They are less likely than whites to have regular physical examinations and early prenatal care and are more likely to obtain treatment in emergency rooms. Because they receive less preventative health care, they are more likely to die from diseases like breast cancer. Many African Americans also work at jobs that put them at greater risk of injury and illness. Add to these factors the violence that needlessly claims the lives of many young black men, and one can readily explain these trends.

Racial differences in life expectancy have important policy implications. For example, African Americans collect less from Social Security and Medicare over their life span because they die earlier than whites. Any cuts in programs like Social Security will further reduce their return from their tax contributions to these programs.

Geographic Distribution

Issues about population aging affect some parts of the country more than others, for the aged population is not evenly dispersed. A disproportionate number of older people reside in the area known as the Sunbelt, which includes states in the West and South. States with especially high proportions of elderly include Florida, Arizona, Nevada, New Mexico, and North Carolina. Between 1970 and 1985, each of these states experienced an increase of 75 percent in its population aged 65 and over (Siegel, 1993). Other states, especially those in the declining industrial areas sometimes called the Rustbelt—Michigan, Ohio, Illinois—as well as in the farming regions, have a high proportion of older people because young people have moved away. Thus, two patterns make a region "old." The elderly in the Sunbelt are migrants from colder climates who have moved to states with moderate weather. Older people in the Midwest are more likely lifelong residents whose children have left because they can't find jobs. In both instances, one finds large pockets of elderly people without family nearby.

A large elderly population in a given region, whether due to outmigration of the young or inmigration of the old, creates fiscal and political issues for states and city governments. Who will provide the services—health care, transportation, housing—that they need? And who will pay for them? The migration patterns of older people also create issues for families, as middle-aged children find themselves coping with the health care crises of aging parents long distance.

HEALTH AND THE HEALTH CARE SYSTEM

Over the past century, there has been a decline in infectious disease among people of all ages, but because people are living longer, there has been an increase in chronic diseases. Presently, the majority of people over age 65 have at least one chronic condition—arthritis, hypertension, hearing impairments, or heart disease; many have several (Markson, 1991).

The fact that older people are at greater risk for chronic illness shows up in statistics on the use of health services. Compared to younger people, people 65 and older have more hospital stays per year, longer lengths of stay, and more physician visits (Kane and Kane, 1990). People suffering from chronic illnesses also require long-term help with activities of daily living, whereas those with acute illnesses require short-term medical interventions. Among people 85 and older, 55 percent report finding it difficult to perform the basic tasks of daily living. The problem in meeting these needs is that our health care system emphasizes treatment in the hospital and, increasingly, the nursing home as a place where individuals recover from long bouts of illness. About 40 percent of people over age 65 will spend some time in a nursing home before they die (Kane and Kane, 1990). The reliance on nursing homes is determined by payment systems. Medicaid will pay for nearly unlimited care for the elderly poor in a nursing home but for only limited care at home.

As more people live longer, the need to reevaluate how health care is organized will become more pressing. A system organized around hospitals and geared toward acute illness simply cannot provide the best care for people with chronic ailments who prefer to remain in their own homes.

WORK AND RETIREMENT

Increased life expectancy owing to improvements in health care and the treatment of chronic diseases has brought about a significant reorganization of the life course. This reorganization has had profound implications for the prevalence and timing of key transitions at all life stages, but particularly for the transition into old age. In industrialized countries, the most important indicator of old age is the transition from work to retirement.

Over the last fifty years, the rates of labor force participation among individuals over age 60 have steadily declined (Clark, 1993). The overall decline would have been steeper were it not for the entry of women into the labor force. These trends are not unique to the United States but are occurring in all Western nations. Why are people leaving the labor force at increasingly younger ages?

For the United States, the decline in the labor force participation of older men and women is partly due to the availability of Social Security benefits. By 1993 fewer than 16 percent of men over age 65, the age of eligibility for full Social Security benefits, were in the labor force. However, the availability of Social Security benefits cannot explain why only 78 percent of men aged 55 to 59 were working (U.S. House of Representatives, 1994). In the United States, private pensions have been responsible for the retirement of younger men. In some occupations, like automaking, the military, or federal service, people can retire as young as age 50 if they have worked twenty or thirty years.

In other countries, the pattern is similar to that of the United States, but private pensions are not responsible for these labor force exits. In Germany the main income source for older workers who leave the labor force has been the disability system; in France it has been the unemployment compensation system (Guillemard and Rein, 1993).

Regardless of the source of income, the departure of so many workers at relatively young ages raises important questions. Why is this trend occurring? Who will pay for the retirement benefits and health care costs of these young retirees? Are there enough younger workers to compensate for the loss of older workers? At present, no one has all the answers.

Despite the trend toward early retirement, the majority of men and women aged 55 to 65 are working. How do older workers fare? Some evidence implies that older workers are a privileged group because they have relatively low rates of unemployment, are least likely to be employed part-time when they prefer full-time work, and are least likely to be fully employed but have income below the poverty line (Doeringer, 1991). On the other hand, older workers have been especially vulnerable to downsizing resulting from declines in manufacturing, take longer to find a new job if they become unemployed, and are likely to end up in a lower status, lower paying job once they do find work.

The answer to whether older workers are a privileged or a vulnerable group depends on *which* older workers are being discussed. Women and minorities are least likely to have private pension coverage and most likely to be employed in low-wage, part-time jobs. Older, white males are more likely to be the privileged older workers. Even among older white men, however, a job loss in the middle years usually signifies downward mobility (Meier, 1986).

The conditions under which people retire play a large role in determining the amount of satisfaction they will have out of life. Most researchers agree that the material conditions of retirement—what people can do physically and what they can afford to do financially—are crucial for a satisfactory retirement experience. Men and women who have adequate income, good health, a comfortable home, and access to an adequate social support system are more likely to be satisfied with retirement than those who do not (Beck, 1982; Seccombe and Lee, 1986). The relationship between material factors and retirement satisfaction is straightforward: a life-style that is both more financially secure and more enjoyable should be a source of satisfaction. The dilemma for society is how to guarantee that all older people, regardless of race, income level, or gender, have the opportunity for a satisfying old age.

THE POLITICS OF AGE

For most of the twentieth century, older people have been viewed as deserving recipients of social benefits. High levels of poverty and unemployment among the elderly created support for the Social Security Act of 1935. As late as 1960, one-third of older men and 40 percent of older women had incomes below poverty level (Duncan and Smith, 1989). Over the past two decades, poverty rates among the elderly have declined, while their relative economic well-being has increased. Much of the improvement in the economic status of older people has been brought about by changes in Social Security. In 1972 Congress increased Social Security benefits by 20 percent and added automatic cost-of-living increases. For the first time in the nation's history, elderly people were guaranteed that inflation would not erode the value of their benefits (Derthick, 1979). Since then, the politics of age has been framed around debates about the Social Security system.

The first phase in the debate about Social Security began in the early 1970s when the economy began to falter. The year 1971 marked the first trade deficit of the century, followed by the energy crisis of 1973 and a combination of high unemployment and high inflation. Within a few years the Social Security trust fund began running a shortage. Critics contended that the program depressed private savings and reduced economic growth (Myles, 1985). The trust fund shortage was readily resolved in 1983 when Congress passed amendments to the Social Security Act that raised taxes slightly.

During the 1980s a new theme appeared. This time the issue was framed in terms of "generational equity." The elderly were accused of squandering the nation's limited resources and impoverishing children.

Recently, attacks on Social Security have taken the form of a plan to reduce the federal deficit through entitlement reform. Entitlements are programs like Social Security and Medicare that are not under the control of yearly decisions by Congress. The idea of entitlement reform is based on the argument that these programs are gobbling up money for other social needs and propelling the nation toward bankruptcy. The solution, according to proponents of entitlement reform, is to cut Social Security benefits and to provide benefits only to the poor or near poor (Peterson, 1993).

Whether the issue has been the solvency of the trust fund, generational equity, or the federal deficit, public support for Social Security has remained high. A 1987 survey conducted by the American Association for Retired Persons concluded that there are "no signs of waning support for programs targeted for the elderly." Even among young adults (aged 21 to 29), 77 percent believed the government should spend more on Medicare, 74 percent favored higher Social Security benefits, and 76 percent said the government was not doing enough for older people (Quadagno, 1991). Still, today's college students aren't convinced that when they retire, Social Security will be there for them. Confidence in the nation's most important source of income security can only be gained by education, so that young people can base their opinions on knowledge, not rumors.

CONCLUSION

Societal aging has become a topic of increasing concern, in terms of both academic knowledge and public policy. The timely articles in this book by some of the most prominent people in the field of social gerontology address key issues associated with population aging.

We have chosen topics and readings with the student in mind. We have tried to select pieces that address these issues in a readable fashion unhampered by complex statistics or laden with academic jargon. Our goal is to cast light on the crucial questions that face the United States today so that students will be capable of making informed judgments about our nation's future.

REFERENCES

Beck, Scott. "Adjustment to Retirement and Satisfaction with Retirement." *Journal of Gerontology* 37(1982):616–624.

Clark, Robert. "Population Aging and Work Rates of Older Persons: An International Comparison." In Olivia Mitchell (ed.), *As the Workforce Ages*. Ithaca, NY: ILR Press, 1993.

Derthick, Martha. *Policymaking for Social Security*. Washington, DC: Brookings Institution, 1979.

Doeringer, Peter. *Turbulence in the Workplace*. New York: Oxford University Press, 1991.

Duncan, Greg, and Ken Smith. "The Rising Affluence of the Elderly: How Far, How Fair and How Frail?" *Annual Review of Sociology* 15(1989):262.

Guillemard, Anne-Marie, and Martin Rein. "Comparative Patterns of Retirement: Recent Trends in Developed Societies." *Annual Review of Sociology* 19(1993):469–503.

Kane, Robert, and Rosalie Kane. "Health Care for Older People: Organizational and Policy Issues." In Robert Binstock and Linda George (eds.), *The Handbook of Aging and the Social Sciences*. Beverly Hills, CA: Sage, 1990.

Markson, Elizabeth W. "Physiological Changes, Illness and Health Care Use in Later Life." In Beth Hess and Elizabeth Markson (eds.), *Growing Old in America*. New Brunswick, NJ: Transaction Press, 1991.

Meier, Elizabeth. "Employment Experience and Income of Older Women." Washington, DC: American Association of Retired Persons, 1986.

Myles, John. "The Trillion Dollar Misunderstanding." In Beth Hess and Elizabeth Markson (eds.), *Growing Old in America*. New Brunswick, NJ: Transaction Press, 1985.

Peterson, Peter G. *Facing Up: How to Rescue the Economy from Crushing Debt and Restore the American Dream*. New York: Simon and Schuster, 1993.

Quadagno, Jill. "Interest Group Politics and the Future of U.S. Social Security." In John Myles and Jill Quadagno (eds.), *States, Labor Markets and the Future of Old Age Policy*. Philadelphia: Temple University Press, 1991.

Quadagno, Jill, and Melissa Hardy. "Work and Retirement." In Robert Binstock and Linda George (eds.), *The Handbook of Aging and the Social Sciences*. Orlando, FL: Academic Press, in press.

Seccombe, Karen, and Gary R. Lee. "Gender Differences in Retirement Satisfaction and Its Antecedents." *Research on Aging* 8(1986):426–440.

Siegel, Jacob S. *A Generation of Change: A Profile of America's Older Population*. New York: Russell Sage Foundation, 1993.

U.S. House of Representatives. *Green Book: Overview on Entitlement Programs*. Committee on Ways and Means. Washington, DC: U.S. Government Printing Office, 1994.

I

THEORIES OF AGING

Although the social sciences have a deep theoretical tradition extending back to the sixteenth century, the formal study of age and aging is fairly recent. Only in the last thirty or forty years have social scientists begun to develop theoretical models that explain both the experiences of aging individuals and their relationship to society. The role of theory in social gerontology is integral to any systematic analysis of aging. Social theories of age and aging structure seek to identify, describe, classify, and explain the dimensions of the aging process (Hendricks and Hendricks, 1986).

EARLY THEORIES OF AGING: FOCUS ON THE INDIVIDUAL

Early social gerontological theories focused primarily on the individual experiences of older people. Consequently, these models often emphasized psychological and microsocial aspects of aging. Among the earliest was Cumming and Henry's (1961) disengagement theory, which proclaimed that the aging process involved an inevitable, progressive withdrawal from earlier roles and social relationships. Disengagement was not only inevitable but also functional. It had benefits for the aged individual and for society: an individual's progress toward inevitable decline and death was eased by this gradual withdrawal from social roles; society benefited as the withdrawal of the old freed up positions for the young.

Disengagement theory elicited criticisms from other gerontologists, who challenged the presumption that older people inevitably and voluntarily withdraw from social roles. Their criticism led to the formulation of a counter thesis, activity theory. Activity theorists argued that core personality attributes were set early in life and that normal aging involved maintaining the activities, behaviors, and attitudes of middle age for as long as possible (Havighurst, 1963).

The debate over what constitutes normal aging highlights the role that theory plays in building knowledge about aging processes. Theoretical models are developed to provide frameworks that explain particular problems or issues of interest to researchers. As research based on a particular theoretical framework is brought to fruition, social scientists attempt to apply the model to other cases or to develop alternative models that build upon, qualify, or refine the original model. Because theories, however elaborated, are only tentative and subject to verification, the process of theory building in social gerontology is as dynamic as the aging process itself.

LATER THEORIES OF AGING: FOCUS ON SOCIETY

Theoretical models focusing on the societal factors that shape the lives of the elderly have become more salient, as modernization and industrialization have transformed the status of the elderly within Western democracies. Although debates have emerged over the timing and the precise nature of this transformation, there is general agreement that increased government intervention in the provision of economic security, the expansion of new technologies, and the decline of manufacturing have altered the position of the older people in the economy and in the family (Fischer, 1978; Haber and Gratton, 1994).

One of the first researchers to attempt to systematically theorize issues regarding the status of the aged was Matilda White Riley, who constructed her classic statement of age stratification. Building on insights from class stratification theorists, Riley argued that society is also hierarchically organized around age and that people not only move up or down the class structure but also across the age structure. Since then, others have continued to study how processes of aging, cohort membership, and personal history entwine to structure human lives (Riley, Johnson, and Foner, 1972). The reading by Matilda White Riley and John W. Riley in this volume represents the most recent contribution to decades of theory building around the concept of age stratification.

Another macrolevel approach to social gerontological theory emphasizes how political and economic institutions shape the nature of old age. Proponents of the political economy theory of aging contend that the social and economic status of the elderly is not primarily defined by biological age but rather by the division of labor that produces structural inequality (Phillipson, 1982; Walker, 1986). While early political economy approaches concentrated primarily on class relationships, recent research in this tradition has also asked how race and gender affect economic security and well-being in old age (Harrington Meyer, 1994; Harrington Meyer, Street, and Quadagno, 1994).

Although other disciplines (notably anthropology and psychology) have developed theories of aging, most social gerontological theories have been elaborated within the sociological tradition. The reading by Patricia M. Passuth and Vern L. Bengtson provides an overview of dominant theories in social gerontology and locates these theories within a broader sociological framework.

REFERENCES

Cumming, Elaine, and William H. Henry. *Growing Old.* New York: Basic Books, 1961.

Fischer, David Hackett. *Growing Old in America.* New York: Oxford University Press, 1978.

Haber, Carole, and Brian Gratton. *Old Age and the Search for Security.* Bloomington: Indiana University Press, 1994.

Harrington Meyer, Madonna. "Gender, Race, and the Distribution of Social Assistance: Medicaid Use among the Frail Elderly," *Gender & Society* 8, no. 4 (1994):8–28.

Harrington Meyer, Madonna; Debra Street; and Jill Quadagno. "The Impact of Family Status on Income Security and Health Care in Old Age: A Comparison of Western Nations." *International Journal of Sociology and Social Policy* 14, no. 1/2 (1994):53–83.

Havighurst, Robert J. "Successful Aging." Pp. 299–320 in Richard H. Williams, Clark Tibbits, and Wilma Donahue (eds.), *Processes of Aging: Social and Psychological Perspectives.* New York: Atherton Press, 1963.

Hendricks, Jon, and C. Davis Hendricks. "Theories of Social Gerontology." Pp. 80–122 in Jon

Hendricks and C. Davis Hendricks (eds.), *Aging in Mass Society: Myths & Realities*. 3rd ed. Boston: Little, Brown and Co., 1986.

Phillipson, Chris. *Capitalism and the Construction of Old Age*. London: Macmillan Press, 1982.

Riley, Matilda White; Marilyn Johnson; and Anne Foner. *Aging and Society,* Vol. 3. *A Sociology of Age Stratification*. New York: Russell Sage Foundation, 1972.

Walker, Alan. "Social Policy and Elderly People in Great Britain: The Construction of Dependent Social and Economic Status in Old Age." Pp. 143–167 in Anne-Marie Guillemard (ed.), *Old Age and the Welfare State*. Studies in International Sociology, Vol. 28. London: Sage, 1986.

1

Sociological Theories of Aging: Current Perspectives and Future Directions

PATRICIA M. PASSUTH
VERN L. BENGTSON

In this reading, Passuth and Bengtson provide an overview of thirty years of theorizing about aging, locating theories of aging within a broader sociological perspective. They examine the strengths and weaknesses of each theoretical approach and explain what each has to offer to the study of aging. Although they suggest that there may be insurmountable problems that prevent the development of a cohesive multidisciplinary model, they nonetheless contend that two recent theoretical developments within the sociology of age show promise for framing future research. Political economy and social phenomenology models have not yet bridged the gap between micro- and macrolevels of analysis, but these theoretical perspectives do emphasize how the relationships between historical, political, and economic conditions pattern older people's lives, and how the shifting social constructions of the meaning of old age shape the individual's experiences.

In the past decade there has been a significant growth in the amount of research in the sociology of aging. At the same time, there has also been greater concern for the theoretical underpinnings of aging research. While early social gerontological theories focused primarily on individual difficulties in adjusting to old age, later perspectives have taken into account broader issues regarding social aspects of age and aging. We feel this is an appropriate time for an assessment of current theoretical perspectives as well as prospects for future developments in the sociology of aging.

The purpose of this chapter is to examine the utility of current theories for explaining social aspects of aging and suggest possible directions for future theoretical analysis. In so doing, we will link theoretical perspectives in social gerontology[1] to major theoretical traditions in the field of sociology. While the study of aging has drawn upon sociological theories in general, it has lagged behind in its theoretical development. We will emphasize which perspectives show the greatest promise for understanding the aging experience. Moreover, in light of recent interest in the development of a multidisciplinary theory of aging, we will address the problems and prospects for a multidisciplinary perspective. We conclude with a call for a more richly contextualized analysis of the aging process.

Within the field of sociology of aging, theoretical perspectives vary greatly with respect to the relative importance given to a number of factors, including consensus, conflict, the self, social structure, and language use. No single theory explains all social phenomena; each focuses on particular aspects of social behavior, offering minimal explanations for other features of social life. This is evident, for example, in considering the level of analysis examined by each of the various aging theories. While some perspectives focus on macro-structural conditions in seeking to explain the aging process, others are more interested in immediate social relations, or the micro-social level of analysis. In the next section we examine the major sociological theories of aging in terms of their central explanatory focus and assess the ability of each to explain social phenomena associated with aging.

MAJOR THEORETICAL DEVELOPMENTS IN THE SOCIOLOGY OF AGING

Sociological theories of aging have emerged, implicitly or explicitly, from five general sociological perspectives: structural functionalism, exchange, symbolic interactionism, Marxism, and social phenomenology.[2] Figure 1-1 organizes the major theoretical perspectives in social gerontology according to the theoretical traditions in sociology.

As Figure 1-1 shows, structural functionalism informs, to varying degrees, the disengagement, modernization, and age stratification theories of aging. Exchange theory has been directly applied to the experiences of the elderly. Symbolic interactionism has influenced three additional perspectives of old age: activity, social competence/breakdown, and subculture theories. The Marxist tradition is the major influence for a political economy approach to aging. The social phenomenological approach also has been used to study the aging process.[3] We now turn to an analysis of the theories of aging according to the major sociological theories from which they derive.

Structural Functionalist Theories of Aging

Structural functionalism (Parsons, 1951) has been an important influence on theorizing in aging. In part, this has reflected the prominence of functionalism in the development of American sociology during the 1940s and 1950s. The theory argues that social behavior is best understood from the perspective of the equilibrium needs of the social system. The approach views social behavior in terms of its function within the structure of society. Key concepts in functionalism include norms, roles, and socialization. Norms are shared rules about appropriate behavior. Roles are the set of behavioral ex-

MAJOR SOCIOLOGICAL THEORIES   MAJOR THEORIES OF AGING

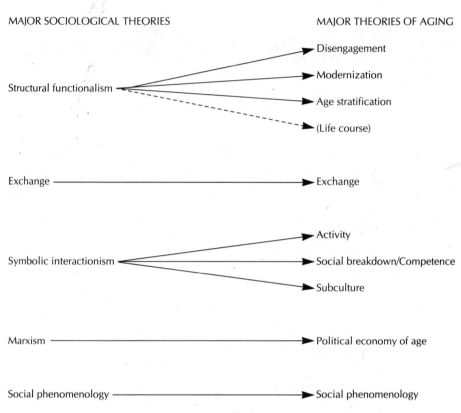

FIGURE 1-1   The influence of sociological theories on theories of aging.

pectations that constitute a particular status. Socialization is the process by which individuals learn and internalize the norms and values of society. Individuals, in turn, become part of the social order, carrying out the needs of the system. As such, the process enables the smooth and efficient functioning of society. In emphasizing the normative aspects of social order, the functionalist perspective focuses on consensus and conformity, rather than conflict, as major features of social order.

Structural functionalist influences on theories in aging can be seen in formulations regarding disengagement (Cumming & Henry, 1961), modernization (Cowgill, 1974; Cowgill & Holmes, 1972), and, to a lesser extent, age stratification (Riley, 1971, 1987; Riley, Johnson, & Foner, 1972). Each of these is informed by a functionalist concern for the ways in which societal norms structure the roles available to different age groups.

Disengagement Theory   Disengagement theory (Cumming & Henry, 1961) represents the most explicit application of structural functionalism to the condition of the elderly in terms of their social and psychological reactions to aging. The term *disengagement* refers to the universal, mutual, and inevitable withdrawal of older people from the configuration of roles characteristic of middle age. The theory examines the aging process in terms of the needs and requisites of society; individuals are conceived as passive agents of the social system (Gouldner, 1970). In effect, elderly persons recognize, as fully socialized members, their readiness to disengage on behalf of society.

In support of their argument, Cumming and Henry (1961) present data to indicate a decreased level in the number and frequency of social interactions as well as decreased emotional involvement in old age. Disengagement theory argues that this process is functional to both society and the individual; it enables society to make room for more efficient young people while, at the same time, allowing the elderly time to prepare for their eventual total withdrawal from social life—death.

Following its emergence in the literature, disengagement theory was criticized on empirical, theoretical and logical grounds (Hochschild, 1975, 1976; Maddox, 1964; Palmore, 1968). In terms of theory, perhaps the most penetrating critique is Hochschild's (1975, 1976) analysis of the logical flaws in the disengagement presentation. She summarizes these as the "escape clause," the "omnibus variable," and the "assumption of meaning" problems.

The "escape clause" refers to the fact that the theory is unfalsifiable. For example, contrary evidence (which Hochschild found in Cumming and Henry's own data) indicates that a significant proportion of older people do not withdraw from society. However, according to Cumming and Henry (1961), this does not refute the theory since these older people are described as either "unsuccessful" adjusters to old age, "off time" disengagers, or members of a "biological or psychological elite."

The "omnibus variable" problem refers to the overinclusiveness of the variables *age* and *disengagement* in Cumming and Henry's model of aging. That is, age is a broad term that encompasses such multifaceted processes as developmental changes, physical decline, and changes in social relations (e.g., retirement, widowhood). The disengagement variable includes numerous psychological and social processes including, for example, a trend toward fewer, less frequent, and less intense social contacts. Hochschild (1975, 1976) argues that the use of these two variables to explain adjustment to old age obscures the diverse processes that the variables represent.

The "assumption of meaning" problem refers to the theory's preference for imputing compliance without measuring it. For example, the theory argues that elderly individuals willingly withdraw from society; yet Cumming and Henry do not include data addressing the validity of this concept.

Despite the limitations of disengagement theory, it has had a profound effect on the field of social gerontology. It was the first formal theory that attempted to explain the process of growing older. The theory encouraged the development of opposing theories of the aged (Hochschild, 1975) and, eventually, the entire aging process. Disengagement theory's challenge to what was termed activity theory resulted in an enduring interest in explaining the "life satisfaction" or "morale" of older people in social gerontological research. Although the original explication of disengagement theory has been roundly criticized, elements of the perspective—especially society's role in excluding the elderly from valued social roles—have been revived and applied in new ways.

Modernization Theory   Modernization theory (Cowgill, 1974; Cowgill & Holmes, 1972) attempts to explain variations in age status both historically and across societies.

It focuses on the macro-structural conditions of the elderly in varied sociocultural settings. It is a functionalist perspective in that it suggests that the status of the elderly derives from their relationship to evolving systems of social roles which vary across societies depending on the degree of industrialization (or "modernization"). From this perspective, structural changes in a society occur in a particular way, regardless of historical or cultural context.

Modernization theory argues that the status of the aged is inversely related to the level of societal industrialization. Whereas in earlier preindustrial societies the elderly held high status by virtue of their control of scarce resources and their knowledge of tradition, they have lower status in present industrialized societies. In an elaboration of this theory, Cowgill (1974) outlines four elements of modernization—health technology, economic technology, urbanization, and mass education—that result in the lowered status of the aged. Palmore and Manton (1974) found that these elements of modernization were generally related to the status of the elderly in various societies.

Cowgill's evidence is based on 20th-century nonindustrial societies (see Simmons, 1945) that are intended to represent past societies. It has been argued that modernization theory presumes a "golden age of aging" in which the elderly lived in multigeneration households where they held much power, controlled many of the resources in the larger society, and were the source of societal tradition and information. Laslett (1965) refers to this romanticization of the past as "the world we have lost" syndrome. Modernization theory incorporates this popular view into a formal theory of the aged. Recent historical analyses (Haber, 1983; Quadagno, 1982; Stearns, 1982) challenge this belief of an ideal existence for preindustrial elderly as well as the notion of a simple, linear relationship between degree of industrialization and status of the elderly. These histories of old age emphasize variations in the experiences of the elderly depending on gender, race, ethnicity, social class, region, and historical period (Stearns, 1982).

Age Stratification   The age stratification model (Riley, 1971, 1987; Riley, Johnson, & Foner, 1972) has become one of the most influential perspectives in the emerging sociology of aging. Its intellectual roots can be traced primarily to structural functionalism. This model examines the movement of successive birth cohorts across time, known as "cohort flow." A birth cohort is a group of people born at the same time in history who age together. Each cohort is unique because it has its own characteristics (e.g., size, gender, and social class distribution) and each experiences particular historical events which affect its members' attitudes and behaviors. For example, Elder (1974) has shown that the cohort of children who grew up during the Great Depression had different values as adults, depending on such factors as relative economic loss and gender. Research on the age stratification perspective further argues that the age structure of roles organizes society into a hierarchy, the consequences of which can be viewed much like social class (Riley, 1971). Foner (1974, 1986), in particular, has examined how one's location within an age structure influences opportunities for societal power and rewards.

In several ways, the age stratification perspective represents a major advance over previous theories in social gerontology. First, it brings to the study of aging conceptual tools of mainstream sociology, in particular those from the areas of social stratification and demography. Second, the model emphasizes that there are significant variations in older people depending on the characteristics of their birth cohort; this suggests the need for a more explicit analysis of historical and social factors in aging. Third, age stratification's emphasis on the relations of cohorts within the age structure of society offers a useful analytic framework for distinguishing between developmental age changes and cohort historical differences. This has led, in part, to the reexamination of much research on presumed developmental changes including, for example, declines in IQ scores in old age (Schaie, 1979) and greater political conservatism with advanced age (Cutler, 1983).

There are, however, several limitations of the age stratification model. Its analogy to social class overstates the power of age status in explaining the distribution of rewards in society (Cain, 1987; Hendricks & Hendricks, 1986; Streib & Bourg, 1984). Although indicators of social class, such as income, may systematically change with age, it has not been demonstrated conclusively that the age structure [as opposed to, for example, the class system (cf. Olson, 1982)] is the causal mechanism driving the reward structure.

While the concept of cohort is a powerful tool for understanding the experience of aging, it also tends to reify chronological age or birth year. That is, people are defined largely in terms of chronological age per se, ignoring the subjective age dimension [cf. Mannheim's (1928/1952) analysis of generational units]. Age stratification's emphasis on differences between cohorts has resulted in a lack of attention to variations within cohorts. The assumption of cohort analysis is that people born in a particular year (subdivided by specific intracohort characteristics such as gender, social class, and race) experience age the same way. Accordingly, situational factors in the day-to-day lives of individual members within a given cohort, which may make for very different aging experiences, play little or no role. Yet a number of studies (e.g., Frankfather, 1977; Matthews, 1979; Ross, 1977; Stephens, 1976) have shown that individuals of the same age group often experience age in a wide variety of ways, depending on the relevant social context. These situational variations among cohort members are not seriously taken into account in the age stratification model.

Life Course Perspective   The life course perspective (Cain, 1964; Clausen, 1972; Elder, 1975; Neugarten & Hagestad, 1976), which has been influenced by the age stratification model, is a recent conceptual development within social and behavioral analyses of aging. Much of the research conducted within this framework incorporates functionalist assumptions about the role of social norms in shaping behavior (e.g., Clausen, 1986; Hogan, 1980, 1981; Neugarten, Moore, & Lowe, 1965). The life course perspective is not a theory per se but a conceptual framework for conducting research and interpreting data. Key elements of this framework include the acknowledgment that (1) aging occurs from birth to death (thereby distinguishing this theory from those that focus exclusively on the elderly); (2) aging involves social, psychological, and biological processes; and (3) aging experiences are shaped by cohort-historical factors.

Hagestad and Neugarten (1985) describe the life course perspective in terms of three research emphases. These are (1) the study of the timing of adult role transitions (e.g., getting married, finishing school, completing military service, and getting a job); (2) the analysis of age norms; and (3) the study of perceptions of age (e.g., at what age is a person "middle-aged"). Recent work within this perspective has suggested the increasing institutionalization of the human life course (Dannefer, 1987; Kohli, 1986; Lawrence, 1984). The lack of explicit links of the life course perspective to sociological theories raises a potential problem in that the term *life course* is used so loosely in the sociology of aging that it is referenced for practically any type of research on adulthood and aging. As such, the perspective, in its current form, loses much of its theoretical explanatory power.

Exchange Theory of Aging

Exchange theory (Blau, 1964; Homans, 1961) applies a rational, economic model to the study of social behavior. From this perspective, social life consists of a collection of individuals involved in ongoing social exchanges. Individuals' reasons for interacting with others depends on their calculations of the costs and benefits they derive from continued social interaction. That is, individuals engage in interactions that are rewarding to them and, conversely, withdraw from interactions that are costly. As such, social order exists as a byproduct of "profit-maximizing" individuals.

Exchange Theory   Dowd (1975) draws from Homans's (1961) and Blau's (1964) exchange theory in examining the experiences of the elderly. His analysis attempts to explain why older people tend to withdraw from social interaction. He argues that the aged have less power in encounters with younger people because they possess fewer resources (i.e., lower income, less education, poorer health); continued interactions with the elderly become more costly for younger age groups. The outcome is that older people decrease their participation in social life. Only those elderly who have the necessary resources to sustain a relationship with other age groups remain actively engaged in ongoing social affairs.

Exchange theory adds a new dimension to the study of aging by focusing on the immediate interactions between older people and other age groups. However, the perspective's purely economic, rational model results in certain limitations. While ongoing interactions may indeed include a give-and-take element, the theory sees all interactions from a rational point of view. For example, an attempt is made to redefine nonrational entities, such as love, strictly in economic and behavioral terms [see Blau's (1964) "Excursus on Love"]. Moreover, the theory overlooks the *quality* of exchange relations, defining social interaction solely in terms of the number of interactions initiated. Although Dowd (1975) acknowledges that the subjective dimension is important, he does not attempt to incorporate it. As such, his focus on the quantification of exchanges overlooks the fact that individuals variously define and redefine the meanings of rewards and costs in ongoing exchange relationships.

Symbolic Interactionist Theories of Aging

Symbolic interactionism (Blumer, 1969; Mead, 1934) emphasizes the dynamic and meaningful processes of social interaction. From this perspective, individuals develop a sense of self through interpreting others' responses to their behavior. Individuals attempt to understand how others see their behavior by "taking the role of the other." Social order is contingent on the shared meanings that develop in ongoing interaction. Activity, social competence/breakdown, and subculture theories of aging are influenced, to varying degrees, by symbolic interactionism.

Activity Theory   Activity theory (Cavan, 1962; Cavan, Burgess, Havighurst & Goldhamer, 1949; Havighurst & Albrecht, 1953; Lemon, Bengtson, & Peterson, 1972), in direct contrast to disengagement, argues that the more active elderly persons are, the greater their satisfaction with life. In its original formulation (Cavan et al., 1949; Havighurst & Albrecht, 1953), activity theory was not explicitly framed within a symbolic interactionist perspective. (Indeed, the theory itself was "implicit" until challenged by disengagement theory.) Later analysis (Cavan, 1962), however, has been more directly tied to symbolic interactionism, placing a greater emphasis on ongoing social interaction in the development of self-concept among the elderly.

The activity perspective argues that one's self-concept is related to the roles one holds. With old age comes a loss of roles (e.g., retirement, widowhood). The theory states that in order to maintain a positive sense of self, elderly persons must substitute new roles for those lost in old age. Thus, well-being in late life results from increased activity in newly acquired roles.

Activity theory provides a conceptual justification for a central assumption underlying many programs and interventions for the elderly—that social activity in and of itself is beneficial and results in greater life satisfaction. At the same time, however, the theory assumes that all older persons need and desire high levels of social activity. The activity perspective also overlooks variations in the meaning of particular activities in the lives of older people. Lemon et al. (1972), for example, in their attempt to frame activity theory in terms of symbolic interactionism, found that the relationship between well-being and activity in old age depends on the type of activity: formal, informal, solitary. Moreover, researchers have shown that the effect of activity norms on older people's life satisfaction is related to the age concentration of various environments (Bultena, 1974; Messer, 1967).

Social Competence and Breakdown Theory   Social competence/breakdown theory (Kuypers & Bengtson, 1973) is another application of interactionist theory which attempts to explain both normal and problematic aspects of aging. This perspective borrows from several other theoretical traditions in explaining the interdependence between older people and their social worlds [including labeling theory in sociology and psychiatry, Lawton's (1983) environmental press theory in psychology, and general systems theory]. As originally proposed, the social breakdown syndrome (Zusman, 1966) refers to the process by which a psychologically vulnerable individual receives negative messages from his or her social environment, which are then incorporated into the self-concept, producing a vicious spiral of negative feedback.

Kuypers and Bengtson (1973) have applied these ideas to the social competence of the elderly and to the negative consequences—breakdowns—in competence that can accompany the crises that often occur with advancing age (e.g., loss of health, loss of spouse). They suggest that a negative spiral of feedback can occur: (1) An elderly individual, whose self-concept may already be vulnerable because of role loss or negative stereotypes concerning aging, experiences a health-related crisis; this leads to (2) labeling of the older person as dependent by the social environment—health professionals or family; (3) atrophy of previous competency skills occurs; and (4) the individual adopts the self-concept of sick, inadequate, or incompetent. This leads to further vulnerability, and the negative cycle occurs again, with further consequences to social and psychological competence.

Kuypers and Bengtson (1973) suggest that the spiraling breakdown of competence in elderly individuals can be reversed through what they term a *social reconstruction syndrome*. By improving environmental supports while facilitating an expression of personal strength, a sense of increased competence can be fostered (see also Gubrium, 1973). More recently, Bengtson and Kuypers (1986) have adapted this model to problems facing the aging family. Families are frequently unprepared for the sudden dependency of an aged member, and problems of caregiving (Brody, 1985) create many strains on family competence (as well as on individual competences). However, an awareness of the cyclical nature of individual–environmental interactions affecting the sense of competence can help identify inputs that may improve family functioning, thus reducing the sense of helplessness that many caregivers feel. While useful as a heuristic device (Hendricks & Hendricks, 1986) and for sensitizing practitioners in dealing with problems of aging (Lowy, 1985; Sherman, 1981), the social competence/breakdown model has yet to be tested in empirical studies.

Subculture Theory   Although the subculture theory of aging (Rose, 1964, 1965) includes a functionalist concern for social norms, its main thesis is that these norms develop in interactions with others. The theory holds that the aged are developing their own subculture in American society. This results from (1) older people's exclusion from interactions with other age groups, (2) their increased interaction with each other as a result of age-segregation policies (e.g., retirement, age-homogeneous housing), and (3) their common beliefs and interests (e.g., health care). As a subculture, the elderly create their own norms and values specific to their group. The aged subculture cuts across other status distinctions—gender, race, social class—so that the elderly develop a group identity.

Rose's contention that a subculture is developing can be found in the creation of age-activist groups such as the Gray Panthers and the American Association of Retired Persons (AARP). However, questions arise about whether the elderly constitute a minority group (Streib, 1965). While Rose asserts that the subculture is developing, some research indicates that the aged do not yet share a strong group consciousness, whether measured in terms of voting patterns or similar attitudes and values (Streib, 1985).

Symbolic interactionism is an important addition to the study of aging because it corrects the overly static, passive image of interaction found in functionalist approaches. Symbolic interactionism views the individual as a more active participant in social interaction. An individual does not just become his or her role, as structural functionalist perspectives argue, but rather engages in a process of "role-taking," adjusting his or her behavior depending on the responses of others. Perhaps the major limitation of the symbolic interactionist approach is that its primary focus on the micro level of analysis fails to recognize fully the structural component of social behavior.

While individuals are confronted by others' perceptions, the systematic, structural constraints placed upon individual behavior are not addressed (Dannefer, 1984). At the same time, symbolic interactionism, at least as applied to theories of aging, does not seriously examine the ongoing interpretive process in everyday social affairs.[4] This concern, however, is explicitly dealt with by social phenomenology, which we look at later in the chapter.

Marxist Theories of Aging

Marx's (1867/1946) theory of capitalist development emphasizes the constraining features of social order. The perspective argues that the social distribution of power and resources in a capitalist society is embedded within the context of the social relations of production. In the ongoing organization of the economic sphere, people confront the existing social organization of their relations with others (class structure), providing a number of opportunities for some, while excluding the majority of others. The differential class interests make for ongoing strains between competing factions in social life.

The Political Economy of Age   It is only in the last ten years or so that the political economy perspective has been applied to the study of old age. Drawing upon Marxism, this perspective (Estes, 1979; Olson, 1982; Phillipson, 1982; Quadagno, 1982; Walker, 1981) focuses on the state and its relation to the economy in a capitalist society to explain the plight of the elderly. In examining the creation of particular social programs directed toward the elderly, for example, political economists maintain that the effects of such programs have been much more beneficial to capitalist interests than to the elderly themselves, often having adverse effects on older people. Estes (1979) explains the development of government welfare programs for the elderly as helping to increase the number of service-oriented jobs—fueling the capitalist economy—without fundamentally providing for a decent standard of living for needy older people. Other research that has examined the political, social, and economic forces surrounding the conditions of the elderly include Olson's (1982) analysis of the development of a social security system in the United States, Quadagno's (1982) study of the formation of a pension system in England, and Guillemard's (1983) analysis of the welfare state in France.

The political economy perspective is a promising recent addition to the study of aging. In looking at the political and economic conditions that give rise to problems of growing old, this perspective encourages gerontologists to stand back and ask whose interests are really served in the efforts to help the elderly. For example, the issue of generational equity (see, e.g., Kingson, Hirshorn, & Cornman, 1986; Longman, 1985; Preston, 1984) would benefit from a political economic analysis. This debate has been framed in terms of the proportion of Federal monies targeted for children versus the elderly. The political economy perspective, however, would argue that these monies do not directly address the issue of childhood or old-age poverty, given that much of it goes to pay the salaries of those employed by social welfare programs.

While the political economy perspective has expanded the study of aging by focusing on the larger social context of old-age problems, it also tends to overstate the extent to which the elderly, as a whole, are impoverished and disenfranchised—both historically and in advanced industrial societies (Harris & Associates, 1975; Stearns, 1982). Indeed, some researchers suggest that the majority of elderly in contemporary American society constitute a *new old* who are healthier and live in relative economic well-being (Cain, 1967; Neugarten, 1974). Moreover, by focusing on the structure of society itself, the perspective overlooks the role of interpretation and meaning in the everyday experiences of the elderly. As such, the analysis does not address the variety of old-age environments which give rise to their own sets of meanings specific to the elderly's experiences within them (see, e.g., Jacobs, 1975; Myerhoff, 1978; Ross, 1977; Stephens, 1976; Teski, 1979). This issue, however, is explicitly dealt with by another rather recent and promising theoretical development in the sociology of aging—social phenomenology—which we turn to next.

Social Phenomenological Theories of Aging

Social phenomenology is a general term that can be used to encompass a variety of works, in particular the phenomenology of Schutz (1967; 1970) and the ethnomethodology of Garfinkel (1967). The perspective brackets, or puts aside, the question of whether things are real or not and examines the process by which they are socially constructed. While this approach is like symbolic interactionism in that it is concerned with the definitional nature of social life, social phenomenology has a more serious concern with the use of language and knowledge as constitutive elements in everyday realities. For example, researchers have studied the use of developmental discourse by teachers (Cicourel et al., 1974), parents (Speier, 1970), caregivers (Lynott, 1983), social workers and psychiatrists (Pfohl, 1978), among others, in making decisions about other persons' competencies. Their analyses reveal how the course of children's and adults' lives is changed with the interpretive and definitional discussions entered into by decision makers.

Social Phenomenology   As applied to the study of aging, the social phenomenological perspective (Gubrium & Buckholdt, 1977; Hochschild, 1973, 1976; Starr, 1982–1983) examines the emergent, situational, and constitutive features of the aging experience. Gubrium and Buckholdt (1977, p. viii), for example, focus on the practical and ongoing considerations over questions of human development, whereby "the meaning of age is presented and negotiated from moment to moment as people participate in sometimes elusive but serious conversation."

Another focus within the phenomenological perspective has been the critique of positivist research that does not take into account the situated meanings attributed by the social participants. Gubrium and Lynott (1983), for example, have demonstrated that the questions that make up life-satisfaction surveys "instruct" older people to organize their lives in a linear and progressive fashion, regardless of the way they have experienced them. In contrast to the developmental sense of living conveyed in the life satisfaction scales, the authors present evidence from a variety of ethnographic descriptions depicting the contextual and constructed features of life satisfactions among older people. Their critique cautions researchers against findings that do not fit the everyday social realities of elderly persons.

Social phenomenology has brought the study of social construction in everyday life situations to the analysis of the aging experience. Its emphasis on the construction of socially emergent meanings encourages the researcher to pay close attention to ongoing social circumstances. Yet, at the same time, like symbolic interactionism, phenomenology's emphasis on microsocial processes overlooks the structural features of social life. As a result, social phenomenologists tend to minimize the role of power in their analysis of everyday social behaviors (Giddens, 1976).

FUTURE DIRECTIONS IN THEORY BUILDING

Theorizing in the sociology of aging has lagged considerably behind theoretical developments in the field of sociology. There are two primary reasons for this. First, until recently, theoretical development in social gerontology has been dominated by a concern for the predictors of elderly life satisfaction. This was, perhaps, most apparent in the long-running activity-disengagement controversy in the 1960s. As a result of this emphasis on the correlates of life satisfaction, research questions traditionally have been more narrowly focused on the adjustment problems of old age rather than addressing broader theoretical issues concerning the social experiences of aging.

The second reason social gerontology has not kept up with theoretical developments in sociology is that it has been largely dominated by structural functionalism. While the development in social gerontology bears a striking resemblance to the impact of Parsonian functionalism on sociological theorizing in general, its monumental dominance in the field of aging came about much later. As a result, it is only relatively recently that more contemporary perspectives from sociology have been applied to the study of aging.[5] In the remainder of this section we examine two potential directions for future theoretical developments: The prospects for multidisciplinary theories of aging and the promise of a richer, more contextualized analysis of the aging experience.

The Prospects for Multidisciplinary Theories of Aging

More so than many other substantive areas analyzing the human experience, the study of aging has been concerned with the interaction of biological, social, and psychological processes. This has suggested to some the desirability of developing a comprehensive, multiperspective theory of aging. The quest for a grand, interdisciplinary theory encompassing phenomena of aging seems misdirected on several grounds.

There are several obstacles to the formation of multidisciplinary theories of aging. The most critical problem in combining sociological, psychological, and biological approaches is that these disciplines are not unified within themselves. A multidisciplinary approach presumes there is agreement within each discipline concerning how human behavior should be conceptualized. But, as we have shown, there does not exist one sociology (or psychology or biology for that matter). For example, which sociological perspective would one choose in the multidisciplinary study of aging? Structural functionalism? Exchange theory? Symbolic Interactionism? Likewise, which psychological perspective would one choose? Freudianism? Behavioralism? Cognitive theory? Each of these would produce a radically different image of the sociology or psychology of aging. The same is also true, although possibly to a lesser extent, of biology. The existence of many diverse theoretical perspectives in each discipline—and there is little reason to believe this will change in the future—works against the assumption that the social, psychological, and biological influences of aging can be readily combined.

Moreover, the conceptual problems multiply in attempting to merge theoretical perspectives from different disciplines. For example, the individualistic framework of many psychological perspectives is at odds with both macrostructural sociological theories and micro-interpretive perspectives. It is not simply that the theories differ in their units of analysis; their assumptions about human behavior are antagonistic and consequently cannot be combined into a unified theory.

This is not to deny that some psychologists and sociologists share common assumptions about the nature of human behavior. For example, Gergen (1980), a psychologist, and Starr (1982–1983), a sociologist, argue for a similar phenomenological conception of the life course despite their divergent disciplinary training. This example of perspectives that cross disciplinary lines points to one requirement for a comprehensive theory of aging: Self-conscious discussion of the underlying assumptions about human behavior that constitute various theories. Until this discussion is seriously taken up by social theorists of aging, it is probable that any multidisciplinary theory will be combining psychological "apples" with sociological "oranges."

What often occurs with respect to developing a multidisciplinary perspective is that researchers acknowledge the existence of the three processes in aging without fully incorporating each in research. For example, one of the tenets of the life course perspective is that aging involves biological, social, and psychological processes (Featherman, 1983; Riley, 1987). In practice, however, researchers typically study social factors, less often psychological elements (e.g., Clausen, 1986; Elder, 1974), and rarely incorporate biological variables. Even when researchers do explicitly include the three processes in their models, they typically must oversimplify the concepts contained in each discipline (see, e.g., Brim & Ryff, 1980; Costa & McCrae, 1980; Gutmann, 1974). Thus, psychological processes are subsumed under "personality factors" and sociology is operationalized as "social roles," thereby incorporating a rather superficial, watered-down version of each.

Recent efforts in the social sciences to include sociological, psychological, and biological processes in the study of aging (e.g., Featherman & Lerner, 1985) further illustrate the problems posed by such a comprehensive theory of aging. In their efforts to be inclusive, Featherman and Lerner produce a model that is multidimensional (including social, psychological, and biological variables) but also extremely abstract. Early theories in social gerontology were too simplistic when they attempted to explain the aging process with one variable, whether it be disengagement, activity, or modernization. By the same token, it would be a mistake for future theories to go to the other extreme and develop models that are overly inclusive, explaining little in particular.

An approach that has been relatively fruitful involves empirical research which focuses on one substantive concern (or dependent variable) and studies it from the three disciplines. Research on the combined effects of biological, social, and psychological factors in health and life expectancy has been somewhat successful in incorporating multidisciplinary perspectives. A limitation of this empirical approach is that it cannot deal with more complex social phenomena involving, for example, interactional features of the aging process. In addition, the model's major emphasis on biological factors as the outcome variables results in a narrow vision of what constitutes aging, excluding much gerontological research conducted in sociology and psychology. It is unclear how such models relate to the development of multidisciplinary theories of aging. A model that explains life expectancy is not a theory of aging; it implies that aging can be reduced to one dependent variable. Clearly, aging encompasses more than that.

Toward a Contextual Analysis of Aging

In contrast to the current interest in developing multidisciplinary theories of aging, we believe that a fuller understanding of the social aspects of aging would be a more fruitful direction for future sociological theorizing. Toward this goal, we call for future theoretical directions which concretely analyze the social contexts of aging. By social context we do not mean the kind of analysis commonly done by age stratification and life course researchers, which merely examines statistical comparisons of select cohort demographics. Our concern, rather, is with social *experience,* the fluid and dynamic features of social context.

Political economy and social phenomenology are the most promising theories in this regard. While each focuses on different levels of concern—micro versus macro—and, accordingly, has its respective weaknesses, both provide important insights into the broader contextual features of the aging process. Whether focused on the larger social, political, and economic conditions of society, or the changing social realities in the day-to-day lives of society's members, each perspective, in its own fashion, enables one to stand back and analyze the social dynamics—ideological or socially constructive—involved in understanding aging phenomena.

Consider, for example, how research in social gerontology has strayed too far from people's everyday experiences. A major conceptual issue in social gerontology has focused on the roles and norms applied to the elderly. Rosow (1974), writing from a structural functionalist perspective, argues that old age is characterized by a lack of social roles and norms. That is, unlike other age groups, older people have few social roles to occupy and are not bound by norms of appropriate behavior; old age is thus characterized in terms of a "roleless role" (Burgess, 1960). Hochschild (1973), in her book *The Unexpected Community,* uses a more contextual approach in her analysis of a group of elderly widows living in an apartment complex. Contrary to Rosow's rather bleak view of old age, Hochschild demonstrates that these women lead busy, purposeful lives within their group. She found an elaborate set of newly defined social roles and experiences among the women, which included numerous norms regarding appropriate social behavior. Although Hochschild's approach is not directly phenomenological, her analysis illustrates how the aging experience is variously defined against shifting background relevancies of elderly life. Hochschild's work demonstrates that roles and norms are not only indeed a part of old age, but they are socially constructed within the varied worlds of experience in which older people live. Several other studies have documented similar context-specific social behaviors in a variety of old-age "unexpected" communities (e.g., Eckert, 1980; Frankfather, 1977; Ross, 1977; Teski, 1979). The implication of such studies for the theoretical significance of the political–economic and social phenomenological perspectives is that the two theories' broader social contextualizing features promise to provide yet new insights into, and challenge existing conceptions of, the aging process.

CONCLUSION

The purpose of this chapter has been to assess current sociological theories of aging and propose possible future directions. We have examined the influence of the prominent traditions in sociological theory (structural functionalism, exchange, symbolic interactionism, Marxism, and social phenomenology) on nine theoretical perspectives in the sociology of aging: (1) disengagement, (2) modernization, (3) age stratification (including the life course perspective), (4) exchange, (5) activity, (6) social competence/breakdown, (7) subculture, (8) political economy, and (9) social phenomenology.

We have argued that the current effort to develop multidisciplinary theories of aging is misguided, given the incompatibility not only of theories between the separate disciplines, but also within them. We conclude that the most fruitful areas of analysis for social gerontology lie in a more thorough examination of the contextual features which surround the aging process. This includes historical, political, and economic features as well as the ongoing social construction of everyday aging experiences.

The rapid increase in the older population in recent years has encouraged greater attention to understanding the social aspects of aging. This makes for an exciting period in the sociology of aging, in large part because of the increasing interest in theory development. Theoretically speaking, the study of aging may be coming of age.

NOTES

We are especially grateful to Robert Lynott, who provided extensive and insightful comments on several drafts of this paper. We also thank several other colleagues for their comments and suggestions on an earlier draft: James Birren, Dale Dannefer, Anne Foner, John Henretta, Gary Kenyon, Marion Perlmutter, Gary Reker, and Peter Uhlenberg. Preparation of this paper was supported by grants Nos. T32 AG00037 and RO1 04092 from the National Institute on Aging.

1. Throughout this chapter, we will use the term "social gerontology" and "sociology of aging" interchangeably to refer to the study of the social aspects of age, aging, and the aged.

2. We have decided to differentiate theoretical perspectives in this way because these categories are widely recognized within sociology as constituting major theories in the field (see Turner, 1978; Zeitlin, 1973).

3. We use the term *social phenomenology* to refer primarily to the theoretical work of Schutz (1967, 1970), in the phenomenological tradition, and Garfinkel (1967), in the ethnomethodological tradition.

4. While Blumer (1969), in his book *Symbolic Interactionism: Perspective and Method,* does examine the ongoing interpretive process, his treatment of symbolic interactionism has not been incorporated into the field of aging.

5. For example, feminist perspectives are just beginning to be applied to aging issues (e.g.,

Hess, 1985; Troll, Israel, & Israel, 1977), which is surprising given the predominance of women in the older population.

REFERENCES

Bengtson, V. L., & Kuypers, J. A. (1986). The family support cycle: Psychosocial issues in the aging family. In J. M. A. Munnichs, P. Mussen, & E. Olbrich (Eds.), *Life span and change in a gerontological perspective* (pp. 61–77). New York: Academic Press.

Blau, P. M. (1964). *Exchange and power in social life.* New York: Wiley.

Blumer, H. (1969). *Symbolic interactionism: Perspective and method.* Englewood Cliffs, NJ: Prentice-Hall.

Brim, O., & Ryff, C. (1980). On the properties of life events. In P. Baltes & O. Brim (Eds.), *Life-span development and behavior,* Vol. 3 (pp. 65–102). NY: Academic Press.

Brody, E. (1985). Parent care as a normative family stress. *The Gerontologist, 25,* 19–29.

Bultena, G. (1974). Structural effects on the morale of the aged: A comparison of age-segregated and age-integrated communities. In J. Gubrium (Ed.), *Late life* (pp. 18–31). Springfield, IL: Charles C. Thomas.

Burgess, E. W. (1960). Aging in Western culture. In E. Burgess (Ed.), *Aging in Western societies* (pp. 3–28). Chicago: University of Chicago Press.

Cain, L. (1964). Life course and social structure. In R. Faris (Ed.), *Handbook of modern sociology* (pp. 272–309). Chicago: Rand McNally.

Cain, L. (1967). Age status and generational phenomena: The new old people in contemporary America. *The Gerontologist, 7,* 83–92.

Cain, L. (1987). Alternative perspectives on phenomena of human aging: Age stratification and age status. *Journal of Applied Behavior Science, 23*(2), 227–294.

Cavan, R. S. (1962). Self and role in adjustment during old age. In A. Rose (Ed.), *Human behavior and social processes.* Boston: Houghton Mifflin.

Cavan, R. S., Burgess, E. W., Havighurst, R. J., & Goldhamer, H. (1949). *Personal adjustment in old age.* Chicago: Science Research Associates.

Cicourel, A., Jennings, K., Jennings, S., Leiter, K., Mackay, R., Mehan, H., & Roth, D. (1974). *Language use and school performance.* New York: Academic Press.

Clausen, J. (1972). The life course of individuals. In M. Riley, M. Johnson, and A. Foner (Eds.), *Aging and society. Vol. 3. A sociology of age stratification* (pp. 457–514). New York: Russell Sage Foundation.

Clausen, J. (1986). *The sociology of the life course.* Englewood Cliffs, NJ: Prentice-Hall.

Costa, P., & McCrae, R. (1980). Still stable after all these years: Personality as a key to some issues in adulthood and old age. In P. Baltes & O. Brim (Eds.), *Life-span development and behavior,* Vol. 3 (pp. 65–102). New York: Academic Press.

Cowgill, D. O. (1974). Aging and modernization: A revision of the theory. In J. F. Gubrium (Ed.), *Late life* (pp. 123–146). Springfield, IL: Charles C Thomas.

Cowgill, D. O., & Holmes, L. D. (Eds.). (1972). *Aging and modernization.* New York: Appleton-Century-Crofts.

Cumming, E., & Henry, W. E. (1961). *Growing old: The process of disengagement.* New York: Basic Books.

Cutler, N. (1983). Political behavior of the aged. In D. Woodruff & J. Birren (Eds.), *Aging: Scientific perspectives and social issues,* 2nd edition (409–442). New York: Van Nostrand Reinhold.

Dannefer, D. (1984). Adult development and social theory: A paradigmatic reappraisal. *American Sociological Review, 49,* 100–116.

Dannefer, D. (1987). Aging as intracohort differentiation: Accentuation, the Matthew Effect and the life course. *Sociological Forum, 1,* 8–23.

Dowd, J. J. (1975). Aging as exchange: A preface to theory. *Journal of Gerontology, 30,* 584–594.

Eckert, J. (1980). *The unseen elderly.* San Diego: Campanile Press.

Elder, G. (1974). *Children of the Great Depression.* Chicago: University of Chicago Press.

Elder, G. (1975). Age differentiation and the life course. In A. Inkeles, J. Coleman, & N. Smelser (Eds.), *Annual review of sociology,* Vol. 1 (pp. 165–190). Palo Alto, CA: Annual Reviews.

Estes, C. L. (1979). *The aging enterprise.* San Francisco: Jossey-Bass.

Featherman, D. L. (1983). The life span perspective in social science research. In National Science Foundation (Ed.), *Five year outlook on science and technology,* Vol. 2 (pp. 621–648). Washington, DC: National Science Foundation.

Featherman, D. L., & Lerner, R. M. (1985). Ontogenesis and sociogenesis: Problematics for theory and research about development and socialization across the lifespan. *American Sociological Review, 50,* 659–676.

Foner, A. (1974). Age stratification and age conflict in political life. *American Sociological Review, 39,* 1081–1104.

Foner, A. (Ed.) (1975). *Age in society.* Beverly Hills, CA: Sage.

Foner, A. (1986). *Aging and old age: New perspectives.* Englewood Cliffs, NJ: Prentice-Hall.

Frankfather, D. (1977). *The aged in the community.* New York: Praeger.

Garfinkel, H. (1967). *Studies in ethnomethodology.* Englewood Cliffs, NJ: Prentice-Hall.

Gergen, K. (1980). The emerging crisis in life-span developmental theory. In P. Baltes & O. Brim (Eds.), *Life-span development and behavior* (pp. 31–63). New York: Academic.

Giddens, A. (1976). *New rules of sociological method: A positive critique of interpretive sociologies.* New York: Basic Books.

Gouldner, A. (1970). *The coming crisis in Western sociology.* New York: Basic Books.

Gubrium, J. F. (1973). *The myth of the golden years: A socio-environmental theory of aging.* Springfield, IL: Charles C. Thomas.

Gubrium, J. F., & Buckholdt, D. R. (1977). *Toward maturity: The social processing of human development.* San Francisco: Jossey-Bass.

Gubrium, J. F., & Lynott, R. J. (1983). Rethinking life satisfaction. *Human Organization, 42,* 30–38.

Guillemard, A. M. (Ed.), (1983). *Old age in the welfare state.* Beverly Hills, CA: Sage.

Gutmann, D. (1974). Parenthood: A key to the comparative study of the life cycle. In N. Datan & L. Ginsberg (Eds.), *Life-span development crises: Normative life crises* (pp. 167–184). NY: Academic Press.

Haber, C. (1983). *Beyond sixty-five.* Cambridge: Cambridge University Press.

Hagestad, G. O., & Neugarten, B. L. (1985). Age and the life course. In R. Binstock and E. Shanas (Eds.), *Handbook of aging and the social sciences,* 2nd Edition (pp. 35–61). New York: Van Nostrand Reinhold.

Harris, L., & Associates, Inc. (1975). *The myth and reality of aging in America.* Washington, DC: National Council on Aging.

Havighurst, R. J., & Albrecht, R. (1953). *Older people.* New York: Longmans, Green.

Hendricks, J., & Hendricks, C. (1986). *Aging in mass society: Myths and realities,* 3rd Edition. Boston, MA: Little, Brown.

Hess, B. (1985). Aging policies and old women: The hidden agenda. In A. Rossi (Ed.), *Gender and the life course* (pp. 319–331). New York: Aldine.

Hochschild, A. (1973). *The unexpected community.* Englewood Cliffs, NJ: Prentice-Hall.

Hochschild, A. (1975). Disengagement theory: A critique and proposal. *American Sociological Review, 40,* 553–569.

Hochschild, A. (1976). Disengagement theory: A logical, empirical, and phenomenological critique. In J. F. Gubrium (Ed.), *Time, roles, and self in old age* (pp. 53–87). New York: Human Sciences Press.

Hogan, D. (1980). The transition to adulthood as a career contingency. *American Sociological Review, 45,* 261–276.

Hogan, D. (1981). *Transitions and social change: The early lives of American men.* New York: Academic Press.

Homans, G. C. (1961). *Social behavior: Its elementary forms.* New York: Harcourt Brace Jovanovich.

Jacobs, J. (1975). *Older persons and retirement communities.* Springfield, IL: Charles C. Thomas.

Kingson, E. R., Hirshorn, B., & Cornman, J. (1986). *Ties that bind: The interdependence of generations.* Washington, DC: Seven Locks Press.

Kohli, M. (1986). The world we forgot: An historical review of the life course. In V. W. Marshall (Ed.), *Later life: The social psychology of aging* (pp. 271–303). Beverly Hills, CA: Sage Publications.

Kuypers, J. A., & Bengtson, V. L. (1973). Social breakdown and competence: A model of normal aging. *Human Development, 16,* 181–201.

Laslett, P. (1965). *The world we have lost.* London: Methuen.

Lawrence, B. (1984). Age grading: The implicit organizational timetable. *Journal of Occupational Behavior, 5,* 23–35.

Lawton, M. P. (1983). Environment and other determinents of well being in older people. *The Gerontologist, 23,* 349–357.

Lemon, B. W., Bengtson, V. L., & Peterson, J. A. (1972). An exploration of the activity theory of aging: Activity types and life satisfaction among in-movers to a retirement community. *Journal of Gerontology, 27,* 511–523.

Longman, P. (1985, June). Justice between generations. *Atlantic Monthly,* 73–81.

Lowy, L. (1985). *Social work with the aging: The challenges and promises of the later years.* New York: Longman.

Lynott, R. (1983). Alzheimer's disease and institutionalization: The ongoing construction of a decision. *Journal of Family Issues, 4,* 559–574.

Maddox, G. (1964). Disengagement theory: A critical evaluation. *The Gerontologist, 4,* 80–82.

Mannheim, K. (1928, 1952). The problem of generations. In D. Kecskemeti (Ed.), *Essays on the sociology of knowledge* (pp. 276–322). London: Routledge and Kegan Paul.

Marx, K. (1867, 1946). *Das Kapital.* New York: Modern Library.

Matthews, S. H. (1979). *Social world of old women.* Beverly Hills, CA: Sage.

Mead, G. H. (1934). *Mind, self, and society.* Chicago: University of Chicago Press.

Messer, M. (1967). The possibility of an age-concentrated environment becoming a normative system. *The Gerontologist, 7,* 247–250.

Myerhoff, B. (1978). *Number our days.* New York: Simon and Schuster.

Neugarten, B. L. (1974). Age groups in American society and the rise of the young old. *Annals of the American Academy of Political and Social Science, 415,* 187–198.

Neugarten, B. L. & Hagestad, G. O. (1976). Age and the life course. In R. Binstock & E. Shanas (Eds.), *Handbook of aging and the social sciences,* 1st edition (pp. 35–55). New York: Van Nostrand Reinhold.

Neugarten, B. L., Moore, J., & Lowe, J. (1965). Age norms, age constraints, and adult socialization. *American Journal of Sociology, 70,* 710–717.

Olson, L. K. (1982). *The political economy of aging.* New York: Columbia University Press.

Palmore, E. B. (1968). The effects of aging on activities and attitudes. *The Gerontologist, 8,* 259–263.

Palmore, E. B., & Manton, K. (1974). Modernization and status of the aged: International correlations. *Journal of Gerontology, 29,* 205–210.

Parsons, T. (1951). *The social system.* New York: Free Press.

Pfohl, S. (1978). *Predicting dangerousness.* Lexington, MA: Lexington Books.

Phillipson, C. (1982). *Capitalism and the construction of old age.* London: Macmillan.

Preston, S. (1984). Children and the elderly: Divergent paths for America's dependents. *Demography, 21,* 435–457.

Quadagno, J. S. (1982). *Aging in early industrial society.* New York: Academic Press.

Riley, M. W. (1971). Social gerontology and the age stratification of society. *The Gerontologist, 11,* 79–87.

Riley, M. W. (1987). On the significance of age in sociology. *American Sociological Review, 52,* 1–14.

Riley, M. W., Johnson, M., & Foner, A. (1972). *Aging and society, Vol. 3: A sociology of age stratification.* New York: Russell Sage Foundation.

Rose, A. M. (1964). A current theoretical issue in social gerontology. *The Gerontologist, 4,* 46–50.

Rose, A. M. (1965). The subculture of aging: A framework for research in social gerontology. In A. M. Rose and W. A. Peterson (Ed.), *Older people and their social world* (pp. 3–16). Philadelphia: F. A. Davis.

Rosow, I. (1974). *Socialization to old age.* Berkeley, CA: University of California Press.

Ross, J. (1977). *Old people, new lives.* Chicago: University of Chicago Press.

Schaie, K. W. (1979). The primary mental abilities in adulthood: An exploration in the development of psychometric intelligence. In P. Baltes & O. Brim (Eds.), *Life-span development and behavior,* Vol. 2 (pp. 68–117). New York: Academic Press.

Schutz, A. (1967). *The phenomenology of the social world.* Introduction by George Walsh. Evanston, IL: Northwestern University Press.

Schutz, A. (1970). *On phenomenology and social relations.* (trans. by H. Wagner). Chicago: University of Chicago Press.

Sherman, E. (1981). *Counseling the aging: An integrative approach.* New York: Free Press.

Simmons, L. (1945). *The role of the aged in primitive society.* New Haven, CT: Yale University Press.

Speier, M. (1970). The everyday world of the child. In J. Douglas (Ed.), *Understanding Everyday Life.* Chicago: Aldine.

Starr, J. M. (1982–1983). Toward a social phenomenology of aging: Studying the self process in biographical work. *International Journal of Aging and Human Development, 16,* 255–270.

Stearns, P. N. (1982). *Old age in preindustrial society.* New York: Holmes and Meier.

Stephens, J. (1976). *Loners, losers, and lovers.* Seattle, WA: University of Washington Press.

Streib, G. F. (1965). Are the aged a minority group? In A. Gouldner & S. Miller (Eds.), *Applied sociology* (pp. 311–328). New York: Free Press.

Streib, G. F. (1985). Social stratification and aging. In R. Binstock & E. Shanas (Eds.), *Handbook of aging and the social sciences,* 2nd edition (pp. 339–368). New York: Van Nostrand Reinhold.

Streib, G. F., & Bourg, C. J. (1984). Age stratification theory, inequality, and social change. *Comparative Social Research, 7,* 63–77.

Teski, M. (1979). *Living together.* Washington, DC: University Press of America.

Treas, J., & Passuth, P. (in press). The three sociologies: Age, aging, and the aged. In E. Borgatta and K. Cook (Eds.), *The future of sociology.* Beverly Hills, CA: Sage.

Troll, L., Israel, J., & Israel, K. (1977). *Looking ahead: A woman's guide to the problems and joys of growing older.* Englewood Hills, NJ: Prentice-Hall.

Turner, J. (1978). *The structure of sociological theory* (2nd ed.). Homewood, IL: The Dorsey Press.

Walker, A. (1981). Towards a political economy of old age. *Aging and Society, 1,* 73–94.

Zeitlin, I. (1973). *Rethinking sociology: A critique of contemporary theory.* New York: Appleton-Century-Crofts.

Zusman, J. (1966). Some explanations of the changing appearance of psychotic patients: Antecedents of the social breakdown syndrome concept. *Millbank Memorial Fund Quarterly, 64,* 63–84.

2

Age Integration and the Lives of Older People

MATILDA WHITE RILEY
JOHN W. RILEY, JR.

Riley and Riley argue that our currently age-differentiated society will give
way to an age-integrated one. Age will lose its power to constrain people's
entry, exit, and performance in such basic social institutions as education,
work, and retirement. Revolutionary changes toward age integration are
needed to reduce the "structural lag," in which the dynamism of human
aging is outpacing the dynamism of structural change. To guide these
changes, research on aging must complement existing knowledge about
human lives with new and deeper understanding of the social structures that
shape and are shaped by them.

In this article we postulate—as a theme for continuing discussion—a veritable revolution in the age structure of society. Over the next several decades, the familiar social structures of work, retirement, and education will be virtually transformed. Age will have lost its current power to determine when people should enter or leave these basic social structures; nor will age any longer constrain expectations as to how people should perform. This structural revolution can mean a greater *age integration* of society. Beginning with older people, it can enhance the lives of people of every age.

We present this theme as a challenge toward current planning for future research, public policy, and professional practice. While the prediction may be visionary, our argument is not without scientific guidance. It rests on a basic proposition from the sociology of age: that, in all known societies, human aging and changing social structures are distinct but interdependent dynamisms. Each influences the other (Riley, Johnson, & Foner, 1972). In modern societies, however, a perplexing problem has been developing for many decades: the dynamism of aging has been outrunning the dynamism of structural change. This is the problem we call "structural lag" (Riley, 1988). Essentially, there is an imbalance between the mounting numbers of long-lived people (the unprecedented transformation of aging) and the lack of productive and meaningful role opportunities—or places in the social structure—that can recognize, foster, and reward these capacities. We draw attention now to the need for age integration, before the 21st century inundation of "baby boom" cohorts can exacerbate the structural lag and over-whelm the societal order.

Structural Lag

The 20th century has experienced a revolution in people's lives, now well-known and documented. With increases in longevity at birth, nearly three decades have been added to the average length of life, more than was previously added in all of human history. These added years have been accompanied by dramatic alterations in the ways people grow up and grow old. For older people, nearly one-third of adult life is now spent in what has become "modern" retirement (cf. Torrey, 1982). Yet ironically, only a minority of older people are so frail or disabled as to need support *from* society; instead, the majority are comparatively "robust" (to use Richard Suzman's term) and capable of making con-tributions *to* society. Figure 2-1 gives graphic evidence of the overwhelming numbers of older people today who are robust (neither fully disabled nor institutionalized)—and of

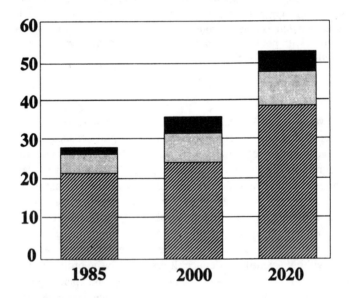

■ In nursing home

▨ Disabled, still at home

▨ No serious disability

FIGURE 2-1   Frail vs "robust" older people 65 and over (population in millions). *(Source: Manton, Stallard and Singer, 1992)*

the greatly enlarged numbers who will be robust in the 21st century (cf. Suzman, Harris, Hadley, Kovar, & Weindruch, 1992). The projections do not include the most recent indications that, on the average, age-specific functioning may be improving.

In contrast to the revolution in people's lives, however, there has been no comparable revolution in the age structures of society. To be sure, many changes have been made in ways of caring for the frail and disabled, but meaningful and institutionalized role opportunities for the robust and capable have lagged behind. Thus, a structural revolution now awaits the 21st century. Increasing numbers of capable, motivated, and potentially productive older people cannot long coexist with empty role structures. Something has to give.

There is a message here: imminent changes (to use Sorokin's term) are underway that can help to offset the structural lag. These changes—though latent—are intrinsic to the continuing societal interplay between changing lives and changing social structures. In this article, we first examine such revolutionary changes by counterposing two ideal types of age structures: a familiar or "age-differentiated" type which is characterized by the lag, and a new or "age-integrated" type which theoretically has the potential to reduce it. We then note a few evidences of age integration in the structures of modern societies, and propose that further scientific, professional, and policy attention be paid to these evidences and their implications.

"IDEAL TYPES" OF AGE STRUCTURES

These "ideal types" of age structure, as schematized in Figure 2-2, are but heuristic devices to aid understanding. In Max Weber's sense, they are artificially simplistic. They may never exist in reality, but are idealized selections from it. Yet they prompt us to think of key elements of one type as reflective of the reality of the recent past, and key elements of the other as potentially prophetic of real directions for the future. Let us be more specific.

Age-Differentiated Structures

At one extreme (at the left of Figure 2-2), age-differentiated structures divide societal roles into three parts: retirement or leisure for older people, work roles for the middle-aged, and educational roles for the young. This type of structure is commonplace today. It so closely approximates the actual experiences of the 20th century as to allow detailed scientific analysis (e.g., Henrichs, Roche, & Sirianni, 1991; Mayer & Schoepflin, 1989). Today, however, we believe that these age-based structures and norms can often be seen as vestigial remains of an earlier era when most people had died before their work was finished or their last child had left home. For example, age 65, established as the criterion for insurance eligibility in 19th-century Germany, is still widely used under utterly changed contemporary conditions.

Despite its failure to accommodate people's changing lives, this conventional age differentiation is continually reinforced. It has been appropriate for societies where paid work is the predominant role, and achievement (or material "success") the predominant value. In particular, this age-differentiated type is bolstered by "ageism," the mistaken but stubborn belief in universal and inevitable decline because of aging: e.g.,

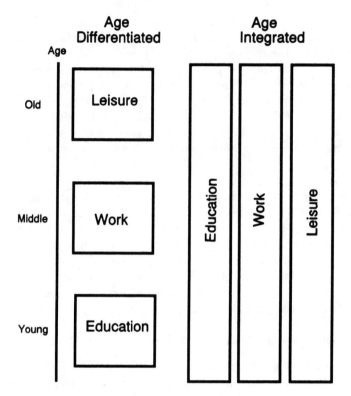

FIGURE 2-2   Ideal types of social structures.

older workers, even those in their 50s, are erroneously believed to have inevitably lost their efficiency. Moreover, the familiar age-based divisions among education, work, and retirement offer many advantages: they provide orderliness as they have become "institutionalized" in people's lives; they are a societal convenience; and they are typically accepted without question. Examples of their persistence are easy to find. Thus, as the baby boom cohorts in the United States flooded entry-level jobs in the work-force, there were heavy social pressures and corporate inducements for older people— well before age 60—to make room for them through "early retirement." Paradoxically, while the age of exit from work has been declining, the age of exit from education and entry into work has been rising. Martin Kohli (1988), writing about the "tripartite" division of the life course, states the absurd extreme this way:

> If we extrapolate the trend of the last two decades, we shall, somewhere in the second half of the twenty-first century, reach the point where at the age of about 38, people move from the university directly into retirement.

Yet, history is not unidirectional and trends in one direction cannot persist indefinitely. Lives are changing, but structures lag behind.

Age-Integrated Structures

Age-integrated structures, at the right of Figure 2-2, stand in sharp contrast to the ideal type of age-differentiated structures. Here (within the limits set by biology) the age barriers are removed. Role opportunities in *all* structures—education, work, and leisure—are open to people of *every* age. This means that throughout society people of all ages are brought together—they are "integrated." Neither teenagers nor retirees are excluded from worksites because of age. There are nursery schools for the very young, and universities are open to adults of all ages, including the old. Extended opportunities for leisure and freedom from work are available even to those in the typically overburdened middle years, rather than being reserved almost exclusively for the "roleless role" of older people, to use Ernest Burgess's well-known expression.

Ideally, such age-integrated structures would have revolutionary consequences. They would open to older people the full range of role choices. And, in changing the opportunities for older people, new opportunities would be unlocked for everyone. For the middle-aged, there would be reductions in the strains imposed by multiple roles—when work is combined with family, homemaking, and health care, as well as with leadership in politics, religion, and community service. Ideally, too, such age-integrated structures would lead to the often proposed "reconstruction of the life course," providing options for people over their entire lives to intersperse periods of work with periods of education and of leisure. And for the society, these structures would broaden the economic base for support of that minority of older people who are frail and needy.

In reality, as ideal types confront real-world exigencies, we have little first-hand experience for specifying the nature of age integration under modern conditions. For example, how might an age-integrated society cope with the widely shifting economic balance between demand and supply for labor (e.g., Sheppard, 1989)? Can mechanisms be designed for spreading more evenly across the range of ages those jobs that are actually available at particular times? Or if age criteria were no longer to control access to work roles, or to other roles in education, family, and health care institutions, what new criteria—of achievement or of need—could be fashioned to replace them (cf. Riley & Schrank, 1972)? Such issues have not gone unnoticed in the gerontological literature: witness, for example, the earlier discussion of an "age irrelevant" society by Bernice Neugarten (Neugarten & Hagestad, 1976); or Barbara Silverstone's (1992) call for a "new view of aging" that would raise to 75 the age of eligibility for Social Security in the United States.

Fuller analytical understanding of how these ideal types might correspond to reality is needed—and urgently. Already the increases in numbers of capable retired people are far outstripping the numbers of younger people who are actively contributing to the economy (cf. Binstock, 1992). And already the metamorphoses in longevity and technology, and the long-range shift toward "contingent" rather than lifetime careers, are pressing toward the flexible boundaries that would characterize age-integrated structures. Paradoxically, while the typical life course becomes *longer,* the half-life of most occupations becomes *shorter.* Medical doctors and nurses, after many years of training, find themselves out-of-date after only a few years of practice. As workers over their lifetime change jobs (and sometimes occupations) as many as eight times, engineers, insurance salespersons, taxi drivers, bankers, computer operators, practicing gerontologists—indeed everyone—is required to relearn and to seek ways of interspersing periods of work with periods of learning and retraining. Thus, strong pressures are already operating to alter societal structures in the age-integrated direction.

TOWARD AGE-INTEGRATED STRUCTURES

Where does this typology leave us? It alerts us, we believe, to real tendencies toward age integration which are already emerging, and which hold far-flung implications and issues for both individuals and society.

Alterability

Parallel to the fallacious belief that the aging process is fixed and immutable is another belief—also fallacious—that social structures, because they ordinarily persist beyond the lifetimes of the individuals passing through, are impervious to alteration. Yet institutions and roles continually change and can often *be* changed, as history has demonstrated. Familiar evidences of structural alterability are the changing ages for marrying, bearing children, leaving school, or leaving the labor force. Somewhat less familiar is the variability in the United States in the age of entry into school. Historians (cf. Angus, Mirel, & Vinovskis, 1988) tell of 19th century "infant schools" where 3-year-olds were taught to read and precocity was encouraged. This was followed, however, by a drastic raising of the age of "reading readiness" as a fear of early learning, even leading to insanity, developed. Only recently has this age criterion for school entry relaxed again, with the current development of nursery schools and infant day care. Even less well-known are the historical changes in age criteria for serving in the military: during the American Civil War, soldiers were reported to range in age from 11 to 61 (Vinovskis, 1989), a far cry from the age requirements in the military today. Such evidences of alterability in the past make clear the future possibilities for age flexibility in social structures.

Evidences of Change

Today, in many countries and in diverse domains, research is beginning to disclose numerous evidences that structures are indeed changing, that the familiar age barriers are weakening, and that deliberate interventions to offset structural lag are feasible. Various aspects of the ideal type of an age-integrated society may not after all be purely visionary. Here are a few examples:

In education, roles are no longer confined largely to the young. Opportunities are being made for older people to engage in teaching (e.g., teaching adults who cannot read, or immigrants who cannot speak the language). Other opportunities are being made for older people to go back to school. For example, according to some U.S. reports, nearly 1,000 colleges now make plans for students over age 65. And, as such structural interventions are focused on older people, they tend to integrate people of all ages. Thus, in a college classroom, making room for older adults brings them together with traditional students who are younger, and with teachers who too are often younger.

Similarly, at work, roles are less exclusively confined to the middle years. Given the ups and downs in the economy, and the recent reorganization of firms to increase productivity per worker, the age patterning of work has become more variable (Henretta, 1992). In the late 1980s in the U.S., various reports showed that 44% of all employers had programs for part-time work, 14% sponsored sabbatical leaves, 40% made "flextime" available (Dychtwald, 1989). Some companies have model programs for "unretirement," rehiring retired employees, providing part-time employment, retraining older adults or preparing them for new occupations. There are opportunities for some older people to become entrepreneurs, and for others to "moonlight" in work that is not officially reported. There are growing demands for older people in the role of care*giver* (rather than care*receiver*). There are increasingly varied and significant opportunities for many kinds of volunteer jobs.

At the other end of the age range, many teenagers work part-time, often alongside middle-aged and older workers who may serve as mentors. Despite its rigidity as a "tracking" system, the German model of combining schooling of the young with on-the-job apprenticeship to the mature is having an impact on educational systems elsewhere. The rising numbers of working mothers often mean that even very young children have assigned tasks along with their elders in the home; and educators are discovering the reciprocal advantages of children teaching children.

Particularly important for the emergence of age integration are public policies and their latent consequences. As one example, Anne-Marie Guillemard (1990) has analyzed reports from several European countries that show how the pathways leading from work to retirement are being rerouted because of the transformation of the welfare system. Public pension plans, which once sustained *age-differentiated* structures, are breaking down with the rise of insurance programs for disability and for unemployment—which operate irrespective of age. As Prof. Guillemard puts it, age criteria for leaving work are giving way to functional criteria, and "old age, retirement, and withdrawal from the labor force no longer coincide."

All such structural interventions are tending to produce new and more flexible roles; and this means wider options for people of every age, and in particular for the competent elderly. If given such options, some old people will opt to remain in the economic mainstream of society. (One U.S. study shows that substantial minorities of early retirees would prefer to work if opportunity afforded; see Harris, 1990.) Other older people will choose education. Others will opt for leisure activities, often combined with householding. Still others will undertake volunteer roles. Today, older people are widely heterogeneous (cf. Nelson & Dannefer, 1992); ideally, they require a wide diversity of roles. But one thing is clear: the wish of *all* older people is *not* for roles in which they are disregarded, denigrated, or dependent.

Unintended Consequences

Many such considerations, then, are providing the fuel for the imminent changes which are operating below the surface of our conventional age-differentiated society. These changes show that the difficulty of reducing the structural lag lies, not in any inevitable inflexibility of age structures, but rather in understanding how the changes occur and how particular *interventions* can operate to benefit, rather than damage, both individuals and society (Riley & Riley, 1989). Unguided interventions to reinforce the inherent tendencies toward age integration can sometimes have unintended, even undesired, consequences. For example, if flexibility of age criteria were pushed too far, the well-known dangers of exploiting the labor of children or older people could rear their ugly heads. Or, entitlements to leisure and relaxation in retirement—as these might be distributed more fairly than at present—could be threatened. Clearly, a broad vision of the future and a sound knowledge base are essential here for guiding interventions—as interventions, explicit or implicit, are continually being undertaken through public or private policies, professional practice, or people's everyday lives.

OTHER SOCIETAL CHANGES IMPLICATED

Social science theories point immediately to other revolutionary aspects of this broad vision. Among them, we conclude this article by noting forms of societal integration and change that are implicated in the potentially emerging ideal type of an age-integrated society, and that raise future issues of gerontological concern.

Most immediately, age integration emphasizes that older people cannot be viewed in isolation. Changes affecting older people tend to ramify throughout the society to affect those of every age and, in turn, to have further consequences for older people themselves (cf. Foner, 1982; Riley, 1978). Lessons learned from aging research disclose many primordial truths about humanity.

Moreover, age integration evokes new forms of *institutional integration*. As roles in work, education, or leisure intersect with roles in other social institutions, old structures give way to new hybrids. For example, corporations become integrated with schools as they provide worker education, and also with families as they provide day-care for employees' children and frail parents, or as technological advances allow jobs to be performed in the home.

Gender integration is already being produced by the extraordinary increases in women's participation in the labor force which bring men and women together at work as well as in the family. Yet the changes in women's roles have primarily affected the years of adulthood prior to retirement. Thus the dual burdens of work inside and outside the home are heavily concentrated among the middle-aged. And the structural lag is exacerbated.

In addition, age integration raises critical issues of *values,* as the norms to which today's middle-aged people have been socialized encounter the exigencies of old age in an utterly changed future society. What changes in achievement values and consumption aspirations would be needed in an age-integrated society if many older individuals, rather than retiring, were to undertake new assignments that bring rewards and benefits lower than their former levels of pay or prestige? What added increments of social involvement would justify the economic decrements? Already in the U.S., some companies have been experimenting with programs to convince middle-aged employees, even business school graduates, that they can find rewards and satisfaction by moving laterally, rather than upward, on occupational ladders. For the future, is it likely that nonmonetary rewards of "success" and "consumerism" will be modulated by renewed emphases on other rewards, such as new types of recognition in the world of work, affection and response from family and friends, recognition for cultural pursuits, or pleasure in new adventure? Is it likely that the current principle of "rights" for older people will be counterbalanced by the principle of "responsibilities" for those capable older people who are competent and motivated to be active participants in society? Resistance to such change is illustrated by the abortive efforts by the International Federation on Aging, in preparing for the 1992 World Assembly on Aging, to include "responsibilities" along with "rights" in its declaration.

FUTURE ISSUES

In this brief research-based essay, we have outlined possible revolutionary changes from a social structure that is primarily age-differentiated toward one that may encompass major elements of age integration. We have suggested that changes toward age integration will implicate broader changes as well: institutional integration, gender integration, changes in values. We have noted latent tendencies that, if they in fact coalesce toward a new societal integration, will reduce structural lag. These inherent tendencies will mean that many people in their later years will be productive assets, rather than burdens, on the economy. And in turn, these inherent tendencies will also unlock future potentials for people's lives: providing wider options for shaping the entire life course; reducing middle-age burdens of piled up responsibilities of work and family; protecting against ageism and discrimination for those elders still wanting to work; enhancing the health and well-being which comes (as massive gerontological research has shown) from all types of sustained active participation.

Like other structural changes sweeping through the world today, such tendencies toward structural integration raise new issues demanding new attention. These tendencies will reach their potential only through innovative, even radical, policies and practices that emanate from laborious and often unglamorous scientific research, and from evolving understandings. In our time, few efforts have been made to reach such understandings (but see Riley, 1978; Riley & Riley, 1991). While much has been learned about aging processes and the dynamic aspects of human lives (cf. Riley & Abeles, 1990; Riley & Riley, 1992), relatively little has been learned about the roles, institutions, and cultural norms that shape these lives and, in turn, are shaped *by* them. One current effort in search of deeper understandings is the Program on Age and Structural Change (PASC) at the National Institute on Aging. Involving a network of scholars, PASC focuses on this neglected area: it aims toward understanding *structural* opportunities and constraints (in Robert Merton's sense) that affect the quality of aging from birth to death.

We salute this objective, and we seek suggestions, criticisms, and help from interested members of the gerontological community.

Some of the ideas in this article were presented at the 1990 Madrid meetings of the International Sociological Association. We appreciate comments on earlier versions of the manuscript from David P. Willis, Anne Foner, Karyn Loscocco, Karin Mack, and other members of the PASC Network, and from anonymous reviewers.

REFERENCES

Angus, D. L., Mirel, J. E., & Vinovskis, M. A. (1988). Historical development of age stratification in schooling. Columbia University, *Teachers College Record, 90,* 211–236.

Binstock, R. H. (1992). The oldest old and "intergenerational equity." In R. M. Suzman, D. P. Willis, & K. G. Manton (Eds.), *The oldest old* (pp. 394–417). New York: Oxford University Press.

Dychtwald, K. (1989). *Age wave: The challenges and opportunities of an aging America.* Los Angeles: Jeremy P. Tarcher.

Foner, A. (1982). Perspectives on changing age systems. In M. W. Riley, R. P. Abeles, & M. S. Teitelbaum (Eds.), *Aging from birth to death: Vol. II, Sociotemporal perspectives.* (pp. 217–228). AAAS Selected Symposium 79, Boulder, CO: Westview.

Guillemard, A.-M. (1990). Reorganizing the transition from work to retirement: Is chronological age still the major criterion determining definitive exit from work? Paper presented at the XII World Congress of Sociology, Madrid, July 9–13.

Harris, L., & Associates (1990). *Aging in the eighties: America in transition.* Washington, DC: National Council on the Aging.

Henretta, J. C. (1992). Uniformity and diversity: Life course institutionalization and late-life work exit. *The Sociological Quarterly, 33,* 265–279.

Henrichs, C., Roche, W., & Sirianni, C. (1991). *Working time in transition.* Philadelphia: Temple University Press.

Kohli, M. (1988). *New patterns of transition to retirement in West Germany.* Tampa, FL: International Exchange Center on Gerontology, University of South Florida.

Manton, K. G., Stallard, E., & Singer, B. H. (1992). Projecting the future size and health status of the U.S. elderly population. *International Journal of Forecasting, 8,* 433–458.

Mayer, K. U., & Schoepflin, U. (1989). The state and the life course. *Annual Review of Sociology, 15,* 187–209.

Nelson, E. A., & Dannefer, D. (1992). Aged heterogeneity: Fact or fiction? *The Gerontologist, 22,* 17–23.

Neugarten, B. L., & Hagestad, G. O. (1976). Age and the life course. In R. H. Binstock & E. Shanas (Eds.). *Handbook of Aging and the Social Sciences* (pp. 35–55). New York: Van Nostrand Reinhold Company.

Riley, M. W. (1978). Aging, social change, and the power of ideas. *Daedalus, 107,* 39–52.

Riley, M. W. (1988). The aging society: Problems and prospects. *Proceedings of the American Philosophical Society, 132,* 148–153.

Riley, M. W., & Abeles, R. P. (1990). *The behavioral and social research program at the National Institute on Aging: History of a decade.* Working Document. Bethesda, MD: Behavioral and Social Research, National Institutes of Health.

Riley, M. W., & Bond, K. (1983). Beyond ageism: Postponing the onset of disability. In M. W. Riley, B. B. Hess, & K. Bond (Eds.) *Aging in society: Selected reviews of recent research* (pp. 243–252). Hillsdale, NY: Lawrence Erlbaum.

Riley, M. W., Johnson, M., & Foner, A. (1972). Aging and society. Vol. III. *A sociology of age stratification.* New York: Russell Sage Foundation.

Riley, M. W., & Riley, J. W., Jr. (1989). The lives of older people and changing social roles. In M. W. Riley & J. W. Riley Jr. (Eds.). *The quality of aging: Strategies for interventions,* special issue of *The Annals* of the American Academy of Political and Social Science (pp. 14–28). Newbury Park, CA: Sage.

Riley, M. W., & Riley, J. W., Jr. (1991). Vieillesse et changement des roles sociaux. [The lives of older people and changing social roles]. *Gerontologie et Societe, 56,* 6–14.

Riley, M. W., & Riley, J. W., Jr. (1992). Die individuellen und gesellschaftslichen potentials. In P. Baltes (Ed.), *Das Alter and und die Zukunft der Gesellschaft.* [Individual and social potentials]. Berlin: Walter de Gruyter.

Riley, M. W., & Schrank, H. (1972). The work force. In M. W. Riley, M. Johnson, & A. Foner

(Eds.), *Aging and society, Vol. III: A sociology of age stratification* (pp. 160–197). New York: Russell Sage Foundation.

Sheppard, H. L. (Ed.) (1989). *The Future of older workers.* Tampa, FL: International Exchange Center on Gerontology, University of South Florida.

Silverstone, B. (1992). A gerontological perspective on the 1992 presidential election and beyond. Beattie Award Lecture, conference of the State Society on Aging of New York, Albany.

Suzman, R. M., Harris, T., Hadley, E. C., Kovar, M. G., & Weindruch, R. (1992). The robust oldest old: Optimistic perspectives. In R. M. Suzman, D. P. Willis, & K. G. Manton (Eds.), *The oldest old* (pp. 341–348). New York: Oxford University Press.

Torrey, B. B. (1982). The lengthening of retirement. In M. W. Riley, R. P. Abeles, & M. S. Teitelbaum (Eds.), *Aging from birth to death: Vol. II: Sociotemporal perspectives.* Boulder, CO: Westview Press.

Vinovskis, M. A. (1989). Have historians lost the Civil War? Some preliminary demographic speculations. *Journal of American History, 76,* 34–58.

II

HISTORICAL PERSPECTIVES

Until the mid-1970s, sociological research on the status of the elderly was based on theoretical claims that had little basis in historical evidence. The dominant paradigm was established by modernization theorists who argued that in the past the old had held power within extended family households, had ruled government councils, and had been venerated for their wisdom. With modernization came a loss in their status as a result of four factors: health technology, economic technology, urbanization, and mass education. Modern health technology extended life expectancy and multiplied the number of older people; economic technology created new occupations and made the skills of older workers obsolete; urbanization brought the young to the cities and destroyed the extended family unit; and the growth of mass education undermined the wisdom of age (Cowgill and Holmes, 1972).

Modernization theory was challenged on a number of fronts. Its critics argued that extensive variation in the treatment of the aged could be documented among societies at all levels of development, that the position of the aged was never so universally exalted, and that modernization had positive as well as negative consequences for older people (Quadagno, 1982).

THE CHALLENGE OF HISTORY

The most direct attack on modernization theory came from historians. The first to take up the challenge was David Hackett Fischer (1978). Fischer agreed with modernization theorists that older people were venerated in the past and that their status had declined in more recent times, but he argued that the decline occurred well before industrialization or modernization had any effect. Instead, according to Fischer, the "cult of age" disappeared between 1770 and 1820, as the ideals of the French Revolution of equality and liberty spread to American society. The ideal of equality destroyed the hierarchical conception of the world on which the authority of age had rested, while the ideal of liberty dissolved the communal base of power. A once firmly established gerontocracy gave way to a society that favored youth.

In his book *Old Age in the New Land* (1978), W. Andrew Achenbaum agreed with Fischer that cultural beliefs rather than political or economic change determined the social worth of older people, and that veneration of the aged had been replaced by more negative perceptions. He disagreed, however, on when the turning point in age relations had occurred. According to Achenbaum, it wasn't until after the Civil War that negative views of the elderly became more prominent. Between 1790 and 1860, the elderly were perceived as indispensable. They provided valuable insights about healthful longevity and served as ideally qualified moral exemplars. Although most Americans were also aware that afflictions like declining health or economic insecurity accompanied aging, they believed that the ability of the aged to overcome these difficulties only increased their value to society. The reading by W. Andrew Achenbaum provides evidence of the positive view of age that dominated American culture before 1860.

THE DIVERSITY OF OLD AGE

Although the historian's challenge to modernization theory undermined some faulty theoretical premises, a unified vision of the aged in the past was perpetuated, in what the British historian Peter Laslett (1976) termed "the world we have lost syndrome." Other historical research has since demonstrated that, even in the colonial period, wide variation in the treatment of the aged existed.

The type of evidence used determined whether the elderly were seen as universally venerated or whether there was greater variation in the position of the aged. When the emphasis was on cultural beliefs about the elderly, the conclusions were more positive. When historians turned from cultural evidence to the kind of social and economic indices more commonly used by social scientists, it became clear that in every historical period, some elderly always fared better than others. In the nineteenth century, for example, some older men continued working until they died, often moving from good jobs to increasingly poorer, lower paying jobs. Others became unemployed and never found new jobs. A privileged few retired comfortably. Widows nearly always faced economic hardships.

Similarly, studies of the family life of older people revealed complex patterns of family structure. Some older people resided with their spouse and children, some lived alone, while others lived in institutions. The reading by Carole Haber and Brian Gratton from their book *Old Age and the Search for Security,* describes the family life of the aged from the colonial period to the twentieth century.

Increasingly, the questions asked by historians and the kind of evidence they use to answer these questions have corresponded with the concerns of social scientists. Simultaneously, social science research has become better informed by history, and the ahistorical assumptions of deterministic theories have been abandoned. We now know that the premodern period was neither golden nor uniform, and that in every historical period older people who possessed few assets or economic resources received no automatic rewards with advancing age.

REFERENCES

Achenbaum, W. Andrew. *Old Age in the New Land.* Baltimore: Johns Hopkins University Press, 1978.
Cowgill, Donald, and Lowell Holmes. *Aging and Modernization.* New York: Appleton-Century-Crofts, 1972.

Fischer, David Hackett. *Growing Old in America.* New York: Oxford University Press, 1978.

Haber, Carole, and Brian Gratton. *Old Age and the Search for Security.* Bloomington: Indiana University Press, 1994.

Laslett, Peter. "Societal Development and Aging." Pp. 87–116 in Robert Binstock and Ethel Shanas (eds.), *Handbook of Aging and the Social Sciences.* New York: Van Nostrand Reinhold, 1976.

Quadagno, Jill. *Aging in Early Industrial Society: Work, Family and Social Policy in Nineteenth Century England.* New York: Academic Press, 1982.

3

The Usefulness of Old Age

W. ANDREW ACHENBAUM

In this reading, Achenbaum argues that, from 1790 to 1860, the elderly were highly valued. Not only did they provide exemplars of life-styles that promoted longevity and morality, but they also contributed to American society through their participation in varied and valuable roles in economic, domestic, and political life. Achenbaum's historical evidence contradicts the notion of other historians that the United States was a "young land for young people."

Many images of old age that circulated in the United States from 1790 to 1860 resemble those that flourish today. Etchings, photographs, and prints of that period generally reveal the same gray hairs and deeply lined faces. They sometimes accentuate the economic and physical problems we still associate with being old. Graphics also confirm that the circumstances and experiences of pre–Civil War elderly Indians, blacks, and whites were no less diverse and that their various difficulties were no less acute than they are in the 1970s. Furthermore, the writings of the era—ranging from classic literature to popular almanacs and from poems to public documents—indicate that, like us, people faced the eternal advantages and hardships of growing old with a mixture of fear, dismay, and joy, acceptance, ambivalence, and reluctance. Visions of happiness and personal fulfillment as well as the specter of misery and despair were just as "real" then as they are now. And yet, for all these similarities, it becomes quickly apparent that some fundamental changes have taken place over time.

One of the most striking differences is in the way early Americans defined older people's place in society. Our predecessors would have been surprised to learn that the elderly as a group would be described one day as roleless and unproductive persons who inevitably and willingly disengage from active life. In sharp contrast, Americans between the Revolutionary and Civil wars believed that their infant republic depended upon the commitment and ability of men and women of all ages to work together in creating a new society. An orator elaborated on this idea during groundbreaking ceremonies for a new canal in Ohio on 4 July 1825. The state's ability to tap the resources of all its citizens, he remarked, provided it "at once, all the vigor and firmness of youth, the strength and firmness of manhood, and the wisdom of age. Great as is the undertaking, your powers are equal to its completion; be but united, firm and persevering, and if heaven smile on your labors, success is sure."[1] Americans claimed that the elderly, by complementing other age groups' assets, were indispensable in establishing a *novus ordo seclorum*—a new order of the ages—as the Great Seal of the United States proudly declared. Indeed, ministers, scientists, essayists, and editors among others asserted in their writings that a lifetime of experience made older persons remarkable promoters of healthful longevity, ideal custodians of virtue, and seasoned veterans of productivity.

In large measure, the basic exigencies of nation building coupled with the articulated values and priorities prevailing before 1860 account for the (comparatively) favorable estimation of the aged's usefulness then expressed in this country. It is essential to remember that when the Constitution was ratified, America was an underdeveloped nation. The truly important political, economic, and social networks operated at the local, state, and regional levels. The federal government could barely muster the military force and diplomatic influence necessary to defend its national borders and maintain more than a low profile on the international scene. "Even after two centuries of struggling," Henry Adams observed long ago in his magisterial study of the Jeffersonian era, "the land was still untamed; forest covered every portion, except here and there a strip of cultivated soil; the minerals lay undisturbed in their rocky beds and more than two-thirds of the people clung to the seaboard within 50 miles of tidewater, where alone the wants of civilized life could be supplied."[2] Despite the striking economic and demographic growth and fundamental societal transformations that took place during the first half of the nineteenth century, the United States was still in the formative stages of its long-term development. By 1860, it had not yet achieved a well-integrated, functional, nationwide structure or assumed a role as a world power.

Commentators during the period were acutely aware of their country's perilous situation. From our perspective, especially with the bicentennial observances lingering in our minds, it is sometimes difficult to recognize and comprehend the sense of cautiousness and vulnerability that counterbalanced early Americans' avowed hopes and boasts of success in the proximate and indeterminate future. Yet the creators and heirs of the American Enlightenment, steeped in classical traditions and contemporary social theories, "had a keen sense of the precariousness of the felicity that they enjoyed, of the moral and social conditions which made its continuation possible, and of the ultimate likelihood of its dissipation."[3] And while the next generations clearly celebrated their apparently boundless resources as they envisioned and attained their seemingly "manifest destiny," they also were alarmed by the rampant individualism and other ominous trends unleashed by new forces in their midst.

Given the particular ways they defined "reality" and given their desire to establish those values, norms, and modes of behavior that would best serve their collective interests and private ambitions, writers prescribed and referred to a variety of methods to increase chances for national and personal success. In this context, Americans between 1790 and 1860 respected the wisdom of years and considered it appropriate to rely on the elderly's experiences and expertise, not because they were living in a bucolic elysium, but because they considered it sensible and worthwhile to do so. If this interpretation is correct, then there probably was *not* a fundamental alteration in age relations occurring immediately after the Revolution, which made old age seem increasingly worthless in young America. Rather, in the minds of their countrymen and in their own self-perceptions, the old should—and could—play useful roles in society. Thus under a specific set of historical circumstances, Americans judged the assets and liabilities of being old invaluable in shaping the cultural and social life of their new land.

To be sure, there were limits to such explicit esteem for the aged's worth. While the evidence strongly indicates that the elderly were ascribed important social roles because of their past accomplishments and presumed current utility, it does not necessarily follow that Americans exalted (or even preferred) old age more than any other stage of life, or that every older person found life rewarding. One can, after all, acknowledge the claims and achievements of age without invariably liking elderly people or even looking forward to growing old; material comforts and social responsibilities do not guarantee personal satisfaction in later years. Furthermore, no one suggested that *only* the aged were capable of performing essential tasks. "Youth" and "manhood," as the Ohio orator noted, also had important roles to play. Above all, the frequent references to the honor due age do not mean that the elderly *in fact* wielded vast power or held extraordinarily prestigious positions; I presently am analyzing *perceptions* of older persons' relative value, not reconstructing their actual social status. (It is conceivable that prevailing descriptions of the aged accurately elucidate most older people's true circumstances. But it is also possible that the ideas typically expressed by observers did not really carry over into the realm of behavior; precepts clearly were not always practiced.) For the moment, I shall explore in some detail the precise ways Americans defined the elderly's overall worth, and the reasons why they valued those who conformed to certain cultural norms and expectations and contributed to the well-being of their fellow citizens.

THE ELDERLY PROVIDE VALUABLE INSIGHTS ABOUT HEALTHFUL LONGEVITY

Americans before the Civil War regarded people who enjoyed a "ripe old age" with respect because they believed that living a long and fruitful life was a worthwhile achievement. Popular and scientific writers claimed that "longevity has always been highly estimated by man."[4] In a world in which sickness, injury, and death plagued all age groups, those who attained the biblically inspired "three-score-and-ten" seemed remarkable. In fact, the number of elderly people in the United States became a powerful ideological weapon to demonstrate that the New World environment was conducive to human existence and societal progress. During the early years of the republic, it was generally believed that the frequency of persons surviving to old age provided a valid measure of the impact of the civil and natural environment on human health. "Tables of longevity may be everywhere considered the touchstones of government," the Frenchman J. P. Brissot de Warville remarked in 1788, "the scale on which may be measured their excellencies and their defects, the perfection or degradation of the human species."[5]

Accordingly, scientists such as William Barton, a nephew of the astronomer David Rittenhouse, gathered bills of mortality and constructed elaborate tables to "prove" that life expectancy was greater in the United States than in Europe. In his *Observations on the Progress of Population and the Probabilities of the Duration of Human Life, in the United States of America* (1791), Barton recounted earlier studies and proceeded to "mention a few remarkable instances of longevity . . . to corroborate the truth of the position, that the people of this country are long lived."[6] (His "few" examples, fully documented from all sections of the country, fill six pages!) Comparing his data with European evidence, Barton deduced that the likelihood of a person living past eighty was greater here than abroad. Although few tried to replicate Barton's methodology, many reached the same sanguine conclusion. Almanacs featured items about Americans living to advanced ages because publishers deemed such information appropriate reading material.[7] Hezekiah Niles, editor of the most widely circulated and authoritative weekly magazine in the early nineteenth century, regularly reported the names and occupations of very old citizens. Finding it too overwhelming to print all of the cases of long life he received from correspondents, Niles decided in 1823 to limit his reporting to listing centenarians. He believed that even these figures confirmed American superiority over England in prolonging life, especially since the data seemed more conclusive with each passing year.[8]

Critics, geographers, and medical scientists among others contended that such empirical evidence justified their belief that America's environment promoted vigorous long life. One of the *Resources of the United States*, John Bristed argued in 1818, was that

> the aggregate salubrity of the United States surpasses that of Europe; the males are, generally, active, robust, muscular, and powerful, capable of great exertion and endurance; the females display a fine symmetry of person, lively and interesting countenances, frank and engaging manners. . . . The Americans average a longer life than the people in Europe, where only *three* out of every thousand births reach the ages of eighty to ninety years; whereas, in the United States, the proportion is *five* to every thousand.[9]

Jeremy Belknap, in his *History of New Hampshire* (1813), credited the country's fresh air, moderate climate, and rich soil as part of the reason why the very elderly mainly succumbed only to "the gradual decay of nature."[10] Dr. Benjamin Rush, one of America's earliest and most famous students of old age, went a step farther and asserted that life in the new land actually may have enabled some to live longer than they had anticipated. In the course of his studies of people who lived past eighty, Rush "observed many instances of Europeans who have arrived in America in the decline of life who have acquired fresh vigour from the impression of our climate, and of new objects upon their bodies and minds, and whose lives in consequence thereof, appeared to have been prolonged for many years."[11] Americans extolled their seemingly greater likelihood for a long, healthy life as a source of national pride: it indicated to them that the new republic was beginning to reap its natural advantages.

Needless to say, interest in life expectancy—and people who lived long lives—extended beyond debates over the relative effects of political and natural environments on shortening or prolonging human existence. Questions about longevity per se attracted considerable attention. Three important treatises published by William Godwin,

Antoine-Nicolas de Condorcet, and Thomas Robert Malthus during the 1790s stimulated decades of speculation about the possibility and desirability of prolonging life.[12] Regardless of whether they thought life expectancy could or should be increased, most Americans believed that trying to live a long, fruitful life was a significant personal goal. "The art of preserving life has become an important study," Anthony F. Willich commented in his *Domestic Encyclopedia* (1821), "and ought to form part of the education of every individual."[13] Determining why and how some people lived longer than others was considered a matter of utmost importance.

As they searched for ways to prolong life, Americans recognized that some factors affecting life expectancy were beyond human control. It was well established, for instance, that people who lived to very great ages often were descended from those who had themselves enjoyed a long life. Compilers such as William H. Hall noted, in *The New Encyclopedia* (1797), that "there is a great reason to believe that longevity is in great measure hereditary."[14] Investigators corroborated eighteenth-century beliefs that a temperate climate, rural setting, and abundant food supply improved chances for a long life. Over time, in fact, commentators gave more and more prominence to variations in longevity. Examining the causes of death for people at all stages of the life cycle led observers like Dr. John Bell, a member of the American Philosophical Society and professor at the College of Physicians and Surgeons in Philadelphia, to conclude that women's chances for long life were better than men's.[15] Racial differences in life expectancy also attracted increasing attention in antebellum America. While there seemed to be many reasons why blacks did not live as long as whites, investigators uncovered variations in life expectancy among blacks as well as whites. For example, Dr. Charles Caldwell, in *Thoughts on the Effects of Age on the Human Constitution* (1846), noted that there were more black than white centenarians in North Carolina. This statistic, Caldwell argued, appeared to contradict Benjamin Rush's observation that "none but men of very active minds attain to a high degree of longevity."[16] It did not challenge, however, the indisputable influence of heredity on life expectancy.

In addition, limitations in the then existing scientific thought and practice precluded applying ideas and means that would enable later generations to improve their overall life expectancy. Classifying, explaining, and treating diseases either in terms of a simple pathogenic condition, an imbalance of humors, or a loss of vital forces frustrated efforts to reduce the mortality rates associated with common contagious illnesses. A galaxy of partially valid but often contradictory theories about the external causes of diseases further limited the possibility of promoting longevity by improving public hygiene and preventing epidemics. Some concerned citizens gathered data and promoted sanitary reform measures, but no state established a public health department before the Civil War.[17]

Other obstacles kept scientists and doctors in the United States from embracing theories and techniques associated with the Paris School of Medicine, which were gaining vogue in Europe after 1820. Because most on this side of the Atlantic remained suspicious of the emerging concept of disease specificity and were indifferent to basic research, doctors' ideas about the best ways to promote a long and healthful life changed remarkably little between 1790 and 1860. Even those native-born doctors versed and skilled in the latest trends in European medicine lacked the opportunity and milieu necessary to influence and alter many of their colleagues' viewpoints and practices. For it is worth noting that scientists generally lacked the laboratory procedures, instruments, and facilities as well as the professional motivation and organizations essential for clinical studies. Furthermore, before orthodox practitioners would make real headway in improving health, they had to convince a skeptical and often disillusioned public that their education and therapies guaranteed better results than those offered by uneducated domestic doctors who dispensed patent medicines, by quacks who sold nostrums, and by sectarians such as the Grahamites, homeopaths, phrenologists, and mesmerists.[18] Indeed, to many patients before the Civil War, home remedies and herbs seemed just as effective (or illusory) in curing illnesses and restoring health as treatments recommended by doctors with years of training.

While acknowledging that heredity, gender, and race affected life expectancy and admitting that no magic drugs or arcane medical techniques guaranteed continuous vim and vigor, Americans before 1860 nonetheless claimed that people could improve their own chances for a healthful long life. Commentators agreed that one could increase the likelihood of attaining a ripe old age by learning and adhering to certain "general principles."[19] Encyclopedists invoked the example of Luigi Cornaro, a sixteenth-century Venetian noble who claimed at eighty-five that virtuous living was the *Sure and Certain Method of Attaining a Long and Healthful Life.* Contemporary newspapers, almanacs, and periodicals printed and reprinted this time-tested piece of advice. Medical doctors also confirmed the therapeutic advantages derived from observing elementary rules of sensible living. Many of the maxims stressed the importance of fresh air, regular exercise, cleanliness, a moderate diet, and sleeping only long enough to restore strength to the body. Cultivating proper attitudes, including a cheerful disposition and an ability to endure disappointments with courage and resignation, was considered essential.

Precisely because most Americans believed that one's mental outlook and personal habits affected chances for living a full life, older men and women were ascribed an important function to perform: the aged, it was said, demonstrated which lifestyles were more effective than others for promoting healthful longevity. The elderly seemed to prove that following certain rules could mean the difference between a short or long life and a comparatively fit or disease-ridden existence. As Thomas Bailey pointed out in *Records of Longevity* (1859),

> I mean—notwithstanding the instances which will be found in these records to the contrary—to establish the truth . . . that temperance, industry and exercise are the three great elements of longevity. A few slothful men have attained to extreme old age, and so have a few gluttons and drunkards, or at least, hard drinkers; but for the most part, and in an incomparably greater proportion, long livers have been distinguished for their sober and industrious habits.[20]

Scientists and popular commentators alike emphasized that the elderly proved the efficacy of temperance, moderation, industry, and exercise in prolonging life and promoting health. In so doing, they underscored the value of the aged's example.

Believing that most older persons exemplified a desirable code of behavior, Americans by and large attributed to the aged a second important societal role. Moderation and industry, Dr. Charles Caldwell among other pre–Civil War writers claimed, "do much more than merely contribute to the preservation of health and the attainment of long life. They are the most effectual *preventives of vice* and promoters of *virtue* and *good* conduct that nature affords."[21] Since it seemed clear to them that virtue was associated with longevity, Americans concluded that the elderly could teach others how to live morally and healthfully.

THE ELDERLY SERVE AS GUARDIANS OF VIRTUE

Poets, essayists, scientists, and others writing between 1790 and 1860 claimed that, with few exceptions, the aged's moral faculties were highly developed. The presumption that virtue in old age was attained mainly through the cumulative effect of righteous living led to the conclusion that older people of all stations generally were paragons of virtuous behavior. Convinced that the elderly's advice was instructive, Americans prior to the Civil War considered it advantageous to rely on elderly men and women to help direct and safeguard the moral development of the young nation.

The stature gained from years of experience, it was generally agreed, made society's oldest members ideally qualified moral exemplars. Physical and moral well-being at advanced ages appeared to hinge in large part upon successfully avoiding the pitfalls and dangers at each stage of life. Abraham Shoemaker poetically declared in his 1797 *U.S. Almanack*, for instance, that

> as in the succession of seasons, each, by the invariable laws of nature, affects the productions of what is next in course; so, in human life, every period of our age, according as it is well or ill spent, influences the happiness of that which is to follow. Virtuous youth gradually brings forward accomplished and flourishing manhood; and such manhood passes of itself, without uneasiness, into respectable and tranquil old age. But when nature is turned out of its regular order, disorder takes place in the moral just as in the vegetable world . . . so if youth be trifled away without improvement, manhood will be contemptible, and old age miserable.[22]

According to the "invariable laws of nature," a respectable old age resulted from a life of virtue and benevolence. That nature was not false to itself was revealed in the fact that it endowed older men and women with the "nobleness of humanity."[23]

Not only did Americans believe that a long and upright life conditioned people's moral sensibility, but contemporary medical research indicated that the human capacity for virtue did not decline after a certain age. For instance, Dr. Benjamin Rush supported this proposition in his *Medical Inquiries on Diseases* (1812): "The moral faculties, when properly regulated and directed, never partake of the decay of the intellectual faculties in old age, even in persons of uncultivated minds."[24] Subsequent investigations conducted in both the north and south uniformly confirmed Rush's observation on this point even though they disagreed with one another on other matters. Scientific observation thus corroborated the widely held popular opinion that moral faculties could improve with age regardless of a person's prior education or current social standing.

Indeed, Americans described older persons as the most trustworthy counselors on moral matters because they believed that the unimpaired wisdom of age was essential to the well-being of the nation. We should not discount references to the elderly's desirable virtues and moral insights as mere propaganda designed to instill those values and instincts necessary to combat the decline in faith and increase in materialism and corruption many politicians, clergymen, and writers felt were perverting the ideals of Revolutionary America.[25] Some writers who characterized the older generation as custodians of virtue probably did hope that exhorting their fellow citizens to follow the aged's advice would have a stabilizing effect and a conservative influence on the young republic. And yet, just as people's fascination with the size of the elderly population went beyond its worth as evidence proving that human life did not invariably degenerate in the New World environment, so too recognition of and appreciation for the elderly's moral counsel and decorum were not based simply on their possible usefulness as an antidote to actual or imagined social ills.

In light of the special way they perceived "reality," most Americans before 1860 thought that the moral instruction offered by people who had lived long and upright lives was valuable because it had been proven successful. The presumption that people could attain virtue only through righteous living led to the conclusion that the elderly's opinions should be heeded. Hence, when "Senex" argued that properly educating young people was crucial because "the purity of *their* morals and the prudence of their conduct, the weal and permanence of this infant republic were essentially depending" upon it, readers assumed that they were hearing the sensible advice of a wise old man. The elderly could perform an important social role by actively engaging in the diffusion and enforcement of the "undoubted laws of virtue."[26]

The elderly's moral expertise, writers emphasized, was particularly valuable to youth. The Reverend Cortlandt Van Rensselaer elaborated on the significance of this function in a sermon on *Old Age* (1841):

What a blessed influence the old exert in cherishing feelings of reverence, affection and subordination in families; in warning the young against the temptations and allurements of the world; in detailing the results of experience, in exposing the fallacies of worldly maxims; in rebuking the recklessness of indiscretion and the experiments of enthusiasm; in imparting judicious counsel in church and State and private life;—in short, how much good of every kind is accomplished by the tranquilizing, wise and conservative influences of age.[27]

Since older Americans were deemed well equipped to give sound advice on how to live in a respectable manner and to avoid or overcome worldly temptations, the beneficial relationship between age and youth was a favorite theme not just of ministers but also of social critics, novelists, and poets. "It was meant . . . that youth and age should exert upon each other a mutual benefit."[28] Aged men and women were thought to serve the rising generation by admonishing against levity, vanity, and idleness, and by instilling a sense of integrity, honesty, and responsibility. Youth repaid age by offering its companionship and sharing its joys. Mutual benefits, moreover, entailed reciprocal responsibilities. The elderly were obliged to set an appropriate model of decorum. The young, in turn, were expected to pay deference to the aged's virtue.[29]

Indeed, the belief that years of experience made older persons sagacious and exemplary was so widespread in pre–Civil War American culture that references to "venerable" old age were an unobtrusive part of everyday language. For example, in compiling *An American Dictionary of the English Language* (1828), Noah Webster illustrated his definition of the verb "to venerate" with the following examples: "We *venerate* an old faithful magistrate; we *venerate* parents and elders; we *venerate* men consecrated to sacred office; we *venerate* old age or gray hairs; we *venerate*, or ought to venerate, the gospel and its precepts."[30] Webster believed that Americans were ambivalent only in their veneration of Scripture. He assumed honor and respect for magistrates, ministers, parents, and older persons were prevailing cultural norms. Webster apparently was not alone in this judgment: the adjective "venerable" was often used in the writings of the era to identify relatively obscure aged men and women who were considered upright and respected members of their community. And white Americans did not think their value system was unique in this regard; other races in the United States were said "to venerate" their elders. Missionaries and hunters, for instance, duly noted "that respect for age and long experience, for which the Indians are remarkable."[31] Regardless of whether owners were kind or cruel to their aged slaves, considerable evidence from both white and black observers indicates that younger blacks generally endeavored to provide their "aunts" and "uncles" with emotional and physical security and treated them with dignity.[32] While far more research must be done before we can determine to what extent contemporaries actually contradicted and conformed to this prescribed "veneration" dictum, such honorific references to older people offer an important measure of the emphasis placed on the aged's role as wise and virtuous counselors.

This does not mean, however, that the elderly's usefulness was merely titular, confined to the comparatively passive tasks of dispensing recommendations on ways to live a healthful existence and/or offering advice concerning matters of morality. In the minds of their compatriots, older persons also had active roles to fulfill. Assuming that everyone shared a responsibility to serve his or her fellow citizens, writers entreated all age groups to work together harmoniously in building the new nation. Most Americans believed, in fact, that the practical knowledge and moral expertise accrued through years of experience enabled the aged to contribute to society in a variety of essential ways.

THE AGED ACTIVELY SERVE
OTHERS IN MANY CAPACITIES

Like everyone else, the elderly were expected to remain economically and socially useful as long as they were physically able to work. Neither structural obstacles, such as mandatory retirement, nor social prejudice denied men and women because of their advanced age the right to engage in any trade, profession, or vocation (except for a few state judicial posts) before the Civil War. In fact, Americans considered it foolish for the elderly to quit their jobs merely on account of age: medical and popular writers noted that deterioration in later years less often resulted from natural decay than from disuse.[33] The prevailing notion that the old were seasoned veterans of productivity, whose advice and participation enhanced prospects for successfully accomplishing many tasks, justified ascribing to aged persons a variety of important societal tasks to perform.

For example, Americans between 1790 and 1860 fully appreciated older people's usefulness in farming. Evidence in almanacs and rural journals indicates that the aged's presumed importance in rural America was not merely a figment of genteel urban writers' imagination: those who worked in the fields claimed that the elderly's agricultural expertise made them living domestic encyclopedias.[34] The well-known *Farmers Almanac*, originally compiled by Robert B. Thomas, regularly featured suggestions by "Father Simkins" on shoeing horses, caring for farm implements, and keeping account books in order. Among "The Contents of an Old Man's Memorandum Book" in an edition of the *U.S. Almanack* was advice on naming sons and daughters, teaching children to be ambidextrous, traveling efficiently, exchanging ideas with friends, and selecting the best time to wind a watch. Writers indicated that the aged possessed helpful insights about nearly every aspect of farm life—a significant fact, since roughly sixty percent of all gainfully employed persons and a vast majority of all workers over sixty actually were farmers prior to the Civil War.[35]

Furthermore, the election and appointment of men to high public office in their later years attest to the favorable opinion of the elderly's value in government as well as on the farm. In the early years of the republic, septuagenarians were serving as chief warden of the ports of Philadelphia and Boston, and as administrators in Connecticut, Pennsylvania, and South Carolina; a number remained politically active at the city, state, and federal levels beyond the age of eighty.[36] Eleven of the twenty-one highest-ranking naval officers in 1839 were over sixty; seven others were fifty-nine years old.[37] Senior statesmen often held congressional seats. For example, two years after losing a reelection bid for the presidency, John Quincy Adams in 1830 won a seat at the age of sixty-four. Adams continuously represented his home district for the next seventeen years until he suffered a fatal stroke. "When persons of mature age and eminent for their experience, wisdom, and virtue" were elected to Congress, Hezekiah Niles, reflecting popular sentiment, editorialized, "it is a subject for gratitude and congratulation."[38] Americans believed that elderly candidates' political sagacity had been ripened by many years of service.

Voters clearly considered older men fit and even uniquely qualified for the presidency, as William Henry Harrison's 1840 bid aptly illustrates. After Ol' Tippecanoe was nominated to be the Whig standard bearer, opponents seized on his prior illnesses and age as campaign issues. Frank Blair's *Globe*, the Democratic party's most influential voice, declared that Harrison's "garrulity" could not be masked by appeals to log cabins and hard cider; one opposition bulletin blasted Harrison as a "superannuated and pitiable dotard."[39] Whigs tried to turn their candidate's "green old age" into a political asset by describing Harrison as a vigorous guardian of a simpler era's homespun virtues. When Democrats charged that he was an "old granny," Whigs countered that the voters wanted an "experienced and skilful 'granny' to deliver our young and beautiful mother of a nest of vipers, who are preying upon her vitals, and hurrying her to a premature grave."[40] Ol' Tippecanoe won 53.1 percent of the popular vote and 234 of

the 294 electoral votes cast. And despite Harrison's untimely death a month after taking office, antebellum Americans continued to nominate and elect elderly men to the
presidency. Old age often seemed to enhance rather than to reduce a candidate's attractiveness.[41]

In fact, prior to the Civil War, laws disqualified men from voting and holding hun-
dreds of offices because they were too young, but there were only a few specific judicial posts throughout the land in which men over a certain age could not serve. Most
places required men to be at least twenty-one to cast a ballot; no jurisdiction, however,
disenfranchised any potential voter on account of advanced age. The Constitution established minimum ages for election to Congress and the White House, but there were
no maximum age restrictions for any elected or appointed office at the federal level.
States barred young but not elderly men from running for governor or the legislature.
Unlike the federal constitution, however, a few states did impose definite limits on the
number of years a person could serve as a justice. Some followed a 1780 Massachusetts constitutional precedent, and required that licenses to justices of the peace be renewed every seven years.[42] (Such restrictions, of course, were designed to guard
against incompetency in general, not to discriminate against senior justices in particular.) In addition, seven states imposed upper age limits on holding judicial office. To
avoid the problems experienced when a colonial chief justice became senile on the
bench, New York state's 1777 Constitution prescribed that "the Chancellor, the judges
of the supreme court, and the first judge of the country court of each county hold their
offices during good behavior, or until they shall have respectively attained the age of
sixty year." Revisions in the 1792 New Hampshire, 1819 Connecticut, and 1851 Maryland constitutions established seventy as the maximum age for judges and justices of
the peace. Although none had imposed old-age restrictions in earlier constitutions, Alabama (1819), Missouri (1820), and Maine (1820) inserted maximum limits for judicial posts when they became states.[43] These are the *only* instances of discrimination
against older men's rights to serve as justices before the Civil War. No other jurisdiction in the remaining twenty-six states making up the nation before the Civil War restricted elderly men from holding any other elected or appointed office.

Although prohibiting the aged from judicial office was an unusual custom between
1790 and 1860, even its limited practice aroused considerable opposition. John Adams
found the removal of competent judges from office at seventy offensive: "To turn out
such men to eat husks with the prodigal or grass with Nebuchadnezzer ought to be tor-
menting to the humanity of the Nation."[44] But it was the clause in the New York Constitution, which removed men from judicial office at sixty, that especially aroused
waves of outcry. In 1788, Alexander Hamilton argued in Federal Paper 79 that the
measure needlessly discriminated against able magistrates and denied elderly men the
right to be useful and remain financially independent:

> when, in addition to this circumstance, we consider how few there are who out-
> live the season of intellectual vigor and how improbable it is that any consider-
> able portion of the bench, whether more or less numerous, should be in such a
> situation at the same time, we shall be ready to conclude that limitations of this
> sort shall have little to recommend them.[45]

Chancellor James Kent's forced resignation on his sixtieth birthday in 1823 sparked another outburst. At a banquet in his honor at Harvard, Kent was toasted: "The James Kent—with better machinery, greater force, and greater safety than any other boat, yet constitutionally forbidden to take another trip." New York was criticized at the same time: "The Constitution of New York—we hear that it diverts the operations, but we see it neither abates the force nor obscures the splendor of intellectual light."[46] Both toasts proved to be accurate prophecies. Three years after his removal from office, Kent began publishing his famous *Commentaries on American Law* (1826–30), establishing him as the American Blackstone. He did not become infirm until a few months before his death at eighty-four, in 1847. Kent's continued eminence and Chief Justice John Marshall's vigorous performance on the Supreme Court considerably beyond the age of sixty prompted periodic barbs at the New York age limitation. Finally, the state dropped the restriction when it revised its constitution in 1846.[47]

There was no comparable controversy in the private sector because mandatory retirement simply did not exist. No profession, industry, business, craft, or trade organization prior to 1860 required people to leave the labor force because they had reached a predetermined chronological age. Thus we must be careful not to attribute twentieth-century connotations to the ways that Americans of the period used the word "retirement": the idea that a person automatically stopped working at a prescribed age is absent from pre–Civil War definitions of the word. Men and women of all ages, not just the elderly, retired under different sets of circumstances. Farmers, according to almanacs, annually "retired" from winter's storms to their family circles. Noah Webster wrote in a 1790 essay "that the morals of young men, as well as their application to science, depend much on retirement."[48] In the first edition of *An American Dictionary* (1828), Webster defined retirement as "1. The act of withdrawing from company or from public notice or station. 2. The state of being withdrawn. 3. Private abode; habitation secluded from much society, or from public life. 4. Private way of life."[49] While the aged conceivably could be "retired" in any one of these uses of the word, no definition necessarily applied only to older people.

It is essential to note, however, that there were two limits to the pervasive cultural norm that the aged should play an active role in society. On the one hand, debilities and infirmities restricted some older persons' employment options. Declining health, for instance, reduced Daniel Boone and Natty Bumppo, perhaps the period's favorite symbols of energetic extreme old age, from hunters to trappers and guides. Indeed, Noah Webster's definition of the verb "superannuate" connotes the critical importance of health: "To impair or disqualify by old age and infirmity."[50] Increasing physical handicaps often prevented people from continuing in their jobs. On the other hand, the elderly had to assess honestly the strengths and liabilities of their years on all their activities. As Hugh Henry Brackenridge reminded readers in *Modern Chivalry* (1804), an old horse that trotted was respectable, but one that tried to speed would be contemptible. "The great secret of preserving respect is the cultivating and showing to the best advantage the powers that we possess, and the not going beyond them."[51] Older Americans were expected to know when it was time to let others assume more and more of their regular duties.

And yet, even those who curtailed previous occupations at advanced ages did not have to cease being useful. Antebellum Americans did not believe that people in- evitably became obsolete as they grew older. Writers throughout the period echoed a theme Isaac Bickerstaff thoughtfully declared in the 1794 edition of his *New-England Almanack*:

> mankind is one vast republic, where every individual receives benefits from the labour of others, which, by labouring in his turn for others, he is obliged to repay; and that where the united efforts of all are not able to exempt all from misery, none have a right to withdraw from their task of vigilance, or be in- dulged in idle wisdom, and solitary pleasures.[52]

As long as evil and misery existed in the world, it was claimed, the aged had construc- tive roles to play.

Americans between 1790 and 1860 invariably extolled the elderly's contributions in the home. Widely circulated magazines and almanacs were frequently illustrated with essays, vignettes, etchings, and poems about the aged's value in performing do- mestic duties. For example, after leaving the bench, Judge Jeremiah Smith spent the next twenty-two years serving as a trustee of the local academy, reading, offering his seasoned advice to others, and sharing the pleasures and pains of his family circle. "We may even question," a reviewer in the *North American Review* observed, "whether he was ever more useful to his fellow-men than in this genial autumn of his days."[53] Artists working in all media capitalized on the theme. Stephen Foster sold about 130,000 copies of "Old Folks at Home" (1851) within three years; others prof- itably wrote imitations of the song. John Rogers created a statue of a family scene fea- turing the grandparents. Currier and Ives issued a large folio print of "Old Age" in 1868.[54] Such sentimental portraits not only enjoyed phenomenal financial success but they also reinforced in popular thought the value of special services older men and women fulfilled in the household. Among other things, observers pointed out that the elderly taught manners and served as models of behavior. Children and grandchildren also depended on their elders' recollections for biographical details about their ances- tral roots.

But according to contemporary accounts, the aged's worth as oral historians usually extended beyond recounting family histories: to younger generations, the elderly seemed to be living monuments of the past. Those attaining old age between 1790 and 1830, in particular, provided their countrymen with a symbolic tie to the nation's revo- lutionary heritage. Magazine and newspaper editors occasionally reprinted the stories anonymous veterans told. The following incident appeared in the 1 October 1825 issue of *Niles Register*:

> "Here, boys, are the marks of war," said an old veteran the other day as he opened an old revolutionary vest, full of bullets and bayonet holes, and showed the scars on his breast. He was wounded, dreadfully wounded, *nine* times wounded, in the battle of Fort Griswold. His breast was literally torn open by bayonets and musket-balls, so that the beating of his heart was distinctly seen. . . . The young soldier unexpectedly recovered and is now a venerable and re- spected inhabitant of this town. "Here, boys, are the marks of war," and his

whole soul seemed beaming from his keen eye, as he exhibited his numerous wounds to a group of youths who had gathered around, and gazed with admiration on one, who in olden time, arose, as it were, from the dead.[55]

Americans believed that older people's first-hand accounts of heroic bravery and steadfast loyalty to the revolutionary cause were uplifting examples of patriotism for everyone to follow. Fourth of July festivities and ground-breaking ceremonies were not complete until audiences heard speeches by Revolutionary War veterans and acknowledged the presence of other survivors in the crowd.[56] The public activities of Charles Carroll of Carrolton, the last surviving signer of the Declaration of Independence, illustrates this ritualistic use of the elderly. Before he died in 1832 at the age of ninety-five, Carroll presided over the laying of the cornerstone of the Baltimore and Ohio railroad, served as president of the American Colonization Society, and rode a steamboat named in his honor. Carroll and his contemporaries thus served as a crucial link between America's past and present that inspired optimism about the future.

Nor did the elderly's role as repositories of the past diminish once the last Revolutionary War survivors died. Aged antebellum Americans remembered and retold the stirring episodes learned from those who had lived through the early years of the republic. During yarn-spinning sessions, in meeting houses and taverns, obscure inveterate storytellers dominated or attracted gatherings with their mixtures of fact and fiction.[57] Some people demanded that the elderly be accurate in recounting the past. John Greenleaf Whittier, for instance, relied upon his elders' memory of colonial folklore and incorporated experiences from their lives in his *Legends of New England*.[58] Writers of children's stories and other works, including Nathaniel Dodge, Nathaniel Hawthorne, and Hannah More, often made older men and women narrators in their books, since readers were accustomed to hearing the aged's sagas about the past. Essayists and poets recorded the visions their elders purportedly held of former days because they thought such materials were exciting, entertaining, or edifying.[59]

Because the elderly could synthesize and share vital lessons garnered from the past and present ages, Americans between 1790 and 1860 considered it practical to heed an older person's counsel and to utilize his or her talents even in periods of rapid change. "By respecting the advice of an old man, we not only gratify the individual by making him feel that he is not living in vain, but we insure to ourselves a great chance of success in the matter at hand; for age advises us from experience, and not from untested theory."[60] The experience and wisdom of years seemed indispensable in nurturing the well-being of the republic. For this reason, most people before the Civil War believed that the aged, except those whose unseemly behavior provoked contempt, made essential contributions to their contemporaries.

It should not be altogether surprising, therefore, that early Americans chose the image of a sinewy old man with long white hair and chin whiskers to symbolize their new land. Dressed in red and white striped pantaloons and a blue coat bespangled with stars, and sporting an unabashedly old-fashioned plug hat, "Uncle Sam" seemed to personify the honesty, self-reliance, and devotion to country so deeply cherished in the early decades of our national experience. Debate persists about whether the sobriquet and character were inspired by a certain Samuel Wilson of Troy, New York, who served as an inspector of provisions for the U.S. Army during the War of 1812. Yet there is little doubt that the nickname caught on before the Battle of New Orleans and that by the 1830s, "Uncle Sam" had joined the bald-headed eagle as one of this country's favorite symbols.[61] "Uncle Sam" not only epitomized the hopes of young America but he also seemed to demonstrate that the nation could be wise and experienced even in its formative years.

NOTES

1. *Niles Register* 28 (30 July 1825): 346.

2. Henry Adams, *History of the United States during the Administration of Thomas Jefferson* (1889; reprint ed., New York: Albert and Charles Boni, 1930), p. 1. See also Richard D. Brown, *Modernization* (New York: Hill and Wang, 1976), pp. 95–96, 100; and Robert F. Berkhofer, Jr., "From Colonial Communities to Modern Mass Society: A Social Evolutionary Model of American History" (Paper delivered at the 1976 American Historical Association convention, Washington, D.C., 29 December 1976).

3. Stow Persons, "The Cyclical Theory of History in Eighteenth Century America," in *The American Culture*, ed. Hennig Cohen (Boston: Houghton Mifflin Co., 1968), p. 121; see also Henry Steele Commager, *Empire of Reason* (Garden City: Anchor Press/Doubleday, 1977), esp. ch. 4.

4. See, for example, Christopher Wilhelm Hufeland, *The Art of Prolonging Life* (1797; reprint ed., New York: Thomas O'Kane, 1873), p. iii; Anthony F. Willich, *Domestic Encyclopedia*, 2d American ed., 3 vols. (Philadelphia: Abraham Small, 1821), 2: 453, 480; Wooster Beach, *Family Physician*, 16th ed. (Boston: B. B. Mussey Co., 1854), p. xli; H. Holland, "Human Longevity," *Living Age* 53 (25 April 1857): 203–6.

5. Quoted in James H. Cassedy, *Demography in Early America* (Cambridge, Mass.: Harvard University Press, 1969), p. 263.

6. William Barton, *Observations on the Progress of Population and the Possibilities of the Duration of Life, in the United States of America* (Philadelphia: Aitken, 1791), p. 20.

7. This observation is based on a survey of more than a hundred different almanacs, published between 1790 and 1860 in diverse parts of the nation, housed in the Clements Library at the University of Michigan, Ann Arbor.

8. For illustrative examples, see *Niles Weekly Register* 9 (1815): 98, 300, 402, 404, 430; ibid. 14 (1818): 151, 296; ibid. 23 (1823): 145, 354; and ibid. 41 (1832): 448.

9. John Bristed, *Resources of the United States of America* (New York: James Eastburn & Co., 1818), pp. 20, 453.

10. Jeremy Belknap, *History of New Hampshire*, 3 vols. (Boston: Bradford and Read, 1813), 3: 171–73, 188–90.

11. Benjamin Rush, "An Account of the State of the Mind and Body in Old Age," in *Medical Inquiries and Observations*, 4 vols. (1793; reprint ed. Philadelphia: Thomas Dobson, 1797), 2: 300.

12. William Godwin, *Enquiry concerning Political Justice, and Its Influence on Morals and Happiness*, 2 vols. (1793; reprint ed., Toronto: University of Toronto Press, 1940); Antoine-Nicolas de Condorcet, *Outlines of an Historical View of the Progress of the Human Mind* (Ann Arbor: Edwards Brothers, [1795]); Thomas Malthus, *On Population* (1798; reprint ed., New York: Modern Library, 1960). For an essential discussion of these writers and attitudes about longevity in general, see Gerald J. Gruman, *A History of Ideas about the Prolongation of Life: The Evolution of Prolongevity Hypotheses to 1800* (Philadelphia: The American Philosophical Society, 1966).

13. Willich, *Domestic Encyclopedia*, 2: 453, 480.

14. *The New Encyclopedia*, 3 vols., 3d ed. (London: William H. Hall, 1797), s.v. "longevity"; *Encyclopedia Brittanica*, 1st American ed., s.v. "longevity"; Frederick Marryat, *A Diary in America* (1839; reprint ed., Bloomington: Indiana University Press, 1960), pp. 121–22;

Daniel Harrison Jacques, *Hints toward Physical Perfection* (New York: Fowler and Wells, 1859), pp. 209–14.

15. John Bell, *On Regimen and Longevity* (Philadelphia: Hasnell & Johnson, 1843), pp. 389–91; Jacques, *Physical Perfection*, p. 219; Elliot G. Storke, *The Family Farm and Gardens* (Auburn: Storke, 1859), pt. 2, p. 249. Marriage, it was said, also promoted longevity.

16. Charles Caldwell, *Thoughts on the Effects of Age on the Human Constitution* (Louisville: John C. Noble, 1846), p. 19. See also "Oldest Negro Yet," *Frank Leslie's Illustrated* 3 (20 December 1856): 44.

17. Lester Snow King, *The Medical World of the Eighteenth Century* (Chicago: The University of Chicago Press, 1958), pp. 193–226, 263–96; Richard H. Shryock, *Medicine and Society in America, 1660–1860* (New York: New York University Press, 1960), pp. 61–66; Barbara G. Rosenkrantz, *Public Health and the State* (Cambridge, Mass.: Harvard University Press, 1972), ch. 1–2.

18. Charles E. Rosenberg, *The Cholera Years* (Chicago: The University of Chicago Press, 1962), pp. 73, 154–157; Richard H. Shryock, *Medicine in America* (Baltimore: The Johns Hopkins University Press, 1966), pp. 72–89; Joseph F. Kett, *The Formation of the American Medical Profession* (New Haven: Yale University Press, 1968), pp. 156–57.

19. Hufeland, *Prolonging Life*, pp. i–ii, 104.

20. Thomas Bailey, *Records of Longevity* (London: Darton and Co., 1859), pp. 4–5. See also David Ramsay, *History of South Carolina*, 2 vols. (Newsberry, S.C.: David Longworth, 1809), 2: 233; Belknap, *New Hampshire, 2: 174; Niles Weekly Register* 29 (10 September 1825): 27; *Atkinson's Casket* 12 (May 1835): 282–83; *North American Review* 55 (July 1842): 272; Andrew Jackson Davis, *Harbinger of Health* (New York: A. J. Davis & Co., 1842), pp. 180–81; Joel Pinney, *How to Attain Health and Long Life* (London: S. Highley, 1839), p. 138.

21. Caldwell, *Effects of Age*, p. 22; Bell, *Regimen*, p. 387; Robert B. Thomas, *Farmer's Almanac for 1853*, p. 37; idem, *Farmer's Almanac for 1858*, p. 38; Bailey, *Records of Longevity*, pp. 4–6, 29, 33; "The Length of Human Life," *Littell's Living Age* 41 (7 July 1855): 3–8.

22. Abraham Shoemaker, *U.S. Almanack* (Elizabeth-town, N.J.: Abraham Shoemaker, 1797).

23. Orville Dewey, *The Problem of Human Destiny*, 2d ed. (New York: James Miller, 1854), p. 122. See also Thomas Bernard, *The Comforts of Old Age*, 5th ed. (London: John Murray, 1820), pp. 31–32; *Cramer's Pittsburgh Almanack* (1807), p. 10; G. G. Foster, "The Old Man Returned Home," *Graham's Magazine* 20 (April 1842): 225; "Youth and Age," *Littell's Living Age* 49 (1856): 99.

24. Benjamin Rush, *Medical Inquiries and Observations, upon the Diseases of the Mind* (1812; reprint ed., New York: Hafner Publishing Co., 1962), p. 297.

25. On this point in general, see Gordon Wood, *The Rising Glory of America* (New York: George Braziller, 1971), pp. 1–22; Arthur M. Schlesinger, Jr., "America: Experiment or Destiny," *American Historical Review* 82 (June 1977): 507–14.

26. The first quotation comes from Senex, "On Education," *Balance, and Columbian Repository* 1 (1802): 370; the second quotation comes from S. Reed, "A Review," *North American Review* 24 (January 1827): 56–57. Reed did not limit this role to the old.

27. Cortlandt Van Rensselaer, *Old Age: A Funeral Sermon* (Washington, D.C.: By the author, 1841), pp. 10–11; Albert Barnes, *Life at Three-Score: A Sermon*, 2d ed. (Philadelphia: Parry and McMillan, 1859), p. 9.

28. Dewey, *Human Destiny*, p. 123. See also "Youth and Age in America," *Harper's Magazine* 20 (January 1860): 264–67; "Life's Lessons," *Knickerbocker Magazine* 21 (June 1842): 505; E. Gallaudet, "Youth and Old Age," ibid. 26 (November 1845): 414; James Pritchett, "The Old Man and the Children," *Littell's Living Age* 51 (October 1856): 256; L. Maria Child, *The Mother's Book*, 6th ed. (Chicago: C. S. Francis & Co., 1844), pp. 114–15.

29. James Fenimore Cooper, *American Democrat* (1838; reprint ed., New York: Alfred A. Knopf, 1931), p. 146; William Mountford, *Euthanasy*, 2d ed. (Boston: W. Crosby and H. P. Nichols, 1850), p. 2; "Outlived Her Usefulness," *Littell's Living Age* 48 (January–March 1856): 317; T. S. Arthur, "The Old-Time Grandfather," *Godey's Lady's Book* 56 (April 1858): 320–21.

30. *An American Dictionary of the English Language*, 1st ed., s.v. "venerate." The definition of "venerate" did not change in successive editions of Webster's dictionary for fifty years. Richard M. Rollins ("Words as Social Control," *American Quarterly* 28 [Fall 1976]: 415–31) argues that Webster used his dictionary as a vehicle to express his concern about social authority and control. This may be so, but it should not be inferred from this important finding that Webster was the only person who described the aged as "venerable" or that his contemporaries necessarily shared his fears or his philosophy. For other examples of "venerable," see *North American Review* 2 (November 1815): 142; *Niles Register* 17 (30 November 1819): 192; ibid. 19 (9 December 1820): 225; ibid. 22 (18 May 1822): 192; Robert B. Thomas, *Farmer's Almanac* for 1805 and 1812, and the *Orwigsburg Almanac for the Year of Our Lord 1830*, p. 50.

31. Maria Leach and Jerome Fried, eds., *Dictionary of Folklore, Mythology and Legend*, 2 vols. (New York: Funk and Wagnalls, 1949), 2: 818; George Lyman Kittredge, *The Old Farmer and His Almanack* (Boston: William Ware and Company, 1904), pp. 333–35.

32. Eugene Genovese, *Roll, Jordan, Roll* (New York: Vintage Books, 1974), pp. 522–23; Mitford M. Mathews, *A Dictionary of Americanisms on Historical Principles*, 2 vols. (Chicago: The University of Chicago Press, 1951), 2: 52, 1793; Leslie H. Owens, *This Species of Property* (New York: Oxford University Press, 1976), pp. 139, 203, 209; Herbert Gutman, *The Black Family in Slavery and Freedom* (New York: Alfred A. Knopf, 1976), esp. ch. 2–4. This does not mean, however, that whites who referred to aged blacks as "Uncle" or "Aunt" invariably did so out of respect. Bertram Wyatt-Brown has suggested, in "The Ideal Typology and Ante-bellum Southern History," *Societas* 5 (Winter 1975): 17, that such possessive labels may also have signified a black person's powerlessness. (See also Owens, *Property*, pp. 47–48 on this point.) Clearly, far more work must be done before we can establish whether respect for aged blacks mollified racial animosity.

33. Caldwell, *Effects of Age*, pp. 6, 14–18; Oliver Wendell Holmes, *Autocrat of the Breakfast Table* (1858; reprint ed., Boston: Houghton Mifflin Co., 1883), pp. 150–63. See also Robert B. Thomas's *Farmer's Almanac* for the years 1846 (p. 25), 1857 (p. 39), and 1864 (p. 2).

34. Kittredge, *Old Farmer*, p. 313; Jedidiah Morse, *The American Universal Geography*, 7th ed., 2 vols. (Charlestown: Lincoln & Edmands, 1819), 2: 291–92. See also Robert Thomas's *Farmer's Almanack* for February 1813, July 1815, December 1820, September 1822, February 1824, and December 1827. "The Contents" are in the 1797 edition of John Nathan Hutchins's *United States Almanack*.

35. P. K. Whelpton, "Occupational Groups in the United States," *Journal of the American Statistical Association* 21 (September 1926): 340. See also Chapters 4–5, below.

36. *Niles Register* 15 (14 November 1818): 196; ibid. 31 (2 December 1826): 222; ibid. 31 (13 January 1827): 308; *Knickerbocker* 2 (August 1833): 160.

37. *Niles National Register* 58 (14 September 1839): 48.

38. *Niles Register* 19 (2 September 1820): 1; ibid. 39 (18 November 1830): 186; ibid. 74 (19 July 1848): 36–37.

39. Robert Gray Gunderson, *Log Cabin Campaign* (Lexington: University of Kentucky Press, 1957), p. 220; *Tippecanoe Almanac* (Philadelphia, 1841), p. 39.

40. Ibid., pp. 49–50; Charles Spelman Todd and Benjamin Drake, *Sketches of William Harrison* (Cincinnati: U. P. James, 1840), p. 165; Isaac Rand Jackson, *Life of Major General Harrison* (Philadelphia: Gregg & Elliott, 1840), p. 89; Samuel Jones Burr, *The Life and Times of William Henry Harrison* (New York: L. W. Ranson, 1840), p. 257. For a typical barb against Harrison, see U.S., Congress, House, *Congressional Globe*, 26th Cong., 1st sess., 1840, app., p. 240.

41. It is important to note that Harrison's death was attributed, not to the infirmities of age, but to "the vanity of man and the mutability of things temporal." See, for example, Horatio Potter, *Discourses on the Death of William Henry Harrison* (Albany: Hoffman, White and Visscher, 1840), p. 257.

42. Francis Newton Thorpe, *Federal and State Constitutions, Colonial Charters and Other*

Organic Laws, 1492–1908, 7 vols. (Washington, D.C.: Government Printing Office, 1909), 3: 1906.

43. See ibid., 4: 2486, for New Hampshire; ibid., 1: 543, for Connecticut; ibid., 1: 107, for Alabama; ibid., 4: 2158, for Missouri; ibid., 3: 1727–28, for Maryland; and ibid., 5: 2647, for New York: For Maine, see Benjamin Perley Poore, *The Federal and State Constitutions*, 2 vols. (1924; reprint ed., New York: Burt Franklin, 1972), 1: 796.

44. John Adams to Thomas Jefferson, July 12, 1822, in *The Adams–Jefferson Letters*, ed. Lester J. Cappon, 2 vols. (Chapel Hill: Institute of Early American History and Culture, 1959), 2: 582.

45. Alexander Hamilton et al., *The Federalist Papers*, no. 79 (New York: New American Library Edition, 1961), pp. 474–75.

46. John Theodore Horton, *James Kent* (New York: D. Appleton-Century Co., 1939), pp. 249–50, 264–66. See also New York State, *Court of Chancery* 7 (1837): 346–47, for a bitter postscript written by Kent's clerk on the day the chancellor retired.

47. Thorpe, *Federal and State Constitutions*, 5: 2634. For Marshall's vitality, see "Chief Justice Marshall," *North American Review* 42 (January 1836): 236–37; and *Niles Register* 48 (25 July 1835): 369–70.

48. For farmers retiring, see Robert B. Thomas, *Farmer's Almanack* (December 1810), n.p. The Webster quotation comes from Wood, *Rising Glory*, p. 159.

49. *An American Dictionary of the English Language*, s.v. "retirement."

50. See the 1828 edition of Webster's *American Dictionary* for the definition of "superannuate"; cf. the definition of "green healthy old age" in James Morison, *Family Adviser*, 4th ed. (London: College of Health, 1833), p. 340. For eyewitness descriptions of Boone in old age, see *Niles Register* 15 (26 December 1818): 328, and ibid. 19 (1820): 152, 263. Daniel Bryan (*The Mountain Muse* [Harrisonburg, Va.: Davidson and Bourne, 1813], bk. 7, ll. 799–811) apotheosizes Boone in his old age. James Fenimore Cooper refers to Boone in *The Prairie* (1827; reprint ed., New York: Holt, Rinehart & Winston, 1965), p. 3. Cooper's novel, in fact, overflows with descriptions of advanced old age and reasons why Bumppo's experience and continued activities ensure him respect.

51. Hugh Henry Brackenridge, *Modern Chivalry*, ed. Lewis Leary, 2 vols. (1804; reprint ed., New Haven: College and University Press, 1965), vol. 1, bk. 1, ch. 2, p. 34. See also Thomas Jefferson to John Adams, 27 June 1822, in *Letters*, ed. Cappon, 2: 580.

52. "Solitude," *New England Almanack* (Isaac Bickerstaff, 1794); Morse, *Geography*, 2: 294; Henry Giles, *Christian Thoughts on Life* (Boston: Ticknor, Reed and Fields, 1850), p. 108; Thomas M'Kellar, "Life's Evening," *Graham's Magazine* 26 (November 1844): 202; *Godey's Lady's Book* 23 (December 1841): 262–63.

53. "Morison's *Life of Jeremiah Smith*," *North American Review* 61 (July 1845): 108–12. See also Nathan Daboll, *New England Almanac* (1851), pp. 23–24; Thomas, *Farmer's Almanac* (1855), p. 36; ibid. (1862), p. 2; Sarah Josepha Hale, *American Sketches*, 2d ed. (Boston: Putnam & Hunt, 1830), p. 26; *Niles National Register* 57 (1 August 1839): 16; ibid. (7 December 1839): 239; *Littell's Living Age* 48 (February 1856): 576.

54. John Tasker Howard, *Stephen Foster* (New York: Thomas Y. Crowell, 1934), pp. 192–205; Clyde Griffen, "The Progressive Ethos," in *The Development of American Culture*, ed. Stanley Coben and Lorman Ratner (Englewood Cliffs: Prentice Hall, Inc., 1970) pp. 130–33; Ann Douglas, *The Feminization of American Culture* (New York: Alfred A. Knopf, 1977).

55. *Niles Register* 29 (1 October 1825): 70–71. See also ibid. 14 (28 February 1818): 15; ibid. 21 (15 September 1821): 34; *United States Magazine and Democratic Review*, 3 (September 1838): 26–28.

56. *Niles Weekly Register* 14 (11 July 1818): 329; ibid. 29 (19 November 1825): 177; ibid. 46 (2 August 1834): 384. On Charles Carroll, see *Niles Register* 34 (12 July 1838): 317 and ibid. 38 (19 June 1830): 395. See also Robert Middlekauff's suggestive essay, "The Ritualization of the American Revolution," in *Development of American Culture*, ed. Coben and Ratner, pp. 31–44, and Fred Somkin, *The Unquiet Eagle* (Ithaca: Cornell University Press, 1967), p. 175.

57. "An Old Lady's History," *Littell's Living Age* 20 (January–March 1849): 550; "An Old

Man's Reminiscence," *Knickerbocker Monthly* 22 (October 1843): 298. See also Nathaniel S. Dodge, *Sketches of New England* (New York: E. French, 1842), p. 61.

58. John Greenleaf Whittier, *Legends of New England* (1831; reprint ed., Gainesville: Scholars' Facsimiles and Reprints, 1965), pp. 27–28, 66, 75, 117–18. See also John Brainard's poem, "Connecticut River," at the frontispiece.

59. See, for example, Nathaniel Hawthorne, *Grandfather's Chair* (1850; reprint ed., Boston: Houghton Mifflin, 1883), p. 25, and the review of Walter Scott's *Tales of a Grandfather* in *North American Review* 94 (January 1862), pp. 269–70. See also Singleton, "An Old Man's Records," *Knickerbocker* 6 (October 1835): 336; Rosa, "An Old Man's Musings," *Graham's Magazine* 47 (September 1855): 248–49.

60. "Shakespeare's Sixth Age," *Knickerbocker* 12 (August 1838): 113–18. See also "Old People," *Boston Weekly Magazine* 2 (26 October 1839): 60–61; "Comforts of Age," *Harper's Magazine* 9 (September 1854): 705; *North American Review* 79 (July 1854): 249–50.

61. Mathews, *Americanisms*, 2: 1793. See also B. A. Botkin, ed., *A Treasury of American Folklore* (New York: Crown Publishers, 1944), p. 286; *Encyclopedia Americana*, s.v. "Samuel Wilson."

4

The Families of the Old

CAROLE HABER
BRIAN GRATTON

This reading explores the family life of the old from the colonial era to the present day. Haber and Gratton demonstrate that, while the family has always been a source of protection in old age, the family life of the elderly has changed dramatically over time. Where once most older people lived in nuclear households with their children, now most reside only with their spouse or live alone. Some historians underscore the role culture has played in shaping family dynamics; others highlight changing demographics. Haber and Gratton emphasize the diversity of family life, paying special attention to race, class, gender, and regional differences.

Throughout American history, the family has been central to the lives of elderly. Before recent decades, most aged persons lived out their days surrounded by kinship members. In their last years, the majority of older people remained in their own households, accompanied by their spouse and maturing children. Even aged spinsters and elderly bachelors often found shelter in the homes—and family networks—of their relatives or neighbors. Such household arrangements reflected economic and demographic constraints as well as cultural expectations. Until the mid-nineteenth century, few individuals lived beyond the maturity of all their children; even as they approached old age, they often remained responsible for adolescent offspring. Moreover, the family served as a source of economic and emotional support. Before the establishment of Social Security, only the most impoverished and isolated looked to private or public charity. Most needy individuals maintained kinship networks that provided for their financial needs.

In recent decades, however, the family life of the elderly has taken on a radically new form. Increases in longevity have had a dramatic impact upon the daily experiences of the old. In contrast to the preindustrial period, the elderly are likely to live long enough to become intimately acquainted with several generations of family members. They are apt to survive well into the middle age of their children, who routinely leave parental households to establish their own homes. No longer surrounded by growing offspring, the old now live alone or with their spouse in the empty nest household.

This modern household structure has provoked considerable anxiety among contemporary social analysts about the place of the elderly in the family. Pointing to the fact that a large proportion of older people live apart from their kin, critics charge that the American family has lost its traditional integrity and compassion. The existence of large numbers of solitary elders, these critics claim, is proof that family members exhibit far less respect and concern for their aging kin than they once displayed.

Such charges are hardly new.[1] Since the industrial era, social analysts have focused on the apparent decline in status of the elderly as conclusive evidence of the deterioration of the modern family. According to their narratives, in the classical family of Western nostalgia, the rural elderly presided over complex, extended households full of generations of attentive and loving kin.[2] In modern times, however, these families' ties have broken. No longer honored or respected, the elderly have been deserted by their kin, left alone to fend for themselves.

As we have seen, however, the traditional view of the family has been challenged by recent historical studies. Across American history, most households have been "nuclear," composed only of husband, wife, and children; few were extended to include grandparents, grandchildren, or other relatives or nonkin.[3] In many eras, demographic conditions made it unlikely that three-generational households could ever be formed. Although the complex household did exist in the preindustrial period (perhaps more commonly than revisionists have claimed), it never was the predominant form.

Moreover, the current highly isolated arrangements of the old cannot be labeled a sign of loathing for the elderly. Recent studies have found that intergenerational exchange between the aged and their children continues to be extremely important and vibrant. Indeed, scholars have characterized their findings of interdependence and intimacy as a modified form of the "extended" family, even if three generations rarely choose to live in the same house.[4]

Given these apparently contradictory findings, the family history of the elderly demands a new and careful treatment.[5] In the pages that follow, we suggest that demography, economics, and cultural expectations created a dynamic history of the elderly in their families. In the preindustrial era, most aged persons resided with their children in nuclear households. Rarely did they live to see all their children grown and married. Often depending on economic strategies that encouraged co-residence with maturing children, they relied on both cultural expectations and promises of inheritance to insure the children's continued assistance. In the industrial era, the family structure of the old became increasingly complex. Many Americans still employed family-based economic strategies. But economic growth and especially demographic change broadened familial possibilities. Race, class, ethnicity, and gender influenced the establishment of a variety of household structures. Moreover, as we shall see, the elderly's family varied according to locale. On the farm, in the city, and in the small villages of the United States, the elderly established distinctive types of households. In the village of the industrial era, in fact, large numbers followed a strikingly "modern" family structure. Living alone or simply with their spouse, they created the empty nest household.

As today, however, this arrangement did not necessarily reflect desertion by kin. Instead, during the industrial era, many older people finally had the financial capability to establish a long-preferred model of separate rather than extended or complex households. While popular beliefs consistently emphasized the importance of assisting needy family members, U.S. cultural admonitions have also stressed the primacy of the distinct nuclear family.[6] As we shall see, throughout the elderly's family history, two cultural paradigms have played a key part in influencing household structure. On one hand, families have continuously attempted to meet kinship responsibility; on the other, they have striven to maintain autonomous living. Individual strategies for fulfilling these ideals have been influenced by economic, demographic, and regional constraints. In the industrial era, for example, farmers and urban workers often extended their households to care for their aged kin. In contrast, retired village couples, as well as the increasingly affluent middle class, resided in nuclear households yet were able to retain intimate intergenerational contact.

In recent decades, the ideal of autonomous living has become a widely shared reality. For the first time, guaranteed Social Security benefits, growth in real income, and increased longevity have made it possible for most older Americans, especially elderly women, to establish separate households while maintaining a close and rewarding family life. In the past, few could achieve these aspirations; only today have economic and demographic conditions supported the dual realization of intimacy at a distance. Rather than being scorned by their kin, the old may in fact be experiencing the most satisfying chapter in the long history of their family relationships.

PREINDUSTRIAL AMERICA

In the seventeenth century, individuals generally lived their entire life spans as members of family households. Few, whether young or old, resided alone. For individuals in colonial America, the family played a multitude of roles. Within the household, families educated their children, taught vocations to adolescents, provided the needy with welfare, and worked together to meet basic necessities.[7]

The multiple roles of the family were dictated by pressing economic realities. In a preindustrial agrarian system, the family served as the basic unit for production. The old as well as the young contributed to the economic well-being of the kinship group. No well-established lines marked the point at which the elderly ceased to be contributing family members. Nor did sharp demographic boundaries distinguish the last stages of life for an elderly family member. Until the mid-nineteenth century, the average age at which women bore their last child was near forty. Well into old age, therefore, men and women remained active parents whose transition to old age was quite ambiguous. Retirement at a fixed age was uncommon; few distinctive exits marked aging adults as having completed one stage of life and begun another. Most aged persons did not experience the empty nest in which all the children had grown and departed. Few were ever simply grandparents without parental responsibilities of their own. Quite commonly, as Table 4-1 suggests, the elderly's youngest children and oldest grandchildren would be of the same age. Having become parents in middle age, older people had adolescents of their own in the home.[8]

The demographic structure of the family, therefore, supported the elderly's roles as

TABLE 4-1 Demographic Life Cycle in America, 1650–1950

	1650	1700	1750	1800	1850	1890	1950
Men							
Mean age at							
First marriage	24	25	26	25	26	26	23
Last birth	42	42	43	42	37	37	29
Last child comes of age	63	63	64	63	58	57	50
Last child marries	65	64	66	67	61	59	50
Death	52	52	c.52	c.56	62	66	77
Women							
Mean age at							
Menarche	n.a.	n.a.	n.a.	15.2	14.6	14.2	12.8
First marriage	20	21	23	22	24	23	20
Last birth	38	38	39	39	35	32	26
Last child comes of age	59	59	60	60	56	53	47
Last child marries	60	61	63	64	59	56	48
Death	c.50	c.50	c.50	c.56	61	71	81

SOURCE: David Hackett Fischer, *Growing Old in America.*

parents, household heads, and active family members. In seventeenth-century America, however, the patriarchal power of the old hardly extended beyond the immediate nuclear family of parents and children; the old rarely ruled over extended households with multiple generations of kin. Few such families existed because, quite simply, not enough people survived to experience the maturity and marriage of all their children. As a result, the early colonial family was generally nuclear in form: an elderly couple resided with their unmarried offspring. If younger heads of household included others in their homes, they were likely to have children, servants, or apprentices under their roof rather than their elderly parents. In Bristol, Rhode Island, in 1689, extended households accounted for the living arrangements of only 3 percent of the population; in 1698 in Bedford, New York, only 6 percent.[9]

Few married elderly Americans appeared to have sought refuge in the residences of their young, or themselves provided shelter to numerous generations of married children and grandchildren. Instead, they remained in their own homes, supported by the presence—and labor—of at least one younger family member. The status of the aging couple was linked to their persisting functions and responsibilities as parents and household heads in a nuclear household.

Legal and cultural prescription also dictated that the young would not desert the home of their aging parents. From birth, children were taught to respect their parents. Biblical injunctions and community laws warned that insolence or neglect would be treated harshly. In colonial Massachusetts, adolescents over the age of sixteen could by law be put to death for striking or cursing their parents. Although it is unclear whether anyone ever actually met this dire end, the command to "honor thy father and mother" was taken quite seriously.[10] The magistrates of communities did not hesitate to interfere in family matters when they felt the children were not properly treating their elders or providing their basic necessities.[11] In 1690, for example, the selectmen of Boston warned James Barbor that unless he cared more properly for his father, "you may expect wee shall; prosecute the Law upon you [sic]." Nor did religious leaders shun the tasks of castigating their congregations if they failed to meet their filial obligations. "Children," thundered Reverend Samuel Willard, "that have been the Charge of the Parents, to bring them up to be capable of doing something, should not presently, in hope of doing better from themselves, desert their helpless Parents, as thinking it now time to look to themselves, and left them [to] shift as they can."[12]

But it was not only religious and legal decrees that held the family of the old together. Aged landholders often maintained their control of the young through significant economic power that diminished little with advancing years. Male heads of household rarely disposed of their property before their deaths. The continued possession of land and assets assured the status of the aging couple in the family. They controlled their children and guaranteed their enduring support by holding out the promise of valued estates.[13]

Custom and inheritance patterns dictated that at least one child remain with the aging couple. Generally, this individual would not marry and sire a new generation while in the home of the old. Rather, in return for the homestead or a larger portion of the estate upon the death of the parents, an individual—whatever his or her age—remained a "child," providing aging parents with labor and support. Only upon the death of the landholder would the child become an adult and be financially able to begin a family of his or her own.[14]

For elderly widows, the ownership of land also ensured a continued role in the family. In colonial wills, an elderly man often listed the care that was to be bestowed upon his widow and the assets that, upon his death, would become her possessions. This list could be as broad as simply giving her one-third of the assets (the "widow's share") or as specific as the names of cows and sheep she was to receive and the room in the home in which she was to sleep. Children were often warned that failure to respect and esteem the wife would mean the loss of the homestead or the forfeiture of valued and hard-earned possessions.[15]

Colonial wills often granted power to the widows by making them guardians of the children and trustees of the estate. Despite the numerous barriers in the seventeenth century to women's legal equality, these documents could bestow considerable power upon an elderly widow. Once granted the control of children or land, she, like men, could threaten her children with grave consequences if they were to desert her. Even the woman who was granted only the traditional "widow's third" was given the opportunity to control some assets—and exert some power—over her kin in her old age. Offspring who one day looked forward to the possession of her realty or the financial gain from its sale would be likely to treat her with continuing respect.[16]

Every colonial widow, however, did not find authority and prosperity in her family relationships. While some clearly retained influence over their offspring and even added materially to their husbands' estates, others experienced considerable hardship in their final days. Richer men often dictated precise wills that reduced a widow's expected share in favor of certain children. Granting only a portion of the assets to the widow, such documents clearly limited the woman's authority among her kin. Moreover, if the will stipulated, as many did, that she would lose the assigned assets upon remarriage, her power was further constricted. To a great degree, therefore, the detailed bequest marked a significant reversal in the family hierarchy; relegated to specific rooms and possessions, she relinquished the status of household head to her adult children.[17]

The living arrangements of widows, in fact, were markedly different from those of their married counterparts. While few elderly couples lived with their married children and their offspring, the widowed old—both male and female—often resided with the young. In late-seventeenth-century Bedford, New York, for example, two of the town's six elderly citizens lived in extended households. Both aged individuals had experienced the death of their spouse; in their last years, they sought shelter in homes headed by their adult children.[18]

Yet, while cultural and legal admonitions assumed that the family would support such needy relatives, the existence of three generations within the home did not always lead to harmonious kinship relations. Although ministers warned their congregations to respect and shelter their aged mothers, they cautioned that power now rested with the new generation. Aging adults who interfered with the upbringing of their grandchildren were sure to do the youngsters irreparable harm. Some middle-aged adults simply avoided the problems of the extended family by boarding their elderly relations in the homes of others, assuming only a financial responsibility for them. Even the most resourceful of mothers, like the admirable midwife Martha Ballard, found children disrespectful and selfish, unwilling to make a parent's old age more comfortable. Such behavior led Ballard to remark bitterly that her children ought to "Consider they may be old and receiv like Treatment. [sic]"[19]

Not all elderly individuals, of course, had children to provide them with the necessary labor or to contribute to their support. While colonial New England society encouraged all to wed, some men and women remained unmarried; others failed to reproduce the requisite offspring; many experienced the early death or desertion of their spouse and children. Even these persons, however, generally did not reside alone. Communities quickly placed elderly spinsters and bachelors, as well as widows and widowers, in the homes of neighbors and kin or assigned others to live with them.[20] Able and propertied aging women became the proprietors of boarding houses. Such establishments provided them both an acceptable kinship structure and a necessary source of financial support. Those physically unable to operate such institutions often became boarders themselves.[21]

Yet even in colonial America, demographic and economic realities tended at times to challenge the traditional family support and authority of the old. Especially in seventeenth-century New England, individuals often lived to great age. In Plymouth Colony, 68 percent of all twenty-year-olds reached at least their sixtieth birthday; in Ipswich, Massachusetts, the proportion rose to 72 percent. While adult mortality in the South was higher, by the mid-eighteenth century the chance of obtaining advanced age had become far greater even in this region. Such extensive life spans may have led to significant strains within the family: children who remained in the household, waiting for their parents to die and pass on the estate, found their stay far longer than anticipated.[22]

Moreover, across the eighteenth century, the division of land reduced the size and potential of estates; the portion that the elderly adult could promise the young—or use to ensure authority—became greatly diminished. By the eighteenth century, elderly couples often deeded the land to their children before their deaths. No longer able to dictate the continued labor or residence of the young, the aged came to rely on financial assets and annual rents to support their own final days.[23] Widows, too, may have been less able to exert power within the family. Unlike their counterparts a century earlier, they were not always named in the will as the guardians of their children or the executrixes of their husbands' estates. Especially among richer households, the widows' power was often shared by kin, acquaintances, or court-appointed representatives.[24]

Such changes may account for the growing concern of ministers and magistrates over the plight of their communities' aged widows. In the eighteenth century, customary forms of family support for the old met the needs of most and provided considerable power to some. But for a small and increasingly visible minority, the system did not operate successfully. Large cities such as Boston, Philadelphia, New York, and Charleston established poorhouses that offered shelter to poverty-stricken and dependent elderly; within these asylums the aged poor and debilitated often made up a quarter of the inmate population. Yet the founders of these institutions viewed the establishments within the traditional system of family welfare. The asylums now provided the needy with the "kin" that they were obviously lacking.[25] In the industrial era, this institutional response would become increasingly important. Yet even in this later period, for the great majority of the old the family remained the most important resource against an impoverished, debilitated, or simply solitary old age.

THE INDUSTRIAL ERA

As the colonial family of the elderly does not meet the extended, patriarchal profile projected by a sentimental and nostalgic view of the past, their household and family patterns in the industrial era did not follow a simple pattern of degeneration. According to the early-twentieth-century advocates for the elderly as well as some modern-day scholars, industrialization disrupted "traditional" family relationships and severed the old from their kin. All alone in the city, the elderly experienced isolation and impoverishment. Only on the farm, individuals such as Abraham Epstein and Isaac Rubinow declared, could the old retain the stable and supportive familial relationships that ensured continued financial and emotional support.

Historical evidence, however, tells a far more intricate and varied tale. Beginning in the mid-nineteenth century, wide-scale demographic changes dramatically affected the nature of the U.S. population and broadened the possible combinations of family patterns. Declines in mortality, both for infants and for women at childbirth, meant that a larger proportion of individuals survived to old age. Earlier marriages and earlier ages for childbearing increased the probability that three generations of family members would be alive simultaneously. In the midst of the industrial transformation, many more families had the opportunity to create three-generational arrangements.[26]

Such residences, however, remained the exception rather than the rule. In the late nineteenth and early twentieth centuries, they comprised perhaps one-fifth of all U.S. households. By 1900, 70 percent of all individuals age sixty and over lived as the head of the household or the spouse of the head; 22 percent, most of whom were older women, resided as a relative to the householder; and only 8 percent lived outside the family, often with a nonrelative, as a boarder in a lodging house, or as an inmate of an institution.[27]

For those who did live in complex households, such arrangements generally did not rely on sheer sentiment. Complex structure was very strongly related to the particular economic circumstances faced by elderly individuals and their families. Complex family relationships were often founded on economic agreements. For many older people, a prosperous old age depended on the continued contribution of offspring to family resources. Reliance on the wages of children, the pressing dependency of the sick or incapacitated elderly, and cultural norms that demanded that children assist their aging kin meant that the elderly rarely lived alone. While few aging married couples extended their households to include subfamilies, their homes commonly included an adult child, an arrangement that could be considered only technically "nuclear."[28] Among the elderly, older women without spouses were the most likely to live in households extended to three generations. In the homes of their married children, such women took their place as dependents of the younger generation.

For the middle class, economic considerations determined whether their household structure would be extended. With increasing assets, relatively affluent individuals were able to provide for their relatives, even if they did not contribute to the family's resources. Such limited prosperity allowed both the elderly and the nonelderly to shelter their dependent kin and apportion their resources efficiently. For every class, complex structures surely were as much a product of necessity as of desire. In organizing their families, Americans found themselves torn between two important and quite contradictory values. While they clearly believed that family members had a duty to support each other, they also saw the small nuclear family as the ideal household. For those who opened their homes to their kin as well as for those who chose to live in nuclear families, the ideal of familial responsibility often came into conflict with a parallel belief in separate households.

The Public Use Sample of the 1900 U.S. Census allows us to examine the diverse arrangements of the industrial period and especially to assess the effects of gender, race, and ethnicity. It reveals as well that household structure was determined according to the location of the older people's residences. Three very different and highly significant locales existed: farm, village, and city. In 1900, 38 percent of Americans aged sixty and over lived on farms. Another 25 percent lived in nonurban areas with fewer than 2,500 residents, although they did not reside on farms. This group we shall refer to as village residents. The remaining 37 percent lived in larger towns and cities. The most important distinctions in these settings are displayed in Table 4-2. As the subsequent discussion reveals, no continuum in family circumstances carried from farm to village to city. The farm offered no special refuge for the elderly; the city rarely marked the dissolution of kinship alliances. By contrast, the village was hardly an interim step, but appears almost modern in its familial structure.

TABLE 4-2 Household Characteristics by Locale for Males and Females Aged Sixty and Over, 1900

	Farm		Village		City	
	M(%)	F(%)	M(%)	F(%)	M(%)	F(%)
Relationship to household head:						
Head	82	13	74	32	77	30
Wife		44		36		31
Parent	13	36	6	18	11	25
Other relative	4	6	2	5	2	4
Nonrelative	2	1	18	9	10	10
Extended household						
Yes	41	61	26	42	31	47
Up to parents	12	29	6	14	10	21
Down to child	19	16	13	16	14	13

SOURCE: Public Use Sample of the 1900 U.S. Census.

Old Folks on the Farm

The farm family of the nineteenth century evokes an image of old people gently rocking on well-worn porches, surrounded by extensive generations of loving and supportive kin. In reality, the final days of the aged—especially those of widowed farm women—may have been quite different. Gender, marital status, and economic standing controlled farm-family experience. The myth of the extended farm household had some validity for the wealthy, married, and native-born. Aging male farmers generally retained the role of household head. Their valued property encouraged younger members to remain in the household and provide their assistance. At the turn of the century in a rural county of Kentucky, for example, a great majority of old men remained married, gainfully occupied, and heads of their households. Two-thirds of the Kentucky aged, in fact, continued to have children living in their homes. Moreover, their families had become increasingly complex; more than half of the men aged sixty-five to seventy-four resided with the family of one of their children or lived with a secondary, nonrelated individual in their households.[29]

Poorer families, however, exhibited different patterns of family structure. The less affluent struggled as hired hands and subsistence farmers; they were far less likely to own valuable property. Additional family members did not necessarily contribute to their financial well-being or allow for an adequate distribution of limited resources. Rather, such extended support networks existed generally among individuals of moderate wealth. They, rather than the poor, possessed the ability to offer support and shelter to dependent relatives and the capacity to use extra hands efficiently. Among elderly farmers in mid-nineteenth-century Erie County, New York, the richer the farm, the more likely it had an extended family; the value of the estate predicted household structure.[30]

These findings reveal the importance of both economics and demography. In contrast to the relatively attenuated colonial family, extended and complex households arose in the industrial era partly because they were finally demographically possible: earlier ages of marriage along with a decline in adult mortality meant that three generations more often existed simultaneously. Moreover, relative economic success permitted the elderly to support nonproductive kin. On the large farm, landholders were able both to sustain additional family members and to hold out the promise of estates to kin in exchange for their labor and assistance.

But census records also suggest that the elderly on the nineteenth-century farm had begun to accept a significant change in their roles and responsibilities. Sheltered within a multi-generational home, the old traded the status of household head for sustenance and gradual retirement. In the farm regions of nineteenth- and early-twentieth-century America, households that included aging parents and adult children had more sons in residence than did urban households, where adult daughters predominated.[31] When older men gave up headship, their male heirs took over the operation of their valuable farms. In contrast to inheritance patterns of colonial America, the transmission of authority may even have occurred while the older farmers were still active and registered as the heads of household. Although their property still served as a vehicle for support in old age, nineteenth-century farmers did not necessarily wait for death or extreme debility to cede control.[32]

Such significant shifts of power were often spelled out in deeds that legalized the transfer of land from one generation to another. These settlements were based on strict guarantees that ensured continued care of the elderly. Children promised that in return for ownership of the family farm, they would provide room, board, clothing, and medical attention to their aging parents and assure them of a proper burial. The new complex families that were formed, therefore, were based on a well-defined understanding of transformed functions and obligations.[33]

Such patterns, however, were not universal. Like the poorer native-born elderly, aging farmers of foreign birth had less access to arrangements based on wealth and were less often found in their children's households. Foreigners were, in fact, the least likely of any group to live in extended households. Their housing arrangements were complex, however, in that they relied on the continued presence of an adult child. In contrast to 65 percent of the native-born heads of farm households, 75 percent of foreign-born male farmers still had a child present in the home. The continued status of the old as household head may be due to ethnic and cultural norms—as its consistency among locales suggests—but it also reflects economic demands. The foreign born were among the poorest of all white farmers. Having fewer resources by which to attract and retain kin outside the nuclear family, the elderly depended upon the willingness of children to remain unmarried and continue to assist them.[34]

The households of African Americans varied still more dramatically from their white counterparts, whether rich or poor. Over 45 percent of aged black men on farms lived in extended households, in contrast to only 37 percent of aged foreign-born men. One-third of these African-American households were extended to younger generations. Thus, unlike native-born white farmers who sacrificed headship, the kinship networks of African Americans tended to be extended *down,* with men heading households well into old age, at rates higher than any other group.[35] Having little wealth to offer their children, who had few assets to offer them in return, black men and women rarely had adult children in their homes or lived as dependents in their offsprings' households.[36] But because of a need for laborers, aged blacks extended their households to include a wide variety of individuals: grandchildren, nieces, nephews, other kin, and even nonrelated persons who might be described as fictive kin. The sharecropping system in southern states, where 90 percent of all African Americans lived in 1900, explains the unique family arrangements of elderly blacks. Contractual, noncash tenancy demanded that older men be able to deliver a large labor force to the landholder.[37]

The most significant difference among farm families, however, was related to gender. For most aged male farmers, the land continued to provide authority, or at least support; for elderly farm widows, however, power quickly passed to the next generation. The widow who acted as head of household was extremely rare.[38] In contrast to their counterparts in both villages and urban areas, farm widows were least likely to exert the power and responsibilities inherent in managing the estate. One consequence was that fewer aged women than men lived in farm households—only 35 percent of the elderly female population, in contrast to 41 percent of all aged men. If a widow continued to live on the farm, she usually assumed the part of a dependent, reliant on the support of the next generation. Although a widow was as likely as other women to have children present in her home, she was far less likely to be considered the head of household. As Table 4-2 shows, while 25 percent of aged urban women and 18 percent of aged female villagers endured the status of dependent ("parent"), 36 percent of all aged farm women spent their last years as dependents in the household of kin. Once widowed, they either left the farm or passed their final years as the mother or mother-in-law in the homes of middle-aged landholders.

Village America

Not all Americans had to choose between the farm and the city. The village provided an alternative, one with important implications for life in old age. Village residents had diverse roots; a middle class of merchants, teachers, industrialists, businessmen, and professionals was joined by employees of rural firms, railroad workers, independent mechanics, and farm laborers living away from the farm. In addition, during the nineteenth century, an increasing number of farmers chose to sell or rent their property and settle down to the gentler life of the village.

The decision of elderly farmers to liquidate their estates and to provide for their own retirement marked a significant change in inheritance patterns. In the early colonial period, elderly farmers often held onto their land until death, assuring themselves of continued power. Members of later generations often deeded the land to their children, continuing to live in the established homestead and legally guaranteeing themselves the support of their offspring. In the late nineteenth century, however, aging farmers with sufficient property began simply to sell or rent their land, utilizing the funds to support themselves. Dependence on the benevolence—or the control—of their children was replaced by establishing their own retirement capital.

In Bucks County, Pennsylvania, for example, a significant evolution in inheritance patterns occurred in the course of two centuries. During the colonial period, 87 percent of all testators passed their farm or other businesses to their heirs; in the 1790s, the proportion had fallen to 71 percent. By 1890, a dramatic change had taken place. Only a little more than a third of all who made out a will bequeathed the property to their offspring.[39]

The conversion of estates, the creation of a retirement "nest egg," and the movement of village youth into the cities help to explain the distinct household structure of the village elderly. Half of all the male heads of village households lived without offspring in their homes, as opposed to one-third in other locations. Even in extreme old age, therefore, they retained their independence as household heads and resided either with their wives or alone. And if they lived with children, they generally did not relinquish their position of authority. If their households were extended, they tended to be extended down. Table 4-2 shows that only 6 percent of all aged village men (in contrast to 11 percent in cities and 13 percent on farms) lived as parent to the household head.

Nor was the role of household head in small communities limited to males. While farm widows appeared to have had a difficult time retaining authority, in rural nonfarm settings more than two-thirds of all women aged sixty and over were listed by census takers as either married to the household head (36 percent) or themselves head of the household (32 percent). On the farm, only 57 percent of all aged women maintained these statuses; in the city, the proportion was 61 percent. For elderly village women, even widowhood did not necessarily lead to dependence. In the village, 56 percent of widows were able to retain their authority as household heads, in contrast to 48 percent in the city, and a mere 24 percent on the farm.

The comparative autonomy of village women was a result of both their relative affluence—they had retained property or retired on their assets—and the shortage of children upon whom they could rely. In contrast to their counterparts on farms and in cities, they were least likely to have a child present. Table 4-2 indicates that 18 percent of all older women in villages lived in households in which they were the mother or mother-in-law of the household head, half the farm rate. In the small village rather than the farm or even the city, elderly women often lived as self-reliant individuals.

For both elderly men and women, therefore, the village seems to have offered an unusually independent, stable, and, by household standards, isolated experience. Unlike the farm, and, to a lesser degree, the urban dwelling, the village home did not represent a valued economic asset. Not expecting to inherit a farm or to share valued urban real estate, the children of the elderly had little reason to co-reside with their parents; they searched for opportunities elsewhere. But the village also offered elderly individuals a new opportunity to establish independent households. Especially for the native-born white elderly, the autonomous village household may have provided a setting for self-sufficiency, achieved through years of economic planning. This setting may also have been the primary residential choice of Civil War veterans, whose receipt of a regular, guaranteed income in old age allowed them to retire.[40] Able to afford to live by themselves, they chose to retain the position of household head and, within the individual household at least, did not rely on co-residence with generations of offspring. Such kinship arrangements, however, did not mean that the village elderly had severed all ties with their families or did not consider them important to their own well-being.[41] Rather, village household structure reveals that when economic circumstances permitted, these elderly individuals preferred to live in separate households.

Urban America

In the village, the households of the elderly began to take on a compact, relatively isolated shape. This rural structure has largely been ignored in the modern indictment of familial irresponsibility. Traditionally the city has been blamed for the solitude and isolation of the elderly. Here, critics assumed, the family life of the old was torn apart. Deserted by children who joined the incessant migration of workers from place to place or who, lured by high wages, left the household and began their own families, the old spent their last years with little family contact. Urbanization supposedly transformed a vibrant intergenerational life into an isolated and solitary experience.

In reality, the family life of the urban aged in the industrial era bore little similarity to this depiction. Historians have often found that urbanization *increased* the likelihood that the old would live with their children. In key cities of Massachusetts, for example, urban growth strengthened rather than weakened ties among generations. Between 1860 and 1880 in Salem, Lawrence, and Lynn, the percentage of the elderly who headed households inhabited by adult children increased. Moreover, a higher proportion of urban elders lived with their children than did elders in nonurban areas of Essex County. Similarly, in early-twentieth-century New York, a majority of the urban old lived with their children, while only a minority of rural elderly did so.[42]

The urban environment affected the structure of the household in another important way. As Table 4-2 reveals, only 11 percent of urban men aged sixty and over lived as dependents in their children's home, a rate slightly lower than that of men living on the farm. The city offered aging men who experienced the death of a spouse a variety of strategies for remaining in control of the home. Some took in boarders; others, more affluent, hired servants. Wealth in the city, like prosperity on the farm, allowed older men and women to bring more kin into their households. In 1900, the wealthier of the elderly—defined as those with servants—were more likely than the poor to reside with at least one child.[43] Their relative affluence often allowed them the privilege of both paid help and the continued residence of their offspring.

For women, urban family life also differed significantly from that of the farm or village. Upon the death of their husbands, widows did not necessarily forfeit authority and become dependents in the homes of the children, a common fate for farm women. Rather, towns and cities provided many elderly women with the means by which to remain heads of households. In contrast especially to the farm, which many widows abandoned, urban areas attracted large numbers of widowed women in search of economic independence. As a result, a larger percentage of older women than men lived in towns and cities. Whether native-born white, foreign-born white, or African American, such women discovered that the urban environment provided a better arena than the farm for finding employment and remaining in control of the household.[44] In 1900, only 29 percent of all city women lived as dependents in households, compared to 42 percent of aged women on farms. Nearly half of the urban widows remained heads of their households.

Many of these independent women relied on the wealth accumulated by themselves and their husbands; in native-born white households, they often resided with a servant. Other women managed to support themselves and maintain their independence through the operation of boarding and lodging houses. In 1900, 15 percent of widows who remained heads of households ran such establishments. For these individuals, their residences not only represented a place for them to live but also provided a highly valuable asset. In the mid-nineteenth century, boarding houses played a significant part in the life cycle of many city dwellers. For young migrants, they provided a suitable shelter; for the old they offered a source of needed revenue. As children matured and left the house, vacant rooms could be turned to economic gain. Especially for women approaching old age, therefore, managing a boarding house constituted a viable and legitimate occupation and gave them a way to retain their autonomy.[45]

As with farm dwellers, ownership of a home represented a substantial economic asset for the urban elderly, but its effects on household structure were significantly different. In the city, ownership of a dwelling did not lead automatically to the transferral of power to the next generation. When farm families included three generations, they tended to be extended *up;* middle-aged males had taken control of the land, and with it, the dominant role in the family. In contrast, urban families often continued to be headed by the old. Table 4-2 shows that 14 percent of the households in which urban aged men lived extended down to a younger generation, while only 10 percent were extended up to the aged. In addition, urban elderly commonly lived with adult daughters rather than with sons. Young women remained in the households of their parents or, if another family lived with the old, it was their daughters' husbands and children.[46] Most commonly, urban households headed by the aged were not extended but complex in structure: adult children—usually female—remained in their aged parents' home.

In urban settings, complex relationships came to serve critical functions for both the old and their children. The elderly and their children employed numerous family strategies to deal with the demands of urban, industrialized society. The establishment of complex families brought measurable benefits to both generations: highly desirable living space could be shared and income combined. Moreover, in cities, where the elderly were far more likely to own property than the young, the adult children sought lodging in homes already established by the older generation.[47]

As in the countryside, however, complex structures were not products of impoverishment. Rather, they were formed by those who could afford to live together and pool their resources; the poorest of the old had the least opportunity to sustain independent, complex households. Middle-class older people had the resources necessary to support additional kin; working-class elders had the greatest reason to encourage adult children to remain unmarried and contribute to the family income. Daniel Scott Smith's study of the 1900 census showed that complex families were more often formed by middle-class persons.[48] In 1900, while 68 percent of all urban middle-class individuals aged 55 and older resided with at least one child, the percentage among the urban working class was only 61.[49] Richer people had the resources—especially the ownership of a home—necessary to bring others into their households. The actions of the most affluent may have been charitably inspired; for those of lesser means, the arrangement was a way of using resources in realty to combine income and reduce per capita expenditures. The elderly were more likely to possess the assets necessary to achieve these objectives.[50]

Despite differences in household arrangements—by locale, class, and gender—the most striking feature at the turn of the century was an increasing complexity in household structure and higher rates of extension. To some degree, the appearance of large numbers of such households in the nineteenth century was the result of broad demographic change; for the first time, a large number of Americans survived long enough to reside in multi-generational households. Except in the village, where independent households were most likely, the particular form of household varied greatly: many elderly individuals lived in homes with downward extension; other households were extended up; some aged resided with distant kin, fictive kin, or even unrelated individuals. But the result for elderly people outside the village was clear: most individuals shared a dwelling with other individuals; few resided alone or even with their spouse in the empty nest household.[51]

The Decline of Complex Households

Although the demographic conditions upon which these new household structures were built did not dissipate, the tendency toward extended and complex forms quickly eroded after 1900. By the second decade of the twentieth century, the likelihood that members of the middle class would extend their households to accommodate kin began to weaken. For the first time, a considerable proportion of middle-class children and their elders established separate residences.[52] Between 1900 and 1940, the proportion of men aged sixty-five and over who lived as dependents in their children's home declined from 16 percent to 11 percent; for women the percentage fell from 34 to 23.[53] While this decline may have reflected a cultural shift marking a deterioration of the desire of generations to live together, the discovery that prosperous village elders had previously established autonomous households challenges the theory of the creation of a new cultural preference. The decrease in residential dependency may instead have been based on rising opportunities that allowed a significant number of Americans to realize a longstanding ideal of autonomous living. Rather than exposing neglect on the part of the young or a sudden dislike of their elders, such living arrangements were largely the result of economic prosperity. Increased wages and additional wealth allowed some families to achieve an ideal of separate dwellings. Among the more prosperous families, elderly individuals could amass sufficient wealth in the course of a lifetime to live independently, without depending on their children's support. As in the villages of the nineteenth century, assets in the form of pensions, investments, or savings accounts provided these persons with the option of living without their relatives. By 1915, in fact, a new pattern began to emerge: fewer middle-class families formed complex households while in the working-class, extension and modification became more common.[54]

One explanation may be found in the economic conditions of industrialization. The average income levels of the working class rose to the standards that the middle class had achieved decades before. As a result, the more prosperous workers secured wealth sufficient to provide housing and support for relatives, although inadequate for separate residences.[55] The "luxury" of kinship co-residence, once only available to the middle class, now became a pattern among laborers. Moreover, the additional high wages of family members increased the financial well-being of the group. In 1880 in Erie County, New York, for instance, the inclusion of extended family among the unskilled generally diminished family wealth. By 1915, this loss of average income was no longer the case. The extended family, in fact, was likely to signal an improvement in the economic status of the unskilled worker.[56]

The middle class, on the other hand, now began to follow a different pattern. Before 1900, even white-collar workers were impoverished by present-day standards. Despite their comparatively higher economic status, they were often unable to establish separate living quarters for aged relatives. In the twentieth century, however, their increased well-being allowed them to live independently. This strategy was not entirely new; it had long been followed by the upper class and the fortunate elderly who resided in U.S. villages.

The growing isolation of the middle-class household not only reflected its superior economic basis but was supported as well by evolving cultural expectations. In the mid-nineteenth century, middle-class sentiment proclaimed the family to be the foundation of all social order, responsible for the development of an individual's personality, values, and character.[57] Few questioned that the family was ultimately accountable for the support of its members. The care of the dependent relative, and especially the widowed mother, was a moral obligation that went beyond economic considerations.[58] In dealing with their own families as well as in defining the correct welfare policy for the poor, the nineteenth-century middle class continually espoused the primary importance of family responsibility.

Despite such beliefs, as in the preindustrial era, co-residence with an elderly relative did not always imply peaceful coexistence, nor the absence of an alternative vision of what might be better. Within complex households, the lines of authority often led to conflict and dissension.[59] In the mid-nineteenth century, Julia and Bildad Merrill, Jr., of Utica, New York, moved into the household of Bildad's elderly parents. Faced with growing disability, Bildad Merrill, Sr., and his wife, Nancy, traded their independence for the support of the younger generation. Yet this economic strategy did not translate into harmonious relations; the elderly couple found it difficult to relinquish their authority to their offspring. Both mother and daughter-in-law claimed command over the servants and preeminence with the children. Ultimately, their dispute led to an outbreak of violence between the two women and an ignominious church trial. After public apologies and resolutions, they returned to share the same abode—and many of the same generational tensions.[60]

The Merrills' household arrangements reflected their emerging middle-class status. Their relative level of affluence allowed them to support the elderly in times of need and to sustain the belief that the family was fulfilling one of its primary responsibilities. For such individuals, the neglect of relatives would have been a sure sign of little breeding or refinement; to share possessions and space was part of the cultural code of the bourgeoisie. Like the Merrills, therefore, few middle-class individuals would have questioned the necessity of assisting kin, if such assistance was required. Before the advent of the welfare state, resorting to public welfare was viewed as ultimate failure; the family rather than the state was responsible for the well-being of its relatives.[61]

Such beliefs, however, were not immune to demographic pressures. Although widows with small families could expect to live with their offspring in old age, they were not as confident of co-residence as their counterparts with many children. In 1910, 63 percent of all white widows over the age of sixty-five who had only one surviving child lived with that offspring. For those with five or more offspring, co-residence reached 85 percent.[62]

But it was not only the elderly who experienced the changing demographics of the family in the United States. The decline in family size also placed greater burdens on the children, presenting a much larger share of them with often-difficult living arrangements. In large families, children had a relatively low expectation of co-residence with an aging mother; in contrast, an only child had little hope of avoiding the complex household. As the number of offspring decreased, the risk for the existing children increased, and the predicament of how to provide for the needs of the elderly parent was shared by more Americans.[63] The aged could not select the most congenial environment; nor could the children decide which of several siblings might bear primary responsibility for aging parents. Especially for urban daughters, care of the old became an obligation they were increasingly likely to face as they themselves entered middle age.

Given the decline in the number of siblings, such middle-aged women often found themselves forced to choose between two powerful and enduring norms. On one hand, they had a preference for separate residences—a desire shared by both young and old. On the other, they continued to be committed to the support of needy aged parents. Thus, while the decline in family size did not lead to the abandonment of the old, it raised the potential for even greater tensions within the family group. In the early 1930s, an anonymous female writer recalled the problems of three-generational households. "When I was a child," she wrote,

I took it for granted that a grandmother or grandfather should live in the house of nearly everyone of my playmates. Soon I came to take it for granted, also, that these houses should be full of friction. The association of grandparents with friction took such a hold in my mind that I called myself lucky because my own were dead![64]

Despite her antagonism to such residence patterns, in adulthood the author found herself with little choice but to take her aging mother into the household. The results, she reported, were disastrous. "Harmony is gone. Rest has vanished." Her daily routine, the lives of her children, and the stability of her marriage, she asserted, had been reduced to sheer chaos. Nor, she argued, was she alone. Numerous friends and acquaintances similarly reported the demise of their family and social life upon the residence of an aging parent. "The intrusion," she argued, "is probably a common cause of divorce, and most certainly of marital unhappiness and problems in children."

The anonymous author's complaints reflected her struggle between opposing values and norms. Her conviction that her elderly mother could not be abandoned conflicted with her strong desire to reside only with her husband and children. Although she felt obligated to open her home to her widowed mother, she strongly objected to the situation. "So strong is the tradition," she wrote, "so strong the sense of duty which we carry on for generation to generation," that she found herself with little choice. The only happy families, she concluded, were those who were financially secure enough to allow aging parent and adult children to live in separate residences.

The author's expressed desire for different dwellings hardly marked her as unique. Even in eighteenth-century England, elderly individuals who were financially able chose to live apart from their offspring. Wealth allowed both the old and their adult children the luxury of separate dwellings.[65] By the twentieth century, this preference—clearly visible in the nineteenth-century village, in the Merrills' conflicts, in the unhappiness of the magazine writer, and, perhaps most apparent, in the continuing effort of older Americans to remain heads of households—began to find expression as a "modern" cultural prescription. While the ideology of supporting the old was never rejected, twentieth-century social critics and advocates of proper family behavior began to stress the centrality of the small private household.

According to their recommendations, few institutions better served society than the nuclear family. Even in the nineteenth century, this arrangement had been at the center of the kinship ideology: the father, the mother, and the children, rather than maiden aunts or mothers-in-law, comprised the central elements in the family circle. Social theorists expressed the concern that the addition of relatives into the hallowed circle would bring dissension and ultimate ruin. Samuel Butler was only one of many anxious English and American analysts. "I believe," he wrote in 1885,

> that more unhappiness comes from this source than from any other—I mean from the attempt to prolong the family connection unduly and to make people hang together artificially who would never naturally do so. The mischief among the lower classes is not so great, but among the middle and upper classes it is killing a large number daily. And the old people do not really like it so much better than the young.[66]

Such pronouncements revealed three central middle-class concerns. First, by the early decades of the twentieth century, scores of social critics were convinced that the enclosed nuclear family was the ideal—and most congenial—arrangement for family members. Abraham Epstein, the pension proponent and expert on aging, asserted that the happiest families were those without extended kin. In 1928, he declared that "we all know among our acquaintances, some people whose young lives have been made pitiably wretched, and in some instances totally ruined, by the constant 'pestering' of an old father-in-law or mother-in-law."[67] Both the elderly and their children, he seemed confident, would be far happier if they could afford to live in separate dwellings.

Second, family experts viewed nuclear households as the proper environment for raising children and ensuring their moral upbringing. Nowhere was this belief expressed with greater vehemence than in the early-twentieth-century attack on the practice of boarding. According to a 1910 report of the U.S. Bureau of Labor, for example, the custom of boarding had little proper place in the American home. The practice, the report explained, was extremely detrimental to family members: "the close quarters often destroy all privacy, and the lodger or boarder becomes practically a member of the family. . . ."[68] The institution, which for so long had been an accepted part of middle-class life and an important source of revenue to the aging, was now seen as a sign of working-class immorality. It was, social analysts declared, an outright attack on the primacy of kinship relations.

Finally, welfare advocates were concerned about the economic impact of extended families. Middle-aged adults, it was feared, were constantly being forced to make irreconcilable economic judgments over the allocation of valued resources. In supporting their elders, they robbed the young; in providing for their children, they dismissed the longstanding obligations they owed to their elders. According to welfare authorities, members of extended families seemed to be faced with an insurmountable predicament: either they provided for their children's growth and education or they saved the old from the shame of the almshouse. Epstein's state pension argument emphasized the economic problems of trying to support the elderly. "It seems cruel," he wrote,

> to force any father or mother in this twentieth century to decide between supporting old parents and contenting themselves with a little less food, less room, less clothing, and the curtailment of their children's education, or sending their parents to the poorhouse or to charitable agencies to accept the stigma of pauperism, and thus assure themselves of more food, more room, more clothing and a better education for their children which would help them become more proficient workers.

In contrast, Epstein asserted, a state pension would "increase filial affection and respect for parents," who were no longer a burden to their middle-aged children.[69]

The concern over the quality of life within the complex family was not limited to "experts." Even the old themselves reported that they would be far happier in separate households. In a 1937 article published in *Saturday Evening Post* and reprinted in *Reader's Digest,* the anonymous author, a seventy-three-year-old woman, wrote, "when declining health and declining finances left me no alternative but to live with my daughter, my first feeling was one of bitterness." The author pledged to make herself as little of a burden as possible through numerous rules: "I must not be around when she was getting her work done, or when she had her friends in. I must ask no questions and give no unasked advice. I resolved to spend the greater part of each day alone in my room."[70]

Given such middle-class views, family experts and welfare advocates came to view complex family settings with increasing hostility. Not surprisingly, perhaps, their criticisms gained credence as the middle class moved away from such households and working-class populations grew affluent enough to adopt them. By the early twentieth century, the extended family no longer seemed a sanctuary of middle-class love and affection. Its value for children, and even for the old, had been seriously challenged. In the experts' views, such family arrangements came to symbolize working-class impoverishment. Only the poor and the immigrant, it was assumed, would live in this manner; all others would choose to reside independently.

The impact of the changing middle-class family, however, should not be exaggerated. Before the development of the welfare state, the family remained the key support for the old and the central agency for their relief should they become dependent. In the working-class family economy, the aged were best served if they could persuade an adult child to remain in the home and contribute wages into the family fund. In the middle class and among the most prosperous of working-class families, older people might amass sufficient assets to retire and maintain independent households, allowing their children to dwell in their own residences. Even for these fortunate aged, however, life was not completely secure; sickness, a sudden loss of assets, or widowhood could undermine even the best of plans.

THE SOCIAL SECURITY ERA

For the families of the middle and working classes alike, the Great Depression had a dramatic and often uncontrollable impact. Severe economic dislocation led to the failure of a fifth of the nation's commercial banks and to the loss of nine million families' life savings.[71] For the elderly, economic collapse spelled disaster as they watched their hard-won assets vanish, and with them their hopes for an independent and secure old age. In city after city, urban dwellers, unable to pay their debts, had to forfeit their homes.[72] In rural areas, the family's inability to meet even its property taxes and ordinary bills led to the repossession and auction of thousands of family farms. Real estate in farm, village, and city had, of course, served as the elderly's protection for old age. It often represented the only important asset among farmers and in the working class. The collapse in the value of property and widespread forfeiture symbolized only too well the insecurity of old age in the United States in the twentieth century.

The dramatic rise in unemployment also challenged traditional means of care of the old. Widespread unemployment meant that families that had prospered through shared incomes were no longer able to meet the needs of all, and certainly had no hope of generating surpluses. Nuclear families were shattered; by 1940, over 1,500,000 married women lived apart from their husbands.[73] Moreover, families that had been able to establish independent households found the retention of such homes difficult. In many cities, families "doubled up" to cut expenses; they relinquished the ideals of separate households and privacy for simple subsistence.

Nowhere was this more true than in the South. There, as many as one-sixth of all urban dwellers shared apartments. The case of Ruby and Elton Cude of San Antonio, Texas, illustrated well the plight of the suddenly impoverished middle class. From 1932 to 1936, the Cudes and their two young children struggled to live independently in their own home. By 1936, however, the financial burdens had become too great, and they were forced to move to Ruby's parents' residence. The house sheltered not only her parents but also her two younger sisters, an unemployed uncle from Mississippi, another uncle with his wife and two children, and a boarder. Although the Cudes were middle class in upbringing and life-style, their experience during the Depression undermined their ideal family structure and challenged their hopes for the future.[74]

The real or incipient collapse of individual households helps to explain the widespread popularity of Social Security. The Depression hit directly at the traditional means of establishing family security. It stripped individuals of their savings and property; it forced families into complex—and often highly stressful—living arrangements that they had long worked to avoid. It even threatened the most respected with the ultimate disgrace: if all family resources were gone, the elders might be forced to take their place among the paupers in the nation's almshouses.

Social Security directly addressed these fears and met the widespread desire for financial and residential independence. Guaranteed monthly checks removed the anxiety over family failure and assured steady if limited support in old age. In their increasingly generous provisions after 1950, however, Social Security benefits had far greater implications. The family economy, which had so long determined household structure, no longer controlled intergenerational transfers. For the first time, the independent household—first realized in the nineteenth-century village, then increasingly favored by the twentieth century's prosperous middle class—came within the grasp of all but the poorest Americans. Rising real incomes after the Second World War released many from the demands of the family economy, which had required co-residence with children. Even among the working class, higher Social Security benefits permitted retirement, security, and the formation of the autonomous household.

The consequent change in the typical household structure of the elderly was far reaching. In 1900, more than 60 percent of all persons aged sixty-five and older resided with their children. Whether as household head or as a dependent of their offspring, the elderly shared residences with the young, uniting their assets and abilities as well as their conflicts. In the 1950s, however, the recipients of Social Security began to establish a clear pattern of separate residences.[75] The allocation of pensions brought on two new related trends: steep declines in complex family living arrangements and striking increases in independent, autonomous households. By 1962, the proportion of the old who lived with their children had dropped to 25 percent and by 1975 to only 14 percent.[76]

While the trend to independent households has affected men, the most significant transformation occurred in the residence patterns of widowed and single women. In 1940, 58 percent of elderly women who were not living with husbands resided with kin; by 1970, only 29 percent of these individuals shared homes with relatives.[77] In the past, widowhood generally had presented women with difficult residential choices. Upon the death of their husbands, many had been forced to restructure their lives in the homes of their kin. In doing so, they had lost their authority as head of household and become dependent; they had found themselves reliant upon the good will and financial support of their offspring. With Social Security, such radical changes were no longer necessary or expected. By the 1950s, most aged women had the financial resources necessary to continue residing in their own dwellings.

Such stable residence patterns for old women conflict with the interpretation of modern old age presented by some sociologists and historians. Several scholars have focused on the dramatic changes that occur in the life of the present-day elderly, marked by abrupt exits such as retirement and the empty nest. Yet they have generally failed to consider that, in the past, aging women often experienced a dramatic break that required great adaptation. Upon the death of their husbands, they shifted from being the spouse of the head of household to being dependent upon the generosity of their children. Rather than marking the continuity of old age, such alterations in roles and residences represented a radical change. Social Security allowed the majority of older women to maintain an autonomy often lost in previous eras.[78]

The independent residential patterns of the old do not imply a modern neglect of the elderly. Rather, they reflect a longstanding preference of most individuals to live autonomously. Contemporary investigations confirm that when able, the elderly choose to live in their own households. In one study, three-quarters of the elderly African Americans and nine in ten of the white elderly persons opposed residing in a multigenerational household. In the survey, nearly all elderly individuals agreed that "it usually does not work out too well for older people to live with the children and grandchildren."[79]

The desire for an autonomous household is hardly new; it has long been the model of preference for most Americans. The recent popularity of the independent household structure means neither that the elderly have been deserted by their families nor that the young devote far less attention and care to the old than in earlier eras. As we noted earlier, contemporary investigations of the elderly's family life have found intergenerational exchange to be vibrant, instrumental, and essential to the elderly's well-being. Independent residency does not equal abandonment; the number of people within the household is certainly not equivalent to the strength of the family or the importance of intergenerational exchange. Children continue to provide assistance to older people in amounts far greater than any government-sponsored programs, while the secure economic standing of most of the elderly allows many to give aid to their offspring.[80] The circumstances of both old and young permit them to exchange resources and support while maintaining independent households.

In the past, guarantees of such independence were rare. Many older people were forced to rely on the family in more direct and intimate ways. Although only a minority lived in extended households, others formed complex living arrangements. Adult children or nonkin, such as boarders and lodgers, occupied the same houses as the elderly. Within the household itself, goods and services were exchanged to assure individual subsistence. In the preindustrial era, most adults spent their lives as parents of children and adolescents; few survived to witness the maturity and family formation of all their offspring. In the nineteenth century, however, a decline in adult mortality and earlier childbirth meant that a far greater number of aged individuals saw their children establish their own families. Complex household structures, then, were most commonly found in the industrial era, when demographic conditions first made such family arrangements highly likely. Rising life expectancy translated into the survival of more individuals into old age who then shared their homes with relatives.

But complex household arrangements were also influenced by economic conditions.

For blacks in the South, extension was dictated by the constraints of sharecropping. Contracts were awarded to those who could provide numerous family members as laborers. For the working class in the industrial era, the family economy relied on keeping older laboring children in the household. Upon the death of their husbands, women were especially likely to become dependents in their children's households, as autonomous economic survival became increasingly tenuous.

As economics shaped the complex and extended household, relative wealth also determined which families were least likely to establish such households. Generally, complex family structures did not occur among the very poor. In most periods, such individuals lacked the resources necessary to respond to family needs and exchange desired necessities. Nor were such arrangements likely to be found among the very wealthy. Their considerable affluence had always allowed them to meet the ideal of the separate household. Autonomous arrangements also became prevalent in the nineteenth-century villages of the United States, where older men and women had fewer offspring upon whom to rely and had amassed the resources necessary to live independently.

By the first decades of the twentieth century, rising levels of wealth extended the opportunity for autonomous households to more and more Americans. But as the Great Depression of the 1930s demonstrated, the permanence of such arrangements remained perilous; ill fortune, bad health, or economic decline could force the newly autonomous middle class into co-residence with their relatives. For working-class families, the Depression had still more severe consequences. Even before the 1930s, they had a pervasive fear of the almshouse and hostility for the condescending private charities of the pre–New Deal era. With the Depression, these anxieties often became reality, forcing families to revert to household arrangements and intrafamilial support that they had assumed were no longer necessary. The Depression's broad impact weakened middle-class objections to public welfare and encouraged the enactment of Social Security. Undoubtedly the most popular of all New Deal measures, it was also the most transforming, for it revolutionized the household and family relationships of the elderly. For the first time, most aged individuals were assured sufficient income to support independent households. Increases in Social Security allocations firmly established the present-day trend of living in isolated, autonomous dwellings.[81]

These changes in household arrangements were supported by cultural assumptions and prescriptions. American ideology has always stressed the centrality of the family and its role in supporting kin. Seventeenth-century ministerial injunctions as well as nineteenth-century middle-class ideology reinforced a belief that the family should give aid and shelter to its members; to rely upon public welfare was a certain sign of moral and economic failure. As a result, when necessary and economically feasible, families pooled income, shared living space, and supported dependent family members. In the twentieth century, however, families more commonly observed another longstanding ideal: separate residences became the basis for enhanced kinship relationships.

The establishment of the autonomous household, however, has not led to the desertion of the old. The continued strength of family relations discovered in recent studies attests to the importance of family networks rather than household arrangements. Although adult children are now less likely than their historical peers to remain in parents' households or to take a needy parent into the home, they are much more likely to have an aging parent depend upon them for some type of assistance. While the pressures upon these adult children are different in nature from those of the industrial era, they are likely to occur with far greater incidence. With the aging of the population and the declining number of children, greater proportions of middle-aged persons must provide some form of assistance to their elderly kin, even as their own families demand their attention. The magnitude of such care has, in fact, raised great concern. Significant and often expensive obligations for the support of elderly family members fall primarily upon middle-aged women, who are already responsible for children, husbands, and, often, their own careers.[82]

In the mid-twentieth century, therefore, the elderly and their families face new challenges. As in the past, demographics and economics determine the range of choices, while the two cultural norms, which balance family responsibility against autonomous living, set the stage for debate. If the family can meet the demands of a larger and older population, it will have realized the goals that history suggests have always guided it: close and instrumental kinship relationships without members of the extended family being forced to share the same household.

NOTES

1. In 1886, for example, the directors of Boston's public institutions complained that "the people of to-day are too prone to wish to get rid of the old father and mother . . . when they become helpless in their old age"; see the Twenty-Ninth Annual Report of the Board of Directors for Public Institutions, *Documents of the City of Boston* (DCB) 1, no. 16, p. 34.

2. In this discussion, the term *extended* will be confined to households that include three generations in a family; *complex* will denote these and other household arrangements such as the inclusion of siblings, cousins, fictive kin, or nonkin, as well as households in which older persons retain headship but adult children reside. The classical family and traditional theory can be found in William J. Goode, *World Revolution and Family Patterns* (New York: Free Press, 1963).

3. This is the famous contention of the Laslett school. See *Household and Family in Past Time*, ed. Peter Laslett (Cambridge: Cambridge University Press, 1972).

4. Lillian E. Troll, in "The Family of Later Life: A Decade Review," *Journal of Marriage and the Family* 33 (May 1971), claimed that the fundamental achievement in social gerontology in the 1960s was the recognition of the centrality of the "modified extended family structure" (p. 264). In an influential collaborative work, Ethel Shanas maintained that "the modified extended family, rather than the nuclear, conjugal family, has emerged as the ideal type in present-day Western society." See Ethel Shanas, Peter Townsend, D. Wedderburn, H. Friees, P. Milhoj, and J. Stehouwer, *Old People in Three Industrial Societies* (New York: Atherton Press, 1968), p. 227. For a recent summary, see Marvin B. Sussman, "The Family Life of Old People," in *Handbook of Aging and the Social Sciences*, ed. Robert H. Binstock and Ethel Shanas, (New York: Van Nostrand Reinhold, 1985).

5. A convincing history of the family faces the imposing difficulty of characterizing the *family* relationships of the old, while the historical evidence almost invariably simply reflects *household* conditions. The "family" is rarely confined to those who live in the same residence; the kinship network, in its emotional and functional aspects, ranges well beyond the dwelling. In addition, our evidence is usually drawn from one moment in time—rarely does it trace families and households across time. See David I. Kertzer, "Future Directions in Historical Household Studies," *Journal of Family History* (Spring 1985): 98–105.

6. According to Tamara Hareven, "The predominance of nuclear residence reflects an over-all commitment in American society to the separation of the family of orientation from the family of procreation"; see her *Family Time and Industrial Time: The Relationship between the Family and Work in a New England Community* (Cambridge: Cambridge University Press, 1982), p. 165.

7. John Demos, *A Little Commonwealth: Family Life in Plymouth Colony* (New York: Oxford University Press, 1970); Edmund S. Morgan, *The Puritan Family: Religion and Domestic Relations in Seventeenth-Century New England* (New York: Harper and Row, 1944).

8. David Hackett Fischer, *Growing Old in America* (New York: Oxford University Press, 1977), appendix, table VI, p. 228; Robert V. Wells, "Demographic Change and the Life Cycle of American Families," in *The Family in History*, ed. Theodore K. Rabb and Robert I. Rotberg, (New York: Harper and Row, 1971), p. 87; Carole Haber, *Beyond Sixty-Five: The Dilemma of Old Age in America's Past* (New York: Cambridge University Press, 1983), pp. 10–11.

9. Steven Ruggles, *Prolonged Connections: The Rise of the Extended Family in Nineteenth-Century England and America* (Madison: University of Wisconsin Press, 1987), p. 4.

10. Demos, *A Little Commonwealth*, pp. 101–3; Morgan, *The Puritan Family*, p. 78.

11. *A Report of the Record Commissioners of the City of Boston containing Miscellaneous Papers*, City Document 150, 3 May 1692 (Boston: Rockwell & Churchill, 1886), p. 62.

12. Samuel Willard, *A Compleat Body of Divinity*, Sermon 64, p. 608.

13. John Demos, "Old Age in Early New England," in Michael Gordon, ed., *The American Family in Social-Historical Perspective*, 2d ed. (New York: St. Martin's Press, 1978), pp. 220–56; Philip J. Greven, Jr., *Four Generations: Population, Land, and Family in Colonial Andover* (Ithaca, N.Y.: Cornell University Press, 1970); Daniel Scott Smith, "Old Age and the 'Great Transformation,'" in *Aging and the Elderly*, ed. Stuart F. Spicker, Kathleen M. Woodward, and David D. Van Tassel (Atlantic Highlands, N.J.: Humanities Press, 1978), pp. 294–95; John J. Waters, "Patrimony, Succession and Social Stability: Guilford, Connecticut, in the Eighteenth Century," *Perspectives in American History* 10 (1976): 157–58.

14. Joseph Abbot of Andover, Massachusetts, was chosen to inherit the family residence upon the death of his father. The elder Abbot did not die until 1731, at the advanced age of seventy-three. Until that time, his son remained a "child" in the family home. Only after his father's demise did Joseph, at age forty-five, marry and inherit the house. See Greven, *Four Generations*, p. 142. See also J. H. Plumb, "The Great Change in Children," in *Rethinking Childhood*, ed. Arlene Skolnick (Boston: Little, Brown, 1976), p. 205.

15. Demos, *A Little Commonwealth*, p. 238; Haber, *Beyond Sixty-Five*, p. 20; Alexander Keyssar, "Widowhood in Eighteenth-Century Massachusetts: A Problem in the History of the Family," *Perspectives in American History* 8 (1974): 108.

16. Carole Shammas, Marylynn Salmon, and Michel Dahlin, *Inheritance in America: From Colonial Times to the Present* (New Brunswick, N.J.: Rutgers University Press, 1987), pp. 51–55.

17. Ibid., pp. 55–60.

18. Robert V. Wells, *The Population of the British Colonies of America before 1776: A Survey of Census Data* (Princeton, N.J.: Princeton University Press, 1975), p. 132.

19. Haber, *Beyond Sixty-Five*, pp. 23–24; *A Report of the Record Commissioners of the City of Boston containing Records of the Boston Selectmen 1701–1715* (Boston: Rockwell & Churchill, 1884), p. 68: Laurel Thatcher Ulrich, *A Midwife's Tale: The Life of Martha Ballard, Based on Her Diary, 1785–1812* (New York: Vintage, 1991), p. 263.

20. Morgan, *The Puritan Family*, pp. 145–46.

21. *Report of the Record Commissioners of the City of Boston containing Miscellaneous Papers* (1707), p. 177.

22. Demos, *A Little Commonwealth*, p. 192; Allan Kulikoff, *Tobacco and Slaves: The Development of Southern Culture in the Chesapeake, 1680–1800* (Chapel Hill: University of North Carolina Press, 1986), chap. 5; Greven, *Four Generations*, p. 229.

23. Greven, *Four Generations*, chaps. 7 and 8.

24. Shammas et al., *Inheritance in America*, pp. 55–60.

25. David J. Rothman, *The Discovery of the Asylum: Social Order and Disorder in the New Republic* (Boston: Little, Brown, 1971), pp. 36, 38–39; Gary B. Nash, "Poverty and Poor Relief in Pre-Revolutionary Philadelphia," *William and Mary Quarterly* 33, 3d ser. (January 1977), pp. 6, 9; Charles Lawrence, *History of the Philadelphia Almshouses and Hospitals*, (Philadelphia: Charles Lawrence, 1905), pp. 39–40.

26. Ruggles, *Prolonged Connections*, pp. 60–83.

27. Unless otherwise indicated, findings presented in the text are based on our analysis of the Public Use Sample of the 1900 United States Census (Center for Studies in Demography and Ecology, University of Washington, Seattle, 1980). For somewhat different calculations, see Daniel Scott Smith, "Accounting for Change in Families of the Elderly in the United States, 1900–Present," in David D. Van Tassel and Peter N. Stearns, eds., *Old Age in a Bureaucratic Society* (Westport, Conn.: Greenwood Press, 1986): 87–110. The distributions varied sharply by sex: 61 percent of females lived as spouse or household head, 32 percent lived as "dependents," and 7 percent lived outside the family. For men, the corresponding percentages were 78, 13, and 9.

28. For a useful introduction to different propensities to include single or married kin, see Steven Ruggles, "Availability of Kin and the Demography of Historical Family Structure," *Historical Methods* 19 (Summer 1986): 93–102.

29. Thomas A. Arcury, "Rural Elderly Household Life-Course Transitions, 1900 and 1980 Compared," *Journal of Family History* 11, no 1 (1986): 55–76.

30. Ruggles, *Prolonged Connections*, p. 40.

31. According to Smith ("Accounting for Change," p. 103), 29 percent of all old farmers lived with their son or sons; only 18 percent resided with a daughter. In middle-class urban neighborhoods, however, 35 percent of older persons lived with a daughter, while only 18 percent lived with a son.

32. The interchange of power and the reciprocity of relations between generations are certainly underestimated by household data, since intergenerational exchange in farming families most often occurred outside the household sphere. See Jill Quadagno and J. M. Janzen, "Old Age Security and the Family Life Course: A Case Study of Nineteenth-Century Mennonite Immigrants to Kansas," *Journal of Aging Studies* 1 (Spring 1987): 33–49.

33. Hal S. Barron, *Those Who Stayed Behind: Rural Society in Nineteenth-Century New England* (New York: Cambridge University Press, 1984), p. 95.

34. Elizabeth H. Pleck, "Challenges to Traditional Authority in Immigrant Families," in Michael Gordon, ed., *The American Family in Social-Historical Perspective,* 3d ed. (New York: St. Martin's Press, 1983), pp. 514–15. In *Family Time and Industrial Time* (p. 180), Hareven argues that while economic factors contributed to this pattern among the foreign born, so also did "the strong sense of familial solidarity that stemmed from premigration traditions."

35. In native-born white households, about one-quarter were extended down; among the foreign-born, approximately 15 percent. Such extension rates, however, did not include the common practice, especially among the foreign-born, of an adult child remaining in the household. For different reasons, downward extension also distinguishes African-American families in our own time, in particular the extension of older females' households to grandchildren. See Brian Gratton, "Familism among the Black and Mexican-American Elderly: Myth or Reality?" *Journal of Aging Studies* 1 (Spring 1987): 19–32.

36. Only 5 percent of African-American elderly males lived as parent to the household head, in contrast to 12 percent of the native-born white and 16 percent of the foreign-born white males. On this point, see Daniel Scott Smith, Michel Dahlin, and Mark Friedberger, "The Family Structure of the Older Black Population in the American South in 1880 and 1900," *Sociology and Social Research* 63 (April 1979): 544–49. On the African-American family in the South, see also Jacqueline Jones, *Labor of Love, Labor of Sorrow* (New York: Basic Books, 1985), pp. 81–95, 340–41, and Orville Vernon Burton, *In My Father's House Are Many Mansions: Family and Community in Edgefield, South Carolina* (Chapel Hill: University of North Carolina Press, 1985), pp. 230, 260–311, 409.

37. Brian Gratton, "The Labor Force Participation of Older Men, 1890–1940," *Journal of*

Social History 20 (Summer 1987): 689–710. See also Steward A. Tolnay, "Family Economy and the Black American Fertility Transition," *Journal of Family History* (1986): 269. The lack of adult children in black elders' households and the presence of more distant kin appear almost immediately in the postbellum period. See Burton, *In My Father's House,* figs. 7–1, 7–3; table 7–1; and pp. 263–83.

38. According to Arcury's study of a rural county in Kentucky ("Rural Elderly Household Life-Course Transition"), only 29 percent of women aged sixty-five to seventy-four lived with a spouse in a nuclear family. Forty-eight percent resided in complex families, while 24 percent lived in a nonfamily setting.

39. Shammas et al., *Inheritance in America*, pp. 106–108.

40. Jon R. Moen, "Rural, Nonfarm Households: A New View of the Labor Force Participation Rate of Men 65 and Older, 1869–1980," *Social Science History* (in press).

41. The rare historical evidence that surveys households in proximity to one another shows that family contact and household structure were not equivalent. Kin often lived close to older persons' homes, especially in rural and farm areas. In rural North Carolina in the mid-nineteenth century, 24 percent of men over seventy who headed their own households "resided just next door to someone with the same surname as their own," and many more lived near kin with a different surname. In 1900, more than 15 percent of the elderly heads of households had same-surname kin living in close proximity. See Robert C. Kenzer, *Kinship and Neighborhood in a Southern Community: Orange County, North Carolina, 1849–1881* (Knoxville: University of Tennessee Press, 1987), p. 20. See also Daniel Scott Smith, "Life Course, Norms, and the Family System of Older Americans in 1900," *Journal of Family History* 4, no. 2 (1979): 285–98. Smith, however, finds that "kin propensity declined across the nineteenth century"; see his "'All in Some Degree Related to Each Other': A Demographic and Comparative Resolution of the Anomaly of New England Kinship," *American Historical Review* 94 (February 1989): 44–79.

42. Michael Anderson first stressed the role urbanization played in increasing rather than decreasing the tendency toward complex households; see his *Family Structure in Nineteenth-Century Lancashire* (London: Cambridge University Press, 1971). In Salem, Lawrence, and Lynn, 64 percent of men and 61 percent of women aged fifty-five and over lived with children; in nonurban areas of Essex County, the corresponding proportions were 47 and 35 percent. These figures, we presume, combine both rural towns and farms into one rural configuration. As we have argued, such a formulation may hide the rather substantial differences between farm and village families. See Howard P. Chudacoff and Tamara K. Hareven, "Family Transitions into Old Age," in *Transitions: The Family and the Life Course in Historical Perspective,* ed. Tamara K. Hareven (New York: Academic Press, 1978), pp. 217–43, and "From the Empty Nest to Family Dissolution: Life Course Transition into Old Age," *Journal of Family History* 4, no. 1 (Spring, 1979): 69–83; Tamara K. Hareven, "Life Course Transitions and Kin Assistance," in Van Tassel and Stearns, eds., *Old Age in a Bureaucratic Society*, pp. 110–25; and N. Sue Weiler, "Family Security or Social Security? The Family and the Elderly in New York State during the 1920s," *Journal of Family History* 11, no. 1 (1986): 77–95.

43. Smith, "Accounting for Change," pp. 87–109.

44. As an example, in 1880, 79 percent of all urban African-American women aged fifty-five and over were widows. In rural areas, the proportion was only 60 percent—surely a product of the movement of African-American rural widows to the cities. See Janice L. Reiff, Michel R. Dahlin, and Daniel Scott Smith, "Rural Push and Urban Pull: Work and Family Experiences of Older Black Women in Southern Cities, 1880–1900," in Sharon Hurley, ed., *The Urban Experiences of Afro-American Woman* (Boston: G. B. Hall, 1981).

45. John Modell and Tamara K. Hareven, "Urbanization and the Malleable Household: An Examination of Boarding and Lodging in American Families," in Gordon, ed., *The American Family in Social-Historical Perspective*, 2d ed., pp. 51–68. For the very old in the city, boarding houses played another essential role. In chap. 4, we show that many such establishments were de facto nursing homes for the elderly; some even specialized in taking in older residents. Settled

into a boarding house, the elderly person without kin became part of a complex household. In the 1900 sample, about 4 percent of those sixty and older lived as boarders.

46. In middle-class urban neighborhoods, 17 percent of persons over fifty-five lived with unmarried daughters; 15 percent lived with a married daughter. The combined figure of 32 percent greatly exceeded the 18 percent who lived with sons. As already discussed, the proportions were far different on the farm. See Smith, "Accounting for Change," p. 103.

47. "Report on Farms and Homes: Proprietorship and Indebtedness," *Eleventh Census of the United States (1890): Housing* (Washington, D.C.: Government Printing Office, 1895); Anderson, *Family Structure in Nineteenth-Century Lancashire.*

48. Smith, "Life Course, Norms, and the Family System," pp. 285–98, and "Historical Change in the Household Structure of the Elderly in Economically Developed Societies," in Peter N. Stearns, ed., *Old Age in Preindustrial Society* (New York: Holmes and Meier, 1982), 248–73.

49. Smith, "Accounting for Change," p. 101. Smith confirms the presence of a third locale: in cities with a population less than 25,000, only 56 percent had a child in their homes.

50. Ruggles, *Prolonged Connections*, pp. 30–59.

51. In 1900, only about 4 percent of Americans fifty-five and over lived alone; 29 percent of the married lived with a spouse in an empty nest. See Michel Dahlin, "Perspectives on the Family Life of the Elderly in 1900," *Gerontologist* 20, no. 1 (1980): 99–107. See also Smith, "Life Course, Norms, and the Family System." A declining age of last childbirth strongly influenced whether a period of life without children would occur. Among eighteenth-century Quakers, the median age at which women bore their last child was thirty-eight; in a cohort of women from the 1920s, the median age was 30.5. The age at which the last child married and left home was determined by the child's age and by the propensity to leave home. Robert V. Wells estimates that the empty-nest period for Quakers began at age sixty, for an 1880–89 cohort at fifty-six, and for a 1920 cohort at fifty-two; see his "Demographic Change and the Life Cycle," p. 93.

52. According to Ruggles, *Prolonged Connections* (p. 35), in Erie County in 1880, 41 percent of all families with servants lived with extended kin; by 1915 the proportion was only 20.2 percent.

53. Smith, "Historical Change in the Household Structure of the Elderly," p. 266.

54. Ruggles, *Prolonged Connections*, p. 44. For some scholars, the shift away from providing household shelter to kin outside the nuclear unit shows that cultural norms, largely lost today, strongly influenced behavior. See Smith, "Life Course, Norms, and the Family System," p. 294. For a more moderate position, however, see Smith, "'All in Some Degree Related to Each Other.'"

55. For the relative poverty of the working class in 1900, see Brian Gratton, *Urban Elders: Family, Work and Welfare among Boston's Aged, 1890–1950* (Philadelphia: Temple University Press, 1986), pp. 55–60. On their ability to accumulate wealth in the twentieth century, see chap. 3 of the present study.

56. Ruggles, *Prolonged Connections*, pp. 43–45.

57. Carl Deglar, *At Odds: Women and the Family in America from the Revolution to the Present* (New York: Oxford University Press, 1980), chap. 5.

58. Tamara K. Hareven and Randolph Langenback, *Amoskeog: Life and Work in an American Factory City* (New York: Pantheon, 1978).

59. On such tensions, see the work of John Bodnar: *Workers' World: Kinship, Community, and Protest in an Industrial Society, 1900–1940* (Baltimore: Johns Hopkins University Press, 1982), and *The Transplanted: A History of Immigrants in Urban America* (Bloomington: Indiana University Press, 1985). In *Family Time and Industrial Time*, Hareven notes (p. 185) that disputes between generations over the dual ideals of assistance and autonomy "often generated conflicts of interests within the family."

60. Mary Ryan, *Cradle of the Middle Class* (Cambridge: Cambridge University Press, 1981), pp. 38–39, 91. For another family history contrary to the "sentimental image of several

generations living harmoniously under one roof," see Emily K. Abel, "Parental Dependence and Filial Responsibility in the Nineteenth Century: Hial Hawley and Emily Hawley Gillespie, 1884–1885," *Gerontologist* 32, no. 4 (1992): 519–26.

61. Tamara K. Hareven, "Life Course Transitions and Kin Assistance in Old Age: A Cohort Comparison," in Van Tassel and Stearns, eds., *Old Age in a Bureaucratic Society*, pp. 110–25.

62. Ellen A. Kramarow, "Living Arrangements of the Elderly, U.S., 1910: Explorations of Demographic Influence," paper presented at the annual meeting of the Population Association of America, Washington, D.C., March 1991.

63. Gratton, *Urban Elders*, pp. 58–59. On recognition of this problem in the first decades of the twentieth century, see I. M. Rubinow, *The Care of the Aged* (1930), reprinted in *The Aged and the Depression*, ed. David J. Rothman (New York: Arno, 1972), pp. 8–9.

64. Anonymous, "Old Age Intestate," *Harper's*, May 1931, p. 715. The cultural preference was shared by others; see Tim B. Heaton and Caroline Hoppe, "Widowed and Married: Comparative Change in Living Arrangements, 1900–1980," *Social Science History* 11 (Fall 1987): 261–80.

65. Peter Laslett, *Family Life and Illicit Love in Earlier Generations: Essays in Historical Sociology* (Cambridge: Cambridge University Press, 1977), pp. 212–13.

66. Samuel Butler, *Note-Books* (ca. 1885), cited by Ruggles, *Prolonged Connections*, p. 3.

67. Abraham Epstein, *The Challenge of the Aged* (New York: Arno, 1976 [originally published 1928]), p. 147.

68. Cited by Modell and Hareven, "Urbanization and the Malleable Household," p. 53.

69. Epstein, *The Challenge of the Aged*, pp. 147, 210.

70. "I Am the Mother-in-Law in the Home," *Reader's Digest*, November 1937, pp. 11–14.

71. Steven Mintz and Susan Kellogg, *Domestic Revolutions: A Social History of American Family Life* (New York: Free Press, 1988), p. 135.

72. By 1934, more than half of all homeowners in Indianapolis and Birmingham had defaulted on their loans; ibid., p. 135.

73. Ibid., p. 136.

74. Ibid., p. 137; Julia Kirk Blackwelder, *Women of the Depression: Caste and Culture in San Antonio, 1929–1939* (College Station: Texas A & M University Press, 1984), p. 50.

75. Alvin L. Schorr, *Filial Responsibility in the Modern American Family* (Washington, D.C.: Government Printing Office, 1958), pp. 19–20.

76. Smith, "Historical Change in the Household Structure of the Elderly," p. 260.

77. Frances E. Kobrin, "The Fall in Household Size and the Rise of the Primary Individual in the United States," *Demography* 13 (February 1976): 127, 138; Charles H. Mindel, "Multigenerational Family Households: Recent Trends and Implications for the Future," *Gerontologist* 19 (1979): 461.

78. On modern-day role exits, see Zena Smith Blau, *Old Age in a Changing Society* (New York: Franklin Watts, 1973), p. 155. For the notion of continuity in the lives of the nineteenth-century old, see Chudacoff and Hareven, "From the Empty Nest to Family Dissolution."

79. Patricia L. Kasschau, *Aging and Social Policy* (New York: Praeger, 1978), pp. 183–84. The study noted, however, a significant difference among Mexican Americans. As a group, they were far more likely to assume that they would eventually live with offspring (32 percent) and that such arrangements would be satisfactory (51 percent). See also Leopold Rosenmayr and Eva Kockeis, "Propositions for a Sociological Theory of Aging and the Family," *International Social Science Journal* 15 (1963): 410–26, and Ethel Shanas, "Social Myth as Hypothesis: The Case of the Family Relations of Old People," *Gerontologist* 19 (1979): 3–9.

80. Victor G. Cicirelli, *Helping Elderly Parents: The Role of Adult Children* (Boston: Auburn House 1981), pp. 3–4.

81. Currently, only the poorest elderly in the population live in three-generation households. In these, however, assistance usually passes from the elderly to the children and grandchildren. The households of elderly African-American women thus exhibit high rates of extension to subfamilies of unmarried daughters and their children. See Gratton, "Familism among the Black and Mexican-American Elderly."

82. Judith Treas, "Family Support Systems for the Aged," *Gerontologist* 16, no. 6 (1977): 486–91. A recent study finds that gender differences in caregiving have been exaggerated; female caregivers were, however, more likely than males to carry out personal care and household tasks. Baila Miller and Lynda Cafasso, "Gender Differences in Caregiving: Fact or Artifact?" *Gerontologist* 32, n.4 (1992): 498–507.

III

CULTURAL PERSPECTIVES

The meaning of age varies considerably from one society to another. Anthropological research on aging focuses on identifying how different cultures define the aging process and how they delineate the parameters as individuals move from one age to another. Lessons from anthropological research are not limited to the unique cultures anthropologists study, however, for all social gerontologists can benefit from recognizing diversity in the aging experience.

DEFINING OLD AGE

Every society has some criteria for defining people as old. Some use chronological age. In the United States, for example, 65, the age of eligibility for Social Security, is generally acknowledged as the transition to old age. Others, however, use functional criteria based on whether an individual can still perform certain tasks. In Canada, for example, Chipewyan Indians accord older men low status because they are no longer able to hunt and provide their own subsistence. In contrast, older Chipewyan women lose less status in old age, since they are still capable of carrying out domestic duties (Sharp, 1981). Still other societies use the transition to new social roles such as retiring or becoming a grandparent as the marker of old age. Regardless of which criteria are used, growing old is accompanied by rights, privileges, and duties, which are incorporated into the cultural values of particular social groups (Hooyman and Kiyak, 1988).

CULTURE AND THE GERONTOLOGICAL RESEARCHER

Social gerontologists have long acknowledged the role that political and economic institutions play in the social construction of old age (Walker, 1986; Walker and Phillipson, 1986), but seldom have they self-consciously acknowledged how these institutions, in concert with cultural values, shape and guide their research (Green, 1993). Yet the very questions that social scientists address in their research are affected by their cultural milieu. Values and norms shape the way gerontologists identify problems they want to research, and circumscribe the definitions they formulate about what age and aging mean and about who "the" elderly are (Green, 1993). The first reading in this section is a call to practice culturally informed gerontology. Mark R. Luborsky and Andrea Sankar argue that critical gerontology, coupled with culturally informed inquiry, will strengthen gerontological research. Of particular importance, they argue, are the roles that cultural values play in shaping public policy for the elderly.

AGING AND CROSS-CULTURAL RESEARCH

In the second reading in this section, Nancy Foner reviews the literature on intergenerational caring and the bonds of reciprocity across several nonindustrial cultures to explore the meaning of the informal contract between the elderly and their children. In most societies, a norm of reciprocity over the life course makes care for the elderly part of the younger generation's duty. Sometimes, however, the implicit contract fails, and the elderly are left alone. This is most likely to occur when older people have no children, when resources are scarce, or when social change happens at such a rapid pace that cultural values lag behind. Foner points out that the failure of the intergenerational contract in nonindustrial cultures parallels in important ways the failure of intergenerational bonds in industrial societies. Foner's interest in the nature of this contract in nonindustrial cultures is informed, at least in part, by her interest in the dilemma of finding satisfactory methods of caring for the frail elderly in the United States.

One need not travel around the world to find cultures that maintain unique patterns of care for the elderly. Within the boundaries of most Western nations that outwardly appear homogeneous, there remain unique subcultures that retain their own traditions, traditions that sometimes conflict with those of the wider society. The reading by Peter Woolfson examines the status of the Quebecois, who traveled from Canada during multiple waves of immigration into northern New England and Louisiana. Woolfson notes that while caregiving traditions have been altered by contact with the broader community, many rituals remain intact.

REFERENCES

Green, Bryan S. *Gerontology and the Construction of Old Age: A Study in Discourse Analysis.* New York: Aldine de Gruyter, 1993.

Hooyman, Nancy R., and H. Asuman Kiyak. *Social Gerontology: A Multidisciplinary Perspective.* Boston: Allyn and Bacon, 1988.

Sharp, H. "Old Age Among the Chipewyan." Pp. 99–110 in P. Amoss and S. Harrell (eds.), *Other Ways of Growing Old.* Stanford, CA: Stanford University Press, 1981.

Walker, Alan. "Social Policy and Elderly People in Great Britain: The Construction of Dependent Social and Economic Status in Old Age." Pp. 143–167 in Anne-Marie Guillemard (ed.), *Old Age and the Welfare State.* Sage Studies in International Sociology: 28. London, 1986.

Walker, Alan, and Chris Phillipson. "Introduction." *Ageing and Social Policy: A Critical Assessment.* Aldershot, UK: Gower Publishing, 1986.

5

Extending the Critical Gerontology Perspective: Cultural Dimensions

MARK R. LUBORSKY
ANDREA SANKAR

Luborsky and Sankar outline how the emerging framework of critical gerontology (CG) may be enhanced by a greater emphasis on understanding the influences of culture on research and practice in gerontology. They argue that
the multidisciplinary nature of social gerontology makes it an apt example of
how routine research practices, including the formulation of topics and the
definition of problems for study, are influenced by cultural components. The
approach Luborsky and Sankar detail goes beyond the technical and analytic
concerns that characterized early gerontological research, toward a culturally
informed critical gerontology. This critical approach would include attention
to neglected topics, the study of the concepts guiding critical studies, and the
refinement of current research methodologies. A culturally informed critical
gerontology would invigorate gerontological research by challenging its
"taken-for-granted" aspects.

Our first advances in gerontology were founded on empirical studies of common
myths about the elderly at home and abroad. For example, the seminal NIMH Human
Aging Study that identified undiagnosed disease conditions among elderly persons led
to differentiating healthy aging from disease-related impairments formerly attributed to
"normal" aging. Similarly, the putative high esteem of aged people in technologically
simple societies was shown by actual fieldwork to be an inaccurate idealization (Glascock, 1990; Maxwell, Silverman, & Maxwell, 1982).

Today, gerontology has advanced to the point where it can benefit by applying this
same critical gaze inward to examine its main topics of attention and the development

"Expanding the Critical Gerontology Perspective: Cultural Dimensions" by Mark R. Luborsky and Andrea
Sankar, from *The Gerontologist*, 33 (1993):440–443. Copyright © 1993 by The Gerontological Society of
America.

of research and policy agendas. For example, research shows that the definitions of variables such as health, illness, ethnicity, family, and self are not universal. Instead, each culture provides its own definition of these constructs (Sankar, 1984). Even within cultures, there is diversity in how various subgroups define those constructs. Further, previously unrecognized ethnic and social class differences in health, morbidity, and mortality have shaped our knowledge of what constitutes "normal" aging; these factors are only now coming to be understood (Dannefer, 1988; House, Kessler, & Herzog, 1990; Longino, 1991). We propose that a modest increase in awareness of how gerontology is practiced will provide benefits by broadening our knowledge base and perhaps identifying unrecognized avenues for research and for policy options.

This introduction suggests ways to extend the critical gerontology framework (Moody, 1988) to include such issues. They do so by developing insights into how wider American culture influences the conduct of gerontology. To understand and appreciate how cultural and historical factors pattern analytic constructs and the topics of study, we need to examine shifts in the nature of the definition of problems and the range of conceivable solutions. Such pursuits are a gap in the gerontological perspective which is gradually receiving wider recognition as a part of the rehabilitation and the aging enterprises (Gritzer & Arluke, 1985; Minkler & Estes, 1991; Moody, 1988).

EXTENDING THE CRITICAL GERONTOLOGY PERSPECTIVE

While the myths and realities approach in gerontology (e.g., Hendricks, 1986) continues to be productive, the time is ripe for more critical and cultural perspectives. We suggest the concepts and methods of critical studies be more widely introduced. The main goal of the critical gerontology (CG) approach is to identify wider societal influences on the problems that are examined, to explore how theorizing is done, and to analyze the consequences of different patterns of research and theory building. The CG approach is useful to other disciplines in that it shows how cultural categories enter into the world view of gerontology as well as the people it studies.

Critical Theory

Critical theory provides a starting point for critical gerontology. Contemporary critical theory is associated with the Continental philosophical and political movements of the Frankfurt school (Habermas, 1988; Slater, 1977) that rose to influence at mid-century. They argued from the stance that scientific and philosophical constructs are enmeshed in and serve to recreate the wider socio-historical settings. In gerontology, the moral and political economy paradigm builds from this perspective. Cogent reviews of the limitations of critical theory are offered by Hammersley (1992) and by Honneth (1987). The challenges it poses for gerontology are described by Moody (1988). More general versions of such a critical theory program have been described as "critical research" (Mishler, 1986) or "analytic induction" (Strauss, 1990; Denzin, 1989). The critical theorists' primary concern with social structure and order did not provide a clear view of the ways that dynamic interactions and competition among social groups lead to social change and shifts in cultural world views. Nor was the individual conceptualized as a willful autonomous person. Instead, individuals were viewed as social norm or "rule-bound zombies" (Stuchlik & Holy, 1981) and were defined simply as the sum of their family, work, and community roles. Critical theory lacked models for important diversities in families and communities at the local level of knowledge (Geertz, 1983), for the nature of personal experience, or for individuals as proactive agents within social systems (Ortner, 1984). These lacunae are being addressed by qualitative researchers in gerontology. However, the inquiry developed here has not yet been made: the coupling of empirical studies of key constructs with culturally informed inquiry into the formation and consequences of the sense of what is problematic for study.

Cultural Dimensions

Culture patterns our knowledge by way of the basic building blocks of science. Two examples may clarify this view. From an anthropological view, sparse attention is devoted to asking how the growing body of knowledge embodies our cultural worldviews. We are accustomed to treating variables and scientific procedures as value-free, a point contested by critical theorists. Yet even the language of science expresses basic cultural values. A critical gerontology points out the deep moral vein in our work: we are instructed to construct and carefully protect "independent" and "dependent" variables, the statistical "power" of our designs; we "control" variables and enhance people's sense of control. We judge if constructs and data are right and "valid" or "invalid" (the latter word also denotes disability). Further, we share with the subjects the search for "themes" in our life and in the data. Second, it can be suggested that the prevailing negative attitude toward "medicalization" as a form of social control is not shared at all levels of society. The medical attention may be welcomed by people whose lifelong poverty excluded them from full participation in mainstream society including adequate healthcare. The universal entitlements provided by Medicare may serve as a welcome avenue to greater social equality.

Basic analytic constructs (e.g., independence, stress, family, frailty, self) are also cultural concepts, not value-free absolute variables. The constructs bring shared cultural assumptions about the world into the research process and the course of the discipline (Achenbaum, 1978; Cole, 1986; Estes & Binney, 1990; Rubinstein, 1990) as Moss and Moss (1989) document in the case of the disenfranchisement of death and grief from mainstream gerontology. Less explicitly, the constructs carry with them an implicit script or teleology for maintaining society and for individual development that replicates current values or social roles and intergroup structures. Cohen and Sokolovsky (1989) describe how the dire conditions faced by aged men in the Bowery get defined in terms of individual adjustment problems, and not in terms of the wider societal and political factors that create the problems for individuals.

Briefly, we propose that the CG perspective can be enhanced by greater attention to the cultural components in the routine practice of gerontology and in the definition of problems for study. Following critical theory's concern with sociocultural values immanent in analytic constructs, CG aims to show how conventional formulations of problems and constructs lead to expectable kinds of findings. The latter, in effect, directs us to seek out the implicit teleology or blueprints (e.g., the acorn is destined to be an oak tree) that replicate the vision for future society that is coded into traditional sociopolitical and scientific paradigms.

We argue that the field of gerontology is a particularly apt demonstration of these processes of cultural patterning by virtue of its multidisciplinary approach. It is important to clarify such cultural and historical processes as gerontologists assume a greater advocacy and policy role for a public that wrestles with the emerging "aging society," and are called upon to propose new visions for aging individuals, society, and political-economic institutions.

EXTENDING CRITICAL GERONTOLOGY CONCEPTS AND METHODS

A culturally informed critical gerontology may begin as follows. The extended CG engages in two modes of analyses. In the one, it examines the cultural contexts of the conduct of contemporary gerontology. In the other, it examines the nature of contextualization itself.

In one mode, culturally informed CG engages in contextualization of gerontology. First, perhaps most familiar to all gerontologists, CG asks about how the routine practice and basic constructs in our field are situated in and respond to particular historical, demographic, and sociocultural contexts. For example, family caregiving studies became ascendant (Abel, 1991a) in the context of a Conservative political ideology oriented to family responsibility and the divestiture of government from individual lives. In a second mode, CG engages in examining the very method of "contextualization," that is, the wider settings within which an event or process occurs (cf., Ochs, 1990; Crapanzano, 1991). We recognize that contextualization is a pervasive feature of qualitative research but observe that is has not received the same careful study as other analytic techniques or concepts. Specifically, we see a need to formulate explicit criteria for the conduct of contextualization, its goals, methods, and standards for evaluating its adequacy. These proposed developments will be directly relevant by specifying guidelines to help evaluate the adequacy and caliber of qualitative-quantitative publications, research, and program evaluations.

Outline for CG Studies

The generalized approaches for conducting CG studies can be briefly outlined. We begin with an overview and then describe some studies that applied the CG framework. The CG method rests upon the systematic pursuit of a set of clearly articulated questions. Quantitative and qualitative methods are used as dictated by the kind of problem being investigated. CG is characteristically based upon the hermeneutic style of a continuing dialogue between the theoretical and empirical approaches to a problem within each study.

CG studies include four general components. First, a clear definition of a key concept or problem formulation in gerontology is presented. Second, a description of how the construct is currently conceptualized is stated, and that formulation's place in the continuing (past to present) thought about the issue is summarized. Third, the current definition is critiqued to reveal several gaps and limitations in the concept/problem formulation's ability to explain the phenomena it focuses on, and other problems that it does not highlight. In particular, we ask in what ways are the problems defined for study consonant with the wider sociopolitical climate of that time, and in what ways do they implicitly embody visions for future social organization and values in human life. Fourth, the researcher conducts the empirical research and presents the data that is now informed by the analytical and historical critique. CG results are in the form of new data as well as new questions and analytic frames for thought.

Examples of Findings and Issues

Results and new questions developed from the extended CG framework were discussed during symposia chaired by the authors at the 1990 and 1991 meetings of the Gerontological Society of America. Several basic concepts were examined using data from ongoing research. Jaber Gubrium (1991) draws data from his study of caregivers of dementia patients to question the assumption that survey respondents are the passive vessels of answers to which researchers pose the questions. Instead, he shows how respondents create their answers through a process of questioning the question. That is, they actively examine and reexamine their lives in light of the posed question and consciously create their response. Using ethnographic work with dementia patients residing in nursing homes, Karen Lyman (1991) probes the construction of caregiving problems as disease based. Lyman's participant observation study suggests, in contrast, that caregiving should be analyzed as a power relationship and that care settings be seen as institutions invested in both care and social control. Based on research with caregivers of the dying and of dementia patients, Andrea Sankar (1991) argues for a rethinking of the dyadic formula in social support theories. Instead of the stimulus-response dynamic which favors a dyadic model, she suggests a systemic approach to understanding the dynamics and effects of positive and negative support. In her analysis of the diaries and letters of 19th century women caregivers, the historian Emily Abel (1991b) reconsiders the assumption that caregivers require professional support and guidance. She attributes the present need to historical shifts in local availability of support for women and in the legitimacy for women's knowledge of caregiving. This later development she links with the increased professionalism of the medical establishment. Similarly, Tamara Hareven and Kathleen Adams (1991) used data from their multigenerational study of a New England industrial town to question the ahistorical tendency of gerontology to focus its analysis on the present. This is particularly the case in its examination of patterns of intergenerational assistance. Instead, they suggest an evolutionary model in which patterns of assistance change over the life course and evolve with conditions in historical time. Linda Mitteness and Judith Barker (1991) described findings from a study of the management of chronic disease and argued that elderly people manage health problems by setting up hierarchies of relative disorder, placing any single health problem in the context of their life environment and other illnesses. The difference in hierarchies of priorities between patients and physicians leads to considerable conflict and miscommunication. Full articles presenting culturally informed critical gerontology studies of life themes by Mark Luborsky and of needs assessment by Ann Dill are presented in this symposium.

Initial results of applying the culturally extended CG perspective have revealed major domains of problems to grapple with in future studies. The issues represent what we believe to be several cutting-edge concerns for gerontology. The issues are formulated as questions or needs for future work. What theory and practice guidelines direct the technique of contextualization? How do we conceptualize the impetuses or motive power for change, at the level of individual action or agency, or of macrosocial structures? What criteria need to be applied to evaluate the claims of qualitative and critical gerontology? What are the implicit scripts for sociopolitical life in critical studies themselves? In multidisciplinary work, what are the implicit logical and theoretical incongruities created by the "creative" blending of conceptual categories and frameworks drawn from differing assumptions and traditions, and what are the implications for theory building and implementation of findings? Answers to these and other questions emerging from CG studies may offer vital new insights to advance gerontology.

In each study reported, contextualization is an important analytic method but is conducted differently. Studies of macro-level institutional processes and phenomena (e.g., systems of health care) are asking how to make sense of these higher order things in terms of individual lives and in concrete social settings. Conversely, the studies of individual phenomena (e.g., life histories) move toward asking how to make sense of the individual life enterprise as a phenomenon of general cultural and historical settings. Contextualization emerges as a continuing challenge as well as an analytic technique. Thus, another contribution is to clarify the problematic nature of contextualization; solutions remain elusive.

FINAL REMARKS

We are not proposing that scientific progress in gerontology is dictated by cultural or historical facts. Clearly, there are many internal and external sources of change and insights into aging in our discipline. Scientific advancements are provided by the cumulative weight of new scientific knowledge and by the emergence of competing scientific paradigms that open new areas of description, study, and hypotheses testing. Also, as a civilization there is a stream of economic and political processes altering the landscape of social life within which concerns about aging are formulated and applied. These processes are fueled by a conceptualization of aging issues in terms of concerns about the shifting profile of age demographics, the social systems costs, and an evolving morality in post-industrial economies. Further, fashions and fads in intellectual perspectives, some transient and others enduring, enter into the discourse of gerontology. So, too, as one multidisciplinary cluster among many American scientific and political interest groups, gerontology works to position itself and to legitimate claims to a political-economic and intellectual territory. It acts as the "town-crier" on aging. Charismatic individuals or special interest groups contribute to progress, as do shifts in developmental and life-stage specific concerns among leaders in the field (Riley, 1988; Lawton, 1990).

In historical view, the early decades in gerontology attended to technical and data analytic concerns. It is now time to help in the maturing and future planning of the field by developing critical insights into the habituated modes of gerontological thought and practice. Future directions for a more culturally informed critical gerontology include studies of other topic areas, of the concepts guiding critical studies, and refinement of the current first generation of methodologies. It is vital to consider the "taken-for-granted" aspect of our sense of problems for gerontological study and how we practice theory building and application if we are to invigorate gerontological practice in the pursuit of basic and applied knowledge. The extended view of CG we propose suggests that gerontology develop a rigorous view of the cultural constructing of the field's orienting questions and concepts. Should we as a field demur from this task, we may miss opportunities to develop new perspectives and modes of practice, thereby serving as exponents for cultural and historical processes rather than proponents of new directions and knowledge.

REFERENCES

Abel, E. (1991a). *Who cares for the elderly: Public policy and the experiences of adult daughters.* Philadelphia: Temple University.

Abel, E. (1991b, November). *A new look at interventions for caregivers.* Paper presented at the 44th Annual Scientific Meeting of The Gerontological Society of America, San Francisco, CA.

Achenbaum, A. (1978). *Old age in a new land.* Baltimore: Johns Hopkins University.

Cohen, C., & Sokolovksy, J. (1989): *Old men of the bowery: Strategies for survival among the homeless.* New York: The Guilford Press.

Cole, T. (1986). *What does it mean to grow old? Reflections from the humanities.* Durham, NC: Duke University.

Crapanzano, V. (1991). The postmodern crises. *Cultural Anthropology, 6,* 431–446.

Dannefer, D. (1988). Differential gerontology and the stratified life course. In G. Maddox & M. P. Lawton (Eds.), *Annual Review of Gerontology and Geriatrics. Varieties of Aging.* New York: Springer.

Denzin, D. (1989). *Interpretive biography.* Newbury Park, CA: Sage.

Dill, A. (1993): Defining needs, defining systems: A critical analysis. *The Gerontologist, 33,* 453–460.

Estes, C., & Binney, E. (1990). The biomedicalization of aging: Dangers and dilemmas. *The Gerontologist, 29,* 587–597.

Geertz, C. (1983). *Local knowledge.* New York: Basic Books.

Glascock, T. (1990). By any other name it's still killing: A comparison of the treatment of the elderly in America and other societies. In J. Sokolovsky (Ed.), *The cultural context of aging: Worldwide perspectives.* New York: Bergin & Garvey.

Gritzer, G., & Arluke, A. (1985). *The making of rehabilitation: A political economy of medical specialization, 1890–1980.* Berkeley: University of California.

Gubrium, J. (1991, November). *The life as narrated experience?* Paper presented at the 44th Annual Scientific Meeting of The Gerontological Society of America, San Francisco, CA.

Habermas, J. (1988). *Theory and practice.* Cambridge: Polity Press.

Hammersley, M. (1992). *What's wrong with ethnography?* London: Routledge.

Hareven, T., & Adams, K. (1991, November). *Intergenerational assistance in later life: A life course perspective.* Paper presented at the 44th Annual Scientific Meeting of The Gerontological Society of America, San Francisco, CA.

Hendricks, J. (1986). *Aging in mass society: Myths and realities.* Boston: Little, Brown.

Honneth, A. (1987). Critical theory. In A. Giddens & J. Turner (Ed.), *Social theory today.* Stanford: Stanford University.

House, J., Kessler, R., & Herzog, R. (1990). Age, socioeconomic status, and health. *The Milbank Quarterly, 68,* 383–411.

Lawton, M. P. (1990). An environmental psychologist ages. In I. Altman & K. Christensen (Eds.), *Environmental & behavior studies: Emergence of intellectual traditions.* New York: Plenum Press.

Longino, C. (1991, November). *Keeping an eye on both social theory and social policy in the 1990s.* Paper presented at the 44th Annual Scientific Meeting of The Gerontological Society of America, San Francisco, CA.

Luborsky, M. (1993). The romance with personal meaning in gerontology: Cultural aspects of life themes. *The Gerontologist, 33,* 445–452.

Lyman, K. (1991, November). *Impaired models for dementia: Alzheimer's disease and the iceberg of dementia.* Paper presented at the 44th Annual Scientific Meeting of The Gerontological Society of America, San Francisco, CA.

Maxwell, R., Silverman, P., & Maxwell, E. (1982). The motive for gerontocide. *Studies in Third World Societies, 22,* 67–84.

Minkler, M., & Estes, C. (1991). *Critical perspectives on aging.* New York: Baywood.

Mishler, E. (1986). *Research interviewing.* Cambridge: Harvard University.

Mitteness, L., & Barker, J. (1991, November). *Hierarchies of disorder in the management of chronic illness.* Paper presented at the 44th Annual Scientific Meeting of The Gerontological Society of America, San Francisco, CA.

Moody, H. (1988). Toward a critical gerontology. In J. Birren & V. Bengtson (Eds.), *Emergent theories of aging.* New York: Springer.

Moss, M., & Moss, S. (1989). Death of the very old. In K. Doka (Ed.), *Disenfranchised grief: Recognizing hidden sorrow.* Lexington, MA: Lexington Books.

Ochs, E. (1990). Indexicality and socialization. In J. W. Stigler, R. A. Shweder, & G. Herdt (Eds.), *Cultural psychology: Essays on comparative human development.* Cambridge: Cambridge University Press.

Ortner, S. B. (1984). Anthropological theory since the Sixties. *Comparative Studies in Society and History, 26,* 126–166.

Riley, M. (1989). *Sociological lives.* Newbury Park, CA: Sage.

Rubinstein, R. (1990). Nature, culture, gender, age: A critical review. In R. Rubinstein (Ed.), *Anthropology and aging.* Boston: Kluwer Academic Publishers.

Sankar, A. (1991, November). *A critical approach to social support.* Paper presented at the 44th Annual Scientific Meeting of the Gerontological Society of America, San Francisco, CA.

Sankar, A. (1984). "It's just old age," old age as a diagnosis in American and Chinese medicine. In D. Kertzer & J. Keith (Eds.), *Age and anthropological theory.* Ithaca: Cornell University.

Slater, P. (1977). *Origin and significance of the Frankfurt school.* London: Routledge.

Strauss, A. (1990). *Basics of qualitative research: Ground theory.* Newbury Park, CA: Sage.

Stuchlik, M., & Holy, L. (1981). *The structure of folk models.* New York: Academic Press.

6

When the Contract Fails: Care for the Elderly in Nonindustrial Cultures

NANCY FONER

Unlike industrialized countries where the government provides economic security and health care in old age, in nonindustrial cultures older people rely
on informal agreements with kin and other associates to meet their needs.
Nancy Foner shows that broad cultural values, internalized by both young
and old, support a strong ethic of intergenerational caregiving in most nonindustrial societies. However, limited resources, the absence of children, or
rapid social change undermine this implicit contract and lead to neglect of
the elderly. Foner points out that cultural beliefs also play a role in understanding neglect and mistreatment in nonindustrial societies. Although nonindustrial cultures are markedly different from the United States, similar forces
motivate children in both types of societies to care for—or to neglect—their
parents.

As the number and proportion of the elderly in American society continue to rise,
alarms have been sounded about how they will be provided for in the future. Of special
concern are the frail elderly. Suffering physical or mental losses, they can no longer
fend for themselves and need special care. At the macro- or societal level, there is a
growing concern as to whether—and how—the government can maintain the level of
support now offered to the elderly through various entitlement programs in social security and health care. At the microlevel, there are questions about whether families will
be able to care for the rapidly growing number of old people who will live, for many
long years, in a disabled and weakened state.

In the face of the enormity of this apparent "aging crisis," there is a temptation to
look longingly to less complex societies where, it is imagined, old age is less of a problem. In these cultures, it is often believed, the weak, sick aged are cared for willingly,

---

faithfully, and lovingly in the bosom of their families. This nostalgia for a golden age or, as Nydegger (1983) puts it, golden isles, crystallizes our cultural concept of the good life and expresses our desires and anxieties. But the idyllic picture of the young faithfully carrying out their caretaking duties seriously distorts reality.

To be sure, the elderly in nonindustrial cultures often do receive tender and loving care. Where government does not provide social welfare benefits and where services cannot be hired, people of all ages, including the old, must rely on kin and other associates in times of need. Indeed, a number of factors act as powerful incentives motivating many young people to carry out their caretaking duties.

Yet problems arise. In fact, the lot of the frail elderly in nonindustrial cultures is sometimes extremely unpleasant and difficult. As part of a broad analysis of inequalities between old and young in nonindustrial societies, I have shown elsewhere how tensions may develop between incapacitated elders and their younger caretakers. (Even more serious conflicts arise between still active elders at the top of the age hierarchy who are powerful and privileged, and subordinate juniors; Foner, 1984a, 1985.) My concern here is different. The issue is not whether intergenerational relations are hostile or amicable. Rather, why is it that in many cultures the elderly may be neglected, mistreated, even sometimes abandoned? Why, in other words, does the informal contract or agreement between the generations—concerning the obligations young people owe the elderly—fail?

Beyond exploding simple and idyllic myths about care for the frail elderly in nonindustrial cultures, this analysis has additional implications. By pointing to factors underlying care—and neglect—in places where the old have nowhere else to turn but their kin and neighbors, it highlights, in bold relief, some of the forces involved in caregiving in our own society as we approach the next century.

THE CONTRACT FULFILLED

A look at ethnographic reports for a wide range of nonindustrial cultures shows that, in many cases, the informal contract with the elderly is, in fact, fulfilled. Children, kin, and neighbors frequently tend to the needs of the physically incapacitated aged for many years, often up until the end. This is so even in some mobile hunting-and-gathering societies, where meeting the needs of the helpless elderly could endanger the very existence of the family or band.

What causes younger people to fulfill their obligations to elderly parents? As in our own society, the answer is less often a matter of formal ethics than of emotional or practical considerations. Many children feel deep affection for aged parents and look after them with loving concern. Indeed, the senior generation often carefully nurtures good relations with their children, or grandchildren, with an eye to old-age support. Navajo grandmothers say that it is the duty of the older generation to teach their children that a "good Navajo" will care for the elderly. The grandmothers admit to having a vested interest in spoiling and coaxing grandchildren into becoming emotionally attached to them. The old women say that those who receive no aid and protection in old age ignored such precautions when younger; having made no attempt to establish warm, loving relationships with their grandchildren in the past, they are now paying the price of isolation (Shomaker, 1990, p. 28). Another related factor can come into play. By looking after their own aged parents and grandparents, younger caretakers may be consciously setting an example for their children so that they will not be abandoned in the future.

Then there is the notion of delayed reciprocity—sometimes referred to as lifetime reciprocity. Sons and daughters frequently see the care they give mothers and fathers as repayment for the gifts, provisions, and care the old people provided them in the past. In words echoed in many ethnographic reports, a man among the Gonja of West Africa said: "When you were weak [young], your mother fed you and cleaned up your messes, and your father picked you up and comforted you when you fell. When they are weak, will you not care for them?" (Goody, 1973, p. 172). From the elders' perspective, they are now rewarded for having met their earlier responsibilities. "Now you sit and eat," is how Samia elders of Kenya view the years when they can no longer work. Now sons and daughters feed them just as they fed their children when the children were too young to work (Cattell, 1990).

Broad cultural values—which young as well as old people have internalized—may also be involved. These may be moral or ethical values about the kind of care or obligations the young owe their elders. As Rosenberg (1990, p. 29) puts it for the !Kung of Botswana, entitlement to care may be "naturalized" within a culture. In other words, cultural norms are so deeply embedded that it seems "natural" that young people will care for elders, especially parents, when they become very old. By the same token, the cultural code also includes ideas about what is unacceptable behavior. Among Australian aborigines, for example, it is considered callous and reprehensible for family members to desert an ailing old person (Reid, 1985). In general, old people in nonindustrial societies often demand care as a publicly acknowledged right—and young people often feel it is the elders' due.

Whatever their origins, once cultural conceptions and attitudes about the elderly come into existence, they have a life of their own and cast a particular light over the solid features of social life. In Geertz's (1966) phrase, they are a model for, as well as a model of, action. In societies where the elderly are respected and admired—for their accumulated practical and ritual expertise, for example, their control of material resources, or their sheer age and seniority[1]—young people may believe that elders deserve to be looked after when they are weak and ill. Indeed, the physically frail (but mentally alert) may still be valued for their experience and knowledge and still control considerable economic resources. Meeting the needs of the frail old may be viewed, at least in part, as an extension of the obligations and respect young people have long owed to senior kin.[2]

When I asked a colleague who had lived for four years with the Twareg pastoralists of Niger how they treated the frail elderly, her initial response mirrored the way the Twareg themselves saw it: Old people should be served and fed. And, indeed, they were. Despite a severe 3-year drought in the 1980s and extreme scarcity of food, the physically weak elderly continued to be fed. When they were sick and dying, a daughter or granddaughter would minister to their needs. The elderly, including the extremely frail, were among the most respected individuals in the society: They had nurtured the young, were founts of wisdom about history and genealogy, and had, by this time in their lives, gained considerable status from years of giving substantial gifts of livestock to others (B. Worley, personal communication, October, 1990).

Cultural values may even dictate that the needs of frail elders come before those of the young. In a study of the Akamba of Kenya, traditional healers and health workers were asked what they would do if a dying old man over 60 and a dying 25-year-old man came for treatment but there was only enough medicine or herbs to cure one person. Many favored saving the old man, even where the young man was first in line (Kilner, 1984).

Complaints by the elderly forcefully remind young people of their duties, thereby greasing the wheels of the system of mutual responsibility and caregiving. Such complaints are a conscious or unconscious strategy to maximize support—an effort to bring about positive consequences by accentuating the negative, as when public complaints prod the young into fulfilling their duties. Despite being well looked after, !Kung elders constantly grumble and denounce others for neglecting them: "Can't you see that I am starving and dressed in rags?" is one typical comment in what Rosenberg (1990) calls !Kung complaint discourse. By negative example—often in melodramatic tales of neglect and woe—complaint rhetoric restates the social contract of caregiving obligations.

In many societies, moreover, there is an economic inducement to look after frail parents. The son or daughter who cares for the old couple receives, in exchange, special treatment in the division of property. Among the Kirghiz herders of Afghanistan, studied in the 1970s, most of the responsibility of looking after aged parents fell on the younger son (and his wife and children). That son never left the parental household, but as compensation he inherited the family herd, tent, and camping ground (Shahrani, 1981). In the past, in parts of Europe and France, the child who sat by the hearth received similar property benefits; if there were no sons, an unmarried daughter might stay and inherit the whole tenement (Goody, 1976).

If sentiments of affection and obligation or the promise of economic benefits are not enough, negative sanctions may be applied, ranging from the threat of disinheritance to community disapproval or even supernatural punishment. In small, closely knit communities, where people live together in continuing face-to-face contact, public opinion matters very much to an individual, so that collective opinion is an important spur to duty. Those who neglect obligations to the elderly may come in for severe criticism, as Reid (1985) mentions for the Yolngu of Arnheim Land, Australia. There family members are expected to mobilize to provide comfort, care, and material support for sick and feeble elders. In many African societies, the fear of the anger of deceased ancestors, who are believed to cause all manner of disasters, may also reinforce norms of respect and obligation. In Nigeria, children who fail to support their elderly parents when they are deemed able to do so earn the wrath of both their parents and the community. They risk a parental curse or perhaps a community accusation of witchcraft (Peil, Bamisaiye, & Ekpenyong, 1989).

The burden of supporting the elderly may be spread over the whole community, as in societies, like the !Kung, with a tradition of communal food sharing and food distributions. Where the sharing ethic is strong, those who are generous to the old may be honored and applauded. And finally, in societies where certain foods are taboo to younger people, the elderly are sure to be given those foods.

THE CONTRACT FAILS

If a variety of factors assure that the informal contract between the generations is often fulfilled, other variables may intervene to upset the balance. Pressures of limited resources and the absence of children are perhaps most important in explaining why the frail elderly may be neglected, forsaken, even abandoned and killed. Also playing a role in poor treatment are broad cultural values and expectations. Indeed, some anthropologists have suggested that far from being a violation of the social contract, the neglect of extremely incapacitated old people is, in some societies, a fulfillment of this contract. The elderly themselves may acquiesce in—sometimes even request—death-hastening treatment.

The state of childlessness or sonlessness (in many societies, it is a son's duty to care for elderly parents) is a terrible misfortune in nonindustrial societies. Parenthood is a crucial aspect of adult status. Children remember and honor their parents when they die—and are expected to care for them when they are incapacitated and can no longer look after themselves. Old people without children (or sons) face the dilemma of being forced to depend upon more distant kin, with whom the bonds of affection and obligation are not so close. The aged will have provided fewer services in the past to more distant relatives than to immediate kin, and they lack the strong moral, jural, or economic authority that they could exert over children.

Admittedly, family arrangements in many societies are flexible enough so that couples unable to bear children of their own can rear youngsters who will support them in old age. Formal adoption occurs in many European and Asian societies; foster parenting, which involves no permanent change in identity, is common in Africa. In societies where daughters are supposed to leave home at marriage, couples who bear only daughters can sometimes arrange a marriage in which the daughter and her husband remain with her parents to support them later on. Yet the best of plans do not always succeed. Foster or adopted (as well as natural) children sometimes die before their parents do, or are unable to care for them for other reasons.

In nonindustrial as well as industrial societies, old men are often cared for by their wives, since men are typically older then their spouses. Where men have several mates, younger wives may still be around by the time their much older husbands need care. Even then, however, sons (or sons-in-law) may be essential for herding, farming, or hunting, so that a sonless or childless old man may find himself in difficult circumstances whether or not he has a young wife to look out for him.

Childless elderly have a peripheral identity among the Gende of Papua New Guinea; they are neglected, often suffering isolation and shame and sometimes even outright physical abuse. Without children to assist them in financing interclan exchange competitions and ceremonies and repaying bride-price loans, they are regarded as "rubbish persons" who have failed to maintain exchange relations in good order. When they become frail and ill, few feel obligated to care for them or sacrifice pigs to restore their strength. When they die, their death is unimportant and unattended (Zimmer, 1987).

To reach old age and have no adult sons is an unfortunate state in many African farming and herding societies.[3] In his classic account of the Tallensi, Fortes reported that sons—own sons or, second-best, proxy sons—were old men's chief economic asset. A son was morally bound to look after and farm for his father. "Yet how can I leave him since he is almost blind and cannot farm for himself?" asked one man who had just quarreled bitterly with his father. "Can you just abandon your father? Is it not he who begot you?" (Fortes, 1970, p. 177). Old men, no matter how incapacitated, still exercised authority over sons, who had an interest in their fathers' land. Old men without adult sons had to depend on the unreliable assistance of kin and neighbors for help on their farms, and as a result they were unlikely to have more than a "minimum of food and other necessaries." When they became too weak to farm at all, relatives ordinarily gave them shelter and food. However, although refusing gifts of food to needy kin was viewed as an offense against the ancestors, people were not bound to be overgenerous to kin who did not contribute to the common pool (Fortes, 1949, pp. 216–217).

Like sonless old men, old women without sons are also at a disadvantage in many African societies. Among the Gusii of Kenya, sonlessness is a disaster second only to barrenness; an old woman needs at least one son who will care for her and whose wives will work for her (LeVine, 1980, p. 94). A case history from another Kenyan group, the Samia, makes this painfully clear. Miriamu was a blind old woman in her late 80s. Of the four children to whom she gave birth, only two grew to maturity, but the son died in 1965. The surviving daughter was married and lived a day's journey away. By the late 1980s, Miriamu could not move about at all and lay naked in her house, save for a dirty, ragged blanket. Sometimes a co-wife or the co-wife's son, who lived nearby, sent food; other kin helped a little. Her daughter did what she could, sending a little money and visiting once or twice a year to clean the house and do a few odd jobs. Some days, according to the anthropologist, Miriamu "sits and eats," but too often she sits cold, and the food does not come (Cattell, 1990).

Even those who do have sons may be without their help. Sons may be alive and well but living far away, often working in towns. Zimmer (1987, p. 72) speaks of "de facto childlessness" among the Gende of Papua New Guinea in cases where parents were left childless when migrant children reneged on their obligations. Even if they do send gifts and financial help, migrant children are not available to attend to the daily, physical needs of aging and sick parents (although in some societies grandchildren are occasionally sent home to provide services or the elderly themselves are brought to live in town) (Peil et al., 1989).

Sons may not be around because they have quarreled with their parents. Moore (1978) tells of an old Chagga man, Siara, who was in his midseventies when she knew him. Siara had no living sons nearby to rely on in old age. His firstborn had died. His eldest living son, a Catholic priest, came home only on holidays. According to Chagga custom, the youngest son, Danieli, should have stayed at home, looking after his old parents and caring for their needs. In return, he would ultimately inherit their garden and whatever was attached to it. Relations between Siara and Danieli had long been marked by conflict, however. In the late 1950s, Danieli left the community. At the time of the study, in 1974, he lived far away and had not even been home to see his father in 14 years.

It is not that the sonless or childless are totally isolated or alone; in small communities, they usually have considerable contact with kin and neighbors, most of whom they have probably known since childhood. Among the Chagga, hardly any of the elderly were alone in their homesteads, and all lived near relatives who were obligated to care for them. However, those who lacked nearby sons had to depend on kin whose interest in them was "secondary rather than primary in the Chagga hierarchy of intensity of relationship and obligation" (Moore, 1978, p. 73). To younger people who must help support distant kin or neighbors, the obligation tends to be seen as a particularly heavy burden, especially if they must also support their own parents as well. The childless or sonless old must often beg for help from people who resent giving, and in some societies such old people are ridiculed, neglected, or even accused of witchcraft. There are some indications that they also run a risk of being abandoned or killed. Zimmer (1987) describes two older Gende men, without wives or children, who depended on their brothers' reluctant help and contributed little to communal festivities. According to villagers, men such as these, in precontact days, before whites imposed their law, would have been thrown from a cliff into the river when they were no longer able to fend for themselves.

RESOURCES

Even the frail elderly who have children can end up neglected, mistreated, and sometimes abandoned and killed. Why some societies make more elaborate provisions for the care of the elderly than others—and why some provide only the bare minimal necessities—is unclear. What we do know is that old people's control of valuable resources (people, property, and knowledge) as well as their drain on the group's resources play a role.

In societies where old people control property, they can use these rights to compel others to support them or provide them with goods and services (Amoss and Harrell, 1981). The extent of old people's political influence or family authority can affect the degree of support they get and the grace with which it is provided. Take the case of the Hopi, as described in the 1930s. As long as aged men controlled property rights, held special ceremonial offices, or were powerful medicine men, they were respected. But "the feebler and more useless they become, the more relatives grab what they have, neglect them, and sometimes harshly scold them, even permitting children to play rude jokes on them." Sons might refuse to support their fathers, telling them, "You had your day, you are going to die pretty soon." Aged Hopi were heard to remark, "We always looked forward to old age, but see how we suffer" (Simmons, 1945, pp. 59, 234). It should be noted, too, that personal qualities can affect a person's fortunes in old age. The basic needs of irascible and querulous elders may be met, but they are less likely than the good-tempered to attract the spontaneous concern and goodwill of younger relatives (e.g., Reid, 1985; Simic, 1978).

Resources affect neglect in another way. There is the problem of limited resources, for basic food and survival, in the community or family—and the drain the incapacitated elderly place on these resources. This is what is sometimes referred to as the cost/contribution balance between what the aged contribute to the resources of the group, on the one hand, and the cost they exact, on the other (Amoss & Harrell, 1981, p. 6). No longer essential workers, or contributors to subsistence, the frail elderly may sap limited resources and be regarded as a burden by the young. This is especially so in societies where subsistence is precarious and/or where there is frequent mobility. In this regard, old women sometimes fare better than old men. Old men who lose physical vigor can no longer do strenuous male productive work such as hunting or farming. Frail old women, however, can still perform useful women's work, performing light domestic chores.[4]

Even with the best intentions, younger people cannot always give elderly parents the kind of attention they expect. They are often too busy with productive or other tasks. And environmental factors beyond anyone's control, such as drought or low food reserves, often require decisions that result in difficulties for the elderly. A poor harvest among the Gwembe Tonga in Zambia, for example, meant that many households simply did not have enough food. To reduce the number of bellies dependent on household granaries, the very old were sometimes sent to live with relatives in distant, more prosperous regions (Colson & Scudder, 1981, p. 128).

In allocating limited resources, young adults may be torn between obligations to parents and to their own children. As land has become scarcer and consumer needs have escalated, the problem has become more serious, leaving the young with less to spare for the old at a time when the elderly are making increased cash demands. "It is a difficult job to look after them," one Kikuyu man from Kenya said of his aged parents. "They are often as unreasonable as children. They forget what it is like to have nine children and little land" (Cox & Mberia, 1977). A study of urban Nigerian workers found them to be torn between the duty to send food and money to their parents, on the one hand, and the expectation to maintain a life style commensurate with their occupational status, on the other. The result was that many did a little of each: often skimping on support for parents and feeling, at the same time, that they had compromised their own quality of life (Togonu-Bickersteth, 1989).

The problems posed by limited resources and old people's dependence are sometimes resolved in an extreme way: killing, abandoning, or exposure of the elderly— what anthropologists call gerontocide. Cross-cultural studies show that such treatment is more common than we might suppose. Maxwell and Silverman found evidence of gerontocide in a little over 20% of 95 societies in a worldwide sample (Silverman, 1987). Glascock uncovered abandonment of the elderly in 9 of the 41 nonindustrial societies in his sample—and reports of killing old people in 14 of these societies (Glascock, 1990).

Both studies found that gerontocide tends to occur in societies that can be characterized as technologically simple—hunting and gathering, pastoral, and shifting horticultural, as opposed to those with intensive agriculture. "The need for the social group to move frequently," Glascock writes, "poses a threat to the elderly as does the inability of most of these societies to store sufficient food to allow all members to survive severe food shortages" (1990, p. 56). A decline in health and strength results in old people becoming a burden on other members of the social group.

Details concerning the killing of the elderly are largely lacking in ethnographic material so that we do not know how the elderly themselves viewed their fate. My own guess is that they sometimes had mixed, perhaps angry, feelings about being killed or left to die, but they felt unable to resist pressures to acquiesce in the decision. What evidence is available, however, shows that far from invariably fighting against such treatment, old people in many societies accepted their fate, or at least did not actively resist it. Indeed, part of the informal contract between old and young in a number of societies is a tacit understanding, accepted by the elderly as well as the younger generation, that when the old become a drain on the community's resources it is time to go. This is much like Durkheim's (1951) description of altruistic suicide, where people have an obligation or duty to the social group to kill themselves. Gerontocide, according to the evidence, is usually a family affair. Typically, children and the elderly individual jointly decide that the time is right to die. Where killing is involved, commonly the son carries out the act (Glascock, 1990).

In some places, anthropologists have found, the disabled elderly were abandoned upon their request. Among the Mardudjara hunters and gatherers of Australia, the incompetent old were fed and spared the difficulties of moving too often, but when frequent travel became unavoidable, some of the elderly asked to be left behind to perish (Tonkinson, 1978). In the past, among the Eskimos of northern Canada, the old person usually initiated the abandonment process. During a storm or when the family was busily occupied, the aged parent would quietly slip off into the tundra to die from exhaustion and exposure (Guemple, 1977).

In some societies, being buried alive was considered an honorable way to die. In earlier times in Samoa, an old and ailing chief was able to orchestrate his own funeral. He told his children and friends to get ready to bury him, thus ending his life amid the acclaim of his family and community in an elaborate mortuary ceremony. In much the same way, extremely frail elders among the Yakut of Siberia would, in ancient times, beg their relatives to bury them. Before being led into the wood and thrust into their graves, they were honored at a three-day feast (Simmons, 1945, pp. 236–237). Such dignified ceremonial deaths, Myerhoff suggests—where the dying person is the "hero, the death not an intrusion but a fulfillment of his life" (1978, p. 229)—are far preferable to the isolation and loneliness of dying that most Americans experience in modern hospitals and nursing homes.

Sometimes, younger people help the death process along when the elderly are in pain and discomfort. In this sense, death hastening can offer an escape from intense suffering (Logue, 1990). A Hopi man told of the time when his uncle—a man who had been frail and sick for several years—was finally dying ("his breath is about the length of my finger and he is getting cold"). After the dying man's face was covered with a blanket, the nephew propped him against the wall "so that the breath will escape quickly . . . he is too old and weak to feel any pain; and it is better for him to be on his way" (Simmons, 1945, p. 234).

Cultural attitudes toward death may soften the blow or make the aged indifferent to dying. In the past, elderly Eskimos in northern Canada were willing to be abandoned when they became weak or ill because they did not believe they would really die. They were convinced that their "name substance"—"the essential ingredient of a human being which includes the personality, special skills, and basic character"—would live on, and would enter the body of a newborn child (Guemple, 1983).

Cultural Beliefs

The Eskimo case makes clear that, critical as social and economic factors are in explaining neglect and mistreatment, cultural beliefs may also be involved.

In an intriguing analysis of aging on the Polynesian island of Niue, Barker (1990) argues that religious beliefs concerning death and the ancestors help explain why the disabled elderly were treated so poorly. Despite free and easily available medical services, caretakers did not bother to ask for medical help for physically ill elders. The demented and incontinent were left unattended and received minimal care. Little effort was made to bathe them, clean their homes, or provide them with material comforts. Old people who were bent over or who walked oddly were figures of fun. When blind or unstable elders hurt themselves, they were ridiculed and teased.

Such mistreatment Barker admits is, in part, a response to the economic burden the frail elderly place on the able-bodied. On Niue, with its fragile ecosystem, there is not much surplus available for nonproducers, and periodic droughts bring food scarcities. Yet younger handicapped people—also an economic burden—are not subject to neglect or special ridicule. The disabled elderly are singled out for neglect, Barker argues, because of Niuean cultural conceptions of death, the life cycle, and spirits of the dead. Old people who no longer look or behave like competent adults are believed to be dangerous and threatening. Courted by spirits of the dead, they are in transition— the nearly dead—inhabiting a twilight world of not-quite-human-but-not-quite-ancestor. By abandoning the nearly dead or limiting contact to the point of neglect, younger adults prevent being contaminated by ghostly influences from beyond, and distance themselves from powerful and potentially dangerous transformations.

Social Changes

Like our own society, nonindustrial societies are not static. The social patterns anthropologists observe at one point in time are not fixed or permanent and can undergo significant change. Brought up to expect that care will be forthcoming, the elderly may find that, when frailty sets in, changes have undermined or reduced the strength of social arrangements, cultural values, and resources that, in the past, guaranteed care.

A reduction in old people's control over productive resources, for example, may affect the willingness of the young to look after them—and the kind of care that is provided. With growing consumer needs and scarcer land in many societies, young people, as I already noted, may have less to spare for elderly parents. And new ideas, values, and conceptions may give legitimacy to young people's neglect—as well as reduce the effectiveness of mystical sanctions at old people's command.

Also crucial is that increased migration to new cities and towns removes many potential caretakers from the scene. Children are less likely to be around to provide care, leaving the elderly in difficult straits when they become frail and ill. The case of the

Gende of Papua New Guinea is pertinent here. Since they were first contacted in 1932, there has been a steady increase in migration away from the area, with many moving to work in town or on plantations. Indeed, in the 1980s, about one quarter of the population—two thirds of whom were men and women between the ages of 18 and 45—were absent. The consequences for the elderly have been devastating. With more and more daughters living at a distance and sons away in town, Zimmer (1987) writes, the daily needs of aging and sick parents are likely to go unattended.

CONCLUSION: LOOKING AHEAD

This bleak scenario is not inevitable. Social changes do not always leave the frail elderly in the lurch, a point that must be emphasized. Too often anthropological writings on aging and change assume that the position of the old will invariably deteriorate as their societies become more economically developed and integrated into the "modern" world. I have argued elsewhere that such predictions must be challenged: The worsening of old people's position is only one possible outcome (Foner, 1984a, 1984b). This is true for the frail as well as for the hardy elderly.

There is no better proof than the very fact that most ethnographic reports describing young people meeting their caretaking obligations—and having a strong sense of filial duty—are based on data collected in societies that have already experienced extensive contact with Western industrial powers, some based on very recent research. Thus, drawing on fieldwork conducted among the Samia of Kenya throughout the 1980s, Cattell (1990) concludes that despite the stresses from labor migration, geographic separations, poverty, and other factors associated with modernization, families still struggle to meet their obligations to the senior generation. Children remain the prime source of old-age security, allowing many elders who can no longer work to achieve the cultural ideal of sitting by the fire and having food brought to them. Indeed, throughout less developed parts of the world, the absence of old-age pensions for most of the rural population—a situation that, given the high costs, is unlikely to change for a long time—means that children continue to be the main support of the frail old.

There are some cases where change has actually led to improvements for the disabled old, as in a number of cultures where pensions have been introduced or where the elderly attract much-needed overseas remittances. Before old-age pensions were introduced among the Western Apache, the very old were poor and economically dependent on the young. When Goodwin lived among them in the 1930s, however, old people who received monthly army pensions were often the wealthiest members of their families, and young relatives came to them for money. The very frail old usually received better care. Younger people had an interest in keeping old relatives alive: When they died, the pensions ceased (Goodwin, 1942, p. 517).

When we turn to our own society, it is difficult to foretell exactly how changes in the next decades will affect care for the frail elderly. What is clear is that dire predictions about the abandonment of elderly family members are unfounded. As in the nonindustrial world, children here are likely to continue to feel strong obligations to look after and help their elderly parents.

True, there are marked differences from nonindustrial cultures. The advent of Social Security and other government programs has reduced pressure on children to support their parents financially. Unlike nonindustrial cultures, where the elderly have long been used to, indeed have demanded, material and other help from their children, there is, as Clark (1973) puts it, a strong cultural imperative for most elderly Americans to be self-sufficient and economically independent. Old people in American society are generally reluctant to live with their children or even to ask them for financial help (see Keith, Fry, & Ikels, 1990). Moreover, a wide array of nonfamilial long-term care arrangements, including large numbers of nursing homes, are available. Nonetheless, children in American society will doubtless still play an important role in caregiving—ranging from providing actual day-to-day care to regularly visiting nursing homes and managing paid home-care arrangements long-distance.

Many of the same forces that motivate children in nonindustrial societies to look after their parents operate and are likely to continue to operate here: emotional bonds between children and parents; cultural norms of filial obligation and duty; and younger people's sense that they owe parents care in repayment for help and assistance parents provided them over the years (see Rossi & Rossi, 1990). Indeed, increased longevity may well strengthen emotional ties between the generations as parents and children have more years of shared lives. Occasionally, the lure of inheritance is a factor underlying care for frail parents. And the opinion of others may play a role. This includes their own children, for whom adult caregivers may be consciously or unconsciously providing a model to guarantee their own care in the future.

If looking at nonindustrial societies points to factors motivating care, it can also reveal some of the reasons why the elderly can be neglected when they most need help and attention. The lack of children who are alive and available is, as we saw, crucial. In our own society, spouses are the first line of defense for the elderly in times of need; children are the second (Bould, Sanborn, & Reif, 1989). The childless run a much greater risk of institutionalization; about 40% of nursing home residents have no living children, compared to less than 20% in the community (U.S. Senate Special Committee on Aging, 1987–88). As we look to the future, the proportion of the elderly with no living children is expected to increase as the low-fertility baby boomers become old. In fact, voluntary childlessness—unheard of in nonindustrial cultures—is on the rise here. Also, with increasing rates of female labor force participation, adult daughters are apt to be less available to their aged parents. Add to this the complications from increased geographic mobility as well as divorce. Moreover, the aging of the population means that chronically ill parents, themselves extremely old, will be more likely to have children who are already retired and who are limited in their ability to provide help due to their own low income or health problems.

The pressure of resources is also an issue. As in nonindustrial cultures, children here are often torn between the demands and needs of their parents, on the one hand, and those of their spouses and children, on the other. This may be especially difficult in times of economic downturns, when financial resources are scarce. How these resources are allocated will vary from case to case, but the sick elderly are likely to suffer when there is not enough to go around or to pay for the kind of care they require.

As more and more middle-aged women are forced to juggle care for a disabled parent with responsibilities to dependent children as well as a job, they may simply be unable to provide the kind of attention and assistance that the parent needs or wants.

It is at the societal, rather than family, level that the question of resources has received the most attention in this country. The frail elderly, many claim, are already monopolizing too much of the nation's resources at the expense of the young—and this will get much worse in the future as costs mount for the rising numbers of elderly.[5] Callahan (1987) puts it bluntly when he says that the full provision of health care, by government funds or institutions, for the ever-growing number of elderly—who are being kept alive for an ever-longer period of time—promises to be insupportable. His controversial solution is to call for a revamping of our obligations to the elderly and our cultural conception of a "natural life span." He proposes rationing health care by age: denying life-extending health care to those who have completed this natural life span, somewhere in their late 70s or early 80s.

This, ironically, brings us back to nonindustrial societies. In the wake of the miracles of modern medicine, which is able to keep large numbers of people alive in grossly incapacitated states, and the problem of scarce government resources, many Americans may well look at practices in nonindustrial cultures with a different eye. Once popularly condemned as savage and barbaric, ceremonial killings and the abandonment of the severely ill aged in these societies may, at the other extreme, come to be glorified as enlightened acts of kindness.

As modern-day anthropologists remind us, the way we interpret different cultures reflects our own concerns, ideas, and predilections. This is true of scholarship as well as popular thought. The very emphasis in this chapter on analyzing failures in the caregiving contract in nonindustrial societies is a response to dilemmas facing the frail elderly in this country. Yet, this analytical process is a dialectical one, as the discussion has also suggested. Much as our views of different cultures are shaped by our own concerns, these views can, at the same time, allow us to reflect back on our customs, values, and attitudes in a slightly different way. Indeed, a cross-cultural perspective can provide a different angle or lens for, and perhaps bring into sharper focus, problems and processes concerning caregiving and relations between the generations that are of such critical importance in our own society.

NOTES

1. Because they have lived a long time, the elderly in preliterate societies are (as long as they are mentally alert) regarded as possessors of knowledge, wisdom, and experience. It is they who know about the past and how things should be done—and they are valued for their expertise and advice. Growing old also usually brings with it certain ritual powers and knowledge. And with aging comes the opportunity to establish durable relations with kin, descendants, social debtors, and allies—and sometimes control over material resources as well. In many nonindustrial societies, age and seniority are, in themselves, bases for deference—juniors may have to greet or speak to elders in a respectful manner or allot them the best or largest portion of food at public ceremonies (see Foner, 1984a).

2. Providing the senior generation with material support and help, moreover, is nothing new. In nonindustrial societies, the dramatic role reversals of later life observed in our own society occur less often. Because services cannot be hired and government does not provide social wel-

fare benefits, people must rely on kin and other associates not just in their later years but throughout their lives in times of danger, emergency, and disaster. In these societies, children are a major human resource, and they usually contribute to their parents' material support, in good and bad times, for much of their lives. This is unlike the situation in middle-class America, where material exchanges between parents and children typically involve parents as the main givers, with a startling shift occurring in late old age if aged parents must turn to adult children for support.

3. In practice, much of the son's obligation of providing day-to-day care usually falls on his wife (or wives) and children.

4. In societies where men have many wives, however, they may have a definite edge in that when they reach an advanced age they often have at least one wife to bring them food and look after them (see, for example, Cattell, 1990, on the Samia of Kenya, and Reid, 1985, on Australian aborigines).

5. For an alternative conceptualization of this issue as it relates to pensions, see Walker (1990). Walker argues that an economic and demographic imperative has been manufactured to facilitate restructuring the welfare state.

REFERENCES

Amoss, P., & Harrell, S. (1981). Introduction: An anthropological perspective on aging. In P. Amoss & S. Harrell (Eds.), *Other ways of growing old* (pp. 1–24). Stanford: Stanford University Press.

Barker, J. C. (1990). Between humans and ghosts: The decrepit elderly in Polynesian society. In J. Sokolovsky (Ed.), *The cultural context of aging* (pp. 295–314). New York: Bergin & Garvey.

Bould, S., Sanborn, B., & Reif, L. (1989). *Eighty five plus: The oldest old.* Belmont, CA: Wadsworth.

Callahan, D. (1987). *Setting limits: Medical goals in an aging society.* New York: Simon & Schuster.

Cattell, M. (1990). Models of old age among the Samia of Kenya: Family support of the elderly. *Journal of Cross-Cultural Gerontology, 5,* 375–394.

Clark, M. (1973). Contributions of cultural anthropology to the study of the aged. In L. Nader & T. Maretzki (Eds.), *Cultural illness and health* (pp. 78–88). Washington, DC: American Anthropological Association.

Colson, E., & Scudder, T. (1981). Old age in Gwembe District, Zambia. In P. Amoss & S. Harrell (Eds.), *Other ways of growing old* (pp. 125–154). Stanford: Stanford University Press.

Cox, F. M., & Mberia, N. (1977). *Aging in a changing village society: A Kenyan experience.* Washington, DC: International Federation on Ageing.

Durkheim, E. (1951). *Suicide.* New York: Free Press.

Easterlin, R. A. (1980). *Birth and fortune: The impact of numbers upon personal welfare.* London: Grant McIntyre.

Foner, N. (1984a). *Ages in conflict: A cross-cultural perspective on inequality between old and young.* New York: Columbia University Press.

Foner, N. (1984b). Age and social change. In D. Rertzer & J. Keith (Eds.), *Age and anthropological theory* (pp. 195–216). Ithaca, NY: Cornell University Press.

Foner, N. (1985). Old and frail and everywhere unequal. *Hastings Center Report, 15,* 27–37.

Fortes, M. (1949). *The web of kinship among the Tallensi.* London: Oxford University Press.

Fortes, M. (1970). Pietas in ancestor worship. In M. Fortes (Ed.), *Time and social structure and other essays* (pp. 164–200). London: Athlone Press.

Geertz, C. (1966). Religion as a cultural system. In M. Banton (Ed.), *Anthropological approaches to the study of religion* (pp. 1–46). London: Tavistock.

Glascock, A. (1990). By any other name, it is still killing. A comparison of the treatment of the elderly in America and other societies. In J. Sokolovsky (Ed.), *The cultural context of aging* (pp. 43–56). New York: Bergin and Garvey.

Goodwin, G. (1942). *The social organization of the Western Apache.* Chicago: University of Chicago Press.

Goody, E. (1973). *Contexts of kinship.* Cambridge: Cambridge University Press.

Goody, J. (1976). Aging in nonindustrial societies. In R. H. Binstock & E. Shanas (Eds.), *Handbook of aging and the social sciences* (pp. 117–129). New York: Van Nostrand Reinhold.

Guemple, L. (1977). The dilemma of the aging Eskimo. In C. Beattie & S. Crysdale (Eds.), *Sociology Canada: Readings* (pp. 194–203). Toronto: Butterworth.

Guemple, L. (1983). Growing old in Inuit Society. In J. Sokolovsky (Ed.), *Growing old in different societies* (pp. 24–28). Belmont, CA: Wadsworth.

Keith, J., Fry, C., & Ikels, C. (1990). Community as context for successful aging. In J. Sokolovsky (Ed.), *The cultural context of aging* (pp. 245–261). New York: Bergin and Garvey.

Kilner, J. F. (1984). Who shall be saved? An African answer. *Hastings Center Report, 14,* 18–22.

LeVine, R. (1980). Adulthood among the Gusii of Kenya. In N. Smelser & E. Erikson (Eds.), *Theories of work and love in adulthood* (pp. 77–104). Cambridge, MA: Harvard University Press.

Logue, B. J. (1990). Modernization and the status of the frail elderly: Perspectives on continuity and change. *Journal of Cross-Cultural Gerontology, 5,* 345–374.

Moore, S. F. (1978). Old age in a life-time social arena: Some Chagga of Kilimanjaro in 1974. In B. Myerhoff & A. Simic (Eds.), *Life's career—aging* (pp. 23–75). Beverly Hills: Sage.

Myerhoff, B. (1978). *Number our days.* New York: Dutton.

Nydegger, C. (1983). Family ties of the aged in cross-cultural perspective. *Gerontologist, 23,* 26–32.

Peil, M., Bamisaiye, A., & Ekpenyong, S. (1989). Health and physical support for the elderly in Nigeria. *Journal of Cross-Cultural Gerontology, 4,* 89–106.

Reid, J. (1985). "Going up" or "going down": The status of old people in an Australian aboriginal society. *Ageing and Society, 5,* 69–95.

Rosenberg, H. (1990). Complaint discourse, aging, and caregiving among the !Kung San of Botswana. In J. Sokolovsky (Ed.), *The cultural context of aging* (pp. 19–41). New York: Bergin and Garvey.

Rossi, A. S., & Rossi, P. H. (1990). *Of human bonding: Parent-child relationships across the life course.* Hawthorne, NY: Aldine de Gruyter.

Shahrani, M. N. (1981). Growing in respect: Aging among the Kirghiz of Afghanistan. In P. Amoss & S. Harrell (Eds.), *Other ways of growing old* (pp. 175–191). Stanford: Stanford University Press.

Shomaker, D. (1990). Health care, cultural expectations and frail elderly Navajo grandmothers. *Journal of Cross-Cultural Gerontology, 5,* 21–34.

Silverman, P. (1987). Comparative studies. In P. Silverman (Ed.), *The elderly as modern pioneers* (pp. 312–344). Bloomington: Indiana University Press.

Simic, A. (1978). Winners and losers: Aging Yugoslavs in a changing world. In B. Myerhoff & A. Simic (Eds.), *Life's career—aging* (pp. 77–103). Beverly Hills: Sage.

Simmons, L. (1945). *The role of the aged in primitive society.* New Haven: Yale University Press.

Togonu-Bickersteth, F. (1989). Conflicts over caregiving: A discussion of filial obligations among adult Nigerian children. *Journal of Cross-Cultural Gerontology, 4,* 35–48.

Tonkinson, R. (1978). *The Mardudjara aborigines.* New York: Holt, Rinehart, and Winston.

U.S. Senate Special Committee on Aging. (1987–88). *Aging America.* Washington, DC: U.S. Department of Health and Human Services.

Walker, A. (1990). The economic "burden" of ageing and the prospect of intergenerational conflict. *Ageing and Society, 10*(4), 377–396.

Zimmer, L. (1987). "Who will bury me?": The plight of childless elderly among the Gende. *Journal of Cross-Cultural Gerontology, 2,* 61–77.

7

Cross-Cultural Families:
The Franco-Americans
PETER WOOLFSON

Franco-Americans who migrated from Canada to northern New England and Louisiana have sustained a tradition of strong intergenerational bonds, with older women occupying the position of clan matriarch. This tradition places responsibility for care of the aged on the younger generation, especially on adult, single children. Although these practices have gradually been eroded by contact with the wider society, there remains an avoidance of the nursing home and a desire to care for the frail elderly within the family.

The Franco-Americans are Americans of French descent who live in the United States. For the most part these people are the descendants of the 65,000 French people who remained in Canada after the French government ceded Canada to the English in the Treaty of Paris of 1763. There were two different populations of French people in Canada in what had been known as *New France*: one in Quebec and the other in Nova Scotia; the former became known as *Quebecois,* the latter as *Acadians.* These two major French populations in North America have had quite different histories and display many cultural differences. However, both groups in the Northeast could be considered cousins, while the Acadians of Louisiana, called *Cajuns* are more distant relatives. The Cajuns differ from the Acadians of New England as they are culturally southerners with a whole set of behaviors and attitudes revolving around the large black population of the state.

There are Franco-Americans throughout the United States—from Maine's 292,279 Franco-Americans to California's 1.3 million. In the Southwest Texas has 500,000. Louisiana continues to have its French flavor with close to a million Cajuns and Creoles. The majority of people claiming French ancestry live in the northeastern United States: the seven states comprising New England and New York: 3,158,992 persons in that region reported that they had at least one parent with French-Canadian, Acadian,

Cajun, or French-Creole background—some 22 percent of the nation's 13.6 million people claiming some French descent.

In spite of active interest in historical roots, Franco-Americans retain contact with a restricted group of kinspeople. Events like baptism, confirmation, marriage, and death involve participation of multigenerational kin. Grandparents, traditionally, played an important role at the birth of a child. It was often the custom to have the grandparents serve as godparents for a first-born child: paternal grandparents for a boy, maternal grandparents for a girl, although the reverse occurs as well. Siblings and cousins form the backbone of the network of relatives who share informal and intimate events: it is this group from which, in most cases, friendship choices develop (P. Woolfson, 1983).

The most important social unit for the French-Canadians and Franco-Americans is the household: a man, his wife, his children, and any other close relatives who happen to live with them—his parents, younger siblings, perhaps a maiden aunt. In farming communities, when a man retired, the son who had been designated as heir to the farm moved downstairs to indicate symbolically the change in status to head of household. Arrangements were often made for parents to move upstairs: the father continued to work on the farm as long as he was able and the mother helped the daughter-in-law with the household. As the parents aged, they might decide to move into a local village in order to be closer to the church for more regular attendance. Younger siblings often stayed with their brother to help with the farm work until the farmers' sons were old enough to shoulder much of the responsibilities of farm duties.

Franco-Americans, if they are financially independent, tend to marry earlier than their French-Canadian counterparts. This is true in both Louisianan Cajun and New England Franco-American society. Financial independence is not, however, the major issue, in the multigenerational farm families described above since resources continue to be shared. Traditionally mature daughters, even those with full-time jobs, were expected to remain at home with their parents well into their middle twenties or so long as they were not married.

Similar to the tradition of Irish-Americans, one of the unmarried daughters was expected to stay at home, unmarried, to take care of incapacitated or elderly parents. The Franco-Americans in New England and the Louisiana Cajuns both felt very strongly about the responsibility of relatives to care for the frail and elderly (M. R. Esman, 1985). Placement of elders in nursing homes is opposed unless absolutely necessary. If there were no daughters available, unmarried sons might choose to remain living at home to care for the parents. The elderly siblings may also join in care-giving roles. For example, an elderly nun came from Quebec to Vermont to assist her sister-in-law and niece with the care of her convalescing brother. This situation, temporary or long-term, illustrates how some multigenerational families continue to extend assistance across the national border when there is a family need.

Marriage is still performed in the parish of the bride and like other events concludes with the celebration of the Mass. Employed wives continue to work at their jobs after marriage. But there is the tendency not to delay having children. Some opt to quit work in order to take care of their small children. This is becoming more common, given maternity leave benefits. Wives who go back to work tend to rely on their mothers to help them with child care. Louisianan grandmothers feel a strong obligation to help their daughters take care of their grandchildren. They firmly believe that families can offer better child care than that provided by strangers (Esman, 1985). Likewise, Franco-American grandmothers feel strongly about helping their daughters. They often raise questions about the quality of care available in day care centers and show concern about daughters having to leave their infants in the care of others while working, but they are largely resigned to their daughter's financial realities of trying to live on the son-in-law's income.

Children today are more mobile than their parents and are choosing where they live on the basis of job opportunities rather than on proximity to their families. Consequently daughters often live too far from their mothers to involve them in child care. Except for vacations, often for the Christmas holidays, families stay in touch by telephone rather than by visiting. Older Franco-Americans, if they can afford to, are spending the winter months in Florida. It has been suggested that there are as many as 250,000 French-Canadians who spend six months or more in that state. One retired Franco-American felt that the ideal retirement life would include a trailer in Vermont for the spring and summer and a trailer in Florida for the fall and winter. This mobility also limits the amount of time mothers and fathers can spend with their children and grandchildren and offer concrete assistance.

Old age brings few changes in living arrangements for those fortunate to be in reasonably good health and to have a family support system at hand. Fifty years residency in the same house is not uncommon. However, other Franco-American elderly, like their nonethnic counterparts, find it impossible to continue this pattern. Winooski, Vermont, has a very large concentration of Franco-Americans who have retired from working in local mills. Fanny Allen Hospital, their personally identified health center, has instituted a system where monitors are placed in the home so that help can be summoned at the touch of a button. Many Franco-American elderly express great relief at having this system. They have faith in this small community hospital: it is still operated by an order of nuns originally from Canada, who continue to use personalized approaches, as compared to the more bureaucratic professional approach at the local university medical center. There are also some nursing homes that have a substantial Franco-American patient population who are very aged, largely alone, without families, and incapacitated.

In Louisianan Cajun and Franco-American communities, old people are treated with respect. This pattern is especially strong for elderly priests and nuns who remain in the local area. Respect is further displayed in fiftieth wedding anniversaries that are very important in the Franco-American tradition. Children and extended family often make elaborate parties for their parents in catering halls following the celebration of a special Mass to honor the occasion. In the Poutre home in Beecher Falls, Vermont, for example, there is a special scroll on the wall carefully calligraphied and ornately decorated to honor the occasion. It was a gift from the nuns who teach at the parish school.

After retirement, men and women do more things together than they did when working. Women, however, spend more time in social activities than their husbands. At La Société des deux Mondes, a Franco-American group in Burlington, Vermont, most of the activities are planned by women: dances, potluck suppers, quilting bees, and special events like talks on I.R.A.s and gardening. The men often find themselves volunteering to set up chairs and tables for banquets or cleaning up after events. It should be noted, however, that for much of its history, the president of the association was a man (Woolfson, 1983).

Death by tradition occurs two hours after a person has been declared dead by a medical authority. When someone is on the verge of death, if it is possible, a priest is called to administer the rites of Extreme Unction. A 60-year-old man in Burlington, Vermont, who recently had a massive stroke and is now recovering, reports that the priest was called in. Because the doctors believed death was imminent, the family allowed the priest to give only a brief benediction. The family during this crisis debated whether to bury him in Vermont or the family plot in Quebec. This decision illustrates the continued attachment that some French families living in the United States still have to Quebec.

After death the body is laid out, most likely for three nights in a funeral home. Frequently the coffin remains open; the body, if male, is dressed in a dark suit with tie; the hands are folded over the chest and clasping a rosary. When Louis Beaudoin, a well-known Franco-American fiddler, died, his family surrounded his coffin on the first night and sang hymns, an indication of the importance of music in the lives of Franco-Americans. Often photographs are taken of the deceased while they are lying in their coffins, and the photos kept in the ubiquitous family album. If the person was an American veteran, those participating in the funeral salute the body with rifle fire and the body is draped in an American flag. After the burial the participants go back to the local American Legion Hall to drink to the deceased (L. French, 1980).

There are many activities of a folk or quasi-religious nature which many Franco-Americans practice. An important manifestation of the relationship between health and religion are the miraculous cures. An older Franco-American woman recalls that when she was a child, her knees were deformed and she could not walk correctly. Her doctors put her in a cast from the waist down in order to minimize further deterioration, but they held out little hope for her condition to improve. Given the hopelessness of the case, her father decided to take her to the famous French-Canadian healer, Frère André at St. Joseph's Oratory in Montreal. She remembers that her father walked on his knees up the steps of the basilica, carrying her on his shoulders and saying a Hail Mary on each step. After Frère André touched her, she was taken to the hospital and her cast removed—she was completely cured.

TRADITIONAL VALUES AND ORIENTATIONS

Within the French-Canadian system of values, two themes appear to be central: *la survivance* and *l'indépendence*. Although both themes appear as national goals—i.e., the preservation of the French language, the moral values of the faith, the culture, and the protection of the group from the interference of foreigners (*les étrangers*), these themes have most relevance within the family household. The survival of the family and its protection from outside harm becomes a central theme that influenced the move from Canada to the United States. Sometimes groups of families came together, or younger members would follow older siblings. Cultural values about family, marriage, and responsibility to children were central to these families. (P. Chasse, 1975).

Of the cultural values considered most important to maintain was what Hughes (1963) called the *individualism of the family*. That is, although strictly personal interests that do not affect other members of the family are given due respect, the individual is expected to subordinate his or her personal interests for the good of the family as a whole.

Chasse (1975) and J. Searles (1982), who have studied the contemporary Franco-American family, report on the struggle to maintain traditional values, especially the value of individual sacrifice for the family. This value competes directly with more current values of economic and social independence from the family. Franco-American mill families, often living eight or nine in a small apartment a few decades ago, required a spirit of cooperation and interdependence that reinforced Quebec farm family values (Woolfson, 1982). That pattern reinforced family bonding. Respect for authority was also part of this familial tradition, with fathers and grandfathers serving as the model for this pattern of behavior.

However, authority is not always adhered to slavishly. J. Ducharme (1980) writes about the intense individuality of the Franco-American, "who is after all a Frenchman. You know the Frenchman is perfectly content with authority so long as he feels that he can be independent of it any time he wants" (1980, p. 259). With their orientation to familial and parochial models for interpersonal relationships, it is not surprising that many Franco-Americans feel uncomfortable in dealing with bureaucracies and impersonal social agencies.

Both men and women take pride in work. Elderly women saw their primary vocations as wives and mothers: they took pride in having well-fed, well-clothed children and a spotless home. Traditionally the French-Canadian housewife took her home apart every spring for the *grand ménage* (spring cleaning). H. Miner (1937) comments that all women of the family cleaned the house a room at a time. Everything was removed and wooden walls, ceiling, and floor were all scrubbed. It required several weeks for the women to complete the ménage (1937, p. 146).

Men took pride in doing their job well—working hard, producing prodigiously, and doing it with craftsmanlike skills. D. Hendrickson (1980) writes about the attitudes held by the men who worked as weavers in the mills and took meaning and pride in their tasks. In the era of the 1920s Franco-American men of the working class did not give education priority. They frequently left school to start work, for example, at age fourteen to earn eleven dollars a week.

Working-class Franco-American parents saved their money without the expectation that it would be used to further their children's postsecondary education. L. French (1980) notes that these families avoided long-term loans and mortgages. Money was saved by renting and avoiding purchase of expensive unnecessary items and the families traditionally did not indebt themselves by spending money on their children in a prolonged adolescence. Even though working-class Franco-Americans did not put a high value on education, Franco-Americans as a group have been very active in founding 264 colleges, high schools, and primary schools.

ACCULTURATION

Elderly Franco-Americans are products of cultural contacts between the French-Canadian culture and its American counterpart. As an immigrant group, their lives and intergenerational families have been affected through confrontation with differences in language, political structure, and the reorganization of familiar religion. Language usage is probably the most powerful acculturation force. In the 1970 census only 9.5 percent of Vermont's population claimed to have French as their major language, but in the 1980 census only 5 percent reported using French in the home.

Many of the elders experienced the battle between the use of English and French in their own parishes. As early as 1934 the religious life of those attending St. Joseph's Church in Burlington, Vermont, was confronted with the bilingual realities when their priest was given permission by the bishop to deliver a sermon in both French and English (Woolfson, 1979).

The eldest generation of Franco-Americans who did not develop English-speaking skills encountered many barriers. Some became estranged in their own religious life because French was no longer used in the local parishes because of the unavailability of French-speaking priests. They found themselves unable to participate fully in intimate daily family life because their grandchildren spoke only English and the parents reinforced this pattern for young children in the home. French-speaking elders also encountered ever greater numbers of English-speaking and fewer numbers of bilingual people in their neighborhoods and communities.

Some community agencies, where there is still a concentration of Franco-American elderly with very limited or no English, attempt to maintain a bilingual nonprofessional staff, but this is far from ideal when communicating with some aged. This language problem is especially evident when these elders must receive medical care. Sometimes nonprofessional people must be brought in to translate into French medical or counseling vocabularies foreign to them. The professional practitioners, speaking only English, are forced to rely on third-party translators; this results in an unsatisfactory rapport. Practitioners working in institutions and community programs having contact with this segment of the aging community recognize their own difficulties when attempting to evaluate dementia and aphasia or other basic life needs not easily communicated in any language.

The social life of some older Franco-Americans centered on the Franco-American societies. As mentioned earlier, coupled with family and church these organizations were sources of cultural and social stimulation. The societies have always varied in membership and continuity. The Fédération Féminine Franco-Américaine established in 1951 now unites 14,000 women throughout New England (P. Chasse, 1975). It continues to be a resource for older women; at the local level groups such as the La Société des deux Mondes in Burlington, Vermont continue even though younger people consider them organizational relics.

The economic life of the Franco-Americans who owned farms on the American side, particularly along the border and in nearby rural communities, has been affected by the changes in farm and family life. Data from the 1930s indicated that Canadian French in Vermont had an average family size of nine children, but by the 1970 census the average family size was four. Many of these older modest farmers were not able to handle the trends of agribusiness that began in the 1950s. When family farms were sold outside the family, there was a significant social displacement for the older farmer and his wife. In some cases when a son continued to own the farm, the elderly parents remained, but under somewhat different arrangements. J. Albert (1979) reports that for Acadian families with a farm inheritance a contract was drawn up between parents and son and daughter-in-law that specified terms of intergenerational obligations extending into directives for matters such as burial instruction. These conditions were taken seriously by adult children.

Economic, social, and cultural impacts were felt by the older Franco-Americans when the cotton and woolen mills throughout northern New England began to close, never to reopen. For some workers it created a form of involuntary preretirement. For others it was the loss of a mill work environment that had always offered much reinforcement for the traditional Franco-American community since French was spoken in the shops. After the mill closings both men and women found themselves in unemployment lines; many had to leave their *petits Canadas* to find work farther afield. This cast them into the melting pot of work. Yet for the older Franco-American mill workers the mill has remained a focal point even in very recent years. Searles (1982) reports that it was a common reference point in homes for the aged with Franco-American residents. If these older residents were not fortunate enough to find other Franco-Americans to share their cultural bond and memories about the textile mills, they could easily experience social isolation (D. Hendrickson, 1980). As a group, older Franco-Americans have struggled under changing circumstances and, even in the face of advanced age, they have always sought to maintain independence (T. Hareven and R. Langenbach, 1980).

Smaller families and the dispersal of family members far away from their parents and grandparents has affected family life and traditional activities. One student describes the historical importance of gatherings in his own farm family, especially during festive periods from Christmas to Lent. In rural Vermont as in other areas, families had designated holidays filled with personal traditions, religious observations, reminiscences, food, and festivity. Cultural events such as rites of intensification which strengthened family ties are increasingly rare, as is the family farm that housed these gatherings.

The older Franco-American woman feels strongly the ending of her traditional role as matriarch of a large clan. French (1980) writes that if both grandparents survived, it was the female who held the higher status. To the extent that their higher status was linked to traditional roles, most of these aging women cannot expect to now plan the large *soirées* and *veillées* that were so important in their past. Their household traditions, such as the *grand ménage,* are no longer practiced to any extent as a result of poor health. This is a common reason for giving up the home and moving into retirement. Widowed mothers maintain close associations with their children if they live close by. Otherwise, travel, including throughout the region and into Canada, can be very expensive and difficult.

Historically the only social agency of any consequence to this group has been the Catholic Church. Parishes that continue to have some elderly Franco-Americans in their congregations serve this community through offering senior citizen programs. They offer parish outreach through community visitations by the priests and younger congregation members. That form of contemporary ministry has many traditional elements, such as visitation to the homebound and sick and support to families in times of crisis or death. Churches sometimes offer trips to special healing shrines such as Ste. Anne de Beaupré in Quebec, and these are still popular with the elderly.

The attitudes Franco-Americans hold about Social Security benefits are generally receptive, as they believe this is their due as former workers in America, but many remain distrustful of governmental services. That reservation is most apparent among the rural Franco-American aged. Their values require expected help to come from very interpersonal relationships, and they feel uncomfortable and stigmatized when encountering large impersonal service sources.

Overall the extent of the acculturation process, as experienced by any elderly individual, is dependent upon where he or she was raised—in Quebec or the United States—the ties maintained to the French language and culture, and the connections with family still in Canada. Intergenerational and multigenerational visitation patterns among these cross-national families help reinforce French-Canadian cultural aspects. The lack of contact—sometimes due to a loss of fluency in French, to self-consciousness on seeing relatives, or to a general mistrust of the highly urbanized Quebec society—weakens those connections.

THE FUTURE

The population of the United States is aging, and the Franco-American population is aging with it. However, the generation of elderly that is most traditionally French-Canadian is dying out. Acculturation of Franco-Americans had its greatest impact in the years following World War II. The labor shortages of the war offered a way for Franco-Americans, like other ethnic groups, to become prosperous. With prosperity, growing ambitions, and changes in mass media, there has been a growing dependence on television for information and entertainment. This is especially the case since access to French broadcasting is limited in much of New England and New York.

The future need to deal with the older Franco-American as a special linguistic and cultural problem is limited. One can look ahead to a time—perhaps only twenty years from now—when French-dominant, culturally distinct Franco-Americans will not require services distinctive to their group. Even now, few people in the health and social services industries are aware of the special needs of the Franco-American patients and clients; they blend into the background so well.

Since the 1970s there has been a resurgence of interest in ethnicity in the United States, reinforced by the surge of patriotism at America's bicentennial in 1976. The Franco-Americans are no exception to other ethnic groups in this country. Searles (1982) documents some of the major interest in reviving the Franco-American heritage that has been facilitated by federal and state funding. Programs offering bilingual education, Franco-American festivals, special public television programs, and university-based Franco-American and Canadian Studies programs (sometimes in English and sometimes in French) are all having some impact on a resurgence of interest and knowledge.

These kinds of activities have been duplicated throughout New England, New York, and Louisiana. While there is little chance to recreate the *petits Canadas,* the resurgence of interest in Franco-American traditions has led to a change in status for the older Franco-American—from rejected cultural baggage to respected cultural resource. One student in a high-school project that used members of a Franco-American Senior Citizens Group in Augusta, Maine, discovered how useful talking to older people can be:

Raissa St. Pierre, a junior from Massachusetts, summed up the feeling of our class:

The French-Canadians went out on a limb, moving to another country and not knowing what to expect. I didn't understand how or what kept them going. After listening to their stories, I wanted to find that kind of confidence and faith in myself (Searles, 1982, viii).

REFERENCES

Albert, J. (1979). The Acadians of Maine. In R. Albert (Ed.), *The Franco-American Overview.* Volume 1 (pp. 151–215). Manchester: Nation Materials Development Center for French.
Chasse, P. (1975). *The Family.* Worcester: Franco-American Ethnic Heritage Studies Program. Assumption College.
Ducharme, J. (1980). The Shadows of the Trees: Religion and Language. In M. Gigue (Ed.), *The Franco-American Overview.* Volume 2 (pp. 255–260). Manchester: National Materials Development Center for French.
Esman, M. R. (1985). *Henderson, Louisiana: Cultural Adaptation in a Cajun Community.* New York: Holt, Rinehart and Winston.
French, L. (1980). The Franco-American Working Class Family. In M. Gigue (Ed.), *The Franco-American Overview.* Volume 2 (pp. 173–190). Manchester: National Materials Development Center for French.
Hareven, T., & Langenbach, R. (1980). *Amoskeag.* New York: Pantheon Books.
Hendrickson, D. (1980). *Quiet Presence.* Maine: Gannet Publishing.
Hughes, E. C. (1963). *French Canada in Transition.* Chicago: University of Chicago Press.
Miner, H. (1937). *St. Denis: A French Canadian Parish.* Chicago: Phoenix.
Searles, J. (1982). *Immigrants from the North.* Bath, Maine: The Hyde School.
Woolfson, P. (1979). The Rapid Assimilation of Canadian French in Northern Vermont. In R. Albert (Ed.), *The Franco-American Overview,* Volume 1 (pp. 211–215). Manchester: National Materials Development Center for French.
Woolfson, P. (1982). The Rural Franco-American in Vermont. *Vermont History, 50* (pp. 151–162).
Woolfson, P. (1983). The Franco-Americans of Northern Vermont: Cultural Factors for Consideration by Health and Social Service Providers. In P. Woolfson and S. J. Senecal (Eds.), *The French in Vermont: Some Current Views. Occasional Paper 6* (pp. 1–26). Burlington: University of Vermont.

IV

STEREOTYPES AND AGEISM

Sociologists have long studied how stereotypes about the elderly shape our attitudes and behavior toward older people. On one hand, stereotypes can be fairly efficient ways of categorizing individuals about whom we have little information. Because we notice a characteristic that an unknown individual shares with some other group of people about whom we have some knowledge, we use stereotypes as frameworks for organizing information. More often, however, stereotypes provide an inaccurate basis for making judgments, because they ignore individual differences. Grouping all people with a particular characteristic (whether age, race, or gender) into a single category disregards the real diversity that exists among individuals within categories. When this happens, stereotypic thinking can lead to overly simplistic (in its least harmful form) or prejudicial (in its more negative form) conclusions about members of particular social groups, even in the face of contradictory evidence.

THE NATURE OF STEREOTYPES ABOUT THE ELDERLY

We live in a symbolic world in which the meanings of objects are determined socially through interaction with others. The self is one object whose meaning is socially determined. The notion of the self-concept refers to the organization of qualities that the individual attributes to his or her self. An individual has many attributes that comprise the self-concept, and one of the more salient is that of age. As people grow older, their self-concept, and thus their sense of self-worth, are shaped by evaluations others hold about the nature of aging. Some of these evaluations are based on fact, but much of what we understand as characteristics of aging are based on stereotypes. One recent study identified three kinds of stereotypes people hold about the elderly: (1) those associated with physical characteristics such as having gray hair, wrinkled skin, or vision and hearing impairment; (2) negative social characteristics such as perceiving older people as complaining, inflexible, forgetful, or dependent; or finally, (3) positive social characteristics, the view that older people are happy, wise, useful, generous, healthy, and active (Schmidt and Boland, 1986). Obviously, many elderly individuals might exhibit characteristics from each of these three types of stereotypes.

Some researchers have devised innovative ways to measure how stereotypes affect attitudes toward elderly people. In one study, college students were shown pictures of the same man at age 25, 52, and 73. The students rated the 73-year-old man significantly more negatively on a number of dimensions than the younger men (Levin, 1988). Other researchers have used "quizzes" to try to identify what facts—and myths—people "know" about the elderly (Palmore, 1977). These quizzes demonstrate that many people hold erroneous ideas about the elderly. People believe that most older people experience a high degree of social isolation, that levels of poverty in old age are high, and that few older people are interested in sex. All of these stereotypes are untrue for the majority of older people. Stereotypes are not constant, however, for personal contact or education can counteract stereotypic attitudes (Levin and Levin, 1981).

CHANGING STEREOTYPES OF AGING

Because stereotypes are shaped by our beliefs, attitudes, and cultural values, they can vary over time. Political scientist Robert H. Binstock (1983) has noted that, from the 1930s through the late 1970s, stereotypes of the elderly were compassionate ones. These compassionate stereotypes were based on the belief that the elderly were (1) poor, frail, and required assistance; (2) that they were politically ineffective; and (3) that they were among the "deserving poor" whose needs should be met by a wealthy nation. According to Binstock, by the early 1980s, stereotypes about the elderly had changed dramatically. The elderly were newly perceived as relatively well off, politically potent, and self-interested. Because of their sheer numbers, they now represented a threat to the future financial stability of the country. While the earlier compassionate stereotype identified elderly people as socially marginal (but deserving assistance), the new stereotype threatened to undermine public support for social programs like Social Security and Medicare that primarily benefit older people. This emergent stereotype has made the elderly scapegoats, often held responsible for "busting the budget" (Binstock, 1983, p. 140). It has also made it possible to pit the elderly against younger generations in the public rhetoric surrounding social policy debates.

STEREOTYPES AND AGEISM

When stereotypes become the basis for action, they result in discrimination. Robert N. Butler (1969) coined the term *ageism* to describe the practice of discrimination against aged individuals. Butler characterizes ageism as a disease, requiring intervention to produce a "cure." Butler's reading in this book examines current manifestations of ageism. Butler suggests that, although knowledge is the best "treatment," growing recognition of older people as consumers may counteract some of the negative effects of ageism.

Prejudice against the aged is neither new in history nor bounded by geography. The fact that ancient Greeks and Romans attributed many negative characteristics to elderly people suggests that ageism has likely existed throughout history. Steve Scrutton's reading traces the historical antecedents of ageism and locates the social basis of contemporary ageism within a British context. Scrutton, too, suggests strategies to counteract ageist practices within the context of the British experience.

Ageism does not affect all elderly people equally. For instance, unusually wealthy or powerful elderly people may not be subject to the same stereotypes as their poor or less powerful counterparts. Ann E. Gerike's reading deals with the intersection of ageism and sexism. Her feminist perspective drives home the fact that aging women face a double risk of stereotyping—on the basis of gender *and* age.

REFERENCES

Binstock, Robert H. "The Aged as Scapegoat." *The Gerontologist* 23, no. 2 (1983): 136–143.
Butler, Robert N. "Age-ism: Another Form of Bigotry." *The Gerontologist* 9 (1969): 243–246.
Levin, Jack, and William C. Levin. "Willingness to Interact with an Older Person." *Research on Aging* 3 (1981): 211–217.
Levin, William C. "Age Stereotyping: College Student Evaluations." *Research on Aging* 10, no. 1 (1986): 134–148.
Palmore, Erdman. "Facts on Aging: A Short Quiz." *The Gerontologist* 17 (1977): 315–320.
Schmidt, Daniel F., and Susan M. Boland. "Structure of Perceptions of Older Adults: Evidence for Multiple Stereotypes." *Psychology and Aging* 1 (1986): 255–260.

8

Dispelling Ageism:
The Cross-Cutting
Intervention
ROBERT N. BUTLER

In this reading, Butler challenges all of us—policymakers, practitioners, scientists, members of the medical profession, the public at large—to intervene in the most basic of all problems of old age: "ageism." Butler begins with a history of ageism as a disease (in the metaphorical sense). He specifies many of its manifestations, which still linger despite years of efforts to allay false stereotypes about older people. In defining ageism as a disease, Butler argues that knowledge is the most basic intervention for dispelling erroneous but widely held beliefs. He concludes with a brief litany of a few crucial interventions, including support for older people's sense of mastery, provision of specially designed self-help books, and the recognition that older people not only constitute an important market but also contribute to the productive capacity of society.

It is increasingly within our power to intervene directly in processes of aging, with prevention, treatment, and rehabilitation. It is also within our power to intervene in social, cultural, economic, and personal environments, influencing individual lives as well as those of older persons en masse. If, however, we fail to alter present negative imagery, stereotypes, myths, and distortions concerning aging and the aged in society, our ability to exercise these new possibilities will remain sharply curtailed. Fortunately, we can treat the disease I call "ageism"—those negative attitudes and practices that lead to discrimination against the aged.

THE DISEASE

I originally coined the term "ageism" in 1968. As chairman of the District of Columbia Advisory Committee on Aging, I had been actively involved in the acquisition of public housing for older people. Stormy opposition arose against the purchasing of a high

"Dispelling Ageism: The Cross-Cutting Intervention." by Robert N. Butler, from *Annals of the American Academy of Political and Social Sciences,* 503 (1989): 138–147. Reprinted by permission.

rise in northwest Washington. The causes for neighbors' negativism were intermixed, for not only were many of the future tenants black, they were also old and poor. In the course of a *Washington Post* interview, I was asked if this negativism was a function of racism; in this instance, I thought it more a function of ageism.[1]

As I originally defined it,

> Ageism can be seen as a systematic stereotyping of and discrimination against people because they are old, just as racism and sexism accomplish this with skin color and gender. Old people are categorized as senile, rigid in thought and manner, old-fashioned in morality and skills. . . . Ageism allows the younger generation to see older people as different from themselves; thus they subtly cease to identify with their elders as human beings.[2]

Not incidentally, in my original formula I was just as concerned with older people's negativism toward young people as I was with young people's negativism toward old people.

I saw ageism manifested in a wide range of phenomena, on both individual and institutional levels—stereotypes and myths, outright disdain and dislike, simple subtle avoidance of contact, and discriminatory practices in housing, employment, and services of all kinds.

Lately, we have seen a rising chorus of voices further criticizing the aged, suggesting that they have had too many advantages. These views come from powerful quarters: politicians, scientists, and philosophers. Interestingly enough, however, these rumblings of intergenerational conflict are not the views of the people at large. National polls and surveys reveal just the opposite, that persons of all ages wish to see older persons keep their entitlements or even have them expanded. An excellent case in point is the recent spectacular rise of the long-term-care issue on the nation's agenda in both the halls of Congress and the recent presidential race.

In light of these surveys, which do not support intergenerational conflict but, rather, reaffirm the needs of older persons, how can we justify the continuation of the practice of ageism? On the one hand, I do believe that the last decade has witnessed a steady improvement in the attitudes toward the aged, in part a consequence of general public education, increased media attention, the expansion of education in the community, colleges, and universities, and the continuing growth of gerontology. On the other hand, the success is uneven, of course. Residual pockets of negativism toward the aged still exist, most occurring subtly, covertly, and even unconsciously. Like racism and sexism, ageism remains recalcitrant, even if below the surface. But it can be—and has been—churned up from its latent position.

To ensure a reasonable place for older persons in society, we need to review some of these contemporary myths, stereotypes, and distorted facts, which must be dispelled or reduced.

CURRENT MANIFESTATIONS

Unfortunately, even the medical profession is not immune to ageism. Medical ageism is contracted in medical school. In fact, it was there that I first became conscious of prejudice toward age, there when I first heard the term "crock"—originally applied to patients with no organic basis for disease thought to be hypochondriacal—applied to middle-aged women and older people. Other terms abounded as well: "gomer" ("get out of my emergency room"); "vegetable"; and "gork" ("God only really knows" the basis of this person's many symptoms).

Medical schools do everything to enhance this virus. The first older person that medical students encounter is a cadaver. Fresh out of college, young people are confronted with death and their own personal anxieties about death, yet they are not provided with group or individual counseling. Not long after, they are exhausted with sleeplessness and hostility for not learning everything fast enough; by the time they are in their third or fourth year of medical school, they are ripe for cynicism. Then comes the internship, and they are working in excess of eighty hours per week, up in the middle of the night—and there is still one of those "gorks" to see.

Few medical school graduates enter the field of geriatrics. In fact, on the whole, physicians do not invest the same amount of time in dealing with elderly patients as they do in their younger counterparts. Doctors question why they should even bother treating certain problems of the aged; after all, the patients are old. Is it worth treating them? Their problems are irreversible, unexciting, and unprofitable.

Then, too, the disease manifests itself in the hospitals themselves. A New York geriatrics professor, currently working at a hospital that, like others, is financially hemorrhaging, fears that his hospital will begin to view the elderly as quite unattractive once administrators see a recent report compiled by accountants tabulating the costs of each diagnosis-related group. Their report gave two tabulations—one for those over 70 and one for those under 70. They correctly concluded that the over-70 group costs the hospital more.

The severe cutback of services following the $750 billion tax cut inaugurated by the Reagan administration has brought steady criticism that Social Security and Medicare provide entitlements for older people yet deny them for the young. Newspapers report that the elderly's median income has risen significantly more than that of any other age group, basically due to Social Security benefits. From such distorted figures has emerged what one author has termed the "New Ageism,"[3] a dangerous viewpoint that envies the elderly for their economic progress and, at the same time, resents the poor elderly for being tax burdens and the nonpoor elderly for making Social Security so costly.

Capitalizing on such distorted figures, many are prepared to churn up these worst views of old people. Not long ago, a cover article of the *New Republic* criticized our society for pampering our "affluent" elderly population, the "greedy geezers." The article began:

Thirty percent of the annual federal budget now goes to expenditures on people over the age of 65. Forty years from now, if the present array of programs and benefits is maintained, almost two-thirds of the budget will go to supporting and cosseting the old. Something is wrong with a society that is willing to drain itself to foster such an unproductive section of its population, one that does not even promise (as children do) one day to be productive.[4]

Groups such as the Americans for Generational Equity promote displacement of Social Security. Wall-Streeter Peter Peterson, former U.S. secretary of commerce, vehemently opposes Social Security; media commentators, seeing the aged as an affluent group, urge Social Security "bashing" and call for privatization of one's retirement planning, which would benefit business and, hence, Wall Street.

Daniel Callahan, expounding the old-age-based rationing of health care originally suggested by former Colorado Governor Richard Lamm in 1983, sees older people as "a new social threat . . . that could ultimately (and perhaps already) do great harm."[5] Programs that benefit the elderly, says Callahan, consume an ever increasing percentage of our taxes; health care expenditures, especially, are becoming extremely disproportionate and costly as the number of our elderly grows. We should use our money to help a sick child live rather than waste it on the old, who have already lived full lives.

It is noteworthy that this sense of renewed threat or concern about the number and proportion of older persons comes in a century of extraordinary increase in average life expectancy. Indeed, in the United States alone there has been a gain of 28 years of life expectancy since the year 1900, nearly equal to what had been attained over the preceding 5000 years of human history. Eighty percent of this gain derives from marked reductions in maternal, childhood, and infant mortality rates. The remainder comes from reductions in death from heart disease and stroke. Although there is considerable chronic disease and disability at later ages, the expanding average life expectancy has yielded large numbers of increasingly vigorous, healthy, and productive older people.

Ageism may bear a relationship to the proportion of older persons in a society. A threshold that might be regarded as an achievement has, instead, become regarded as a burden. Ironically, the long-sought-for gain in life has been met by anxiety. What should have been a celebration has become a sense of threat. What should have been a message of hope has become a matter of despair.

Indeed, my impression, gained from wide travels in varied societies, cultures, and political systems—the Soviet Union, the People's Republic of China, Sweden, France, Argentina, Canada, Mexico, Israel—is that these concerns are universal, in response to the increasing numbers and proportions of older persons. Societies are afraid this increasing older population will become unaffordable, lead to stagnation of the society's productive and economic growth, and generate intergenerational conflict.

TREATMENT

Georges Bernanos wrote, "The worst, the most corrupting lies are problems poorly stated." Let us then state these problems as they really are, putting various myths and distortions into their proper perspectives. In order to treat this disease, we first need to realize what is really true about persons. One antidote to ageism is knowledge.

Knowledge, the Primary Intervention

The belief that neither societies nor individuals will be able to deal with the avalanche of age is reminiscent of the ancient Greek saying, When the Gods are angry with you, they give you what you want. Presumably, human beings wanted an extended life. But the truth is, there has been no extension of the natural inherent life span from the beginning of time, as far as is known. What has happened is an increased survivorship. More and more persons have been able to live out a full life.

Another myth is that all old people are senile and debilitated. But senility is not inevitable with age; rather, it is a function of a variety of brain diseases, most notably Alzheimer's disease and multi-infarct dementia. Nor are the great majority of older people so afflicted. Unfortunately, there may always be some residual gerontophobia and ageism resulting from discomfort and distaste for age and its disabilities. Some profound and pervasive disorders of old age—mobility problems, dementia, and incontinence—are unattractive and provoke disgust and fear.

Then there is the myth that all old people are affluent. Although the elderly are about as likely to be poor as younger populations, income and assets are distributed more unevenly among the elderly, concentrated highly among the rich old. In our rich nation, only 5.6 percent of older people have incomes in excess of $50,000 a year.

Simply stated, the old are, on the whole, the poorest of adults. Of our 28.0 million Americans aged 65 and over, 2.6 million fall below the parsimonious government-recognized poverty line. Two-thirds of them live alone on incomes of less than $104 a week; the other third are couples sharing $131 a week. Additionally, 4.5 million elderly are near-poor. Half of these live alone, existing on between $104 and $156 a week; the other half—elderly couples—live on between $131 and $195 a week.[6] Those in the oldest category—85 years and older—have the lowest income and the greatest percentage of chronic illness. They are more likely to require medical services but less able to afford the care they need.

Widows are the primary victims of elderly poverty and thus bear the brunt of ageism's assault. Their luck in living longer than men has, paradoxically, compounded their problems. Of elderly women, 41 percent are near-poor, contrasted with 17 percent of elderly men. The fact that 75 percent of the poor elderly are women reflects their lower wage levels during their working years, inadequate and inequitable Social Security coverage, and the increased risk of financial devastation from widowhood. Their poverty rate increases with age, from 15 percent for those 65–74 years old to 26 percent for those 85 and older. Of those over 85, 8 percent—50,000 widows—are forced to live on less than $76 per week. Two-thirds of the noninstitutionalized elderly who live alone are widows; over half of them became poor after their husbands died, probably due to consuming medical and funeral expenses and lost pension income.[7] Thus it is really women that New Ageists are referring to when they talk about denying health care to the elderly.

Like sexism, racism, too, is interrelated with ageism. Incomes of the minority elderly are significantly below those of their white counterparts. Black men between 65 and 69 have median incomes 47 percent lower and Hispanic men 40 percent lower than white men. Black and Hispanic women also have lower median incomes than white women, 35 percent and 29 percent lower, respectively. Poverty rates are also much higher among the minority elderly: 31.5 percent for blacks and 23.9 percent for Hispanics as compared to 11.0 percent for whites.[8] In addition, it is primarily minority women and children who suffer most from poverty.

The increases in the elderly population, together with the already large number of poverty-ridden elderly in need of health care, have led to the fear that our older population is unaffordable. After all, our country already has a huge deficit. But Canada is able to provide total health care access to all its people and does so at 2 percent less of its yearly gross national product than the United States. Sweden, East and West Germany, and others already have a higher percentage of older people than does the United States, and they are surviving quite well. In comparison with the rest of the world, Sweden has the highest proportion of people over 65—17.0 percent—and people over 80—3.5 percent. Yet, during the recent Swedish elections, the Conservatives as well as the Social Democrats came out for stronger financial support of older people. All parties are in agreement and Sweden is not falling apart; in fact, its economic situation is quite favorable. The People's Republic of China already has 80 million people over 60, and this situation will become even more dramatic, for China will have 240 million over 60 about the year 2045. Yes, China is a very poor country, but its economic position is not due to its elderly population. Thus the concept that nations will become bankrupt by their growing older populations is not accurate.

How about the myth that our Social Security system is bankrupt, that when young people reach the criterion age, they will not receive Social Security benefits? Social Security is not bankrupt. Rather, trust funds are becoming enormous; they will be in the trillion-dollar range at the turn of the century and will have $12 trillion when all of the baby-boomers are 65 years of age and over.

The dependency ratio is misunderstood. Not everything is given to the elderly. It is true that there is an increasing number of retirees compared to nonretirees. But if one looks at the total dependency ratio, that is, including both people under 18 and people 64 and above, there has been a steady decline in the total dependency-support ratio since the year 1900, and this decline will continue to the year 2050. The reason is the low birthrate—just below zero population growth.

Income transfers do not simply go from young to old through the public means of Social Security, Medicare, and related entitlements. Medicare *in toto* is not an entitlement. Only Part A is an entitlement. Part B is voluntary, not universal, and partially paid for by a premium. By law, 25 percent of the expenditures under Part B are derived from premiums. That is, older people themselves pay for it. Moreover, in 1988 the annual Part B premium increased by 38 percent, from $212 to $298. Two-thirds of poor elderly people receive no coverage under Medicaid, which is, in fact, 50 programs— one in each state—with differing eligibility requirements and benefits. Those elderly living just above the poverty line are often forced into poverty by out-of-pocket medical costs and premiums for private health insurance coverage.[9]

Examination of all income transfers, private and public exchanges, shows that most income, as well as assets and services, go from old to young. In any case, public insurance is an intergenerational compact. Social Security itself is a multigenerational life-long protection system. Benefits are not limited to retirees; in fact, 3 million children receive Social Security benefits.

If one asks more sophisticated questions related to the actual cost of old versus young, one must take care to look at all sources. When one looks only at federal expenditures, the old certainly receive more than the young. But in our system of government, we desire protection from the authority of the centralized state. Education, the great expenditure for the young, is not supported by the federal sector but rather on a community basis through property taxes. For example, in 1986, $140 billion of state and local moneys alone were spent on elementary and secondary public education in the United States. If the New Ageists would look at all the sources, they would see the huge amount of money that goes to children—and should. A policy analysis of the cost of raising a child compared with the cost of caring for an older person still remains to be done.

Data do show conclusively that the condition of children as a group has deteriorated markedly, while that of older people, on the average, has improved. In fact, both children and the old living alone suffer from a 20 percent poverty rate. But the older people have not caused this deteriorating condition. That a society as rich as ours tolerates this suffering is abominable. It is important that the New Ageists realize and emphasize society's failure to deal constructively with the poverty of our children—but correction cannot be at the expense of the older people. We will not improve the welfare of children by tearing down what the elderly have impressively achieved. We need to support intergenerational programs, ones that build a coalition between advocates for the children and advocates for the elderly. One answer to the exploitation of intergenerational conflict has come with the founding of Generations United, which now includes the National Council on the Aging, the Child Welfare League of America, and all those marvelous mainstream organizations that have been advocacy groups for children. We must realize that we really are a group of generations and we must work together, recognizing that today's older persons are yesterday's children and that today's children are tomorrow's elders. We must recognize that there is a continuity and a unity to human life.

Then, too, the high costs associated with old age are not "disproportionate," as so many New Ageists say, but are, in fact, proportionate to age. In 1830, only 1 in 3 babies born in the United States lived to his or her sixties; today, 8 of 10 do. Death has become the harvest of old age. Medical advances have led to people's living longer lives; disease and disability, once affecting the younger population, have been pushed forward and now occur more frequently in old age. This increased longevity has caused high health costs, once associated with maternity, infancy, and childhood, to be shifted to the elderly.

The myth of the high cost of dying needs to be dispelled. Studies show that the aged do not really contribute to rising health costs as much as technology does. And technology, such as that involved in heart transplants, is rarely if ever used in older people. Only 6 percent of U.S. Medicare beneficiaries in their last illness utilize an excess of $15,000 in expenses. Our government needs to create an expanded national center of health services technology to evaluate, monitor, and disseminate information on medical technological innovations.

A Variety of Interventions

Another ageism intervention is the recognition that older people themselves are a market. Japan has the most rapidly growing population of older people in the world, as well as the highest life expectancy. When its Ministry of International Trade and Industry became excited by the "silver community concept"—establishing communities for their older citizens in other countries—there was considerable negative reaction in Japan. When Spain heard this plan, however, it pricked up its ears, for it saw this as a source of jobs. But if "silver communities" are economically valuable for Spain, then they are economically valuable for Japan itself—and for the United States. There is a lot of "gold in geriatrics," as the *Wall Street Journal* once wrote, when one considers capitalism as a connection between producers and consumers. Thus this so-called high cost of health and social services produces jobs and consumption. We speak about the rising costs of health care, but, looking at it another way, the health care enterprise is the second largest producer of jobs. We cannot forget that it does contribute to the gross national product. This is true with Social Security as well. Pension funds, the largest source of capital formation in our country, own half of American stocks. The fact that in 1776 the average life expectancy was 35 and today it is 75—a 40-year difference, more than doubling in 200 years—means bigger markets.

Older persons themselves need to be productive and develop a philosophy on aging if we are to fight ageism. Survival is closely associated with individuals' views of themselves, as well as their sense of continued usefulness. In 1963, our multidisciplinary study of community-residing aged men found that people's experience of aging and their adaptation to it are influenced not only by disease, social adversity, economic deprivation, personal losses, and cultural devaluation, but also by their personalities and their previous life experiences.[10]

In a land where self-help books are plentiful, we need self-help books on aging. Contemporary older persons are rather like pioneers. They do not have a wisdom book to turn to. We need life reviews, reminiscences by the elderly that will help teach others the kinds of lives our older citizens have lived. There are few landmarks, few signposts on the highway, to describe the meaning and character of the new longevity.

Mastery is another important intervention. The simple ability of older people to have some control over their own lives will consequently become evidence to younger populations that the older population is not unproductive, depressed, disengaged, inflexible, or senile—myths that need to be dissipated in the attack on ageism. In fact, in the National Institute of Mental Health Human Aging Studies (1955–66), we found that older persons with life goals and some organization in their daily lives survive; those who do not have such goals and organization do not survive.[11] People need autonomy; in fact, studies show that the relation between health and a sense of control may grow stronger as one ages.[12] When older people's control of their activities is restricted, there are detrimental effects on their health; on the other hand, interventions that enhance their opportunities for control over their activities, circumstances, or health promote health.

Heavy investment in biomedical, behavioral, and social research is the ultimate cost containment, the ultimate disease prevention, and the ultimate service. When we eliminate Alzheimer's disease, the polio of geriatrics, we will empty half of our country's nursing home beds. Spending a few dollars now will dramatically affect the image of senility and debility as inevitable in old age. Through research we can gain freedom from senility and further improvement in the strengthening of the social network that helps sustain people in grief. A better understanding of what accounts for the difference in life expectancy between men and women and the development of a means to assist men to catch up with women by living longer will do much to overcome many of the problems of age, as well as ageism.

CONCLUSION

In conclusion, the war against ageism, even the New Ageism, is largely showing signs of success. The remaining issues are more of social class and race. This does not mean, however, that there must not be continuing vigilance against the possibilities of rationing and denial of care and income. Ageism is a primitive disease, and, unfortunately, our fears about aging are so deep that ageism will probably never totally disappear. But there are interventions we can make now to treat its painful assault.

From the social perspective, certainly, the treatment is to tap those sources responsible for maintaining a dignified and healthy old age. These include the individual, who should remain productive for as long as possible and be attentive to his or her health; the family, which, in fact, in the United States remains the most important caretaker of older persons; and the community, which is rich with strong informal networks of friendly visitors and volunteers and businesses. Union pressures in the 1930s, and particularly during World War II, also played their role in developing fringe benefits that include pensions and health care.

Finally, government needs to be involved at all levels. Legislation such as the Age Discrimination in Employment Act and various other protections, including entitlements and long-term care, are antidotes for ageism. Deciding how to balance all these sources of responsibility is one of the challenges of these next decades.

NOTES

1. Carl Bernstein, "Age and Race Fears Seen in Housing Opposition," *Washington Post,* 7 Mar. 1969.
2. Robert N. Butler, "The Effects of Medical and Health Progress on the Social and Economic Aspects of the Life Cycle" (Paper delivered at the National Institute of Industrial Gerontology, Washington, DC, 13 Mar. 1969), pp. 1–9; idem, "Ageism: Another Form of Bigotry," *Gerontologist,* 9:243–46 (1969).
3. Harold Sheppard, "The New Ageism and the 'Intergenerational Tension' Issue" (Manuscript, International Exchange Center on Gerontology, University of South Florida, 1988).
4. Henry Fairlie, "Greedy Geezers," *New Republic,* 28 Mar. 1988, p. 19.
5. Daniel Callahan, *Setting Limits: Medical Goals in an Aging Society* (New York: Simon & Schuster, 1987).
6. "Aging Alone: Profiles and Projections" (Report, Commonwealth Fund Commission on Elderly People Living Alone, 1988).
7. Ibid.
8. Ibid.
9. "Medicare's Poor: Filling the Gaps in Medical Coverage for Low-Income Elderly Americans" (Report, Commonwealth Fund Commission on Elderly People Living Alone, 20 Nov. 1987).
10. Robert N. Butler, "The Facade of Chronological Age: An Interpretive Summary of the Multidisciplinary Studies of the Aged Conducted at the National Institute of Mental Health," *American Journal of Psychiatry,* 119:721–28 (Feb. 1963), reprinted in *Middle Age and Aging: A Reader in Social Psychology,* ed. Bernice L. Neugarten (Chicago: University of Chicago Press, 1968).
11. Robert N. Butler, "Aspects of Survival and Adaptation in Human Aging," *American*

Journal of Psychiatry, 123(10):1233–43 (Apr. 1967); Robert D. Patterson, Leo C. Freeman and Robert N. Butler, "Psychiatric Aspects of Adaptation, Survival, and Death," in *Human Aging II: An Eleven Year Biomedical and Behavioral Study,* ed. S. Granick and R. D. Patterson, U.S. Public Health Service monograph no. (HSM) 71-9037, 1971, reprinted 1976.

12. Judith Rodin, "Aging and Health: Effects of the Sense of Control," *Science,* 233:1271–76 (19 Sept. 1986).

9

Ageism: The Foundation
of Age Discrimination
STEVE SCRUTTON

Steve Scrutton examines the historical and cultural bases of ageism. He notes that ageism is not a new phenomenon, but rather a practice that has changed in accordance with specific historical circumstances and cultural values. Scrutton uses examples from his own experiences as a social worker, as well as from social structural and cultural evidence in contemporary Great Britain, to illuminate his discussion of how pervasive ageism negatively affects the lives of older people. He concludes his reading with some strategies that, if undertaken in Great Britain, could counteract ageist attitudes and practices.

My father died in 1979, aged 76. After a period of normal grieving, my mother, who was then 74, decided that she wanted to travel from Norwich to Northamptonshire to visit me, a journey of about 100 miles. Previously, she would have been driven by my father, but she announced that it was her intention to travel, alone, by train. My first reaction was that she was to do no such thing. I would go to Norwich and bring her myself. My second reaction was to let her do as she wished. After all, what were the reasons for not allowing her to travel alone? Indeed, she insisted on it, and did the entire trip by herself.

My initial reaction had been a prime, although mild, example of ageism in operation. My mother was quite capable of making the journey but, because of her age, I had felt that it would be wrong for me to allow her to undertake it. Such a decision, if carried through, would have been debilitating for my mother, who would have been made to feel dependent, no longer capable of making decisions for herself, or acting independently. Instead, she had not been a burden, either in my mind or, more importantly, in her own. She had demonstrated her independence and proven conclusively that her age was not a barrier.

This form of patronizing ageism is common where there is genuine care for ageing people. We do not allow older people to work, because they are old. We protect older people from harm, real and imaginary, because we do not believe they can protect

"Ageism: The Foundation of Age Discrimination" by Steve Scrutton, from *Age: The Unrecognized Discrimination*, Evelyn McEwen, ed. Copyright © 1990 by Age Concern England.

themselves. Our concern restricts their ability to fend for themselves. We clean their homes, fetch their shopping, ferry them to where they wish to go; and we do all this without thinking that our care might be undermining their independence, even their morale. We prevent them from taking risks, discourage them from taking physical exercise, and even deny their sexuality.[1] In many subtle ways our care demonstrates that we believe the ageing process makes independent action impossible. The reason we do so is entirely based on our perception of what older people should and should not be allowed to do for themselves—at their age.

There is another, more pernicious form of ageism. This is the ageism that arises from neglect, and from discounting the needs of older people. It is not based on compassion. Instead it deprives older people of social status and role, undermines their self-esteem, and denies them a fair share of social resources. Why else do we insist that older people cannot be employed after a certain age? Why else do we ensure that when they retire they receive subsistence-level pensions? Why else do we frequently talk of the "demographic trends," implying that older people are a burden? Why else is the care of frail, dependent older people in hospitals and residential care so frequently a disgrace? And why else has the abuse of older people failed to become more of a social issue?

WHAT IS AGEISM?

The attitudes which dominate any society usually reflect the interests of the most powerful and influential social groups. Such attitudes may not be shared by everyone, but are accepted by most people without question. Where the assumptions made about old age are negative they lead to ageism, which treats older people not as individuals but as a homogeneous group which can be discriminated against. Ageism creates and fosters prejudices about the nature and experience of old age. These usually project unpleasant images of older people which subtly undermine their personal value and worth. Commonly held ideas restrict the social role and status of older people, structure their expectations of themselves, prevent them achieving their potential and deny them equal opportunities.

Ageism, so defined, is broader than age discrimination. The reason for the discriminatory practices described throughout this book cannot be fully understood and tackled without reference to the concept of ageism.

THE SOCIAL PROCESS OF AGEISM

Each society defines and reacts to older people in ways which are often subtly, sometimes fundamentally, different from each other. The popularly held view of old age today is of very old people, usually women, living alone, socially isolated, managing on inadequate incomes, poorly housed, suffering ill health, dependent on younger carers, yet isolated from their families. Unhappy, withdrawn, but at the same time not interested in making new friends, they have lost their energy, enthusiasm and drive, and are no longer concerned with education or personal development. Their deteriorating physical and mental health offers only the prospect of further decline and the ultimate sentence of old age—death.

This depressing but widely held view of life in old age is the foundation upon which judgments are made about individual worth. It pervades the outlook and expectations of young and old alike, influencing their understanding and appreciation of the nature of old age. It forms the basis for contempt on the part of the young and strong for the old and weak, and the increasing fear of human mortality which old age seems to represent so vividly. Older people have absorbed these attitudes which they once held as young people, and lead their lives in ways which confirm the stereotyped images, and perpetuate the myths of ageism from generation to generation.

Racism, classism, disablism and sexism have developed through similar social processes. While they have much in common, ageism is perhaps different in two major respects. First, older people do not form an exclusive group, but one of which every individual will eventually become a member. The white racist will never be black; the male sexist will never be female; but the young ageist will grow old. Second, the discrimination which emanates from ageism can appear to result from the natural process of biological aging rather than social creation. It is important to emphasize that the concept of ageism does not deny the aging process, but rather seeks to distinguish between—on the one hand—aging as a process of physiological decline and—on the other—the social phenomenon which forms the basis of the disadvantage and oppression of older people. Any consideration of ageism has to be clear about the difference.

THE SOCIAL CREATION OF AGEISM

If different cultures, at different times, value older people in different ways, it indicates that our stereotypes are socially rather than biologically created. It is useful to confirm this in order to counter the popular idea that discrimination against older people arises entirely from the nature of old age.

Former civilizations have regarded and treated older people in very different ways. The historian Minois[2] has delved systematically into the changing status of older people in history, and he has been able to link these changes to the dominant social ideas and circumstances of the time. In ancient Greece, the cult of youth and beauty, and the reverence for the elderly Homeric sage, created an ambivalence which has typified attitudes toward older people throughout history. In the Roman Empire, this ambivalence was demonstrated by the important role played by senior citizens, on the one hand, and their cruel subjection to the literary satire of the time on the other. In the Christian tradition, the image of the revered holy sage was contrasted with the condemnation of the aging sinner.

Throughout history, two main factors have contributed to these historical fluctuations in the fortune of older people: physical strength, and the value placed on acquired knowledge and experience. Physical strength has always been highly regarded. The theory of the "survival of the fittest" predicts that the old and weak must eventually succumb to the young and strong, and that this is necessary for the future vitality of the species. Social life based on this condition can hardly be favorable to older people, and the more turbulent and anarchical the times, the worse their condition and status has been. It is the loss of strength associated with old age that has permitted and continues to permit the abuse of older people.

The respect once given to older people for their knowledge and experience has suffered as a result of several factors: the decline of custom, the acceleration of change and the loss of oral traditions. Civilizations which pass on their learning and experience verbally have to rely on older citizens to provide the vital link between generations. The development of writing and the widespread circulation of books undermined the importance of memory, thereby destroying one of the most useful social functions provided by older people.

For these reasons, prejudice against age is certainly not new. Aristotle (384–322 BC), in his *Rhetoric*, accused older people of every conceivable fault. He described them as cowardly, hesitant, selfish, timorous, suspicious, fearful, parsimonious, miserly, small-minded, ill-humored and avaricious. This form of ageism has probably always existed. It is unlikely that there has ever been a golden age, in which elders have been respected solely for their age. There has always been a close correlation between the status of older people and their personal achievement. The greater the past achievement and the higher the social class, the more status individuals have been able to maintain in old age. Among the poor the situation has always been more difficult. When older people were no longer able to fend for themselves, they became a burden of no further value, and often ended their lives despised and in extreme poverty.

Despite these disadvantages, many older people have been able to maintain their social status by remaining active, alert and healthy. The ability to maintain physical and mental powers has allowed some individuals to pursue their chosen careers regardless of their age. They are the exceptions that prove the rule, "the rule" being the dominant expectations of the time. The evidence of Western civilization suggests that the status of older people has been generally low, but variably so. While it was low in ancient Greece, it was higher in the Hellenistic world. Similarly, it was higher during the early centuries of the Roman republic than in the later Empire period, and while it was low during the turbulence of the early Middle Ages, it reached a peak in the fourteenth and fifteenth centuries, when the importance of older people was enhanced by their ability to survive the plagues of the era.[2]

Thus, although capitalism is blamed by many workers for the treatment older people receive today, it is clear that ageism has a history which long predates this form of social organization. However, the human disruption caused by the agricultural and industrial revolutions did produce in the West a social environment which was particularly unfavorable to older people. If they were unable to take part in hard productive work, they became surplus to the manpower requirements of the new industrial society. This led to two main developments. Initially, older people were removed from the community supports which traditionally looked after them and subjected to the rigors of a "work or starve" philosophy. Subsequently, nineteenth-century philanthropy sought to protect older people from the worst impacts of the economic climate, and such efforts culminated in the introduction of pension legislation. Unfortunately, through fixed ages for the receipt of pensions, these reforms also forcibly prevented older people from being productive members of the society and thereby reduced their social status.

Longevity was once a rarer phenomenon than it is in the late twentieth century. As such, it evoked curiosity and some awe. In a time when birthrates are decreasing in

TABLE 9-1. The Elderly Population in Great Britain: Past, Present and Future[3]

	65+	%	75+	%	85+	%
1901	1734	4.7	507	1.4	57	0.15
1931	3316	7.4	902	2.1	108	0.24
1951	5332	10.9	1731	3.5	218	0.45
1961	6046	11.8	2167	4.2	329	0.64
1971	7140	13.2	2536	4.7	462	0.86
1981	7985	15.0	3053	5.7	552	1.03

Projections for the Future (made in 1987)

	65+	%	75+	%	85+	%
1987	8624	15.6	3699	6.7	746	1.3
1991	8838	15.8	3925	7.0	875	1.6
2001	8984	15.6	4309	7.5	1144	2.0
2011	9425	16.1	4372	7.5	1291	2.2
2021	10642	18.0	4699	7.9	1287	2.2
2027	11472	19.2	5308	8.9	1326	2.2

In the first column of figures, the size of the population is given *in thousands*.

In the second column, the number is expressed as a percentage of the total population of the country.

many countries, it creates fear. In Britain where there has been a continuing decline in the birthrate this century, politicians who talk about the "burden" of old age reveal their concern that a smaller working population will be forced to support a growing number of retired people. This number will grow dramatically as the baby boom generation reaches retirement in the twenty-first century (see Table 9-1).

In the next 30 years, Britain expects the number of people over 65 to increase by 20% and the number of people over 84 to increase by 47%. This prospect has led to a retrenchment in state pension provision and an emphasis on informal caring systems, two attempts to reduce the need for society to foot the bill of its aging population.

The status of older people is also dependent on the social context in which people live, and this is made apparent by the wide variation in aging patterns in different ethnic, geographic and socio-economic sub-cultures.[4] In some cultures, older people are deprived of esteem, suffer severe neglect and, in extreme cases, the frail and weak are simply left to die.

Far Eastern cultures appear to be the most favorable in which to grow old. Elders are widely respected and have high social status. Yet even here deference for old age is not universal or unconditional but is based upon personal achievements or the special knowledge and skills that the individual can offer. Moreover. when these societies become industrialized and urbanized another set of values begins to undermine these time-honored traditions. The respect for elders in Japan is gradually waning as a result.

A similar weakening of traditional cultural values can be witnessed in Britain, where Asian communities have now been subjected to dominant Western values for several generations. There has developed what has been described as a "transition trap," experienced by the generation which has cared for their elders in the traditional manner, but whose children have increasingly embraced Western lifestyles, and fail to fulfill customary expectations about caring for their parents.

This pattern of cultural change is one of the clearest indications of the powerful impact that dominant social attitudes and values have on the status and treatment of older people. Both historical and cultural comparisons indicate that the ideas we have about old age are *as* important, probably *more* important than biological aging in determining the way old age is perceived, and how older people are treated. Where the status of older people is low, it is because these attitudes determine that it will be low, not because it is a natural consequence of the aging process. This raises the important question of where our ageism originates.

AGEISM AND THE PROCESS OF SOCIALIZATION

From birth onwards we are all presented with unflattering images of old age. There has never been a time more conscious of chronological age than our own. Life is presented as a succession of "ages": from birth, through babyhood, infancy, childhood, adolescence, adulthood, middle age and finally old age. Youth represents potential for future growth and development, a time of hope and expectation. Thereafter all is decline, with an increasing if unspoken fear of aging. It is this process of socialization—the gradual adoption of values and norms associated with social roles—which generates ageism. Infants do not discriminate on the basis of age. Their judgment of people is based entirely on whether they are treated gently or harshly, kindly or unkindly, with love or with disdain. It is socialization that transforms aging into something that is to be feared and leads us to believe that older people are to be pitied.

Many school textbooks, from the earliest readers, portray older people as clumsy, frail, pathetic, and needing to be helped across roads, while younger members of the family are happily enjoying an exciting and glamorous life. Many pre-school poetry collections include material which presents negative images of older people.[5] These early influences are probably the first to make an impression on the minds of young children, and this impression is confirmed in later school years, not least in classic literature. In Shakespeare's *As You Like It*, for example, the melancholy Jacques describes old age as:

> . . . second childishness and mere oblivion,
> Sans teeth, sans eyes, sans taste, sans everything.[6]

Our education system also subtly confirms the ageist idea that older people are not educable and are not interested in personal development. The very foundation of our modern system, the 1944 Education Act, discusses the education of "the people" but effectively means the education of those between 5 and 16 years. Adults have no statutory rights to education and, as one educational gerontologist writes, "if adult education is marginalised then the education of older adults is marginalised to the margins of the margin."[7]

Language is another powerful method of structuring attitudes about old age. In this area our language is highly expressive and almost invariably derogatory, infantilizing or pitying. Words and phrases in common usage, such as "mutton dressed as lamb," "dirty old man," "silly old woman," "old fogies," "old ducks," "old biddy," "old codger," "old dears" and "old folk" all conjure up images which leave little doubt about the nature and experience of old age.

Nor is the impact confined to popular expressions. *Roget's Thesaurus*, a classic English text which seeks to arrange words "according to the ideas which they express," describes old age by such nouns as "senility, grey hairs, climacteric, declining years, decrepitude, hoary age, caducity, superannuation, second childhood, dotage, decline of life" and, even more graphically, by the adjectives "senile, run to seed, declining, waning, past one's prime, grey, hoary, venerable, time-worn, antiquated, doddering, decrepit, superannuated, stricken in years, wrinkled, having one foot in the grave."

The assumption that old people are rigid, less capable, less willing to adapt to new developments, and unable to change is firmly rooted in modern psychological theory. The father of modern psychology, Sigmund Freud, believed ". . . psychiatry is not possible near or above the age of 50; the elasticity of the mental processes on which the treatment depends is as a rule lacking—old people are not educable."[8]

This view has had an influential impact on psychology, and although some might now consider such ideas outmoded, they continue to have an enduring effect on public perceptions of old age. The association between age, adaptability, and psychological theory remains one of the major factors that disables older people, particularly within a society in which "change" and "progress" are increasingly important.

Ageism is also firmly rooted in our pervasively influential religious beliefs. Many religions encourage the idea that our current condition is temporary, and that old age should be a time of looking toward our place in the next life which is more important. Suffering is part of our preparation for the hereafter. Death, our link to a better world, is to be welcomed rather than feared. Happiness and fulfillment will be abundantly available in heaven, valhalla, or nirvana.

The impact of religious belief on the attitudes to life of older people is particularly strong. These attitudes in Christian tradition can be traced back to ideas which linked old men with the image of sin, and old age as a curse and a punishment.[9] In Western tradition, the belief that a normal lifespan was the biblical "three score years and ten" has shaped the expectations of older people, and justified a lack of social provision.

Medical opinion is another influential source of dominant social attitudes, and its views on aging are central to the expectations we have about the "normal" conditions of older people. A common image of health in old age is one associated with the loss of energy and personal drive, significantly greater need for rest, long and increasing periods of sickness, permanent experience of pain and discomfort, increasing immobility, the gradual loss of personal control and responsibility, the onset of incontinence, with the resulting loss of dignity and self-respect, increasing confusion, and ultimately the most feared condition of all, senility.

The image of old age as a time of pain, illness and disease has often implied that older people actually owe their continuing existence to medical expertise alone. Unfortunately, comments made by some doctors to older people nurture and encourage the view that pain, illness and disease are an unavoidable feature of normal aging. The biological assumptions involved in such statements are based on a series of half-truths about the aging process, extended so that they appear to support explanations about the nature of life and health in old age that are not justified by the facts. For instance, while brain cells do die and are not replaced, their loss is not an explanation for senility. Yet through such biological "explanations," dementia is perceived as part of the normal, natural process of aging. Moreover, once this premise is accepted there is less reason to seek to cure it; pain, illness and disease become an accepted consequence of old age.

The association between youth and beauty has been evident throughout history, particularly in ancient Greece and during the Renaissance. It is equally apparent today when many people go to considerable lengths to maintain the appearance of youthfulness by the use of vitamins, beauty preparations of all descriptions, hormone treatment, plastic surgery and much else besides. The link that is assumed between beauty and youth implies a link between old age and ugliness, and is detrimental to older people. It supports the belief that aging makes people unattractive, and no longer physically or sexually interesting. The impact on older women is greater than for older men, as dominant sexist ideas have created the belief that being attractive is more important for women. Consequently, dual standards are applied. Eyebrows are raised considerably higher by the idea of an older woman with her "toy boy" than an older man with a much younger girlfriend.

STRUCTURAL AGEISM

The most pernicious aspect of ageism is not that which is present in the minds and attitudes of individuals, but that which is confirmed and reinforced by the functions and rules of everyday social life. The structural analysis of aging has become increasingly prominent in recent years.[10] The close association between productivity and social status within the "work cultures" of Western capitalist societies has been well documented. Marx believed that capitalist values were completely determined by considerations of productivity. Weber saw capitalism as characterized by an emphasis on work and activity and highlighted the effect this had on the moral as well as the economic and political development of a society. Durkheim recognized this too when he defined the "division of labor" as a system of moral integration as well as economic production.

This analysis has had important implications for older people. Compulsory retirement enforces non-productivity, depresses social status, and promotes the idea of old people as a burden. It is the basis for age discrimination through neglect. Medical, educational and social service provision becomes a low priority if it is considered that there is only a marginal return on such investment. The result is that ageism is at its most vicious when older people compete for limited resources, for they are often denied equal access—solely by virtue of their age.

The structural confirmation of ageism is vitally significant. If age discrimination was entirely a matter of individual attitudes it could be more easily tackled. It is when ageist attitudes become part of the rules of institutions, govern the conduct of social life, and blend imperceptibly into everyday values and attitudes that they have a drastic effect on the way older people lead their lives. . . . Older people, on the basis of chronological age, are progressively removed from economic life, which provides them not only with income, but structures their daily routines and integrates them into regular social relationships. Compulsory retirement places older people in a no-win situation; they are not allowed to work in order to earn their living; nevertheless, their enforced lack of productivity makes them a "burden," and serves to devalue them.

The most immediate effect of retirement is a dramatic reduction in living standards. Our welfare state encourages, even ensures, poverty among retired people. State pensions have remained fixed at subsistence levels. Non-means-tested welfare benefits display many features of structural ageism. The maximum social security payments for older people living in residential care homes are lower than for younger, physically handicapped people. Other disablement benefits cannot be claimed once an individual has reached pensionable age, implying that disability is a normal part of old age. The perception that disability is age-related ultimately influences the take-up rate of these benefits, for many older frail people fail to claim allowances to which they are entitled because they assume that their problems result from old age rather than disability.[11]

The structural neglect of older people reaches its peak when they become frail or dependent. Ageist attitudes ensure that caring for dependent and vulnerable older people is regarded as a low prestige, low priority enterprise by both health professionals and social workers. The low standards of residential care have been a topic of concern for many years. There have been a number of major scandals, the most significant being the Nye Bevan Lodge investigation in 1988, in which residents were found to have been illegally deprived of their money, made to queue naked for baths, and subjected to other practices which included physical and sexual assault. It was widely recognized at the time that these practices were the tip of a much larger iceberg of old-age abuse.

I was personally involved in the investigation of a private residential home for older people in Northampton, in which gross practices against residents were uncovered. Neither of these events, nor other similar ones, have hit the imagination of the media or the public with the same force as the similar serious scandals involving children.[12]

Weaker members of society are always vulnerable to mistreatment. Abuse of children has been recognized as an important concern because children are seen to represent the future; to abuse them is to abuse the future welfare of the nation. Child protection has therefore been given priority status, resulting in a plethora of legislation, directives, regulations and procedures, all adopted to protect the well-being of children.

The abuse of older people has not attained equal priority. The Northampton investigation centered on an elderly woman, suffering dementia, who was found to have a double fracture of the jaw. There was no acceptable explanation for the injuries, and the injuries were consistent with a single blow. Yet the medical authorities would not clearly state this, nor did the police believe that they had a case capable of being taken further, not least because the abused woman could not tell us how it had happened. While I was personally convinced that abuse had taken place, it appeared that no further action was likely.

The contrast between this inactivity and the action which would have been taken had the injured individual been a young child was a stark one. There would have been more medical concern. The social services would have had powers to protect not only the injured party (even without evidence that could be proven in court), but also all the other children, probably by their removal from the home. Public concern, legislation, departmental procedures, and pressure on professional staff would have combined to ensure that effective action was taken. In contrast, lack of public concern, the absence of legislation and departmental procedures, and a general lack of professional concern seemed to conspire in the opposite direction with regard to this elderly woman. In his survey, the social worker Mervyn Eastman states that "society does not even accept that old-age abuse takes place, let alone appreciate the reasons why it happens."[13] His view seems to be undeniable in this situation, and it serves to convince me that ageism will never be tackled unless recognition of the problem is followed by the introduction of positive measures.

Yet, Eastman's statement leads to another vital question that needs to be addressed. Why is it that structural ageism sanctions discrimination against older people and enables it to continue unnoticed on a daily basis, and remain unchanged over many years? Further, how can this situation occur in a society which would consider itself to be both civilized and compassionate in its dealings with older people?

THE DENIAL OF AGEISM AND THE MYTH OF PHILANTHROPY

Despite the widespread ageism which exists at both the individual and structural level, there remains widespread social ignorance and denial of its impact. The result is that the evidence for ageism remains unaltered, and the assumptions upon which ageism is based are preserved and perpetuated.

In its place has developed the myth of philanthropy. This is based upon the belief that older people are treated with greater compassion now than ever before. To confirm this, more comfortable images of old people have been created, enabling us to believe that older people are leading lives which are happy, contented and fulfilled. These are images of older people as kindly and inoffensive, sitting in front of their fires, or enjoying winter in hotels on the Costa del Sol. When they do need support, there is the comforting notion that the welfare state and National Health Service are looking after their needs better than ever before.

The denial of ageism can go further, with older people often being blamed for their own situation. Many professional people, including some gerontologists, consistently emphasize physical, psychological and social decline above all other factors in the characteristics and capacities of older people.[14] In doing so, they reveal how accustomed they have become to working with entrenched and unquestioned assumptions that such loss and decline is caused by age alone. We have even constructed elaborate theories to make us feel better about the lives older people lead. The theory of disengagement[15] has led us to believe that it is a normal feature of growing old to withdraw from social life, that isolation and loneliness is a chosen path and not the product of enforced retirement, low income, low status and inadequate social provision. The result is a tendency to "blame the victim," a belief that older people have caused the plight in which they find themselves.

More convincing is the idea of "structured dependence,"[16] which suggests that dependency in old age is more usually a social than a biological or individual creation. The idea is graphically summarized by Alison Norman: "We are all familiar with the advertisements and Christmas begging letters which ask for money in terms which suggest that old people are in danger of hypothermia or social isolation simply because they are old—not because they do not have sufficient incomes to heat and repair their homes or to pay for a taxi or telephone."[17]

The situation of older people from ethnic-minority communities can be worse. The assumption that they are not neglected, and that cultural values ensure they will be cared for adequately, has been challenged by Norman.[18] Her concept of "triple jeopardy" demonstrates that elders from such groups suffer from dominant Western social values in three distinct ways: psychologically, bureaucratically and financially.

The myth of philanthropy is quickly discredited by a realistic look at how older people lead their lives. However, the myth is constantly perpetuated in subtle ways; for instance, through apparently "charitable" views of old age. In responses to a recent questionnaire from members of Age Concern England's governing body,[19] it was notable that few saw concessionary entitlement to services as discriminatory and patronizing, only necessary in a society which implicitly recognizes that older people are not treated fairly. The special treatment that concessions represent removes from older people the dignity associated with being able to function independently without the need for subsidy or support.

All forms of charity can have the same unfortunate, unintentional impact. The value of charity is twofold: it is aimed at helping the recipient, but it is also beneficial to the giver. Charity salves our conscience, allows us to feel that something is being done, that what is being done is sufficient, and that we have played our part in doing it. This is an integral part of the denial of ageism. We have old age pensions; but they are not sufficient. We have a National Health Service; but it does not deal adequately with the illnesses of old age.

In similar vein, dare it be said that the charitable function of Age Concern serves this dual function? To what extent does its dependence on charitable donations make it an involuntary party in the game of denial? If it were more forcefully to challenge the ageism that underlies the social structure, would it be in danger of provoking a backlash from those of its supporters who do not wish to be reminded that all is not well, despite their charity? Is Age Concern contributing to the idea that something effective is being done? Does it address the issue that it is the impact of social structures on older people that needs to be challenged, and that any amount of charitable good work is not going to fundamentally alter this situation? Is it strident enough in stating that not enough is being achieved? Despite its undoubted contribution in the past 50 years, perhaps these are questions that it needs to address now it is embarking on the journey of its centenary.

The consequence of the widespread denial of ageism is a strong social taboo surrounding the subject of old age, decline and death. Simone de Beauvoir asserted that "society looks upon old age as a kind of shameful secret that it is unseemly to mention."[20] Young people frequently dismiss remarks which older people may make about their impending or eventual death. Such thoughts are usually considered to be unnecessarily morbid, although the subject is probably more painful for younger people than those who more closely and personally face their own decline and death. For many older people this taboo is unhelpful and leads to difficulties, including an inability to prepare for and come to terms with the realities of old age, with physical and mental decline, and ultimately with death itself.[21]

COUNTERING AGEISM

Ageism surrounds us, but it passes largely unnoticed and unchallenged. Moreover, just like racism and sexism, it is so engrained within the structure of social life that it is unlikely to be challenged effectively by rational argument or appeals to the more philanthropic side of human nature.

There are a number of general strategies which are useful in combating ageism. Increased awareness is the basis on which they can be developed. Only when we are more aware of our personal attitudes can we become active in confronting ageism wherever it is encountered.

Ageism-awareness campaigns and anti-ageist strategies, while essential, are not sufficient to bring about the level of change which is required. Age discrimination is so intertwined with the social fabric that legal action must become the major objective. There are no statutory safeguards against ageist practices, no equivalent of the Race Relations Act or Equal Opportunities legislation. Legislation will not end ageism, but it will bring the issues into sharper focus and force a reappraisal of current social practices. There are several areas in which legal protection is required. The first of these is in the field of employment. Legislation is needed to protect the right to employment of older people by outlawing discriminatory practices in advertising and filling job vacancies. Individuals should also have the right to choose their own time of retirement. The second area requiring legislation is where older people have been discriminated against to such an extent that they have been put in jeopardy. Legal safeguards are necessary to protect their money and property, and a way should be found to provide security of tenure for dependent older people in residential care. There should also be legislation which will protect older people against bad practice and abuse in both private and public residential care and nursing homes and in hospitals.

These defensive and protective proposals could be reinforced by a single measure, brilliant in its simplicity, which would guard against old-age discrimination more effectively than any other. This would be to outlaw general references to age in all current and future legislation where it is used to imply frailty or the need for services. Such a measure would have a dramatic impact. For example, the right to work would depend solely upon individual ability to do the job; the renewal of an annual driving license after the age of 70 would have to be replaced by measures which are not triggered simply by people reaching a certain age.

The use of the word "age" in legislation has helped to create age discrimination. Age was put alongside grave chronic disease, infirmity or physical incapacity as a qualifier in the 1948 National Assistance Act, and to this day the word continues to be used in legislation as a blanket term to imply dependence. This practice encourages the belief that old age is a condition similar to disability. To ban the use of the word in legislation would encourage the awareness that age is not an illness or a disability. It would encourage the idea that to be old and disabled is not so different from being young and disabled; that dementia is a mental *illness*, not an inevitable feature of old age. It would stress that it is the circumstances and condition of individuals, not their age, that is significant.

Such a move would force a reappraisal of ageist assumptions and encourage more positive attitudes which judge individual ability according to performance rather than chronological age. Pessimism about the nature of old age is perhaps the greatest enemy of a happy and fulfilled old age. To develop more positive images of aging in this way is not a contrived attempt to pursue attitudes which are unreal, but an effort to seek redress to the current imbalance created by ageism. The starting point is to accept that each individual develops and evolves throughout life, and that the final stages of life are as important as any other. As Gore has said: "Life lived as a continuum, is a garnering and enriching experience. It becomes a process of addition rather than subtraction; of a growing maturity rather than a loss of youth, of evolution rather than dissolution. It removes the pernicious, if subconscious obsession with calendar age, which precludes some of us from learning new things, or undertaking new tasks, or taking a new interest in the world around us."[22] Legislative change would bring about a positive reassessment of the social role of older people. It would help to create a more responsive social climate, enabling them to fulfill their potential and conclude their lives with dignity.

Moreover, legislation could galvanize the power of older people, countering the ageist idea that they cannot represent their own interests. The "Grey" movement, in the shape of organized pensioners' groups, is becoming stronger. I hope they will challenge the images which restrain and persecute older people at present, and seek to shift public attitudes about the nature of old age. Collectively, older people need to exploit the full potential of their influence, which will only increase as their numbers grow, in order both to maintain responsibility for their own lives, and to demand their full social, political and economic rights.

REFERENCES

1. Greengross, W and S (1989) *Living, Loving and Ageing*, Age Concern England, London.
2. Minois, G (1989) (also reference 9) *The History of Old Age: From Antiquity to the Renaissance*, Polity Press/Blackwell, Oxford.
3. Office of Population Censuses and Surveys (1901–1981 census data). Population projections by the Government Actuary (1987–2027), pp2, no 16, HMSO, London.
4. Ory, M and Bond, K (eds) (1989) *Ageing and Health Care: Social Science and Policy Perspective*, Routledge, London.
5. Tyler, W (1986) (also reference 7) Structural Ageism as a Phenomenon in British Society. *Journal of Education Gerontology*, Keele.
6. *As You Like It* (II, vii).
7. Tyler, W (1986) (reference 5).
8. Freud, S (1905) *On Psychotherapy*, Hogarth Press, London.
9. Minois, G (1989) (reference 2).
10. Townsend, P (1981) (also reference 16) The Structural Dependency of the Elderly: A Creation of Social Policy in the 20th Century. *Ageing and Society*, 1, 6–28, London.

Phillipson, C (1982) (also reference 16) *Capitalism and the Construction of Old Age*, Macmillan, London.

Myles, J (1984) *Old Age in the Welfare State: the Political Economy of Public Pensions*, Little/Brown, Boston.

Phillipson, C and Walker, A (1987) *Ageing and Social Policy: A Critical Assessment*, Gower, Aldershot.

11. Evandrou, M and Falkingham, J (1989) Benefit Discrimination, *Community Care*, 25 May.

12. Scrutton, S (1989) Time to Treat Elderly People Like Children? *Social Work Today*, 10 August, Birmingham.

13. Eastman, M (1984) *Old Age Abuse*, Age Concern England, London.

14. Levin, J and Levin, WC (1980) *Ageism: Prejudice and Discrimination Against the Elderly*, Wadsworth, Belmont, California.

15. Cummings, E and Henry, WE (1961) *Growing Old: the Process of Disengagement*, Basic Books, New York.

16. Townsend, P (1981) (reference 10). Phillipson, C (1982) (reference 10).

17. Norman, A (1987) *Aspects of Ageism: A Discussion Paper*, Centre for Policy on Ageing, London.

18. Norman, A (1985) *Triple Jeopardy: Growing Old in a Second Homeland*, Centre for Policy on Ageing, London.

19. Age Concern England (1989) Retirement Forum: Responses to Questionnaire (unpublished).

20. Beauvoir, S de (1972) *Old Age*, Deutsch/Weidenfeld and Nicholson, London.

21. Scrutton, S (1989) *Counselling Older People: A Creative Response to Ageing*, Age Concern England/Edward Arnold, London.

22. Gore, Irene (1979) *Age and Vitality*, Allen and Unwin, London.

10

On Gray Hair and Oppressed Brains
ANN E. GERIKE

It is not surprising, in societies where the effects of sexism are pervasive, that women's experiences of ageism differ from those of men. Gerike's reading focuses on the interconnections of ageism and sexism in regard to a widespread cultural phenomenon routinely practiced by older women: dyeing gray hair. In this discussion of a subject seldom addressed by feminists, Gerike describes the sexual, social, and economic pressures to color hair and deny age. She concludes that attitudes toward gray hair are slowly beginning to change, and she discusses the political and personal advantages of graying naturally.

Gray hair is universally viewed as an indication of advancing age, though the age at which hair begins to gray varies widely among individuals. Changes in hair color begin sooner than most people realize. A study of Australian blood donors in 1965, for example, revealed that, by the time they were twenty-five, 22 to 29 percent of the men in the group and 23 to 35 percent of the women had some obvious graying (Parachini, 1987). The age at which people begin to gray seems to be genetically determined, as are the graying patterns.

Much of the gray effect is produced by the mixture of light and dark hairs, though as dark hair loses its color it is genuinely gray for a time. Blond hair, of course, "grays" much less noticeably than darker hair. The proportion of white to dark hairs has to be well over 50 percent before it begins to show decisively.

Little research has been done on the graying of hair, so most of what is known about it is assumption and guesswork. But the basic process appears to be the following:

Each of the 100,000 hairs on the head is controlled by a hair bulb below the follicle at the deepest part of the root system. It is through the hair bulb that a variety of complex substances are channeled, creating each hair, mainly composed of a biochemical substance called keratin.

In the hair roots and in the epidermis, millions of protein-producing pigment cells, called melanocytes, produce chemicals that determine the coloring of hair and skin. . . . The melanocytes, in turn, are responsible for chemistry that colors the hair that takes shape in the follicle and grows long enough, eventually, to be seen. . . .

Melanin, the pigmentation chemical, has two components. The two basic colors predispose a hair to be dark or light or a shade between, depending on the proportion of each pigment that is genetically introduced into the hair-making process. Coloration is influenced by racial and ethnic factors, but virtually no research has been done on the existence of such influences in graying. . . .

The color chemistry changes with age so that even a person who has no gray may find his or her natural hair coloring changing with advancing age. Many people experience a darkening in their coloring—directly attributable to the maturing function of the melanocytes and the varying production of melanin.

With time . . . the melanocytes weaken and their pigment-producing chemistry begins to shut down. It is a gradual process and, for the period that the melanocyte is still functioning at reduced capacity, the bulb may produce a hair that is gray, or incompletely colored. In time, though, the melanocyte stops working and the hair bulb produces white hair. The process can also be influenced by a variety of diseases that prematurely—and sometimes reversibly—reduce enzyme chemistry and interfere with pigment cells. In the vast majority of cases, age and the natural evolution of melanocytes—culminating in their cessation of function—cause graying. (Parachini, 1987, p. 2C)

However interesting that explanation may be as a description of biological process, the graying of hair is interesting primarily for sociological, not biological reasons. For of course millions of women, and increasing numbers of men, color their hair because of the negative myths and stereotypes about aging which form the basis of ageism in our society. These negative attitudes are implicit in our language: "old" is assumed to connote incompetence, misery, lethargy, unattractiveness, asexuality, and poor health, while "young" is used to imply competence, happiness, vitality, attractiveness, sexuality, and good health. People are told they're "as young" (or "only as old") as they feel, and they are admonished to "keep themselves young." When they are ill, they are said to have aged; when they recover, they're told they look younger.

The coloring of gray hair disguises the physical feature associated with aging that is most obvious and most easily changed. Such hair dyeing, in our youth-oriented culture, represents the attempt of aging people to "pass" as members of a group with greater power, privilege, and prestige than the group to which they in truth belong. In that, it is similar to the widespread use of skin lighteners by many blacks in the time preceding the Civil Rights movement.

In a patriarchal society, the power and privilege of women reside in their utility to men. They must be able and willing to bear children, and be willing to remain in a subservient position. In such a society, women beyond the menopause are useless; they obviously cannot bear children. They may also be dangerous: with the growing assertiveness that often comes to women as they age, many are unwilling to remain subservient (Melamed, 1983; Rubin, 1981). If a woman's choices are to be either useless or dangerous as she ages, it is perhaps no wonder many women prefer to use hair color as a means of concealing—or at least underplaying—their age.

Since traditional male socialization does not encourage men to acknowledge their "weaker" feelings, women have often taken on the role of caring for men's emotional as well as their physical needs. A 54-year-old man interviewed by Barbara Gordon for her book *Jennifer Fever* says: "Men are emotionally underdeveloped, and they want women to handle the emotional side of life for them" (Gordon, 1988, p. 100). In discussing feelings of vulnerability, Jean Baker Miller argues that "women provide all sorts of personal and social supports to help keep men going and to keep them and the total society from admitting that better arrangements are needed" (Miller, 1976, p. 32).

The fact that women expend far more time, money, and effort in attempts to retain a youthful appearance than do men may well represent an aspect of such emotional caretaking. By providing men their own age (usually their husbands, but sometimes their lovers) with a false-faced mirror of youth, they may be attempting to protect such men from the emotional reality of aging and eventual death. In the film *Moonstruck* a white-haired Olympia Dukakis asks, "Why do men chase women?" and answers herself: "Because they fear death." I once heard a man say to his gray-haired wife, without rancor: "I only feel old when I look at you."

At the same time, of course, the woman may be protecting herself, or at least attempting to do so. A gray-haired or white-haired woman is often seen as motherly, and sexual attraction to the mother is taboo. In *About Men*, Phyllis Chesler writes:

> When a wife grows "old"—*as old as his mother once was*—a man must renounce his interest in Her once again. Only the blood of strange women, the blood of ever-younger women, can be pursued without incestuous guilt. (Chesler, 1978, p. 80)

If a woman believes that maintaining a youthful appearance in itself will enable her to attract or "keep" a man, however, she may well be disappointed. In Gordon's reports on a series of interviews with older men who are in relationships with younger women, she extracts their reasons for preferring such women: adoration, which they are unlikely to receive from an age peer; "liberation backlash"; the "scarring factor" of unhappy long-term marriages to women their own age; and "innocence." A 60-year-old lawyer says:

> I want someone young to love me. I want someone young and fresh and new to be attracted to me. I don't want a forty-five-year-old woman who looks great for her age, young for her age. No matter how great she looks, she's still forty-five. (Gordon, 1988, p. 100)

Fortunately, not all older men are so emotionally retarded. It will be interesting to see what kinds of attitudes today's young men, having grown up in a world where gender arrangements are changing, will have toward older women when they themselves grow old.

The assumption that women are no longer sexual beings when they have passed their childbearing years is clearly an aspect of patriarchy. The desexualizing effect of gray hair is well illustrated by the experience of a friend of mine, who had grayed in her late teens and had never colored her hair. When she was in her late thirties she dyed her hair black, on a dare. The next day, when she went to the gym she had been attending for some time, she suddenly materialized for men who had not previously noticed her.

Such magical invisibility is not only sexual; it is pervasive, similar to that noted long ago for blacks by Ralph Ellison in *Invisible Man* (1952) and James Baldwin in *Nobody Knows My Name* (1961). The title of Barbara Macdonald's powerful treatise on ageism, *Look Me in the Eye* (1983), addresses the fact that, in most social circumstances, women as well as men seldom make eye contact with the old, whom they simply do not see. If old women are not ignored, they are often subjected to a condescending head-patting kindliness which suggests that its recipient is unintelligent, uneducated, and incompetent. That women should want to avoid such treatment as far as possible is understandable, and they may be able to avoid it for a time by coloring their gray hair.

Sexism in combination with ageism also causes women problems in the job market as they age. Many women dye their hair because their fear, perhaps with good reason, that they might lose their jobs, or find it difficult to obtain jobs, if their gray hair were visible. In many professional circles, gray hair on women is considered unprofessional. Office workers in particular are often chosen for youthful physical appearance. A story frequently heard from highly competent female clerical workers in their forties and fifties is of waiting for a job interview in competition with young inexperienced women, and seeing one of those women selected for the job (Leonard, 1982).

Interestingly, however, gray hair can be an advantage for a woman who is already in a position of authority. For example, a friend of mine who was a medical resident found her students much easier to manage when she let her naturally gray hair appear. I myself suspect that my almost-white hair gives me "clout," even though I entered my profession, clinical psychology, late in life. (One might assume that having gray or white hair would be an advantage for those working with an older population, as I do; but the majority of older women I know who work with the elderly dye their hair—perhaps out of fear of being identified with their clients?)

In the personal sphere, if not in that of employment, lesbians would seem to have less incentive than their straight sisters to dye their gray hair; lesbian women are less likely to be obsessed with youth and appearance than are heterosexual women (Doress & Siegal, 1987). But prejudices against *old* women are intact among most lesbians, as indicated in Macdonald's *Look Me in the Eye* (1983) and Baba Copper's *Over the Hill: Reflections on Ageism Between Women* (1988). Copper writes:

> Lesbian youth worship differs little from heterosexual youth worship. The deprivation of sexual recognition between women which takes place after middle age (or the point when a woman no longer passes for young) includes withdrawal of the emotional work which women do to keep the flow of social interactions going: compliments, questions, teasing, touching, bantering, remembering details, checking back, supporting. (Copper, 1988, pp. 29–30)

Considering the combination of ageism with sexism, it is not surprising that far more women than men color their gray hair—45 percent of women in their forties and fifties (Doress & Siegal, 1987) and 8 percent of men (La Ferla, 1988). In a description of male and female ideals in advertising, the ideal woman's hair is "not gray," while that of the ideal man is "any color, even gray" (Melamed, 1983, p. 121). Hollywood "stars" over the age of fifty are living testimony to the sexist aspect of ageism: almost all of the men that age are gray or white-haired (and/or balding), while almost all of the women are blondes, brunettes, or redheads. Since women begin to gray sooner than men, that is obviously not a natural gender difference. Barbara Stanwyck, now gloriously white-haired, is one of the few film actresses who has never attempted to hide her age, by either word or deed.

Most of the older female actors on television dye their hair, including the woman most often cited as a role model for older women, 63-year-old Angela Lansbury, the star of "Murder She Wrote." Of the four older women on "Golden Girls," the two characters who do not color their hair are Sophia, a rude and inconsiderate woman in her eighties (whose rudeness is presumably funny because she is old), and her daughter Dorothy (Bea Arthur), who is very tall, deep-voiced, and powerful—clearly not the essence of traditional femininity.

The belief that aging is more negative for women than for men has a long history. Lois Banner, in *American Beauty*, her study of attitudes toward American women's physical appearance, quotes a *Harper's Bazaar* article from 1892 which noted that men did not have to look young to be appreciated; they could be considered attractive at any age. For women, "on some level their physical appearance would be judged and their approximation to a youthful standard measured" (Banner, 1983, p. 225).

Despite the advances of feminism, the ageist standards of appearance were seldom challenged before the last few years—probably because the majority of women in the latest wave of the movement could, until relatively recently, have considered themselves young. Now that the Baby Boom generation is entering middle age, however, that situation is beginning to change; the Boston Women's Health Collective, for example, with the publication of the excellent guide, *Ourselves, Growing Older*, has now acknowledged that women beyond menopause have both bodies and selves (Doress & Siegal, 1987).

In general, increasing attention is being paid to the "older [i.e., middle-aged] woman," with innumerable magazine stories and newspaper articles about well-known women (such as Diahann Carroll, Joan Collins, Jane Fonda, Ali McGraw) turning forty or even fifty, proclaiming that they have no problems with growing older. The message they give about age, however, is a mixed one: "It's all right to get older as long as you look as young as possible." (Can one imagine a Civil Rights movement with the slogan "Black is beautiful as long as you look as white as possible"?) That the normal physical signs of age, particularly wrinkles and gray hair, are unattractive is usually assumed without question. The assumption that women "lose their looks" as they age is implicit in the frequent description of a woman as "good-looking for a woman her age."

The film *Moonstruck* also contains a somewhat mixed message about gray hair. When Cher, as a supposedly dowdy woman, goes to her hairdresser to become transformed, the entire salon breathes a sigh of relief that they can finally get rid of her "awful gray hair." But the Nicholas Cage character fell in love with her when her hair was still gray.

Another example of this ambivalence about age is the new magazine "for the woman who wasn't born yesterday," *Lear's*. Founded by Frances Lear, the ex-wife of the television producer Norman Lear, and launched in early 1988, it is a glossy magazine for "women over 40"—wealthy women. (As such, of course, it ignores the reality that the weighted mean of pooled median incomes for women age 45 and over is $7,550—Wang, 1988.) Though it does regularly include women's ages, and does indeed show faces with some visible wrinkles, gray hair is not in particular abundance. Frances Lear herself, as photographs indicate, is flamboyantly white-haired. But an examination of the first five issues reveals only one "cover woman" who may possibly have a few gray hairs; four have dark brown hair, and one light brown. Among the hundreds of women in the stories and advertisements, there are photographs of only thirty obviously gray-haired or white-haired women. (This total counts as one a photographic essay of a gray-haired yoga teacher—with a slim, taut, flexible body—in the second issue.) The possibility of progress is suggested by the sixth issue (January/February 1989), which includes four full-page closeup photographs of gray- and white-haired women in their sixties and seventies, with pores, wrinkles, and age lines attractively visible. (Interestingly, the second issue also contains an article about a totally dark-haired 70-year-old Mike Wallace. And three of the issues contain photo essays with full-page photographs of "good men," where wrinkles, gray and white hair, and baldness abound.)

One cannot, of course, blame editorial policy alone for the absence of women's gray hair in *Lear's*; many of the stories are about women who almost certainly color their hair. In that sense the magazine is simply reflecting a reality. Magazine articles which state that "Madison Avenue has given its OK for hair, at least, to look its age" (Salholz, 1985), and newspaper stories with titles such as "Gray definitely OK, more women believe" (Beck, 1988), appear occasionally, but the women who are cited in them as models of acceptable gray hair are most often relatively young women—the 34-year-old television news reporter Kathleen Sullivan, and the 27-year-old model Marie Seznec, for example. The oldest gray-haired woman mentioned in any of them is 45-year-old Tish Hooker, who models for Germaine Monteil.

But there is no doubt that mainline fashion magazines no longer consign gray hair to total oblivion. As long ago as 1984, in a *Harper's Bazaar* issue headlined "Forty and Fabulous: How to Look Younger Every Day," two expert hair colorists recommended "making the gray work for the woman rather than fighting it." One of them suggested coloring the rest of the hair in imaginative ways and letting "one or two gray hairs show" ("Sensational Hair," 1984, pp. 238–239). They even included, at the suggestion of the magazine, advice for the occasional woman who might not want to cover her gray hair.

Older gray-haired models are not readily accepted for everyday fashion assignments. Kaylan Pickford, the top "mature" model in the country, says there is not enough work for her to earn a living. Despite her slim figure, she says she is most in demand for ads about laxatives, aspirin, denture cream, and arthritis or osteoporosis medications (Lindeman, 1988).

Ultimately, the coloring of gray hair by women is an endorsement of both ageism and sexism. It also serves to perpetuate both those forms of discrimination. The world is full of gray- and white-haired women who are living testimony to the advantages of age for women, but the power of their testimony is greatly muted by their dyed hair. Older women entering the job market would probably find it much easier to be hired if the older women in the work force were more visible.

I am not aware of any overt attempts by feminists to raise consciousness specifically on the issue of gray hair, and I am aware of no published feminist research on the subject. Elissa Melamed, in her book on ageism and its effects, *Mirror, Mirror: The Terror of Not Being Young* (1983), talks at length about cosmetic surgery and skin treatment and their ageist implications, but dismisses hair dyeing with one sentence: "Covering gray is so simple and commonplace that there is no longer much emotional charge about it" (p. 134). (It is interesting, however, that in her fantasy about a pilot for a television series, the 50-year-old heroine's hair is gray.)

Internalized ageism, an acceptance of the status quo, is no doubt one reason little has been written about gray hair; at earlier points in time, a male-dominated world was also considered "simple and commonplace." Another reason may be a reluctance to "blame the victim." Women clearly are the victims of ageism, and older women may be struggling to do their best in a world where they are disproportionately the victims of poverty. While it might theoretically be better for them to challenge ageism, they may be fighting other battles which consume most of their energy.

When most women reach their sixties and seventies (like the women in the sixth *Lear's* issue noted above), they are likely to give up on pretense and become more willing to look like their gray-haired and white-haired selves. (The fact that suicide rates for white women peak between the ages of 45 and 54—Melamed, 1983—and drop steadily thereafter is perhaps significant here.) Several shampoos are marketed especially to enhance gray and white hair. The advent in the White House of a defiantly white-haired First Lady may well increase the social acceptability of "old" hair.

One might postulate that feminist women, being more aware of sexism and the patriarchy, would be less likely than nonfeminist women to color their gray hair. Again, I know of no research on the subject. It does seem to me that I see many more gray-haired women in Minneapolis and St. Paul, a Mecca for feminists, than I did in Houston, where I lived previously. As women increasingly accept the reality that they have value in themselves, beyond their youth and their serviceability to men, they will naturally be less likely to attempt to hide the normal effects of their age. Just as women have produced a less sexist world, so they can challenge ageism to produce a world in which women do not feel compelled to hide their age with hair dyes, face lifts, and other expensive stratagems.

The advantages of leaving gray hair untouched are many. It saves a considerable amount of both time and money. The natural affinity of hair and skin color is preserved. Skin tone also naturally changes with age, and women who color their hair usually have to expend considerable time and effort to make their faces match their hair. Unfortunately, the combination of old face and young hair is often discordant.

Hair may gray in interesting patterns, which are lost when the gray hair is colored. Women who allow their hair its natural changes also often find themselves able to wear colors that did not suit them in their younger-haired days. And they can preserve both their hair and their health: the use of hair dyes can contribute to hair loss, especially when combined with other harsh hair treatments (Winning the Battle, 1984), and petroleum-based dyes, usually in dark shades, cause cancer in laboratory animals and may pose a danger to users (Doress & Siegal, 1987).

The greatest advantage, however, is that a woman who allows her hair to gray naturally is accepting herself for who she is. She is also, in effect, challenging the ageism of a society that tells her she should be ashamed of her age and should make every effort to disguise it. Just as blacks took a physical feature associated with their blackness—naturally kinky hair—and flaunted it in the Afro, challenging the limited white standards of physical attractiveness, so aging women can flaunt their graying and white hair, challenging the blinkered standards of an ageist society.

In her fortieth year, talking about her hair (not about its grayness but its blackness), Alice Walker wrote:

Eventually, I knew precisely what hair wanted: it wanted to grow, to be itself, to attract lint, if that was its destiny, but to be left alone by anyone, including me, who did not love it as it was. . . . The ceiling at the top of my brain lifted; once again my mind (and spirit) could get outside myself. (Walker, 1988, p. 53)

She calls her essay "Oppressed Hair Puts a Ceiling on the Brain."

REFERENCES

Baldwin, J. (1961). *Nobody knows my name: More notes on a native son.* New York: Dial Press.

Banner, L. (1983). *American beauty.* New York: Knopf.

Beck, B. (1988, February 3). Gray definitely OK, more women believe. Houston (Texas) *Chronicle.*

Chesler, P. (1978). *About men.* New York: Simon & Schuster.

Copper, B. (1988). *Over the hill: Reflections on ageism between women.* Freedom, CA: Crossing Press.

Doress, P. B., & Siegal, D. L. (1987). *Ourselves, growing older: Women aging with knowledge and power.* New York: Simon & Schuster.

Ellison, R. (1952). *Invisible man.* New York: Random House.

Gordon, B. (1988, September). Why older men chase younger women. *New woman.* From *Jennifer fever: Older men, younger women.* New York: Harper & Row.

La Ferla, R. (1988, January 17). Under cover: Going gray is going out. *New York Times Magazine.*

Leonard, F. (1982), with T. Sommers and V. Dean. *Not even for dogcatcher: Employment discrimination and older women.* Gray Paper No. 8. Washington, D.C.: Older Women's League.

Lindeman, B. (1988, February). Midlife beauty: The road to success for older models is a rough one. *Active Senior Lifestyles.* Kaylan Pickford has an autobiography, *Always a woman* (New York, Bantam), 1982.

Macdonald, B. (1983), with C. Rich. *Look me in the eye: Old women, aging and ageism.* San Francisco: Spinster's Ink.

Melamed, E. (1983). *Mirror, mirror: The terror of not being young.* New York: Simon & Schuster.

Miller, J. B. (1976). *Toward a new psychology of women.* Boston: Beacon Press.

Parachini, A. (1987, October 14). Scientists still haven't got to roots of gray hair. Minneapolis *Star-Tribune,* reprinted from the Los Angeles *Times.* All factual information about hair presented here is from this article.

Rubin, L. B. (1981). *Women of a certain age: The midlife search for self.* New York: Harper & Row.

Salholz, E. (1985, January 28). The look of a "certain age." *Newsweek.*

Sensational Hair (1984, August). *Harper's Bazaar.*

Walker, A. (1988, June). Oppressed hair puts a ceiling on the brain. *Ms.*

Wang, C. (1988). *Lear's* magazine, "For the woman who wasn't born yesterday: A critical review." *The Gerontologist, 28,* 600–601.

Winning the battle against hair loss (1984, August). *Harper's Bazaar.*

V

LIFE COURSE
TRANSITIONS

Much of the recent research on the life course has focused on the relationship between social differentiation and inequality on one hand and patterns of adult development on the other. One focus has been on stratification over the life course, with the primary emphasis being on the historical and institutional factors that allocate resources and status across major demographic categories—age, birth cohort, employment status, and gender. A second focus has been on the within-cohort differences in processes of status achievement and loss across the major life roles linked with age, that is, education, family, work, and retirement (O'Rand, 1990).

These studies have largely ignored the role of the state in shaping life course transitions. Yet the history of the American welfare state demonstrates that it was closely linked to assumptions about the typical life course, and that the policies derived from these assumptions affected individual lives and family structure.

THE LIFE COURSE AND THE WELFARE STATE

The American welfare state was constructed around the Social Security Act of 1935, which established a national program of social insurance for retired workers (and four years later a spouse benefit), unemployment insurance for wage workers with steady employment patterns, and a program of aid for widowed or single mothers with children (Quadagno, 1988). Built into these programs were assumptions about the nature of the family and the structure of the life course: that the typical family consisted of a "monogamous, life-long marriage with the female as full-time housewife and the male as primary provider" (Popenoe, 1993, p. 528), and that the wages of an industrial worker could adequately support that family except during crises of the business cycle or as a result of illness or old age. Eligibility rules in each program reproduced this family type (Sapiro, 1990).

These programs reinforced a pattern of work and social protection that political theorists term the "Fordist life cycle." As John Myles (1990, p. 273) explains, "it involved the creation of a system of wage stabilization to smooth the flow of income to workers over the life course and the flow of profits to corporations over the ups and downs of the business cycle." In 1960, 42 percent of all families had a sole male breadwinner. In addition, only 38 percent of married women with children aged 6 to 17 and only 19 percent of married women with children under age 6 were in the labor force (Popenoe, 1993). It was possible for a young man without a college education to support a family on his wages from a blue-collar job. If he became unemployed, he received unemployment benefits. When he retired, he received Social Security benefits for himself and a modest spouse benefit for his wife. If he had been employed in certain industries such as automobile manufacturing or steel, his income would be supplemented by a private pension. When he died, his widow continued to receive her share of the Social Security benefit, albeit a significantly reduced amount (Harrington Meyer, 1990).

These policies had consequences for the opportunities available to men and women to work and retire. The reading by Melissa Hardy examines how public policies that were designed to shape the labor force and redistribute the burden of unemployment also placed an increasing number of older people outside the productive core of economic activity.

THE TRANSFORMATION OF THE LIFE COURSE

Since 1960, the structure of the family and the path of the life course have altered dramatically. The high-paying manufacturing jobs that supported the Fordist life cycle have declined both relatively and absolutely, replaced by low-wage, unstable jobs in the service sector. By 1990, less than 15 percent of all families had a sole male breadwinner; more than 60 percent had two earners (Levy, 1992). Many of the low-wage workers in the expanding service sector were women, who between 1960 and 1990 increased their rates of labor force participation significantly. The presence of children, previously an impediment to female labor force participation, has become increasingly irrelevant. By 1990, nearly 70 percent of mothers with school-age children, and nearly 50 percent of mothers with children under 6, were working. Equally important was the rise of single-parent households. In 1990, 24 percent of all children and 55 percent of black children lived in households headed by women (Popenoe, 1993).

During the same period, male labor force participation rates declined (Doeringer, 1990). Between 1965 and 1988, the labor force participation rates for men aged 55 to 64 dropped from 85.7 to 78.7 percent (Guillemard and Rein, 1991). Unlike European nations, where public unemployment and disability programs have encouraged early retirement, in the United States most of the decline in male labor force participation has been triggered by incentives in private pension programs (Guillemard and Rein, 1991). The reading by Anne-Marie Guillemard describes the pathways out of the labor force—disability systems, unemployment systems, and pension systems—that have been constructed in different nations, and discusses how these programs are now restructuring the life course.

THE CONCEPT OF AGE NORMS

While life course transitions are shaped in the context of structural opportunities, there is still considerable individual variation in the timing of these transitions. In the past, the life course for women was traditionally timed more in relation to family events—marriage, childbearing, and childrearing—than the patterns of men which have been tied more to occupational events. As women have entered the labor force, however, their life course patterns have increasingly come to resemble the male model (O'Rand, 1990).

The third reading in this section, by Bernice L. Neugarten, Joan W. Moore, and John C. Lowe, is based on research conducted in the 1960s. It reflects gender-based expectations concerning age-appropriate behavior and the timing of life cycle events. Although some of the life course events may be less gender-differentiated today than they were thirty years ago, this classic article still alerts us to the way age norms form a pervasive set of expectations regarding age-appropriate behavior.

REFERENCES

Doeringer, Peter. *Bridges to Retirement.* Cornell University: ILR Press, 1990.

Guillemard, Anne-Marie, and Martin Rein. "Comparative Patterns of Retirement: Recent Trends in Developed Societies." *Annual Review of Sociology* 19 (1991): 469–503.

Harrington Meyer, Madonna. "Family Status and Poverty Among Older Women: The Gendered Distribution of Retirement Income in the United States." *Social Problems* 37 (1990): 552–563.

Levy, Frank. "U.S. Earnings Levels and Earnings Inequality: A Review of Recent Trends and Proposed Explanations." *Journal of Economic Literature* 30 (1992): 1340–1376.

Myles, John. "States, Labor Markets and Life Cycles." In R. Friedland and S. Robertson (eds.), *Beyond the Marketplace: Rethinking Economy and Society.* New York: Aldine de Gruyter, 1990.

O'Rand, Angela. "Stratification and the Life Course." In Robert Binstock and Linda George (eds.), *Handbook of Aging and the Social Sciences.* New York: Academic Press, 1990.

Popenoe, David. "American Family Decline, 1960–1990: A Review and Appraisal." *Journal of Marriage and the Family* 55 (1993): 527–555.

Quadagno, Jill. *The Transformation of Old Age Security: Class and Politics in the American Welfare State.* Chicago: University of Chicago Press, 1988.

Sapiro, Virginia. "The Gender Basis of American Social Policy." In Linda Gordon (ed.), *Women, the State and Welfare.* Madison: University of Wisconsin Press, 1990.

11
Vulnerability in Old Age: The Issue of Dependency in American Society
MELISSA HARDY

The American focus on the importance of self-sufficiency and independence stands in contrast to recent economic trends. These trends of the past several years have led to an increased number of adults standing outside the productive core of economic activity. This "burden of dependency" has been manufactured by public policies designed to reconstitute the labor force and redistribute the burden of unemployment largely through the growth in retirement. Recently, the success of income maintenance programs developed to improve the financial viability of retirement for older workers has begun to undercut the legitimacy of their status as dependents. Hardy's reading examines that role of dependency. She argues that the social processes that produce dependency among older people are not substantively different from the processes that affect younger age groups. Consequently, the questions of distributive justice that are involved in the dependency of the elderly are questions that relate to members of all age groups who occupy positions of disadvantage in the economic structure.

The American people have long valued the principles of individualism and self-reliance. Our literature, folklore, and politics venerate the success of self-made men and women, and in those individual successes, the American people have taken collective pride, for what was possible for one to achieve became a possibility for all. Success was a measure of the person, a testimony to strength and intellect, the reward of the deserving. But the glorification of independence and self-sufficiency has another side, for an emphasis on individuals as discrete, separate entities has overshadowed our recognition of the interrelatedness of our lives with the lives of others. The issue of dependency has never been easy for Americans to resolve. Our emphasis on self-sufficiency teaches us that dependency is weakness, and our focus on individualism

"Vulnerability in Old Age: The Issue of Dependency in American Society" by Melissa Hardy, from *Journal of Aging Studies*, 2 (1988): pp. 311–320. Copyright © 1988 by JAI Press, Inc.

argues that the cause of that weakness is in ourselves—that the dependency of adults stems from their own poor decisions, their lack of initiative, and the absence of proper planning. That emphasis leads to a discounting of the importance of social and economic structures in the production of dependency, and to the devaluation of the complex networks of interdependency that more accurately reflect the content of our lives.

Americans live in a society where an increasing proportion of adults stand outside the core of productive activity. Although a decline in fertility has reduced the proportion of children in our population, our own economic policies have increased the proportion of adults who depend on public programs for their incomes. The vast majority of these dependents are elderly. They are retired workers and their spouses, and most of them rely on Social Security as their major source of income. That dependence creates vulnerability, and the fewer personal resources on which an individual can draw, the more vulnerable he or she becomes to a change in social consciousness, to a redefinition of distributive justice, and to a change in the political or economic climate.

THE CREATION OF DEPENDENCY

The creation of dependency among the elderly is accomplished by two kinds of processes (Walker 1980; Estes 1986). One process relates to the physiological changes that can occur with aging—changes that can undermine an individual's ability to perform certain activities—changes that can reduce a person's capacity to handle everyday tasks. This dependency is one of physical necessity, and it characterizes not only the old, but all those who find their functional capacity diminished by illness. This kind of dependence therefore does not create a vulnerability specific to the elderly; however, because the risk of having a chronic illness or a disabling condition increases markedly with age, this form of dependency is often seen among the elderly. But as the process that defines dependency, physiological decline affects fewer elderly than one might expect.

Although chronic health conditions are common among persons age 65 and older, the vast majority of elderly are still able to carry on with normal activities. The need for help does increase with age; estimates place the proportion of noninstitutionalized older persons age 65 and older who require functional assistance at 19%, ranging from 13% among those age 65–74 to 46% of those age 85 and older (Fowles 1985).

The second process that creates dependency is a social process that limits access to the means of maintaining what we like to refer to as "financial independence." In modern industrial societies, the predominant structural cause of dependency is nonemployment and the shifts in the productive capacities of many of our industries that have limited the number of workers who can be actively employed at any given time. Firings, layoffs, and retirement are all mechanisms that sever the ties between workers and their jobs. Firings are more common among younger workers; layoffs more common among prime-age workers (Schervish 1983). Retirement serves as the mechanism for removing older workers from the labor force. Younger workers without jobs typically maintain a marginal attachment to the labor force by occupying the status of unemployment, moving in and out of jobs as positions become available. But older workers who lose their jobs have greater difficulty relocating in suitable positions.

Both of these processes show that dependency is a relational status: It implies access to the means of achieving self-support through employment and the functional capacity to effectively utilize those means. In our society self-support is achieved through work because the occupational structure is the major means of income distribution. By this definition, the dependency of the elderly is not substantively different from the dependency of other age groups. Dependent populations are not advantageously located in the occupational structure; either they have no jobs at all, or the jobs they perform fail to provide them with a reasonable standard of living. What makes the dependency of young and old similar, at least to this point in history, is that both groups have been universally defined as "deserving." Within the intermediate age range, however, the definition of "deserving" is less clear-cut. The major differences between the dependency of the elderly and the young lie in the management of their support and the social view of their lifecourse stage. In the majority of cases, the dependency of the young is a matter of family responsibility. Therefore the question of when (i.e., at what age) the child ceases to be a legitimate dependent and thereby ceases to deserve significant financial support is a family decision. In the case of the elderly, however, the dependency is relative to the collectivity (the tax-paying public). The question of legitimacy is therefore one of social definition, and the decision to cease financial support is a matter of public policy.

The second difference in how the dependency statuses of young and old are socially constructed lies in the assessment of the merits of their potential contributions. In part, the decision to accept the dependency of children for so many years lies in a desire to prepare them for their "adult responsibilities." The "labor" of children, it was argued in the early part of this century, should not be in the factories, but in the schools. Their major task should be to learn basic information, to develop sound habits, to master specific skills—for it is on their abilities that the now-adult generation must rely in old age. This reliance exists at the level of family structure, as parents rely on their own children, but it also exists at the level of the collectivity. As the pattern of cohort succession replaces one generation with the next, the burden of responsibility is shifted onto different shoulders. As a society, their development is subsidized because their potential is seen, and the importance of their future contributions is anticipated.

In the case of the elderly, however, the designation of them as a "deserving" group was made with a backward glance, not a forward view. Financial support programs were made available in recognition of the contributions that older workers had already made and linked to labor policies that discounted their potential for continuing contributions. The willingness to accept their dependency was largely one of reward, not one of investment.

THE ROLE OF PUBLIC POLICY IN DEFINING AGE AND DEPENDENCY

But our redefinition of childhood and old age was a matter of national policy, as well (Graebner 1980; Mirkin 1987). By the turn of the century, unemployment had become a recurring problem in the American economy. Labor policies designed to control unemployment have typically attempted to increase the demand for labor (or certain categories of labor) and/or to redefine the supply of workers by organizing their market availability. In this century the favored strategy for dealing with a rising level of unemployment has been to limit the working lives of individuals by delaying the entry of younger workers into the labor force and by routinizing the exits of older workers from the labor force. Therefore the decision to accept retired older workers and their families as dependents was based not only in a recognition that self-support outside the labor force generally meant poverty; it was a collective choice to reallocate unemployment on the basis of age, to rename it *retirement*, and to associate with retirement a claim to current and future income on the basis of work history.

In spite of all the claims of self-sufficiency and independence, it becomes clear that by introducing the historical dimension to intergenerational relationships, either within families or across cohorts, the issue of dependency is not so much a question of either/or; it is a question of when. The population dynamic is one of interdependence. Yet the rhetoric remains one of extremes—one of alternative locations at either end of the continuum. And the question of the legitimacy of the designation is continuously raised. As the economy tightens, we look for ways to cut back on collective responsibilities and wonder whether our collective benevolence to these dependent groups has not become excessive (Wolfe 1981).

The Question of Legitimacy

A recent article in *Forbes* magazine titled "The Old Folks" captures this sentiment all too well (Flint 1980).

The myth is that they're sunk in poverty.
The reality is that they're living well.
The trouble is, there are too many of them—
    God bless 'em

What is the evidence that fuels such comments? Is it the case that *all* elderly are "living well"? Such remarks are often buttressed by a historical contrast that emphasizes the significant improvements in financial status of the elderly during recent decades. In addition, the changing demographic composition of the population provides younger generations with a different repertoire of experiences with the elderly—one that makes it easier to overlook the problems that continue to exist.

During the early part of this century rates of unemployment and poverty among the elderly were much higher than they are today. Changes in the labor process and in the incentive structures used by management negatively affected the demand for the labor of older workers. Before the enactment of Social Security, it was estimated that as many as half of all male wage earners age 65 and older were unemployed (Olson 1982, p. 37) with the same proportion of elders relying on family or public relief for some financial assistance (Lubove 1968). But by 1984, the poverty rate for persons age 65 and older was quoted as 12.4%, somewhat lower than the poverty rate for younger persons. An additional 9% of the elderly were classified as "near-poor" (having an income between the poverty level and 125% of the poverty level), and of the approximately 11%

of the elderly who were in the labor force, only 3% were unemployed. Income maintenance programs have clearly been successful: both poverty rates and unemployment rates among the elderly have been impressively reduced. Reduction in poverty rates is largely attributable to the availability of Social Security benefits to replace wage income among retirees. Reduction in unemployment rates can be similarly attributed to the availability of retirement benefits and the related reduction in the supply of older workers to the labor market. The lower unemployment rates of older workers are not proof that older workers are having an easier time finding employment when they seek it.

The demographic fuel for these comments comes from both the increasing proportion of the elderly in the general population, and from the changing composition of the elderly with regard to income, health, and labor force characteristics. Even though better than one in five people age 65 and older is poor or near-poor, four out of five are not. So typical encounters with elderly people do not bring us into contact with the disadvantaged elderly. In addition, the incidence of poverty and unemployment has become localized in subpopulations that are often residentially and socially segregated from the mainstream of society, and this segregation further reduces opportunities for contact.

Poverty and the Elderly

It is clear that old age policies have had considerable success. They have managed to rescue millions of middle-class older Americans who would have been unable to avoid poverty once their ties to the labor force had been severed. But they have been unable to offer the same salvation to the very groups whose marginal attachments to the labor force at earlier ages have made them most vulnerable to the physical and financial difficulties of old age. This failure is a failure by design; it is a function of the way we calculate the benefits; it is further indication that, although we have been willing to redistribute income across generations, redistributing income across class boundaries is another matter.

Although it may once have been the case that bases of stratification were less pronounced among the elderly than among younger age groups, recent research has supported the notion that there is a continuity to socioeconomic differences across the lifecourse (Auletta 1981; Duncan and Coe 1981). The choice of the word *continuity* rather than *determinism* is an important one; *determinism* implies that individuals face neither risk of losing their advantages at birth, nor any hope of overcoming their disadvantages. The empirical evidence shows far less certainty in lifecourse patterns. Yet there is a regularity to the process, a structure of probabilities that makes some outcomes more likely than others. It is therefore not a question of certainty—it is a matter of odds.

The elderly who remain poor or near-poor in spite of current old age policies are a group that is disproportionately black and disproportionately female. Although the poverty rate for older whites in urban areas is down to 11%, one in three elderly urban blacks lives in poverty. In rural areas, the poverty rate for blacks is as high as 50%. And poverty rates for Hispanics are not as high as those for blacks; their rate of poverty is still more than twice as high as the poverty rate for whites. What is consistent across all race-ethnic groups is the fact that single men and women (those who are divorced, widowed, or never married) have higher poverty rates than married couples. Because the number of nonmarried women is so much higher than the number of nonmarried men, single older women comprise a large proportion of the elderly poor.

In their volume, *Income of the Population 55 and Over, 1984*, the Social Security Administration reports poverty rates for aged units by marital status, gender and race-ethnicity (Grad 1985). Among units 55 and older, the poverty rate increases with age, with 15% of units age 65 and older falling below the poverty line and 25% falling below 125% of the poverty line. The comparable rates for married couples, however, were only 6% and 11% respectively, showing the advantage of two-person households (and two benefit checks from Social Security) in maintaining a level of household income that exceeds the poverty level. The situation of nonmarried women in this age group is, however, considerably worse; their reported poverty rate was 21%, with 35% of all nonmarried women age 65 and over being poor or near-poor. As alarming as those figures are, the race-ethnic breakdown of these rates makes clear the combined disadvantage suffered by nonwhite females. Among the 65 and older, 35% of black units were below the poverty level, and an additional 14% were near-poor. Among older, black, nonmarried women, 58% were poor or near-poor.

Work, Careers, and Retirement

Such apparent disparities in the economic status of the elderly call into question this nation's general success in accomplishing the goals set forth in the Older Americans Act of 1965. As one of the major features of Lyndon Johnson's Great Society legislation, the Older Americans Act set forth what were considered to be the legitimate expectations of older people in this society. Among its objectives was to provide older workers with "equal opportunity to the full and free enjoyment of . . . retirement in health, honor and dignity" (U.S. Department of Health, Education, and Welfare 1976). However, as was the case with many of the programs developed during this period, proclaiming equal opportunity was easier than producing it, because any attempt to provide equality of access to retirement in "health, honor, and dignity" would have to begin by addressing the major source of the current inequality in retirement statuses; we would have to begin by addressing the structures of opportunity and constraint that characterize different locations in the occupational structure as well as the distribution of opportunities to gain access to the more favorable locations. It is necessary to look at earlier stages of the career because security in retirement is frequently determined by the circumstances of the retirement transition, and the extent to which the individual worker can exercise control over the nature and timing of this transition. The ability of a worker to control his or her exit from the labor force is a function of the resources he or she has been able to accumulate throughout his or her career.

It is only fairly recently in our history that retirement has been defined as a positive status, and dependency on the social welfare benefits generated by the Social Security program has been defined as an earned right that could be coupled with considerable independence in expenditure decisions. As the social view of retirement has become more favorable and the retirement policy supporting this view has provided more security, the retirement ages of older workers have steadily declined. These retirements created vacancies for younger workers, allowed businesses to replenish their labor forces, and provided older workers with the opportunity to enjoy leisure activities after years of hard work. The separation of the older worker from his or her job, however, does not always occur at the right time, from the worker's point of view. In such cases, "retirement" is not fundamentally different from any other form of involuntary job termination.

Recent research on retirement has reported increases in voluntary retirement, a decrease in the proportion of workers who retire because of ill health, and an increase in the importance of pension eligibility for the timing of the retirement transition. Although these empirical patterns provide evidence of a shift in the normative pattern of retirement, they do not attest to the elimination of involuntary retirement. Older workers typically have the lowest unemployment rates of any age group; but one reason for this may be that older workers who are initially unemployed soon drop out of the labor force when they are unsuccessful in finding jobs. In that sense, unemployment rates understate the number of workers who want jobs. Although it is possible for workers of any age who are unsuccessful in finding employment to leave the labor force, it is primarily for older workers and the disabled that exiting the labor force can be a permanent transition rather than a temporary state. Whereas unemployed younger workers must continue to search for jobs in order to qualify for earnings-replacement income in the form of unemployment benefits, older workers have available to them an alternative status—retirement.

In Florida, for example, a recent study examined the factors that distinguish successful and unsuccessful labor force reentry among retired older workers and found that many of the factors that define positions of disadvantage in the labor market among younger workers are reproduced as predictors of unsuccessful reentry into the labor force after retirement (Hardy 1988). Race, gender, and age all significantly affected the ability of older workers to reenter the labor force, with blacks, women, and older workers having less success. In addition, workers who had last worked in lower-status jobs and whose retirements had been involuntary (i.e., prompted by a plant closing, a relocation, or a mandatory retirement policy) were more likely to have failed at reentry. Although the racial difference in success rates appears to be largely due to the earlier locations of the workers in the occupational structure (and, relatedly, to the different levels of skill and reward those locations represent), the lower success rate for women remained unchanged when these additional structural indicators were introduced. The fact that poverty among the elderly remains a disproportionately female problem makes the unsuccessful reentry of older women workers into the labor force particularly troublesome.

Persistent Poverty by Design

The poverty rates cited earlier not only reflect the fact that the poor elderly are unable to supplement their retirement incomes with enough earned income to keep them above the poverty line. These rates also reflect work histories that are characterized by spells of unemployment and intermittent work activity in low-wage jobs that offer little in the way of job security or retirement benefits. But then those differences in income maintenance are by design, not by accident. For although policymakers have been willing to accept the legitimacy of income redistribution from younger generations who are active in the labor force to older generations who are not employed, they have traditionally been unwilling to aggressively advocate the rights of other categories of "dependents" when that advocacy required a significant transfer of income to the persistently poor.

The Social Security system was initiated as two separate programs—one for "deserving" older workers who had made significant contributions to the economy during their careers; the other as public assistance for the poor elderly. Whereas the former did not incorporate means-testing or annual reevaluations of the retirees' eligibility, the public assistance component incorporated all the negative rituals we tend to associate with programs of public welfare. Even within the Old Age Insurance component of Social Security, concerns have traditionally focused on maintaining a benefits schedule that reproduces the income inequities that existed earlier in the lifecourse. A concern for the poor and for the question of the adequacy of minimum-level benefits has usually been contingent on a rate of economic growth that is high enough to fund improved levels of public assistance by new increments of productivity rather than by straightforward redistribution (see, e.g., Olson 1982).

AVOIDING MANUFACTURED CLEAVAGES

Unfortunately the evidence of the success of social programs designed to maintain the incomes of the elderly during their retirement has begun to overshadow the awareness of problems that remain unaddressed. Rather than gaining encouragement from what has already been accomplished and continuing to search for ways to improve the conditions of those who remain disadvantaged, questions are being raised about the size of the commitment already made (Margolis 1987). And it is in that questioning that the elderly share in the vulnerability of all dependent groups, for the claim they have to income is just that—a claim based on a socially produced understanding of what is fair treatment.

The income security that has been provided for the majority of the elderly is based in public policy and norms of distributive justice, both of which can change. And the change will come as a challenge to the legitimacy of the dependency status, as a question of the relative merits of the groups requiring assistance, as an evaluation of the needs of one group compared to another (Taylor 1985). The rhetoric of change already casts the needs of the elderly against the needs of our children. Writing in the *Atlantic Monthly*, Philip Longman (1985) points out that poverty-stricken children outnumber poverty-stricken elders 4:1. Rather than subsidize the rich in order to aid the poor, policymakers have begun to argue for means-testing in Social Security benefits. And in that argument is the unraveling of Social Security—making Social Security indistinguishable from poverty-relief programs, wiping out the legitimacy of the claim that a lifetime of work activity entitles an older worker to share in the continuing productivity of the nation. It begins the transformation of our public policy into a zero-sum game that casts one generation in opposition to another, and views the gains of one age group as the losses to another. It is an unnecessary and destructive division.

If there is an element of truth in the *Forbes* statement, it does not lie in the fact that we have "too many" elderly; it lies in the fact that we have too automatically delegated our elderly to the status of dependents and therefore to positions of vulnerability. The creation of dependency reflects the ageism in our society. Our old age policies have attempted to compensate for the negative effects of growing old, even though many of those negative effects grew from our own decisions to limit economic access—formally and informally—on the basis of age. We as a nation were successful in implementing health care and income maintenance programs for the elderly because historical evidence coupled old age with sickness and poverty. In that process we have inadvertently perpetuated the ageism behind the patterns of disadvantage. Improvements in health care systems and the success of income maintenance programs have altered the picture such that these negative consequences are experienced only by a minority of elderly; therefore the focus has shifted to the fact that, among the poor elderly, there are too many faces that are female, too many who are not white. But the point is not only to address the race-gender composition of the poor elderly. We do not succeed if we can only claim that all race, ethnic, and gender groups are proportionately represented among the poor—if we can only claim that poverty does not discriminate. Because if that is all we do, we have only renamed the victims.

Our strategy must be to attack the social processes that produce and reproduce—generation after generation—millions of elderly poor. But to address the issues of poverty in old age, the issues of the vulnerable elderly, we must address the problems of poverty and vulnerability, per se. Progress on this broader front does not require that we eliminate or distort the programs that currently protect the elderly. It does not require lines of conflict across generations. What it does require is a general commitment to expand the opportunities of young and old, to accept as a social responsibility the care and maintenance of dependent people, and to reshape the social processes that produce dependency in the first place.

To return one last time to the *Forbes* quotation, let me offer my version of the situation. The myths are that all elderly are living well, that poor elderly deserve no better, and that achieving the goal for all elderly *to* live well must prevent younger people from doing the same. The facts are that rates of poverty among the elderly remain too high, that poverty in old age is often an extension of poverty at younger ages, and that our resolve to deal with poverty and vulnerability grows weaker as our rate of economic growth becomes smaller. The problem is that we are beginning to define the elderly *as* the problem, that we are beginning to place generations in competition with each other, and that we are losing sight of what should be our collective goals, our shared strategies, our interdependence. The challenge is for us to resist the pressure to make the *divisions* among dependent groups more important than the commonalities, for all these groups have a common interest in finding solutions to the socially and structurally produced vulnerability they face.

REFERENCES

Auletta, K. 1981. *The Streets Were Paved with Gold.* New York: Random House.

Duncan, G.J., and R. Coe. 1981. *The Dynamics of Welfare.* Ann Arbor: Survey Research Center, University of Michigan.

Estes, C.L. 1986. "The Politics of Ageing in America." *Aging and Society* 6: 121–134.

Flint, J. 1980. "The Old Folks." *Forbes* 125(4): 51–56.

Fowles, D. 1985. *A Profile of Older Americans: 1985.* Program Resources Department, American Association of Retired Persons and Administration on Aging.

Grad, S. 1985. *Income of the Population 55 and Over, 1984.* Social Security Administration Publication No. 13-11871. U.S. Department of Health and Human Services, Washington, DC: U.S. Government Printing Office.

Graebner, W. 1980. *A History of Retirement: The Meaning, Function of an American Institution, 1885–1978.* New Haven, CT: Yale University Press.

Hardy, M. 1988. "Unemployment and Retirement: Where Do You Draw the Line?" Paper presented at the annual meetings of the American Sociological Association, Atlanta, Georgia.

Longman, P. 1985. "Justice Between Generations." *Atlantic Monthly* (June).

Lubove, R. 1968. *The Struggle for Social Security.* Cambridge, MA: Harvard University Press.

Margolis, R. 1987. "The Elderly Poor: Down and Out on Easy Street." *Democratic Left* (May/August).

Mirkin, B.A. 1987. "Early Retirement as a Labor Force Policy: An International Overview." *Monthly Labor Review* (March): 19–33.

Olson, L. 1982. *The Political Economy of Aging: The State, Private Power and Social Welfare.* New York: Columbia University Press.

Schervish, P. 1983. *The Structural Determinants of Unemployment: Vulnerability and Power in Market Relations.* New York: Academic Press.

Taylor, P. 1985. "The Coming Conflict as We Soak the Young to Enrich the Old." *Washington Post* (December 17).

U.S. Department of Health, Education, and Welfare; Office of Human Development; Administration on Aging; Older Americans Act of 1965 as Amended and Related Acts, Bicentennial Compilation (March) 1976: 2–3.

Walker, A. 1980. "The Social Creation of Poverty and Dependency in Old Age." *Journal of Social Policy* 9(1): 49–75.

Wolfe, A. 1981. *America's Impasse: The Rise and Fall of the Politics of Growth.* New York: Pantheon.

12

The Trend Toward Early
Labor Force Withdrawal and the
Reorganization of the Life Course:
A Cross-National Analysis
ANNE-MARIE GUILLEMARD

Guillemard's reading focuses on how changes in labor force participation in recent years represent a substantial reorganization of the adult life course. Using data from Japan, the United States, and several Western European countries, she provides evidence that new pathways from work to retirement have evolved over the past two decades. Guillemard argues that retirement systems are declining in importance as a means of regulating withdrawal from work life. Instead, new institutional arrangements such as unemployment and disability are becoming more important as pathways to exit from work. Guillemard's international evidence supports her argument that, despite country-specific qualitative differences in the processes of exit from work, the life course is becoming "deinstitutionalized," characterized by more flexible transitions from work to retirement than in the past. Her study predates the unification of Germany, and she therefore refers throughout to "West Germany," which is now part of Germany.

For the last fifteen years labor force participation rates for persons aged 55 to 64 years old have been rapidly decreasing in most developed industrial societies. This trend first engulfed the 60–64-year-old age group and now embraces 55–59-year-olds. Significant changes have taken place in the pathways and calendar of definitive withdrawal from the labor force. In this article I shall use international comparisons of how people leave the labor market in order to shed light on the social implications of this massive trend, which is marking out new boundaries between work and retirement.

THE THEORETICAL FRAMEWORK OF SOCIOLOGICAL INQUIRY INTO LABOR FORCE WITHDRAWAL

Two main objectives have guided this inquiry into this trend: first, to analyze how the life course and the welfare state are being reorganized: and second, to interpret the institutional arrangements regulating definitive labor force withdrawals as social constructions both of age categories, in particular of old age, and of the relationship between the life course and work.

The changes in definitive labor force withdrawal provide special evidence for examining the inter-relations between the reorganization of the life course (how various socially defined ages are assigned the functions of work, education and leisure) and the reorganization of social policies (notably how the internal boundaries between various welfare subsystems are being modified). Given the first objective, this sociological research has focused on the presumptive significance of these changes, particularly as embodied in the institutions providing coverage following definitive withdrawal, and the presumed meaning of what is considered to be a trend that is undermining our societies' model of the life course.

Should the changes now affecting the end of "working life" be interpreted simply as following from an enlarged application of the life course model that has been slowly developed during the industrialization of our societies? In this threefold model, there is, successively, a time for education, a time for work and, finally, a time of rest. If this interpretation holds, the phenomenon of early withdrawal from the labor force, like that of the late entry of young people into the labor market, merely amounts to concentrating the time spent working on an ever-narrower group of adults. Accordingly, a person's life still takes shape around his working life; and the major social determinant is still employment, the problem of jobs. Therefore, the chronological thresholds separating the three phases, though variable, are still set by the first entrance into and the last exit from the labor force. It follows that the meaning of work and, therefore, of its counterpart, retirement, have not been altered.

Another interpretation is possible. The changes under way can be taken to be signs that the threefold model of the life course is being deinstitutionalized. This interpretation has guided the hypotheses underlying this research. The boundaries between economic activity and "inactivity" seem to be shifting as a result less of simply applying the retirement logic to younger age groups (with, as a consequence, early withdrawal) than of relinking the welfare system and the life course (with, as a consequence, the eventual overthrow of the threefold model).

As for the second objective, the institutional arrangements ensuring the transition out of the labor force can be taken to be the means of defining the relationship between age and employment. They give a meaning to growing old, to aging, to acquiring an "inactive" economic status. The rules governing these arrangements and the eligibility requirements under them provide evidence of how the transition toward economic inactivity is being socially redefined.

Working Hypotheses

At first glance, one might suppose that the present rapid lowering of the age for definitive labor force withdrawal results from the acceleration of an age-old trend that started when pension systems were set up and has continued as coverage has been expanded. Accordingly, the date for admission into the third phase of life has simply advanced without any other change of importance. It is necessary to show why this interpretation does not fit the facts. A comparative analysis of several countries leads to another interpretation, one that sees these changes as a trend, and this trend as a radical transformation of the end of the life course, as the milestones are torn up that used to chronologically mark ages, give direction to career paths and point out the limits wherein individuals could draw up their plans. The meaning of this trend has to do not with reinforcing the threefold model of the life course but with "dechronologizing" and deinstitutionalizing it. After presenting the data that prove that the labor force participation rates of 55–64-year-olds have dropped considerably, the institutional arrangements used to handle labor force withdrawal in the countries under study will be compared. In general, definitive withdrawal corresponds to entry into a (public or private) welfare subsystem. The most common of these subsystems will be described, and their eligibility requirements will be examined so as to clarify the principles governing how work and non-work are being redistributed in the later years of life. Examining these principles leads, in conclusion, to an analysis of how the life course is being socially reorganized.

Of course, a fundamental question comes to mind: how are old-age insurance funds and pension systems involved in this trend? If they have lost the power to regulate definitive withdrawal from the labor force, then may not both our conception of retirement and the underlying idea of a contract between generations be coming up for reassessment? Is a new conception arising of what is just in exchanges from one generation to another?

EARLY WITHDRAWAL: A MAJOR TREND IN DEVELOPED INDUSTRIAL SOCIETIES

The OECD's data on labor force participation rates during the past fifteen years for persons from 55 to 64 years old reveal a general, massive, downward trend. From 1975 to 1985, the rates for men fell, as Figure 12-1 shows: from 75 to 50 per cent in France, from 80 per cent to 53 per cent in the Netherlands, from 82 per cent to 58 per cent in West Germany and from 80 to 60 per cent in the United States.[1] Since these rates have been calculated by counting job-seekers as part of the labor force, the decrease has been even sharper than we might imagine by looking at the figure. This remark holds, in particular, for Great Britain which, if we take into account only those who have jobs, joins the list of countries whose labor force participation rates have plummeted (see Table 12-1, Employment activity rates). By comparison, Sweden (as well as Japan) has not been swept up in this trend. On the question of women, a cross-sectional analysis is not very revealing since large numbers of women have entered the labor market during this period; an identical trend toward early labor force withdrawal can be clearly seen through a cohort analysis (Jacobs *et al.*, 1989). Given that data about men are more interpretable, the following remarks will be based primarily on them. Likewise, five countries were selected where the early withdrawal trend is the most noticeable; and Sweden was added to the sample as evidence of the contrary. In effect,

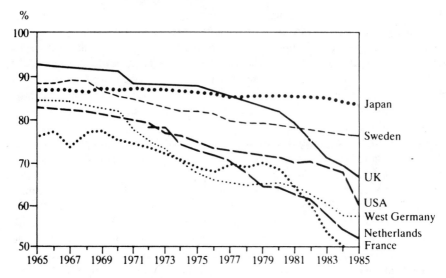

FIGURE 12-1   Labor force participation rates from 1965 to 1985 for men from 55 to 64 years old. *(Source: OECD,* Labour Force Statistics, Paris, 1984–86.)

the boundaries between work and retirement in Sweden have shifted but only slightly in comparison with the other five.

After a slow evolution over nearly half a century that gradually set the retirement age at 65 (the most common age of entitlement to a full old-age pension), the chronological thresholds used both to determine personal identities throughout the life course and to organize the transition to old age have been torn up during the last fifteen years. The age when persons stop working has been lowered significantly. This change affected, at first, the 60–64-year-old age group (see Figure 12-2); its labor force participation rate has fallen by about 50 per cent over the past twenty years. By 1979–80 in most countries, excepting Sweden (and Japan), this change concerned 55–59-year-olds (see Figure 12-3); their economic activity rate fell by an average of 20 per cent.

COMPARATIVE ANALYSIS OF THE INSTITUTIONAL ARRANGEMENTS ENSURING EARLY WITHDRAWAL

Given this lowering of the threshold for definitive withdrawal from the labor force, it is necessary to examine the institutional arrangements that have authorized this shift in the boundary between inactivity and activity if we want to understand the meaning of this trend and to propose an interpretation. The nature and characteristics of these arrangements can be studied as being the means used to socially construct the relationship between the life course and work. The rules governing these institutions and the eligibility requirements under these arrangements reveal how the transition toward retirement is being socially redefined. Analyzing these institutional arrangements can shed light on the principles that govern how work and non-work are distributed in the later years of life. This analysis also helps explain how the elderly are socially categorized as a group, and how old age is socially constructed.

The institutional arrangements to be taken into account cannot be defined a priori; they must be discovered and examined country by country. At the start, this meant studying each country to observe the principal pathways by which persons withdraw early from the labor force and the complicated institutional arrangements that have opened these pathways. The following analysis brings together the principal results of this empirical investigation of the six countries under review here. The aim is, above all, to see the similarities in the operation of such institutional arrangements. These cross-national points of convergence provide significant evidence of how national welfare systems are being reorganized with, as a consequence, a reorganization of the life course.

Two lessons can be drawn from the systematic examination of how institutional arrangements in these six countries are converging. First of all, old-age pension systems are declining as the means of regulating exits from the workforce. In all six countries, people are leaving the labor market long before they start receiving such pensions: exit from the workforce, in most cases, no longer corresponds to a direct entry into the old-age pension system. In fact, only a small minority of persons now receive old-age pensions upon retirement immediately after they stop working: in these countries, excepting Sweden, only about 20 per cent of men still fit into this pattern. Second, and as a consequence, the new institutional arrangements now regulating definitive withdrawal bring into play other subsystems of the welfare system than old-age insurance. These new arrangements connect, in original ways, various of these subsystems so as to create unprecedented and unstable possibilities for moving out of the labor market and reaching the moment of entitlement to an old-age pension. These arrangements, their rules and requirements, both govern passage toward inactivity and set the threshold of old age as a period of life after work.

The Decline of the Retirement System as a Means of Regulating Withdrawal

A crucial change is that retirement systems are no longer as important for managing definitive exit from work. The generalization of old-age pensions has been, during the development of industrial society, a major factor in the institutionalization of the life course following a model of three ordered phases: education–work–retirement. Retirement has served as a compensation for the alienation of work, a time when people rest at the end of their lives; after contributing to production, they are entitled to rest. Work has thus been placed at the center of the individual's life to the point that we talk about his "working life." It conditions the right to this time of rest. Analyzing retirement as an "element of the moral economy" in industrial societies, Martin Kohli (1987) considers it to be a pivotal means of social control. He sees the institutionalization of the three-phase life-course model as a major means of socialization in industrial society. Retirement has significantly contributed to the "chronologization" and "standardiza-

TABLE 12-1 Labor Force Participation Rates and Employment Activity Rates from 1965 to 1985 for Men 55 to 64 Years Old in Industrialized Countries

	1970	1971	1972	1973	1974	1975	1976	1977	1978	1979	1980	1981	1982	1983	1984	1985
Labor force participation rates: age 55–64/male																
USA	80.7	80.0	79.1	76.9	76.2	74.6	73.3	72.8	72.3	71.8	71.2	69.9	70.2	68.8	67.9	59.7
Japan	86.6	87.1	86.6	86.8	86.3	86.0	85.9	84.8	85.0	85.2	85.4	85.0	84.9	84.7	83.8	83.0
France	75.4	74.6	73.4	72.1	70.8	68.9	67.9	69.4	68.8	69.9	68.5	64.3	*59.8	53.6	50.3	50.1
West Germany	82.2	77.8	75.2	73.4	70.5	68.1	66.5	65.7	65.1	65.4	65.5	64.5	62.6	60.2	57.6	57.5
Netherlands	—	80.8	78.7	77.2	74.6	73.0	72.5	71.3	68.3	65.7	63.6	60.8	59.1	57.8	55.9	53.8
Sweden	85.4	84.7	83.5	82.7	82.0	82.0	81.3	79.7	79.1	79.2	78.7	78.1	77.7	77.1	76.2	76.0
UK	91.3	*88.4	88.2	88.0	87.9	87.8	86.8	85.7	84.4	83.3	81.8	79.1	75.1	71.0	69.2	66.4
Unemployment rates: age 55–64/male																
USA	2.8	3.3	3.2	2.4	2.6	4.3	4.2	3.5	2.8	2.7	3.4	3.6	5.5	6.1	5.0	4.3
Japan	2.1	2.1	2.1	1.8	2.1	3.2	3.8	3.8	4.3	4.4	3.7	4.3	4.3	5.0	5.0	5.0
France	1.9	2.2	2.6	1.9	2.1	2.6	3.1	3.6	4.3	4.0	4.7	4.8	*5.3	6.0	6.2	6.7
West Germany	0.9	1.2	2.0	1.6	2.3	3.9	3.9	3.7	4.0	4.3	4.3	5.4	7.0	8.5	10.0	10.2
Netherlands	—	—	—	2.4	2.4	3.1	3.6	3.5	3.3	3.2	3.3	3.9	5.2	13.7	11.9	5.3
Sweden	1.5	2.3	2.3	2.1	1.9	1.6	1.4	1.1	1.8	1.8	1.6	2.2	3.1	4.0	4.2	3.5
UK	5.0	*5.9	6.6	5.7	5.4	6.3	7.6	7.8	8.2	8.1	9.5	15.2	*17.6	13.9	13.3	13.4
Employment activity rates: age 55–64/male																
USA	78.4	77.4	76.6	75.1	74.2	71.4	70.2	70.3	70.3	69.9	68.8	67.4	66.3	64.6	64.5	57.1
Japan	84.8	85.3	84.8	85.2	84.5	83.2	82.6	81.6	81.3	81.5	82.2	81.3	81.2	80.5	79.6	78.9
France	74.0	73.0	71.5	70.7	69.3	67.1	65.8	66.9	65.8	67.1	65.3	61.2	*56.6	50.4	47.2	46.7
West Germany	81.5	76.9	73.7	72.2	68.9	65.4	63.9	63.3	62.5	62.6	62.7	61.0	58.2	55.1	51.8	51.6
Netherlands	—	—	—	75.3	72.8	70.7	69.9	68.8	66.0	63.6	61.5	58.4	56.0	49.9	49.2	50.9
Sweden	84.1	82.8	81.6	81.0	80.4	80.7	80.2	78.8	77.7	77.8	77.4	76.4	75.3	74.0	73.0	73.3
UK	86.7	*83.2	82.4	83.0	83.2	82.3	80.2	79.0	77.5	76.6	74.0	67.1	*61.9	61.1	60.0	57.5

*Break in time series

SOURCE: OECD, Labour Force Statistics, Paris, 1984, and our calculations.

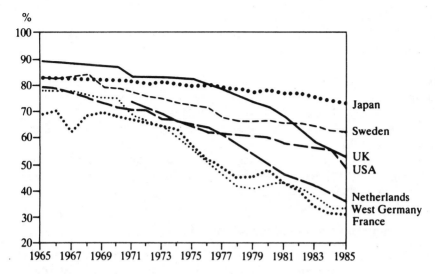

FIGURE 12-2   Labor force participation rates from 1965 to 1985 for men from 60 to 64 years old. *(Source: OECD,* Labour Force Statistics, *Paris, 1984–86.)*

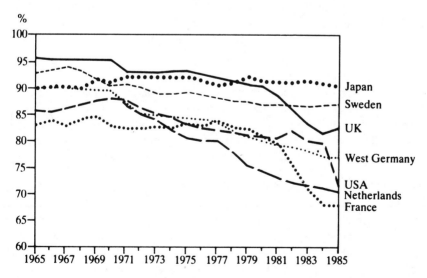

FIGURE 12-3   Labor force participation rates from 1965 to 1985 for men from 55 to 59 years old. *(Source: OECD,* Labour Force Statistics, *Paris, 1984–86.)*

tion" of the life course: as old-age pension coverage was generalized, the lifespan has been chronologically marked with reference to it (the age of entitlement to a full pension, the number of years of contributions necessary for entitlement, etc.)

Given the way retirement has helped construct a life-course model, what are the implications of its decline? Does it not imply that this model is also waning? The fact that retirement systems are losing control over early withdrawal runs counter to the interpretation that the latter amounts to a change of calendar, a sign of the acceleration of an age-old trend toward lowering the retirement age. On the contrary, this decline is evidence in favor of another interpretation, namely, that the threefold organization of the life course is coming apart. This hypothesis will be used to examine the new institutional arrangements that are taking over, from the retirement system, the management of definitive withdrawal from the labor force.

The New Institutional Arrangements and Their Implications

As old-age insurance and the pension system no longer fully manage the transition out of the labor force, other welfare subsystems have become significantly involved in redefining the boundary between working life and life after work. The principal subsystems are unemployment compensation and disability insurance. In France, the Netherlands and West Germany, definitive withdrawal has been managed through new measures within the framework of unemployment compensation and/or disability insurance. The same holds for Sweden and England, but not to the exclusion of all other arrangements. In the United States, public welfare programs have had little effect on labor force departures; but many companies have adopted early withdrawal policies, notably the Early Retirement Incentive Program (ERIP), which has spread widely since the early 1980s (Meier, 1986). All this has taken place despite the 1986 amendment to the Age Discrimination in Employment Act, which forbids age discrimination with regard to dismissals as well as to retirement. Let us look at the two principal means of handling early withdrawal and examine their implications.

The Disability Insurance Pathway   Disability insurance provides one of the major pathways out of the labor force in the Netherlands, West Germany, Sweden and Great Britain. It has, in some cases, been used along with other arrangements, particularly under unemployment compensation, so as to complete the bridge from the workforce across early withdrawal till the normal retirement age. The building of this bridge has usually involved, as we shall see, broadening eligibility requirements under disability insurance.

In the Netherlands, the most common pathway for early withdrawal led until the late 1970s through disability insurance, and this is still a well-used route. The number of beneficiaries increased 130 per cent from 1973 to 1979; in 1979 nearly 60 per cent of persons receiving disability benefits were over 50 years old. Under these arrangements, health insurance covers the first stretch of fifty-two weeks; and then, if total disability is recognized, disability insurance takes up the remainder. The impact of these arrangements increased after 1973, when eligibility requirements under disability insurance were broadened. Accordingly, partial, even minimal, disability can be reclassified as total if the applicant is unable to find, in the local labor market, a job adapted to both his qualifications and handicap. According to a Dutch study (Van den Bosch and Petersen, 1983), one-third of persons receiving disability benefits in 1978 could be described as having a purely "economic disability" that had nothing to do with any medical criterion. After 1980, two other sorts of arrangements began competing with disability insurance. First, early retirement provisions (VUT) have been placed in collective agreements; this arrangement was, at the start, financially encouraged by the Dutch government, which saw it as a means of transferring the costs of early withdrawal from public funds (disability insurance) toward the private sector. However, these VUT provisions have limited scope and concern but a fraction of potential beneficiaries from 60 to 64 years old. A second sort of arrangement, involving unemployment compensation, has been developed since 1975 and has covered as a result a significant proportion of 55–59-year-olds. Its success signals the failure of the government's effort to transfer the cost of early withdrawal toward firms.

In the Federal Republic of Germany, the prevailing pathway for early withdrawal has operated through disability insurance since the early 1970s. In 1984, 47.7 per cent of new admissions at the normal age into the retirement system had passed through disability insurance (Jacobs *et al.*, 1987). As in the Netherlands, the success of this arrangement has come from broadening eligibility requirements beyond strictly medical criteria, so as to take into account variables related to the labor market. Since 1976 a partially disabled person may receive full disability benefits if there is no part-time job adapted to his situation. Consequently, this arrangement has been widely used by 55–59-year-olds, an age group that cannot enter the retirement system and whose situation in the labor market is, owing to age, precarious. Although the tightening of eligibility requirements since 1985 has somewhat narrowed this pathway, it is still important, despite the passage of a May 1984 Act in favor of "pre-retirement" contracts that seeks to involve private companies in the cost of early withdrawal. In 1987 about 30 per cent of new beneficiaries of old-age pensions had still taken the pathway via disability insurance.

In Sweden and Great Britain, disability insurance has not been expanded as far as in the Netherlands and West Germany. Nonetheless, it has been used to cover more and more early withdrawal cases.

In Sweden, eligibility requirements under disability insurance were slackened in favor of aging jobless persons; a criterion of "employability" was added on to strictly medical ones. Since 1976, a jobless person at least 60 years old may, if he does not find a job corresponding to his qualifications, claim disability benefits till the normal retirement age of 65. Companies have not missed the chance to incorporate this early withdrawal arrangement into their personnel strategies. The opportunity thus presented should not be underestimated since the target population is, on one hand, very often the least productive age group in the workforce, and, on the other, the group that both has the best legal protection against dismissal and benefits from an active public policy for keeping aging workers in the labor force (Casey and Bruche, 1983). This country, though characterized by such an active public policy, has opened a breach in this system of protection, since it has broadened the definition of disability. This new pathway for early withdrawal has, since 1980, come into competition with a "partial" retirement program. This program, which has been very successful since it was set up in 1976, makes it possible to adjust the time an aging person spends working by combining a part-time job with part-time retirement. However, expanding disability insurance has opened a pathway for getting around this active policy in favor of job flexibility for aging workers: it authorizes total early definitive withdrawal from the labor force and could thus threaten the retirement system by limiting its essential function of regulating definitive withdrawal. For the time being, however, what characterizes Sweden is both the relative stability of labor force participation rates for persons over 55 years old and the maintenance of the retirement system's power over definitive withdrawal. The linkage in Sweden between the lifespan and the welfare system has not changed much during the period under study, unlike in the five other countries where new welfare subsystems have been set up to regulate exits from the labor force.

In Great Britain, a growing number of aging workers have also withdrawn early from their jobs under disability insurance, which, however, has not been purposefully restructured, nor its eligibility requirements broadened as in the other countries. A British study (Piachaud, 1986) has revealed a strong correlation between the number of persons receiving disability benefits and the jobless rate. In effect, physicians are responsible for judging whether persons are unfit for work, and they apparently take into account conditions in the labor market. Nonetheless, only a small proportion of aging wage-earners—mainly manual workers over 60 years old—have been capable of negotiating this sort of arrangement.

As the above cases show, disability insurance has become a predominant means of early withdrawal in countries where eligibility requirements have included, besides purely medical criteria, the criterion of the "employability" of aging workers given the situation in the labor market. Disability has been redefined in terms that are more economic than medical. What is often the result of age discrimination by employers is now euphemistically called worker's disability.

In several countries, a large percentage of definitive withdrawal cases are now regularly handled by arrangements under disability insurance instead of provisions under the retirement system. This means that the criteria for definitive withdrawal have been redefined; they are no longer a function of the age of entitlement to a pension but of the inability to work. Functional criteria, not age itself, are the basis for admission; disability benefits are acquired following procedures that have nothing to do with chronological age: the condition for receiving them is to be unfit for work. This change in definitive withdrawal can be interpreted as a new way of marking the end of the lifespan with functional labels rather than chronological milestones. It may reflect a "dechronologization" of the life course, a process that inevitably involves "destandardizing" it. Since a person's ability to keep working as he grows older depends upon the social group to which he belongs, these functional criteria lead to major differences among individuals in the timing of transitions between phases of the life course. Another consequence is the emergence of a new social construction of age and of its relationship to work. The aging worker is no longer primarily someone said to be close to the age of entitlement to retirement; instead, he is defined as being unable to work. When, as in West Germany or the Netherlands, nearly half of those who reach retirement age have previously been managed by disability insurance programs, economic inactivity no longer means having the right to rest; it means being unfit for work.

The Unemployment Compensation Pathway   Unemployment compensation is another welfare subsystem that has decisively redefined the boundary between working life and life after work. Toward the mid-1970s special procedures were adopted, almost everywhere in Europe, for compensating older unemployed persons for lost jobs. Of the six countries under study, this holds for France, the Netherlands, West Germany and Sweden.

In France, arrangements under unemployment compensation were a principal and massive means of managing early withdrawal: a guaranteed income scheme was set up in 1972 for persons over 60 years old dismissed from their jobs and was extended in 1977 to those who resigned. Other measures introduced in 1982 provided similar treatment for wage-earners over 55. Under agreements between the government and firms, wage-earners at the age of 56 years and 2 months (and sometimes at 55) can be dismissed but will be covered by a special allocation from the National Employment Fund until the normal retirement age (fixed in 1982 at 60 for persons who have contributed to the Old Age Fund for thirty-seven and a half years).

The Netherlands adopted a new rule in 1975 stipulating that anyone between 60 and 64 years old who receives unemployment benefits (WWV) should continue receiving them till the legal retirement age of 65. Under these new rules, persons can leave the labor force at the age of 57 years 6 months. Unemployment insurance and unemployment welfare assistance together successively provide benefits to such jobless persons till the age of 65, the normal age for receiving an old-age pension.

West Germany has gradually loosened the conditions for providing unemployment benefits to jobless persons over 54. In 1987, given the maximal length of coverage, a person at the age of 57 years and 4 months who is dismissed from his job can receive unemployment benefits until he is 60, the age that entitles him to a normal retirement pension, as a long-term unemployment case. Hence, the so-called "59er rule," which has worked as a means of early withdrawal for a long time and ever more intensively since 1975, has become, *de facto*, a "57er rule" (Kühlewind, 1988). In 1986, 11 per cent of new retirees had withdrawn from their jobs under arrangements with unemployment compensation.

In Sweden, a combination of arrangements under the unemployment and disability insurance funds opens the way to definitive withdrawal as early as the age of 58 with unemployment benefits till 60 and then disability benefits till 65, the normal age for receiving an old-age pension. In comparison with the five other countries, however, this pathway is still not often taken.

In Great Britain, no special protection has been offered to the aging jobless; and no particular pathway opened for early withdrawal under unemployment compensation. However, unemployment assistance compensation for cases of long-term unemployment are very often provided so as to supplement the incomes of aged "discouraged" workers (Laczko, 1987) who have stopped working early either owing to partial disability or thanks to occupational old-age pensions that are paid early. Occupational pension funds are one of the major means of early withdrawal in Britain.

In all six countries under study, facts are linked in the same way. Making it easier for older workers to receive unemployment compensation also makes it easier for companies to dismiss, first of all, those who benefit from better coverage. Firms can thus get rid of such workers at the least economic and social cost. Adopting measures that compensate older workers for lost jobs is a factor that reinforces age discrimination in the economy, all the more so as the economic situation worsens.

The growing importance of unemployment compensation and/or disability insurance as a means of regulating definitive withdrawal from the labor force has considerable significance and meaning. Three implications will be pointed out. First of all, the new boundary between economic activity and inactivity is more directly modified as a function of the labor market and of the definition of age groups thus produced. Early withdrawal under unemployment compensation depends on the employer and his power to dismiss, not on the employee and his claim to a right to rest. Even though it is optional in some cases (for example, the French guaranteed income scheme), this recourse to unemployment compensation mainly depends on companies' employment policies. Second, the right to receive social transfer payments (disability and/or unemployment benefits) entails surrendering the right to a job. In contrast, the principle of the retirement system is to separate the right to a job from the right to a pension; in general, a person does not have to give up his job in order to receive a pension. Using unemployment compensation, or disability insurance, to manage labor force withdrawal has considerably weakened the older worker's right to a job. Third, with respect to the life course, replacing the retirement system with these other two sorts of arrangement has opened a gap between the individual's working life and his life after work. He loses control over the transition to the later years of his life. There is greater age specialization. After a working life comes the time when one is denied the right to work and forced to stop working (Guillemard, 1985a). To continue working at an advanced age becomes morally questionable by public opinion in a context of high unemployment (Guillemard, 1986a). Meanwhile, the transition toward the last phase of the life course is less foreseeable. The chronological reference marks of retirement have been swept away and, with them, any principle providing for an orderly transition out of the labor force. There is more flexibility in organizing the end of the lifespan, which is increasingly governed by the labor market and companies' employment policies. The subsystems of unemployment compensation and disability insurance are handy; they are, in each country, constantly being reworked in relation to the labor market.

The Decline of the "Pre-retirement" Pathway   The description of the institutional mechanisms used to manage early withdrawal would not be complete without mention of "pre-retirement" arrangements. These have been the third principal pathway out of the labor force in most of the countries under study: solidarity pre-retirement contracts in France, the Pre-retirement Act in West Germany, the Job Release Scheme in Great Britain, and the VUT in the Netherlands. The main characteristic of pre-retirement arrangements is that they are intended to improve the situation in the labor market by proposing voluntary early withdrawal to aging wage-earners and, in many cases, by stipulating that such departures must be replaced by new hirings of jobless young people. Despite their diversity (whether they derive from public policy or come out of collective agreements, how they are financed, etc.), such measures tend to manage labor force exits similarly to the retirement system: age remains an essential eligibility requirement, and the choice of whether to go on pre-retirement is left up to the aging worker himself. Although eligibility requirements have changed frequently as a function of the labor market, they nonetheless provide for a regulated transition out of the workforce without placing beneficiaries in successive, precarious positions, as arrangements under unemployment and disability insurances do.

Significantly, pre-retirement schemes have, in most cases, either been abandoned (in France in 1986 and West Germany in 1988) or been restrictive (such as the British Job Release Scheme). Only the Dutch VUT program is still in effect, and even that has apparently been called into question.

This decline of pre-retirement schemes corroborates the interpretation advanced herein of changes in definitive labor force withdrawal. These changes should not be taken to be simply the result of lowering the age of withdrawal. The tendency to let pre-retirement schemes expire furthers the decline of the retirement system since the former, like the latter, uses chronological criteria to manage a regular transition out of the labor force. This too is a sign of the dechronologization of the life course.

THE DEINSTITUTIONALIZATION OF THE LIFE COURSE AND CROSS-GENERATIONAL TRANSFERS

This attempt to interpret international data reveals the scope of the changes under way. Although we might, at first, think that these are simply a means of setting the calendar of retirement ahead, they turn out, after analysis, to be a deep trend that upsets the way the life course is organized along with the welfare system.

The retirement system has lost its central function of regulating labor force withdrawal. The other subsystems (principally unemployment compensation and disability insurance) that now do this introduce their own logic for regulating the transition from work to non-work. As a result of this replacement of retirement, the chronological milestones that used to mark the life course are no longer visible; and functional criteria have assumed importance in organizing the later years of life. This change is especially noticeable when disability insurance has thus replaced retirement. Other observations than those presented here reinforce this interpretation. For instance, the US law against age discrimination in employment can be interpreted as indicating a different way of organizing the lifespan, one that places less importance on the age criterion but greater emphasis on functional criteria based on the individual worker's capabilities and effectiveness: only these criteria can now be legally used by employers to dismiss or retire employees.

This dechronologization entails destandardizing the life course, undoing the threefold model with which we are familiar. The transition to the last stage of life is being rearranged more flexibly, but this new flexibility does not mean that individuals have more freedom of choice. In fact, the large majority of early withdrawals are not voluntary (Guillemard, 1986b, p. 288; Casey and Laczko, 1988, p. 13). This early withdrawal trend is a reflection of the employment situation and of companies' strategies in relation to it. As pointed out, the new boundaries being drawn between economic activity and inactivity are directly modulated by conditions in the labor market and the definition of age groups thus produced. Given the broader eligibility requirements under disability insurances or unemployment compensation, early withdrawal mainly depends on a judgment about the "unemployability" of older wage-earners, a judgment that comes out of negotiations about jobs. The time for definitive withdrawal from the labor force is, for the individual, no longer fixed ahead of time; it is not predictable. Since the chronological milestones of retirement are being torn up, the threefold model, which placed the individual in a foreseeable life course of continuous, consecutive sequences of functions and statuses, is coming apart. As a consequence, an individual's working life now ends in confusion.

Jobless aging persons' conceptions of their situation provide evidence of this fundamental change. A minority of this new "inactive" population between 55 and 65 years old identify themselves as "retirees." There is clear evidence of this for France (Guillemard, 1986), but also for Great Britain. According to Casey and Laczko (1988) (using the results of the *Labour Force Survey*), one-quarter of the aging jobless British population between 60 and 64, and only 12 per cent of those between 55 and 59, classify themselves as retirees; the rest define themselves mainly as being unemployed or "discouraged" workers no longer looking for a job. These data measure the impact that the previously described institutional arrangements for early withdrawal have had on the organization of the life course. Retirement is no longer the unifying principle, which gives a homogeneous meaning to a third phase of life that opens with departure from the labor force. The elderly no longer have a clearly defined social status. Definitive withdrawal, old age and retirement no longer concur with each other: occupational old age begins with definitive withdrawal, well before retirement and physical old age. The life course as an institution is coming undone. Retirement is no longer a central means of socialization that determines the identities and symbolic universes of individuals. There is less and less of a definite order to the last phases of life. The life course is being deinstitutionalized. It would, by the way, be interesting to compare the results of the numerous studies about how people enter the labor force with those of the scarcer studies about how they leave it so as to see if the interpretation advanced herein would be confirmed.

Deinstitutionalizing the life course undermines not only the possibility of forming a continuous, foreseeable idea of one's life but also the system of reciprocity across generations. Doubt is being cast not only on retirement but also on the underlying contract of the commitments binding generations together. What are the prospects of this long-term contract involving several *successive* generations? The reciprocity of commitments across generations is no longer so reliable in a society where time is accelerating, where the lifespan is no longer part of a long run with fixed, standard chronological milestones, where, on the contrary, flexible diversified models are taking shape that provide for unpredictable life courses. People still working are starting to doubt whether coming generations will pay for their pensions as willingly as they are now paying for those of current retirees. In effect, the temporal strategy underlying this transfer implies that compensation for the alienation of work be delayed in exchange for the right to rest at the end of life. But the motivations behind this strategy are weakening since the life course no longer makes individuals part of a foreseeable continuity.

The passage from a society of "managed time" (Roussel and Girard, 1982) to an ephemeral society, from a society that tries to control the future to one that is running beyond time and has no future, tends to give rise to a new conception of solidarity among generations. Short-term solidarity with immediate reciprocity *between* generations is now preferred to long-term solidarity *across* generations. As a consequence, the equity of such exchanges tends to be evaluated only over the short run, here and now. An alarming example of this is the pressure group Americans for Generational Equity (AGE), which criticizes the redistribution of social transfer payments in favor of the elderly (Jones, 1988; Preston, 1984). In current debates about the equity of *inter*generational exchanges, the transfer of public funds among various age groups is measured instantaneously in order to denounce imbalances; no thought is given to the long-term *cross*-generational reciprocity of which these transfers provide but a partial image.

The institutional arrangements used to ensure early definitive withdrawal from the labor force provide evidence that the contract binding generations is being focused on the present. This early withdrawal trend has often been justified by the argument that the transfer of work between old and young balances the transfer of money (in the form of pensions) from young to old (Commissariat Général du Plan, 1986). This intergenerational solidarity involves an immediate reciprocity that has been given form through these new institutional arrangements. Rather than work being shared, it has, in most countries, been transferred from one generation to another, as older persons have seen their right to a job restricted. As a consequence public expenditures on the aging, economically inactive part of the population have exploded. In France, for instance, half of what was spent on unemployment compensation in 1985 went to beneficiaries at least 55 years old (Ragot, 1985). In all the countries under study, public authorities have been attempting to shift the costs, but without much success, toward the private sector (Casey, 1987).

Yet another consequence has been how society now constructs the reality of aging. Younger generations now see the aged as a relatively privileged, excessively costly group who accumulate the right to both social benefits and free time, an image that is all the stronger insofar as the other part of this exchange—transferring jobs from old to young—has not been up to expectation (Franck *et al.*, 1982). Older generations thus appear to be well off and to have free time whereas the prospects of younger generations are not so bright, given the aging of the population. This new conception of an immediate balance of intergenerational exchanges can be taken to be the result of re-modeling the organization of the life course, in particular from the labor force toward retirement. As a consequence, the cultural base underlying retirement and legitimating the contract binding generations is cracking. We are thus forced to recognize the long-term instability of the organization of cross-generational transfers. Changes in retirement should not be considered, as they too often are, to be the mechanical effect of demographic aging, nor should the future of old-age pension systems be predicted merely in terms of the cost analysis of a growing proportion of old people in the population. In effect, the processes of legitimation and the quest for meaning are just as decisive as budgetary considerations for shedding light on the prospects of the retirement system and for understanding how the welfare state is being restructured in relation to the life course.

(Translated from the French by Noal Mellott, Centre National de la Recherche Scientifique, Paris)

NOTE

1. These graphs and tables were drawn by an international research group (Anne-Marie Guillemard, Martin Kohli, Martin Rein and Herman Van Gunsteren) that has worked on six countries (the United States, the Netherlands, France, West Germany, Sweden and Great Britain) in collaboration with F. Laczko and C. Phillipson (for Great Britain), Harold Sheppard (for the United States) and E. Wadensjö (for Sweden). The information thus gathered is the basis of a personal interpretation of the changes under way, one that reflects my own point of view.

REFERENCES

Casey, B. (1987), "Early retirement: the problems of instrument substitution and cost shifting and their implications for restructuring the process of retirement," *International Social Security Review*, IV.

Casey, B. and Bruche, G. (1983), *Work or Retirement*, London, Gower.

Casey, B. and Laczko, F. (1988), "Recent trends in labour force participation of older men in Great Britain and their implications for the future," paper given at the *Futuribles* conference on "The Ageing of Population in Europe: Trends, Challenges and Policies," Paris, 4–5 October.

Commissariat Général du Plan (1986), *Vieillir solidaires*, Paris, Documentation Française.

Franck, D., Hara, R., Magnier, G. and Villey, D. (1982), "Entreprises et contrats de solidarité de préretraite-démission," *Travail et Emploi*, XIII (July–September).

Guillemard, A. -M. (1985a), "Préretraite et mutations du cycle de vie," *Futuribles*, LXXXVIII, pp. 31–8 (May).

Guillemard, A. -M. (1985b), "The social dynamics of early withdrawal from the labour force in France," *Ageing and Society*, V, 4, pp. 381–412 (December).

Guillemard, A. -M. (1986a), "State, society and old age policy in France from 1945 to the current crisis," *Social Science and Medicine*, XXIII, 12, pp. 1319–26.

Guillemard, A. -M. (1986b), *Le déclin du Social: formation et crise des politiques de la vieillesse*, Coll. Sociologies, Paris, Presses Universitaires de France.

Jacobs, K., Kohli, M. and Rein, M. (1987), "Early exit from the labor force in Germany: country report," paper presented at the international conference on "Early Exit from the Labor Force," Tampa, Florida, November.

Jacobs, K., Kohli, M. and Rein, M. (1989), "The evolution of early exit: a comparative analysis of the labor force participations of the elderly," in M. Kohli, M. Rein, A. -M. Guillemard and H. Van Gunsteren (eds.), *Time for Retirement*.

Jones, J. R. (1988), "Conflit entre générations aux Etats-Unis," *Futuribles* (October).

Kohli, M. (1987), "Retirement and the moral economy: an historical interpretation of the German case." *Journal of Aging Studies*, I, 2, pp. 125–44.

Kühlewind, G. (1988). "Age and procedures of retirement in Germany: present situation, past evolution and forecast," paper presented at the *Futuribles* conference on "The Ageing of Population in Europe: Trends, Challenges and Policies," Paris, 4–5 October.

Laczko, F. (1987), "Older workers, unemployment and the discouraged worker effect," in S. di Gregorio (ed.), *Social Gerontology: New Directions*, London, Croom Helm, 1987, pp. 239–51.

Meier, E. (1986), *Early Retirement Incentive Programs: Trends and Implications*, Washington DC, AARP Public Policy Institute.

Piachaud, D. (1986), "Disability, retirement and unemployment of older men," *Journal of Social Policy*, 2, pp. 145–62.

Preston, S. H. (1984), "Children and the elderly in the US," *Scientific American*, CCLI, 6, pp. 36–41 (December).

Ragot, Maurice (1985), *La cessation anticipée d'activité salariée*, rapport présenté au nom de la section du travail, Conseil Economique et Social, Paris (June).

Roussel, L. and Girard, A. (1982), "Régimes démographiques et ages de la vie" in *Les Ages de la Vie*, Proceedings of the 7th Conference on Demography, vol. 1, Paris, Presses Universitaires de France, pp. 15–23.

Van den Bosch and Petersen (1983), "An explanation of the growth of social security disability transfers," *De Economist*, CXXXI, 1, pp. 65–79, quoted in B. de Vroom and M. Blomsma, *The Netherlands: An Extreme Case*, Working Paper, Leyden Institute for Law and Public Policy.

13

Age Norms, Age Constraints, and Adult Socialization

BERNICE L. NEUGARTEN
JOAN W. MOORE
JOHN C. LOWE

Expectations regarding age-appropriate behavior form a pervasive system of rules, which govern the timing of major life events and constrain social interaction. This reading by Neugarten, Moore, and Lowe first lays out a theory of age norms and then analyzes empirical evidence about the pertinence of age norms for various age groups. Their research demonstrates that belief in the relevance and validity of age norms increases over the life span, with older people more likely than younger people to believe that age is a reasonable criterion for evaluating behavior and establishing limits.

In all societies age is one of the bases for the ascription of status and one of the under-lying dimensions by which social interaction is regulated. Anthropologists have studied age-grading in simple societies, and sociologists in the tradition of Mannheim have been interested in the relations between generations; but little systematic attention has been given to the ways in which age groups relate to each other in complex societies or to systems of norms which refer to age-appropriate behavior. A promising group of theoretical papers which appeared twenty or more years ago have now become classics,[1] but with the exceptions of a major contribution by Eisenstadt and a provocative paper by Berger,[2] little theoretical or empirical work has been done in this area in the two decades that have intervened, and there has been little development of what might be called a sociology of age.

The present paper deals with two related issues: first, with the degree of constraint perceived with regard to age norms that operate in American society; second, with adult socialization to those norms.[3] Preliminary to presenting the data that bear upon these issues, however, a few comments regarding the age-norm system and certain illustrative observations gathered earlier may help to provide context for this study.

"Age Norms, Age Constraints, and Adult Socialization" by Bernice Neugarten, Joan Moore and John Lowe, from *American Journal of Sociology*, 70 (1965). Reprinted by permission.

BACKGROUND CONCEPTS AND OBSERVATIONS

Expectations regarding age-appropriate behavior form an elaborated and pervasive system of norms governing behavior and interaction, a network of expectations that is imbedded throughout the cultural fabric of adult life. There exists what might be called a prescriptive timetable for the ordering of major life events: a time in the life span when men and women are expected to marry, a time to raise children, a time to retire. This normative pattern is adhered to more or less consistently by most persons in the society. Although the actual occurrences of major life events for both men and women are influenced by a variety of life contingencies, and although the norms themselves vary somewhat from one group of persons to another, it can easily be demonstrated that norms and actual occurrences are closely related. Age norms and age expectations operate as prods and brakes upon behavior, in some instances hastening an event, in others delaying it. Men and women are aware not only of the social clocks that operate in various areas of their lives, but they are aware also of their own timing and readily describe themselves as "early," "late," or "on time" with regard to family and occupational events.

Age norms operate also in many less clear-cut ways and in more peripheral areas of adult life as illustrated in such phrases as "He's too old to be working so hard" or "She's too young to wear that style of clothing" or "That's a strange thing for a man of his age to say." The concern over age-appropriate behavior is further illustrated by colloquialisms such as "Act your age!"—an exhortation made to the adult as well as to the child in this society.

Such norms, implicit or explicit, are supported by a wide variety of sanctions ranging from those, on the one hand, that relate directly to the physical health of the transgressor to those, on the other hand, that stress the deleterious effects of the transgression on other persons. For example, the fifty-year-old man who insists on a strenuous athletic life is chastised for inviting an impairment of his own health; a middle-aged woman who dresses like an adolescent brings into question her husband's good judgment as well as her own; a middle-aged couple who decide to have another child are criticized because of the presumed embarrassment to their adolescent or married children. Whether affecting the self or others, age norms and accompanying sanctions are relevant to a great variety of adult behaviors; they are both systematic and pervasive in American society.

Despite the diversity of value patterns, life styles, and reference groups that influence attitudes, a high degree of consensus can be demonstrated with regard to age-appropriate and age-linked behaviors as illustrated by data shown in Table 13-1. The table shows how responses were distributed when a representative sample of middle-class men and women aged forty to seventy[4] were asked such questions as: "What do you think is the best age for a man to marry? . . . to finish school?" "What age comes to your mind when you think of a 'young' man? . . . an 'old' man?" "At what age do you think a man has the most responsibilities? . . . accomplishes the most?"[5]

The consensus indicated in the table is not limited to persons residing in a particular region of the United States or to middle-aged persons. Responses to the same set of questions were obtained from other middle-class groups: one group of fifty men and

TABLE 13-1 Consensus in a Middle-Class Middle-Aged Sample Regarding Various Age-Related Characteristics

	Age Range Designated as Appropriate or Expected	Percent Who Concur	
		Men (N = 50)	Women (N = 43)
Best age for a man to marry	20–25	80	90
Best age for a woman to marry	19–24	85	90
When most people should become grandparents	45–50	84	79
Best age for most people to finish school and go to work	20–22	86	82
When most men should be settled on a career	24–26	74	64
When most men hold their top jobs	45–50	71	58
When most people should be ready to retire	60–65	83	86
A young man	18–22	84	83
A middle-aged man	40–50	86	75
An old man	65–75	75	57
A young woman	18–24	89	88
A middle-aged woman	40–50	87	77
An old woman	60–75	83	87
When a man has the most responsibilities	35–50	79	75
When a man accomplishes most	40–50	82	71
The prime of life for a man	35–50	86	80
When a woman has the most responsibilities	25–40	93	91
When a woman accomplishes most	30–45	94	92
A good-looking woman	20–35	92	82

women aged twenty to thirty residing in a second midwestern city, a group of sixty Negro men and women aged forty to sixty in a third midwestern city, and a group of forty persons aged seventy to eighty in a New England community. Essentially the same patterns emerged in each set of data.

THE PROBLEM AND THE METHOD

Based upon various sets of data such as those illustrated in Table 13-1, the present investigation proceeded on the assumption that age norms and age expectations operate in this society as a system of social control. For a great variety of behaviors, there is a span of years within which the occurrence of a given behavior is regarded as appropriate. When the behavior occurs outside that span of years, it is regarded as inappropriate and is negatively sanctioned.

The specific questions of this study were these: How do members of the society vary in their perception of the strictures involved in age norms, or in the degree of constraint they perceive with regard to age-appropriate behaviors? To what extent are personal attitudes congruent with the attitudes ascribed to the generalized other? Finally, using this congruence as an index of socialization, can adult socialization to age norms be shown to occur as respondents themselves increase in age?

The Instrument

A questionnaire was constructed in which the respondent was asked on each of a series of items which of three ages he would regard as appropriate or inappropriate, or which he would approve or disapprove. As seen in the illustrations below, the age spans being proposed were intended to be psychologically rather than chronologically equal in the sense that for some events a broad age span is appropriate, for others, a narrow one.

- A woman who feels it's all right at her age to wear a two-piece bathing suit to the beach:
    When she's 45 (approve or disapprove)
    When she's 30 (approve or disapprove)
    When she's 18 (approve or disapprove).

Other illustrative items were:

- A woman who decides to have another child (when she's 45, 37, 30).
- A man who's willing to move his family from one town to another to get ahead in his company (when he's 45, 35, 25).
- A couple who like to do the "twist" (when they're 55, 30, 20).
- A man who still prefers living with his parents rather than getting his own apartment (when he's 30, 25, 21).
- A couple who move across country so they can live near their married children (when they're 40, 55, 70).

The thirty-nine items finally selected after careful pretesting are divided equally into three types: those that relate to occupational career; those that relate to the family cycle; and a broader grouping that refer to recreation, appearance, and consumption behaviors. In addition, the items were varied systematically with regard to their applicability to three periods: young adulthood, middle age, and old age.

In general, then, the questionnaire presents the respondent with a relatively balanced selection of adult behaviors which were known from pretesting to be successful in evoking age discriminations. A means of scoring was devised whereby the score reflects the degree of refinement with which the respondent makes age discriminations. For instance, the respondent who approves of a couple dancing the "twist" if they are twenty, but who disapproves if they are thirty, is placing relative age constraint upon this item of behavior as compared to another respondent who approves the "twist" both at age twenty and at age thirty, but not at age fifty-five. The higher the score, the more the respondent regards age as a salient dimension across a wide variety of behaviors and the more constraint he accepts in the operation of age norms.[6]

The Sample

A quota sample of middle-class respondents was obtained in which level of education, occupation, and area of residence were used to determine social class. The sample is divided into six age-sex cells: fifty men and fifty women aged twenty to thirty, one hundred men and one hundred women aged thirty to fifty-five, and fifty men and fifty women aged sixty-five and over. Of the four hundred respondents, all but a few in the older group were or had been married. The great majority were parents of one or more children.

The only known bias in the sample occurs in the older group (median age for men is sixty-nine; for women seventy-two), where most individuals were members of Senior Citizens clubs and where, as a result, the subsample is biased in the direction of better health and greater community involvement than can be expected for the universe of persons in this age range. While Senior Citizens is a highly age-conscious and highly age-graded association from the perspective of the wider society, there is no evidence that the seventy-year-old who joins is any more or any less aware of age discriminations than is the seventy-year-old who does not join.[7] The older group was no more or less homogeneous with regard to religious affiliation, ethnic background, or indexes of social class than were the other two age groups in this sample.

Administration

To investigate the similarity between personal attitudes and attitudes ascribed to the generalized other, the questionnaire was first administered with instructions to give "your personal opinions" about each of the items; then the respondent was given a second copy of the questionnaire and asked to respond in the way he believed "most people" would respond.[8]

In about half the cases, both forms of the instrument were administered consecutively in personal interviews. In the remainder of the cases, responses on the first form were gathered in group sessions (in one instance, a parents' meeting in a school), and the second form was completed later and returned by mail to the investigator.

The two types of administration were utilized about evenly within each age-sex group. No significant differences in responses were found to be due to this difference in procedure of data-gathering.

FINDINGS

The findings of this study can be read from Figure 13-1. The figure shows a striking convergence with age between the two sets of attitudes.

1. Age trends within each set of data are opposite in direction. With regard to personal opinions, there is a highly significant increase in scores with age—that is, an increase in the extent to which respondents ascribe importance to age norms and place constraints upon adult behavior in terms of age appropriateness.
2. With regard to "most people's opinions" there is a significant decrease in scores with age—that is, a decrease in the extent to which age constraints are perceived in the society and attributed to a generalized other.

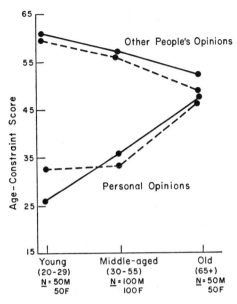

FIGURE 13-1   Perception of Age Constraints in Adulthood, by Age and Sex. An analysis of variance for the data on "personal opinions" showed that age was a highly significant variable (*F* is statistically reliable beyond the .001 level); and the interaction between age and sex was significant (*F* is reliable at the .05 level). For the data on "other people's opinions," age alone is a significant variable (*F* is reliable beyond the .001 level). Dotted line, women; solid line, men.

3. Sex differences are minimal with the exception that young women stand somewhat outside the general trend on "personal opinions," with scores that differentiate them from young men but not from middle-aged women.

DISCUSSION

The difference shown in these data between personal attitudes and attitudes attributed to the generalized other (a finding that holds true for all but the oldest respondents) implies that age norms operate like other types of norms insofar as there is some lack of congruence between that which is acknowledged to be operating in the society and that which is personally accepted as valid. It is noteworthy, on the one hand, that age norms are uniformly acknowledged to exist in the minds of "most people." While the data are not shown here, on each one of the thirty-nine behavioral items some 80 percent or more of all respondents made age discriminations when asked for "most people's opinions." In other words, general consensus exists that behaviors described in the test instrument are age-related. On the other hand, respondents uniformly attributed greater stricture to age norms in the minds of other people than in their own minds. This difference was reflected in the scores for every respondent as well as in the mean scores.

These findings indicate that there is an overriding norm of "liberal-mindedness" regarding age, whereby men and women consistently maintain that they hold more liberal views than do others. In many ways this situation is reminiscent of the phenomenon of pluralistic ignorance, in which no respondent's personal view of the attitudes of others is altogether correct.[9] In other ways, however, this may be a situation in which respondents tend to exaggerate, rather than to misconstrue, the opinions of others. A young person who says, in effect, "I am not strict about age norms, but other people are," is indeed correct that other people are stricter than he is (as shown in these data on "personal opinions"); but he exaggerates, for other people are not so strict as he thinks. Similarly, when an old person says, in effect, "I think this is the norm, and other people think so, too," he is also partly correct that other old people agree with him, but he ignores what *young* people think.

These partial misconceptions have at least two implications: first, when a person's own opinions differ from the norms he encounters, he may exaggerate the differences and place the norms even further away from his own opinions than is warranted. Second, it may be that in considering age norms, the individual gives undue weight to the opinions of persons who are older or stricter than himself and ignores the opinions of others who are younger or less strict. In both instances, the norm image is not the average of all opinions encountered but the image of the "ideal" norm. In the case of age norms, the "ideal" norms may well be those held by older persons.

The findings of this study are also of interest when viewed within the context of adult socialization. Cross-sectional data of this type must be interpreted with caution since the differences between age groups may reflect historical changes in values and attitudes as much as changes that accompany increased age itself. Still, the findings seem congruent with a theory of adult socialization: that personal belief in the relevance and validity of social norms increases through the adult life span and that, in this instance, as the individual ages he becomes increasingly aware of age discriminations in adult behavior and of the system of social sanctions that operate with regard to age appropriateness. The middle-aged and the old seem to have learned that age is a reasonable criterion by which to evaluate behavior, that to be "off-time" with regard to life events or to show other age-deviant behavior brings with it social and psychological sequelae that cannot be disregarded. In the young, especially the young male, this view is only partially accepted; and there seems to be a certain denial of age as a valid dimension by which to judge behavior.

This age-related difference in point of view is perhaps well illustrated by the response of a twenty-year-old who, when asked what he thought of marriage between seventeen-year-olds, said, "I suppose it would be all right if the boy got a good job, and if they loved each other. Why not? It isn't age that's the important thing." A forty-five-year-old, by contrast, said, "At that age, they'd be foolish. Neither one of them is settled enough. A boy on his own, at seventeen, couldn't support a wife, and he certainly couldn't support children. Kids who marry that young will suffer for it later."

Along with increased personal conviction regarding the validity of age norms goes a decreased tendency to perceive the generalized other as restrictive. The over-all convergence in the data, a convergence which we have interpreted in terms of adult social-ization, may reflect status and deference relationships between age groups in American society, where high status is afforded the middle-aged and where social enforcement of norms may generally be said to be vested in the mature rather than the young. The young person, having only recently graduated from the age-segregated world of ado-lescents, and incompletely socialized to adult values, seems to perceive a psychologi-cal distance between himself and "most people" and to feel only partially identified with the adult world. This is evidenced by the fact that when asked, "Whom do you have in mind when you think of 'most people'?" young adults tended to answer, "Older people."

Only for old people is there a high degree of congruence between personal opinions and the opinions ascribed to others. This may reflect not only the accumulated effects of adult socialization and the internalization of age norms, but also a certain crystal-lization of attitudes in the aged. Older respondents volunteered the most vehement and the most opinionated comments as they moved from item to item, as if to underscore the fact that their attitudes with regard to age and age-related behaviors are highly charged emotionally. Under these circumstances, there is likely to be a blurring of dis-tinctions between what the respondent himself regards as right and what he thinks other people would "naturally" regard as right.

With regard to sex differences, the fact that young women perceive greater con-straints regarding age-appropriate behavior than do young men is generally congruent with other evidence of differences in socialization for women and men in our society. Young women are probably more highly sensitized to the imperatives of age norms than are young men, given the relatively more stringent expectations regarding age at marriage for women.

It should be recalled that the present study is based upon quota samples of middle-class respondents and that accordingly the findings cannot be readily generalized to other samples. Nevertheless, the findings support the interpretation that age norms are salient over a wide variety of adult behaviors and support the view that adult socializa-tion produces increasingly clear perception of these norms as well as an increasing awareness that the norms provide constraints upon adult behavior.

NOTES

This article is adapted from the paper "Age Norms and Age Constraints in Adulthood," pre-sented at the annual meeting of the American Sociological Association, September 1963. This study has been financed by research grant No. 4200 from the National Institute of Mental Health (Bernice L. Neugarten, principal investigator). The authors are indebted to Mrs. Karol Weinstein for assistance in the collection and treatment of the data.

1. Following the classic article by Karl Mannheim ("The Problem of Generations," *Essays on the Sociology of Knowledge* [New York: Oxford University Press, 1952], pp. 276–322), these include Ralph Linton's discussion in *The Study of Man* (New York: Appleton-Century, 1936); Ruth Benedict, "Continuities and Discontinuities in Culture Conditioning," *Psychiatry*, I (1938), 161–67; Kingsley Davis, "The Sociology of Parent-Youth Conflict," *American Sociological Review*, V (1940), 523–35; and Talcott Parsons, "Age and Sex in the Social Structure of the United States," *American Sociological Review*, VII (October 1942), 604–16. Anthropological classics include Arnold Van Gennep (1908), *The Rites of Passage* (Chicago: University of Chicago

Press, 1960); Robert H. Lowie (1920), *Primitive Society* (New York: Harper & Bros., 1961). More recently, A. H. J. Prins, *East African Age-Class Systems* (Groningen: J. B. Wolters, 1953) has presented a critical analysis of concepts and terms in use among anthropologists.

2. S. N. Eisenstadt, *From Generation to Generation* (Glencoe, Ill.: Free Press, 1956); and Bennett M. Berger, "How Long Is a Generation?" *British Journal of Sociology*, XI (1960), 10–23.

3. With some exceptions, such as the work of Robert K. Merton, *Social Theory and Social Structure* (Glencoe, Ill.: Free Press, 1957), sociologists have as yet given little attention to the broader problem of adult socialization.

4. The sample was drawn by area-probability methods (a 2 percent listing of households in randomly selected census tracts) with the resulting pool of cases then stratified by age, sex, and socioeconomic status. Using the indexes of occupation, level of education, house type, and area of residence, these respondents were all middle class. The data were gathered in connection with the Kansas City Studies of Adult Life, a research program carried out over a period of years under the direction of Robert J. Havighurst, William E. Henry, Bernice L. Neugarten, and other members of the Committee on Human Development, University of Chicago.

5. For each item in the table, the percentages that appear in the third and fourth columns obviously vary directly with the breadth of the age span shown for that item. The age span shown was, in turn, the one selected by the investigators to produce the most accurate reflection of the consensus that existed in the data.

The way in which degree of consensus was calculated can be illustrated on "Best age for a man to marry." Individuals usually responded to this item in terms of specific years, such as "20" or "22," or in terms of narrow ranges, such as "from 20 to 23." These responses were counted as consensus within the five-year age range shown in Table 13-1 on the grounds that the respondents were concurring that the best age was somewhere between twenty and twenty-five. A response such as "18 to 20" or "any time in the 20's" was outside the range regarded as consensus and was therefore excluded.

6. For each item of behavior, one of the ages being proposed is scored as the "appropriate" age; another, the "marginal"; and the third, the "inappropriate" (the age at which the behavior is usually proscribed on the basis of its transgression of an age norm). A response which expresses disapproval of only the "inappropriate" age is scored 1, while a response which expresses disapproval of not only the "inappropriate" but also the "marginal" age receives a score of 3. The total possible score is 117, a score that could result only if the respondent were perceiving maximum age constraint with regard to every one of the thirty-nine items. A response which expresses approval or disapproval of all three ages for a given behavior is scored zero, since for that respondent the item is not age-related, at least not within the age range being proposed.

The "appropriate" age for each item had previously been designated by the investigators on the basis of previous findings such as those illustrated on Table 13-1 of this report. That the designations were generally accurate was corroborated by the fact that when the present instrument was administered to the four hundred respondents described here, more than 90 percent of respondents on successive test items checked "approve" for the "appropriate" one of the three proposed ages.

7. On the other hand, members of Senior Citizens are more likely to be activists and to regard themselves as younger in outlook than persons who do not join such groups. If this is true, the age differences to be described in the following sections of this paper might be expected to be even more marked in future studies in which samples are more representative.

8. The problem being studied here relates to problems of conformity, deviation, and personal versus public attitudes. As is true of other empirical research in these areas, the terms used here are not altogether satisfactory, in part because of the lack of uniform terminology in this field. For example, while age norms are in some respects related to "attitudinal" and "doctrinal" conformity as posed by Robert K. Merton ("Social Conformity, Deviation, and Opportunity Structures: A Comment on the Contributions of Dubin and Cloward," *American Sociological Review*, XXIV [1959], 177–189), these data do not fit that analytical framework because age norms are

less clear-cut than the norms Merton discusses, and the realms of attitudinal and doctrinal conformity are less prescribed.

Similarly, the projection of personal attitudes upon the generalized other has been studied by Jacob W. Getzels and J. J. Walsh ("The Method of Paired Direct and Projective Questionnaires in the Study of Attitude Structure and Socialization," *Psychological Monographs*, Vol. LXXVII [Whole No. 454, 1958]); but their theoretical model is not altogether applicable because in the present research the phenomenon of projection cannot be demonstrated. The same lack of fit exists with the concepts used by Milton Rokeach, *The Open and Closed Mind* (New York: Basic Books, 1960); and with the concepts of social norms, norms of common consent, and personal norms as used by Elizabeth Bott, *Family and Social Network* (London: Tavistock, 1957). The *self, generalized other* terminology is therefore regarded as the most appropriate for describing the present data.

9. Floyd H. Allport, *Social Psychology* (Boston: Houghton Mifflin, 1924).

VI

LIVING ARRANGEMENTS

Living arrangements are more diverse for elderly Americans than for younger individuals. Like most younger adults, most older people live independently in single-family homes or apartments. However, substantial numbers, particularly the very old, share homes with children, other relatives, or friends. Some move to retirement communities or live year round in recreational vehicles; others live in congregate facilities that offer a range of services to their residents. Among widows, when physical frailty overwhelms the resources of their support networks of family and friends, the result is often a move to a nursing home. And, although no reliable estimate of their numbers exists, for some elderly people there is no home at all—they are among the nation's homeless (Population Reference Bureau, 1986). In the first reading of this section, Stephen Golant provides an overview of the living arrangements of elderly Americans.

RESIDENT OWNERS

Most older people fervently hope to remain independent householders. For many that dream has been realized. Between 1940 and 1980, homeownership among those 65 to 74 increased from 48 to 70 percent (Chevan, 1987). By 1987, 75 percent of the over-65 population lived in owner-occupied homes (Siegel, 1993). The ethic of independent home residence is so deeply ingrained, and the symbolic importance of remaining in one's home so strong, that even when the homes of the elderly are small and defective, most report that their homes meet their needs and that they have no desire to move (Montgomery, Stubbs, and Day, 1980). Over 90 percent of older homeowners have paid off their mortgages (Struyk, 1987), and their homes are their single largest asset.

Although, on the whole, the housing units occupied by older persons are of similar quality to those of younger persons, this is not true for the rural elderly. Older people who live in rural areas are more likely to live in deficient housing than are younger rural residents (Siegel, 1993). And elderly married-couple households occupy housing of better quality than other elderly households (Soldo, 1981).

CHALLENGES FOR RESIDENT HOMEOWNERS

Despite the advantages of owning one's own home, ownership can pose a number of disadvantages as people grow older. One disadvantage for older resident homeowners is that they may find themselves *overhoused*. As people age in place after other family members have died or moved away, they remain in dwellings that are more suitable for a large family than a single individual (Siegel, 1993). And the older the occupant, the older the housing unit is likely to be. Larger than necessary, older homes can mean high maintenance costs; this presents a challenge for older people living on fixed incomes. For other elderly people, remaining in the same home throughout old age poses other problems. For example, the physical decline that often accompanies old age may mean that, for some householders, their traditional home has physical barriers that make daily activities difficult. If an elderly person has mobility problems, ramps instead of stairways and hand grips in bathrooms may be necessary for safe movement; however, these renovations can be expensive and beyond the means of those who are "asset rich but income poor older owners" (Struyk and Soldo, 1980).

REVERSE ANNUITY MORTGAGES

Reverse annuity mortgage programs are recent innovations that allow elderly homeowners to supplement their current incomes by tapping into the equity of their homes. Typically, the lender takes title to the home; in return, the homeowner receives a monthly payment from the lender and remains in the house until he or she dies. Once that happens, the house is sold. The lender then retires the loan and receives a portion of the home's appreciated value. It is important to note that reverse annuity mortgages primarily benefit middle-class and upper-class whites whose properties are in neighborhoods desirable to mortgage lenders (Siegel, 1993). Although reverse annuity mortgages offer substantial potential to help elderly homeowners remain financially independent and in their own homes, institutional barriers to reverse mortgages still exist, and many older people are reluctant to encumber their estates (Jacobs, 1986).

RENTERS

Although most elderly Americans own their own homes, a substantial minority rent their accommodations. Because rents are likely to be raised periodically, they strain the resources of individuals on fixed budgets. Since renters do not control the buildings in which they live, they may be forced to move if their landlord sells their building or converts it to condominiums. Renters' annual housing costs represent a substantially larger share of household income than is the case for homeowners. Among the lowest income elderly, over half of their annual income goes for rent (Siegel, 1993).

The second reading of this section focuses on some of the housing problems faced by the elderly. In a chapter from his book *Risking Old Age in America*, Richard Margolis emphasizes the critical shortage of adequate housing assistance for elderly individuals. The struggles faced by the men and women Margolis interviewed for his book underscore the shortcomings of national housing policy in the United States.

REFERENCES

Chevan, Albert. "Homeownership in the Older Population: 1940–1980." *Research on Aging* 9, no. 2 (1987): 226–280.

Jacobs, Bruce. "The National Potential of Home Equity Conversion." *The Gerontologist* 26 (1986): 496–504.

Montgomery, James E.; Alice C. Stubbs; and Savannah S. Day. "The Housing Environment of the Rural Elderly." *The Gerontologist* 20 (1980): 444–451.

Population Reference Bureau. "Counting The U.S.'s Homeless." *Population Today* 14, no. 10 (1986): 86–91.

Siegel, Jacob S. *A Generation of Change: A Profile of America's Older Population.* New York: Russell Sage Foundation, 1993.

Soldo, Beth J. "The Living Arrangements of the Elderly in the Near Future." Pp. 491–512 in Sara B. Kiesler et al. (eds.), *Aging: Social Change.* New York: Academic Press, 1981.

Struyk, Raymond J. 1987. "The Economic Behavior of Elderly People in Housing Markets." *Housing Studies* 2, no. 4 (1987): 221–236.

Struyk, Raymond J., and Beth J. Soldo. *Improving the Elderly's Housing: A Key to Preserving the Nation's Housing Stock and Neighborhoods.* Cambridge, MA: Ballinger, 1980.

14

Problems in Conventional Dwellings and Neighborhoods

STEPHEN GOLANT

Most elderly Americans remain in independent households, living in their own homes and neighborhoods as they age. In this chapter from his book *Housing America's Elderly*, Stephen Golant provides a comprehensive overview of the predominant form of housing for elderly Americans, and the advantages and disadvantages the elderly encounter in conventional dwellings and neighborhoods. He highlights the diversity of living arrangements among the elderly and underscores potential problems for elderly people living in conventional housing.

Older Americans are attributed with having a wide range of residential problems—from dwellings in physical disrepair to difficulties maintaining independent accommodations because of mental and physical impairments. These problems are documented in an eclectic group of sources: scientifically designed research studies, case studies by various advocacy groups, government testimony, private consultants' focus groups, design and market analyses, and a multitude of anecdotal comments from the elderly themselves.

The discussion of these problems will be organized under the following 10 topics:

1. The views and assessments of older people.
2. The physical conditions of dwellings and buildings.
3. The affordability of residential accommodations.
4. The amount of dwelling space used or needed.
5. The distinctive situations of owners and renters.
6. The desirability of the neighborhood.
7. Physical and mental disabilities that threaten independent living.
8. The effects of living alone.
9. Changes in life-style.
10. The housing plight of the socially marginal elderly.

THE VIEWS AND ASSESSMENTS OF OLDER PEOPLE

Why Listen to Older People

It is advantageous to examine first what older people themselves consider are their major housing needs. How older people define and prioritize their problems can help professionals determine which helping strategies will be more positively received and successful. Professionals must recognize, however, that the elderly tend to understate their housing problems and sources of dissatisfaction (Golant, 1986; Lawton, 1985; Rabushka & Jacobs, 1980). Several factors appear to be responsible (Golant, 1984; Lawton, 1977, 1980):

- Older people, like persons of any age, have personalities, life-styles, and capabilities that differently influence what they consider to be significant in their lives. For some elderly, noisy children next door may be a more serious problem than any physical deficiencies afflicting their dwellings. Neighborhood concerns may be greater for elderly who have difficulty getting around and lack automobile transportation. A fear of crime may bring greater consternation to the older woman who lives alone.
- Older people may cope with their problems by denying or ignoring them to make tolerable a living situation from which they see little escape.
- Older people's longtime occupancy in the same place may desensitize them to what were once felt to be deficiencies; they may have accumulated a wealth of positive memories that they draw on to deal with adversity.
- Longtime older residents are thoroughly familiar with all aspects of their dwelling—including the problems. This awareness gives them strong compensating feelings of security and confidence.
- Older people have lowered their expectations and aspirations regarding their prospects of occupying better housing.
- Older people may have strong emotional attachments to their dwellings—whatever the inadequacies.
- Compared to other troublesome aspects of their life—health, income, family affairs—the material problems of the dwelling may be considered minor and relatively insignificant.
- Older people may accept a poorer quality dwelling because of its affordability, which in turn allows them to spend more income on their health or recreation needs.

Two National Assessments

In 1986 and 1989 the American Association of Retired Persons commissioned nationwide surveys of older adults (in 1986 over the age of 59; in 1989 over the age of 54), asking about housing satisfaction and concerns (American Association of Retired Persons, 1990). The findings, summarized in Table 14-1, emphasize that the majority of older people are satisfied with their current housing arrangements. Still, a significant minority is displeased with the high cost of home utilities, property taxes, and homeowner's insurance; the lack of public transportation; and financial security generally (Table 14-2). Topping the list of residential worries are concerns about keeping homes

TABLE 14-1 Housing Satisfaction of the U.S. Elderly (in percentages)

Housing Aspects	Very Satisfied	Somewhat Satisfied	Don't Know	Somewhat Dissatisfied	Very Dissatisfied	Total
Cost of your utilities relative to your income	35	34	5	15	11	100
Cost of your property taxes relative to your income	32	28	19	13	8	100
Availability of public transportation to stores, doctors, relatives, or friends	54	18	14	7	7	100
Cost of homeowners insurance relative to your income	32	36	15	11	6	100
Your financial security in general	41	42	4	8	5	100
Cost of your mortgage or rent payments relative to your income	39	12	44	2	3	100
Neighborhood or location of your home	75	18	0	5	2	100
Physical condition of your home	71	23	0	5	2	100
Your personal security or safety in your home	74	20	1	3	2	100
Type of home you live in— house, apartment, condo, townhouse, or mobile home, etc.	76	19	1	3	1	100
General comfort of your home, heating, lighting, and getting around	80	16	1	2	1	100
Cost of upkeep or maintenance on your home relative to your income	44	33	13	7	3	100

SOURCE: American Association of Retired Persons (1990). Used with permission.

in good condition, failing health, losing independence, having to take care of a sick or impaired loved one, and having to live with other people not of one's choosing. Comparison of the 1986 and 1989 survey responses reveals some clear shifts in perspectives:

- "Older Americans are more likely to want to 'age in place,' with 86% of those surveyed in 1989 wanting to stay in their present home and never move, compared to 78% in 1986."
- "Respondents in 1989 (40%) are more likely than those in 1986 (32%) to prefer a 'senior citizen' building to one for all age groups. Consistent with this, they are

TABLE 14-2 Housing Concerns of the U.S. Elderly (in percentages)

Housing Concerns	Very Concerned	Somewhat Concerned	Don't Know	Not Too Concerned	Not at All Concerned	Total
Having my health fail	61	19	2	9	9	100
Losing my independence as I grow older	56	18	2	12	12	100
Keeping my home in good condition	59	25	2	7	8	100
Having to live with other people if I don't want to	47	16	3	14	20	100
Having to take care of a loved one if he or she becomes ill	44	21	4	12	19	100
Having to move from my present home	42	19	2	16	21	100
Having to move away from my family and friends	42	17	3	16	22	100
Having enough money to live on	38	25	2	18	17	100
Having to live alone if I don't want to	32	21	3	18	26	100
Leaving something for my family after I am gone	29	22	1	22	26	100
Selling, giving away, or storing my possessions	18	18	3	27	34	100

SOURCE: American Association of Retired Persons (1990). Used with permission.

less likely (31% in 1989 and 41% in 1986) to say they would like to live in a household with people of all ages."

- "Two-thirds (65%) of those in the recent survey anticipate needing help in the future with outdoor maintenance, compared to 40% in 1986. Likewise, over one-half (55%) of those surveyed in 1989 foresee needing assistance in the future with heavy housework, while only one-third (33%) of those in the previous survey anticipated needing such help." (American Association of Retired Persons, 1990, p. 8)

PHYSICAL CONDITIONS OF DWELLINGS AND BUILDINGS

Table 14-3 identifies an array of physical conditions that can jeopardize the health, safety, and security of older residents, making it difficult or uncomfortable for them to occupy and use their residential accommodations (Hiatt, 1985, 1990; Lawton, 1975; Regnier & Pynoos, 1987). A home accident often signals to family members that their loved one's ability to live independently is in jeopardy. Although physical frailty and sensory problems (e.g., difficulty seeing) are key predisposing factors, unsafe home features are often responsible. Accidents represent the fifth leading cause of death for persons over age 65. They predominantly occur in the home and primarily result from

TABLE 14-3 Housing-Related Problems of the U.S. Elderly

Physical Health Problems of Dwelling or Building

Dwelling lacks workable plumbing facilities
Dwelling lacks adequate provision for sewage disposal
Dwelling lacks some or all kitchen facilities
Inadequate electrical power or outlets
Inadequate heating or air conditioning systems
Temperature of one or more rooms is too hot or too cold
Poor room ventilation
Poorly insulated walls or windows
Excessive room drafts
Presence of insects or rodents

Safety Problems in Dwelling or Building

Slippery walking/standing surfaces (e.g., floors, tubs, doormats), especially in bathroom
  and kitchen
Lack of grab bars to maintain balance in bathrooms
Torn or worn carpeting, unsecured throw rugs, turned-up floor materials, raised floor
  tiles, obtrusive thresholds or other floor obstacles contributing to falls
Steep staircases
Tread edges of stairs unclear or confusing
Stair floor coverings with bold geometric patterns are visually confusing
Absence of contrasting colors demarcating edges of steps, doorway entries
Absent or loose railings on stairs
Abruptly changing or uneven floor surfaces
Insufficient light or too much glare leading to falls
Cluttered rooms making maneuvering difficult
Elevator doors close too quickly
Exposed electrical outlets, wires, inappropriate light bulb wattage
Fuses or circuit breakers blow frequently
Deteriorated or faulty electrical wiring
Unsafe stove or burner design
Unsafe fireplaces, space heaters
No simple means in apartment units or public areas to get help in case of emergency
Window or door exits of dwelling blocked or difficult to open or manipulate
Inadequate electronically monitored smoke/fire alarms
Protruding sharply cornered counter edges
Building management neglects or ignores maintenance needs of residents (e.g., upkeep
  of common areas)

Security Problems of Dwelling or Building

Poor defenses against home break-ins (e.g., inadequate or inoperational locks on doors
  or windows, breakable door glass)
Outside design of house and/or landscaping facilitates hiding by prowlers
Semiprivate spaces such as mail areas, elevators, laundry rooms, lobbies, outside parking areas, and outside recreational areas are poorly lit and vulnerable to the
  intrusion of dangerous outsiders

(continued)

TABLE 14-3   (Continued)

Security Problems of Dwelling or Building (Continued)

Resident unable to screen visitors to home without opening door
Lack of outside private, secured areas for socializing or recreation
Lack of electronically monitored security/intercom system or full-time security staff

Use or Accessibility Problems in Dwelling or Building

Plumbing controls, kitchen appliances, cabinets, mailbox, electrical outlets,
    thermostats, emergency call buttons, cupboard shelves, or counters not easy to reach
    or require bending or stooping
Shelving cannot be adjusted
Poorly marked light switches/electrical outlets or absence of night lights
Kitchen appliance dials, faucets difficult to read
Telephone unavailable or difficult to use
Design of seats (chairs, sofas, toilets, etc.) or bed makes getting up or sitting down
    difficult
Tub or shower difficult to get into or out of
Utensils, food containers, appliances, cupboards, lamps, windows, doorknobs, faucets,
    or other residential objects are difficult to turn on, open, or manipulate
Insufficient storage/shelf/counter space for food, clothing, cleaning supplies, prosthetics
Insufficient space to administer in-home care
Floors or walls difficult to clean
Difficulty moving from one part of the house to another because of the presence of
    steps/stairs (e.g., two-story dwelling's entry way has several steps above sidewalk
    level)
Difficulty negotiating ramps (in lieu of steps)
Porch area of house one step below main living area
Multistory building lacks operational elevator
Bathroom difficult to reach on second story of house
Floor surface (e.g., thick shag carpet) restricts use of wheelchair or walker
Areas/pathways in dwelling (rooms, hallways, appliances, tables, toilet) are
    inaccessible by wheelchair
Wheelchair maneuverability is difficult (e.g., moving within or between rooms, fitting
    under tables)
Pathways or floors within apartment/townhouse building poorly demarcated
Furniture arrangement restricts mobility
Room design inconsistent with everyday activity patterns
Too much bright light, unshielded light, or glare from natural or artificial lighting
Inadequate light from natural or artifical lighting within dwelling unit, in common
    areas of building, in task performance areas, in outside building areas, and on steps
Inadequate, nonexclusive, or difficult-to-reach parking areas
Outside parking areas difficult to reach or restricted by inclement weather (e.g., icy
    surfaces)

Financial Stress of Housing Costs

Costs of occupying dwelling burdensome (i.e., rent, mortgage payment, property taxes,
    insurance)

(continued)

TABLE 14-3 (Continued)

Financial Stress of Housing Costs (Continued)

Costs of maintaining dwelling in good condition burdensome (i.e., making repairs, replacing outmoded systems such as electrical, heating, plumbing, air conditioning)
Costs of utilities and related structures burdensome (i.e., heating and cooling, replacement or insulation of windows)
Costs of alternative housing options too great (i.e., either in-dwelling modifications or new dwelling opportunities)
Moving costs too high
Costs of home-based or community-based services and benefits too great (e.g., home care, adult day care)
Costs of accessing community-based services too great (i.e., transportation costs)
Cost of living in community or region too high
State or local taxes too high
State inheritance taxes too high

Use or Accessibility Problems in Neighborhood or Community

Inadequate, difficult-to-use, or overly expensive transportation options
Fear or reality of crime prevents or discourages activities outside dwelling
Unsafe (poor walking conditions, too much traffic) streets, walking areas
Lettering for signs or directions difficult to read
Inclement climatic conditions discourage or prevent activities outside the dwelling
Specific home- or community-based services/benefits unavailable or lack openings
Lack of complete or accurate information provided about home- or community-based services and benefits addressing older people's needs
Services/benefits difficult to use because of overly complex or conflicting rules, regulations, standards

Security Problems of Neighborhood or Community

Streets, sidewalks, or pathways unsafe to walk because of threat and reality of criminal activity
Streets, sidewalks, or pathways unsafe to walk because of heavy traffic conditions
Poor street lighting
Abandoned or boarded-up dwellings in immediate neighborhood

Autonomy Problems in Dwelling or Building

Dependence on the regular assistance of others to maintain independent living quarters
Unavailable or inadequate congregate services to facilitate independent living
Unavailable or inadequate personal care services to facilitate independent living
Lack or inadequacy of caregivers (family, friends, acquaintances) in neighborhood or community

Social Problems

Loneliness
Few persons living nearby with similar interests or life-style
Clashes with other occupants in the same dwelling unit that derive from personality or life-style differences (e.g., home-sharing arrangements involving strangers or family)

(continued)

TABLE 14-3 (Continued)

Social Problems (Continued)

Other residents in building or neighborhood practicing behaviors or life-style that clash with older resident (e.g., loud stereos, children playing too loudly, drug activity, fighting)

Other household members or housemates cannot serve as confidants

Incompatible neighbors because of income, race/ethnicity, age

Lack of persons living in or near dwelling to provide emotional/psychological supports

Gossiping and nosiness by other building or neighborhood residents

Life-Style Problems

Bad weather (large number of days without sunshine, too much snow, ice, rain)

Urban way of life is considered undesirable

Rural way of life is considered undesirable

Inadequate or poorly organized neighborhood- or community-based group activities (e.g., bingo, exercise, religious activities, adult education classes, social clubs, and discussion groups)

Inadequate opportunities to pursue leisure or recreational interests

Lack of different or challenging experiences; insufficient stimulation

Aesthetically unattractive dwellings or buildings nearby

Rooms and wall surfaces have drab or dreary appearance

Noxious smells from nearby neighborhood dwellings (e.g., from poor garbage pickup, industrial/commercial land uses)

Too much noise from traffic, other people, commerical/industrial activities

Poor window views of the outside

Background noise (from machines, appliances, heating and ventilating equipment, other people's conversations) preventing hearing of immediate voice conversations or adversely affecting sleep patterns

Unattractive landscaping

Unattractive building lobby

Room sizes too small

Room arrangement inappropriate

Insufficient inside-dwelling space for entertaining

Insufficient display space for knickknacks

Absence of balconies in apartment units

No suitable place in dwelling or building complex to carry out hobbies or other leisure activities

Lack of space or equipment for exercise

Toilet situated outside of bathroom in first-floor living area for accessibility is both visually and olfactorily distasteful

Lack of place for gardening

Lack of places in or around building complex to sit comfortably and to enjoy spontaneous communications with others or to observe the activities of others

Lack of comfortable seating areas immediately outside building

Neighborhood public services poorly maintained

Building management fails to involve or elicit the views of building's residents in management policies and "building rule" decisions (e.g., decoration of public areas)

Rental building converted to condominiums necessitates involuntary relocation falls on stairways, floors, and bathtubs (Pynoos, Cohen, Davis, & Bernhardt, 1987; Tinetti, Speechley, & Ginter, 1988). Older women are at greater risk because of their involvement with household duties. Accidents also result from burns or scalds from fires, hot liquids such as hot water and grease, and hot surfaces (e.g., heaters). Accidental poisoning from medication now ranks third among the most prevalent home accidents (Czaja & Guerrier, 1991).

Older people's occupancy of older dwellings places them at greater risk of experiencing physical deficiencies. As of 1987 about 3 out of every 10 older households were living in housing built before 1940, over 41% in housing built before 1950. Elderly homeowners are especially likely to occupy such older housing (U.S. Bureau of the Census, 1990a). The tendency of older people to stay put largely accounts for their living in older housing. Over 40% of elderly homeowners have not relocated in over 30 years and almost 25% of elderly renters have lived in their same buildings for over 15 years (U.S. Bureau of the Census, 1990a).

Studies that have estimated the extent to which older people occupy housing with physical deficiencies have largely depended on data from the American Housing Survey. Now conducted nationally every 2 years by the U.S. Bureau of the Census (1990a), this survey is administered to a scientifically selected sample of U.S. households of all age groups and contains a comprehensive set of enumerator-based assessments of both dwellings and neighborhoods. Estimates of poor housing conditions depend largely on what groupings of indicators are used to define deficiencies or problems (Table 14-4). A report by two nonprofit organizations (Lazere, Leonard, Dolbeare, & Zigas, 1991) found that in 1989 16% of elderly households living below the poverty level occupied physically deficient housing, compared with 6% of nonpoor elderly households. A U.S. Congressional Budget Office study (1988) found that in 1985 10% of elderly renters and 4% of elderly homeowners (or 5.4% of both groups) lived in dwellings that required rehabilitation. In an earlier analysis of 1983 data, Struyk, Turner, and Ueno (1988) reported that about 11% of elderly renters and 7% of elderly owners (8.3% of both groups) occupied physically deficient housing.

Along with renters being more likely than owners to live in physically deficient housing, most studies agree that certain subgroups of elderly are more likely to live in poor housing. These include the oldest (over age 75), minority groups (especially African-Americans but also Hispanics), single-person as opposed to married households, rural dwellers, and the very low income elderly (Redfoot & Gaberlavage, 1991). On a more positive note, during the late 1970s and the 1980s, smaller percentages of older people—both owners and renters—were reported to be occupying physically deficient housing (Redfoot & Gaberlavage, 1991; Struyk et al., 1988).

AFFORDABILITY OF RESIDENTIAL ACCOMMODATIONS

The Economic Status of the Elderly Population

Various factors contribute to the financial difficulties of older people. Low lifetime earnings and a failure to save adequately for retirement are prime causes. But even those with initially adequate postretirement savings may experience financial hardship—a result of living longer than actuarially expected, increases in the cost of living,

TABLE 14-4 Indicators Identifying Dwellings in Poor Physical Condition

House or building boarded up, sagging roof, missing roof materials, holes in roof,
    missing wall or siding materials, broken windows, or crumbling foundations
Lack of complete kitchen facilities (installed sink, fridge, oven/burners)
Lack of complete plumbing facilities (hot/cold piped water, flush toilet, shower/bath)
No conventional means of sewage disposal
Room heater (gas, oil, kerosene) without vent or flue or no heating equipment
No air conditioning of any kind
Water leaks into dwelling from outdoors in past 12 months
Open cracks or holes in inside walls or ceiling or holes in floors
Walls with broken plaster or peeling paint over one square foot
Signs of rats or mice in house or building in past 90 days
Faulty electrical outlets, blown fuses, or exposed electrical wire
Inside water leaks in past 12 months
Two or more water breakdowns of 6 hours or more in past 90 days
Two or more toilet breakdowns of 6 hours or more in past 90 days
Two or more sewer breakdowns of 6 hours or more in past 90 days
No working elevator in building where dwelling unit is two or more floors up or down
Some or all of building's public hall light fixtures are not working
Loose, broken, or missing steps in common hallways of building
Missing or poorly attached railings on common stairways

SOURCE: U.S. Bureau of the Census (1990a).

and large medical and long-term health care costs. The death of a spouse may create money problems when life insurance coverage fails to compensate for lost income.

Although the majority (over 80%) of older homeowners no longer have mortgage payments to make, they nonetheless must deal with property taxes, utility costs, insurance, and home repair, all very sensitive to inflation. The upkeep and maintenance costs of homeownership can be especially burdensome to older persons who need to hire outside labor. They also may have high residential energy expenditures because of their need to compensate for their greater sensitivity to very cold or hot weather. Heating costs during the winter months in particular can consume a high percentage of the fixed monthly incomes of elderly solely dependent on Social Security benefits or on Supplemental Security Income (especially the unmarried). The elderly may also be especially vulnerable because they are living in older dwellings that are poorly weatherized and are heated by energy-inefficient equipment (National Consumer Law Center, 1989).

Renters are not immune from these trends. They also must confront the prospects of steady rent increases and rising utility bills. During the 1980s the older renter population consisted increasingly of the very poor, the very old, and racial and ethnic minorities. During this period the financial difficulties of low-income older renters were accentuated by the shrinking number of affordable rental units (Redfoot & Gaberlavage, 1991), reflecting the removal from the housing stock of the most deteriorated (and least expensive) rental apartments and the rise in construction costs and borrowing rates that put a large share of newly built rental housing out of economic reach. Projections for the 1990s suggest that the low construction rate of unsubsidized housing charging lower rents is likely to exacerbate the problems of this group (Apgar, Di Pasquale, Cummings, & McArdle, 1991).

Generalizations about the availability of alternative elderly housing options in most communities must necessarily be cognizant of these economic realities. When most advocates speak of the lack of adequate housing accommodations for older people, they necessarily imply the inadequacy of *affordable* housing accommodations. Robert Atchley expressed the problem this way:

> In areas of life where there is sufficient profit to be made, private enterprise serves us very well. As a result, people in the upper third of the income distribution have few serious difficulties purchasing the housing they need. As we go down the income ladder, however, the prices people can afford to pay for rent simply will not provide the return on investment necessary to attract private capital to construct or operate housing. (American Society on Aging, 1989, p. 3)

Even this generalization oversimplifies. When we examine the availability of affordable housing options for older people, the lowest-income elderly are sometimes less disadvantaged than moderate-income elderly. This somewhat topsy-turvy situation occurs because it is usually only the poorest elderly who can qualify for many government-sponsored subsidized housing and service programs. In contrast, those who have incomes just above poverty levels find they cannot afford private-sector alternatives, yet their modest incomes disqualify them from receiving most government benefits.

Economic Patterns and the Incidence of Elderly in Costly Housing

Insights into the economic status of older people are summarized in Tables 14-5, 14-6, and 14-7. Older persons who are chronologically older and unmarried have especially low monthly incomes. Other disadvantaged elderly subgroups are listed in Table 14-6. But as Tables 14-5 and 14-7 reveal, monthly income statistics offer only an incomplete look at the elderly population's economic well-being. The equity that most older people have in their homes is an important source of their wealth. In this regard, African-Americans and Hispanics are especially disadvantaged.

The aforementioned nonprofit organization study (Lazere et al., 1991) found that in 1989 60% of elderly renters and 22% of elderly homeowners were paying more than 30% of their income on their housing costs. The U.S. Congressional Budget Office study (1988) reported the comparable figures of 58% and 23% for the year 1985. These and other studies (e.g., Apgar et al., 1991; Redfoot & Gaberlavage, 1991; Struyk et al., 1988) have shown that both owners and renters who are very poor, owners who still are paying off their mortgages, and African-American and Hispanic minority groups are especially likely to live in overcostly housing.

These studies may still be understating the size of the elderly population experiencing financial burdens. They do not consider homeowners who have to make large one-time expenditures, such as for a new roof or new heating system, and large out-of-pocket home care and medical costs. They also hide the extent to which some elderly occupants cope with inadequate funds by not using electricity (heating, lamps, stoves,

TABLE 14-5 Wealth of U.S. Households, 1988

Population Group	Median Monthly Income	Median Net Worth Including Home Equity	Median Net Worth Excluding Home Equity
Age			
Under 35	$2,000	$6,078	$3,258
35–44	2,500	33,181	8,993
45–54	2,604	57,466	15,542
55–64	2,071	80,032	26,396
65–69	1,497	83,478	27,482
70–74	1,330	82,111	28,172
75+	977	61,491	18,819
65+	1,211	73,471	23,856
Elderly (65+) Households			
Married couple	1,733	124,419	45,890
Unmarried males	1,023	48,863	15,914
Unmarried females	780	47,233	10,693

SOURCE: U.S. Bureau of the Census (1990b).

etc.) to the detriment of their health. They also gloss over the variable costs of living in different places.

At the same time, estimates of financial burden may be overstated because of inadequate assessments of the economic worth or wealth of elderly persons (Table 14-7) or their in-kind benefits (e.g., food stamps, Medicare assistance). One study (Radner, 1987) estimated that unearned income by the elderly population may be underreported by 20% to 50%.

TABLE 14-6 Percentage of Selected U.S. Age 65+ Population Groups Below the Poverty Level, 1989

Characteristics	Percent
Black women living alone	60.6
African-Americans	30.8
Women living alone	23.3
Living alone	22.0
Not completed high school	20.7
Hispanics	20.6
All persons 85+	18.5
Nonmetropolitan	15.4
Women	14.0
Central city	13.8
All persons 65 and older	11.4

SOURCE: U.S. Senate, American Association of Retired Persons, Federal Council on the Aging, and U.S. Administration on Aging (1991).

TABLE 14-7 Composition of U.S. Elderly Households' Net Worth, 1988 (in percentages)

Total net worth	100.0
Own home	40.4
Interest-earning assets	29.2
Rental property/other real estate	9.3
Stocks/mutual fund shares	8.2
Other financial investments*	3.5
Vehicles	3.1
Business or profession	3.0
IRA or KEOGH accounts	2.8
U.S. savings bonds	0.6
Checking accounts	0.5
Unsecured liabilities**	−0.5

*Includes mortgages held from sale of real estate, amount due from sale of business and unit trusts.

**Because net worth is the value of assets less liabilities, unsecured liabilities are subtracted from the distribution of net worth and are shown as negative.

SOURCE: U.S. Bureau of the Census (1990b).

THE AMOUNT OF DWELLING SPACE USED AND NEEDED

Because older people do not always relocate in response to the shrinking size of their households (e.g., after children leave, spouse dies), they often occupy dwellings that are identified as excessively large. This can result in larger than necessary housing expenses (e.g., excessive cooling, heating, maintenance and repair expenses, everyday upkeep and housekeeping, larger insurance and property tax bills). From a societal perspective, these older residents are also restricting the housing opportunities of younger and larger families who could better utilize these larger homes.

One study (Lane & Feins, 1985) estimated that over one-third of U.S. elderly households are overhoused; that is, they had at least one extra bedroom and more than two extra nonsleeping rooms given the size of their household (e.g., a single woman living in a two-bedroom house with kitchen, living room, and dining room; or a married couple in a three-bedroom house with kitchen, living room, dining room, and family room). Predictably, older widows living alone are the most likely to occupy such overhoused accommodations.

The characterization of older people as overhoused should not be overstated, however. The costs of maintaining these dwellings—because of their low monthly rent or paid-up mortgage—may still be less than if they moved to smaller accommodations. Furthermore, their life-style may demand extra rooms to accommodate return visits by children or a home office, a hobby room, a place to display belongings, or storage. The potential also exists for the so-called surplus space to be used for an in-law suite or accessory apartment. Finally, the emotional attachments formed in a familiar house might simply override the disadvantages of excessive space. As to the argument that others might better utilize the space, few guarantees exist that subsequent nonelderly occupants might not themselves also live in overhoused situations (Lane & Feins, 1985).

DISTINCTIVE PROBLEMS OF OWNERS AND RENTERS

Homeownership Prevails

As of 1990, 75.5% of older households owned their dwelling. The homeownership rate of the married elderly was 89%, dropping to 63% for the unmarried. Of the age 65 to 74 group, 79% were owners; of those 75 and over, 71% were owners (Apgar et al., 1991). Elderly homeownership rates are especially high in suburban (80%) as opposed to central city locations (64%; U.S. Bureau of Census, 1990a). Historically, elderly homeownership has steadily increased, up from around 70% during the 1960s.

Being in Control

The need to feel in control of one's life is especially important in old age (Langer, 1983). This control is often more available to homeowners than renters. For example, the homeowner can personally regulate the heat and air conditioning of his or her dwelling, alter its physical layout or design, and choose who will inherit the property. The ability to take care of a home is perceived as evidence of continued personal capabilities. The homeowner can also ignore the visible signs of an aging and deteriorated housing unit, avoid dealing with the unwelcome vigilance of an apartment landlord, and escape from the numerous restrictions found in a renter's lease.

However unrealistic it might be, older homeowners find considerable comfort in their belief that they can remain "forever" in their current residence. In contrast, the continued occupancy status of the older renter is always in doubt, subject to the whims of the landlord who chooses not to renew the lease or to renew it with such an exorbitant increase in rent that relocation is the only alternative. Renters also face the prospect that their long-occupied apartment buildings will be converted to condominiums, leaving them to choose between the two undesirable alternatives of the formidable cost of ownership or the disruption of relocation.

The owner's fear of impoverishment and financial dependence may also be considerably less than a renter's. Because most elderly homeowners own their home free and clear, they always consider that they have the option, however unrealistic, of selling or refinancing their dwellings to realize a major source of income.

Homeownership may better buttress older persons from the sense of loss they experience after retirement or the death of a spouse. Homeownership in the United States is clearly linked with achievement and social status. Thus it may provide an important material basis by which the elderly person can maintain a positive self-image in the face of personal adversities.

By the same token, homeownership can accentuate one's sense of vulnerability. Because of the usual problems that beset older dwellings, elderly homeowners may confront a greater share of shelter problems than older renters. Older people who lack either the personal energy or finances to remedy such deficiencies can become enslaved to their dwelling. If homeownership crises occur unexpectedly and too frequently, this form of residential tenure will only confirm the uncertainties and vulnerabilities of old age. In contrast, the competence of older renters may be enhanced by a vigilant, thoughtful, and helpful landlord or building superintendent.

Unique Problems of Condominium and Cooperative Residents

At the end of the 1980s, 5% of elderly households were living in condominiums or co-operatives. Most (about 82%) were homeowners (U.S. Bureau of the Census, 1990a).

Although their ownership rights differ in some important respects, both condo and coop residents have two occupancy characteristics in common (Clurman, Jackson, & Hebard, 1984). First, they live in some type of multiple-unit building complex, such as a low-rise or high-rise building or a cluster of townhouses or mobile homes. Second, although they hold ownership rights to their dwelling unit, they share ownership (with the other condo or coop residents) of common facilities, such as the lobby, hallways, exterior walls and roof, the grounds, parking areas, utility buildings, and inside and outside recreational and social areas. Typically, each dwelling occupant pays a monthly fee for the daily maintenance and insurance protection of these common areas. Some part of the monthly maintenance fee may also be placed in a reserve fund to cover the costs of large or unusual maintenance expenses (e.g., replacing the building's roof, repainting the building's hallways, or replacing the carpeting in the common areas).

Older people attracted to condo or coop living obtain relief from homeowner tasks such as cutting grass, removing snow, removing garbage, cleaning a pool, and fixing leaking pipes or a damaged roof. This relief, however, comes only with a price. Inevitably, they sacrifice some of their individual rights, because the care and upkeep of the building's common areas are no longer under their exclusive control. Residents may disagree about the necessity of repainting a recreation area, resurfacing the parking lot, or enlarging a swimming pool deck. A building's everyday upkeep and maintenance may seem shabby. Residents may face restrictions regarding the kinds of physical modifications they can make to their dwellings (e.g., enlarging doors for a wheelchair, knocking out an interior wall) and to whom they can sell their units. They may disagree with rules that prevent them from having pets, guests, or a permanent live-in helper.

Monthly housing costs may also be more unpredictable. Although a condominium's monthly maintenance fee may steadily increase over time because of the usual inflationary increases, costs may also increase because of poor management decisions or the greater physical upkeep and maintenance demands of an aging building. Residents may be required to make large extra payments to cover the costs of these periodic maintenance problems when the building's reserve funds are insufficient. If these charges are too frequent, some occupants may find themselves financially stressed.

Ironically, some of the dissatisfactions experienced by elderly condo or coop occupants may have little to do with their unique ownership arrangements, but result from living in a high-rise, multifamily building. Older people who have been homeowners most of their lives may find that apartment living requires them to tolerate higher noise levels, unfriendly or incompatible neighbors, insect problems (as in the case of living next door to someone with an infested apartment), or sharing common facilities such as a laundry room. Inevitably, residents lose some control over their living arrangements.

Older persons who purchase a coop or condo unit that was converted from a rental building face other potential problems. They may find that the developer has shoddily upgraded and remodeled the building, is unwilling to remedy renovation-related problems, and has underestimated the monthly assessments.

THE DESIRABILITY OF THE NEIGHBORHOOD

Older people themselves link the inappropriateness of their neighborhoods to the following six factors (Carp & Carp, 1982; Golant, 1984a; Struyk & Soldo, 1980; Ward, LaGory, & Sherman, 1988):

1. A poor location, in which it is difficult and inconvenient to reach leisure and recreational opportunities and needed services and facilities
2. Alternative transportation options, namely transit and walking access, unavailable or inconvenient for nondrivers
3. Lack of nearby (in the same neighborhood) alternative housing arrangements that would be more compatible with changing life-styles and capabilities
4. Displeasure over the kind of people who live nearby
5. High crime levels
6. Poorly maintained houses and apartments that are in violation of building codes, vacant or abandoned buildings, the encroachment of noxious nonresidential land uses (bars, strip joints), trash or litter, and the absence of dependable public services (e.g., garbage collection, sidewalk repair, police and fire protection)

Some of these problems are familiar consequences of declining neighborhoods that have lost their social and economic desirability. A very different set of problems may beset older residents whose neighborhoods have become revitalized or gentrified and have attracted younger, middle-class professionals as residents (Varady, 1986). Some argue that older residents in these rejuvenated neighborhoods suffer from these revitalization efforts. Apartment rents, property taxes, and the costs of everyday neighborhood goods and services often increase. In the face of large rent increases, outright eviction, or the conversion of their rental apartments to unaffordable condominiums, older people may be forced to move (Stegman, 1986). This leads not only to the destruction of important place attachments but to the usual difficulties associated with trying to find comparably priced housing elsewhere. Even if they are able to afford the higher cost of residential living, some of their close friends and neighbors will have left the area. Alternatively, they may need to deal with new neighbors with different life-styles and social values.

Actual findings as to how a revitalized neighborhood impacts its elderly residents are mixed and sometimes difficult to interpret. Some studies demonstrate that significant numbers of older people (estimates reach as high as 30%) are displaced from their long-standing dwellings as a result of events linked to revitalization. But not all researchers agree. Varady (1986), for example, argues that the elderly are not disproportionately displaced, maintain their neighborly ties, and do not experience excessive increases in their housing expenses. Rather, the majority of older people welcome the positive changes associated with revitalization efforts (Zais & Thibodeau, 1983).

Such optimistic findings are discounted by critics who emphasize that the most disenfranchised elderly have already left their dwellings before the commencement of any study. Proponents of revitalization retort that without rejuvenation, the neighborhood would decline to a point at which most elderly residents would have to move anyway because of building decay, disinvestment, abandonment, and an exceptionally hostile living environment.

PHYSICAL AND MENTAL DISABILITIES
THAT THREATEN INDEPENDENT LIVING

Substantial percentages of older people are afflicted by such chronic conditions as arthritis (48%), hypertension (38%), hearing impairments (29%), heart disease (28%), physical deformities (16%), cataracts (16%), chronic sinusitis (15%), and diabetes (9%) (U.S. Senate, Special Committee on Aging, 1991). Over 6% of the aged 75 and older population has some trouble controlling bowel or bladder movements. Symptoms of depression affect as many as 15% of the elderly (U.S. Senate et al., 1991). Over 4% of the community-residing elderly and almost a quarter of the disabled elderly (i.e., with one or more ADL or IADL disabilities—see below and next section) suffer from cognitive impairments—deficits of perception, thinking, and memory (Spector, 1991, p. 54). These result from Alzheimer's disease and other dementias, Parkinson's disease, strokes and aphasia, along with lifelong impairments such as mental retardation. Some estimates of the incidence of Alzheimer's disease among the elderly residing in the community are especially high—more than 10% (Evans et al., 1989).

Although these health problems are closely linked to the incidence of physician visits, hospital stays, and mortality, they inadequately predict older people's ability to live independently. As Leon and Lair (1990) put it: "There is no direct correspondence between the presence of chronic illness and a person's ability to function" (p. 4).

Recognizing that level of functioning is a more important basis for measuring the capacity for independent living, professionals have focused on the extent to which older people with mental or physical health problems have more difficulty performing activities within two broad categories: *activities of daily living* (ADLs) and *instrumental activities of daily living* (IADLs) (Short & Leon, 1990). ADLs include bathing, dressing, toileting, feeding, transferring from a bed or chair, and walking; IADLs include using the telephone, shopping for personal items, transportation, managing money, light housework, and preparing meals. As the number of either ADLs or IADLs increases, a person is considered more dependent. Dependencies in IADLs are considered less serious than dependencies in ADLs.

These functional difficulties not only threaten older people's ability to live autonomously and increase their reliance on others, but they also increase their risk of having various of the housing problems identified in Table 14-3 (Newman, 1990). That is, they will have more difficulty obtaining everyday ordinary goods and services, will be more vulnerable to accidents within and outside the home (Tinetti, Speechley, & Ginter, 1988), will have greater difficulty using or accessing their dwellings or the facilities and services in their community, and will be easier prey for the criminal element.

Disabilities can increase the real housing costs of older residents. They may require hired labor to perform repairs or maintenance previously done by themselves or find it necessary to modify their dwellings to help them compensate for their disabilities. Dwelling modifications may be relatively minor—as in installing more reachable cupboards—or quite substantial—as in the instance of converting space in the dwelling into an accessory apartment or in-law suite to allow a housemate to live in the same house.

The social lives of older people may also be adversely affected. Along with not being able to get out of the house as frequently to socialize, older people may also find that their disabilities have made them less desirable friends or neighbors. Greater loneliness may result. Relationships with family members may suffer because the usual parent-child relationship becomes reversed. The children increasingly perform as caregivers and the parents become dependents.

When their physical or mental impairments become unmanageable, older people may have to leave long-occupied homes and seek more appropriate accommodations. This may be a cause of stress and anxiety, especially if such a move is involuntarily imposed without adequate preparation or planning (Pastalen, 1983). Indeed, the mere anticipation of moving to alternative quarters may have a negative impact on an individual's psychological well-being (Tobin & Lieberman, 1976).

The Incidence of Older People's Impairments

Tables 14-8 to 14-11 summarize the incidence of functional impairments among the U.S. elderly who are not living in institutions (e.g., nursing homes). The patterns are mostly self-evident, but the following points deserve emphasis (Leon & Lair, 1990):

1. About 13% of the noninstitutionalized elderly population has difficulty with at least one ADL task or in walking (Table 14-9).
2. Only a small percentage of this group can perform these tasks or walking without help.
3. Help usually involves assistance from other people, especially for bathing or dressing; only a minority of older people can function with the help of equipment alone.
4. The most frequent difficulties are with bathing and walking.
5. Performing these common everyday activities becomes more difficult with increasing age, especially after age 85.
6. Almost 18% of the noninstitutionalized elderly population has difficulty with at least one IADL task. The most frequent problems are getting about the community and shopping. Very few older people with IADL difficulties manage without help.
7. Almost 20% of the noninstitutionalized elderly population has difficulty with at least one ADL *or* IADL task.

Along with the very old, certain groups appear to be more at risk of experiencing ADL or IADL difficulties: blacks, the poor, the unmarried without children, and persons living alone (Leon & Lair, 1990).

Focusing only on these functional impairments understates older people's likelihood of experiencing other housing problems by failing to capture age-related physio-

TABLE 14-8 Overall Severity of Functional Impairments of the Noninstitutionalized U.S. Elderly Population by Age and Sex, 1987

Population Group	Number (in thousands)	Percent with at Least One ADL* or IADL** Difficulty	Percent with at Least One ADL* Difficulty	Percent with Number of ADL* Difficulties		
				1	*2 or 3*	*4 or more*
65+	27,909	19.5	11.4	5.2	3.8	2.4
65–69	9,361	9.9	5.9	2.4	2.1	1.3
70–74	7,525	13.2	7.9	3.4	3.0	1.5
75–79	5,389	19.9	11.5	6.2	3.3	2.0
80–84	3,361	34.1	18.6	8.0	7.5	3.2
85+	2,274	56.8	34.5	15.6	9.7	9.2
Males						
65–69	4,097	8.0	5.0	1.7	1.8	1.4
70–74	3,359	9.2	6.3	2.3	2.3	1.7
75–79	2,167	15.5	8.7	4.2	2.7	1.8
80–84	1,175	29.5	17.4	7.4	6.6	3.4
85+	743	51.5	26.3	13.0	9.2	4.1
Females						
65–69	5,264	11.3	6.5	2.9	2.4	1.3
70–74	4,165	16.5	9.2	4.3	3.5	1.3
75–79	3,222	22.9	13.3	7.6	3.7	2.0
80–84	2,186	36.6	19.3	8.3	7.9	3.1
85+	1,531	59.3	38.4	16.9	9.9	11.7

*Activity of Daily Living.
**Instrumental Activity of Daily Living.
SOURCE: Leon and Lair (1990).

logical decrements predisposing the older person to physical injury. For example, physical changes in the eyes often distort vision and impair perception of height, width, and depth (e.g., the depth and height of stairs or uneven sidewalk surfaces). Because older persons may also experience decreased sensitivity to contrast (as between colors or between light and dark), signs may be more difficult to read or stairs more difficult to negotiate. These visual problems may make driving more difficult, increase the risk of home accidents, and increase older people's fears about tripping or falling, in turn leading to their unconsciously limiting their activities (Tinetti et al., 1988). Age-related hearing losses may limit older people's acquisition or understanding of new information relevant to their maintaining independent living quarters. The frequency of their social contacts may also decline because their friends or family suddenly find them to be withdrawn or uncommunicative.

These national impairment studies may also understate the impact that cognitive impairments have on living independently. Older people may require greater supervision in their homes (especially if they display wandering or disruptive behaviors) and more reminders to perform their everyday tasks, such as taking their medicines or looking after their hygiene (Kane, Saslow, & Brundage, 1991).

TABLE 14-9 Noninstitutionalized U.S. Elderly Population with Specific Functional Impairments, 1987

Population Category	Aged 65 and Older Population Impaired with Respect to						
	Walking or at Least One ADL*	Bathing	Bed/Chair Transfer	Dressing	Toileting	Feeding	Walking
Number (in thousands)	3,601	2,492	1,635	1,437	975	316	2,152
Percent of non-institutionalized aged 65+ population	12.9	8.9	5.9	5.1	3.5	1.1	7.7

Percent of the Aged 65 and Older Community Population That Is

Functioning without help	1.8	0.9	1.4	0.6	0.2	0.1	0.6
Functioning with help: Equipment only	2.9	1.1	1.1	0.1	0.9	0.0	3.6
Personal assistance only	3.5	4.5	1.7	4.1	0.9	0.6	0.6
Both	4.7	2.4	1.2	0.3	1.0	0.1	1.5
Unable to perform activity with or without help	0.0	0.0	0.5	0.0	0.5	0.3	1.4

*ADLs or Activities of Daily Living include Bathing, Bed/Chair Transfer, Dressing, Toileting, and Feeding; walking or mobility is considered a separate functional impairment category.

SOURCE: Leon and Lair (1990).

ADL and IADL measures may also provide only a partial view of the problems of living independently, because they fail to account for how older people themselves personally interpret and respond to their disabilities. Some older people cling more tenaciously than others to their autonomous way of life.

Events Happening to Other People

If they have the option, most older people deal with their impairments by relying on the personal assistance of others. Many married older persons, for example, feel confident that they can rely on their spouse to assist them if necessary with their usual activities of daily living and home management tasks. They take comfort in knowing someone is available to share both emotional highs and lows. Others have confidence in the help they would receive from other family members—a child or sibling—or an extremely close friend or neighbor. Because they hold these beliefs firmly and confidently, whatever the actual validity, their conception of their own competence be-

TABLE 14-10 Overall Severity of Home Management Impairments of the Noninstitutionalized U.S. Elderly Population by Age and Sex, 1987

Population Group	Number (in thousands)	Percent with at Least One IADL* Difficulty	Percent with Number of IADL* Difficulties		
			1	*2 or 3*	*4 or more*
Total	27,909	17.5	5.0	5.7	6.8
65–69	9,361	8.4	2.7	2.4	3.4
70–74	7,525	11.6	3.5	3.9	4.2
75–79	5,389	17.3	5.7	5.8	5.9
80–84	3,361	31.4	10.0	10.8	10.6
85+	2,274	54.4	10.4	17.3	26.7
Males					
65–69	4,097	6.9	2.3	1.8	2.8
70–74	3,359	7.8	1.7	1.7	4.5
75–79	2,167	12.1	4.5	3.1	4.6
80–84	1,175	25.8	9.4	5.3	11.1
85+	743	50.1	11.9	17.9	20.3
Females					
65–69	5,264	9.5	3.0	2.8	3.7
70–74	4,165	14.7	5.0	5.8	3.9
75–79	3,222	20.8	6.6	7.6	6.7
80–84	2,186	34.4	10.3	13.7	10.4
85+	1,531	56.4	9.7	17.0	29.8

*Instrumental Activity of Daily Living (includes persons with or without ADL and walking problems).
SOURCE: Leon and Lair (1990).

comes inseparably linked with the personal resources of these significant others. The existence of such interindividual alliances helps to explain why the moving away of an only daughter or the death or institutionalization of a spouse constitutes such a devastating experience for some older people and may trigger the onslaught of a whole host of housing-related problems. Part of the individual's basis for autonomy has been ripped away.

Risk of Institutionalization

Most older people and their family members concur in considering the worst housing problem to be the need to move into a nursing home. It is the definitive notice that one has lost the ability to live independently. Currently, about 5% of the U.S. population aged 65 and older is in nursing homes, ranging from 1% of those aged 65–74, to 6% of those aged 75 to 84, to 22% of those aged 85 and over (U.S. Senate, Special Committee on Aging, 1989).

The actual lifetime risk of nursing home occupancy is much greater. About 43% of persons who turn age 65 in 1990 are expected to enter a nursing home at least once before they die (Kemper & Murtaugh, 1991). A majority of this group, however, will oc-

TABLE 14-11 Noninstitutionalized U.S. Elderly Population with Specific Home Management Impairments, 1987

Population Category	Aged 65 and Older Population Impaired with Respect to						
	At Least One IADL*	Use of Telephone	Handling Money	Shopping	Getting About the Community	Preparing Meals	Doing Light House-work
Number (in thousands)	4,884	1,237	1,758	3,072	3,774	2,090	2,823
Percent of noninstitu-tionalized aged 65+ population	17.5	4.4	6.3	11.0	13.5	7.5	10.1

Percent of the Aged 65 and Older Community Population That Is

Functioning without help	1.3	1.1	0.3	0.3	0.6	0.5	0.8
Functioning with help	6.8	1.7	2.8	3.9	8.9	1.9	3.3
Unable to perform activity with or without help	9.4	1.6	3.2	6.8	4.0	5.1	6.0

*IADLs or Instrumental Activities of Daily Living are referred to here as home management tasks.

SOURCE: Leon and Lair (1990).

cupy these institutions for less than one year because they will require only short-term recovery or rehabilitation assistance, they will return to a hospital, or they will die. Most elderly are admitted into a nursing home directly from another health care facility, typically after a short stay in a hospital.

The characteristics of the elderly who are in nursing homes are well known: This population is dominated by very old (over age 80) women, who are living alone, widowed, and white. They require regular assistance with several activities of daily living (especially toileting, feeding, and ambulation) and they are likely to be disoriented or exhibit some memory impairment (afflicting over 60% of nursing home residents). Compared to a decade ago, the elderly population in nursing homes has become older and more physically and mentally impaired, a trend likely to continue.

That a particular subgroup of elderly makes up much of the nursing home population does not necessarily imply that it has a high risk of institutionalization. The elderly population as a whole may simply be numerically dominated by this subgroup so that even a low percentage of its members becoming institutionalized results in a large representation. Several key individual attributes can be identified, however, as "sentinels, markers, risk factors, or predictors" of admittance into a nursing home (Branch, 1984, p. 33).

Representative results come from a Massachusetts study (Branch & Jette, 1982). Those elderly most at risk were very old (aged 80–99), lived alone, used ambulation aids, were mentally disoriented, and needed assistance in performing activities of daily living (ADLs) and instrumental activities of daily living (IADLs). At the same time, this study reported that "elders who are widowed, have no relatives nearby, those with general physical disability, and those who are Medicaid-eligible are at no increased risk of entering a long-term care institution" (p. 1376).

Other studies have shown that the white elderly are at more risk than African-American elderly (Kemper & Murtaugh, 1991; Newman, 1990). Recently hospitalized disabled elderly are also shown to be at greater risk, because of their subsequent need for rehabilitation therapy and a longer recovery period. The elderly person's financial status usually emerges as a relatively small risk factor. Nor are the at-risk elderly more likely to be occupying poorer quality housing, paying off a mortgage (and thus be financially stressed), or living in nonmetropolitan areas where services may be unavailable, inadequate, or inconvenient (Newman, 1990).

Researchers assessing the risk of institutionalization often use sophisticated methodologies. Yet, they have had difficulty identifying accurately those elderly persons most at risk of institutionalization and thus in need of more assistance or supportive residential arrangements. Statistically, the risk predictors have generally explained less than 20% of the variability in the elderly population's nursing home admission rates.

THE EFFECTS OF LIVING ALONE

About 16% of elderly (aged 65 and older) males and 42% of elderly females live alone. It is the dominant living arrangement for women over the age of 75, and well over 50% of this group live alone.

Very different circumstances can produce this outcome: marriage never occurring; divorce or separation in middle or late life; the loss of a spouse in early old age; and the loss of a spouse in late old age. It is likely that the types and incidence of housing problems differ among these groups of the alone, but researchers have not made these distinctions. Unquestionably, however, for this group overall, the prevalence of a whole host of housing-related problems is higher. A study conducted on behalf of the Commonwealth Fund Commission on Elderly People Living Alone (Louis Harris, 1987) concluded:

The elderly person living alone is often a widowed woman in her eighties who struggles alone to make ends meet on a meager income. Being older, she is more likely to be in fair or poor health. She is frequently childless or does not have a son or daughter nearby to provide assistance when needed. Lacking social support, she is at high risk for institutionalization and for losing her independent life style. Finally, like one-half of all elderly people living alone, she may have lived alone for ten years or more.

Many elderly people living alone are poor: One-quarter have incomes below the federal poverty level. The elderly living alone are likely to be dependent on Social Security; overburdened with health care bills; lack pensions; are less likely to own their own home; and are unlikely to be receiving Supplemental Security Income assistance and Medicaid. (p. i)

CHANGES IN LIFE-STYLE

Changing life-style preferences can result in a very different set of residential problems (see Table 14-3). On retirement, older people sometimes find that their leisure and recreational pursuits simply are not compatible with their current residential situations. Moreover, they are no longer required to live in a dwelling accessible to their workplace. Given this new block of unstructured time and a new sense of locational freedom, their long-occupied residence may come under new scrutiny as a place to live.

THE HOUSING PLIGHT OF THE SOCIALLY MARGINAL ELDERLY

The Homeless

The homeless are defined as those persons lacking a permanent residence whose accommodations at night are a public or private emergency shelter or a place not intended to be a shelter, such as a train station. Nationwide, persons over the age of 60 comprise at least 2.5% to 9.0% of the homeless (Institute of Medicine, 1988); some estimates are as high as 19% (Keigher, Berman, & Greenblatt, 1989).

If the elderly population is less likely than other age groups to suffer from homelessness, the reasons are unclear. Perhaps they have lower survival rates or are less apt to seek out emergency shelter and thus are left out of most studies. It may also be that the aged are more likely to have guaranteed minimum government income supports and medical coverage than other age groups, or have more rent-subsidized housing opportunities.

Studies of the elderly homeless have produced conflicting findings, and uncertainty exists whether this group is dominated by men or women, or by younger as opposed to older elderly persons (Cohen & Sokolovsky, 1983; Keigher et al., 1989). Most studies find that elderly African-Americans are overrepresented.

Housing experts and social advocates have argued that a lack of affordable housing (including government-subsidized rental accommodations) is the chief cause of homelessness (U.S. Senate, Special Committee on Aging, 1990). Certainly, housing unavailability is fundamental, but elderly homelessness results from multiple factors. The most important include: extreme poverty; unemployment; impaired mental functioning (mental illness, depression, dementia, alcohol, drug abuse); poor physical health; a paucity of social resources (relatives or friends); a history of evictions, relocations, or emergency shelter episodes; occupancy of rundown housing that is demolished or converted to other uses; the demise of single room occupancy hotels; and the decline in the availability of inexpensive, skid row neighborhood services (e.g., slop joints, used clothing stores).

One common situation is described below (Lurie, 1989):

> Tom, a retired sailor, is 75 years old. He had been living on his pension in a hotel in San Francisco's Tenderloin district since he retired at age 50. Despite arthritis and mild hypertension, he was relatively comfortable. He had friends in the hotel, enough money to pay his rent and a strong sense of independence—until a fire broke out in the middle of the night. Tom was forced to evacuate, leaving behind his clothes, possessions and what was left of the month's pension. (p. 1)

One expert on the elderly homeless, Beverly Ovrebo, argues that it is important for practitioners in aging to get Tom rehoused as quickly as possible so that he can "recreate what he's lost." Knowledge of what options are available for persons like Tom becomes essential. For example, it would be good to know "What are the single room occupancy hotels (see below) in the neighborhood, who are the good managers, where are the vacancies, so that one is as ready as possible, to rehouse the person" (Lurie, 1989, p. 2). Ovrebo cautions, however, that this is not a straightforward task: "Because Tom has lost a network of life supports, he is likely to resist the efforts of service providers to find him replacement housing. Ironically, the greater his need, the more symbolic the home he has lost, the more resistant he may be to receiving help" (Lurie, 1989, p. 1).

The Elderly in Single Room Occupancy (SRO) Hotels and Rooming Houses

SRO accommodations consist of relatively low priced, furnished one-room rental units in residential hotels, rooming houses, or transient hotels located in the inner city, skid row, or edge of the urban downtown. They usually have only communal or shared bathroom facilities, but often provide 24-hour desk clerk service, linens, and housekeeping.

Elderly hotel occupants are predominantly male, white, with no more than elementary education, living in poverty, unmarried, and living alone. They typically have few people (either family or friends) they can count on outside the helping network of the hotel. They often feel alone (Monk, 1988) and often suffer from numerous health problems (podiatric, vision, hearing aid needs, dental problems, psychiatric disturbances, alcohol-related problems, and nutritional deficiencies). The majority seek this housing because other options are financially unfeasible or inconsistent with their unconventional life-style (Eckert & Murrey, 1984; Ehrlich, 1986; Keigher et al., 1989; Minkler & Ovrebo, 1985). Still, generalizations must be made carefully. As pointed out in one study (Felton, Lehmann, & Adler, 1981):

> A small-town SRO with a benign management and a population of tenants who have lived a skid row existence for most of their adult lives cannot be assumed to be similar in social life or in tenant-management relations to a large-city SRO hotel located in a semi-residential area with a newly arrived and apathetic management and a clientele of formerly middle-class older tenants for whom hotel life offers a preferred alternative to suburban exile or congregate living in a home for the aged. (p. 271)

Considering the SRO hotel in a chapter on housing problems is bound to be controversial: These accommodations are frequently pointed to as essential for the poorest and most socially marginal elderly who seek to live independent, self-reliant, and private lives.

Supporters list many virtues of these accommodations: tolerance for a broad range of "erratic and antisocial" life-styles (Felton et al., 1981); their operators' perceptions of seniors as "desirable residents"; their "inside" safety (as opposed to their often unsafe neighborhoods); their provision of basic housekeeping services (laundering, bed linens, cleaning, bathrooms); their convenience to secondhand clothing stores, cheap restaurants, small grocery stores, discount drug stores, beauty and barber shops, soup kitchens, pawn shops, and other necessities of life; their closeness to the energy or pulse of city life; and their socially supportive attributes (e.g., other hotel residents, hotel manager, or housekeeping staff who "watch out for each other" and sometimes assist with the incidental instrumental activities of daily living). Advocates argue that the cost of rehabilitating and subsidizing SRO hotels is less than the cost of providing new low-rent conventional apartments for single people (Franck, 1989).

More generally, supporters emphasize the "right of citizens to select their own housing and to live in whatever accommodations best suit their preferred style of life" (Felton et al., 1981, p. 269). In turn, society is criticized for imposing standards not held by the occupants of such housing.

These accommodations may constitute the best available alternative that society now offers this segment of the elderly population. Nonetheless, many of these facilities suffer from a host of well-defined problems, including building deterioration with frequent operating and maintenance difficulties with roofs, boilers, gas lines, trash chutes, elevators, plumbing, insensitive physical design (e.g., long or treacherous stairways, heavy doors, poor lighting, inadequate heating and sanitary facilities, lack of elevators, many opportunities for slips and falls); location in crime-infested or gang-ridden neighborhoods; and frequent use for the drug trade and prostitution. These problems are compounded by the general unwillingness of this population to confide in or accept assistance from human service professionals and the unwillingness of many hotel managers to provide other than minimal assistance to their elderly tenants. Altogether, these factors increase the risk of this group of elderly tenants becoming homeless, institutionalized, or dying prematurely.

The long-term availability of the SRO option for older persons is problematic. In the 1970s and 1980s, more than one million SRO rooms in the United States were converted to apartments, condominiums, office space, and tourist hotels or were destroyed as part of urban redevelopment or gentrification. These forces will undoubtedly continue in many urban communities. The development of new SRO hotels (through renovation or new construction) is often discouraged by cost constraints and building codes and regulations. Many inner-city neighborhoods containing SRO hotels have witnessed a decline in the social, health, and nutrition services that contributed to the attractiveness of the SRO option. Many SRO hotels have also increased their rents as these accommodations have become more scarce. The reduced supply of and increased demand for these facilities has led some hotels to go upscale, with operators becoming more choosy about tenants. The less desirable, more marginally functional and more mentally and physically disabled tenants lose out. Furthermore, many hotel owners are unwilling to modify their buildings to conform to city fire codes or new national accessibility standards.

On a more positive note, several communities (e.g., New York, San Francisco, Portland) have taken legal action to stem the loss of SRO units and have established programs designed to preserve and rehabilitate them. Federal support is now available for SRO rent subsidies and renovation efforts (Franck, 1989).

CONCLUSION

This overview of older people's housing problems has both strengths and weaknesses. On the plus side, it captures the voices and views of multiple segments of U.S. society—from experts and interest group advocates to the elderly themselves. On the negative side, this grocery list of inadequacies fails to assess which problems are the most important and urgent to address. Although older people themselves have hinted at such rankings, housing experts have failed to derive comparable assessments. In part, this reflects the difficulty of the task. But more likely the explanation revolves around the very diversity of the elderly population itself. There is not one but multiple sets of important and high-priority housing problems. These differently impact older persons depending on their capabilities and life-style. The wide array of responses and solutions that have emerged from almost every sector of U.S. society is testimony to this diverse consumer market.

Before looking closer at the alternatives, it may be helpful to examine whether the larger presence of elderly persons in some places than in others helps to diagnose those with the greatest needs.

REFERENCES

American Association of Retired Persons. (1990). *Understanding senior housing for the 1990s.* Washington, DC: American Association of Retired Persons.

American Society on Aging. (1989, October/November). *The Aging Connection, 10,* 3.

Apgar, W. C., Di Pasquale, D., Cummings, J., & McArdle, N. (1991). *The state of the nation's housing: 1991.* Cambridge, MA: Harvard University, Joint Center for Housing Studies.

Branch, L. G. (1984). Relative risk rates of nonmedical predictors of institutional care among elderly persons. *Comprehensive Therapy, 10,* 33–40.

Branch, L. G., & Jette, A. M. (1982). A prospective study of long-term care institutionalization among the aged. *American Journal of Public Health, 72,* 1373–1379.

Carp, F. M., & Carp, A. (1982). The ideal residential area. *Research on Aging, 4,* 411–439.

Clurman, D., Jackson, F. S., & Hebard, E. L. (1984). *Condominiums and cooperatives.* New York: John Wiley.

Cohen, C. I., & Sokolovsky, J. (1983). Toward a concept of homelessness in aged men. *Journal of Gerontology, 38,* 87–89.

Czaja, S. J., & Guerrier, J. H. (1991). Enhancing the home safety of the elderly. *Report on Technology & Aging, 1,* 1–3.

Eckert, J. K., & Murrey, M. I. (1984). Alternative modes of living for the elderly: A critical review. In I. Altman, M. P. Lawton, & J. F. Wohlwill (Eds.), *Elderly people and the environment* (pp. 95–128). New York: Plenum.

Ehrlich, P. (1986). Hotels, rooming houses, shared housing, and other housing options for the marginal elderly. In R. Newcomer, M. P. Lawton, & T. Byert (Eds.), *Housing an aging society* (pp. 189–199). New York: Van Nostrand Reinhold.

Evans, D. A., Funkelstein, H., Albert, M. S., Sherr, P. A., Cook, N. R., Chown, M. J., Herbert, L. E., Hennekens, C. H., & Taylor, J. O. (1989). Prevalence of Alzheimer's disease in a community population of older persons. *Journal of the American Medical Association, 262,* 2551–2556.

Felton, B., Lehmann, S., & Adler, A. (1981). Single-room occupancy hotels: Their viability as housing options for older citizens. In M. P. Lawton & S. Hoover (Eds.), *Community housing choices for older Americans* (pp. 267–285). New York: Springer.

Franck, K. A. (1989). Single room occupancy housing. In K. A. Franck & S. Ahrentzen (Eds.), *New households, new housing* (pp. 245–262). New York: Van Nostrand.

Golant, S. M. (1984). The effects of residential and activity behaviors on old people's environmental experiences. In I. Altman, M. P. Lawton, & J. Wohlwill (Eds.), *Elderly people and the environment* (pp. 239–278). New York: Plenum.

Golant, S. M. (1986). Subjective housing assessments by the elderly: A critical information source for planning and program evaluation. *Gerontologist, 26,* 122–127.

Hiatt, L. G. (1985). Understanding the physical environment. *Pride Institute Journal of Long Term Home Health Care, 4,* 12–22.

Hiatt, L. G. (1990). Modifying the home or community setting for people with cognitive impairments. *Pride Institute Journal of Long Term Home Health Care, 9,* 18–27.

Institute on Medicine, Committee on Health Care for Homeless People (1988). *Homelessness, health and human needs.* Washington, DC: National Academy Press.

Kane, R. L., Saslow, M. G., & Brundage, T. (1991). Using ADLs to establish eligibility for long-term-care among the cognitively impaired. *Gerontologist, 31,* 60–66.

Keigher, S. M., Berman, R. H., & Greenblatt, S. (1989). *Relocation, residence, and risk: A study of housing risks and the causes of homelessness among the urban elderly.* Chicago: Metropolitan Chicago Coalition on Aging.

Kemper, P., & Murtaugh, C. M. (1991). Lifetime use of nursing home care. *New England Journal of Medicine, 324,* 595–600.

Lane, T. S., & Feins, J. D. (1985). Are the elderly overhoused? Definitions of space utilization and policy implications. *Gerontologist, 25,* 243–250.

Langer, E. J. (1983). *The psychology of control.* Beverly Hills, CA: Sage.

Laventhol & Horwath (1990). *Retirement Housing Industry, 1989.* Philadelphia: Laventhol & Horwath.

Lawton, M. P. (1975). *Planning and managing housing for the elderly.* New York: John Wiley.

Lawton, M. P. (1977). The impact of the environment on aging and behavior. In J. E. Birren & K. W. Schaie (Eds.), *Handbook of the psychology of aging* (pp. 276–301). New York: Van Nostrand Reinhold.

Lawton, M. P. (1980). *Environment and aging.* Monterey, CA: Brooks/Cole.

Lawton, M. P. (1985). Housing and living environments of older people. In R. H. Binstock & E. Shanas (Eds.). *Handbook of aging and the ageist sciences* (2nd ed., pp. 430–478). New York: Van Nostrand Reinhold.

Lazere, E. B., Leonard, P. A., Dolbeare, C. N., & Zigas, B. (1991). *A place to call home: The low income housing crisis continues.* Washington, DC: Center on Budget and Policy Priorities and Low Income Housing Information Service.

Leon, J., & Lair, T. (1990). *Functional status of the noninstitutionalized elderly: Estimates of ADL and IADL difficulties* (National Medical Expenditure Survey Research Findings 4., DHHS Publication No. [PHS] 90-3462). Rockville, MD: Public Health Service, Agency for Health Care Policy and Research.

Louis Harris & Assoc. (1987). *Problems facing elderly Americans living alone.* New York: Louis Harris.

Lurie, M. (1989). Homelessness increasing among elderly. *Aging Connection, 10,* 1–2.

Minkler, M. & Ovrebo, B. (1985). SRO's, The vanishing hotels for low-income elders. *Generations, 9,* 40–42.

Monk, A. (1988). Aging, loneliness, and communications. *American Behavioral Science, 31,* 532–563.

National Consumer Law Center. (1989). *Energy and the poor—The forgotten crisis.* Washington, DC: National Consumer Law Center.

Newman, S. (1990). The frail elderly in the community: An overview of characteristics. In D. Tilson (Ed.), *Aging in place* (pp. 3–24). Glenview, IL: Scott, Foresman.

Pastalen, L. A. (1983). Environmental displacement. In G. D. Rowles & R. J. Ohts (Eds.), *Aging and milieu* (pp. 189–203). New York: Academic Press.

Pynoos, J., Cohen, E., Davis, L., & Bernhardt, S. (1987). Home modifications improvements that extend independence. In V. Regnier & J. Pynoos (Eds.), *Housing the aged: Design objectives and policy considerations* (pp. 277–303). New York: Elsevier.

Rabushka, A., & Jacobs, B. (1980). *Old folks at home.* New York: Free Press.

Radner, D. (1987). Money incomes of the aged and nonaged family units, 1976–84. *Social Security Bulletin, 50,* 9–28.

Redfoot, D. L., & Gaberlavage, G. (1991). Housing for older Americans: Sustaining the dream. *Generations, 15,* 35–38.

Regnier, V., & Pynoos, J. (Eds.). (1987). *Housing the aged: Design objectives and policy considerations.* New York: Elsevier.

Short, P. F., & Leon, J. (1990). *Use of home and community services by persons ages 65 and older with functional difficulties* (National Medical Expenditure Survey Research Findings 6). Rockville, MD: Public Health Service, Agency for Health Care Policy and Research.

Spector, W. D. (1991). Cognitive impairment and disruptive behaviors among community-based elderly persons: Implications for targeting long-term care. *Gerontologist, 31,* 51–59.

Stegman, M. A. (1986). Urban displacement and condominium conversion. In R. Newcomer, M. P. Lawton, & T. Byert (Eds.), *Housing an aging society* (pp. 151–160). New York: Van Nostrand.

Struyk, R. J., & Soldo, B. J. (1980). *Improving the elderly's housing.* Cambridge, MA: Ballinger.

Struyk, R. J., Turner, M. A., & Ueno, M. (1988). *Future U.S. housing policy.* Washington, DC: Urban Institute Press.

Tinetti, M. E., Speechley, M., & Ginter, S. F. (1988). Risk factors for falls among elderly persons living in the community. *New England Journal of Medicine, 319,* 1701–1707.

Tobin, S. S., & Lieberman, M. A. (1976). *Last home for the aged.* San Francisco: Jossey-Bass.

U.S. Bureau of the Census. (1990a). *American housing survey for the United States in 1987* (Current Housing Reports, H-150-87). Washington, DC: U.S. Government Printing Office.

U.S. Bureau of the Census. (1990b). Household wealth and asset ownership: 1988. *Current Population Reports* (Series P-70, No. 22). Washington, DC: U.S. Government Printing Office.

U.S. Congressional Budget Office. (1988). *Current housing problems and possible federal responses.* Washington, DC: Superintendent of Documents.

U.S. Senate, Special Committee on Aging. (1989). *Aging America: Trends and projections* (Serial No. 101-E). Washington, DC: U.S. Government Printing Office.

U.S. Senate, Special Committee on Aging. (1990). *Developments in aging, 1989* (Vols. 1 & 2). Washington, DC: U.S. Government Printing Office.

U.S. Senate, Special Committee on Aging. (1991). *Developments in aging, 1990* (Vols. 1 & 2). Washington, DC: U.S. Government Printing Office.

Varady, D. P. (1986). *Neighborhood upgrading: A realistic assessment.* Albany: State University of New York Press.

Ward, R. A., LaGory, M., & Sherman, S. S. (1988). *The environment for aging: Interpersonal, social, and spatial contexts.* Tuscaloosa: University of Alabama Press.

Zais, J. P., & Thibodeau, T. G. (1983). *The elderly and urban housing.* Washington, DC: Urban Institute.

15

Shelter: Bring Us to This Hovel

RICHARD MARGOLIS

Although many older Americans now reside in federally subsidized housing, Richard Margolis argues that we have not done enough to serve the housing needs of the elderly. His focus is on the "ill-housed"—those elderly Americans whose very existence is threatened by the housing they occupy. Using a combination of government statistics and extensive interviews with elderly householders, Margolis makes a powerful case for his contention that policy initiatives pursued to improve housing conditions for elderly Americans have not been sufficient for the task.

> Kent: *Gracious my lord, hard by here is a hovel;*
> *Some friendship will it lend you 'gainst the tempest. . . .*
> Lear: *The art of our necessities is strange. . . .*
> *Come, bring us to this hovel.*
>
> —Shakespeare, *King Lear*

Although nearly 3 million older Americans now reside in some kind of federally subsidized dwelling, at least as many could instantly benefit from similar forms of assistance, were they available. It is mainly the ill-housed elderly on whom we shall focus here. Some have literally been left out in the cold: They belong to the ranks of America's homeless. Others have had to settle for makeshift dwellings beyond repair, and often for rents beyond belief. Still others are homeowners trapped in an inflationary cycle of taxes, upkeep, and utility bills.

The trap has many springs for renters and homeowners alike, the most terrifying of which is institutionalization. An aged resident may be too poor or frail to stay put but too scared to move. The authors of a study on older residents of Manhattan's West Side report that many occupy "semi-abandoned buildings lacking heat and hot water," yet they "live in constant worry of eviction. . . . Like a line of dominos, a lost check or a mugging can result in institutionalization."[1]

The elderly, of course, are not the only sufferers. If their residential needs are in some respects unique, they also reflect a national housing malaise that discriminates less by age than by class. The young as well as the old have been victims of a system widely assumed to be capable of healing social ills with profit-oriented remedies. Speculation, inflation, and gentrification have all had their innings, and all have contributed to an alarming shortage of decent, reasonably priced housing.

Bulldozers have widened the affordability gap by toppling old neighborhoods to make room for shopping malls and luxury condominiums. It has been estimated that 2.5 million households are displaced each year, "some through publicly or privately financed redevelopment, others through abandonment."[2]

The White House and the Congress, meanwhile, have done little to intervene. Instead of inventing programs more suitable to the times, they have simply gutted the federal housing budget. Since 1981, Congress has given the Department of Housing and Urban Development (HUD) fewer and fewer dollars to work with. Incredibly, HUD's budget authority over the decade has been cut by 76 percent.[3]

The sharply reduced outlays have turned a vexing problem into a full-blown emergency. As we shall see, it was the elderly who had most to gain from earlier federal housing initiatives. Now, with inertia replacing initiative, it is the elderly who have most to lose.

A bit later in this chapter I shall present an overview of elderly housing conditions nationwide, paying particular attention to strains on the pocketbooks of the poor. Then, in tandem segments called "Digging In" and "Letting Go," I rely largely on elderly voices to recount the hazards of both entrenchment and displacement. A penultimate section traces the history of federal housing programs for the aged, taking into account the breakthroughs achieved as well as the hopes still to be realized. Finally, I consider what is to be done. Solutions are at hand; they only await a firm national commitment.

To begin with, though, it may be helpful to examine the difference that decent housing can make in the life of someone who is old and poor, and by extension, in the life of the general community. Edna Morrison lives in a subsidized apartment in Alexandria, Virginia. The apartment helps her stay productive, not as a job holder, but as a grandmother and a churchwoman. What she mainly produces are vital services to family and friends, considerations of the sort we all rely on to hold things together.

THE VISIT

"Would you like to see my place?" It is a pleasant May afternoon. Edna and I are sipping coffee at a picnic table beneath a flowering dogwood outside St. Martin's Senior Center. We have just met, and although we have hit it off instantly—"You call me Edna and I'll call you Dick"—her invitation surprises me. Few of my new acquaintances have appeared eager to let me see where they live. The quality of their housing has governed the extent of their hospitality.

Edna Morrison is a large black woman who wears leg braces and uses crutches. Locomotion is painful. "You just go ahead," she says as we inch toward my car. "Don't you worry none about me. I came into this world like you see me now: oversize and crippled. I had what they call the rickets. The doctor told my mother it was brought on by soft bones."

In the car she tells me more about her life. She was born in Alexandria in 1915, the youngest of seven children. "We never had money but we didn't think we was poor. My mother took in washing. She was a church person, just like me. She would give away her own money to the poor for food on Christmas and Thanksgiving, just like me. She belonged to the Love and Charity Club.

"All I knew growing up was church and work. I was born again when I was seven, and Mama wouldn't let me go to no parties after that. My father worked on the roads, when there was work. After I finished the eighth grade I went to work, too, 'cause nobody in the family didn't help out. I got a job in the laundry."

Edna married twice and had three children by the second marriage. "Joyce is the oldest and Robert is next—he's thirty-nine. Cindy is my baby. She was the late late show. I have eleven grandchildren. Think of that: *eleven*."

She is warming to her subject. "I didn't have what you'd call a bad life," she says, "just a complicated one. My first marriage was to a minister, but he turned out already married. So I divorced him. My second marriage was to a smooth talker. He'd come home at three in the morning and I'd ask him where he'd been all night. He'd say, 'I ain't been nowhere but window shoppin' to see what you want for Christmas.' I divorced him, too. Well, after eighteen years I was fixin' to marry him again, but the Lord knew best. He took him away."

Edna lived in the same place—"a little house on South Alfred Street"—for forty-eight years, and paid off the mortgage with money she earned working in laundries and kitchens. "But when I got my heart condition I couldn't work no more to keep up the taxes." She sold the house in 1981, and most of the proceeds went for back taxes. Edna gave her children a share of what was left and banked $2,000 against a rainy day.

Then, for the first time in her life, housing became a problem: "At first I moved in with Joyce, but that didn't work out. We kept bumping into each other. Then I found a room on the other side of town and I stayed in it two years. I sat in that dark place and watched the roaches crawlin' around the linoleum. I didn't call nobody and nobody came to see me. I got sicker and sicker. Well, I'd been waitin' for one of those government apartments to open up, and when it did, I moved there quicker than a cockroach. 'Cept for my children getting born, that was the happiest day of my life."

We park in front of a development I shall call Maple Manor, a large brick complex made up of 2,300 apartments. Most of the units command luxury-style rents on the open market, but 300 are subsidized through a federal program called "Section 8," and Edna lives in one of those. She pays $90 a month (30 percent of her income) plus utilities.

We walk through a lilac-scented garden. Edna unlocks a door and we make our way painfully up a concrete staircase. She lives on the second floor. "Well," she says as she ushers me in, "this is my place."

The apartment overlooks the courtyard and gets the afternoon sun. Edna gives me a fast tour. There is a small, carpeted living room full of stuffed furniture, framed family photographs, and electronic devices—a TV set in one corner, a huge stereo in another. "My grandson gave me that stereo," Edna says, "so when he visits he can listen."

A formica-top counter separates the living room from the narrow kitchen, which features a large refrigerator, a gas stove and oven, and a double sink. Edna opens the refrigerator to show it off. It is gleamingly clean—and empty.

"And here's the bathroom," she goes on, opening another door. "I like the shower but I could use a tub." In the bedroom Edna calls my attention to her large closet. She also points out "my new bedroom suit," which she bought with the $2,000 she'd been saving. There is a gorgeous purple-and-orange quilt on the bed, and I ask her where she got it. "That's one I made myself," she answers. "I'm thinkin' of givin' it to this old lady I met at St. Martin's."

Back in the living room Edna invites me to "sit over there on my new couch. I want you to try it out." The couch seats four and is upholstered in a scratchy tweed. I remark on its stylish look.

"I gave the old one to Joyce's first-born when he got married," Edna tells me, "—something to get them started with, you know. And then I went out and got this new one. It cost me over $1,000, but the man lets me pay $73 a month and I don't mind. I needed to buy something beautiful to cheer me up. It gives me a new zeal on life. And it's where my grandchildren sleep. Two of them are coming tonight. They're in their teens, so they don't get on too good at home."

Edna is sitting next to a shiny green telephone. When it rings, she answers without saying hello. "That you, Carla? Thought so. When y'all comin? That soon, huh? No, but I ain't cleaned yet."

"That's my church club," she explains as she hangs up. "We meet every month and it's usually here 'cause here's the best place. Yesterday I got cookies. Today's the day."

I ask Edna if she ever runs out of money, and she laughs. "Uh-huh," she says. "I got the rent and the couch and the 'lectric and the gas and all the medicines I got to take and the fire insurance and the cable TV, and I ain't even mentioned food. Yah, I runs out of money lots of times, 'specially 'round the birthdays and Christmas. That's when I'm hurtin', when I can't give no presents to my grandchildren."

A social worker has told Edna she is not eligible for social security because her employers failed to keep records or put money aside. But she could probably collect Supplemental Security Income if her son Robert, an officer in the U.S. Navy, consented to stop supporting her. At Robert's request the Navy sends Edna $300 each month out of his paycheck. She is proud of his loyalty: "When Robert was in his teens, he said to me, 'Mama, you took care of me when I couldn't take care of myself, and now I won't let you down.' And he never did." But she worries that she has become too much of a burden to Robert and his family. "He has a wife and five little children to feed," she says. "The money should be going to his babies."

I visited Edna several times, and each time I came away with a strong impression that the money we as a nation were spending on her housing—it amounted to about $5,000 a year—bought something very like her salvation. She may have exaggerated the dreadfulness of the room she lived in before moving to Maple Manor ("I sat in that dark room and watched the roaches"), but surely she did not exaggerate her feelings of depression during that difficult time. In her eyes, and perhaps in the eyes of her friends, the room diminished her. Very likely, too, its tawdriness discouraged her grandchildren from coming to see her.

Edna's present apartment affords her a view of the garden, a "pad" for the grand-children, and a gathering point for friends. What such assets finally signify, to use Edna's own word, is her "place"—not only a place of residence but also a place of pur-pose within the larger community. By assuring Edna's continued usefulness to others, by preserving her social identity, the apartment makes it possible for her to keep on struggling.

But not everyone has been so fortunate as Edna Morrison.

THE STATUS OF ELDERLY HOUSING

Housing is a serious problem for a sizable minority of older Americans, who as a group occupy 21 percent of the nation's 88 million dwellings. Among the poor overall, the elderly face disproportionate risks: They make up two of every five low-income households nationwide. To alter the terms slightly, HUD has identified close to 4 mil-lion elderly households with incomes below the official poverty line and another 1 mil-lion whose incomes exceed that threshold by less than 50 percent—the so-called near poor.[4]

About three-fourths of all elderly residences are said to be owner occupied, but in many such cases ownership is no guarantor against hardship, as can be seen from HUD's market-value estimates. Elderly dwellings account for 34 percent of all units valued at less than $40,000—this in a real estate market that is generally booming. The age of the houses, like that of their occupants, seems inversely related to their per-ceived worth: About two-thirds of all elderly residences were built at least forty years ago.

HUD has also tabulated some of the housing deficiencies that beset elderly owners and tenants alike. For instance, more than 1 million of their dwellings lack electrical wiring; about .5 million are without decent plumbing facilities; and some 3 million have no central heating. The elderly account for a third of all households using un-vented room heaters.

In sorting out winners and losers among older households, we can discern a rough pecking order. Broadly speaking, rural residents fare worse than do metropolitan resi-dents; renters worse than owners; and single persons worse than couples. At the lower depths are black older women who live alone and rent, and they account for 17 percent of *all* black elderly households.[5] If the nation ever decides to clean up its elderly hous-ing act, it can begin here, where the keenest sufferers reside.

THE HIGH COST OF HOVELS

For the losers, shelter expenses can be hard to bear. HUD's figures suggest that 2.6 million elderly poor households must spend 50 percent or more of personal income on housing. One way of assessing the scariness of that number is to express it as a propor-tion of older households that are eligible for, but not privy to, federally subsidized housing. In those terms, 56 percent of all unassisted elderly poor households consume at least half their incomes on shelter.

What money remains usually goes for food and medicine, and for little else. As a number of researchers have demonstrated, just the daily expense of keeping warm can overwhelm an aged resident already near the end of her rope. One study focused on households whose sole support came from Supplemental Security Income. Researchers found that in forty states, during the year's three coldest months, home fuel costs consumed nearly one-third of a person's maximum SSI benefit; in nine other states, more than half the maximum benefit; and in Maine, 71 percent of the maximum benefit.[6] The figures underscore the absurdity of the federal definition of poverty, which assumes that groceries, not rents or fuel, are the poor's biggest budget item.

According to Edwin Rothschild of the Citizen/Labor Energy Coalition, some 2.8 million older Americans "who live alone and are in poor health" risk succumbing to hypothermia, or loss of body heat caused by constant exposure to the cold. In Connecticut, the risk loomed so large that sympathetic citizens began knitting "hypothermia kits" consisting of blankets, slippers, hats, and scarves. In Colorado, Rothschild reported, "low-income elderly are living in bathrooms, huddled around kerosene heaters, because they cannot afford to turn on their furnaces." He said his coalition had received "numerous letters from people who spend winters in bed, wrapped in blankets and clothing, because they cannot afford heat."[7]

People who live in the Sun Belt have their own kind of energy problems. Here is Ruth Carlyle, a senior citizen from Tampa, Florida, testifying at the same hearing:

> I will tell you about my energy experience. . . . Last year, while waiting for a bus, I was overcome by heat. My electric bill was only $18 during the winter because we are very lucky, we don't need very much heat. . . . But [that summer] my electric bill went up from $18 to $92. I found myself keeping cool by going to the shopping malls and sitting in ladies' lounges in department stores. I am not going to wave the flag. This country has been very, very good to me, and I don't expect it to support me, but on $289 a month . . . I find it very hard to pay $90 a month [for electricity].[8]

Many of the elderly I interviewed were paying sacrificial sums for the most wretched of shelters. From them I learned just how strange "the art of our necessities" can be, and how much it can cost in courage as well as in dollars. Three sobering examples, plus one that is relatively cheering, must stand here for the whole.

Ivar Peterson, Eighty-six. Income from social security: $357 a month; rent: $135 (38 percent of income). Mr. Peterson lives in a small, spare room in the basement of a brick apartment building near downtown Minneapolis. An iron cot and a narrow wooden chair are his only furnishings. The bathroom, which he shares with three other tenants, is down the hall. There is a large steam radiator bolted to his ceiling, but "it doesn't give much heat," Mr. Peterson says. "I had two coats on yesterday." The only entertainment he can afford is "taking a walk some days." But he complains that the landlord does not always clear the walkway of snow: "I feel a little wobbly sometimes. Once I fell in the soft snow. I didn't want to get up."

Walt and Evelyn, Both in Their Seventies. Combined SSI income: $472; rent: $257 (54 percent of income), plus $40 a month for gas and electricity; total housing expenses: $297 (63 percent of income). Walt and Evelyn live in Hartford, Connecticut, where they occupy cramped quarters—four dirty walls and a damp ceiling. One end of the double bed has been shoved into an open closet: The bed is too long for the room. Walt, a retired janitor, has a cheerful manner. "Most of the pipes leak," he tells me.

"When we sit on the toilet, we have to hold a newspaper over our head to keep dry. It's good exercise. Another way I stay fit is killing roaches."

"What do you kill them with?" I ask.

"My fist," he says with a smile and pounds the wall.

Alfonso and Elizabeth Gutierrez, in Their Late Sixties. Income from SSI and Elizabeth's part-time jobs: $478; mortgage, taxes, and insurance: $219 a month (46 percent of income), plus $30 for electricity, $25 for gas, and $20 for water; total housing expenses: $294 (62 percent of income). Mr. and Mrs. Gutierrez are Cuban refugees. They live on the outskirts of Miami in a four-room cinderblock house their son helped them purchase in 1973. In those days both parents did seasonal work in the tomato fields. Now Mrs. Gutierrez finds occasional factory work. The house is close to adequate, but the roof leaks in three places. Mr. Gutierrez cannot fix it himself—he suffers from emphysema—nor can he afford to hire someone. They are four months behind in their mortgage payments, and Mrs. Gutierrez fears they will lose the house. "We have no extra money," she says. "My husband needs medicine. I did not think being old like this would be so hard."

Susan Williams, Seventy-four, and David Williams, Seventy-five. Income from social security and a veteran's pension: $519; house taxes, utilities, heat, and insurance: $160 (31 percent of income). The Williamses live on Bloom Street in Jackson, Mississippi. Their low-lying area, misnamed "High Towers Neighborhood," is subject to frequent flooding. "Back a few years we had five feet of water in the house," Mrs. Williams says. They bought the house in 1947 for less than $3,000. It is of the type known in those parts as a "shotgun bungalow"—so named, I have been told, "because you can shoot through the front door and the bullet will come out the back door. Nothing but a hallway between doors." Eight persons besides Mr. and Mrs. Williams live there: two daughters, a son-in-law, four grandchildren, and an older brother of Mrs. Williams. At night, with everyone home from work and school, the house gets crowded.

Still, the roof is tight, the rooms are dry and warm, and the mortgage is paid. The difference between this family's circumstances and those of the others is in part due to Mr. Williams's veteran's pension (he fought in World War II) and in part to the job he held at Union Hose Corporation for twenty-nine years. His wages never exceeded $3 an hour, but they were enough to pay off the mortgage before he retired.

DIGGING IN

The Williamses' long tenure on Bloom Street reflects another important trait of many elderly residents: No matter how inadequate the dwelling, they prefer to stay where they are. According to Leo Baldwin of the American Association of Retired Persons (AARP), "Seventy percent of all people who reach the age of 65 will die with the same residential address as the day they reached 65. So we're not talking about a very mobile market."[9] Thoreau would not have been surprised. "Our lives," he commented, "are domestic in more ways than we think."

A prospectus published by the Commonwealth Fund, a New York-based charitable foundation, offers a precise summary of the elderly's domestic attachments: "Most elderly people prefer to remain at home even if their ability to maintain independent life declines. . . . For them, home is the place where families grew and friendships flourished. It is the center of things accessible and familiar. It is the key to a lifetime of feelings and memories."[10]

In Chicago I was told a story by Jerry Riemer, a young, soft-spoken Lutheran minister who runs a neighborhood center called the Uptown Ministry. Most Uptown residents are old and poor. There are eighteen nursing homes in the area.

"There was an old woman," said Riemer, "who was going to be sent to a nursing home in an ambulance. She had been making a fuss—she definitely did not want to go—so I was asked to come along and help smooth the way.

"Well, before we'd gone very far she insisted that we turn around. 'I have to get my things,' she kept saying. 'There is a letter I want to take with me.'"

The place they returned to was a tiny room with four bare walls, and what few things of hers remained did not fill a small paper bag. But she found the letter and she seemed content.

"Did you get a look at it?" I asked Riemer.

"Yes. It was a Christmas card—from a local bank."

It is not surprising that younger Americans change their residences three times more frequently than do older Americans. In youth we turn outward, impatient to spread our wings. In old age our bones demand more predictable consolations: the rosebush in the yard, the family photographs on the shelf, the cat at our feet. Our very walls take on new meaning. In the language of gerontology, we prefer to "age in place," and at times the preference shades into obstinacy. It is then that we dig in for the duration, whatever the cost: We shall not be moved.

But for many older Americans, to age in place is no simple task. The poor in particular must struggle for a firm purchase and then hang on tight. That is why any discussion of elderly housing conditions must take into account the fear of expulsion as well as the solace of stability. The two are part of a single dilemma.

Sisu

The Finns have a word for it—*sisu*—which means to "keep on going," or just "guts." There are quite a few Finns in Houghton County, Michigan, where the elderly make up about 10,000 of the 40,000 residents. As in other parts of rural America, most of the county's aged (four of every five) own their dwellings, but some of these are hovels that lend scant friendship against the tempest.

Houghton County is part of the state's northern peninsula, separating Lake Michigan from Lake Superior. Once it was rich in copper and lumber, but the mines are shut down now and the logging isn't what it used to be. The old people there were never prosperous, not even in their prime; and because the logging bosses they worked for commonly paid them in cash, with no written records to show for it, their minimal social security benefits keep them poor. The housing reflects the poverty.

Michael Aten, a young man, has been living up there for six years, working for the local branch of an international care-giving organization called Friends of the Elderly. One of his responsibilities is to help people move out of their freezing backwoods shacks and into warm, subsidized "senior housing" available at modest rents in towns like Hancock and Laurium. It has not been easy.

I interviewed Aten by telephone the day after Christmas. He said he'd been cutting wood all day and delivering loads to those on his "most in need" list. "It's going to be tough this year. People are running out of wood before the winter's half over. We've had 150 inches of snow this month alone."

Yet none of Aten's clients seemed ready to move. "Rural people like their independence," Aten told me. "There was a man I knew—he must have been in his nineties—who actually had a stroke and still wouldn't leave his place. I found him one day chopping wood *on his knees.* He couldn't even stand up, but he refused to switch to an apartment in town where all he'd have to do for heat was flick the thermostat. I can't really blame him. He knew what he wanted."

Mayme Kemppainen is seventy-six. The house she has lived in much of her life is falling down around her. Part of it caved in after the blizzard of 1984, when she had felt too weary to climb up and shovel the heavy snow off the roof. It took longer for the other side to go—it just seemed to rot away. Now Miss Kemppainen is confined with her dog and two cats to a single room, ten feet by twelve, where she does all her cooking, eating, and sleeping.

The mechanical facilities are not the best, but in Houghton County neither are they the worst. A kerosene space heater works some of the time. Thanks to Aten's diligence, the house has both electricity and running water, though the water is not for drinking because the new well is shallow and sandy. For potable water Miss Kemppainen must travel twelve miles to a public restroom, where she can fill up her six half-gallon milk jugs. She ties the plastic jugs together with string, for easier carrying to and from the bus.

But transportation has proved a problem ever since her arthritis got so bad that she had to start using a walker. The bus won't stop for her any more because the walker slows her down and the driver grows impatient. Now, when she runs out of drinking water, she must wait for Aten or a neighbor to come by in a car.

Every winter Aten reminds Mayme Kemppainen that she doesn't have to endure the isolation, the temperamental kerosene stove, the sagging remnant of a house: She can move into the senior project at Laurium. All she has to do is say the word. And every winter she agrees, promising that this will surely be her last winter in the woods. But then comes the thaw, and with it second thoughts. What will become of her dog and her cats if she moves to town? And what will happen to *her,* tucked away among all those strangers in a citified building with long hallways a person could get lost in? She can name people like herself, folks getting on in years, who tried that peculiar way of life and didn't last two weeks. Quicker than you'd think they'd packed up and gone back to their little cabins. Too much noise, they said. Too many rules.

Well, maybe she won't go to Laurium just yet. Maybe she can tough it out just one more winter. *Sisu.*

A Little Piece of the United States

Thelma Poole was born in Sweden in 1910 and has lived in the same house in Minneapolis for more than half her years. It is a two-story, wooden-frame "fourplex," just a mile south of downtown, which she and her husband bought in 1938 for $2,700. The down payment took all their savings. "My husband was a chauffeur and a gardener for a very rich family," she told me. "We didn't have much money but my husband was smart with his hands. He fixed our house just right."

Her husband died in 1978: "I miss him terrible. Nothing seems to matter any more. All I cared for was . . . was . . . I can't think of the word. It's something like 'togetherness' but that's not it."

I had come to Mrs. Poole's house one wintry afternoon at the suggestion of Julie Gamber, a young woman who worked for the Minneapolis chapter of Friends of the Elderly. "It's not a pleasant place to spend time in," she had warned.

"This lady stays forever in one room. She never goes out. The other three apartments are empty, so it's not as if she gets any rent money. A few months ago a woman on welfare moved into some of the rooms downstairs. She didn't pay rent, she just squatted there with her children and her boyfriend. They played music all day and all night—the kind that thumps. It drove Thelma bats. When you're very old, you're helpless. People can just invade your space and do anything they please. The city finally got them out of there, so now the place is empty again except for Thelma upstairs. I'll take you there."

The front door is unlocked. We walk up the groaning staircase and enter a shadowy room that smells of stale food and urine. My feet find trash at every step—twisted cans, plastic dishes, crushed paper bags. Accidentally I kick something large and round, and it rolls across the floor. It is an empty bird cage.

"I used to have canaries." The voice is Scandinavian and lilting. "Oh, what music they made! Not like those tenants and *their* music. That wasn't music at all—just crazy crazy sounds."

Thelma Poole is lying beneath blankets on a bed in the far corner, her white head resting on a dingy pillow. "Oh, you are a tall one," she says to me, extending a skeletal hand in greeting. She must have been a beautiful woman. Even now her large eyes hold me. They are a deep blue.

Julie says, "Thelma, this gentleman is writing a book. He wants to know how you are getting along in your house."

"Getting along? Well, you see me here. It is a good house. When we bought it, it was just a ramshackle. I said to my husband, 'This house looks like an old pirate's nest, but to us it's a palace.' My friends, oh, how they made fun of it! They wanted to know how in the world we could buy such an old ramshackle. But later they kept quiet. *They* didn't have anything, you see, and we had this house, a little piece of the United States, and when I woke up I could step out on my own little lot."

Mrs. Poole doesn't step out anymore. The doors to her kitchen and bedroom seem permanently shut, and the room we are in, the living room, is indeed the one in which she does all her living. For food Mrs. Poole depends on Meals on Wheels, which delivers two meals each weekday. She does not eat on weekends. Her monthly social security check is mailed directly to the bank where she has a checking and savings account, as are her fuel and tax bills. Mrs. Poole is not much bother to the rest of us. She has outlived all her close relatives; she has no telephone. People from Friends of the Elderly and other agencies look in on her from time to time, but beyond cheering her up and making her comfortable, there seems little they can do.

The house, meanwhile, is slowly reverting to its ramshackle state. There are leaks in the pipes and holes in the plaster. Minnesota storms have cracked several windows and torn away some of the roofing as well as many of the gutters. Nothing gets repaired. One sees a reverse symbiosis at work here, in which house and owner simultaneously deteriorate, growing less and less capable of protecting each other. It is not an uncommon condition in America. Among persons seventy-five years old and older, some 70 percent still reside in their own homes and nearly half the owners have incomes below the poverty line. In tabulations made during the late 1970s, about one-quarter of such dwellings were found to have "persistent deficiencies" such as leaks, unvented room heaters, and inadequate plumbing or electrical wiring. Deficiency rates in rural areas reached 35 percent.[11]

We lack the programs and institutions needed to allow these determined homeowners to age gracefully in place. In Thelma Poole's case, where helpful measures seem feasible, none has been taken. Surely tenants could be found for the vacant apartments downstairs; surely portions of their rent could be paid in essential services—in maintenance work around the house, for instance, and in home care for Mrs. Poole. Such a plan does not appear farfetched, yet it would require initiatives and arrangements for which no agency at present, not even Friends of the Elderly, seems prepared to take responsibility.

So Mrs. Poole remains trapped in her cage. Her alternative—the only real option society has granted her—is to surrender body and soul to a nursing home. It is a recourse at which I gently hint as we take leave. Wouldn't she receive better care, I wish to know, in a different kind of place?

The question astonishes Mrs. Poole. "Why should I want to leave my house?" she finally asks, her eyes opening very wide. "No, I think I die here."

LETTING GO

People cannot always choose their dying places. A few years ago Mary Chambord, now an Uptown resident, wished to stay forever in the West Side apartment she and her family had called home for more than two decades. "It was really the only place I wanted to be," she told me. "I figured sooner or later I'd die in my kitchen. And you know what? I almost did." More recently, she just wanted to die, period—it didn't matter where. There are tales more dramatic than Mrs. Chambord's, but few more representative of her working-class generation's search for a safe harbor amid the geriatric storm.

She is a seventy-year-old Chicagoan, a large red-headed woman whose bifocals keep slipping down her nose. In the summer of '84, desperate for a place she could call her own, she took a single room in a "retirement residence" I shall call Balfour House. It is an old-fashioned stone building with a gilded lobby, an enormous dining room, and a "TV lounge" that Mrs. Chambord likes to frequent. Balfour House is a proprietary enterprise licensed by the state, with a twenty-four-hour telephone switchboard and a trained nurse always on call. For revenue it depends on the tenants' social security and public assistance checks.

Mrs. Chambord went there directly from a nursing home, where she had spent eight years recuperating from a number of serious maladies. Her older brother, she said, had taken a nearby room in the same nursing home.

"I'd been wanting to leave the institution for some time. I kept saying to my brother, 'You make arrangements to get out of here and we can both live together somewhere cheap. We'll manage.' But he never made the arrangements.

"One day the hospital called and told me my brother had had a heart attack, in fact two of them, and they had tried to save him but they couldn't."

The next week she moved into Balfour House. Her tiny rectangle on the fifth floor bulges with massive, dark-brown hotel furniture. The books atop her dresser are piled ceiling-high, covering up a wall mirror; more books lie scattered on the gray linoleum floor. The walls, painted a dull yellow, are bare except for a drugstore calendar hanging from a nail beside the entranceway. There are cans of juice on the windowsill, along with a hot plate and a little pile of pink Sweet 'n Low packets. (She suffers from diabetes.) The day I visited—a very cold January morning—the radiator was bubbling hot and the windows were wide open.

Mrs. Chambord shares a bathroom with her neighbor in the adjoining room. "It's a nuisance," she said, "but I can't be too particular for what I pay." Her rent is $325 a month, which includes three meals a day served in the congregate (communal) dining room. She collects $299 in social security and gets "extra help from welfare" ($103 a month from the state). The $77 that's left after she's paid the rent is "enough to keep me in cigarette money."

She made instant coffee for us on her hot plate, and she was gracious throughout; yet something in her manner struck a melancholy note. Her speech dragged noticeably, like a tape played at too slow a speed.

"My husband was a construction worker from Canada," she told me. "He spoke better French than English, so we never talked much to each other. That was OK. We kept busy."

She had married soon after graduating from high school. They set up housekeeping in a one-bedroom apartment on the West Side, "but after Leonard was born we moved to a bigger place on the same block. When Nicky came along we didn't move. We'd been paying rent so long we felt like it belonged to us. There were sixteen years between Leonard and Nicky. He was what you'd call a surprise child."

Her husband died on Thanksgiving Day, 1975, and some months later Nicky joined the army. Leonard had long since married and settled in Arizona. Suddenly Mrs. Chambord was gazing at an empty nest.

"I began to put on a great deal of weight. I weighed 225 pounds. I had difficulty walking and breathing. The doctor was giving me medicine—I don't know what it was, tell you the truth. Anyway, this is what they tell me: Somebody from the church came over to see me—a woman. They found me on the floor. At the hospital they told me I'd had a heart attack, and after I got better the doctor said to me, 'We don't think you can take care of yourself. We think you ought to go into a nursing home.' So I went to the same one my brother was living in. We always got along, you see.

"That's when I lost all my things—my pictures, my letters, my books, my dishes, my furniture. I just walked out and left everything behind me, because I didn't have anybody to store them with. I imagine the landlady kept most of it; some of the things I had were in very good shape. I always saw to it that the children took good care of their things. There was a sled in the basement that still looked brand new. All the furniture you see here belongs to the hotel. None of it's mine."

Toward the end of our interview I asked Mrs. Chambord how she liked living at Balfour House. Her answer was more than I had bargained for. "There's something I ought to explain to you," she began.

"At first everything was going along fine. Then my other brother died, my younger brother, and I took that very hard. And the woman I shared the bathroom with, she died too. I liked her. We used to sit around evenings and talk about people in general, and I would give her my books to read. Her name was Mary, too.

"Well, one time I sat here—it was in the evening—and I went over to the drawer, got a knife and began sawing on my wrist. I also took an overdose of pills that I had, and I don't remember anything else. However, a nurse found me—we have a nurse here on duty all the time—and I asked her afterward how did she know I needed help. She said, 'because you called me.' I don't remember calling her. Maybe I wanted to live after all."

In the lottery that often determines housing for the elderly poor, Balfour House seems neither the best nor the worst of draws. For Mary Chambord it became a timely haven, a way to shake free of institutionalization's chains while being assured warm shelter, daily sustenance, and even a measure of care. Its round-the-clock nursing service probably saved her life. On the other hand, the dreary and expensive cubicle to which she was consigned, and the loneliness it must have engendered, doubtless deepened her bereavement and contributed to her own brush with death.

ELDERLY HOMELESSNESS

If some displaced older Americans have managed to find more agreeable quarters than those afforded by Balfour House, many have had to settle for considerably less.

One rainy morning Dorothy Lykes, not knowing where else to turn, telephoned the Gray Panther office in New York City.

> Mrs. Lykes was 78, terminally ill with cancer, and weighed 70 pounds. Her husband was in the hospital, also terminally ill. Most of their Social Security was going for his hospital bills. The city had taken possession of their Bronx home, which they bought in the 1950s, because they could not pay the property taxes. Nor could they pay the $300 a month rent the city was asking from them for living in their own home. Mrs. Lykes asked: "Is the next step for me to move to Penn Station?"[12]

Increasingly now, our older residents are being forced to move out of their single rooms, their rented apartments, even their own homes—places and neighborhoods they have lived in for generations. And in more cases than is generally recognized, these refugees have no place to turn. Thus to the pain of relinquishment is added the nightmare of homelessness.

One study of states in the northeast concluded that elderly people there make up about 30 percent of the homeless.[13] An analysis by Mary Ellen Hombs and Mitch Snyder (of the Community for Creative Non-Violence) noted that those who "populate our city streets" are mainly "the old, the sick, the mentally ill, the unemployed, the disabled, the displaced and the disenfranchised." It is not unusual for a single individual to embody all seven traits. Hombs and Snyder emphasized still another characteristic of street people—their invisibility: "Thus, the older woman next to you on the bus may be going nowhere in particular, riding only to keep warm or dry or seated. . . . In the world of the streets, invisibility equals access, and those who can pass unnoticed into public places . . . suffer less abuse and harrassment."[14]

The elderly's street-wise invisibility has been matched by a calculated myopia on the part of federal officials; they have doused the homeless aged with vanishing cream. In 1984 a HUD functionary named Carol Bauer assured a congressional committee that "our current programs are adequate to provide a coordinated package of housing choices designed to prevent the elderly from entering the homeless category."[15] (Bauer's title at HUD would have delighted Nicolay Gogol. She was executive assistant to the deputy assistant secretary for policy, financial management and administration.)

In fact, the range of choices available to poor people of all ages has been shrinking for at least a decade, along with the federal resolve to lend them a helping hand. Certainly for older citizens there is no such thing as "a coordinated package" of affordable housing, only a forlorn heap of once-promising programs lately eviscerated.

But I am getting ahead of my story.

THE FEDERAL COMMITMENT: A HISTORY

It would not be difficult to imagine a rough topographical "picture" of the federal commitment to low-income housing as it has developed over the decades. In the background we might place a large desert to represent the arid years prior to 1937. The desert would yield gradually to more fertile stretches that climb toward the green uplands of the 1960s; then a sudden descent into an almost forgotten valley known as "Nixon's Rest Area" (1973–1974), followed by another hill, which peaks at decade's end. The gulf that yawns beyond could be called "Reagan's Ravine."

But the size of our picture may be misleading, for in the larger scheme of things all the elements would appear as little more than a brush stroke. The truth is that America has never quite accepted the idea of decent housing as a universal right or entitlement; year after discouraging year federal assistance to people in urgent need of shelter has constituted less than 1 percent of the national budget and reached fewer than 25 percent of the poor.

Of this mouselike portion, however, it must be said that older Americans have enjoyed a lion's share. Today they occupy 39 percent of all government-subsidized housing. Only the rural programs, those supported by the Farmers Home Administration, appear to have short-changed the older population relative to other age groups. Of the 1.9 million households assisted by that agency, just 207,000, or 11 percent, are elderly.

The other programs present a very different picture: In public housing, 541,000 older households make up 45 percent of the total; in the two rent supplement programs known as "Section 8," 983,000 elderly units constitute 48 percent of the total; and in the "Section 202" program, which offers building loans to local nonprofit sponsors, older households (188,000) and handicapped households (12,000) make up the entire roster of beneficiaries. The numbers overall suggest that elderly assisted housing is now a large fish in a very small pond.[16]

There was a time when the elderly were nowhere near the pond. The public housing program started in 1937 with passage of the Wagner-Steagall Low Rent Housing Act, and its target was not the elderly poor but the millions of younger families displaced and made destitute by the Great Depression. Reformers back then had a tendency both to identify with and to romanticize the poor. Eleanor Roosevelt characterized the homeless of her day as "the finer people" who had "adventure in their souls." She was struck by "the beauty of some of the children" and their "bright minds."[17]

Early beneficiaries of public housing were seen not as dependents but as people temporarily down on their luck. In Alvin Schorr's words, they were "families who voluntarily sought to improve their housing but could not afford private rentals."[18]

It was not until the massive urban renewal and slum-clearance projects of the 1950s, which dislocated huge numbers of poor people, that the program—to cite the social commentator Chester Hartman—came to be viewed as "'last resort' housing for the economy's cast-offs."[19] The upshot might have been expected but wasn't: an increasingly affluent, largely white America started insisting that public housing projects be placed in neighborhoods far from their own, where they had the effect of augmenting the very slums they had been meant to replace. The sociologist Nathan Glazer would later observe that public housing in the popular mind became "a graveyard of good intentions."[20]

The Greener Uplands

At that critical moment the federal housing pendulum began to swing sharply toward older Americans. In 1956 only 2 percent of the nation's public housing units were occupied by elderly tenants. The proportion rose to 19 percent by 1964 and to 46 percent by 1984. In the interim several new housing programs had been inaugurated, one of them (Section 202) aimed almost exclusively at assisting older tenants. As Jon Pynoos, a University of Southern California gerontologist, has pointed out, "In spite of the limited resources of their interest group, . . . the elderly have been a prime beneficiary of federally subsidized housing programs."[21]

What lay behind the elderly's remarkable gains? Society's interests seemed partly political, partly demographic. To suburbanites who had been rejecting proposals for low-income projects in their towns, the presence of *older* poor people appeared less threatening a prospect and, in the bargain, a convenient appeaser of uneasy consciences. In addition, people had already begun to take note of the old-age population boom and to wonder out loud where all the new senior citizens could find places to live. As far back as 1950 delegates to the First National Congress on Aging had pointed with alarm to the growing demand for elderly housing and had called for swift federal action.

In fact, a handful of pioneer thinkers in the field had been recommending such measures for more than a decade. Among them was a remarkable woman named Marie C. MaGuire (later Thompson), who in many respects can be considered the founding mother of federal housing for older Americans. Her story neatly encapsulates the evolution of elderly housing, both the victories scored and the setbacks endured.

Mrs. MaGuire staked much of her distinguished career on finding ways to build decent shelters for older Americans. The career began in Houston, Texas, where in 1942 the local Public Housing Authority hired her as manager of a new project. She was thirty-eight years old. Early on, she noticed that many of the project's applicants were considerably older than the conventional portrait of public housing tenants had led her to expect. Quite a few were widows or widowers, and their applications were perforce rejected: The law in those days specifically barred single persons from tenancy in low-rent projects.

Those few older applicants who did gain entrance soon discovered that their new apartments had not been designed for the likes of them. "The floors were bare concrete," Mrs. MaGuire recalled when I interviewed her in her Washington, D.C. apartment. "All the old people complained about the cold floors. And there were many accidents. The shelves were too high—people had to stand on chairs, and sometimes they fell off. The frailer tenants couldn't get out of their bathtubs because there were no grab bars. One woman actually drowned in the tub."

Mrs. MaGuire resolved that one day she would plan a project to answer the special needs of older tenants. She edged closer to that goal in 1949, when the city of San Antonio asked her to direct its Public Housing Authority. Now, at least, her voice would be heard in decision-making councils. But she had to wait until 1956 before Congress cleared the way. In that watershed year the lawmakers lifted restrictions on single-person occupancy of low-rent housing and instructed local housing Authorities "to give preference to admission of the elderly. . . . This preference is to be prior to any other preference." Congress also recognized that older residents might require extra amenities: It earmarked an additional $500 in project construction money for every elderly household.

Mrs. MaGuire did not need to be pushed. In an application fired off to Washington, she pointed out that the elderly population in Texas had increased by an astonishing 20 percent in just five years. In Greater San Antonio they numbered 37,000, and nearly one-quarter were living with their children or with other relatives. She proceeded to give Washington officials a short course in housing's role vis-à-vis the elderly. "At varying chronological ages," she wrote, "old age ceases to be academic. Old age is a condition that demands individual attention. Society must provide the setting for such attention." She held out the hope that "enlightened communities" would provide housing that permitted "the aged to live independently, insuring that privacy which equates with personal dignity."

Apparently Washington got the point. The result was a six-story, 184-unit project named Victoria Plaza Apartments, the nation's first low-rent housing complex designed and built exclusively for older citizens. It opened, amid much fanfare, on July 2, 1960, with rents starting at $25.50 a month.

"From the first," noted the authors of a special brochure published eight months after the opening, "the residents were joyful about their new homes." It was easy to see why. The new building was equipped with many of those age-targeted niceties Mrs. MaGuire had found lacking elsewhere: ramps, nonskid floors, grab bars, an elevator with a bench, storage space that required no reaching up or bending down, even "sit-down" showers where one could take one's sudsy ease. (The glass was shatter-proof. The seats were made of Alaskan birch, a wood impervious to water.)

The project, moreover, was within easy walking distance of stores and churches. Mrs. MaGuire had been "aghast" at the placement of some earlier projects: "They were sitting in the middle of meadows, far away from everything." The prime location of Victoria Plaza paid off in tenant morale as well as convenience, a dividend that earlier had been identified by the Senate Committee on Labor and Public Welfare in its ten-volume *Studies of the Aged and Aging*. "Not only do older persons want to be in the center of things," the committee had observed, "but they want to feel they are an active part of community life."

For Victoria Plaza tenants, some of that community life would occur on the premises. The building included a community activities center on the first floor, where a number of city agencies quickly set up shop—for health, recreation, and library services, among others. Here was "the setting" in which elderly people could receive "individual attention."

Less formal activities took place in the lobby. "That's when I found out how important it was to have a large lobby with plenty of seating," Mrs. MaGuire recalled. People enjoyed coming together: "They would start waiting for the mail an hour before it was due to arrive. It wasn't just the mail they wanted—it was the social life." The lobby represented something of an aesthetic triumph as well. Mrs. MaGuire had been able to raise an extra $100,000 from local philanthropists for the purchase of artwork. "I wanted to introduce the thought of beauty," she said.

Victoria Plaza appears to have been a turning point in the development of housing for older Americans: It converted an abstraction into bricks and mortar. Housing officials from cities with problems identical to San Antonio's made pilgrimages there to look and learn. The parade grew so long that Mrs. MaGuire began passing out printed guides. She also mailed out some three hundred architectural blueprints to planners who had written in for information. The seeds thus planted, some of them started to sprout, with Victoria Plaza replicas springing up in many places.

The project was also a turning point in Marie MaGuire's career. The following year she went to Washington to serve as President Kennedy's commissioner of public housing, a position she held through 1966. When the Public Housing Administration became part of the newly created Department of Housing and Urban Development, she stayed on as HUD's special adviser on problems concerning the elderly and handicapped. She retired in 1972.

Mrs. MaGuire's time in office happened to coincide with elderly housing's golden years. The signs could not have been more favorable. Congress had already given its blessing to Section 202 (in the Housing Act of 1959), which helped nonprofit sponsors to build rental and cooperative housing for older Americans. (The law was amended in 1964 to include the handicapped.) In 1963 President Kennedy promised major new housing initiatives for the elderly. Not surprisingly, federal investments in elderly housing quadrupled between 1961 and 1964, and the number of elderly units actually completed during those years increased ninefold. Few doubted Moses J. Gozonsky, a federal housing official, when he boasted, "Housing for the elderly has become a growth industry, but its future growth should dwarf all previous records."[22]

The advent of the Great Society only confirmed the obvious. In a message to the Congress delivered in March 1965, Lyndon Johnson declared his intent "to ensure a steadily increasing supply of federally assisted housing for older Americans." He was as good as his word. By 1968, the annual total of public housing units under construction had risen from 35,000 to 103,000; about one-third were earmarked for older tenants. The new Section 202, meanwhile, had already accounted for 45,000 additional elderly units.

It was a moment worth savoring: Twelve years before, we had falteringly begun to confront the critical shortage of affordable housing for older citizens. Now we were well on our way toward a solution. All we had to do was keep pushing—or so it appeared.

Nixon's Rest Area

In fairness, Richard Nixon did not hold a patent on the ensuing retreat. In 1968, with Johnson a "lame duck" in the White House, HUD decided to phase out all new construction under Section 202 and replace it with a less age-oriented program. The substitute enacted by Congress that year (Section 236) assisted tenants of all ages rather than just the elderly. The 202 program lay buried in HUD until 1975, when Congress exhumed it, rewrote it, and put it back to work. The good repute it enjoys today, however, belies its surprisingly limited impact. Less than 3 percent of poor older households enjoy 202 housing subsidies, yet the Senate Special Committee on Aging has called this form of assistance "the flagship of federal housing programs for the elderly."[23]

At the start of his second term (January 1973), Richard Nixon made a deteriorating situation still worse by announcing a freeze on all shelter construction subsidies, including those for public housing. The moratorium would last nearly two years and would deprive nearly one million low-income households of their chances for adequate shelter.

"I could never understand the Nixon moratorium," Marie MaGuire said in our interview. "They claimed it was to give them time to think up new ideas, but I suspect it was just their way of saving some money. In any case, it was devastating."

HUD's two years of enforced meditation were not entirely wasted. Besides the eventual disinterment of the 202 program, the interlude's happiest effect on older Americans was the drafting of Section 8 legislation, which Congress passed in late 1974 as part of its landmark Housing and Community Development Act. The Section 8 measure came in two parts, one for new or rehabilitated housing and one for old housing. In both instances, low-income tenants were charged rents at below-market levels, with HUD making up the difference through payments to landlords.

As we have seen, the elderly poor have made considerable use of this program. But in 1983, at the Reagan administration's urging, Congress threw out the program's new-housing component—so now the poor must settle for half a loaf. (A wit who works on the Hill has suggested that the program's name be changed to "Section 4.")

As was the case with quite a few other social welfare measures passed in the mid-1970s, the 1974 Housing and Community Development Act marked the end of a more bountiful era. Henceforth, lawmakers would shrink from making further programmatic leaps, while presidents would call for withdrawals along a wide front. In Jimmy

Carter's time the federal housing commitment fell off noticeably, dropping from 517,000 newly completed assisted units in 1976 to 206,000 in 1980. In Ronald Reagan's era the descent grew even more precipitous.

Reagan's Ravine

The chief goals of Reagan's housing policies were "to shrink the growth of programs as far as possible and to replace the solutions . . . with cheaper options."[24] In this he succeeded admirably, but not half so well as he seemed to wish. Congress on the whole temporized, yielding to some of the president's demands while elsewhere digging in its heels. During the last seven years of the 1980s, the White House and HUD requested $465 million in housing assistance; Congress appropriated $62 billion.

The administration may well have felt free to press for wholesale elimination of essential housing programs only because it was certain that Congress would not go along. There is something unappealing about using such a tactic. It brings to mind the little boy who relies on his parents to stop him from being naughty. Before they can intervene, of course, considerable damage may be wrought.

The damage in this case, as Struyk has noted, "is absolutely clear: the poor have lost." In HUD-sponsored programs, "The actual number of newly assisted households was only one-third to one-quarter of that during the Carter years." For the first time in recent memory annual totals of subsidized housing starts dipped below six digits. The drop was dramatic: In 1980, HUD started 183,000 subsidized units; in 1983, 81,000; in 1988, 10,000. Low as those numbers were, they would have been much lower had Congress simply rubber-stamped the president's recommended budgets.[25]

The steep decline in new construction reflected the administration's customarily sanguine view of the marketplace and the miracles it could achieve. Despite a large body of evidence to the contrary, HUD had concluded that there was sufficient housing out there for everyone, even for the poor, who had only to seek in order to find. Neither the record-low vacancy rates being reported by cities from coast to coast nor the alarmingly long lines of applicants awaiting housing assistance were enough to alter the official version of reality.

With an eye to opening up the private market, the administration urged Congress to enact a system of federal housing vouchers that low-income tenants could exchange for a portion of their rent. The plan in due time was supposed to replace what was left of the much-bloodied Section 8 program. Congress responded unenthusiastically, providing demonstration money for only 15,000 vouchers in 1983 and for 42,000 more in 1985.

Congress was more receptive to a rent-hike recommendation that had been on the table since the Carter years. In a characteristic move to make subsidized housing more "cost effective," the lawmakers raised rents from 25 percent of a tenant's income to 30 percent. The seemingly small increment occasioned much distress in federally assisted households, as I learned when I interviewed elderly public housing tenants in New Haven.

Fred Stancill's plight was typical. A seventy-seven-year-old tenant of the Elm Haven public housing project, Mr. Stancill now had to pay $105 a month instead of $87.50. He said the extra $210 a year came directly out of his food budget. "But to tell you the truth," he added, "I'm behind in my rent right now. I got two months owing."

Mr. Stancill was not the only tenant in New Haven to fall behind because of the rent hike. Things got so bad that the Public Housing Authority announced it would impose a $20 penalty on residents who did not pay their rent by the tenth of the month. In the past, wayward tenants had been assessed only 50 cents a day, with a ceiling of $10.50 per month. But the new rule did not appreciably improve collections, and a few months later it was quietly dropped. As one of the commissioners observed, "If a tenant can't pay $10.50, how is he going to pay $20?"

ONWARD

As we bid Reagan's ravine a not-so-fond farewell, we should bear in mind that the hardships it engendered were part of a much larger catastrophe. Reaganomics, after all, did not discriminate among generations or types of deprivation: It exacted tribute from the poor of all ages and along a wide front of public assistance endeavors.

Still, the virtual abandonment of time-tested housing programs represented an especially shabby page in our social-policy annals. For in housing, as perhaps in no other category of elderly support, we had been learning how to do things right. We had found ways of making a positive difference in the quality of elderly lives.

Our newly summoned will to fail can be readily understood if not wholly excused. As with Medicare, inflation has been the problem perceived and cost containment has been the solution attempted. We have allowed our federal housing programs to become indentured to the private market with its soaring rents and out-of-sight land prices. The $5,000 that Edna Morrison's rent supplement cost us in 1986 would in 1976 have been sufficient to subsidize *two* low-income households.

The marketplace may be able to supply us with a plethora of luxuries—it can gentrify vast stretches of America—but one thing it appears unable to supply is adequate housing at affordable prices. If we are serious about finishing the job we began fifty years ago, we shall have to invent a new system of housing and financing that works independently of the old. We need a national housing institution whose functions combine those of a bank with those of a foundation. In the best of all possible worlds that institution would be capable of making construction grants and low-interest loans to churches and other local nonprofit groups prepared to rebuild their communities along compassionate lines.

To make possible the rebuilding, we shall also require measures that can remove selected land parcels from speculative arenas and earmark them for what Chester Hartman has called "social ownership." By social ownership he means "housing that is operated solely for resident benefit and is subject to resident control."[26]

If the initial cost of all this seems excessive, consider the billions to be saved over the long haul from less speculation, lower interest rates, and a more watchful community involved in the housing process. The real issue, one guesses, is not how much it will cost but how much we shall consent to spend on behalf of the poor. Right now we are spending enormous sums on the nonpoor, chiefly in the form of tax deductions for mortgage interest payments and property taxes. Between 1976 and 1990 those accumulated deductions cost the national treasury about $58 billion, which is more than all moneys spent on government-assisted housing programs since the inception of public housing in 1937. Three-fifths of the benefits went to taxpayers in the top 10 percent income bracket.[27]

For the older poor as for the younger poor, much depends on the nature of our prior-

ities. But the elderly, in addition, have uncommon burdens that require special attention. There are, to start with, the diggers-in, the millions like Thelma Poole who will
not be moved. Many of them could use a combination of home care and house care, a
program that will hold together body and soul and domicile. Several federal agencies
do sponsor home repair programs for the elderly (as do some states and municipalities), but their reach is short and the list of suppliants is long. Besides dollars, what is
missing from these scatter-shot efforts is a *plan,* a thoughtful federal home repair and
maintenance policy aimed at helping older Americans stay where they are. The money
saved in Medicaid reimbursements that won't have to be paid to nursing homes may
justify the expense—if the lives saved will not.

Much more will be required on behalf of the elderly displaced, who still await the realization of HUD's phantom "coordinated package of housing choices." A genuine package would offer something other than wrappings: It would contain useful options for the
frail and the hardy alike, choices ranging from Edna Morrison's no-frills residence at
Maple Manor to complex, multiservice versions of Marie MaGuire's Victoria Plaza in
San Antonio. The rule should be special facilities for some, decent dwellings for all.

It is not only a question of money. Poor or affluent, many older citizens lack the
strength to fend wholly for themselves—to cook their own meals, to drive a car, even
to get up in the morning. An assumption that informs this chapter concerns the importance of bringing home-based care and services to the frail and forgotten—not the
"total care" that nursing homes are supposed to provide (and usually don't), but the
kind of day-to-day support that may help someone retain a measure of verve and independence.

"Congregate housing" is the term experts use to describe such residential arrangements, whereby many essential services can be enjoyed right on the premises: meals,
health care, transportation and housekeeping assistance, to name a few. Gerontologists
and housing commentators have been extolling the virtues of congregate housing for at
least forty years. Here is Charles E. Slusser, President Eisenhower's Public Housing
Administration commissioner, speaking on the subject in 1956: "Livability for the elderly must go beyond handrails in bathrooms, low-hung cabinets, non-skid floors, and
ramps instead of stairs. It should also look to the social and recreational needs of our
elderly residents and provide facilities for them."

Slusser's early hopes remain largely unfulfilled, especially for people of limited
means. The dream is barely kept alive nowadays by a scattering of federally funded
demonstration projects—authorized in the Congregate Housing Services Act of
1978—which together serve fewer than 30,000 older residents.

THE LONELY CROWD

If congregate housing were to do no more than dispel loneliness, it would be worth the
price. Elderly loneliness has many causes, but to judge from Edna Morrison's experience, much of it seems a function of place—the place one lives in and the place one is
asked, or not asked, to fill in the community. We are dealing here with a sense of use-
lessness as well as a sense of isolation.

Some of the consequences were spelled out for me by an eighty-year-old Minneapolis widow named Rose Darling, whom I interviewed in her small, neat apartment

in a subsidized senior housing development: "I wake up in the morning and start to get up. Then I ask myself: What for? Because I have nothing to do any more—no dog, no garden, nobody to take care of. And I don't eat. I cook something for the evening and when it is ready, I say ach! I don't want to eat it, and I put it in the refrigerator.

"The other morning I was alone and I thought at least I wish somebody would call me. I sat there waiting for the phone to ring. And then it actually rang. 'Hello, Hello,' I said. They wanted to speak to someone named Steven. It was the wrong number."

What did she do then, I asked.

"I switched on the TV. A game show."

There are well-meaning experts who counsel new kinds of clusterings as alternatives to living alone—small-group housing, retirement villages, and the like. "What has to be done," said Leo Baldwin of the AARP, "is . . . create an atmosphere where we can help older people understand that it is appropriate to move into conditions which will serve them better."[28]

But given America's love affair with self-reliance, it is hard to see how we shall ever succeed in persuading a majority of our older citizens to apply that theoretical truth. And even if we could, the elderly poor would scarcely benefit, for it is a truth beyond their means.

In Minneapolis, at the Cedar Riverside People's Center, a dozen older women were gracious enough to meet with me one morning and speak frankly about their lives. All but one were renting small apartments like Rose Darling's, in the multistory, federally assisted senior developments that dominated the neighborhood landscape. I asked them if they would prefer living in a small group (not necessarily with each other) to living alone. No one welcomed the suggestion. One woman, a retired secretary, seemed to speak for all when she remarked, "I like what I got, and what I got is privacy."

"It's true," another concluded, "that living alone can make you selfish. But don't us oldsters deserve a little peace of mind?"

In place of group living, some of the women proposed more comfortable ways of opening up their lives. They wished for gardens to cultivate in common, more shared space in which to entertain friends and relatives, and more timely transportation services—"to help us get up and get going," one of them said. Not least, they yearned for smaller residential buildings, in which each tenant could be recognized by name. "In a big building," complained the ex-secretary, "you're nothing but a number."

The lesson seems clear. If we hope to be helpful to our older friends and relations, we shall have to listen to their expressed needs. What those women definitely did not want was anonymity and isolation. What they did want was independence-plus—plus mobility, plus conviviality, plus beauty.

No one expects Congress to accomplish such miracles overnight, but Congress *could* resolve to start anew, and this time to finish the job. In gearing up for a fresh start, the lawmakers should plan in an affirmative-action mode, giving priority to those most grievously deprived of shelter. An emergency program for the elderly homeless would be an essential first step, to be closely followed by measures to assist the next-worst-housed contingent—poor black women who live alone and rent.

If the ultimate goal—decent shelter for all the elderly—seems discouragingly distant at times, we should bear in mind that a mere 2 million additional units would finish the job begun thirty-five years ago. The main thing is to restore our sense of urgency, to keep pressing ahead with all deliberate speed. For as Robert N. Butler reminds us, "The old can't wait for housing."[29]

NOTES

1. Denise Hinzpeter and Anita Fischer, *Graying in the Shadows,* New York City Service Program for Elderly People, 1983.
2. Roberta Youmans's testimony, "Homeless Older Americans," Hearing before the Subcommittee on Housing and Consumer Interests, House Select Committee on Aging, May 2, 1984, pp. 101–09.
3. Low Income Housing Information Service, "Special Memorandum," Washington, D.C., March 1989.
4. Unless otherwise noted, the source for all numbers cited here is Department of Housing and Urban Development, *American Housing Survey for the United States in 1985* (Washington, D.C.: Government Printing Office, December 1988).
5. J. P. Zais et al., *Housing Assistance for Older Americans* (Washington, D.C.: Urban Institute Press, 1982), pp. 44–45.
6. The Grier Partnership, "Cold—Not by Choice," National Consumer Law Project, Washington, D.C., April 1984; Typewritten.
7. "Energy and the Aged: The Impact of Natural Gas Deregulation," Hearing before the Senate Special Committee on Aging, March 17, 1983, p. 92.
8. Ibid., pp. 109–10.
9. *Orlando Sentinel* [Fla.], March 16, 1986.
10. "Living at Home Program," Commonwealth Fund, 1985.
11. S. Newman, R. Struyk, and J. Zais, "Housing for Older America," in *The Physical Environment and the Elderly* (New York: Plenum Press, 1982).
12. Roger Sanjek, "Federal Housing Programs and Their Impact on Homelessness," Coalition for the Homeless, New York, 1982, p. 1; Typewritten.
13. Coalition for the Homeless, "An Embarrassment of Riches," New York, 1985, p. 9; Typewritten.
14. Mary Ellen Hombs and Mitch Snyder, *Homelessness in America,* Community for Creative Non-Violence, Washington, D.C., 1983, p. 4.
15. "Homeless Older Americans," pp. 33–48.
16. "Developments in Aging," Vol. 1, A Report of the U.S. Senate Special Committee on Aging, February 26, 1988, pp. 269–75.
17. Quoted in Irving Bernstein, *A Caring Society* (Boston: Houghton Mifflin, 1985), p. 4.
18. Quoted in Harold Wolman, *Politics of Federal Housing* (New York: Dodd, Mead, 1971), p. 31.
19. Chester Hartman, "National Comprehensive Housing Program," working paper, Institute for Policies Study, 1986, p. I-12.
20. Nathan Glazer, "Housing Problems and Housing Policies," *Public Interest,* Spring 1967, p. 37.
21. Jon Pynoos, "Setting the Elderly Housing Agenda," *Policy Studies Journal,* September 1984, p. 175.
22. Moses Gozonsky, "Senior Citizens," *New Jersey Municipalities,* June 1965, p. 27.
23. Senate Special Committee on Aging, "Section 202 Housing for the Elderly and Handicapped: A National Survey," Information paper prepared by committee staff, December 1984, p. 4.
24. R. J. Struyk, N. Mayer, and J. A. Tucillo, *Federal Housing Policy at President Reagan's Midterm* (Washington, D.C.: The Urban Institute, 1983), p. 4.
25. Low Income Housing Information Service, "Special Memorandum," Tables 1 through 4.
26. Hartman, "National Comprehensive Housing Program," p. I-19.
27. Low Income Housing Information Service, "Special Memorandum," Table 6.
28. *Orlando Sentinel* [Fla.], March 16, 1986.
29. Robert N. Butler, *Why Survive?* (New York: Harper & Row, 1975), p. 134.

VII

GENERATIONAL AND FAMILY RELATIONSHIPS

Demographic change has transformed the nature of the family as well as the obligations and responsibilities between generations. Because of increased life expectancy, it is now possible and, indeed, increasingly common for four generations of one family to be alive. Currently, about one-half of all individuals over 65 are great-grandparents. That means that older people today may be part of a complex, multigeneration family in which members of two generations occupy the roles of both parent and child (Hagestad, 1986).

Family ties not only are more complex but also extend for more years than in the past. In the nineteenth century, family size was large, and children were born relatively late in the life cycle. Yet because of high mortality, parents and children may have shared only twenty or thirty years together, grandparents and grandchildren only a decade. In the twentieth century, reductions in mortality and in fertility have changed the nature of family relations. Typical family size is smaller, but parents are likely to be part of their children's lives for half a century; the ties of grandparents to grandchildren may last twenty or thirty years (Bengtson, Rosenthal, and Burton, 1990). These changes not only provide greater opportunity for family bonds to survive over decades but also give rise to new dilemmas regarding the care of older family members.

FAMILY CAREGIVING AND THE STATE

It is part of our mythology that in the past families lived in three-generation households. In fact, in the past as now such households were rare. Usually, when older people lived with children, it was because they were still caring for their own dependent children. Families were a source of support for the infirm elderly, especially older women, who were taken into the households of their children when they needed care (Laslett, 1985). Those without family might spend their final days in the poorhouse (Quadagno, 1988).

The family has been transformed in the twentieth century. Lower fertility coupled with greater life expectancy means that more older people are living on their own. At the same time, higher divorce rates, more single parents, and large numbers of women in the labor force place new pressures on the family. Despite these changes, family members, especially women, still provide about 80 percent of the care to the elderly (Stone, Cafferata, and Sangl, 1987). And there is growing evidence that busy women today don't abandon their parents but rather adjust their work schedules to accommodate their needs (Hagestad, 1986).

Caregiving places demands on time and financial resources as well as psychological stresses on families. Yet many family members also find satisfaction in caring for an elderly parent. The reading by Sandra L. Boyd and Judith Treas discusses both the strains and the positive aspects of caregiving in the twentieth century.

One recent trend has been the shifting of duties formerly performed solely by the family to the state. The reading by Alan Walker examines the relationship between the family and the state in the provision of care for older people. Walker first asks why the family, and women in particular, care for older relatives and second, what impact state intervention has on family relationships.

RECIPROCITY ACROSS GENERATIONS

While much has been written about the burden of caregivers, from a life course perspective there exists greater reciprocity in family relationships—most individuals both give and receive care and support from other family members. Some exchanges are short and concrete—doing home repairs, caring for an ill child, sending a son or daughter through college—while others, like shopping or preparing dinner for one's family, may last a lifetime (Kingson, Hirshorn, and Cornman, 1986). In the classic study of three industrialized countries, Ethel Shanas and her collaborators found that familial ties were complex and extensive. Most older people reported that they had seen at least one child the same day or within the previous week, that they visited frequently with children who lived farther away, and that reciprocity was the norm across generations (Shanas et al., 1968). Subsequent studies have confirmed that, even when families live apart, family ties remain strong. This give and take among family members underscores their interdependence.

Familial interdependence is the topic of the final reading by Margaret Platt Jendrek. Jendrek's study of grandparents who provide daily care to their grandchildren shows how caring for grandchildren alters their lives. The effects of caring range from changes in life-style to changes in relationships with spouses, other family members, or friends.

REFERENCES

Bengtson, Vern; Carolyn Rosenthal; and Linda Burton. "Families and Aging: Diversity and Heterogeneity." Pp. 263–287 in Robert Binstock and Linda George (eds.), *Handbook of Aging and the Social Sciences*. New York: Academic Press, 1990.

Hagestad, Gunhild. "The Family: Women and Grandparents as Kin-Keepers." Pp. 141–160 in Alan Pifer and Lydia Bronte (eds.), *Our Aging Society*. New York: W. W. Norton, 1986.

Kingson, Eric; Barbara Hirshorn; and John Cornman. *Ties that Bind: The Interdependence of Generations*. Washington, DC: Seven Locks Press, 1986.

Laslett, Peter. "Societal Development and Aging." Pp. 199–230 in Robert Binstock and Ethel

Shanas (eds.), *Handbook of Aging and the Social Sciences.* New York: Van Nostrand Reinhold, 1985.

Quadagno, Jill. *The Transformation of Old Age Security: Class and Politics in the American Welfare State.* Chicago: University of Chicago Press, 1988.

Shanas, Ethel, et al. *Old People in Three Industrial Societies.* London: Routledge and Kegan Paul, 1968.

Stone, Robyn; Gail Cafferata; and Judith Sangl. "Caregivers of the Frail Elderly: A National Profile." *The Gerontologist* 27 (1987): 616–626.

16

Family Care of the Frail Elderly: A New Look at "Women in the Middle"

SANDRA L. BOYD
JUDITH TREAS

The phrase "women in the middle" refers to middle-aged women who have multiple responsibilities: for aging parents and for dependent children. These women are often described in negative terms, as trapped between familial and job demands. This reading by Boyd and Treas first describes the demographic changes that have created the coinciding of parent care and child care and then debunks some of the negative stereotypes associated with the concept "women in the middle." Specifically, they argue that most middle-aged women who are responsible for ill, aging parents no longer have dependent children at home, that women do adapt to multiple responsibilities associated with paid employment and parent care, and that while caregiving can be experienced as a burden, it also provides a sense of usefulness.

Unprecedented demographic shifts in this century have profoundly affected the lives of middle-aged and older women. As the population ages, increasing numbers of women provide care to elderly relatives. The elderly population currently is the fastest growing segment of American society. By 1985, average life expectancy at birth was 71.2 years for men and 78.2 years for women.[1] Sixty percent of fifty-five-year-old women could expect to have at least one living parent in 1980, compared to just 6 percent in 1800.[2] It is estimated that 20 percent of a woman's lifetime will be spent with at least one parent over the age of sixty-five.[3]

We now know that offspring do not abandon their elderly parents;[4] family members provide roughly 80 percent of care to the elderly.[5] A vast caregiving literature shows that women in the family—primarily wives, daughters, and daughters-in-law—are most involved in caregiving.

Elaine M. Brody has coined the phrase "women in the middle" to refer to women who "are in their middle years, in the middle of older and younger generations, and in the middle of competing demands."[6] She suggests that long-term parent care has become a "normative" family stress for a growing number of middle-aged women.[7] Other researchers, however, contend that studies based on small, nonrandom samples overstate the prevalence of "women in the middle."[8] Furthermore, the gerontological literature focuses almost exclusively on the negative consequences of caregiving and competing demands; few studies have examined positive aspects.[9]

"WOMEN IN THE MIDDLE": BETWEEN GENERATIONS

Brody's definition embraces two, sometimes overlapping types of "women in the middle": 1) those who are "caught" between older and younger generations and 2) those who combine parental care and paid employment.

Although some women provide both parental care and child care simultaneously, the life cycle provides some insulation against experiencing such dual demands. Table 16-1 shows that 17 percent of women between the ages of forty and forty-four have children under the age of eighteen at home, and 97 percent have parents over the age of sixty-five. But many of these parents can be considered part of the "young-old"; they are under the age of seventy-five, enjoy relatively good health, and are married.[10] Moreover, because money, goods, and services flow down the generational ladder to a greater extent than they flow up,[11] these "young-old" parents are apt to be assets, not liabilities; rather than posing burdens to their children, they provide critical financial help and emotional support.

Sixty percent of fifty-five-year-old women have living parents; unlike the parents of younger women, these often are over the age of seventy-five, many are widowed, and a significant proportion suffer from impairments limiting their daily activities. But only a tiny fraction of women in their mid-to-late fifties still have children at home.

A constellation of factors, including postponed childbearing, "crowded nests," and increased sickness among older persons may mean that child dependency and parent-care overlap more frequently in the future.

Postponed Childbearing and Childlessness

Although some well-educated women are remaining childless altogether, others in recent cohorts have delayed childbearing until their late twenties and thirties.[12] For such women, child rearing may well coincide with parent care. Moreover, responsibilities for grandchildren may impinge on some middle-aged women, especially blacks, as a result of the rise in teenage illegitimacy.[13]

"Crowded Nests"

Declining proportions of adult children over the age of eighteen are married, and increasing proportions either remain in their parental home or return there.[14] Thirty per-

TABLE 16-1 Women with Parents over Age 65 and Children under Age 18 in Household

Women's Ages	Percent with Parent over Age 65[a]	Percent with Children Under Age 18 in Household[b]
40–44	97	17
45–49	92	8
50–54	78	4
55–59	60	2
60–64	35	1
65–74	14	less than 1

[a]Based on estimates applied to a synthetic cohort under 1980 conditions. Susan C. Watkins, Jane A. Menken, and John Bongaarts, "Demographic Foundations of Family Change," *American Sociological Review* 52, no. 3 (1987): 346–58.

[b]Children under eighteen living with one or both parents, all races, 1984. Age of parent was based on the age of the householder, defined as the homeowner or renter. Since homeowners are still more likely to be men than women, and since husbands are somewhat older on average than their wives, these percentages may slightly underestimate the number of children under eighteen living with women. Current Population Reports—Population Characteristics, Series P-20, No. 399, *Marital Status and Living Arrangements*, March 1984.

SOURCE: Women's Studies Quarterly 1989: 1 & 2.

cent of eighteen to thirty-four year olds lived in their parents' households in 1983, compared to 25 percent in 1970. Adult children living at home typically are single and between the ages of eighteen and twenty-two; most are in school rather than in the work force.[15] Adult children aged twenty-three to twenty-nine living in their parents' home typically either are preparing for independent living or have returned temporarily following job loss or failed marriages. The prolonged dependency of adult children may mean that middle-aged women are responsible simultaneously for their children and their parents.

Increasing Sickness of the "Young-Old"

Researchers recently have found a significant increase in the prevalence of chronic disease among the "young-old," though not among the rest of the elderly population; more people suffering from chronic illness are surviving today than in the past.[16] Some women thus may be compelled to provide parental care when their children are still relatively young.

In summary, although many middle-aged women experience competing demands, most are not "caught between older and younger generations." When middle-aged women still have dependent children, their aging parents typically have not reached an age when they are likely to be impaired and in need of assistance. Middle-aged women who do have frail elderly parents tend not to be responsible for children living at home. If future cohorts of middle-aged women care for sicker parents and have younger children or children who remain at home longer, they may be more likely to be "caught in the middle."

"WOMEN IN THE MIDDLE": BETWEEN CAREGIVING AND PAID EMPLOYMENT

In addition to competing family responsibilities, "women in the middle" confront conflicting demands of care for elderly family members and paid work. Between 1947 and 1986, the number of women in the labor force grew from 29.8 to 54.7 percent;[17] the most notable increases occurred for middle-aged married women and mothers of small children. Over 60 percent of married women aged forty to fifty-four are in the labor force.[18] According to data from the National Long-Term Care Survey, 31 percent of all unpaid caregivers also hold paying jobs, including 10 percent of wives and 44 percent of daughters.[19] Some observers fear that women who simultaneously work for pay and care for parents suffer from "burn out" as a result of role strain.

Women who have competing demands from paid work and caregiving adapt in a number of ways, including leaving the labor force, making changes at work, and making changes at home.

Leaving the Labor Force

Although the three generations of women interviewed by Elaine Brody stated that women should not have to quit their jobs to provide care to elderly parents,[20] daughters are much more likely to actually do so than sons. According to a variety of studies, between 12 and 28 percent of caregiving daughters leave the work force to provide care.[21] These women often lose salary and benefits, retirement pensions, social networks, and work satisfaction. Caregiving responsibilities also may compel some women to remain unemployed.[22]

Brody found that women who quit work are older, provide more help to their mothers, and have lower status jobs than those who remain in the work force.[23] Because their family incomes are low, such women may face financial difficulties. Some of these women, however, may prefer caregiving to unrewarding jobs and thus welcome the opportunity to depart the labor force.

Changes at Work

Women who continue to work often make changes on the job to accommodate caregiving obligations. Robyn Stone et al. (1987) reported that 20 percent of caregivers cut back their hours, 29 percent rearrange their work schedules, and 19 percent take time off without pay. The tendency to make such changes is directly related to the level of impairment of disabled parents.[24]

Patricia Archbold (1983) argues that women in higher status positions are more able to accommodate caregiving in their work lives because they have more flexible work schedules.[25] According to Brody, however, the higher status, career-oriented workers feel more conflicted and report more work interruptions and missed job opportunities.[26]

Changes at Home

Many working caregivers give up free time and leisure activities while maintaining rigid schedules.[27] Some also adjust their caregiving responsibilities to alleviate the strain. Although caregivers in the labor force provide the same levels of help as unpaid workers in terms of housework, financial management, and emotional support, they provide significantly less assistance with personal care and meal preparation.[28] Employed caregivers also tend to supplement their own assistance with help from other family members and paid providers.

ROLE STRAIN FROM COMPETING DEMANDS

Most caregiving literature focuses on the negative consequences of providing care, and most studies report at least moderate stress for many caregivers. Researchers have directed considerable attention to women in the middle of paid work and informal caregiving, assuming that role conflict and overload predispose them to stress. Studies suggest that a quarter of caregivers who remain in the labor force do have conflicted feelings,[29] and many suffer from fatigue and strained personal relationships.[30] But employment does not appear to be the most important determinant of stress. The primary predictor of stress is the quality of the relationship between the caregiver and care recipient.[31] Working women providing care to older family members do not systematically exhibit more stress than their counterparts who do not work outside the home.[32] Moreover, contrary to the assumption that an increase in the number of roles is detrimental to psychological well-being,[33] there is some evidence that the ability to handle diverse roles can promote self-esteem. Multiple roles provide women with added sources of satisfaction, not simply increased burdens. Individuals also can compensate for failure in any one sphere by relying on rewards from another. Some caregivers may find that a job provides a respite from the demands, and often failures, of caregiving.

At the same time, caregiving provides a sense of usefulness, compensating for frustrations at work. Although most gerontological literature emphasized the stress of caregivers, many of the findings on caregiving stress come from small samples recruited from service agencies. Families who are most visible to community agencies are those who are experiencing more stress than they can handle and who feel that they need help. As Horowitz notes, "most caregivers can identify at least one positive aspect of caregiving, primarily a feeling of self-satisfaction and increased self-esteem stemming from the knowledge that one is successfully fulfilling a responsibility and coping with a personal challenge."

SUMMARY AND CONCLUSION

Despite warnings about many women being "caught in the middle," the situation is not as grim as many observers would have us believe. The life cycle helps protect women against competing family responsibilities; only a small percentage of women care simultaneously for dependent parents and children. The addition of paid work to caregiving responsibilities may have positive as well as negative consequences. Moreover, many women cope successfully with competing demands. By focusing exclusively on the stress of caregiving, we ignore the tremendous resiliency and adaptive capabilities of many women and send young women a depressing message about their future. Although it is necessary to alert policymakers and employers to the problems of women who do find caregiving overwhelming, we should retain a sense of perspective.

It should be emphasized, however, that those women who are experiencing stress from competing responsibilities do need special assistance. A small but growing number of corporate employers offer "elder care" to assist employees with caregiving obligations. The current wave of corporate interest is encouraging, but more employers could provide programs that help working women deal with family responsibilities, whether child care or elder care. Support groups and counselors can also be a tremendous source of help to caregivers. Women who have been able to balance competing demands successfully may be an important resource to others. Finally, researchers should explore the complexities of different competing demands. Although being a "woman in the middle" may not be a "normative" experience, demographic trends suggest it may become more common in the future.

NOTES

1. National Center for Health Statistics, *Vital Statistics of the United States, 1985* Life Tables, Vol. 11, Sec. 6, Department of Health and Human Services Pub. No. (PHS) 88–1104 (Public Health Service, Washington, D.C.: U.S. Government Printing Office, 1988).

2. Susan C. Watkins, Jane A. Menken, and John Bongaarts, "Demographic Foundations of Family Change," *American Sociological Review* 52, no. 3 (1987): 346–58.

3. Ibid.

4. Ethel Shanas, "The Family as a Social Support System in Old Age," *The Gerontologist* 19 (1979): 169–74.

5. National Center for Health Statistics, *Vital Statistics of the United States, 1973 Life Tables* (Rockville, Md.: U.S. Government Printing Office, 1975).

6. E. M. Brody, "'Women in the Middle' and Family Help to Older People," *The Gerontologist* 21 (1981): 471–80.

7. E. M. Brody, "Parent Care as a Normative Family Stress," *The Gerontologist* 25, no. 1 (1985): 19–29.

8. Sarah H. Matthews, "The Burdens of Parent Care: A Critical Assessment of the Recent Literature" (Revision of a paper presented at the Gerontological Society of America, New Orleans, 1985); Carolyn J. Rosenthal, Victor W. Marshall, and Sarah H. Matthews, "The Incidence and Prevalence of 'Women in the Middle'" (Revision of a paper presented at the Gerontological Society of America, Chicago, 1986).

9. Emily K. Abel, *Love is Not Enough: Family Care of the Frail Elderly*, APHA Public Health Policy Series. (Washington, D.C.: American Public Health Association, 1987); Amy Horowitz, "Family Caregiving to the Frail Elderly," in *Annual Review of Gerontology and Geriatrics, Volume 5*, ed. C. Eisdorfer (New York: Springer, 1985).

10. Rosenthal et al., "Incidence and Prevalence of 'Women in the Middle.'"

11. Vern L. Bengtson et al., "Generations, Cohorts and Relations between Age Groups," in *Handbook of Aging and the Social Sciences*, 2d ed., ed. Robert H. Binstock and Ethel Shanas (New York: Van Nostrand Reinhold, 1986), pp. 304–38.

12. David E. Bloom and James Trussell, "What Are the Determinants of Delayed Childbearing and Permanent Childlessness in the United States?" *Demography* 21, no. 4 (1984): 591–609.

13. Linda M. Burton and Vern L. Bengtson, "Black Grandmothers: Issues of Timing and Continuity of Roles," in *Grandparenthood*, ed. Vern L. Bengtson and Joan F. Robertson (Beverly Hills, Calif.: Sage Publications, 1985).

14. David M. Heer, Robert W. Hodge, and Marcus Felson, "The Cluttered Nest: Evidence

That Young Adults Are More Likely to Live at Home Now Than in the Recent Past," *Sociology and Social Research* 69 (April 1985): 437–41.

15. Jill S. Grigsby and Jill B. McGowan, "Still in the Nest: Adult Children Living with Their Parents," *Sociology and Social Research* 70 (January): 146–48.

16. Eileen M. Crimmins, "Evidence on the Compression of Morbidity," *Gerontologica Perspecta* 1 (1987): 45–49.

17. U.S. Bureau of the Census, *Statistical Abstract of the United States* (Washington, D.C.: Government Printing Office, 1987).

18. U.S. Bureau of Labor Statistics, *Handbook of Labor Statistics,* March 1984 population survey, table #52 (Washington, D.C.: Government Printing Office, 1985), p. 119.

19. Robyn Stone, Gail Cafferata, and Judith Sangl, "Caregivers of the Frail Elderly: A National Profile," *The Gerontologist* 27, no. 5 (1987): 616–26.

20. E. M. Brody et al., "Women's Changing Roles and Help to the Elderly: Attitudes of Three Generations of Women," *Journal of Gerontology* 38 (1983): 597–607.

21. Stone et al., "Caregivers of the Frail Elderly"; E. M. Brody et al. "Work Status and Parent Care: A Comparison of Four Groups of Women," *The Gerontologist* 27, no. 2 (1987): 201–208.

22. Beth J. Soldo and Jaana Myllyluoma, "Caregivers Who Live with Dependent Elderly," *The Gerontologist* 23, no. 6, (1983): 605–11.

23. Brody et al., "Work Status and Parent Care."

24. Robert B. Enright, Jr. and Lynn Friss, *Employed Caregivers of Brain-Impaired Adults: An Assessment of the Dual Role* (San Francisco: Family Survival Project, 1987).

25. Patricia G. Archbold, "Impact of Parent-caring on Women," *Family Relations* 32 (1983): 39–45.

26. Brody et al., "Work Status and Parent Care."

27. A. M. Lang and E. M. Brody, "Characteristics of Middle-aged Daughters and Help to Their Elderly Mothers," *Journal of Marriage and the Family* 45 (1983): 193–202; Brody et al., "Work Status and Parent Care."

28. E. M. Brody and Claire B. Schoonover, "Patterns of Care for the Dependent Elderly When Daughters Work and When They Do Not," *The Gerontologist* 26, no. 4 (1966): 372–81.

29. Stone et al., "Caregivers of the Frail Elderly"; Brody et al., "Work Status and Parent Care."

30. Dorothy A. Miller, "The 'Sandwich' Generation: Adult Children of the Aging," *Social Work* 26 (1981): 419–23; Andrew E. Scharlach, "Role Strain in Mother-Daughter Relationships in Later Life," *The Gerontologist* 27, no. 5 (1987): 627–31.

31. Horowitz, "Family Caregiving."

32. Ibid.

33. W. J. Goode, "A Theory of Role Strain," *American Sociological Review* 25 (1960): 488–96.

17

The Relationship Between the Family and the State in the Care of Older People

ALAN WALKER

Walker focuses on the issue of why the family and female kin in particular care for older relatives. The role of the state in promoting the primacy of family care is discussed with reference to a major empirical study of the care of older people in Sheffield, England. The results of this study are used to highlight the normative basis of the caring relationship. Walker examines alternative forms of care and casts doubt on the simplified assumption of conflict between older people and their caregivers.

INTRODUCTION

The purpose of this article is to examine the relationship between the family and the state in the provision of care to older people. The first question it addresses is *why* does the family (and female kin in particular) care for older relatives? The answer to this question is of enormous significance, both theoretically in the study of social gerontology and social policy, and practically in the realm of public policy. In most industrial and pre-industrial societies the family is the main provider of care to older (and other) relatives in need. For example, in Britain the proportion of severely disabled older people being cared for in their own or relatives' homes is as much as three times the proportion in all health and social services institutions put together (Townsend, 1981). Among confused older people, the group which places particularly heavy strains on carers, four-fifths are cared for in private households (Levin, Sinclair & Gorbach, 1986). In Canada too, despite a higher rate of institutional use than in Britain, recent research shows that the majority of people with dementia are receiving care in the community (MacFadgen, 1987, p. 286; Shulman, 1985). This consistent research finding concerning the primacy of the informal sector among all groups of older people receiving care signals the main factor underlying

"The Relationship Between the Family and the State in the Care of Older People" by Alan Walker, from *Canadian Journal on Aging,* 10 (1991). Copyright © 1991 by the University of Sheffield.

the current interest of the state in all developed and developing societies, in the so-called caring capacity of the community. All national governments are concerned about the cost implications of the unique demographic phenomenon of aging societies, though some are more concerned than others.

This raises a second question: what role does the state perform in the family care of older people? The main concern of this article is not with the direct provision of care by the state but with its role in promoting the primacy of family care—what has been called by feminist writers, the ideology of "familism" or "Familialism" (Barrett & McIntosh, 1982; Dalley, 1988). An examination of this question sheds considerable light on the social foundations of the caring relationship between older people and their families and draws on evidence from recent field research on the caring relationship.

In turning, thirdly, to the question of what alternative forms of caring relationships there are—ones that do not suffer from the same deficiencies as the present system of family care—issue is taken with some feminist analyses that have assumed a conflict between older people and their carers. It is argued that, in fact, the primary conflict is between state and people and is caused by the failure of the former to meet the needs of *both* older people and their carers. Underlying this failure is the state's active perpetuation of a narrow familist ideology which, at best, allows the costs of care to lie where they fall and, at worst, coerces carers and older people into relationships that are physically and emotionally damaging to both parties.

THE FAMILY CARE OF OLDER PEOPLE

The crucial role of the family in providing care for older relatives has been firmly established by research over the last 30 years (see, for example, Townsend, 1957; Shanas et al., 1968; Qureshi & Walker, 1989). It is increasingly widely accepted too that the primary burden of informal caring falls on women and, as a result, the costs associated with care fall predominantly on them. The extent of these four-fold costs—economic, physical, emotional and psychological—has been well-documented (see, for example, Parker, 1985; Joshi, 1987). But while there has been a great deal of research over the last ten years on the impact of caring, particularly on informal carers—which it must be said has redressed a long-standing neglect of their role—there has been very little work on the caring relationship itself and its social foundations. Why does the family (and female kin in particular) care for older relatives? On what basis is the caring relationship founded? It was questions such as these that, six years ago, prompted me to embark on a major empirical investigation of the caring relationship (Qureshi & Walker, 1989).

The Sheffield Study of Family Care

The research was based on a stratified random sample of people aged 75 and over living in Sheffield, England's fourth most populated city. In all, 306 older people were interviewed, at length, on such matters as contact with relatives and others, degree of disability, need for and receipt of formal and informal care, income and attitudes towards disability, dependency and care. The achieved sample closely matched the Census data on people aged 75 and over in Sheffield. Some recent research on people giving care to older relatives had tended, understandably, to present a one-sided picture of this process (see, for example, Nissel & Bonnerjea, 1982, p. 140). It was therefore decided from the outset that, since the caring relationship was the centerpiece of this research, it was necessary to interview those on *both* sides of it. So we followed up 57 people living outside the older person's household and providing sustained informal help to one of the older people in our sample on a regular weekly basis, by means of long semi-structured taped interviews.[1] In cases where more than one informal helper was contributing to the care of the older person an attempt was made to identify a principal carer in terms of the division of the caring labor, which proved possible in nearly all instances. To concentrate on practical assistance, or tending, is not to deny the importance of expressive emotional and moral support between older people and their families (see, for example, Rosenthal, 1987). However, it does serve to concentrate attention on those aspects of caring that might be regarded as substitutable by persons or agencies other than relatives (and, it must be said, the side of the caring coin that can be more reliably measured).

So, the findings reported here are based on a unique (in the British context) study of the two sides of the caring relationship.

Factors Influencing the Provision of Informal Care

At the heart of this investigation of the caring relationship was an attempt to determine the factors contributing to the provision of informal care to older people. But, before outlining our findings concerning provision, we will explore the question, who were the principal informal carers?

Just under half (45%) of the older people in the sample had at least one principal helper; while one-fifth of all older people had two such helpers. Principal informal carers were drawn overwhelmingly from within the older person's own family: only 9 per cent received regular help just from non-relatives and even fewer (7%) received assistance from both relatives and non-relatives. Thus, more than four in five older people with informal carers were receiving this help from relatives only. Furthermore, three in every four of those receiving informal care were receiving this help from outside their immediate household.

In common with previous studies of informal care we found that daughters were the most likely relatives to be providing care: over half (52%) of older people receiving care (just under one-quarter of all older people) had at least one daughter helping. One in four people with carers were being helped by a lone daughter. (Daughters were also the principal providers of expressive support.) The next most common source of family help was a spouse. Just over one-fifth of married older people (16 per cent of those with carers and 7 per cent of all older people) were receiving care from their spouse as a consequence of disability. Spouses were followed by other relatives, mainly siblings (13 per cent of those with carers and 6 per cent of the total population), though most of them were providing help in combination with another family member. Next in line of frequency were sons (11 per cent of older people with carers and 5 per cent of the total population). They were followed closely by daughters-in-law (10 per cent of older people receiving help). In contrast to sons (who were assisted by either their sisters or wives), the majority of the daughters-in-law who were caring were doing so alone. All of the five sons-in-law who were named as carers were assisting their wives (the daughters of the older people concerned) rather than caring alone. Finally a small number of non-relatives were lone carers (though altogether 13 percent of older people receiving help and 4 per cent of all older people were being helped by a non-relative). Thus, out of the seven possible single person categories of helper—spouse, daughter, daughter-in-law, son, son-in-law, other relative, non-relative—we found six operating in practice (the exception being son-in-law). In addition, out of the 27 possible two-person combinations we encountered 13, the most frequent of which were two daughters (8 per cent of older people with carers), a daughter and a son (5%) and a daughter with a son-in-law (4%).[2]

Having established the structural pattern of informal care, it was obviously important to discover whether or not there was any generally observed order of preference among available helpers, apart that is, from the consistent preference for daughters. But it may be argued that attempts to discover detailed normative "rules" determining patterns of care or caring personnel would be a hopeless task because individual social context and idiosyncratic personal history are more important than normative obligations or structural material conditions. For example, it is believed by some authorities within the field of social gerontology that both affect and reciprocity are important determinants of the delivery of informal care (see, for example, Abrams, 1978; Bould, Sanborn & Reif, 1988). We investigated both of these bases for care and our findings suggest that *neither* affect nor reciprocity are necessary conditions for the provision of practical care or tending. This is particularly clear when the carers are the older person's children. Thus we encountered a significant proportion of caring relationships where there was no evidence of affect or reciprocity and, therefore, no sense of individual-level obligation. It is not being argued, however, that reciprocity and affect are unimportant, indeed our data show that they are extremely important factors in determining the quality of the caring relationship. But my primary concern here is with the factors governing the *supply* of informal (family) care to older people.

Was there any generally observed order of preference among available helpers? Since information about living relatives was collected for each older person, it was possible for us to test the results of supposed theoretical decision-making rules against what actually happened in practice. We constructed a simple hierarchical decision model reflecting a traditional (in western cultures) normative preference structure. The rules are that close relatives are preferred to more distant ones, any relative is preferred to a non-relative, and female relatives are preferred to male relatives. In the first instance this decision model was based solely on relationship, but in order to recognize that normative rules are legitimately modifiable in practice by circumstances, such as the geographical proximity and health status of potential carers, this was adapted in subsequent analysis. Thus, the final hierarchy for the selection of principal helpers was:

1. spouse,
2. relative in lifelong joint household,
3. daughter,
4. daughter-in-law,

5. son,
6. other relative (living locally),
7. non-relative.

This admittedly rather simple decision model was applied to each older person to see how well its predicted decisions corresponded with decisions taken in practice. Surprisingly, the decision model predicted the correct carer or carers in 75 per cent of cases (80 per cent of single principal helpers and 67 per cent of pairs of helpers were correctly predicted). The main exceptions derived from our assumptions that other local relatives would step in to assist older people who had no local children and that daughters-in-law would assist spouses and sons, but they did not fulfill our expectations. (However, daughters-in-law themselves often had obligations to their own parents.)

To sum up so far: it can be argued that in making decisions about who provides care people very largely behave as if the hierarchical principles described in the model operate in practice, although these may be overruled by the ill-health of prospective carers. Of course, in ordinary families a "decision" to care in the sense of the culmination of a conscious process of deliberation is rarely made (Lewis & Meredith, 1988, p. 21), the process is more akin to a gradual drift. However, the extent of the continuity of this drift is remarkable. When the choice of carer is not clear-cut, as for example where there are two daughters both emotionally and geographically close to their older mother, the outcome is likely to hinge on an informal process of negotiation within the family.

What the model does not show should also be noted: first, that people themselves believe they have followed the principles implicit in it; secondly, that this structure reflects people's beliefs about what it is right to do. In order to investigate these questions we relied on extensive qualitative information collected from carers.

Why Do People Become Carers?

The decision model was based on a traditional normative preference structure which assumed that behavior in accordance with these established norms needs no explanation. Thus, it was predicted that those carers who perceived their help to be in accordance with such norms would see no need for explanation or elaboration. In fact three in ten carers could not elaborate on questions about whether or not they were the right person to be helping beyond responding "yes, of course." A further two in ten pointed to the fact that there was no-one else: "You see I'm the only one, so there's only me to do it." Among the remaining half of the carers, by far the most common response was a statement of the family relationship, such as "I'm her daughter." In other words, the vast majority accepted without question that caring for their older relative was *their* role.

The comments of non-family carers made it clear that family and particularly children are seen as the first line of assistance for older people:

I didn't think I should be doing it, because I think your family should come first . . . Mrs. Murphy needed somebody, and the family wasn't going regularly enough to see how she is coping day to day, so that was it. I took it on myself more or less. (Friend, daughter-in-law predicted by model.)

All carers who were children felt that they were the right people helping, but a number qualified their answers by indicating that other members of the family *should* do more. This finding accords with other research which found resentment on the part of carers about the lack of help from other relatives (Lewis & Meredith, 1988).

If the model reflects people's views about what is right, then people who are helpers when another family member would be predicted should be particularly prone to offer explanations of this deviation or give accounts of normative conflict, and this proved to be the case:

I don't mind. I don't mind helping his mother and I don't mind doing it because I know John (her husband) can't do it, but it annoys me that his sister doesn't do it. (Daughter-in-law who cares where daughter does not.)

Comments by carers give considerable support to the idea that obligation towards older people falls more strongly on family members, particularly children. But also, given the nature of the tasks required, daughters were expected to discharge obligations to provide domestic assistance directly, whereas some sons might be able to discharge such an obligation through their wives' labor (although the obligation to provide social contact remained).

In most cases individual feelings of affect and reciprocity and normative values are mutually reinforcing. However, some indication of the force of these obligations and of the fact that they are constructed externally to the caring relationship itself can be gained from looking at the position of those who care despite antagonistic individual-level feelings. Isaacs and his colleagues (1973) have commented on these phenomena: even children who had, for example, received little other than abuse from a violent and alcoholic parent still felt an obligation to help, or expressed guilt at their failure to do so. What about those adult children in our study who considered that their relationship with their parent had always been one-sided and who felt no obligation based on individual-level reciprocity? The feelings of the minority of children (one in six) who did not think that they owed any debt to their parents, yet still provided the necessary care, may be illustrated:

No matter what anybody does or says to me, I can't say "right, that's it, I've done, I am going (to stop helping)." I have to go back, my conscience won't let me. I mean some of the things I used to have said and done to me, some people would never have gone to my mother's again. (Daughter)

Also there appeared to be a clear association between the perception that the relationship between the adult carers and their parents had always been one-sided and a lack of emotional closeness, although the numbers were too small for statistical generalization.

The results of this study of family care, reported in outline, correspond with the findings of other recent research into family care including that by Marshall and his colleagues (1987) in Canada, which point to the delicate balance between reciprocity, affection and duty on which the nature of the individual caring relationship depends. However, our research suggests that while the quality of the caring relationship may rest on the outcome of this complex of individual-level factors, its existence owes more to external normative structures. In the first place, choices about who should care for older people are based on rules which derive from stereotyped beliefs about the debts owed by children to their parents and expectations about appropriate gender roles. Although the decision model employed was not sophisticated and requires further validation, it predicted the choice of carer with considerable accuracy.

Secondly, even though, in most instances where care was given, it was clear that people did feel a personalized sense of obligation towards their parents for past help, it was equally clear that a significant minority did not share these feelings, yet felt compelled to help by pressures external to the particular relationship. Indeed, in some instances it was evident that relationships between family members could be far more difficult and emotionally damaging than any other relationships. This raises the question: How are these external normative pressures reproduced? It is to the role of the state in this process that we now turn.

THE STATE AND FAMILY CARE

The state occupies a central role in the social construction of the traditional caring relationship outlined above and, therefore, in the maintenance of the dominant role of the family, and female kin in particular, in caring for older people.

How does the state influence, directly or indirectly, the provision of care by families? A variety of direct methods exist, varying from outright coercion (for example, prosecution for neglect of children) through to the provision of incentives, such as tax allowances or additional benefits for those caring for dependents. Secondly, the state can influence family help less directly by the way it organizes and provides services to individuals in need and by the assumptions it makes about the nature and availability of such assistance in rationing care (Moroney, 1976; Land, 1978; Walker, 1981; Dalley, 1988). Finally, the state's general economic and social policies set the framework of material and social conditions within which individual families find themselves. Thus, broad welfare policy may help to increase or reduce strains in and around the caring relationship by, for example, its response to poverty. In other words care *by* the community depends, in part, on care *for* the community (Walker, 1982). The state may have an observable influence on the provision of family care by the decisions, or lack of them, it makes with respect to public money. However, in most capitalist societies, it is the operation of covert forms of power, particularly at the ideological level, that give the state its primary influence over the lifeworld.

In the field of the care of older people coercion has rarely proved successful. The idea that the state could compel families to offer love and gratitude to their older parents was given little credence even by the administrators of the English Poor Law. They found that even the most obvious needs of older people failed to call forth sufficient informal support, despite coercive measures. This emphasizes the fact that if informal care is unwillingly given it loses its special qualities—particularly the *intrinsic* benefits such as emotional warmth, affection and interest—and can no longer claim to be a superior form of care. Indeed, in this situation it can become rapidly destructive of relationships, inducing resentment and guilt in both giver and receiver.

In Britain the direct involvement of the state in the caring functions of the family is relatively small, despite the existence of community care policies for the last 40 years. Social services departments are primarily concerned with crisis intervention, short-term support, such as respite care and, in cases of severe breakdown, long-term residential care.

In recent years the state has also substantially increased its subsidy, through the social security system, to the private sector of residential and nursing homes for older people. But again these services usually substitute for family care following the breakdown of the caring relationship or where there are no available relatives. The state is obviously committed to a system whereby the bulk of support for disabled older people is provided by relatives. In the first place it has a direct financial interest in doing so: a recent estimate of the economic value of the six million informal carers in Britain put the total at up to £24,000 million, more than the total public sector health and social services budget (Family Policy Studies Centre, 1989). Secondly, therefore, it fears that state intervention would weaken family ties. This position is reinforced by the neo-liberal aversion of the British government to most forms of state intervention in the lifeworld. Thirdly, it must be remembered that the state is a patriarchal state in that it is both dominated by men and by the ideology of patriarchy (Barrett, 1980). This means that the state has a direct interest in supporting traditional, that is, gendered, patterns of caring.

From the late sixteenth century to the nineteenth century, the primacy of family responsibility was enshrined in the Poor Laws by the legal obligation to provide for dependent relatives; and the fear that state help, if too easy to obtain, would undermine family relationships was ever present. The words of an Assistant Poor Law Commissioner in 1834 have a familiar ring today: "social ties . . . (are) now in the course of rapid extinction by the Poor Law." From his study of the evidence Anderson (1977) reached the opposite conclusion:

> . . . the (legal obligation) to assist was often a source of tension between parents and children throughout the nineteenth century. The "quality" of relationships was thus clearly worsened in these cases.

Most American studies have revealed a preference among the general population that long-term financial assistance to older people be provided by the state. However, the concern that "state interference" may threaten family ties by taking over the functions of the family seems to have persisted even in the area of financial help (see, for example, Kreps, 1977). Like the earlier Poor Law fears, this appears to be based on the assumption that intergenerational dependence is essential for the maintenance of family ties. Similar concerns have affected the construction of social policies in Britain: how to strike an appropriate balance between assuming too many responsibilities, and thus run the risk of weakening family ties, and offering too little help, thus causing the family to collapse under the unrelieved burden of providing care (Land & Parker,

1978). On the whole the provision of state services in Britain has been characterized by a norm of non-intervention in the caring relationship. The result is that the organization and distribution of social services has played a key role in reproducing traditional dependencies within the family, based on age and gender.

A Threat to the Family?

However, the assumption that state intervention would undermine family care has little support in contemporary research; indeed there are indications that non-intervention is more likely to put caring relationships under strain. It is assumed by policy-makers and service providers that state help, once offered, would inevitably be preferred (at least by those giving help). But in practice, those older people receiving services from their families are *not* anxious to apply for state help instead. In the Sheffield survey of older people and their families, although there was considerable unmet demand from those not receiving care, less than 10 per cent of those in receipt of weekly practical assistance from relatives or (in a few cases) neighbors, said that they would prefer such tasks to be performed by a home help (Qureshi & Walker, 1989). Most people preferred their existing family help even if a home help would have been available. What of those few who would have preferred a home help? Most frequently, these older people did not exactly prefer formal help but wished to relieve a perceived burden upon their family carer. Most older people felt (and their carers agreed) that family members were the right people to help them.

This research also demonstrated that seeking formal help is only the final stage of a dynamic process in which the available sources of informal assistance have all been considered, and the costs associated with them evaluated, *before* any approach is made to statutory services for assistance. Moreover, judgments about the quality of informal help available are made by those with the most detailed and exhaustive knowledge of the informal network: that is, the members themselves.

Current allocation practices in the social services show little respect for, or insight into, these prior processes in the informal sector. Statutory services are often delivered, and to some extent rationed, on the assumption that other family members, particularly daughters, should help in preference to agents of the state, especially in tasks where no recognized professional expertise is required. Such services as home help and auxiliaries to assist with bathing have been denied to, reduced or withdrawn from older people who have local relatives, particularly daughters, available (Qureshi & Walker, 1989). Also, it has been clearly shown that older people living with relatives are less likely to receive statutory help, no matter what their level of dependency (Charlesworth, Wilkin & Durie, 1984; Levin, Sinclair & Gorbach, 1986).

In the face of the norm of non-intervention, it is important not to lose sight of the fact that the provision of state services can strengthen family ties. Furthermore, it is important to remember that many statutory services are highly valued by recipients. One example is given in a recent study of people caring for older mentally infirm relatives or neighbors (Levin, Sinclair & Gorbach, 1986). Carers who received practical help in the form of home help, day care or community nursing services were *less* likely to suffer stress and more likely still to have the dependent person at home than people who did not receive such assistance. Additionally, it should be noted that the impersonal nature of help delivered through a bureaucratic structure may be seen as an advantage by some of those receiving help. Agents of an outside organization are detached from past family quarrels or disputes, and have no future expectations of return for services rendered. Equally, from the point of view of carers, there are sometimes situations in which an older person behaves less reasonably towards family members than towards agents of the state. A number of carers in the Sheffield study indicated occasions on which their older relative "put on a different face," generally a more cooperative face, for people from outside agencies. Other evidence (Boyd & Woodman, 1978) suggests that this can be carried to the extreme in situations in which an older person's capacity for, or willingness to display, independence drops dramatically as soon as they are returned from a hospital or residential home to the care of their relatives.

The Social Construction of the Caring Relationship

The idea that the family is a private domain is a myth. It is, in fact, the longstanding object of both direct and indirect state intervention (Donzelot, 1979). But the illusion is fundamental in obscuring this intervention and maintaining the status quo. As Moroney (1976, p. 213) has pointed out:

By presenting (existing patterns of responsibility and dependencies and the division of labour) as "normal" or "natural," the state supports and sustains these relationships without appearing intrusive, thus serving the illusion that the family is a private domain.

The norm of non-intervention in some selected aspects of the lifeworld reinforces itself in preventing demand for social services and in ensuring that the family performs certain functions, such as the care of older relatives. In this way the limits to the roles of the family and the state are firmly established not in statute but through the reproduction of "normal" patterns and duties of family life.

At the heart of this process of reproduction, particularly in the field of social care, is the hegemony of what has been called the ideology of familism (Barrett & McIntosh, 1982; Dalley, 1988). That is, the ideological construction of a particular form of individualistic western family organization—with traditional gender division of domestic labor and normative belief systems concerning responsibility for care within the family of procreation and the family of orientation—underlies all contemporary forms of organization of everyday life. This ideology and particularly its prescriptive normative beliefs concerning responsibility for the care of older relatives, as we have seen, are internalized by family members and even when there is no individual-level obligation, they still act according to a general sense of duty. Thus, non-conformity to the hegemony of familism is regarded as deviant (Dalley, 1988, p. 21).

Within this ideology of familism the family is portrayed as a haven from the outside world. Women are located centrally as the providers of nurture and care. They are regarded as "natural" carers and, moreover, their altruism is also portrayed as "natural." Their idealized role conforms to the principles of Victorian womanly values: self-sacrifice and service to others. However, as the Sheffield research demonstrated, female kin are under enormous normative pressure to care and, therefore, their conformity should more properly be regarded as what Land and Rose (1985) call "compulsory altruism."

It is widely accepted that modern welfare states were founded on the unpaid domestic labor of women (and their low paid employment in the institutions of welfare). But it is not simply sexism that underpins the welfare state; it is assumptions about the proper role of women within a traditional family structure, or familism. For example women were said to have "a sense of divine vocation" by the founder of the British postwar welfare state, William Beveridge (Land & Rose, 1985, p. 181).

Not surprisingly, the altruistic housewife featured centrally in Beveridge's proposals for social security. Benefits were structured to reflect the dependent status of married women and their priority to duties in the household and the primary responsibility of men to the labor market. Today social policies, such as community care, reflect and reinforce the ideology of familism by assuming that the family is necessarily the right location for the care of older relatives and that, within it, female kin are the most appropriate carers.

The social security system still retains some remnants of these ideological foundations: for example, the exclusion of domestic tasks from the payment of attendance allowance (a benefit for people with disabilities needing care and attention). Until a European Court ruling against the British government, in 1986, married women caring for their husbands were excluded from receiving invalid carers allowance (a benefit for carers of people with disabilities). The social division of care along gender lines is also reinforced, as we have seen, by the tendency in Britain to limit home help and home care support to older people if there is a daughter living nearby (Finch & Groves, 1983).[3] Thus the state enforces and capitalizes on the subordinate role of women within the family by the reproduction of a traditional familist ideology and through social policies which make caring a social obligation.

The preceding analysis has shown that what has been called a "naturally negotiated" relationship between the old and the young in the family (Johnson, 1972) with regard to care is, in fact, socially constructed on the basis of prescriptive normative ideas and beliefs about the traditional family as the most appropriate form for the social organization of care and the correct division of labor within it. Informal deviations from these norms carry heavy social sanctions, such as guilt and stigma, and formal deviations are rationed by the state. Currently favored community care policies operate to reinforce the compulsory altruism of the family and female kin in particular. Even where there is a choice of care between different family members, decisions about who should help are not freely made but incorporate normative judgments based on gender-role expectations about the appropriateness of the particular tasks required, and the importance which may be attached to other normatively determined obligations. For example, it may be that a man's obligations to his immediate family are assumed to include remaining in full-time employment, whilst a woman's may not be.

As Land & Rose have argued, drawing on Titmuss' analysis of blood donation in *The Gift Relationship* (1970), if the gift is to be safe to be received it must be freely given:

> For women to be free not to give (care) as well as to give requires that there are good alternative services. Only then will they not feel that they have no choice except to sacrifice themselves for another (Land & Rose, 1985, p. 93).

The evidence outlined earlier shows that carers do not give care freely because they, older people and health and social services personnel alike, have all internalized the powerful ideology of familism, and it is this that largely determines the provision of informal care. Of course, the detailed operation of the caring relationship is negotiated between those family members involved but within the structural context of forceful normative expectations and beliefs. Carers' own beliefs about what is right and wrong and their personal struggles to enact these moral beliefs reflect this dominant ideology (Ungerson, 1987). The end result is that, at best, women bear a larger burden of caring labor than men and, at worst, that some of the most destructive relationships imaginable are imposed on both older people and their carers. Because family and other informal carers are constrained by normative obligations it is difficult for change to be achieved at an individual level. Also the large-scale provision of alternatives is a matter for social policy, which brings us to the third and final question of this article: what alternatives are there to the traditional caring relationship?

THE CONFLICT BETWEEN FAMILY AND STATE

The necessity for alternative ways of providing social care to older people and the urgency of the search for them are based on the preceding analysis of the unequal gender division of labor within, and the coercive aspects of, the caring relationship. Three main options are open to policy-makers, although choice between them depends more on ideology than on any perceived benefits to older people and their families (Walker, 1987). Discussion of these alternatives highlights the conflict over the care of older people between the family and the state.

First, there is the policy pursued by neo-liberal governments, as exemplified by the Thatcher administrations in Britain, to encourage greater reliance on the informal sector itself. In the government's own words: "it is the role of public authorities to sustain and, where necessary, develop—but never to displace" informal and voluntary care and support; and "Care *in* the community must increasingly mean care *by* the community" (DHSS, 1981, p. 3). This policy comprises two main elements. On the one hand, already minimal domiciliary provision has been purposely reduced in relation to the growing need among the population aged 75 and over (Walker, 1985). On the other hand, ministers have been appealing to the wider "community" to provide an increased input and have devoted comparatively small sums of money to several initiatives—such as the Helping the Community to Care initiative—designed to encourage it to do so. The fundamental flaw in this approach is that it is based, at best, on an overoptimistic view of the existing and potential contribution of the wider community and is, therefore, bound to increase the burden on family carers and increase the strains on the caring relationship. Therefore the interests of *both* older people and their carers lie in opposition to this development.

Second, it has been proposed that the collective residential services should take over a substantial amount of the care of older people currently provided by the family. Some feminists, doubting the feasibility of the social and economic changes necessary to establish greater gender equality in caring and opposing the individualism of the family, have suggested that residential care represents a preferable alternative as far as female carers are concerned (Dalley, 1988; Finch, 1984; Waerness, 1986). This approach is based on the erroneous assumption that the primary conflict in the social construction of the caring role is between female carers and older people (most of whom are themselves female). In fact the primary division is between *both* carers and older people on the one side and the (patriarchal) state, which is failing to ensure adequate support for either, on the other side. Thus the argument by some feminists for collective forms of care overlooks the point that caring consists of labor and love, that is caring *for* and caring *about* someone. There is no doubt that carers need assistance with caring labor but there is no evidence that this is true for the affective or expressive aspects of care.

Also, proponents of this attempt to rehabilitate the concept of the residential institution apparently do not take into account the long history of research which demonstrates the inhibiting and dependency-creating nature of residential care (for a review, see Townsend, 1981). The compulsory altruism of carers would be replaced by the compulsory dependency of older people. In other words, this approach is one-sided—emphasizing the needs of carers and playing down those of older people—and does not reflect the perceptions of those actually engaged in caring relationships. Thus seven out of ten older people in the Sheffield study either rejected residential care or regarded it as a last resort. At the same time nearly six out of ten carers also rejected the idea (Qureshi & Walker, 1989).

Third, both of these alternatives entail unacceptable costs either for female carers or older people—usually both. Yet the status quo is equally untenable. This conclusion has led a number of policy analysts to propose a greater sharing of caring tasks and responsibilities between the formal and informal sectors (Moroney, 1976; Land & Parker, 1978; Parker, 1981; Bayley, 1982; Walker, 1982). For example, I have argued previously for the introduction of community care policies which support and share the caring activities of families. Such a policy "should not put women under a greater obligation than men to provide care and . . . as far as possible, it should actively encourage men to provide care" (Walker, 1981, p. 37). The aim of this proposal was not to establish sex equality, since this would rest on social and economic changes outside the immediate realm of the caring relationship, but rather to attempt to ensure that sex inequality in caring is not reinforced.

The fundamental principles upon which a policy of shared care should be based are that neither families nor female kin should be put under any external obligation to care for older relatives and, if they choose to do so, the expectation must be that formal supportive services will be available on demand to assist them. For too long families have been left to themselves to organize and deliver care. This burden has fallen largely on daughters, often single-handed and with little sustained formal support. Policy-makers have legitimated non-intervention by the excuse that it is the family's responsibility and, therefore, the domestic sphere has been kept private or "familised." But a genuine commitment to shared care implies the collective provision of resources to supplement and, where necessary, substitute for family care. The policy would be aimed at supporting the caring activities of family and other informal carers while not exploiting their willingness to care.

The three main points at which change must be initiated to promote a policy of shared care may be summarized (for a full account see Walker, 1987). First of all change is required in the organization and operation of the formal services. In order to overcome the rigid division between the formal and informal sectors it might be helpful to think more in terms of "social support networks" than informal support networks (Whittaker & Garbarino, 1983). Social support networks are not necessarily "natural" and may be created to fill a specific need. They may comprise both formal and informal helpers, or professional and non-professional personnel. This broader concept of support networks encourages policy-makers to perceive care in the form of a partnership between people with different skills. Various experimental schemes in Britain suggest that it is possible to increase the sensitivity of the formal sector to family and other informal networks and change traditional roles within the state social services (Qureshi & Walker, 1989, p. 270).

Secondly, change must be initiated in professional values and attitudes within the formal sector if a partnership between the formal and informal sectors is to be developed. This is primarily a matter of increasing the accountability of professionals to both older people and their carers. Although a long-term goal would be the socialization of the health and social services to transform the experience of welfare from a passive one (as clients or patients) to active participation in the definition of need and policy responses to it, there will always be an important role for professional groups.

Thirdly, the goal of shared care must not divert attention from the need to share care within the family. Major social and ideological changes are required to overcome the normative designation of women as carers and the moral imperative on them to care. In the absence of policies to overcome gender inequalities in society as a whole, the best that can be hoped for are social care policies which do not put women under a greater obligation than men to provide care. A start can be made in this direction by ensuring that the availability of female kin is not a criterion for rationing formal care, and that sufficient social services are available to facilitate a choice for female kin.

How likely is it that these sorts of changes will be brought about? In Britain the recent direction of government economic and social policy has increased the likelihood of female kin being expected to care for older relatives in need. At a time when the numbers of very old people requiring care are rising and the pool of family carers shrinking, albeit slowly, the government has reduced the already meagre resources for community-based formal care. In addition to a growth in the coverage of family care, the burdens on individual carers are likely to be increased. We are witnessing the heightening of a major conflict between the state and the people. The needs of both older people and family carers are not being adequately met by policy. The strains and tensions that exist in a caring relationship which is imposed on relatives or which is conducted in an atmosphere of great physical and emotional tribulation, affect *both* sides of the relationship. While the state sustains a casualty-oriented system of care it is effectively supporting the unequal division of labor in care and the detrimental impact this has on carers and older people alike.

CONCLUSION

The research on which this paper is based found the family system of care for older people to be widespread, resilient and extremely efficient in delivering care to where it was most needed. In common with Canadian research we found no loss of community (Wellman & Hall, 1986) among older people. But the caring relationship entails unacceptable costs for carers, primarily women, which also damage the expressive side of the relationship itself (Qureshi & Walker, 1989). This caring relationship, contrary to the biologically determinist assumptions common in this field, was shown to be socially constructed. Its foundation is a set of traditional normative beliefs concerning the role of the family in care and that of women in the family. This ideology goes much deeper than governments of different political persuasions, that may come and go, and is common to all western industrial societies. The insight provided by the feminist analysis of "familism" is essential to understanding this ideological basis of the caring relationship—although as a western model it is culturally specific; however, the policy proposals emanating from this analysis confuse the collective provision of care with collectivized forms of care. The latter would add to the dependency of older people.

In Britain older people with disabilities and their informal carers want to live in their own home, within a familiar community setting, for as long as possible. They prefer "intimacy at a distance" with their relatives. This aspiration seems to be shared by Canadian elders (National Advisory Council on Ageing, 1986). Thus the challenge for policy is to find ways of sharing care more effectively between family and state, ways which do not exploit the willingness of female kin to care but which at the same time maintain the independence of older people and their families. Policy-makers and professionals working with older people should begin to consider the possibility that not all relationships across the generations will be characterized by love, affection or even a sense of personal obligation. People who wish to help should be assisted to do so without a significant personal sacrifice, but perhaps the main principle that policy-makers and society in general must recognize is that not all families should be expected to care.

NOTES

1. Sustained informal help was defined as practical assistance involving the complete performance of tasks such as heavy laundry, shopping or housework at least once a week, or lighter tasks such as cooking and light housework at least three times a week. It was specified that this assistance should not be part of routine household duties, such as were performed by many older wives for their non-disabled spouses.

2. The apparently low level of support provided by spouses is accounted for by the fact that a spouse was only regarded as a principal helper if the division of domestic duties was regarded by the couple as a consequence of one partner's disability rather than a normal state of affairs.

3. Home help/home care services are provided by local authorities to assist with domestic tasks in the older person's own home.

REFERENCES

Abrams, P. (1978). *Neighbourhood Care and Social Policy.* Berkhamsted: Volunteer Centre.

Anderson, M. (1977). The impact on the family relationships of the elderly of changes since Victorian times in government income maintenance. In E. Shanas & M. Sussman (Eds.), *Family Bureaucracy and the Elderly.* Durham, NC: Duke University Press.

Barrett, M. (1980). *Women's Oppression Today.* London: Verso.

Barrett, M., & McIntosh, M. (1982). *The Anti-Social Family.* London: Verso.

Bayley, M. (1982). Helping care to happen in the community. In A. Walker (Ed.), *Community Care: The Family, the State and Social Policy.* Oxford: Blackwell/Martin Robertson.

Bould, S., Sanbourn, B., & Reif, L. (1988). *Eighty-Five Plus.* California: Wadsworth.

Boyd, R. V., & Woodman, J. A. (1978). The Jekyll-and-Hyde syndrome: An example of disturbed relations affecting the elderly. *The Lancet, 8091,* 671–672.

Charlesworth, A., Wilkin, D., & Durie, A. (1984). *Carers and Services: A Comparison of Men and Women Caring for Dependent Elderly People.* Manchester: EOC.

Dalley, G. (1988). *Ideologies of Caring.* London: Macmillan.

DHSS. (1981). *Growing Older* (Cmnd. 8173). London: HMSO.

Donzelot, J. (1979). *The Policing of Families.* London: Hutchinson.

Family Policy Studies Centre. (1989). *Family Policy Bulletin, 6.* London: FPSC.

Finch, J. (1984). Community care: developing non-sexist alternatives. *Critical Social Policy, 9,* 6–18.

Finch, J., & Groves, D. (Eds.) (1983). *A Labour of Love: Women, Working and Caring.* London: Routledge & Kegan Paul.

Isaacs, B., Livingstone, M., & Neville, Y. (1973). *Survival of the Unfittest: A Study of Geriatric Patients in Glasgow.* London: Routledge.

Johnson, M. L. (1972). *Old and young in the family: A negotiated arrangement.* Paper given at the British Society for Social and Behavioural Gerontology Conference.

Joshi, H. (1987). The cost of caring. In C. Glendinning & J. Millar (Eds.), *Women and Poverty in Britain* (pp. 112–136). Brighton: Wheatsheaf Books.

Kreps, J. (1977). Intergenerational transfers and the bureaucracy. In E. Shanas & M. Sussman (Eds.), *Family, Bureaucracy and the Elderly.* Durham, NC: Duke University Press.

Land, H. (1978). Who cares for the family? *Journal of Social Policy, 7,* 3, 357–384.

Land, H., & Parker, R. (1978). Family policy in the UK. In S. Kamermann & A. Kahn (Eds.), *Family Policy: Government and Families in Fourteen Countries* (pp. 331–366). New York: Columbia University Press.

Land, H., & Rose, H. (1985). Compulsory altruism or an altruistic society for all? In P. Bean et al., *In Defence of Welfare* (pp. 74–95). London: Tavistock.

Levin, E., Sinclair, I., & Gorbach, P. (1986). *Families, Services and Confusion in Old Age.* London: Allen & Unwin.

Lewis, J., & Meredith, B. (1988). *Daughters Who Care.* London: Routledge.

MacFadgen, S. L. (1987). The care of irreversible dementia sufferers in the Toronto and Peel regions: Perceptions of service providers. *Canadian Journal on Aging, 6,* (4), 271–289.

Marshall, V., Rosenthal, C., & Dacink, J. (1987). Older parents expectations for filial support. *Social Justice Research 1,* (4), 405–424.

Moroney, R. M. (1976). *The Family and the State.* London: Longman.

National Advisory Council on Ageing. (1986). *Toward a Community Support Policy for Canadians.* Ottawa: NACA.

Nissel, M., & Bonnerjea, L. (1982). *Family Care of the Handicapped Elderly: Who Pays?* London: PSI.

Parker, G. (1985). *With Due Care and Attention.* London: Family Policy Studies Centre.

Parker, R. (1981). Tending and social policy. In E. M. Goldberg & S. Hatch (Eds.), *A New Look at the Personal Social Services* (pp. 17–32). London: PSI.

Qureshi, H., & Walker, A. (1989). *The Caring Relationship: Elderly People and Their Families.* London: Macmillan.

Rosenthal, C. J. (1987). The comforter: Providing personal advice and emotional support to generations in the family. *Canadian Journal on Aging, 6,* (3), 228–239.

Shanas, E., Townsend, P., Wedderburn, D., Henning, F., Milhøj, P., & Stehouwer, J. (1968). *Old People in Three Industrial Social Societies.* London: Routledge & Kegan Paul.

Shulman, K. (1985). Geriatric psychiatry: What's new in old age? *Perspectives in Psychiatry, 4,* (3) 1–4.

Titmuss, R. M. (1970). *The Gift Relationship.* Canada: Allen & Unwin.

Townsend, P. (1957). *The Family Life of Old People.* Harmondsworth: Penguin.

Townsend, P. (1981). Elderly people with disabilities. In A. Walker with P. Townsend (Eds.), *Disability in Britain* (pp. 91–118). Oxford: Martin Robertson.

Ungerson, C. (1987). *Policy is Personal.* London: Tavistock.

Waerness, K. (1986). Informal and formal care in old age? Paper presented to the XIth World Congress of Sociology, New Delhi.

Walker, A. (1981). Community care and the elderly in Great Britain: Theory and practice. *International Journal of Health Services, 11,* (4), 541–557.

Walker, A. (1982). The meaning and social division of community care. In A. Walker (Ed.), *Community Care: The Family, The State and Social Policy.* Oxford: Blackwell/Martin Robertson.

Walker, A. (1985). Care of elderly people. In R. Berthoud (Ed.), *Challenges to Social Policy.* Aldershot: Gower.

Walker, A. (1987). Enlarging the caring capacity of the community: Informal Support networks and the welfare state. *International Journal of Health Services, 17,* (3), 369–386.

Wellman, B., & Hall, A. (1986). Social networks and social support. In V. Marshall (Ed.), *Later Life* (pp. 191–232). California: Sage.

Whittaker, J. K., & Garbarino, J. (Eds.). (1983). *Social Support Networks: Informal Helping in the Human Services.* New York: Aldine.

18

Grandparents Who Parent Their Grandchildren: Effects on Lifestyle

MARGARET PLATT JENDREK

Jendrek's study is based on a screening and in-depth interview with each of 114 grandparents who provide daily care to their grandchildren. Based on the results of her study, she has identified three categories of caregivers: grandparents whose grandchildren live with them and with whom they have a legal relationship; grandparents whose grandchildren live with them but with whom there is no legal relationship; and grandparents whose grandchildren do not live with them but for whom they provide day care. Jendrek shows how providing care for grandchildren affects caregivers' lives by changing their life-styles and their relationships with friends, families, and spouses.

The media refer to some grandparents as the "silent saviors," "the second line of defense," and "the safety net." Highlighted in the media are the grandparents who thought their childrearing days were over and who now find themselves raising their children's children (e.g., Creighton, 1991). I know several grandparents who provide regular care to grandchildren, and have spoken with colleagues who also know such individuals. The idea for this study emerged from my conversations with these grandparents. I was deeply impressed by their ability to improvise, their love and concern for the third generation, their fears and worries, and the policy issues they raised. The part of the study reported here was undertaken to collect both quantitative and qualitative data on the effect of providing care on grandparents' lifestyles. The quantitative data allow for comparisons across respondents and samples; the qualitative data give life to the numbers as the voices of the "silent saviors" are heard.

"Grandparents Who Parent Their Grandchildren: Effects on Lifestyle" by Margaret Platt Jendrek, from *Journal of Marriage and the Family*, 55 (1993): 609–621. Copyright © 1993 by the National Council on Family Relations.

BACKGROUND

The Demographic Context

Grandparents provide regular care to grandchildren either formally (via court orders or decisions) or informally (the grandchild either lives with the grandparent or spends a regular portion of his or her day with the grandparent). The Census Bureau estimates that, in 1991, approximately 3.3 million children in the United States lived with grandparents (Saluter, 1992). This figure refers to homes maintained by grandparents and does not include grandchildren whose parents maintain the home, even though a grandparent lives with them. The 3.3 million figure represents a 44% increase since 1980 in the number of grandchildren living with grandparents. Among these grandchildren, only the mother was present for approximately 50%, neither parent was present for 28%, both parents were present for 17%, and only the father was present for 5% (Saluter, 1992).

In 1991, black children were much more likely to live in a grandparent's home than were white children or children of Hispanic origin; the proportions were 12.3%, 3.7%, and 5.6% for black, white, and Hispanic children, respectively. These figures represent increases of 24%, 54%, and 40% for each group since 1980 (Saluter, 1992). The largest rate of increase occurred among white children, from 2.4% of white children living with grandparents in 1980 to 3.7% in 1991. This research focuses on white families, that segment of the population in which the rate of increase is largest.

The Theoretical Context

Seltzer (1976) defined time-disordered roles as those that arise when "an individual's various social spheres and role sets are not temporally synchronized" (pp. 111–112). Normally, an individual expects congruence in his or her work, family, and age-set spheres. Time-disordered roles result when even one sphere is out of phase with the other two.

In addition to being "off-time," time-disordered roles may create stress in two other ways. First, stress may be created by a dramatic change in the individual's life expectations and in the ability of peers to provide social support (Hagestad & Neugarten, 1985). That is, individuals who have been rehearsing expected roles suddenly find that they cannot play the role in the anticipated manner. The resulting disjuncture between the anticipated role and the actual role may create strain. Second, the individual's traditional support networks of friends and family may be unable to help because they are no longer simultaneously experiencing similar circumstances (Hagestad & Neugarten, 1985; Seltzer, 1976). Thus individuals experiencing time-disordered situations may find that they need to readjust their roles and support groups.

The time-disordered pattern to be examined here is contingent on the life transitions of other family members. Although Hagestad and Neugarten (1985) note that "American society does not have formal norms regarding such interdependencies" (p. 50), informal expectations exist. In the expected pattern, one first becomes a parent and raises children. The children then form their own nuclear families, bearing and raising their own children. Grandparents remain free of parenting responsibilities in relation to grandchildren. That pattern is violated when the grandparent assumes a parenting role for the third generation. How does this pattern violation and the ensuing time-disordered role affect the grandparent?

METHOD

The Interview Schedules

The research is based on two interviews, a screening interview and an in-depth interview. The screening interview (available upon request from the author) briefly examines grandparents' temporal access to grandchildren and their degree of involvement with grandchildren. The screen contains both subjective and objective assessments of the types and amount of care provided by the grandparent. Questions were asked about each grandchild to whom the grandparent provided care. If the grandparent provided routine care to more than one grandchild, he or she was asked whether one grandchild required more care than the other(s). The grandchild receiving the most care became the focus grandchild in the in-depth interview.

Where more than one grandchild could serve as the focus grandchild, I randomly selected the focus grandchild from the screening interview data, using a table of random numbers. The screen was designed to include grandparents who provide regular care to a grandchild and to exclude grandparents who volunteered because they obtained information about the study, for example, the one and only time they took their grandchild to the dentist. The screening interviews were conducted over the telephone and were not taped. Each screening interview lasted approximately one-half hour.

The in-depth interview blends quantitative with qualitative methods to produce a more complete picture of grandparents who provide care to grandchildren. Focusing on one grandchild, this interview contains six sections (available upon request from the author). One section gathers information about the type of care currently provided by the grandparent (adoption, legal custody, temporary custody, guardianship, living with the grandchild but no legal relationship to that grandchild, and daycare) and the type of care, if any, provided previously by the grandparent. Using both open- and closed-ended questions, a second section examines why grandparents provide regular care to grandchildren. A third section focuses on the decision to provide care and on whether pressures were exerted to provide that care. A fourth section concerns grandparents' employment experiences, with emphasis on whether providing care influences either employment or retirement decisions. Grandparents' leisure activities and the effect that providing care to a grandchild may have on lifestyle are the focus of a fifth section, which uses both open- and closed-ended questions. Grandparents' use of service providers (social service agencies, medical practitioners, and lawyers) constitutes the sixth section. Questions pertaining to grandparents' feelings and concerns about providing care to a grandchild are interspersed throughout the interview. Overall, the aim was to gather comparative information via the closed-ended questions and to allow the grandparents' own words to help interpret and exemplify the findings.

All in-depth interviews were taped and either conducted over the telephone or face-to-face. The decision to conduct an interview face-to-face was based on either the respondent's request for such an interview or on my decision to randomly select a group of grandparents to interview face-to-face. Face-to-face in-depth interviews were conducted at a time and place named by the respondent. After taping the first few face-to-face interviews, I found that the quality of the tapes was so poor that the transcriber could not always understand them. Consequently I interviewed most respondents over the telephone. In-depth interviews ranged in length from ½ hour to 3½ hours, depending on the type of care being provided by the grandparent.

The Sample

Locating grandparents. There are no grandparent registration lists and certainly no rosters of grandparents as caregivers. Using courts, medical practices, schools, and advertising, I obtained a nonprobability sample of grandparents who provide regular care to grandchildren in or near Butler County, Ohio. Using the demographic data that were available at the time of selection, I selected Butler County as the study area (although some respondents came from adjacent counties) because many of the pertinent demographic characteristics of Butler County (e.g., the gross birth rate, the percentages of people age 45 or older, the divorce rate, and the percentages of births to mothers under age 20) reflect the demographic characteristics of Ohio and the United States (U.S. Bureau of the Census, 1988). Because of these similarities, the exploratory data generated by the sample may have implications for the rest of Ohio and for the United States.

The Domestic Relations Court judge and the Juvenile Court judge in Butler County agreed to alert grandparents to the study. A court clerk gave a packet of information describing the study to grandparents seeking a legal relationship with a grandchild. The packet contained a self-addressed postcard, which grandparents were to return if they were interested either in learning more about the study or in participating.

I also used other sources to create the sample. I wrote to physicians and dentists in 110 medical practices listed in Butler County telephone book. I visited the 10 practices that agreed to participate and explained the study to the staff member responsible for overseeing the distribution of the information. Each participating practice received about 20 information packets to distribute to grandparents who they knew were providing care to grandchildren.

I sent a packet of information describing the study to principals of each of the 89 schools listed for Butler County. Six principals agreed to participate and allowed me to place a notice about the study in their school newsletter. Packets of information were sent to these principals to distribute to grandparents who they knew provided care to grandchildren.

Miami University's News Bureau released information about the study to local radio stations. My name and telephone number were included so that interested listeners could contact me. Advertisements were also placed in local newspapers.

Caregiver roles. This research is based on the screening and in-depth interviews with 30 custodial grandparents, 4 adoptive grandparents, 2 grandparents who assumed guardianship, 26 grandparents living with a grandchild without having a legal relationship to that grandchild, and 52 grandparents providing regular day care. Three major categories of grandparent care roles emerged from the data: custodial, living with the grandchild, and day-care roles. Throughout the remainder of the analysis, the 36 grandparents who have a legal relationship with the grandchild (adoption, full custody, temporary custody, guardianship) will be combined and called "custodial" grandparents. The 26 grandparents who live with a grandchild but do not have one of the above-noted legal relationships to that grandchild will be called "living-with" grandparents; the 52 grandparents providing regular day care will be known as "day-care" grandparents. These three roles differ from each other both quantitatively and qualitatively.

A legal relationship with the grandchild (adoption, full custody, temporary custody, or guardianship) defines the grandparent's care role as custodial. Legal custody is "the right or authority of a parent, or parents, to make decisions concerning the child's upbringing" (Schulman & Pitt, 1982, p. 540). Legal custody includes, for example, the right to make decisions pertaining to the child's education, medical care, and discipline. Physical custody is "the right to physical possession of the child (i.e., to have the child live with the . . . parent)" (Schulman & Pitt, 1982, p. 541). The physical custodian is responsible for the daily care of the child. Custodial grandparents become the grandchild's legal and physical custodians. Custodial grandparents used the court system and hired attorneys to obtain the transfer of responsibility and authority for the grandchild from the parent(s) to themselves. When the grandchild's parent(s) agreed to the transfer, it generally occurred "smoothly." When the case was contested, the court record contained statements from the grandparent about his or her own child's inability to parent the grandchild and counterclaims about the grandparent's parenting skills made by the child's parent. Contested cases were a source of agony for grandparents, who were forced to announce publicly that their child was an unfit parent. Once a custodial arrangement is obtained, custodial grandparents have full care of their grandchild; they become both the decision makers and the daily caregivers.

Living-with grandparents are defined by their role of responsibility without any corresponding authority. These grandparents have not gone to court to obtain a legal relationship with their grandchild. Therefore, they are not authorized to make decisions about their grandchild; that authority resides with the parent. Living-with grandparents, however, assume responsibility for some, if not all, of the grandchild's daily care. When the parent abandons the grandchild, the grandparent constantly fears the parent's return and the possible impact on the grandchild. When one parent lives in the home with the grandparent and the grandchild, the two older generations must find a way to establish the lines of authority.

Day-care grandparents are not casual baby-sitters; they provide grandchildren with daily care for extended periods. Their days are organized around the arrival and departure of the grandchild. Like the three-generation living-with grandparents, day-care grandparents must resolve differences in childrearing with their grandchild's parent(s). These grandchildren, however, go home at the end of a day.

Overall profile of the sample. The total number of grandparents interviewed was 114. The sample was primarily white (96%) and female (97%). Respondents ranged in age from 41 to 71 years; the mean age was approximately 56 years at the time of the in-depth interview. More than half (55%) of the sample was not currently employed outside the home; 29% worked full-time and 16% worked part-time. The respondents' educational level ranged from completion of the seventh grade to the completion of several Master's degrees; the mean educational level was approximately 1 year of college. The grandparents in the study said they had between 1 and 24 grandchildren; the median number was 3. (These figures include the focus grandchild.)

Slightly more than half (53.5%) of the focus grandchildren in the study were male. The number of grandchildren to whom grandparents provided care ranged from one to five; most (60%) grandparents provided care to only one grandchild. The focus grandchild for the remaining 40% of the grandparents was either the grandchild to whom they said they provided the most care or was selected randomly from the grandchildren to whom they provided care. All of the focus grandchildren were the natural grandchildren of the grandparents rather than stepgrandchildren. Most (67%) grandchildren were related through their mother to the grandparent providing care.

Custodial grandparents. Grandparents seek a custodial relationship because of problems in the grandchild's family, particularly problems involving the mother. The five leading reasons for providing care given by the custodial grandparents were: (a) the grandchild's mother was having emotional problems (72.7%), (b) the grandparent did not want the grandchild in a foster home (53.1%), (c) the grandchild's mother was having a drug problem (52.8%), (d) the grandchild's mother was having a mental problem (48.3%), and (e) the grandchild's mother was having an alcohol problem (44.1%). (For a more complete description of the circumstances of and decisions about providing care to a grandchild, see Jendrek, 1993.)

Custodial grandparents ranged in age from 40 to 62 years at the time of obtaining a legal relationship with their grandchild; the mean age was about 48 years. The grandchildren ranged in age from newborn to 14.5 years at the time when the grandparent obtained the legal relationship; the grandchild's median age was 2 years. The length of the legal relationship at the time of the in-depth interview ranged from 2 months to 13 years; the median length was 3 years at that time.

Custodial grandparents tended to be married (74%) when they began the legal relationship. The length of their marriages ranged from 3 to almost 40 years; the median length was 22.5 years. Three-fourths of the custodial grandparents were related to the grandchild through their daughter.

Most (89%) of the custodial grandparents had provided care to their grandchild before taking legal action. Two-thirds (67%) of the grandparents with temporary custody had lived with the grandchild before obtaining temporary custody. Similarly, almost two-thirds (65%) of the grandparents with custody of a grandchild had lived with the grandchild before obtaining custody; an additional 15% had temporary custody before obtaining full legal custody. The two grandparents with guardianship said they had lived with the grandchild before obtaining guardianship. Two of the adoptive grandparents said they had lived with the grandchild before the adoption; the other two said they had custody of the grandchild before adoption. Only four grandparents had not provided any form of care to the grandchild before obtaining a legal relationship to that grandchild.

Living-with grandparents. In their reasons for providing care, grandparents living with a grandchild focused on parental problems and on their desire to help the grandchild's parents. The five leading reasons given by living-with grandparents for providing care were (a) wanting to help the grandchild's parent(s) financially (65.4%), (b) the grandchild's mother was working full-time (34.6%), (c) not wanting the grandchild in day care or at a babysitter's house (30.8%), (d) the grandchild's mother was having emotional problems (30.8%), and (e) the grandchild's parents were not married when the grandchild was born (29.6%).

Most (85%) of the grandparents who lived with grandchildren had the grandchild living in their home. Only two grandparents (8%) lived with the grandchild in a home maintained by a grandchild's parent(s); only one grandparent said that the home was maintained by both the grandparent and the parent(s). In addition to living with one or both grandparents, 53% of the grandchildren lived with their mother, 30.1% lived with neither parent, and 15% lived with their father.

Grandparents ranged in age from 40 to 65 years when they began to live with the grandchild; the mean age was 52.5 years. Grandchildren began living with grandparents from the time of birth to the age of 9.5 years. Most (65%) grandparents were married when they began living with their grandchild. The length of the marriages ranged from 1 year to 42 years; the median was 31 years. More than two-thirds (69%) of the living-with grandparents were related to the grandchild through their daughter.

Day-care grandparents. Day-care grandparents cited reasons for providing care that were oriented to helping the grandchild's parent(s) or fulfilling their own needs. The five leading reasons given by these grandparents for providing care were: (a) the grandchild's mother was working full-time (70.6%), (b) not wanting the grandchild in day care or at a baby sitter's house (68.6%), (c) wanting to help the grandchild's parent(s) financially (66.7%), (d) the grandchild's father was working full-time (51.0%), and (e) providing care to the grandchild gave the grandparent something to do (35.4%).

Most (81%) of the day-care grandparents provided care in their own home, and most (71%) were not paid for providing that care. Grandchildren ranged in age from newborn to age 3 years when grandparents started to provide day care; the grandchild's median age was about 1 month. Grandparents ranged in age from 39 to 67 years when they began to provide day care; the mean age of the grandparent at that point was about 54 years. Most (89%) of the grandparents were married when they started to provide day care to a grandchild. About half (58%) were related to the grandchild through his or her mother.

FINDINGS

The Effect of Providing Care on Lifestyle

Grandparents were asked a series of closed-ended questions about events and feelings that may have changed because they were providing care to a grandchild. At least half of the total sample reported change on 9 of the 20 lifestyle items.

As shown in Table 18-1, the three leading issues mentioned by a majority of the total sample as undergoing change in the direction of more were: an increased need to alter routines and plans (79.5%), having more of a purpose for living (55.4%), and feeling more physically tired (55.0%). A majority of the total sample report change in the direction of less on three items: having less privacy (58.6%), having less time for oneself (58.0%), and having less time to get everything done (53.6%).

Table 18-2 gives the percentages, according to the type of care provided, for grandparents reporting that a lifestyle item changed in the direction of less. Table 18-3 gives the percentages for change in the direction of more, again by type of care provided.

At least half of the custodial grandparents reported change, either increasing or decreasing, on 13 of the 20 items while, at least half of the living-with grandparents reported change on 6 of the 20 items, and at least half of the day-care grandparents reported change on only 3 of the 20 items. Clearly the lifestyles of custodial grandparents undergo the most change and this is reflected, in part, by the fact that differences in change based on the type of care were statistically significant for 11 of the 20 items. Custodial grandparents reported the most change on 10 of these items. On the *contact with neighbors* item, the living-with grandparents reported the greatest change. Day-care grandparents reported the least change on all statistically significant items.

One item, *the need to alter routines and plans,* although not statistically significant, is particularly interesting because almost three-fourths of the grandparents in each care category said they experienced an increased need to alter their routines and plans because of providing care to a grandchild. The ability to improvise is the hallmark of providing care to another person when the care provider places that person's needs and wants above his or her own at times. Grandparents providing regular care to grandchildren improvise. Often they place the grandchild's needs and desires above their own, thus altering their routines and plans. Effects on lifestyle are discussed below within each category of care.

Custodial grandparents. As shown in Table 18-2, at least half of the custodial grandparents indicated that they have experienced a decline on the following 8 items because of providing care to a grandchild: less privacy (80.0%), less time for self (77.1%), less time to get everything done (62.9%), less time for one's spouse (59.1%), less contact with friends (55.6%), less likely to do things for fun and recreation (55.6%), less attention given to spouse (50.0%), and less money (50.0%). A majority of custodial grandparents reported increases on five items: an increased need to alter routines and plans (85.7%), feeling more physically tired (68.6%), having more of a purpose for living (65.7%), feeling more emotionally drained (60.0%), and worrying more about things (51.5%).

All of these items reflect the change in lifestyle that accompanies a child's entry into one's life and home. Grandparents suddenly must plan vacations around school holidays, babysitters, and children's activities. Many grandparents had entered (or were about to enter) a period when they thought they could plan, not only a day, but a holiday around themselves. Children, especially children viewed as vulnerable, change those plans and the types of activities in which one engages, as well as one's energy level.

The custodial grandparents described quite eloquently how these changes affected them. The following comments by one custodial grandmother reflect the types of issues raised by other grandparents as well:

TABLE 18-1 Percentage of Total Sample Indicating a Change Since Beginning to Provide Care to Grandchildren

		Direction of Change		
	Less	More	Direction Not Given	No Change	Total
Doing things for fun and recreation*	43.4	5.3	8.0	43.4	100.1
Having money*	26.5	1.8	0.0	71.7	100.0
The need to alter routines and plans	.9	79.5	0.0	19.6	100.0
Having contact with relatives	13.3	11.5	1.8	73.5	100.1
Having contact with friends*	37.2	0.0	1.8	61.1	100.1
Having contact with neighbors*	3.6	22.3	1.8	72.3	100.0
Enjoyment of your daily activities*	25.2	18.9	6.3	49.5	99.9
Having your own privacy*	58.6	0.0	0.0	41.4	100.0
Believing that grandparenting is fun*	20.0	15.2	3.8	61.0	100.0
Having time for yourself*	58.0	1.8	1.8	38.4	100.0
Feeling edgy or upset	3.6	36.6	1.8	58.0	100.0
Having time to get everything done	53.6	1.8	.9	43.8	100.1
Having a purpose for living	0.0	55.4	1.8	42.9	100.1
Feeling physically tired	2.7	55.0	.9	41.4	100.0
Feeling emotionally drained*	2.8	41.3	0.0	56.0	100.1
Worrying about things	9.1	40.9	0.0	50.0	100.0
Having time for your spouse[a]	35.7	2.4	2.4	59.5	100.0
Satisfaction with your relationship with spouse*[a]	12.2	15.9	2.4	69.5	100.0
Giving attention to your spouse*[a]	29.3	2.4	2.4	65.9	100.0
Having things in common with your spouse[a]	1.2	25.0	2.4	71.4	100.0

*Statistically significant difference by type of care provided, $p < .05$.

[a]Percentages refer to married grandparents only.

Before, I had all the freedom. I didn't need a baby sitter; I didn't need to check to see if I could go out of the house or when I had to be back or to make 9,000 arrangements to do anything. I don't like her out of her routine, so if I have a . . . meeting I have to be at, I don't take her out during the week. She really thrives best on a routine, so that has definitely cut my leisure, plus the fact that babysitting's expensive. I don't have the money to do that. If I pay the babysitter then I don't have the money to go out.

A grandfather with guardianship of two grandchildren for about 3 years said:

There will be times I can't go places. I would feel guilty—that's my problem—about leaving them with someone else, so rather than going somewhere or doing something, I don't go or don't do it.

A grandmother with custody of two grandchildren said:

TABLE 18-2   Change by Type of Care, Percentage Reporting a Decline

	Type of Care Provided			
	Custodial	*Living-With*	*Day-Care*	*Total*
Doing things for fun and recreation*	55.6	60.0	26.9	43.4
Having money*	50.0	36.0	5.8	26.5
The need to alter routines and plans	0.0	0.0	1.9	.9
Having contact with relatives	22.2	16.0	5.8	13.3
Having contact with friends*	55.6	44.0	21.2	37.2
Having contact with neighbors*	8.3	4.2	0.0	3.6
Enjoyment of your daily activities*	45.7	16.7	15.4	25.2
Having your own privacy*	80.0	75.0	36.5	58.6
Believing that grandparenting is fun*	30.0	26.1	11.5	20.0
Having time for yourself*	77.1	64.0	42.3	58.0
Feeling edgy or upset	2.8	4.0	3.9	3.6
Having time to get everything done	62.9	44.0	51.9	53.6
Having a purpose for living	0.0	0.0	0.0	0.0
Feeling physically tired	2.9	4.2	1.9	2.7
Feeling emotionally drained*	5.7	0.0	2.0	2.8
Worrying about things	12.1	16.0	3.8	9.1
Having time for your spouse[a]	59.1	41.2	22.2	35.7
Satisfaction with your relationship with spouse*[a]	28.6	6.3	6.7	12.2
Giving attention to your spouse*[a]	50.0	33.3	17.8	29.3
Having things in common with your spouse[a]	4.5	0.0	0.0	1.2

*Statistically significant difference by type of care provided, $p < .05$.

[a]Percentages refer only to married grandparents.

Their school activities have quite an impact on us. . . . We try to go to the things that they're in in school and things that they're in in church, and places that they have to be on certain nights, school or church, we try to make at least sure that there are arrangements made for them to get there.

Focusing on other types of changes, a grandmother with custody of her grandchild for about 3 years told me:

There are people that you don't see as much because you're not able to do things with them. Then you're available to do things with other neighbors with small children that you wouldn't have done anything with before. Now I get invited to the children's birthday parties!

And a grandmother with custody for about two years said the following:

I really enjoy doing little things with her. We go out and play in the yard and do a little bit of yard work and play in the leaves. We go to the library . . . and I'm

TABLE 18-3   Change by Type of Care, Percentage Reporting an Increase

	Type of Care Provided			
	Custodial	Living-With	Day-Care	Total
Doing things for fun and recreation*	11.1	0.0	3.8	5.3
Having money*	2.8	0.0	1.9	1.8
The need to alter routines and plans	85.7	84.0	73.1	79.5
Having contact with relatives	13.9	12.0	9.6	11.5
Having contact with friends*	0.0	0.0	0.0	0.0
Having contact with neighbors*'	22.2	41.7	13.5	22.3
Enjoyment of your daily activities*	17.1	20.8	19.2	18.9
Having your own privacy*	0.0	0.0	0.0	0.0
Believing that grandparenting is fun*	6.7	4.3	25.0	15.2
Having time for yourself*	0.0	4.0	1.9	1.8
Feeling edgy or upset	44.4	40.0	29.4	36.6
Having time to get everything done	2.9	0.0	1.9	1.8
Having a purpose for living	65.7	48.0	51.9	55.4
Feeling physically tired	68.6	54.2	46.2	55.0
Feeling emotionally drained*	60.0	50.0	24.0	41.3
Worrying about things	51.5	36.0	36.5	40.9
Having time for your spouse[a]	4.5	0.0	2.2	2.4
Satisfaction with your relationship with spouse*[a]	23.8	12.5	13.3	15.9
Giving attention to your spouse*[a]	4.5	0.0	2.2	2.4
Having things in common with your spouse[a]	22.7	23.5	26.7	25.0

*Statistically significant difference by type of care provided, $p < .05$.

[a]Percentages refer only to married grandparents.

really enjoying it. I feel I need to keep myself physically fit and healthy because someone needs to be here to take care of my grandchild. I think my husband must feel that way too. He's a smoker and . . . he's trying to quit.

Living-with grandparents. As shown in Table 18-2, a majority of grandparents living with grandchildren reported declines in: having privacy (75.0%), having time for self (64.0%), and doing things for fun and recreation (60.0%). The living-with grandparents reported increases in: the need to alter routines and plans (84.0%), feeling physically tired (54.2%), and feeling emotionally drained (50.0%). These issues are similar to those mentioned by the custodial grandparents as changing most. This similarity reflects the fact that both the custodial and the living-with grandparents actually live with their grandchildren and have daily responsibilities for those grandchildren which do not end at the day's end.

One grandmother, whose granddaughter and daughter have lived with her for the last 4 years, said that one of the biggest changes was:

Entertaining here at the house. In the beginning, especially, I didn't have the energy to do it, and because of the way she was, to invite people our age over and to have a crying baby all the time wouldn't have been any fun. It just got to the point where we couldn't do it at all here so we would try to go somewhere else, like to dinner with other friends . . . but now . . . things are getting back on track.

Describing the lack of time for oneself, one grandmother spoke for many others when she said:

It was nonexistent. Now it's getting better too because she's getting older. I couldn't take my eyes off her to do anything. I'd go upstairs to try to get dressed or whatever, and I'd come down and she'd be climbing out the dining room window or she'd be into whatever down here, so you couldn't leave her alone for anything.

Focusing on her enjoyment of her grandchildren, one grandmother, whose two grandchildren and daughter have lived with her for about 5 years, said:

The change in my enjoyment of daily activities has been for the better. . . . They're fun kids. . . . I'm less apt to sit and watch TV; I'm more apt to be sitting down playing Legos.

Day-care grandparents. As shown in Table 18-2, a majority (51.9%) of grandparents providing day care say that they have less time to get everything done because of providing regular day care. A majority of day-care grandparents reported that they have experienced an increased need to alter routines and plans (73.1%) and have more of a purpose for living (51.9%) because of providing care to their grandchild.

The voices of these grandparents can be used to interpret these findings. One grandmother, who previously had her grandson living with her and who now provides him with regular day care, spoke about the need to alter her routines and plans:

I have to be on call. I can't just take off willy-nilly if I feel like it. I have to keep myself on schedule. . . . I think he will be with me all summer . . . I'll get used to it. I don't know what plans we have. We're not thinking about that yet, so I don't know what arrangements. But it does change. It keeps you housebound . . . especially the younger ones, and your free time is not your own.

A grandmother who has provided regular day care to her grandchild for $1\frac{1}{2}$ years spoke for many of the day-care grandparents when she said:

If I know he's going to be here I do go ahead and try to get my usual daily chores around the house finished. . . . I notice that I don't have as much pep, maybe, to follow a little toddler around as what I once did.

And a grandmother who has provided regular day care to her two grandchildren for the last 3 years told me:

Daily activities are more enjoyable when I have the kids. They keep me young or get me young. I probably was settling into middle age before all this came about and I really think that I'm much better off with them. It's the best thing that ever happened. They keep me young. I think that it's just something that most kids don't have grandparents close; it's something that they all miss out on and I feel sorry for them because it's a beautiful experience. I have so much more patience with these kids than I did with my own . . . I can enjoy them a whole lot more than I did my own children.

The Effect on the Friendship Network

More than one-third (38.9%) of the grandparents reported that their contact with friends changed when they began to provide regular care to a grandchild (see Table 18-1). I found a statistically significant difference ($\chi^2[4, n = 113] = 12.3, p < .05$) in contact based on the type of care provided; more than half (55.6%) of the custodial grandparents said that contact with friends declined, compared with 44% of the living-with and 21.2% of the day-care grandparents (see Table 18-2). No respondents said that contact with friends increased because of providing care to a grandchild (see Table 18-3).

One grandfather with a legal relationship to two grandchildren said:

Yes, contact with friends changed. I just don't go places. A friend invited me out . . . it's just easier to stay home. So, friends I don't see as often. . . . But that's just the way it has to be. . . . They [the children] get a little nervous [if I'm gone]—this isn't good.

We pursued the subject of friendship patterns by asking grandparents, "Who were your closest friends before you began to provide care to your grandchild?" and "Who are your closest friends now that you have been providing care?" I compared their answers; if the two sets differed, the respondent was asked whether the difference was the result of providing care to the grandchild. Most (82.6%) of the grandparents reported no change in their close friends. I found, however, a statistically significant difference in the maintenance of close friends by the type of care the grandparent provided ($\chi^2[3, n = 92] = 13.94, p < .05$). Custodial grandparents were more likely to report different friends as a result of providing care than were living-with and day-care grandparents; 37% of the custodial grandparents, compared with 25% of the living-with grandparents, said their closest friends changed. Grandparents who provided day care were unlikely to say that their closest friends changed; only 4.1% reported a change. Once again, these differences reflect the fact that although the day-care grandparents provide care throughout the day, the grandchild goes home at night and the grandparent can interact at that time with his or her friends. Custodial and living-with grandparents are "on" day and night; "childfree" friends may not wish to spend time with a family that has children.

These findings are expressed by the grandparents themselves. One custodial grandmother said:

There's one couple that we used to be very close with. We're just not that close with them anymore. We can't just have them over for dinner by ourselves; there's always the children here. We're still friendly, but just not as close as we were.

Another grandmother, who has been living with a grandchild for about 8 years, used words to describe friendship transitions that were echoed by other custodial and living-with grandparents:

In our age bracket most of our friends don't have [young] children and as a result a lot of times we don't accept invitations to go because our children [the grandchildren] are not invited. . . . Most of the time it doesn't bother me. . . . Our close friends are still the same. We don't see them as often.

I also pursued the subject of friendship patterns by asking grandparents whether they had problems with friends as a result of providing care to grandchildren. Overall, almost three-fourths (71.7%) said they had no problems with friends because they were providing care to a grandchild. I found a statistically significant difference (χ^2[2, $n = 113$)] $= 6.43$, $p < .05$), however, when I compared responses among the three groups. Custodial grandparents were more likely to report problems with friends than were living-with and day-care grandparents: proportions were 41.7%, 32%, and 17.3%, respectively.

Friendship networks change most profoundly for custodial grandparents and living-with grandparents; little change occurs in the friendship networks of day-care grandparents. These changes seem to reflect the fact that the custodial and living-with grandparents are out of phase with their friends. As mentioned before, schedules must be altered to fit the needs of children, babysitters, and finances. "Childfree" friends have a different lifestyle, and grandparents with children have difficulty fitting their "second time around" lifestyle to those of their friends without children.

The Effect on the Family Network

In response to the question, "Did you have problems with family because of providing care to a grandchild?" almost three-fourths (72.6%) of the overall sample said they had no such problems. However, I found a statistically significant difference (χ^2[2, $n = 113$] $= 12.18$, $p < .05$) in the response depending on the type of care provided. Almost half (47.2%) of the custodial grandparents said they had "some" or "a lot of" problems with family because they were providing care to their grandchild. Twenty-eight percent of the living-with and 13.5% of the day-care grandparents said they had such problems.

The types of problems reported by grandparents also vary with the type of care provided. Custodial grandparents reported difficulties with their other children, the siblings of the grandchild's parent. These other children were reported as seeming to be jealous, and as saying, "Don't do this" or "You shouldn't do this at your age." Grandparents reported that they find these statements neither helpful nor supportive. They speculated that their other children's jealousy stems from a feeling that their children (the grandparents' other grandchildren) will not receive equal attention.

Grandparents who live with both a grandchild and one of the grandchild's parents reported tensions over house rules. One grandmother living with her grandchild and daughter said:

> The only problem that my daughter and I really have is [that] when I'm with him [the grandchild] alone everything's fine, but for a while he [the grandchild] used to play one against the other. He'd call her on the phone and have her say "yes." Then we got wise to that [and] she'd say "Do what grandma says." When she comes home she wants to be the sole parent. . . . It's very difficult for me sometimes not to add a word or two, and she resents that.

Day-care grandparents also reported tensions about childrearing practices. One day-care grandmother remarked:

> One of my concerns was the husband [the father] coming into the house [to pick up the grandchild] and seeing what I did with the baby and then going home and complaining to the wife [the mother]: "Well, Mother does it this way," or "You should do it the way Mother does it." I think it would cause a lot of conflict between the two parents. It would have been better, I think, in a lot of ways, if it had been a third party and not a mother.

The Effect on the Marriage

As shown in Table 18-1, most married grandparents reported no change in having time for their spouse (59.5%), in their satisfaction with their relationship with their spouse (69.5%), in giving attention to their spouse (65.9%), or in having things in common with their spouse (71.4%) because of providing care to a grandchild. However, based on the type of care the grandparent provided, there were statistically significant differences on two of these items: satisfaction with the relationship and giving attention to their spouse.

When asked about change in satisfaction with their marital relationship as a result of providing care to a grandchild, overall, almost one-third (30.5%) of the respondents said their satisfaction had changed. I found a statistically significant difference ($\chi^2[6, n = 82] = 12.8, p < .05$) between satisfaction with one's marital relationship and the type of care provided to a grandchild. As shown in Table 18-2, custodial grandparents were more than four times as likely as living-with and day-care grandparents to report declines in their marital satisfaction because they were providing care to a grandchild. More than one-fourth (28.6%) of the custodial grandparents, as compared with 6.3% of the living-with and 6.7% of the day-care grandparents, said that their satisfaction with their marital relationship had declined as a result of providing care. However, as shown in Table 18-3, custodial grandparents were also almost twice as likely as living-with and day-care grandparents to report an increase in their marital satisfaction because they were providing care to a grandchild. Almost one-fourth (23.8%) of the custodial grandparents, as compared with 12.5% of the living-with and 13.3% of the day-care grandparents, said that their marital satisfaction increased because they were providing care to a grandchild.

It appears that most custodial grandparents experience a change in their marital satisfaction because of providing care and that for some that change is positive, while for others it is negative. One custodial grandmother remarked:

> We talked about that once in a while . . . just kidding around, but there are times when it's serious that I'm not giving him [her husband] enough attention. But I do try to do more things and he likes those things. It's give and take, you know. We both wanted her, so we both have to work at this. I can't do it myself.

Another custodial grandmother whose husband has retired and who has had custody of her grandchild for about 2 years said:

> We do things together that we never did before . . . he never participated in raising our children. He never had time to be a parent and I asked him if he missed that and he said "no," and then he said . . . "I have time this time to be involved, and I like it." And I thought wow! . . . We are sharing, we are doing together what I did before.

As shown in Table 18-1, slightly more than one-third (34.1%) of the grandparents said that giving attention to their spouse had changed because they were providing care to a grandchild. There was a statistically significant difference ($\chi^2[6, n = 82] = 15.8$, $p < .05$) in such attention, based on the type of care provided. Custodial grandparents were more likely than living-with or day-care grandparents to report that giving attention to their spouse had declined. Half of the custodial grandparents, as compared with 33.3% of the living-with and 17.8% of the day-care grandparents, said that such attention had declined (see Table 18-2). As shown in Table 18-3, few grandparents reported an increase in giving attention to their spouse because of providing care to a grandchild. One custodial grandmother of two expressed the feelings of many other grandparents:

> Time is between 9 P.M. and 7 A.M. and it's usually, do we have to talk or do we have to do anything? . . . You're either too exhausted, too tired . . . and this is not just with me. It's with both of us.

Married grandparents were asked whether providing care to a grandchild created problems with their spouse. Most (83.1%) of the married grandparents answered "no" to this question, but I found a statistically significant difference ($\chi^2[2, n = 83] = 9.11$, $p < .05$) in problems occurring with a spouse, based on the type of care the grandparent provided. More than one-third (38.1%) of the custodial grandparents said that providing care created problems with their spouse, compared with 11.8% of the living-with and 8.9% of the day-care grandparents. One of the more dramatic problems was described by a grandmother married for about 30 years to a man who had supported their obtaining custody of a grandchild:

He walked out on us [the grandchild and the grandmother]. I think he just felt trapped. It was like he couldn't cope with him [the grandchild]. He loved him very much.

SUMMARY

This research is based on screening and in-depth interviews with 114 grandparents: 36 custodial grandparents, 26 grandparents living with a grandchild without having a legal relationship to that grandchild, and 52 grandparents providing regular day care. The sample is composed of grandparents who responded to advertisements that appeared in the media, schools, medical practices, and courts. This sampling strategy deviates from some of the recent research on grandparents that targets groups of grandparents because of a particular problem. For example, Burton's (1992) research focused on black grandparents rearing children of drug-addicted parents in a drug-addicted environment. Similarly, Minkler, Roe, and Price's (1992) research focused on grandparents rearing crack cocaine babies. This research focuses on white grandmothers who provide care to grandchildren for many different reasons. None of these studies is the definitive study of grandparents who provide care to grandchildren. However, each study increases our knowledge and understanding about the issues facing grandparents who provide regular care to grandchildren under varying circumstances.

A second word of caution regarding the findings should be noted. As previously stated, the final sample was not selected randomly from a list of grandparents. The final sample was composed of grandparents who responded to advertisements about the study and volunteered to participate. Volunteer grandparents may differ from grandparents who choose not to respond. For example, the grandparent volunteers may be more (or less) articulate or more (or less) concerned about their childrearing skills than the grandparents who chose not to participate. Therefore, these findings should be viewed as suggestive of the types of effects that parenting grandchildren has on grandparents' lifestyles.

Together, however, studies such as this one and Burton's (1992) and Minkler, Roe, and Price's (1992) research indicate that, as a group, grandparents who provide care to grandchildren are solvers of what seem to be insoluble problems. Like Burton (1992) and Minkler, Roe, and Price (1992), I found that custodial grandparents attempt to provide a stable environment for their grandchildren when their own children are drug- and alcohol-addicted. I found that grandparents, especially day-care grandparents, attempt to provide their grandchildren with a stable day-care environment when parents work and day-care costs are prohibitive. I found that grandparents evidence strength in the face of adversity, and cope with their own time-disordered relationships, apparently because they feel they must.

Children alter their caregiver's lives, both positively and negatively, especially when they live with their caregiver. Caregivers responsible for a child's daily personal and legal (decision-making) care feel profoundly the effect of providing such care. This study shows that lifestyle changes tend to differ on the basis of the type of care the grandparent provides. As noted earlier, three categories of care emerge from the data: custodial, living-with, and day-care. These three categories differ from one another in regard to legal and physical custody of the grandchild.

Granted a legal right to the grandchild by the court, custodial grandparents assume responsibility for both the daily care of the grandchild and decision making for the grandchild's upbringing. In essence, they assume the functions typically linked to parenthood in our society. Although custodial grandparents assume the functions of the parent, often there are no structural supports to help them assume this unexpected role. These individuals not only are "off-time" but also feel the disjuncture between the anticipated grandparent role and the custodial grandparent role. Some grandparents experience the failure of their traditional support networks because they and their friends are no longer "all in the same boat at the same time." For example, almost half of the custodial grandparents reported problems with family and friends, the first line of defense for most people in times of stress. Oftentimes friends do not have the care of young children, they do not want to include young children in their social activities, and they want to do things on the spur of the moment. The custodial grandparents who were looking forward to spur-of-the-moment adventures are now responsible for the care of a young child; like typical parents, they cannot go anywhere until the grandchild's needs are taken into account. Although the burden of rearing grandchildren often seems heavy, almost two-thirds of the custodial grandparents reported having more of a purpose for living because of providing care to their grandchild; the grandchild keeps them young, active, and "in shape."

The living-with grandparents assume some, if not all, of the daily physical care for the grandchild but do not have legal custody. These grandparents face some of the problems faced by custodial grandparents, but with a twist. There are at least two categories of living-with grandparents: those who have the grandchild's parent living with them and those who do not. The latter function more like custodial grandparents in regard to daily care and decision making, but they never know when the grandchild's parents will take the grandchild back. These grandparents have no way of protecting the grandchild from an unsuitable or even dangerous parent. Many living-with grandparents expressed their fear and concern about this unstable situation but expressed fear and uncertainty about going to court. A court appearance entails a public announcement that the grandparent's child is an unfit parent, and it involves uncertainty about the outcome. Therefore, some grandparents prefer the living-with arrangement.

A three-generation household raises other issues: The grandparents reported feeling that they "walk a thin line," trying to provide a stable environment for the grandchild without overstepping boundaries of authority. The parent clearly retains decision-making responsibility but often leaves the grandparent with the physical care of the grandchild. Such a relationship gives the grandparent great responsibility without any authority. These grandparents also reported a strain between their beliefs about what grandparenting would be like and how it actually is. One custodial grandmother summed up the feelings expressed by many custodial and living-with grandparents when she said:

It's something that I've been trying very hard to overcome but I've been feeling, and I know I've been feeling this a long time . . . very hurt and self-pitying. . . . This is what we had planned and so forth, and it's just not fair for this to happen to us. And I'm not taking anything away from the children or anything like that, but it's just a feeling that we have. . . . I think it's mostly because we are so tired, we do have so much to do, and we did want so much. . . . We know now if we're going to have any of it, we're going to have to try harder, and there are some things which are just not going to happen.

For some grandparents these strains are balanced by the positive changes. Almost half of the living-with grandparents reported an increased purpose for living because of providing care to a grandchild, and about one-fourth said that having things in common with their spouse has also increased.

Day-care grandparents assume responsibility for the regular physical care of their grandchildren and assume no legal responsibility. Although these grandparents arrange their schedules around the grandchild's day, they are least affected by their caretaking role because the children go home at the end of the day. Some day-care grandparents are thrilled to be taking care of their grandchildren; others resent the assumption that they wish to spend their days in this way. Of the three categories, however, these grandparents tend to function more according to our societal definition of grandparents than of parents.

This research highlights some of the lifestyle changes experienced by grandparents who provide regular care to grandchildren. This research also raises many questions. For example, why do some grandparents, rather than others, experience more positive changes in their lifestyle because of providing care to grandchildren? Does the grandchild's age help to explain this difference? Does the grandparent's belief about whether the situation is temporary or permanent help explain different lifestyle changes? Does the parent's complete withdrawal or involvement in the grandchild's life affect the grandparent's lifestyle? More research is needed on this growing segment of the population: grandparents who provide care to their grandchildren.

NOTE

This research was funded by the AARP Andrus Foundation. Special thanks to my consultants, especially Millie Seltzer, for her willingness to play with ideas and her critical review of earlier manuscript drafts. I also want to thank *JMF*'s anonymous reviewers. Thanks also to Kathryn Myles and Jill Wessell for their skilled help in interviewing grandparents. A very special thanks to the grandparents who spent many hours talking with us about their experiences.

REFERENCES

Burton, L. M. (1992). Black grandparents rearing children of drug-addicted parents: Stressors, outcomes and the social service needs. *The Gerontologist, 32,* 744–751.
Creighton, L. L. (1991, December 16). Silent Saviors. *U.S. News & World Report,* pp. 80–89.
Hagestad, G., & Neugarten, B. (1985). Age and the life course. In R. Binstock & E. Shanas (Eds.), *Handbook of aging and the social sciences* (pp. 35–61). New York: Van Nostrand Reinhold.
Jendrek, M. P. (1993). *Grandparents who parent their grandchildren: Circumstances and decisions.* Manuscript submitted for publication.
Minkler, M., Roe, K. M., & Price, M. (1992). The physical and emotional health of grandmothers raising grandchildren in the crack cocaine epidemic. *The Gerontologist, 32,* 752–761.
Saluter, A. F. (1992). Marital status and living arrangements: March 1991. *Current Population*

Reports, Population Characteristics (Series P-20, No. 461). Washington, DC: U.S. Government Printing Office.

Schulman, J., & Pitt, V. (1982). Second thoughts on joint custody arrangements: Analysis of legislation and its implications for women and children. *Golden Gate University Law Review, 12,* 539–577.

Seltzer, M. M. (1976). Suggestions for the examination of time-disordered relationships. In F. J. Gubrium (Ed.), *Time, roles and self in old age* (pp. 111–125). New York: Human Sciences Press.

U.S. Bureau of the Census. (1988). *County and city data book 1988.* Washington, DC: U.S. Government Printing Office.

VIII

WORK AND RETIREMENT

Although we intuitively understand what it means to be retired, agreeing on a definition of retirement has proven difficult, because retirement is not a definitive state. People move into and out of retirement as they exit and reenter the labor force. Many people do retire at a fixed age, usually 62 or 65, and never work again. But it has become more common for workers to reenter the labor force after an initial retirement (Hayward, Grady, and MacLaughlin, 1988). Older workers who reenter occupy "bridge" jobs—jobs that span the interim between employment in a career job and permanent retirement. These jobs generally differ in occupation and industry from career jobs and often involve part-time employment for significantly lower wages (Ruhm, 1989). The reading by Rose C. Gibson discusses the specific dilemmas faced by older black Americans: they experience the highest rates of unemployment in later life, they have the least opportunity to retire with private pension income, and they often spend years in bridge jobs.

Individual decision-making processes are an important factor in explaining retirement patterns. Yet the opportunity to retire is also shaped by job opportunities and by public and private pensions.

THE TRANSITION FROM MANUFACTURING TO SERVICES

From World War II to the 1970s, workers in unionized manufacturing industries achieved a degree of economic security across the life course. In the past two decades, this protection has been undermined by economic restructuring, and the burden has fallen heavily on older workers, who were concentrated in manufacturing industries (Sum and Fogg, 1990).

Although older workers lost ground in manufacturing, they increased their share of employment in the finance, insurance, and real estate industries and in the service industries. The shift in employment of older workers to services has occurred among both men and women, but the growth of service employment has been greater among women (Doeringer, 1991). The new job opportunities that have opened to women have drawn younger women into the labor force and have reduced somewhat the concentration of women in traditional "female" occupations. These opportunities have bypassed working women aged over 55, who in 1987 were still employed mainly in three traditionally female jobs—sales, administrative support (including clerical), and services (Herz, 1988). Older women are underrepresented in the ranks of professional, managerial, and technical employees and substantially overrepresented among administrative support workers (Doeringer, 1991). The selection by Lois B. Shaw describes the special problems faced by older women workers.

JOB OPPORTUNITIES FOR OLDER WORKERS

In the 1980s many employers introduced flexibility to the workplace. Flexibility in labor management provided corporations short-run control over the labor force, thereby reducing labor costs and improving corporate competitiveness. It meant abandoning the model of lifetime affiliation between worker and employer and replacing it with contingent labor. Under contingent employment systems employers alter compensation systems to tie wages and benefits more closely to corporate profits. Employers do not make significant investments in specific workers, contracts cover only a short period of time, and there is also more shifting of workers from one region to another and from one job to another (Belous, 1990). These are typically part-time jobs with few fringe benefits.

At first glance, older workers with limited time horizons of three to five years before retirement seem ideally suited to such temporary or part-time assignments. They present a potential pool of skilled and experienced workers for short-term projects to get a new business spinoff launched or to manufacture a product line with a foreseeable life cycle. Indeed, older workers are more likely to work part time. In 1985, for example, a much higher proportion of men and women over age 65 and in the labor force worked part time, compared to younger workers (Meier, 1986). However, the increase in part-time and part-year employment among older workers has been concentrated in the service sector and in smaller firms, and not in the large-enterprise sector that has been experiencing much of the growth in flexible employment (Sum and Fogg, 1990). Older workers have been recruited in low-wage jobs such as child care and fast foods (Applebaum and Gregory, 1990).

Increasingly, older workers who find themselves out of the labor market, or at risk of losing their positions or being downgraded in their jobs, decide instead to retire. This trend toward increasingly early retirement began in the 1960s and increased more rapidly during the 1970s and 1980s. The reading by Harold L. Sheppard analyzes the changing pattern of labor force participation of older workers and explains why, in the United States, the main early-exit route is through private pension systems.

REFERENCES

Applebaum, Eileen, and Judith Gregory. "Flexible Employment: Union Perspectives." In Peter Doeringer (ed.), *Bridges to Retirement: Older Workers in a Changing Labor Market.* Ithaca, NY: ILR Press, 1990.

Belous, Richard. "Flexible Employment: the Employer's Point of View." In Peter Doeringer (ed.), *Bridges to Retirement: Older Workers in a Changing Labor Market.* Ithaca, NY: ILR Press, 1990.

Doeringer, Peter. *Turbulence in the American Workplace.* New York: Oxford University Press, 1991.

Hayward, Mark D.; William R. Grady; and Steven D. MacLaughlin. "Changes in the Retirement Process among Older Men in the United States: 1972–1980." *Demography* 25 (1988): 271–286.

Herz, Diane. "Employment Characteristics of Older Women, 1987." *Monthly Labor Review* 9 (1988): 3–12.

Meier, Elisabeth L. "Employment Experience and Income of Older Women." American Association of Retired Persons no. 8609. Washington, DC: AARP Public Policy Institute, 1986.

Ruhm, Christopher. "Why Older Americans Stop Working." *The Gerontologist* 29 (1989): 294–300.

Sum, Andrew, and W. Neil Fogg. "Profile of the Labor Market for Older Workers." In Peter Doeringer (ed.), *Bridges to Retirement: Older Workers in a Changing Labor Market.* Ithaca, NY: ILR Press, 1990.

19
The Black American Retirement Experience
ROSE C. GIBSON

Gibson's analysis of the retirement roles and resources of older black Americans is based on her findings from the National Survey of Black Americans (NSBA) data (1979–1980). She analyzes how gender and socioeconomic status affect late-life roles and shape the relationships between source of income, work history, disabilities, and retirement roles. Gibson calls for a new research agenda, one that permits testing across national samples to determine whether blacks and other minorities and whites differ in the experiences that influence late-life roles.

This chapter presents descriptive analyses of the National Survey of Black Americans (NSBA) data (1979–1980) exploring older black Americans' retirement roles and resources and describing the differences by gender and socioeconomic status (SES). Specifically, I analyze differences in late-life roles: differences in the timing of and plans and reasons for retirement, and differences in activities after retirement.

A theoretical framework for understanding black Americans' late-life roles is presented. A literature review follows of blacks' retirement roles and experiences. Then, after presenting the NSBA findings, the chapter concludes with recommendations for approaches to future black American retirement research.

CONCEPTUAL FRAMEWORK FOR STUDYING LATE-LIFE ROLES

The "Unretired-Retired" Concept

Three fairly new social trends are creating a new type of black retiree, referred to as the *unretired-retired* (Gibson, 1986a). The trends for middle-aged and older blacks are: declining labor force participation, increasing physical disability, and increasing disability pay availability. The unretired-retired are individuals aged 55 and over who do not consider themselves retired despite their nonworking status (Gibson, 1986b).

This unretired-retired group appears to be the most deprived of the black elderly (Gibson, 1987a, 1988; J. S. Jackson & Gibson, 1985). The unretired-retired do not meet traditional retirement criteria, and therefore, they are screened by definition from major national retirement research. This excludes them from planning and policy stemming from the research. Whether older blacks view themselves as retired is influenced by their lifetime disadvantaged work patterns, current work income, and psychological or economic need for the disabled worker role. Each of these issues is discussed in turn.

Relationships Between Lifetime Work and Retirement Experiences

Black Americans' disadvantaged work experiences across the life course have been reported in the more than 20 years of published work and retirement literature. These unchanging disadvantaged work patterns, over time, create an unclear line between work and retirement experiences. This ambiguity, in turn, influences late-life role choices.

The current generation of older black Americans is more likely to have worked in low-status jobs characterized by sporadic work patterns and small earnings (Abbott, 1980; Anderson & Cottingham, 1981; Cain, 1976; Corcoran & Duncan, 1978; U.S. Department of Commerce, 1980; Gibson, 1982, 1983; Gordon, Hamilton, & Tipps, 1982; Hill, 1981; Montagna, 1978; Munnell, 1978). These work patterns threaten black Americans' economic well-being as they reach old age (Abbott, 1980). Work in old age in the same low-status jobs becomes a necessity for many (Abbott, 1977). The result is a continuity of disadvantaged work patterns from youth through old age.

Income from paid work rather than from traditional retirement sources also could cause uncertainty as to whether one is working or retired. This complicates blacks' adoption of the retirement role. Blacks' lifetime work experiences have influenced income levels and sources in old age (Abbott, 1980). Restriction to unstable jobs with low earnings and few benefits relates directly to low levels of retirement pensions and social security benefits. Thus, compared to other groups, older blacks' income packages contain a greater proportion of money from work and nonretirement sources (Abbott, 1977; J. S. Jackson & Gibson, 1985; Parnes & Nestel, 1981).

The Retirement Versus the Disability Role

The attractiveness, availability, and appropriateness of roles alternate to retirement may interfere with blacks' adoption of the retirement role. Role theory literature lends additional insights into the reasons blacks might prefer the disability role to the retirement role (see Biddle & Thomas, 1966; Sarbin & Allen, 1968, for analyses of role theory). In general, these theories suggest individuals select new roles under these conditions: when forced out of the old role, when the new role is different from the old role, or when the new role offers greater benefits than the old role. Blacks' inclination to take on the retirement role is interpreted within this general framework.

To begin, William James's (1910/1950) identity theory posits that individuals change their self-identity when changes in the opportunities or demands of current social situations occur. At this point, individuals formulate different sets of expectations of what are appropriate or desirable self-meanings. Changes in demands or opportunities in the work sphere could encourage a search for more appropriate self-meanings, such as the retiree role. Blacks experience few changes in their work spheres in old age and thus may be less likely to search for or take on a new retiree identity.

Stryker (1968), expanding James's identity theory, offered another framework in which to interpret blacks' reluctance to adopt the retirement role. He suggested that individuals have a hierarchy of available roles, with the most salient in priority positions. Individuals change identities by selecting roles from this hierarchy that have the highest probabilities of being invoked across situations and of congruence between the expectations of the individual and the expectations of society in regard to appropriate role behaviors.

Extrapolated to work and retirement, this might mean that when the work role is no longer available, individuals choose the retirement role if (a) the retirement role is the most salient in their hierarchy of roles, (b) the retirement role is applicable across a variety of life situations, and (c) the individual and others agree to the behaviors of the retiree role. For older blacks whose work is still contributing to their income and for whom the line between work and retirement is unclear, the retiree role would not meet these three conditions.

The theory that individuals give up and take on new roles according to the margin of benefits over costs offers yet another framework in which to examine blacks' adoption of the retirement role. Thus blacks would adopt the retirement role if its benefits outweighed the benefits of other available roles. The disability role possibly pays larger benefits to blacks than the retirement role.

The special profits of the disability role for blacks might be explained by new versions of sick-role theory. First, intolerable social and psychological conditions encourage individuals to adopt the sick role as an escape from a less desirable current role (Phillips, 1965; Thurlow, 1971). Second, the secondary *economic* gains of illness encourage adoption and maintenance of sick-role behavior (Lamb & Rogawski, 1978; Ludwig, 1981; Prince, 1978). Chirikos and Nestel (1983) demonstrated that reports of disability are related to economic need. Individuals who expected lower future wages were more likely to say they were work disabled. Interestingly, this influence of expected income on self-reported disability was stronger for blacks than whites.

Ellison (1968) suggested that among blue-collar workers, the sick role is a substitution for the retirement role. Intolerable social and psychological experiences create a "lack of fit" in the retirement role for this group. Considering both the Chirikos and Nestel and Ellison findings, the sick role may have a better fit and greater economic benefits for disadvantaged black workers than the retirement role. Disability pay may be greater than retirement pay in this group. The availability of disability pay cannot be ignored in blacks' failure to adopt the retirement role.

Thus far, it has been suggested that taking on the retirement role among black Americans is a function of lifetime and current labor force experiences; source of income; and the availability, attractiveness, and appropriateness of the disability role. The disability role appears to have larger social, psychological, and economic payoffs than the retirement role.

EMPIRICAL WORK ON LATE-LIFE ROLES

The general unretired-retired conceptual framework and reasons for adopting a disabled-worker instead of a retirement role shaped the existing research on black American late-life roles. Work in this area has progressed from descriptive, to multivariate, to analyses of the very meaning and measurement of the late-life role constructs.

Three studies focused exclusively on black American retirement-role adoption. The first study (J. S. Jackson & Gibson, 1985) examined the possibility that self-definitions of retirement among elderly blacks were complicated by an indistinct line between work patterns earlier in life and work patterns in old age and a large part of income stemming from work. They found those who did not call themselves retired were more likely than those who did to never have had a full-time job in life, to have been lifetime part-time workers, and to be working currently from time to time. These black elderly who did not view themselves as retired also had a large portion of their income coming from their own work. These unretired-retired individuals were more disadvantaged economically and socially than the retired individuals. These findings suggest that two factors are related to ways in which older blacks define retirement for themselves: unchanging disadvantaged work patterns and source of income. This study, however, was descriptive and did not determine the relative or collective effects of factors on adopting a retirement role.

The second study (Gibson, 1987b) extended the earlier J. S. Jackson and Gibson study by exploring the complexity of older blacks' adoption of the retirement role. These multivariate findings, based on logit regression (Hanuschek & J. E. Jackson, 1977), confirmed the descriptive J. S. Jackson-Gibson findings, indicating that four factors decreased the odds of calling oneself retired: (a) having worked discontinuous types of patterns over the lifetime, (b) viewing oneself as disabled, (c) receiving income from one's own work, and (d) receiving income from sources other than retirement pensions, annuities, or assets.

The issues raised by J. S. Jackson and Gibson (1985) and by Gibson (1987b) set the theoretical framework for a third study. Gibson (1991a), using latent variable analyses, explored the meaning and measurement of the retirement and disabled-worker constructs. Gibson identified a role negotiation process:

1. Perceptions of a discontinuous work life, by creating an ambiguity of work and retirement, discouraged adoption of the retirement role.
2. Those in economic need, feeling more compelled to work intermittently, were less inclined to view themselves as retired.
3. The greater economic and psychological rewards of the role encouraged the disabled-worker role.
4. Taking on a disabled-worker role decreased the inclination to take on the retirement role.

Three other findings raise two additional issues. First, the failure to adopt the retirement role may be more a matter of socioeconomic status than race. For example, in the Gibson (1987b) study those black elderly who did not call themselves retired were more economically deprived than those who did. There also were fewer compulsions to work among those receiving retirement pensions. The second issue is that the older-worker roles of black Americans may be more necessity than choice. For example, J. S. Jackson and Gibson (1985) found lower morale among black elderly who were *in* the labor force than among those who were *out* and receiving retirement pensions. The lower worker morale and other characteristics suggest work was a necessity and not a choice.

Both theory and empiricism, then, suggest that late-life roles in the black population are influenced by having to work in old age, perceptions of how little lifetime work patterns have changed, and by the forces of economic and psychological need.

EMPIRICAL WORK ON RETIREMENT EXPERIENCES

For more than 50 years, considerable research has been devoted to the retirement decisionmaking process (see, e.g., Fillenbaum, George, & Palmore, 1985; Morgan, 1980; Streib & Schneider, 1971). Several factors were found to predict retirement: poor health, socioeconomic status, financial readiness, the interaction of poor health and financial readiness, job dissatisfaction, extended periods of unemployment, and work and retirement attitudes (cf. Gibson, 1991c).

Virtually no studies focus on black American retirement experiences. The findings of a few race comparisons do suggest, however, that blacks compared with whites are more likely to: retire at earlier ages, retire because of poor health, have been forced to retire, have been unemployed in the 12-month period prior to retirement, and have reported job dissatisfaction and job search discouragement prior to retirement (cf. Gibson, 1991c). In short, there are race differences in the factors that determine the retirement process and decision. Poor health and disadvantaged labor force experiences are more influential for blacks, whereas financial readiness is more influential for whites.

Life after retirement also has been frequently studied. Researchers have examined such factors as morale, physical and mental health, and leisure and productive activities (Gibson, 1991c). Although this research has increased steadily over the past two decades, little work focuses specifically on black Americans. Earlier descriptive analyses of the NSBA data (Gibson, 1991c) reveal some common responses to a question asking how retired blacks spend their time. In order of frequency these were: housekeeping; leisure activities, such as sports and hobbies; gardening; nothing; sitting; and resting. Only a small percentage of the responses were church or church related, reading, listening to the radio, watching television, visiting, or talking. Even smaller percentages of responses were in the categories of caring for others, clubs, organizations, volunteer work, or travel.

These recent studies of the late-life roles and retirement experiences of black Americans are informative and valuable. They do not, however, explore the possibility that the retirement experience differs within the black population—notably in socioeconomic status (SES) and gender subgroups. We turn now to new descriptive analyses of the NSBA data that begin to identify differences in late-life roles and retirement experiences between men and women and between individuals in income, education, and occupation groups.

LATE-LIFE ROLES: GENDER AND SES DIFFERENCES

About one-third of black Americans ages 55 years and over who are not working refer to themselves as retired (Table 19-1, pp. 316–317). About one-fourth, in spite of not working, view themselves as disabled workers instead of as retired. Another fourth are still working. These findings are consistent with past research (Gibson, 1987a, 1987b, 1991a; J. S. Jackson & Gibson, 1985) and illustrate the heterogeneity of black Americans' late-life roles.

Men were slightly more likely than women to call themselves retired and still to be working. Women, however, were more likely than men to call themselves disabled. Individuals with incomes less than $6,000 were more likely than those with incomes $6,000 and over to call themselves disabled. They also were less likely to be working. The two income groups were about equally likely to call themselves retired.

Those with low levels of education (0–8 years) were more likely than those with higher levels to call themselves disabled workers. Individuals with some college were the least likely of all to call themselves disabled workers. Individuals with low (0–8 years) and high (some college) levels of education were more likely than individuals with mid levels of education (9–12 years) to call themselves retired. Those with less than 9 years of education were the least likely still to be working.

Individuals in blue-collar and service occupations were more likely than those in white-collar occupations to call themselves disabled workers. The three occupation groups were about equally likely to call themselves retired. The most likely to be working were those in white-collar occupations.

In sum, gender seems slightly associated with the work, retirement, and disabled-worker roles in late life; whereas SES is not associated with the retirement role, but rather with the worker and disabled-worker roles.

THE RETIREMENT EXPERIENCE: GENDER AND SES DIFFERENCES

Age at Retirement

Black Americans are least likely to retire "on time" (age 65 years) and most likely to retire at earlier ages (55–64 years) (see Table 19-2, pp. 318–320). There were no notable gender or SES differences in age at retirement. It is interesting to note, however, that about 15% of the sample retired at or after age 70. This was especially true of those with incomes less than $6,000. This supports prior research and theory and also reinforces the idea that the black American older worker role is one of economic necessity. This black elderly group that works well into old age may be the group to which Jacqueline Jackson refers as "dying from, rather than retiring from, the work force."

Retirement Planning

About half the black American elderly retired unexpectedly whereas half planned to retire. Similarly, about half retired willingly and half retired unwillingly. Differences in these two aspects of retirement were clearer by SES than by gender. Occupational level, unlike income and education, however, seemed unrelated to retirement planning and willingness to retire.

Retired men were more likely than retired women to have planned their retirement, whereas men and women were equally likely to be willing to retire. The lowest income and education groups (less than $6,000 and 0–11 years) were more likely than the higher groups ($6,000 or more and 12 or more years of education) to have retired unexpectedly and unwillingly. It is interesting to note that those with mid-level education (9–11 years) were more disadvantaged in regard to unexpected and unwilling retirement than were those with less education (0–8 years).

Reasons for Retirement

Black Americans retired mainly due to poor health. Job-related reasons ranked next, with financial readiness and new interests at the bottom of the list. Age and mandatory retirement were named by a few. Reasons for retirement did not appear to vary that much by gender or SES. There were, however, a few exceptions:

1. Women were slightly more likely than men to retire because of job-related and family responsibilities, and men more likely to retire mandatorily.
2. Those with incomes less than $6,000 were more likely than those with higher incomes to retire for reasons of age.
3. Surprisingly, the more highly educated (some college) were the likeliest to give poor health as the reason for retiring; and those with 12 or more years of education were more likely than those with less than 12 years to give job-related reasons.
4. White-collar workers were slightly more likely than blue-collar or service workers to retire for job-related and mandatory reasons.

Activities After Retirement

The activity most frequently engaged in by the black retired was housekeeping (Table 19-3). Nothing, sitting, or resting were second in rank. About 15% engaged in sports, hobbies, and other leisure activities, and another 10% in gardening. Church, reading, radio, television, visiting, and talking ranked next. Very few were engaged in helping others, clubs, organizations, travel, or volunteer work.

There were practically no gender or SES differences in most retirement activities. There were some exceptions, however, that should be interpreted with caution because percentage bases and percentage differences were small.

1. Women were more likely to be engaged in housekeeping and men in gardening.
2. Those with incomes less than $6,000 were slightly more likely than those with higher incomes to be doing nothing, sitting, or resting.
3. Those with the lowest levels of education (0–8 years) were slightly more likely than those with higher levels (9 or more years) to name keeping house, gardening, nothing, sitting, and resting; but less likely to name sports, hobbies, and other leisure activities.

TABLE 19-1 Late-Life Roles of Black Americans Aged 55–101 by Gender, Income, Education, and Occupation (N = 581)

	Gender			Income		
	Men	Women	Total	<$6,000	≥$6,000	Total
Role						
Retired	86	111	197	96	101	197
	(41.0)	(30.9)	(34.6)	(36.4)	(33.1)	(34.6)
Disabled worker	38	101	139	90	49	139
	(18.1)	(28.1)	(24.4)	(34.0)	(16.1)	(24.4)
Working[a]	76	81	157	34	123	157
	(36.1)	(22.6)	(27.6)	(12.9)	(40.3)	(27.6)
Homemaker	2	16	18	11	7	18
	(1.0)	(4.5)	(3.2)	(4.2)	(2.3)	(3.2)
Other[b]	8	50	58	33	25	58
	(3.8)	(13.9)	(10.2)	(12.5)	(8.2)	(10.2)
Total	210	359	569	264	305	569
	(100.0)	(100.0)	(100.0)	(100.0)	(100.0)	(100.0)

| | **Years of Education** | | | | | **Occupation** | | | |
	0–8	9–11	12	Some College	Total	Service	Blue Collar	White Collar	Total
Role									
Retired	120	25	24	25	194	81	78	27	186
	(38.8)	(24.3)	(26.1)	(45.5)	(34.8)	(32.4)	(40.3)	(40.3)	(36.4)
Disabled	93	20	18	5	136	62	46	9	117
worker	(30.1)	(19.4)	(19.6)	(9.1)	(24.3)	(24.8)	(23.7)	(13.4)	(22.9)
Working[a]	51	42	41	22	156	71	54	29	154
	(16.5)	(40.8)	(44.5)	(40.0)	(27.9)	(28.4)	(27.8)	(43.3)	(30.1)
Homemaker	9	6	2	0	17	6	1	1	8
	(2.9)	(5.8)	(2.2)	(0.0)	(3.0)	(2.4)	(0.5)	(1.5)	(1.6)
Other[b]	36	10	7	3	56	30	15	1	46
	(11.7)	(9.7)	(7.6)	(5.5)	(10.0)	(12.0)	(7.7)	(1.5)	(9.0)
Total	309	103	92	55	559	250	194	67	511

NOTES: Column percentages are in parentheses below each number. Columns fail to add to 581 due to missing data. Blue-collar occupations are craftspersons, operatives, laborers, farmers, and farm workers. Service occupations include all service workers. White-collar occupations are professional, managerial, sales, and clerical.

a. Working 20 or more hours per week.
b. Includes student and welfare recipient.

TABLE 19-2   Age at and Plans and Reasons for Retirement of Black Americans Aged 55–101 Years by Gender, Income, Education, and Occupation (N = 259, the retired only)

	Gender			Income		
	Men	Women	Total	<$6,000	≥$6,000	Total
Age in Years at Retirement						
Less than 55	13	20	33	19	14	33
	(12.9)	(14.4)	(13.8)	(14.7)	(12.7)	(13.8)
55–64	45	62	107	55	52	107
	(44.5)	(44.9)	(44.8)	(42.7)	(47.3)	(44.8)
65	14	13	27	13	14	27
	(13.9)	(9.4)	(11.3)	(10.1) ·	(12.7)	(11.3)
66–69	15	22	37	19	18	37
	(14.8)	(15.9)	(15.5)	(14.7)	(16.4)	(15.5)
70+	14	21	35	23	12	35
	(13.9)	(15.2)	(14.6)	(17.8)	(10.9)	(14.6)
Plans for Retirement[a]						
Planned to retire	54	63	117	48	69	117
	(54.0)	(44.7)	(48.5)	(36.6)	(62.7)	(48.5)
Retired unexpectedly	46	78	124	83	41	124
	(46.0)	(55.3)	(51.5)	(63.4)	(37.3)	(51.5)
Retired willingly	59	84	143	55	88	143
	(56.7)	(57.9)	(57.4)	(41.4)	(75.9)	(57.4)
Retired unwillingly	45	61	106	78	28	106
	(43.3)	(42.1)	(42.6)	(58.6)	(24.1)	(42.6)
Reasons for Retirement[b]						
Job related	7	17	24	16	8	24
	(14.3)	(21.0)	(18.5)	(19.3)	(17.0)	(18.5)
Age	3	4	7	7	0	7
	(6.1)	(4.9)	(5.4)	(8.4)	(0.0)	(5.4)
Poor health	28	40	68	42	26	68
	(57.2)	(49.4)	(52.3)	(50.7)	(55.4)	(52.3)
Other (personal, new interests)	1	1	2	1	1	2
	(2.0)	(1.2)	(1.5)	(1.2)	(2.1)	(1.5)
Family responsibilities	4	11	15	9	6	15
	(8.2)	(13.6)	(11.5)	(10.8)	(12.8)	(11.5)
Financial readiness	0	3	3	2	1	3
	(0.0)	(3.7)	(2.3)	(2.4)	(2.1)	(2.3)
Mandatory	6	5	11	6	5	11
	(12.2)	(6.2)	(8.5)	(7.2)	(10.6)	(8.5)

(continued)

TABLE 19-2   Continued

	Years of Education				
	0–8	9–11	12	Some College	Total
Age in Years at Retirement					
Less than 55	16	4	6	5	31
	(11.2)	(11.8)	(18.8)	(19.2)	(13.2)
55–64	66	15	13	13	107
	(46.1)	(44.1)	(40.6)	(50.1)	(45.5)
65	18	5	1	3	27
	(12.6)	(14.7)	(3.1)	(11.5)	(11.5)
66–69	23	5	4	4	36
	(16.1)	(14.7)	(12.5)	(15.4)	(15.3)
70+	20	5	8	1	34
	(14.0)	(14.7)	(25.0)	(3.8)	(14.5)
Plans for Retirement[a]					
Planned to retire	70	11	17	18	116
	(47.9)	(34.4)	(51.5)	(69.2)	(48.9)
Retired unexpectedly	76	21	16	8	121
	(52.1)	(65.6)	(48.5)	(30.8)	(51.1)
Retired willingly	81	17	20	22	140
	(54.4)	(50.0)	(58.8)	(81.5)	(57.4)
Retired unwillingly	68	17	14	5	104
	(45.6)	(50.0)	(41.2)	(18.5)	(42.6)
Reasons for Retirement[b]					
Job related	13	3	5	2	23
	(16.9)	(13.0)	(29.4)	(22.2)	(18.4)
Age	6	1	0	0	6
	(7.8)	(4.3)	(0.0)	(0.0)	(4.8)
Poor health	41	11	8	6	66
	(53.2)	(47.9)	(47.0)	(66.7)	(52.8)
Other (personal, new interests)	1	1	0	0	2
	(1.3)	(4.3)	(0.0)	(0.0)	(1.6)
Family responsibilities	9	3	2	0	14
	(11.7)	(13.0)	(11.8)	(0.0)	(11.2)
Financial readiness	3	0	0	0	3
	(3.9)	(0.0)	(0.0)	(0.0)	(2.4)
Mandatory	4	4	2	1	11
	(5.2)	(17.5)	(11.8)	(11.1)	(8.8)

(continued)

TABLE 19-2   Continued

	Occupation			
	Service	Blue Collar	White Collar	Total
Age in Years at Retirement				
Less than 55	13	14	5	32
	(12.9)	(15.4)	(15.1)	(14.2)
55–64	44	45	12	101
	(43.5)	(49.4)	(36.4)	(44.9)
65	11	9	4	24
	(10.9)	(9.9)	(12.1)	(10.7)
66–69	15	14	6	35
	(14.9)	(15.4)	(18.2)	(15.5)
70+	18	9	6	33
	(17.8)	(9.9)	(18.2)	(14.7)
Plans for Retirement				
Planned to retire	47	50	17	114
	(46.5)	(53.2)	(54.8)	(50.4)
Retired unexpectedly	54	44	14	112
	(53.5)	(46.8)	(45.2)	(49.6)
Retired willingly	61	56	21	138
	(59.2)	(57.7)	(63.6)	(59.2)
Retired unwilllingly	42	41	12	95
	(40.8)	(42.3)	(36.4)	(40.8)
Reasons for Retirement				
Job related	10	8	4	22
	(18.2)	(17.4)	(25.0)	(18.8)
Age	4	3	0	7
	(7.3)	(6.5)	(0.0)	(6.0)
Poor health	25	26	8	59
	(45.5)	(56.7)	(50.0)	(50.4)
Other (personal, new interests)	1	1	0	2
	(1.8)	(2.1)	(0.0)	(1.7)
Family responsibilities	9	2	2	13
	(16.4)	(4.3)	(12.5)	(11.1)
Financial readiness	1	2	0	3
	(1.8)	(4.3)	(0.0)	(2.6)
Mandatory	5	4	2	11
	(9.1)	(8.7)	(12.5)	(9.4)

NOTES: Percentages are in parentheses below each number. Columns fail to add to 259 due to missing data. Blue-collar occupations are craftspersons, operatives, laborers, farmers, and farm workers. Service occupations include all service workers. White-collar occupations are professional, managerial, sales, and clerical.

a. Categories are not mutually exclusive.

b. Multiple mentions are possible; asked only of those who retired unexpectedly and are currently working less than 20 hours per week.

4. White-collar workers were the most likely to name visiting, talking, and volunteer work; blue-collar workers were the most likely to name gardening, nothing, sitting, or resting.
5. Service workers were the most likely to name housekeeping.

In summary, SES may influence retirement roles, planning, and activities. SES, however, may not influence age at and reasons for retirement. Gender may influence the retirement roles and experiences of the black elderly less than SES. This is in spite of the fact that clear gender differences in these aspects of retirement have been found in the general population. Race differences in the importance of gender in the retirement experience are suggested.

THE FUTURE OF BLACK RETIREMENT RESEARCH

The findings of this descriptive analysis of the NSBA work, retirement, and disability data warrant new multivariate research. In this new research, models of late-life roles and retirement experiences should be developed separately for black and white men and women, and for blacks of lower and higher SES.

Analyzing SES Differences

Because the present findings suggest that late-life roles and retirement experiences vary by income and education, new retirement research should take into account the different circumstances of those in lower and higher socioeconomic status groups. The findings did not differ much by occupation. Is occupation not a valid social class indicator for the present generation of older black Americans? If not, the reason might be that racial discrimination placed a ceiling on their occupational mobility. The increasing validity of occupation as a measure of social class among blacks, then, would be a good barometer of widening occupational opportunities for them.

Analyzing Race Differences in the Effects of Gender

The findings suggest that gender is less important in the late-life roles and retirement experiences of black than white Americans. This may be because black men and women in the present elderly cohort, unlike their white counterparts, had similar work lives. Both black men and women were lifetime workers with discontinuous work patterns. New research should focus on such race and gender differences when examining late-life roles and retirement experiences.

Revising Retirement Definitions

Definitions of retirement need recasting if a most disadvantaged group of the black elderly is to be included in future retirement research, planning, and policy. Findings in this chapter highlight the diversity of black Americans in late-life roles. They are workers, disabled workers, and retirees. Prevailing procedural retirement definitions may be inappropriate for those individuals, although eligible, who do not call themselves retired (the unretired-retired).

This sizable and deprived segment of older blacks by definition could be omitted

TABLE 19-3 Activities of Black Americans Aged 55–101 After Retirement by Gender, Income, Education, and Occupation (N = 245, the retired only)

	Gender			Income		
	Men	Women	Total	<$6,000	≥$6,000	Total
Housekeeping	14 (13.5)	41 (29.1)	55 (22.4)	29 (22.1)	26 (22.9)	55 (22.4)
Gardening	18 (17.3)	6 (4.3)	24 (9.8)	13 (9.9)	11 (9.6)	24 (9.8)
Helping Others	1 (1.0)	6 (4.3)	7 (2.9)	4 (3.0)	3 (2.6)	7 (2.9)
Church Related	10 (9.6)	10 (7.1)	20 (8.2)	10 (7.6)	10 (8.8)	20 (8.2)
Clubs/ Organizations	3 (2.9)	4 (2.8)	7 (2.9)	4 (3.1)	3 (2.6)	7 (2.9)
Sports, Hobbies, Other Leisure	12 (11.5)	25 (17.7)	37 (15.1)	19 (14.5)	18 (15.8)	37 (15.1)
Travel	3 (2.9)	2 (1.4)	5 (2.0)	1 (0.8)	4 (3.5)	5 (2.0)
Reading, Radio, Television	6 (5.8)	10 (7.1)	16 (6.5)	9 (6.9)	7 (6.1)	16 (6.5)
Visiting, Talking	5 (4.8)	10 (7.1)	15 (6.1)	7 (5.3)	8 (7.0)	15 (6.1)
Volunteer Work	1 (1.0)	2 (1.4)	3 (1.2)	1 (0.8)	2 (1.8)	3 (1.2)
Nothing, Sitting, Resting	24 (23.0)	24 (17.0)	48 (19.6)	30 (22.9)	18 (15.8)	48 (19.6)
Other	7 (6.7)	1 (0.7)	8 (3.3)	4 (3.1)	4 (3.5)	8 (3.3)

	Years of Education					Occupation			
	0-8	9-11	12	Some College	Total	Service	Blue Collar	White Collar	Total
Housekeeping	37 (25.0)	6 (18.2)	5 (15.2)	5 (18.5)	53 (22.0)	26 (26.0)	18 (18.8)	6 (18.8)	50 (21.9)
Gardening	20 (13.4)	2 (6.1)	2 (6.1)	0 (0.0)	24 (10.0)	3 (3.0)	19 (19.8)	2 (6.3)	24 (10.5)
Helping Others	4 (2.7)	1 (3.0)	1 (3.0)	1 (3.7)	7 (2.9)	5 (5.0)	1 (1.0)	1 (3.1)	7 (3.1)
Church Related	5 (3.4)	8 (24.2)	4 (12.1)	3 (11.1)	20 (8.3)	9 (9.0)	6 (6.3)	3 (9.3)	18 (7.9)
Clubs/Organizations	4 (2.7)	0 (0.0)	1 (3.0)	1 (3.7)	6 (2.5)	2 (2.0)	2 (2.1)	1 (3.1)	5 (2.2)
Sports, Hobbies, Other Leisure	18 (12.2)	7 (21.2)	7 (21.2)	5 (18.5)	37 (15.4)	19 (19.0)	12 (12.5)	3 (9.3)	34 (14.9)
Travel	4 (2.7)	0 (0.0)	0 (0.0)	1 (3.7)	5 (2.1)	2 (2.0)	2 (2.1)	1 (3.1)	5 (2.2)
Reading, Radio, Television	9 (6.1)	2 (6.1)	3 (9.1)	2 (7.4)	16 (6.6)	8 (8.0)	5 (5.2)	2 (6.3)	15 (6.6)
Visiting, Talking	5 (3.4)	4 (12.1)	1 (3.0)	4 (14.9)	14 (5.8)	5 (5.0)	5 (5.2)	3 (9.3)	13 (5.7)
Volunteer Work	1 (0.7)	0 (0.0)	1 (3.0)	1 (3.7)	3 (1.2)	0 (0.0)	1 (1.0)	2 (6.3)	3 (1.3)
Nothing, Sitting, Resting	37 (25.0)	2 (6.1)	6 (18.2)	3 (11.1)	48 (19.9)	17 (17.0)	23 (23.9)	6 (18.8)	46 (20.2)
Other	4 (2.7)	1 (3.0)	2 (6.1)	1 (3.7)	8 (3.3)	4 (4.0)	2 (2.1)	2 (6.3)	8 (3.5)

NOTES: The figure on top is the number of people who responded in that activity category, and the figure on the bottom is the column percent. Blue-collar occupations are craftspersons, operatives, laborers, farmers, and farm workers. Service occupations include all service workers. White-collar occupations are professional, managerial, sales, and clerical. Columns fail to add to 259 due to missing data.

from retirement research. These are individuals who do not choose to call themselves retired, who have never had a regular job, who do not have pension benefits, and for whom there is no clear cessation of work. Because alternate definitions of retirement change the findings of retirement research (Palmore, Fillenbaum, & George, 1984), expanding current definitions of retirement to include the unretired-retired black elderly could change some of the past findings and paradigms of retirement research.

Toward New Retirement Models

Although discussions in this chapter have focused on relationships among source of income, work history, the disabled worker, and retirement roles, the choice of late-life roles undoubtedly is a more complex social-psychological process. Variables excluded from our discussion are likely to be cognitive-motivational and personality factors such as: ways individuals make sense of their world, values they have (and perceive society has) about retirement, external barriers (real and perceived) to carrying out a full retirement role, and various other psychological costs and benefits of the retirement role. These variables could affect choice of late-life roles and retirement experiences directly, as mediators, or as intervenors, as recent latent variable analyses demonstrate (Gibson, 1991a, 1991b).

The models should be tested across national samples to determine whether blacks and other minorities (Gibson & Burns, 1992) and whites differ in the factors influencing late-life roles and retirement experiences. The models also should be tested in longitudinal data to determine the special effects of social change and civil rights legislation on the late-life roles and retirement experiences of blacks, and to determine the causal ordering of work, disability, and retirement roles. For maximum planning and policy benefit, new research on black American late-life roles and retirement resources should employ similar constructs, personal biographies, and methods of analysis.

REFERENCES

Abbott, J. (1977). Socioeconomic characteristics of the elderly: Some black/white differences. *Social Security Bulletin, 40,* 16–42.

Abbott, J. (1980). Work experience and earnings of middle-aged black and white men, 1965–1971. *Social Security Bulletin, 43,* 16–34.

Anderson, B. E., & Cottingham, D. H. (1981). The elusive quest for economic equality. *Daedalus, 110,* 257–274.

Biddle, B., & Thomas, E. (Eds.). (1966). *Role theory: Concepts and research.* New York: John Wiley.

Cain, G. G. (1976). The challenge of segmented labor market theories to orthodox theory: A survey. *Journal of Economic Literature, 14,* 1215–1257.

Chirikos, T., & Nestel, G. (1983). *Economic aspects of self-reported work disability.* Columbus: Center for Human Resource Research, The Ohio State University.

Corcoran, M., & Duncan, G. J. (1978). A summary of part 1 findings. In G. J. Duncan & J. N. Morgan (Eds.). *Five thousand American families* (Vol. VI, pp. 3–46). Ann Arbor: University of Michigan, Institute for Social Research.

Current Population Reports. (1980). *The social and economic status of the black population in the United States 1970–1978.* (Special Studies Series P-23, No. 80). Washington, DC: Bureau of the Census, U. S. Department of Commerce.

Ellison, D. L. (1968). Work, retirement, and the sick role. *The Gerontologist, 8,* 189–192.

Fillenbaum, G., George, L., & Palmore, E. (1985). Determinants and consequences of retirement among men of different races and economic levels. *Journal of Gerontology, 40,* 85–94.

Gibson, R. C. (1982). *Race and sex differences in the work and retirement patterns of older heads of household* (pp. 138–184). (Minority Research Monograph). Scripps Foundation.

Gibson, R. C. (1983). Work patterns of older black female heads of household. *Journal of Minority Aging, 8*(2), 1–16.

Gibson, R. C. (1986a). *Blacks in an aging society* (pp. 1–41). New York: Carnegie.

Gibson, R. C. (1986b). Blacks in an aging society. *Daedalus, 115*(1), 349–371.

Gibson, R. C. (1987a). Defining retirement for black Americans. In D. E. Gelfand & C. Barresi (Eds.), *Ethnicity and aging* (pp. 224–238). New York: Springer.

Gibson, R. C. (1987b). Reconceptualizing retirement for black Americans. *The Gerontologist 27*(6), 691–698.

Gibson, R. C. (1988). The work, retirement, and disability of older black Americans. In J. S. Jackson (Ed.), *The black American elderly: Research on physical and psychosocial health* (pp. 304–324). New York: Springer.

Gibson, R. C. (1991a). The subjective retirement of black Americans. *Journal of Gerontology, 46*(2), 204–209.

Gibson, R. C. (1991b). Race and the self-reported health of elderly persons. *Journal of Gerontology, 46*(5), S235–S242.

Gibson, R. C. (1991c). Retirement in black America. In J. S. Jackson (Ed.), *Life in black America* (pp. 179–198). Newbury Park, CA: Sage.

Gibson, R. C., & Burns, C. J. (1992). The work, retirement, and disability of aging minorities. *Generations,* Fall/Winter, 31–35.

Gordon, H. A., Hamilton, C. A., & Tipps, H. C. (1982). *Unemployment and underemployment among Blacks, Hispanics, and women.* (U.S. Commission on Civil Rights Clearinghouse Publication No. 74). Washington, DC: Government Printing Office.

Hanuschek, E. A., & Jackson, J. E. (1977). *Statistical methods for social scientists.* New York: Academic Press.

Hill, M. S. (1981, January). *Trends in the economic situation of U. S. families and children: 1970–1980.* Paper presented at the Conference of Families and the Economy, Washington, DC.

Jackson, J. J. (1980). *Minorities and aging.* Belmont, CA: Wadsworth.

Jackson, J. S., & Gibson, R. C. (1985). Work and retirement among the black elderly. In Z. Blau (Ed.), *Current perspectives on aging and the life cycle* (pp. 193–222). Greenwich, CT: JAI.

James, W. (1950). *The principles of psychology.* New York: Dover. (Originally published 1910)

Lamb, H. R., & Rogawski, A. S. (1978). Supplemental security income and the sick role. *American Journal of Psychiatry, 135,* 1221–1224.

Ludwig, A. (1981). The disabled society? *American Journal of Psychotherapy, 35,* 5–15.

Montagna, P. D. (1977). *Occupations and society: Toward a sociology of the labor market.* New York: John Wiley.

Morgan, J. N. (1980). Retirement in prospect and retrospect. In G. J. Duncan & J. N. Morgan (Eds.), *Five thousand American families: Vol. 8. Patterns of economic progress.* Ann Arbor: University of Michigan, Institute for Social Research.

Munnell, A. H. (1978). The economic experience of blacks: 1964–1974. *New England Economic Review,* January/February, 5–18.

Palmore, E. B., Fillenbaum, G. G., & George, L. K. (1984). Consequences of retirement. *Journal of Gerontology, 39,* 109–116.

Parnes, H., & Nestel, G. (1981). The retirement experience. In H. S. Parnes (Ed.), *Work and retirement: A national longitudinal study of men.* Cambridge, MA: MIT Press.

Phillips, D. (1965). Self-reliance and the inclination to adopt the sick role. *Social Forces, 43,* 555–563.

Prince, E. (1978). Welfare status, illness and subjective health definition. *American Journal of Public Health, 68,* 865–871.

Sarbin, T., & Allen, V. (1968). Role theory. In G. Lindzey & E. Aronson (Eds.), *The handbook of social psychology* (2nd Ed., pp. 223–258). Reading, MA: Addison-Wesley.

Streib, G., & Schneider, G. (1971). *Retirement in American society: Impact and process.* Ithaca, NY: Cornell University Press.

Stryker, S. (1968). Identity salience and role performance: The relevance of symbolic interaction theory for family research. *Journal of Marriage and the Family, 30,* 558–562.

Thurlow, H. J. (1971). Illness in relation to life situation and sick role tendency. *Journal of Psychosomatic Research, 15,* 73–88.

20

Special Problems of Older Women Workers

LOIS B. SHAW

Older women workers face quite different problems from the ones that men face. Because of demands arising from family responsibilities, many older women have spent several years entirely out of the labor market or have worked only part time. When they attempt to reenter, they find many barriers to better jobs. This selection describes the impact of such barriers as age and sex discrimination and continuing family responsibilities on job opportunities. Shaw also makes policy recommendations to improve conditions for women at work and in retirement.

The problems faced by older women workers differ substantially from those faced by men. Many of the employment problems of older women stem from their previous commitment to family roles. Most older women have spent many years either entirely out of the labor market or working only part time or intermittently. Older women who are recent labor market reentrants are, of course, at entirely different stages of their work careers than are older men. Even those who have worked part time or intermittently for years may require a reorientation of their work lives and in some cases additional training if they need to become completely self-supporting. As traditional family caregivers, older women are also vulnerable to further work interruptions if their husbands, parents, or adult children become ill and require care.

Problems that affect older workers of both sexes may have a different impact on women and men because of differences in their work experience. Even though age discrimination affects both sexes, the kinds of discrimination they encounter may be different. Because they are more likely to be entering the labor market, women may be more likely to encounter age discrimination at the point of hiring, whereas age-related involuntary terminations may be more important for men. Similarly, layoffs from long-term jobs will affect fewer women than men and may affect women differently when they do occur. Sex stereotyping of jobs and reluctance of employers to hire people for

"Special Problems of Older Women Workers" by Lois Shaw, from *The Older Worker,* eds. Michael Borus, Herbert Parnes, Steven Sandell, and Bert Seidman. Copyright © 1989 by the Industrial Relations Research Association, Madison, WI.

jobs unconventional for their sex may constrain the job choices of both women and men. However, since higher paying jobs tend to be stereotypically male, any such sex discrimination weighs more heavily on women's job opportunities than on men's.

Because the problems of reentering the labor force and advancing beyond entry-level jobs will be a major focus of this chapter, the age range of the "older" workers described may be somewhat broader than that of other chapters in this volume. For example, displaced homemaker programs often use 35 or 40 years as a lower age limit. Most of the research reviewed here will focus on women who are 40 years old or over, but relevant research findings that include somewhat younger women will be mentioned as well.

The women who are the subject of this research have entered the labor market during a period of rapid increase in women's labor force participation and rapid change in norms concerning women's roles. At the upper end of the age range, women who are now age 65 reached age 18 as the Depression of the 1930s was ending. In 1941, as they were reaching adulthood, a survey of city school systems found that about 60 percent had policies of not hiring married women as teachers, and many more would hire them only if they had dependents to support or met other special criteria. During the 1930s, legislation barring married women from employment had been introduced in the legislatures of 26 states, though only one state actually passed such legislation (Oppenheimer, 1970). The contrast for women who are now 40 years old could hardly be greater. These women reached age 18 in 1965, just after the passage of legislation and executive orders making discrimination on the basis of sex illegal. Among the oldest women we are considering, probably few except the poor had themselves had mothers who worked outside the home, whereas for the youngest, working mothers had become a familiar phenomenon.[1] We should keep in mind, therefore, that as the background of women entering middle age changes, the problems of the older woman worker will change—a topic I will consider at greater length in my concluding remarks.

PROBLEMS OF LABOR MARKET REENTRY

Labor market reentry has been a subject of interest to both the research community and to policymakers. The mature women's cohort of the National Longitudinal Surveys of Labor Market Experience (NLS) was initiated with the idea of collecting data to study the problems women encounter when they reenter the labor force after staying at home to rear children (Parnes, 1975). This data set is the source of the most extensive work history information for older women in the United States. The surveys were begun in 1967 with a representative sample of about 5,000 women who were then age 30–44. These women have been reinterviewed at one- or two-year intervals through 1987, and considerable research has been completed using these data through 1982 when the women were age 45–59. The availability of longitudinal data and the use of increasingly sophisticated research methodology have enabled researchers to begin to answer questions about women's work patterns, about the effects of work interruptions on women's earnings, and about the kinds of employment problems middle-aged women encounter.

Women's Varied Work Patterns

The stereotypic view of the reentrant depicts her as a woman who returns to the labor market after many years at home. Reentry is pictured as a one-time event. A woman leaves the labor force to raise children, stays at home until her children are in school or have left home or until she loses her husband. Then she returns to work and continues to be employed until retirement.

Research using work history data and labor force flow data reveals that these stereotypes are inaccurate. Analyses using the NLS show that few women with children have followed the single reentry pattern. Among women age 45–59 in 1982, about 40 percent of white women and 60 percent of black women first returned to work before their first child reached age six (Mott and Shaw, 1986). However, the great majority of these women had additional absences from the labor force, and even women who stayed out much longer often had further work interruptions. Overall only 20 percent of these women had worked fairly continuously from the time they first returned to work until the date of the 1982 interview. A similar result was obtained from life table models of working lives using data from the Current Population Survey. Researchers at the Bureau of Labor Statistics (BLS) estimated that as of 1977 the average 25-year-old woman will enter the labor force 2.7 times during her remaining life (Smith, 1982).

If repeated entries and exits are common, how many women experience long spells out of the labor market? In the NLS slightly more than 40 percent of middle-aged women with children had remained at home for as long as 10 years before returning to work, and about one quarter stayed at home for 15 years or more. The median length of work interruption before first returning to work was about seven years (Dex and Shaw, 1986). Although long interruptions were not uncommon for today's middle-aged woman, most women evidently followed a pattern of several shorter spells out of the labor force. However, these repeated spells, in many cases, added up to a total number of years out of the labor market that was quite large. In 1976 women in the NLS, who were in their forties and early fifties had, on average, spent a total of about 15 years at home and about 11 years at work since leaving school (Shaw, 1979).

The great diversity of work patterns among middle-aged women is striking. In a study of the work patterns of NLS women who were age 45–59 in 1982, Shaw (1986a) found that about one quarter of the sample demonstrated increasing work attachment over the previous 15 years. These women could be considered labor market reentrants who had not worked or, more frequently, had worked intermittently in the first years of the interviews, but had become steadily employed by the last five years of the period. Irregular work patterns with no clear trend toward permanent attachment were about as common as increasing attachment. About 20 percent had worked continuously throughout the 15 years, and about 5 percent appeared to have retired after a lengthy period of employment. The other quarter of the sample had not worked at all or had very minimal work records.

Displaced Homemakers: Myths and Realities

One reason for concern about labor market reentry has been that increasing divorce rates have caused many women to find that they must become self-supporting. The displaced homemaker movement was organized in the early 1970s primarily by middle-class women who had experienced a midlife divorce after many years of marriage.[2] As the term implies, the displaced homemaker was pictured as a woman displaced from her primary job of homemaking and forced to become the primary earner because of divorce, separation, widowhood, or disability of her husband. Having no recent work experience, she had difficulty finding employment. She would not qualify for unemployment compensation because she had no recent work experience, would not qualify for welfare because her children were grown, and would not qualify for Social Security benefits because she was too young. In short, as this description implies, the displaced homemaker was viewed as the stereotypic reentrant.[3]

Legislation to provide job counselling and training for displaced homemakers was a major goal of the movement. Partly as a result of their efforts, federal displaced home-maker legislation was enacted in 1976 in amendments to the Vocational Education Act and in 1978 amendments to the Comprehensive Employment and Training Act (CETA). Funding for programs fell when CETA was replaced by the Job Training Partnership Act (JTPA), but the Carl D. Perkins Vocational Education Act of 1984 provided increased funding. By 1984, 24 states had enacted legislation supporting or providing funds for displaced homemaker programs (U.S. Congress, 1985).

Determining the number of women who might be classified as displaced homemak-ers is not a simple matter. Legislative definitions of the population eligible for services have varied, and privately sponsored programs have also catered to different groups. Understandably, government-sponsored programs have usually had income cutoffs so that only low-income women are served. Some programs have age limits, on the grounds that other programs such as the Work Incentive Program (WIN) serve younger welfare recipients with children, but many programs serve all ages.

The requirement that women must have spent a "substantial" number of years out of the labor force has been incorporated in some of the displaced homemaker legislation.[4] This requirement, if defined restrictively to mean that a woman cannot have worked at all during a period of five, 10, or 15 years, excludes many women who have supple-mented family income with part-time or low-paid employment, but would have diffi-culty in becoming completely self-supporting. In a study of women eligible for the CETA displaced homemaker program, Shaw (1979) found that women who would have been eligible except that they had not been out of the labor force for at least five years were similar to the eligible population in education, wages, and poverty status. Two-thirds of the excluded group were black.

Researchers at the Urban Institute have estimated that about 2.2 million women could be classified as displaced homemakers in 1983 under a definition they developed (O'Brien and Nightengale, 1985; also reported in U.S. Congress, 1985). This defini-tion included women age 35–64 who were widowed, separated, divorced, or had hus-bands who were disabled or long-term unemployed. A small number of single AFDC mothers were also included. Women in these categories were counted as displaced homemakers if they had employment-related problems, including current unemploy-ment and having been unemployed or out of the labor force for at least 26 weeks in the previous year, working part time when a full-time job was desired, receiving pay below the minimum wage, or dropping out of the labor force because of discouragement. Spending a given number of years out of the labor force was not a requirement. Women whose youngest child was age 17–19 and who were receiving a substantial proportion of income from child support, AFDC, or Social Security dependent benefits were also included. The 2.2 million women meeting this definition represented about 6 percent of all women age 35–64. Among divorced, separated, and widowed women at these ages, about 17 percent could be considered displaced homemakers, while only 2 percent of married women were included.

These estimates, though the best available using a national data base, illustrate the difficulties of definition.[5] Because of limited funds, government-sponsored displaced-homemaker programs will probably continue to define the displaced-homemaker population so as to include only those in greatest need. However, using the minimum wage as the cutoff for considering that a woman has an employment problem excludes many women who are in need of further training if they are to become fully self-supporting on a long-term basis. A full-time minimum wage job at present represents a yearly income of slightly under $7,000, which is above the poverty line for one person, but not for a person with one or more dependents. Even for a woman living alone $7,000 does not represent economic security. At this level many jobs do not carry health insurance and few provide pensions. Women who cannot obtain better jobs than these are living near poverty and are at risk of becoming poor if they encounter health problems or if they must rely on Social Security for most of their income when they retire. Obtaining a job at the minimum wage surely should not be taken to mean that an older person's employment problems are at an end. If a more realistic definition of "having an employment problem" were adopted, the estimated numbers of displaced homemakers would be considerably higher than those quoted above.

Even if we accept a particular definition of the number of women who could be classified as displaced homemakers in a particular year, virtually nothing is known about the dynamic aspects of the problem. One estimate placed the yearly flow into displaced homemaker status at 200 to 300 thousand.[6] This estimate is probably too low; if accurate it would suggest that many women remain displaced homemakers over an extended period.

Studies of the characteristics of displaced homemakers have found that about half have not completed high school (Vanski, Nightengale, and O'Brien, 1983; Shaw, 1979). Over 40 percent cite a service occupation as their current or most recent employment. Most had worked at some time in the previous five years, but the majority had less than 10 years of total work experience (Shaw, 1979). Any broadening of the definition of the displaced-homemaker population would probably bring women with more education or work experience into the group. Some privately funded programs do, in fact, serve women who are better prepared than those eligible for government programs.

Effects of Work Interruptions
on Earnings and Job Opportunities

The major problem for reentrants is that the jobs they can obtain are low paid.[7] According to human capital theory, the major determinants of wages are education, vocational training, and work experience, which provides on-the-job training.[8] An interruption in work experience can be expected to have an adverse effect on reentry pay for two reasons. First, any time spent out of the labor market will lessen the amount of work experience a person will have acquired by a given age. Second, job-related skills that are not utilized will depreciate (become rusty or in some cases obsolete).

Empirical research examining the effects of work interruptions on women's wages has consistently shown that the amount of women's previous work experience affects their wages. Support for the skill depreciation hypothesis is less clear. That work interruptions would cause skill depreciation appears plausible for persons holding high-skill jobs, but most middle-aged women who have been the subject of research on work interruptions had left jobs that required little specialized training. The predominant view appears to be that some deterioration in earnings capacity does occur during a work interruption, whether due to skill depreciation, loss of current information about job opportunities, or employers' preferences for hiring people with recent references.[9] Any or all of these factors might make it necessary for a labor market reentrant to take a job below her potential earnings capacity.

Mincer and Ofek (1982) observed a short period of rapid wage growth following reentry, which they attribute to "skill repair." Corcoran, Duncan, and Ponza (1983) point out that the wage growth might be due either to skill repair or to a trial period in which the reentrant's skills are assessed, either by the employer or by the reentrant herself, and a better job match secured. One study found that rapid wage growth was observed only for reentrants who changed employers in the first years after reentry (Shaw, 1984). This finding appears more congruent with an initial job mismatch than with skill repair as the cause of rapid wage growth. Of course, a period of rapid wage growth does not imply that work interruptions are not costly since any time out of the labor force will mean less work experience than would otherwise have been achieved.

Other information on how absences from the work force might affect the jobs reentrants obtain is more impressionistic. Directors of displaced-homemaker centers stress the need to build confidence through counselling and peer support groups, to offer practice in preparing for job interviews, and to provide information about the local job market and job search agencies. However, the fact that some centers offer refresher courses for women seeking clerical and nursing employment suggests that some women who formerly held jobs requiring specialized skills do find it useful to update their training (U.S. Congress, 1985).

BARRIERS TO BETTER JOBS

From the perspective of an older woman worker without much recent work experience or with experience only in low-paid jobs, the outlook for obtaining well-paid employment is not promising. In 1986 the median earnings of all women workers who worked full time for the entire year were about $16,000 compared with nearly $26,000 for men.[10] Nearly one quarter of all year-round, full-time women workers earned less than $11,000. Median earnings for retail sales and service workers were about $10,000, for operatives $12,500, and for clerical workers $15,500. Since these occupations provide nearly 60 percent of employment of full-time women workers and a much higher percent for those without college or other specialized training, becoming self-supporting at a level approaching a middle-class standard of living presents a formidable problem for an older woman without much recent work experience or training.

Although their needs may be less pressing, other middle-aged women besides displaced homemakers are concerned with acquiring new skills and obtaining better jobs. For many couples, financing their children's college education or preparing for financial security in old age may depend on wives' employment. In many black families especially, wives' earnings have been crucial for raising family income above the poverty line or achieving a middle-class standard of living. In addition, whatever the level of need of individual women and their families, we have widespread social consensus that barriers of age, sex, or race should not prevent people from moving into positions for which they are qualified.

The Need for Further Education and Training

The educational level of middle-aged women is well below that of younger women. In 1984 nearly 30 percent of women age 45–64 had not completed high school, compared with less than 15 percent of women age 22–34; only one-quarter of the older women had completed at least one year of college compared with over 40 percent of the younger women (U.S. Bureau of the Census, 1986, Table 9). Older women were also less likely than older men to have completed at least one year of college.

The problem of upgrading the skills of disadvantaged older women is a difficult one. Most federally funded programs for disadvantaged workers have focused on youth or on workers displaced from long-term jobs. Although older women have participated in a variety of government-funded employment and training programs, displaced-homemaker programs provide the only ones specifically geared to the needs of middle-aged and older women.

No systematic research has been undertaken to evaluate displaced-homemaker programs. Studies of other training programs for disadvantaged workers have found that job training increases the earnings of women with little labor market experience (Bassi, 1983; Congressional Budget Office and National Commission for Employment Policy, 1982). However, the programs studied appear to have been less successful in training women for more than entry-level jobs (Harlan, 1985). Research is needed on what aspects of displaced-homemaker programs are most successful and on what kinds of job training provide the best prospects for helping older women to obtain better jobs.

In a survey of experienced directors of displaced-homemaker programs, a major problem identified was that many women find it impossible to work at a full-time job, manage a household, and participate in training even on a part-time basis. Many displaced homemakers need financial assistance to cover basic living expenses if they are to enroll in training programs, but funds for this purpose are very limited (U.S. Congress, 1985). Other problems mentioned include the need for some women to obtain basic literacy and mathematical skills before they can benefit from regular job training and the need for more encouragement for women to enter programs that offer training for nontraditional occupations that are better paid than the traditional jobs that older women tend to choose.[11]

Middle-aged women report considerable participation in job-related training. A study using the NLS found that between 1977 and 1981 about 16 percent of employed women reported participation in some kind of noncollege occupational training program that was not provided by their employers. About one-quarter reported having participated in formal on-the-job training, but much of this training was of short duration, averaging 8 to 12 weeks (Shaw, 1983b). This study showed wage gains for women who had participated in on-the-job training or in some kinds of occupational training. However, occupational categories were too broadly defined to be very useful as a guide for job counselling. Appelbaum (1981) found that training leading to a professional certificate, but not clerical training, increased the wages of women with interrupted work careers.

Many older women have also obtained additional formal education in recent years. A study using the NLS found that about 4 percent of middle-aged women who had graduated from high school but not gone on to college had obtained their high school diplomas at age 35 or later; nearly 10 percent of black women with high school diplomas had obtained them at these ages (Morgan, 1986). A much larger percentage had attended college: 22 percent of women who were age 45–59 in 1982 had attended college at some time in the previous 15 years. However, among those who had attended college, only 15 percent had obtained a degree. In some cases, women may have been attending for recreational reasons or for limited objectives. For example, women whose most recent occupation was teaching or nursing were among those most likely to attend, and these women were probably renewing education or nursing credentials without necessarily wanting another degree. However, some women may have encountered difficulties, either financial or personal, that made continued attendance difficult.

In the past, educational institutions have not catered to the needs of part-time and older students. Returning women students, who are often employed and must attend part time, have faced such problems as lack of financial aid for part-time students, inflexibility in the scheduling of courses, and limited access to services such as counselling and job placement, which may not be available during evening hours.[12] The older woman may also have to deal with her own lack of confidence, uncertainty about career directions, sense of isolation, or opposition from family members.

Although many universities did open centers for the continuing education of women in the 1960s and 1970s, these were years when enrollment of traditional college-age students was soaring, and the needs of part-time and older students were often not adequately met. As the number of traditional students declines, colleges appear to be paying increasing attention to the needs of older returning students. Legislation passed in 1986 that will allow financial aid for part-time students may also make continuing college attendance possible for more middle-aged women who are seeking to upgrade their skills.

Sex Discrimination and the Kinds of Jobs Women Hold

The human capital research previously described has been the basis for attempting to show whether sex discrimination exists. Earnings differentials between women and men cannot be explained by differences in education and work experience alone. Commonly, not more than half of the differential can be explained by these human capital differences; some part of the remaining differential is usually attributed to sex discrimination.[13] However, it is possible that unmeasured productivity differences account for part or all of the unexplained earnings differences. Other differences that have been shown to contribute to wage differentials include occupational differences (Treiman and Hartmann, 1981) and differences in college major and the kinds of rewards sought on the job (Daymont and Andrisani, 1984).

Some researchers believe that because of the heavier burden of household work they perform, women choose jobs that do not require as much effort or work involvement as men's jobs. Support for the view that women may seek less demanding jobs comes from a study of authority on the job, which is shown to be negatively correlated with responsibility for household tasks (D'Amico, 1986). Women's occupational segregation is also thought by some to be a result of the greater ease of combining stereotypically female jobs with family roles.[14] For example, female-dominated jobs may be chosen because they offer more opportunities for part-time employment than do male-dominated jobs (O'Neill, 1985).

Women's occupational choices may also be influenced by their perceptions of sex discrimination. Women may often be reluctant to enter male-dominated occupations; they may take the scarcity of women in an occupation to be a sign that women will encounter barriers to acceptance and advancement. A growing literature on the problems women encounter in male-dominated occupations attests to the relevance of this factor.[15]

Studies of company employment practices provide a different approach to investigating sex discrimination. The use of employee referrals when recruiting new workers, informal networks within companies from which "outsiders" such as women and minorities are excluded, and preferences for homogeneous work groups, which are believed to be more harmonious and productive, are some of the company practices found to limit opportunities for women and minorities (Roos and Reskin, 1984). Different promotion ladders for women and men and nearly complete segregation by job title were found in a study of 400 establishments in California (Bielby and Baron, 1984).

Women who are now past age 45 have undoubtedly encountered much more overt sex discrimination than is now legally possible. Especially at the stage of making initial vocational choices, preparing for nontraditional jobs was not encouraged by schools or by what the woman herself might observe in the labor market. For example, only after the antidiscrimination legislation of the 1960s did it become illegal for employers to specify the desired sex of applicants in job advertisements in newspapers. Many women who are now in their fifties and sixties probably expected to remain full-time housewives as their mothers had. Those who did expect to work were well past the age of making initial vocational commitments before a wider range of occupations began to appear to be reasonable choices. Women in their forties have benefited more from equal opportunity legislation, but most of these women had also completed their educations before the legislation became effective. Although older women have made some advances into managerial jobs in recent years, younger women have accounted for most of the increases in employment in the male-dominated professional and managerial positions (Shaw, 1986a; Beller, 1984).

Whether many older women who have undertaken additional education or training would have gone into nontraditional fields if more training programs and supportive counselling had been available is an open question. With relatively short remaining work lives, older women may be unwilling to risk spending time on training for an occupation in which they might find barriers to entry or an inhospitable work environment.

If older women are, for the most part, already committed to traditionally female occupations, raising wages in these occupations becomes important for improving their earnings. In the 1970s unions such as the American Federation of State, County, and Municipal Employees brought suits charging that job evaluation schemes were systematically biased in their ratings of typical female jobs. Since that time, a number of states have undertaken studies of state employee evaluation schemes and a few have implemented pay increases for low-paid, predominantly female jobs (Aaron and Lougy, 1986).

In the meantime, controversies have proliferated over the merits of mandating equal pay for jobs judged by evaluation methods to be of comparable worth. Proponents of comparable worth believe that sex-biased evaluations are an important reason for women's lower pay, while opponents believe that supply and demand in labor markets produce wages that accurately measure productivity.[16] One concern is that raising pay in female-dominated jobs might lead to increased unemployment among women. A study of the effect of raising minimum wage standards for women's occupations in Australia found rather small employment effects. However, the wage increases occurred at a time of rapid growth in industries that traditionally employ women (Gregory and Duncan, 1981). Some research suggests that the overall impact of pay equity schemes on the male-female earnings gap would be small because only wage differentials within companies or governmental units would be affected. Wage differentials between industries and between different companies within the same industry would remain.[17] However, some women working for companies or state governments that implemented pay equity would undoubtedly benefit. As more implementation occurs, additional research on the impact of comparable worth on wages and employment will be possible.

Age Discrimination

Public opinion polls show widespread agreement that older workers face age discrimination. Even employers agree with this perception, though they are usually unwilling to admit that they themselves practice it (McConnell, 1983). However, the extent of age discrimination and its importance for older women workers is not known. Research in this area is difficult and the little that exists is more likely to consider men than women. One problem is that if systematic differences in pay are found between older and younger workers with similar characteristics, it is hard to determine whether these differences are due to unmeasured differences in productivity or to discrimination. Another is that older workers who can find only poorly paid employment may drop out of the labor force entirely, so that comparisons between older and younger workers may not adequately reflect the disadvantages that older people face.

A few studies have attempted to determine whether wages decline with age after controlling for other worker characteristics, but most of this research pertains to older men. In one study of men and unmarried women, the earnings of older men but not women were found to decline with age (Hanoch and Honig, 1983). However, a study of earnings and promotion in a large company found that, after controlling for level of the first job and other worker characteristics, the age when both men and women first joined the company had a negative effect on their advancement (Rosenbaum, 1984).

Another line of research has attempted to document age discrimination by asking employers to answer questions on whether hypothetical job candidates would be hired or considered for promotion.[18] Again most of these studies have been confined to men. One study, which asked personnel specialists to rate secretaries, found no age-related differences in recommendations for promotion or salary increase (Schwab and Heneman, 1978). On the other hand, employers were less willing to hire 55-year-old than 25-year-old hypothetical applicants and also preferred men to women for semiskilled jobs even though the descriptions of competence were identical (Haefner, 1977). Although research of this kind is often suggestive of discrimination, the limited kinds of occupations involved and small sample sizes make generalization impossible.

Another approach to studying age discrimination is through examination of complaints and lawsuits filed under the Age Discrimination in Employment Act (ADEA). In a study of age discrimination charges filed in 1981, the complaint rate of women was slightly lower than that of men (McConnell, 1983). In a study of actual lawsuits under ADEA, Schuster and Miller (1984) found that women were more likely to be involved in cases concerning hiring, promotion, or wages and fringe benefits, whereas men were more frequently involved in cases of termination and early retirement. Women were found to be more likely to win their suits than men. The authors speculated that this result may have been due to women having the additional protection of legislation against sex discrimination, to courts being more responsive to the kinds of claims brought by women, or to companies being less prepared to defend cases at the clerical level where the majority of female plaintiffs are employed.

If some employers have informal upper age limits on hiring for certain positions or if they have perceptions of appropriate ages for reaching certain job levels, any such hiring or promotion policies based on age would be particularly detrimental for older women who have not been continuously employed. Especially for hiring, this kind of discrimination may be difficult for individuals to detect because most people have little information about other job applicants and their qualifications. There may also be age-related barriers to receiving training. One study found that some offices of the Employment Service were less likely to provide job counselling or suggest training for women age 45 and over than for younger women (Pursell and Torrence, 1980).

Family Obligations That Interfere with Steady Employment

After first reentering the labor market following childbearing, many women have additional work interruptions, often associated with having additional children or with the needs of their families. However, by the time they reach middle age, fewer women have work interruptions associated with family obligations. A study of women age

40–54 in 1977 found that about 20 percent of women workers said they had left their last jobs for family-related reasons (Shaw, 1983a). One family circumstance leading to work interruptions at this age was moving to a different locality—often in response to the husband's job opportunities. Sandell (1977) found that migration led to lower earnings for married women, at least in the short run.

Another cause of work interruption may be a husband's health problem. Although in some cases the effect of husbands' health problems may be in the opposite direction, causing women to assume more responsibility for the family's support, some research suggests that the predominant effect is to cause women to leave the labor force or reduce their hours of work to provide care (Haurin, 1986; Gitter, Shaw, and Gagen, 1986). In 1982 about 4 percent of white married women and 9 percent of black married women age 45–59 said that the ill health of a family member limited their work (Gitter, Shaw, and Gagen, 1986). Although some of the family members with health problems were children and a few were parents, husbands constituted the largest single category.

In recent years with the rising cost of nursing home care and the increasing size of the population over age 75, the group at greatest risk of needing this care, the idea of providing more incentives for home-based care has become popular. The implications for the probable caregivers—most commonly older women—have frequently not been considered. A recent study of the caregivers of noninstitutionalized disabled elderly people found that about three quarters of the primary caregivers were women. Wives and daughters were the major caregivers among women, but husbands also provided a substantial amount of care (Stone, Cafferta, and Sangl, 1988). Women not only provided the major portion of care, but were also more likely to have caregiving responsibilities while still middle-aged. Daughters, especially, were more likely to be employed and to report conflicts between work and caregiving than were either wives or husbands, most of whom were age 65 or older. However, about 12 percent of both spouses and daughters reported having to quit a job to provide care. For some middle-aged women, caregiving for the elderly could come at the expense of being able to provide for their own economic security in old age.

Other Causes of Work Interruptions

Some causes of work interruptions and early retirement are probably not substantially different for women and men. Both sexes encounter health problems that limit their ability to work, and some older workers of both sexes experience displacement from long-term jobs. . . . Here I will mention briefly research pertaining specifically to women workers and suggest ways in which these problems could be somewhat different for women and men.

Health appears to be an important cause of labor market withdrawal for older women (Gitter, Shaw, and Gagen, 1986; Chirikos and Nestel, 1985, 1983; Hanoch and Honig, 1983; Shaw, 1983a). However, the measures of health used in these studies are self-reported. They are thus subject to the same controversies that have surrounded research on men's health as a factor in labor force withdrawal. Because fewer women than men work at jobs that are physically demanding, it might be expected that women would be less likely than men to have health problems that limit their ability to work. One analysis found that among recently retired workers 47 percent of men, but only 29 percent of women, had last worked at jobs with medium or heavy strength requirements (U.S. Department of Health and Human Services, 1986). However, these figures were not adjusted to reflect differences in average strength between women and men.

Most of the research on job loss among long-term workers has focused on men, who are more likely than women to be long-tenured and to be employed in the declining manufacturing industries that have received the most attention. Women job-losers have also generally lost jobs that paid much lower wages than those of male job-losers. A recently completed study of older women job-losers with two or more years of job tenure showed reemployment at lower wages among women who lost better-paid jobs, whereas lower-paid workers showed little wage loss but a much higher probability of remaining unemployed or leaving the labor force (Gagen, 1987). Additional research on this subject should provide insight into the problems of the growing number of women who are long-service workers.

WOMEN AND RETIREMENT

The factors that affect age of retirement are discussed in another chapter of this volume. Here we focus on the relationship between employment at older ages and economic security after retirement. Although most women will be eligible for Social Security benefits either on their own work records or as dependents or survivors, women who do not have other sources of retirement income have a much higher risk of becoming poor in old age than those who have pensions or those who continue to work beyond the usual retirement age. In 1984 the most vulnerable elderly women, those living alone, had an overall poverty rate of 25 percent. However, among those who were either employed or had a pension other than Social Security, only 5 percent were poor (U.S. Bureau of the Census, 1986, Table 11). The importance of pensions as a supplement to Social Security points up the importance of older women being able to move into jobs that provide pensions. The importance of continued employment beyond the usual retirement age raises questions about the kinds of work available to women workers in their sixties and seventies and the continued ability to work at advanced ages.

Problems of Pension Coverage and Entitlement

In 1984, 31 percent of nonmarried women ages 65–69 had pension income other than Social Security either from their own jobs or in the form of survivor benefits from their husbands' pensions. Among married couples in this age range, 54 percent were receiving pension income (U.S. Department of Health and Human Services, 1985). As women who are now middle-aged move into retirement, these percentages may increase. Nearly one half of nonmarried women age 45–59 in the 1982 NLS expected to have pension income either from their own work or from survivor benefits from their husbands' pensions (Shaw, 1986b). Although these expectations may not be completely realized, the greater work attachment of this generation of women, together with recent changes in pension law, will probably lead to somewhat increased pension receipt when they retire.[19] However, some influences may be working in the opposite direction; pension coverage appears to have stabilized for working women and declined slightly for working men between 1979 and 1983 (Beller, 1986).

The most recent source of national data on pension coverage is the 1983 Current Population Survey (CPS) pension supplement. Andrews (1985), using this data set to estimate rates of coverage for all wage and salary workers, found that slightly over half of employed women were covered by pension plans; coverage was defined as working for an employer with a pension plan. However, because some employees are not included in their employers' pension plans, actual plan participation is a more relevant measure.[20] Beller (1986), using the same data to measure actual participation rates in private industry plans only, found that about 41 percent of full-time women workers were participating in a pension plan, but when part-time workers were considered as well, only about one-third of all women workers participated. However, participation is known to be much higher in the public sector. Snyder (1986), using data from the Social Security Administration's 1982 New Beneficiary Survey (NBS), found that 39 percent of women working in the private sector had participated in a pension on their longest job compared with 82 percent of women whose longest job was in the public sector.

In these studies men's coverage or participation exceeded that of women by 7 to 10 percentage points.[21] If only workers who are already vested (i.e., entitled to receive benefits or lump-sum distributions) are considered, the disparity is even larger. In Beller's study, 44 percent of women participants and 55 percent of male participants were vested. These figures include workers of all ages. Among women age 45–64, Beller found that about half of women full-time workers in private industry were participants. Vesting was also higher than among younger workers.

The major reasons that women's coverage, participation, and vesting are lower than men's involve their shorter average job tenure and the greater extent of their part-time employment. The kind of jobs they hold is another important factor. Pension coverage is high in durable goods manufacturing, communications, and utilities—industries that employ relatively few women—and low in retail trade and many service industries where women predominate (Andrews, 1985; Snyder, 1986). Other factors favoring pension coverage include firm size and unionization. Here again, women are less likely than men to work in firms with more than 500 employees, to be covered by a union contract, or to work in industries where coverage is high. In addition, high-wage workers are much more likely to be covered than are low-wage workers (Andrews, 1985).

Although Andrews found no significant difference in coverage between men and women after controlling for the factors discussed above, women and low-wage workers were less likely than men to report actually participating in a pension plan. One reason for this lower participation may be that in some pension plans workers' participation depends on their making contributions; low-wage workers of both sexes may feel unable to contribute, and women may not want to contribute if their husbands have pensions. A second reason may be that under the Employee Retirement Income Security Act (ERISA), employers could exclude up to 30 percent of their employees from pension plans even if they met minimum age and service requirements. No systematic information is available on the characteristics of workers who were excluded, but some researchers believe that women may have been disproportionately affected. The Tax Reform Act of 1986 makes participation rules more stringent, but still allows some workers to be excluded (Congressional Budget Office, 1987). Additional data and research are needed on excluded workers and effects of the new legislation.

Among participants in pension plans, women are less likely than men to become vested largely because of their shorter job tenure. In the past most private pension plans have required 10 years of service before vesting. About 30 percent of newly retired women in the NBS had worked less than 10 years on the longest job they had ever held, as compared with less than 8 percent of men (Snyder, 1986). As part of the 1986 tax reform legislation, most private pension plans will be required in the future to reduce their vesting requirements to five years. This legislation should increase pension receipt among women, but the benefit amounts will probably be quite small in most cases.

A final reason for women's low rate of pension receipt is again related to low wages and short job tenure. Women are more likely than men to receive a lump-sum distribution in lieu of a monthly pension benefit. Over 20 percent of recently retired women, compared with 10 percent of men, covered by a private pension on their longest job received a lump-sum distribution (Snyder, 1986). Under ERISA lump-sum distributions are allowable for defined contribution plans, which are the most common type among small employers, but are allowed under defined benefit plans only if the value of the benefit is below quite low limits.[22]

Although women's pension receipt may continue to increase in the near future as women with more work experience reach retirement age, the long-run outlook for increasing pension coverage and receipt among women is not clear. The shift in employment out of manufacturing into services will affect men's pension coverage more than women's; a continuing decline in unionization would also affect men most. However, any trend toward greater concentration of employment in small firms would adversely affect women's pension coverage as well as men's. Whether increased tenure on jobs that do have pensions will offset such industrial shifts is not clear. Any decline in pension coverage among men will also have an adverse effect on the probability of an elderly couple's having a pension and on widows receiving survivor benefits. If fewer men have pensions in the future, the importance of women's gaining pensions on the basis of their own employment will increase.

When women do have pensions, their benefits are considerably smaller than men's. A comparison based on the 1983 CPS found that women's benefits were, on average, about half those of men (McCarthy, 1986). However, when replacement rates per year of employment were calculated, the median replacement rate for women was 82 percent of that of men, and women's mean replacement rate was actually slightly larger than men's. (McCarthy did not attempt to explain this difference.) In any event, this analysis suggests that the difference between women's and men's benefits is largely explained by differences in wages and job tenure, the two major elements usually determining pension amounts.

Although pension plans cannot incorporate rules that discriminate against women directly, rules that give proportionately smaller pensions to low-wage or short-service workers will have a larger impact on women than on men. One rule that makes pensions relatively smaller for short-tenure workers than for long-tenure workers calls for larger benefit accruals as tenure increases. A second provision that has had an adverse impact on low-wage workers has been the integration of pensions with Social Security benefits. In pension plans with this feature, pensions are reduced by various formulas based on the size of the employee's Social Security benefit or the employer's contribution to the Social Security account of the employee; in the past these rules sometimes caused the pension to be eliminated entirely.[23] The Tax Reform Act of 1986 limited reductions that will be allowable under integration formulas.

A final problem for short-tenure workers is that many pension plans are based on salary in the last few years of employment. Under this kind of pension formula, a person who changes employers several times over the course of a career will have smaller pension benefits than a person who remains with one employer even if vested rights have accrued in all pensions and the total work experience and salary history of the two are the same. This is the case because salaries on earlier jobs are likely to be lower than the salary on the last job, and earlier job salaries are not indexed for inflation. Therefore pensions from the earlier jobs will have low current-dollar values when the person retires.[24] Even women with fairly extensive work experience may have small pension benefits if they have changed employers to accommodate their husbands' careers or upon returning to the labor force following other interruptions.

Working Beyond Normal Retirement Age

The work activity of both women and men decreases rapidly after age 60, and once retired, the majority do not return to work. However, there are a number of differences between women and men who continue to work at these older ages. Although both sexes show increasing employment in sales and service occupations, the largest single employment category for women remains administrative support occupations (primarily clerical work). As the figures on occupational distributions suggest, men are overrepresented in professional and managerial jobs at older ages. Probably many continue to be employed as independent professionals or as high-ranking executives. However, older women are underrepresented in professional and managerial occupations. Few older women hold the kinds of jobs in these categories that older men hold. Most women professionals are teachers or nurses—jobs that are not so easy to continue at older ages. Perhaps in part because of this different job mix, men who continue to work at older ages are more likely than women to work at year-round, full-time jobs.

An interesting perspective on work after retirement can be gained by comparing women and men who continue to work after beginning to receive Social Security benefits. Although labor force participation rates of men are considerably higher than those of women at age 62 and above, if we look only at those who were drawing Social Security benefits as retired workers, women and men were equally likely to continue working; close to 20 percent were employed about a year after first receiving benefits (Holden, 1987; Iams, 1986). Furthermore, if only those who were working shortly before beginning to receive benefits are compared, women were more likely than men to continue working.[25]

There are probably several reasons why women with recent work experience were more likely than men to continue working after receiving Social Security benefits. The most important predictors of continued employment for women were marital status and receipt of another pension in addition to Social Security (Iams, 1986). Over 40 percent of unmarried women and 20 percent of married women without pensions were employed, compared with under 10 percent of both married and unmarried women with pensions. The amount of income other than earnings was also an extremely important predictor of employment, especially for unmarried women. Nearly half of unmarried women with other income of less than $500 per month were employed. These findings suggest that the higher employment rates of female retired workers compared with their male counterparts reflect their lower economic status. Women are less likely to have other pensions, and their Social Security benefits are lower, on average. In addition, because women earn less, they are more likely to be able to continue working, at least part time, without exceeding the Social Security earnings test, currently $6,120 per year before age 65.

Women were more likely to continue working if they had previously worked in sales or service occupations or were self-employed. Private household workers had the highest rate of continued employment, probably reflecting lack of a pension, low income, and the availability of part-time work in private households. Snyder (1987) found that women were more likely than men to remain in the same occupation if they continued to work after retirement. Thus the downward occupational mobility seen in the post-retirement jobs of men is less common for women, partly because many of those who continue to work were already in low-status, low-paying jobs.

Health limitations also influence post-retirement employment of both women and men (Iams, 1986). Especially among unmarried women with limited economic resources, health problems appear to be limiting the possibility of supplementing retirement income, even in the early years of retirement. As these women age, fewer will be able to work. A few may still become eligible for pensions through their continued employment, but many others may be counted among the elderly poor when they are no longer able to work.

SUMMARY AND CONCLUSIONS

The special problems that confront older women workers today are to a considerable extent due to their prior work patterns, which for most women were characterized by work interruptions while raising children. Traditional social norms, widely practiced sex discrimination, and poor economic circumstances when they were young also influenced vocational and educational choices and precluded some kinds of careers for today's older women. Increasing divorce rates meant that women who had not planned for extensive work careers were forced to become self-supporting.

How will the problems of older women workers change in the years ahead when women with very different work backgrounds reach their middle and older years? To answer this question we must first consider how much change has actually occurred. One factor that should improve the employment prospects of future generations is that older women in the future will be much better educated than their counterparts today. Few will have less than a high school education and many will be college graduates.

As to changes in work experience, we sometimes tend to believe that few women will have had work interruptions, but this view confuses high labor force participation rates with steady employment. For example, in 1984 slightly over 60 percent of women whose youngest child was under age 6 had worked during the previous year, but only 27 percent had worked full time for at least 40 weeks, and almost 40 percent had not worked at all (U.S. Bureau of the Census, 1986). Similarly, 72 percent of women whose youngest child was age 6–17 had worked for at least part of the year, but only 42 percent had worked full time for 40 weeks or more, and 28 percent had not been employed at any time. Especially in the years when they have preschool children, most women do not now engage in continuous full-time employment.

When they reach middle age, the next generation of women will undoubtedly have more work experience than older women today. However, a great diversity of work patterns can be expected. Changing patterns can be monitored with data from the younger NLS samples. In one such study of women who were age 24–34 in 1978 (and are now age 33–43), Mott and Shapiro (1982) found that in the approximately seven years after the birth of their first child, only 12 percent of women had worked at least six months in all years and 30 percent had not worked as much as six months in any year. Among women who are still younger than these, the percentage of continuously employed women will surely increase and the percentage with long work interruptions will decrease, but as shown in the CPS figures cited above, many women will continue to experience work interruptions, and intermittent work patterns will continue to be common. The displaced homemaker who has difficulty becoming self-supporting will become less common but is not likely to completely disappear. The trend toward later childbearing could mean that older women in the future have more family responsibilities than older women today; we do not know what effect this trend will have on work patterns and employment problems.[26]

An important consideration is the quality of work experience acquired by women who work intermittently or part time. Do the kinds of jobs they hold provide work experience that would help a woman to become self-supporting, or are they mainly low-skilled jobs that are only viewed as a means of supplementing family income? An important question for further research is whether part-time employment is a viable means of keeping up current work skills or acquiring new ones. Research on older women has tended to show either no earnings growth associated with part-time employment (Corcoran, Duncan, and Ponza, 1983) or considerably slower earnings growth than for full-time employment (Shaw, 1984; Jones and Long, 1979). However, it is possible that the nature of part-time work is changing, and that in the future women who have invested in lengthy training will seek opportunities to continue to work at their usual occupations on less than a full-time basis in order to maintain their skills.[27]

In an economy undergoing industrial transformation, more research is needed on the effects of job displacement for women workers. Textiles, shoes, and electronics, industries that employ many women, are all under intense pressure from foreign competition. A much reduced demand for clerical workers has been predicted, but has so far not materialized.[28] Additional research on what kinds of training are most beneficial for older women could improve programs for both women displaced from long-term jobs and for displaced homemakers.

Research on pensions and retirement will undoubtedly continue to receive much attention as the population ages. More of the research on this subject should focus on the problems of women, who make up 60 percent of the elderly population. Our private pension system receives considerable subsidies from favorable tax treatment. Increasing concern has been expressed as to whether well-paid, long-tenured workers are being subsidized at the expense of lower-paid workers and those who have changed jobs (Congressional Budget Office, 1987). Because of women's employment patterns, this is an important issue for women workers. Research on the effects of the many changes in pension laws recently enacted and currently proposed should consider effects on women as well as men. Finally, the kinds of jobs women hold and their ability to continue working well into their sixties will become an increasingly important area to monitor as the normal age of retirement is increased to 67 under Social Security.

NOTES

1. Further discussion of the changes in the social climate at the time different cohorts of women reached different life-cycle stages may be found in Shaw and O'Brien (1983), Jusenius and Parnes (1976), and Chafe (1972).

2. Shields (1981) provides an interesting account of the displaced-homemaker movement by one of its organizers.

3. The reentry stereotype predates the displaced-homemaker movement. Middle-aged married women first began reentering the labor force in large numbers during World War II (Shaw and O'Brien, 1983). The idea of a second career after childbearing was widely discussed during the 1950s by social scientists such as Myrdal and Klein (1956).

4. The 1978 amendments to CETA used this language, and some state legislation also incorporated it. However, the Perkins Vocational Education Act does not mention either time spent out of the labor market or age (U.S. Congress, 1985).

5. Other estimates of the number of displaced homemakers and comparisons of the assumptions used in making them may be found in Vanski, Nightengale, and O'Brien (1983).

6. This estimate, which used 1976 CPS data, was made by Emily Andrews and is reported in Vanski, Nightengale, and O'Brien (1983).

7. A study of the displaced-homemaker population in 1975 found that having pay below the minimum wage or having to accept part-time employment when full-time work was desired were more common problems than unemployment or dropping out of the labor force because of inability to find work (Vanski, Nightengale, and O'Brien, 1983).

8. One of the first statements of human capital theory may be found in Becker (1964). Blaug (1976) provides a review of human capital research and a discussion of some of the problems with this approach.

9. Large wage losses per year of work interruption were found by Mincer and Ofek (1982) and Mincer and Polachek (1978, 1974). Smaller losses, commonly 3–4 percent per year if measured near the point of reentry and as low as 1 percent or less after a few years of employment, have been found by Corcoran, Duncan, and Ponza (1983), Ferber and Birnbaum (1981), Corcoran and Duncan (1979), and Sandell and Shapiro (1978). A study of middle-aged reentrants found that three quarters had previously worked at occupations requiring less than a year to learn (Shaw, 1982); for these kinds of jobs skill depreciation is unlikely to have much long-term importance.

10. These figures are based on unpublished data from the March 1987 Current Population Survey, furnished by the Bureau of Labor Statistics.

11. One study found that women in CETA training programs had a high probability of receiving training for traditional female jobs even if they expressed a preference for being trained for a traditionally male job (Waite and Berryman, 1984).

12. See Tittle and Denker (1980) and Astin (1976) for overviews of some of the institutional barriers faced by older women students.

13. Excellent reviews of theoretical and empirical research on sex discrimination may be found in Blau and Ferber (1986), Madden (1985), O'Neill (1985), and Cain (1984).

14. Polachek (1981, 1979) has been a major proponent of this view, which he bases on the belief that skills depreciate more slowly in female-dominated occupations. However, other researchers such as England (1984, 1982) and Abowd and Killingsworth (1983) have not found evidence for differences in skill depreciation between male- and female-dominated occupations.

15. See, for example, Kanter (1977) for women in management and Walshok (1981) for blue-collar workers. Also see discussions in Bergmann (1986) and Reskin and Hartmann (1986).

16. In addition to Aaron and Lougy, see Remick (1984), Gold (1983), and Livernash (1980) for further discussion of the arguments on both sides.

17. Johnson and Solon (1984) estimate that even if pay equity schemes were widely mandated, no more than 10 percent of the male-female earnings gap would be eliminated.

18. See Doering, Rhodes, and Schuster (1983) for a review of this literature.

19. For example, the likelihood of receiving survivor benefits from their husbands' pensions may be enhanced by the Retirement Equity Act of 1984, which requires that pension plans offering life annuities must provide survivor benefits unless the spouse waives her (or his) right to the benefit.

20. This use of the terms "coverage" and "participation" appears to be widespread, though by no means universal, among pension analysts. However, common usage probably understands coverage to mean that a person is participating in a pension plan. Hence, use of the term "coverage" without explicit definition can be misleading.

21. Since both the CPS and the NBS depend on self-reporting of pension status, it may not always be clear to respondents whether the question refers to coverage or participation as defined above.

22. The Retirement Equity Act of 1984 allows cashouts of pension benefits that have a present value of less than $3,500.

23. For a discussion of the different kinds of rules under which private pension plans may be integrated with Social Security benefits, see U.S. General Accounting Office (1986) and Bell and Hall (1984).

24. See Congressional Budget Office (1987) for examples of the effects of pension rules on workers who have work and salary experiences that are identical except for the number of employers.

25. For looking at retirement behavior, this kind of comparison is more meaningful than comparison of participation rates because persons with similar pre-retirement work attachments are being compared.

26. However, it is possible that the trend toward smaller families may offset the trend toward later childbearing, so that the average age of women at the birth of their last child will not increase.

27. Kahne (1985) argues that new policies on part-time employment would benefit women and older workers as well as employers. She envisions an increase in part-time jobs that provide for career progression and prorated fringe benefits. She cites the Federal Employees Part-Time Career Act and describes numerous private industry plans as examples of the kind of part-time employment that might become common in the future.

28. An estimate by Leontief shows full office automation reducing the percentage of the labor force employed in clerical jobs from 18 to 12 percent (*Scientific American*, September 1984, p. 82). The major impact would fall on women, who are the majority of clerical workers.

REFERENCES

Aaron, Henry J., and Cameran M. Lougy. *The Comparable Worth Controversy.* Washington: The Brookings Institution, 1986.

Abowd, John, and Mark P. Killingsworth. "Sex Discrimination, Atrophy, and the Male-Female Wage Differential." *Industrial Relations* 22 (Fall 1983), pp. 387–402.

Andrews, Emily S. *The Changing Profile of Pensions in America.* Washington: Employee Benefits Research Institute, 1985.

Appelbaum, Eileen. *Back to Work: Determinants of Women's Successful Reentry.* Boston: Auburn House, 1981.

Astin, Helen S. *Some Action of Her Own: The Adult Woman and Higher Education.* Lexington, MA: D.C. Heath, 1976.

Bassi, Laurie J. "The Effects of CETA on Postprogram Earnings of Participants." *Journal of Human Resources* 18 (Fall 1983), pp. 539–56.

Becker, Gary S. *Human Capital.* New York: National Bureau of Economic Research, 1964.

Bell, Donald, and Diane Hall. "How Social Security Payments Affect Private Pensions." *Monthly Labor Review* 107 (May 1984), pp. 15–20.

Beller, Andrea H. "Trends in Occupational Segregation by Sex and Race, 1960–1981." In *Sex Segregation in the Workplace: Trends, Explanations, Remedies,* ed. Barbara F. Reskin. Washington: National Academy Press, 1984.

Beller, Daniel J. "Coverage and Vesting in Private Pension Plans, 1972–1983." In *The Handbook of Pension Statistics,* eds. Richard A. Ippolito and Walter W. Kolodrubetz. Chicago: Commerce Clearing House, 1986. Pp. 53–118.

Bergmann, Barbara R. *The Economic Emergence of Women.* New York: Basic Books, 1986.

Bielby, William J., and James N. Baron. "A Woman's Place Is With Other Women: Sex Segregation Within Organizations." In *Sex Segregation in the Workplace: Trends, Explanations, Remedies,* ed. Barbara F. Reskin. Washington: National Academy Press, 1984.

Blau, Francine D., and Marianne A. Ferber. *The Economics of Women, Men, and Work.* Englewood Cliffs, NJ: Prentice-Hall, 1986.

Blaug, Mark. "The Empirical Status of Human Capital Theory: A Slightly Jaundiced Survey." *Journal of Economic Literature* 14 (September 1976), pp. 827–55.

Cain, Glen G. "The Economic Analysis of Labor Market Discrimination: A Survey." Special Report No. 37. Madison: Institute for Research on Poverty, University of Wisconsin, 1984.

Chafe, William H. *The American Woman.* New York: Oxford University Press, 1972.

Chirikos, Thomas N., and Gilbert Nestel. "Economic Consequences of Poor Health in Mature Women." In *Unplanned Careers: The Working Lives of Middle-Aged Women,* ed. Lois B. Shaw. Lexington, MA: D.C. Heath, 1983.

———. "Further Evidence on Economic Effects of Poor Health." *Review of Economics and Statistics* 67 (February 1985), pp. 61–69.

Congressional Budget Office. *Tax Policy for Pensions and Other Retirement Saving.* Washington: U.S. Government Printing Office, 1987.

Congressional Budget Office and National Commission for Employment Policy. *CETA Training Programs: Do They Work for Adults?* Washington: Congressional Budget Office, 1982.

Corcoran, Mary E., and Greg J. Duncan. "Work History, Labor Force Attachment, and Earnings Differences Between Races and Sexes." *Journal of Human Resources* 14 (Winter 1979), pp. 3–20.

Corcoran, Mary E., Greg J. Duncan, and Michael Ponza. "A Longitudinal Analysis of White Women's Wages." *Journal of Human Resources* 18 (Fall 1983), pp. 497–520.

D'Amico, Ronald. "Authority in the Workplace: Differences Among Mature Women." In *Midlife Women at Work: A Fifteen-Year Perspective,* ed. Lois B. Shaw. Lexington, MA: D.C. Heath, 1986.

Daymont, Thomas N., and Paul J. Andrisani. "Job Preferences, College Major, and the Gender Gap in Earnings." *Journal of Human Resources* 19 (Summer 1984), pp. 408–28.

Dex, Shirley, and Lois B. Shaw. *British and American Women at Work: Do Equal Opportunities Policies Matter?* London: Macmillan, Ltd., 1986.

Doering, Mildred, Susan R. Rhodes, and Michael Schuster. *The Aging Worker.* Beverly Hills, CA: Sage, 1983.

England, Paula. "Wage Appreciation and Depreciation: A Test of Neoclassical Economic Explanations of Occupational Sex Segregation." *Social Forces* 62 (March 1984), pp. 726–49.

———. "The Failure of Human Capital Theory to Explain Occupational Sex Segregation." *Journal of Human Resources* 17 (Summer 1982), pp. 358–70.

Ferber, Marianne A., and Bonnie G. Birnbaum. "Labor Force Participation Patterns and Earnings of Clerical Workers." *Journal of Human Resources* 16 (Summer 1981), pp. 416–25.

Gagen, Mary G. "Job Displacement of Established Women Workers: Correlates and Employment Consequences." Ph.D. dissertation, The Ohio State University, 1987.

Gitter, Robert G., Lois B. Shaw, and Mary G. Gagen. "Early Labor Market Withdrawal." In *Midlife Women at Work: A Fifteen-Year Perspective,* ed. Lois B. Shaw. Lexington, MA: D.C. Heath, 1986.

Gold, Michael Evans. *A Debate on Comparable Worth.* Ithaca, NY: ILR Press, 1983.

Gregory, R. G., and R. C. Duncan. "Segmented Labor Market Theories and the Australian Experience of Equal Pay for Women." *Journal of Post-Keynesian Economics* 3 (Spring 1981), pp. 403–28.

Haefner, James E. "Race, Age, Sex and Competence as Factors in Employer Selection of the Disadvantaged." *Journal of Applied Psychology* 62 (1977), pp. 199–202.

Hanoch, Giora, and Marjorie Honig. "Retirement, Wages, and Labor Supply of the Elderly." *Journal of Labor Economics* 1 (1983), pp. 131–51.

Harlan, Sharon L. "Federal Job Training Policy and Disadvantaged Women." In *Women and Work: An Annual Review,* Vol. 1, eds. Laurie Larwood, Ann H. Stromberg, and Barbara A. Gutek. Beverly Hills, CA: Sage, 1985.

Haurin, Donald R. "Women's Labor Market Reactions to Family Disruptions, Husband's Unemployment, or Disability." In *Midlife Women at Work: A Fifteen-Year Perspective,* ed. Lois B. Shaw. Lexington, MA: D.C. Heath, 1986.

Holden, Karen C. "Work after Benefit Receipt: Do the Characteristics of Jobs Make a Difference?" Discussion paper, Institute for Research on Poverty, University of Wisconsin, 1987.

Iams, Howard M. "Employment of Retired-Worker Women." *Social Security Bulletin* 49 (March 1986), pp. 5–13.

Johnson, George, and Gary Solon. "Pay Differences Between Women's and Men's Jobs: The Empirical Foundations of Comparable Worth Legislation." National Bureau of Economic Research Working Paper No. 1472, 1984.

Jones, Ethel B., and James E. Long. "Part-Week Work and Human Capital Investment by Married Women." *Journal of Human Resources* 14 (Fall 1979), pp. 563–77.

Jusenius, Carol L., and Herbert S. Parnes. "Introduction and Overview." In *Dual Careers, Volume 4,* R and D. Monograph 21, U.S. Department of Labor, Employment and Training Administration, 1976.

Kahne, Hilda. *Reconceiving Part-Time Work: New Perspectives for Older Workers and Women.* Totowa, NJ: Rowman and Allanheld, 1985.

Kanter, Rosabeth Moss. *Men and Women of the Corporation.* New York: Basic Books, 1977.

Livernash, E. Robert, ed. *Comparable Worth: Issues and Alternatives.* Washington: Equal Opportunities Council, 1980.

Madden, Janice F. "The Persistence of Pay Differentials: The Economics of Sex Discrimination." In *Women and Work: An Annual Review,* Vol. 1, eds. Laurie Larwood, Ann H. Stromberg, and Barbara A. Gutek. Beverly Hills, CA: Sage, 1985.

McCarthy, David. "Private Pension Benefit Levels." In *The Handbook of Pension Statistics 1985,* eds. Richard A. Ippolito and Walter W. Kolodrubetz. Chicago: Commerce Clearing House, 1986. Pp. 119–76.

McConnell, Stephen R. "Age Discrimination in Employment." In *Policy Issues in Work and Re-*

tirement, ed. Herbert S. Parnes. Kalamazoo, MI: W.E. Upjohn Institute for Employment Research, 1983.

Mincer, Jacob, and Haim Ofek. "Interrupted Work Careers: Depreciation and Restoration of Human Capital." *Journal of Human Resources* 17 (Winter 1982), pp. 3–24.

Mincer, Jacob, and Solomon Polachek. "Family Investments in Human Capital: Earnings of Women." *Journal of Political Economy* 82 (March/April 1974), pp. S76–S106.

———. "An Exchange: The Theory of Human Capital and the Earnings of Women: Women's Earnings Reexamined." *Journal of Human Resources* 13 (Winter 1978), pp. 118–34.

Morgan, William R. "Returning to School at Midlife: Mature Women with Educational Careers." In *Midlife Women at Work: A Fifteen-Year Perspective,* ed. Lois B. Shaw. Lexington, MA: D.C. Heath, 1986.

Mott, Frank L., and David Shapiro. "Continuity of Work Attachment Among Young Mothers." In *The Employment Revolution,* ed. Frank L. Mott. Cambridge, MA: MIT Press, 1982.

Mott, Frank L, and Lois B. Shaw. "The Employment Consequences of Different Fertility Behaviors." In *Midlife Women at Work: A Fifteen-Year Perspective,* ed. Lois B. Shaw. Lexington, MA: D.C. Heath, 1986.

Myrdal, Alva, and Viola Klein. *Women's Two Roles.* London: Routledge and Kegan Paul, 1956.

O'Brien, Carolyn Taylor, and Demetra Smith Nightengale. "Programs for Displaced Homemakers in the 1970s." Discussion paper. Washington: The Urban Institute, 1985.

O'Neill, June. "Role Differentiation and the Gender Gap." In *Women and Work: An Annual Review,* Vol. 1, eds. Laurie Larwood, Ann H. Stromberg, and Barbara A. Gutek. Beverly Hills, CA: Sage, 1985.

Oppenheimer, Valerie Kincade. *The Female Labor Force in the United States.* Berkeley: Institute for International Studies, University of California, 1970.

Parnes, Herbert S. "The National Longitudinal Surveys: New Vistas for Labor Market Research." *American Economic Review* 65 (May 1975), pp. 244–49.

Polachek, Solomon W. "Occupational Self-Selection: A Human Capital Approach to Occupational Structure." *Review of Economics and Statistics* 63 (February 1981), pp. 60–69.

———. "Occupational Segregation Among Women: Theory, Evidence, and a Prognosis." In *Women in the Labor Markets,* eds. Cynthia B. Lloyd, Emily S. Andrews, and Curtis L. Gilroy. New York: Columbia University Press, 1979.

Pursell, Donald E., and Willard D. Torrence. "The Older Woman and Her Search for Employment." *Aging and Work* 3 (Spring 1980), pp. 121–28.

Remick, Helen, ed. *Comparable Worth and Wage Discrimination.* Philadelphia: Temple University Press, 1984.

Reskin, Barbara F., and Heidi I. Hartmann. *Women's Work, Men's Work: Sex Segregation on the Job.* Washington: National Academy Press, 1986.

Roos, Patricia A., and Barbara F. Reskin. "Institutional Factors Contributing to Sex Segregation in the Workplace." In *Sex Segregation in the Workplace: Trends, Explanations, Remedies,* ed. Barbara F. Reskin. Washington: National Academy Press, 1984.

Rosenbaum, James E. *Career Mobility in a Corporate Hierarchy.* Orlando, FL: Academic Press, 1984.

Sandell, Steven. "Women and the Economics of Family Migration." *Review of Economics and Statistics* 59 (November 1977), pp. 406–14.

Sandell, Steven, and David Shapiro. "The Theory of Human Capital and the Earnings of Women: A Reexamination of the Evidence." *Journal of Human Resources* 13 (Winter 1978), pp. 103–17.

Schuster, Michael, and Christopher S. Miller. "An Empirical Assessment of the Age Discrimination in Employment Act." *Industrial and Labor Relations Review* 38 (October 1984), pp. 64–74.

Schwab, Donald P., and Herbert G. Heneman III. "Age Stereotyping in Performance Appraisal." *Journal of Applied Psychology* 63 (1978), pp. 573–78.

Shaw, Lois B. "Introduction and Overview." In *Midlife Women at Work: A Fifteen-Year Perspective,* ed. Lois B. Shaw. Lexington, MA: D.C. Heath, 1986a.

———. "Looking Toward Retirement: Plans and Prospects." In *Midlife Women at Work: A Fifteen-Year Perspective,* ed. Lois B. Shaw. Lexington, MA: D.C. Heath, 1986b.

———. "Determinants of Wage Growth after Labor Market Reentry." Special Report to the U.S. Department of Labor. Columbus: Center for Human Resource Research, The Ohio State University, 1984.

———. "Causes of Irregular Employment Patterns." In *Unplanned Careers: The Working Lives of Middle-Aged Women,* ed. Lois B. Shaw. Lexington, MA: D.C. Heath, 1983a.

———. "Effects of Education and Occupational Training on the Wages of Mature Women." Special Report to the U.S. Department of Labor. Columbus: Center for Human Resource Research, The Ohio State University, 1983b.

———. "Effects of Age, Length of Work Interruption, and State of the Economy on the Reentry Wages of Women." Special Report to the U.S. Department of Labor. Columbus: Center for Human Resource Research, The Ohio State University, 1982.

———. "A Profile of Women Potentially Eligible for the Displaced Homemaker Program under the Employment and Training Act of 1978." Special Report to the U.S. Department of Labor. Columbus: Center for Human Resource Research, The Ohio State University, 1979.

Shaw, Lois B., and Theresa O'Brien. "Introduction and Overview." In *Unplanned Careers: The Working Lives of Middle-Aged Women,* ed. Lois B. Shaw. Lexington, MA: D.C. Heath, 1983.

Shields, Laurie. *Displaced Homemakers: Organizing for a New Life.* New York: McGraw-Hill, 1981.

Smith, Shirley J. "New Worklife Estimates Reflect Changing Profile of Labor Force." *Monthly Labor Review* 105 (March 1982), pp. 15–20.

Snyder, Donald C. "Work After Retirement." Unpublished manuscript, 1987.

———. "Pension Status of Recently Retired Workers on Their Longest Job: Findings from the New Beneficiary Survey." *Social Security Bulletin* 49 (August 1986), pp. 5–21.

Stone, Robyn, Gail Lee Cafferta, and Judith Sangl. "Caregivers of the Frail Elderly: A National Profile." *The Gerontologist* (1988).

Tittle, Carol Kehr, and Elenor Rubin Denker. *Returning Women Students in Higher Education: Defining Policy Issues.* New York: Praeger, 1980.

Treiman, Donald J., and Heidi I. Hartmann. *Women, Work and Wages: Equal Pay for Jobs of Equal Value.* Washington: National Academy Press, 1981.

U.S. Bureau of the Census. *Characteristics of the Population Below the Poverty Level, 1984.* Current Population Reports, Series P-60, No. 152. Washington: U.S. Government Printing Office, 1986.

U.S. Congress, Office of Technology Assessment. *Displaced Homemakers: Programs and Policy—An Interim Report.* Washington: U.S. Government Printing Office, 1985.

U.S. Department of Health and Human Services, Social Security Administration. "Increasing the Social Security Retirement Age: Older Workers in Physically Demanding Jobs." *Social Security Bulletin* 49 (October 1986), p. 5–23.

———. *Income of the Population 55 and Over, 1984.* Washington: U.S. Government Printing Office, 1985.

U.S. General Accounting Office. *Pension Integration: How Large Defined Benefit Plans Coordinate Benefits with Social Security.* Washington: 1986.

Vanski, Jean E., Demetra Smith Nightengale, and Carolyn Taylor O'Brien. "Employment Development Needs of Displaced Homemakers." Final Report to the U.S. Department of Health and Human Services. Washington: The Urban Institute, 1983.

Waite, Linda, and Sue E. Berryman. "Occupational Desegregation in CETA Programs." In *Sex Segregation in the Workplace,* ed. Barbara F. Reskin. Washington: National Academy Press, 1984. Pp. 292–307.

Walshok, Mary L. *Blue Collar Women.* Garden City, NY: Anchor Books, 1981.

21

The United States:
The Privatization of Exit

HAROLD L. SHEPPARD

Corporate mergers and economic restructuring have led many corporations to find new ways to downsize their labor force. In recent years, a number of companies have used private pensions coupled with incentives such as lump-sum payments and continued fringe benefits as a way of inducing older workers to retire. As a result of these incentives, men and women are leaving the labor force at earlier and earlier ages. Sheppard describes the impact these programs have had on retirement trends and argues that private-sector policies, supported by tax incentives, appear to be at odds with government Social Security policy, which encourages later retirement.

INTRODUCTION AND HISTORICAL BACKGROUND

The historical aspect of this chapter could begin as far back as the mid-nineteenth century to identify examples of the first prototypes of private and public employer retirement policies and programs—more specifically, pension-age policies and programs. At that time there were a small number of voluntary philanthropic aids of various types for "superannuated" employees. Graebner (1980) in his historically oriented study, *A History of Retirement: The Meaning and Function of an American Institution, 1885–1978*, cites—in agreement with the conventional wisdom of historical gerontologists—the American Express Company as the first U.S. corporation to introduce a pension system. To discuss "retirement" is really to discuss "pensionable age," but Graebner does not inform his readers on the issue critical to us: the age at which employer pensions were available to employees.

The late nineteenth century and the first decade of the twentieth century witnessed the growth of private-sector pensions in the railroads, public utilities, banks, and metal industries. "The year 1910 was a benchmark, for in the decade that followed, new plans were established at a rate of at least 21 per year" (Graebner 1980:133).

The persistent theme in Graebner's perspective is the overwhelming motivation of efficiency and/or labor force control—goals or values of employing organizations—not the more generally popular theme of rewarding men and women for their many years of toil in the workplace, or as some form of social justice. A more balanced approach might recognize an interactive perspective, which would include the desires or demands of employees themselves. But early retirement (retirement in general, for that matter) cannot be explained adequately as an act derived from an individual's own characteristics. Social policy is one of the primary factors in this ever-changing process.

The passage by the U.S. Congress in 1935 of the Social Security Act included a major provision for benefits for workers who ceased work upon reaching age 65. In subsequent years, this was reduced to 62, first for women and later for men. This legislation was designed to tackle the unemployment crisis of the Great Depression in two different forms: (1) Unemployment Insurance, and not merely (2) Old Age or "Retired Workers" Insurance. The dominating drive for the second provision of the Social Security provision was the need to alleviate the high jobless rate, and one way out was to remove "older" men and women from the labor force by transferring them into another social category, namely, the retired population. This does not mean that other reasons and social forces were not at play in this social legislation.

The early decades after World War II were characterized by a high demand for labor, partly met by the beginnings of an expanded female supply source, but also by keeping and hiring older workers (primarily men). The literature of industrial relations and of industrial sociology and psychology, during the period of 1945–65 or so, was replete with emphasis on retraining, job redesign, and so forth, as techniques and measures to assist older adult workers in coping with changing technologies and product markets.

But in the early 1970s, and certainly by the midpoint of that decade, possibly influenced by the entry of larger numbers from the post–World War II "baby boom" and the rapid rate of entry of women, especially married ones (and not just baby boom females), the secular trend of a decline in the labor force participation rates of males was accelerated. What Standing (1986) has called the "progressive marginalization of older workers" began to emerge as a pattern.

For New Deal liberals, writes Graebner, retirement was a way of achieving "certain economic and social goals, rather than a time in a person's life when work would cease in favor of some state of security. There was a good deal of cold-blooded calculation in the process.[1] The benefits of retirement were expected to rebound to the larger society and the young through unemployment relief and job creation, rather than to the aged. Older railroad workers, organized in a powerful national association, might force the society to act; but it was action in the form of retirement, to social security. If this was the welfare state, it was built along lines descended from the limited vision of retirement generated in the progressive era" (Graebner 1980:180).

For a rather long period of time, a core of American workers was assured of relative job security based on seniority and/or a low level of disjunctures in the stability of enterprises and industries. The United States in the 1980s, however, underwent "de-industrialization," international competition for world and domestic markets, and sharp technological shifts. "Restructuring" especially hit older workers, possibly because the industries most affected were old ones, and older industries ipso facto mean an older work force. Older workers thus affected face greater difficulties in finding reemployment, or reemployment acceptable to them.

RECENT DEVELOPMENTS

Recent years (since the early 1980s) have witnessed the visible surfacing of special early-exit incentives—the "golden handshake." This relatively new phenomenon (at least in terms of magnitude) is a symptom or a leading indicator of the economic and industrial "restructuring" of the United States. Given a systematic decision to reduce the work force in various industries, it is understandable why early exit from work has become easier than in past decades. *The Employee Benefit Plan Review* of October, 1986, cites a Wyatt Company (pension consultants) study showing, for example, that among the 50 largest industrial companies there has been a substantial increase in firms that offer early pension provisions without any actuarial reductions. Very often, other attractions are offered the employee, such as lump-sum payments, continued fringe benefits, and so forth.[2]

Indirect Public-Policy Influence on the Private Sector

The General Accounting Office (GAO), an evaluation and inspection agency for the United States Congress, has pointed out that the "federal government has no consistent policy regarding retirement age" (General Accounting Office 1986:10). The popular versions of this lack of consistency typically point to the poor coordination of pension-age policy, if any, between government and the private sector. But it is very important to recognize that the early-exit trends and practices of the private sector (in contrast to recent legislation concerning age discrimination and Social Security retirement age) are made into policy by previous and long-standing government legislation and policy that offer favorable tax provisions to employers whose pension programs *allow and encourage retirement at ages 62 and younger"* (italics not in original). Even individual retirement income plans allow a person to withdraw the funds without any tax penalty as early as age $59^{1}/_{2}$.

In essence, all of the pension programs in the U.S. retirement "system" are subsidized (and/or influenced) in one way or another by the government. The GAO report, in this connection, may be one of the first signs of official recognition of the role of the state in the determination of private-sector policy on retirement age. The private-sector system does not operate outside of rules, norms, and laws set by the state, but this does not necessarily mean that the state has consciously and deliberately selected a given pension age for the private sector. It is instead the recognition—at least by this arm of Congress—that there are some unanticipated consequences of policies and legislation that are not explicitly or directly designed to determine retirement age but nevertheless do have an impact on age at exit.

The GAO cites 1986 estimates that preferential tax exemptions and privileges amount to about $88 billion. Thus, it is not completely correct to claim that the exit-age practices of the private sector are unrelated to policies and practices belonging to the sphere of government. Such an estimate of lost tax revenues is but one measure of the costs of retirement at a public macro-level.

Early exit on the part of greater and greater proportions of a population of "working age" (a term that is itself subject to sociocultural definitions) is made possible by, and is dependent upon, the resources of a society's economy. This raises the issue of the capacity of that economy to support a given population of nonworking adults at a given level of retirement income or its equivalent, or an even larger population of such adults at a lower level of retirement income. The significance of this point about resources and capacity lies in the fact that these two elements (along with societal willingness) set major parameters or conditions within which workers have the "freedom" to exit from work at a certain age or at the earliest pensionable age.

In addition to government, there are organizational "actors" whose views and interests impinge on decisions by the state, for example, labor and management, nonprofit welfare-related organizations, and so forth.[3]

LABOR FORCE PARTICIPATION TRENDS

The following observations characterize the progress of early exit in the United States:

In the 1950s, the labor force participation rate of men aged 60 to 64 began to decline.
In the 1960s, the participation rate for men aged 55 to 59 started its decline.
In the late 1980s, there were some signs of the decline starting as early as 50 to 54.

Whether we use the measure of labor force participation (number of employed *and* unemployed as a percentage of the population) or employment activity rate (number of employed as percentage of the population) of different age groups, we cannot ignore the long-term downward trends in both measures for all men, but especially older ones (starting at about age 45), and the downward trends of women, too, but starting only at about age 60 in the United States. The male–female discrepancy is so great that it is misleading to talk about the decline of older Americans in general when discussing attachment to the work force.[4]

Using age 55 as an arbitrary, potential "early-exit" cutoff point, we should note that the 1970–86 decline in labor force participation rates of men and women varies by age group (Table 21-1).

In general, the older the age, the greater the rate of decline over the 16-year period covered in Table 21-1. The large change in the decline rates of both men and women between age 61 and age 62 is a reflection of the availability of "early retirement" Social Security retired-worker benefits for both sexes at age 62. The average or mean age of retired-worker awards between 1960 and 1985 went down from 66.8 to 63.7 for men (a figure that has remained virtually unchanged since 1982) and from 65.2 to 63.4 for women (also unchanged since 1982). No longer should it be said that 65 is the typi-

TABLE 21-1   Rates of Change in Labor Force Participation Rates, by Single Age for Men and Women, 1970–86

Selected ages	% Decline 1970–86	
	Men	Women
55	−6.6	+6.1[a]
57	−8.9	−0.2
59	−13.6	−1.7
61	−16.6	−0.5
62	−25.5	−12.7
63	−32.9	−6.3
65	−37.9	−26.7
66	−39.4	−22.8
67	−34.5	−21.6

[a]Rates of increase are based on the "Stouffer" method, i.e., % in time 2 − % in time 1/(100% − % in time 1).

SOURCE: Bureau of Labor Statistics unpublished data.

cal or "normal" retirement age in the United States, and the same generalization applies to other countries of the "more developed," industrialized world.

It should be noted that, especially among men, the shift in labor force participation rate between age 61 and age 62 is only partly a function of the latter age being the earliest retirement age under Social Security. This shift also points not only to the possible influence of the unemployment experience but also to the growing coverage of workers by private-employer (and by public-employer) pension plans. Many workers defer exit from work until they are eligible for retirement income from both sources—Social Security and private pensions. But there are also many workers who exit from the labor force before age 62—with and without retirement pensions from sources other than Social Security.

For women in the middle-age group of 40 to 54, during the 20 years from 1965 to 1985, labor force participation showed relatively high rates of increase: It grew from 49 percent to 72 percent for those aged 40 to 44, from 52 percent to 68 percent for those aged 45 to 49, and from 50 percent to 61 percent for those aged 50 to 54. These patterns are clearly different from those for men. The labor force participation rate for women aged 55 to 59 showed only a slight increase in the same 20-year period (from 47 percent to 50 percent), and the rate has remained virtually at a plateau for the group aged 60 to 64—the so-called preretirement age group (a label that may need to be transferred soon to the younger age group of 55 to 59, given the contemporary early-exit trends).

It should be pointed out that, on a longitudinal basis, the decline in the participation rate for women aged 55 to 59 in any given time period has increased since the 1965–70 period. The sharp drops between 1970 and 1975 may partially reflect the severe recession that occurred during that five-year period. The decline rate between ages 55 to 59 and 60 to 64 during that earlier (1965–70) time frame was 23 percent, compared with at least 30 percent in each of the three five-year periods following 1965–70.

Unemployment and Labor Force Participation

The relationship of the unemployment experience to early exit has been shown in several studies.[5] Take, for example, the finding that during the period 1970–5, which encompassed several years of relatively high unemployment, the labor force participation rates of men 50 to 54, 55 to 59, and 60 to 64 years old dropped more steeply than in any of the three five-year periods surrounding the years from 1970 to 1975. Table 21-3 shows a sharp increase from the 1965–70 period to the 1970–5 period in the decline of participation rates. Although the participation rates of women in the same age groups have ordinarily been increasing, this certainly was not the case during the period under discussion. When the general jobless rate for women increased from 3.2 percent to 5.8 percent (at a rate of 2.7 percent),[6] the labor force participation rates of women in the three pertinent age groups declined (Table 21-2). But during the periods 1965–70, 1975–80, and 1980–5, when the female jobless rate either plummeted sharply or increased only imperceptibly, the participation rates of these three "preretirement" age groups actually ascended. It should be noted that during the latest period covered in this analysis, 1980–5, the labor force participation rates of women in the group aged 60 to 64, however, barely rose (by only 0.1 percent). This period, too, included some years with very high overall unemployment.

From 1970 to 1975, unemployment among men 16 and older rose from 4.4 percent to 7.9 percent (at a rate of 3.6 percent over the five years). Over the same period, the participation rates of "younger older" male workers declined at rates well beyond those for the previous and subsequent five-year periods. (Table 21-3)

TABLE 21-2   Changes in Labor Force Participation Rate Relative to General Female Jobless Rate for Four Different Five-Year Periods

Period	Rate of Change in Jobless Rate of Females Aged 16+[a]	% Change in Labor Force Participation		
		50–54	55–59	60–64
1965–70	+0.4	+7.4	+3.6	+3.2
1970–75	+2.7	−0.9	−2.2	−4.4
1975–80	−25.2	+9.6	+1.3	0
1980–85	+0.2	+7.1	+3.3	+0.1

TABLE 21-3   Changes in Labor Force Participation Rate Relative to General Male Jobless Rate for Four Different Five-Year Periods

Period	Rate of Change in Jobless Rate of Men Aged 16+[a]	% Change in Labor Force Participation		
		50–54	55–59	60–64
1965–70	+0.4	−2.0	−0.8	−3.8
1970–75	+3.6	−3.2	−5.7	−12.4
1975–80	−12.7	−0.9	−3.0	−7.2
1980–85	+0.3	−0.8	−2.1	−8.9

[a]Stouffer's method of measuring rates of increase in proportions.

Even though the pattern of an above-average reduction in participation rates accompanying above-average increases in jobless rates prevails among both women and men, it is also important to note that the participation declines for women are substantially below those for men. This difference may be attributable to differences in the industry-occupation mix between men and women, and also to the possibility that in times of high husband joblessness, wives might enter the job market.

Employment Activity Rate

The employment activity rate[7] of older men shows no great drop between ages until the 61- to 62-year-old shift, for obvious reasons (especially the eligibility at age 62 for retired-worker benefits). In 1970 this rate was 81 percent for men aged 61 and 74 percent for men aged 62, an 8.6 percent rate of difference. By 1980 the rates had declined to 70 and 57 percent, respectively, showing a difference rate of 18.6 percent. By 1986 the figures were 66 and 54 percent, an 18.3 percent rate of decline.

Over this 16-year period, accordingly, the employment activity rate of 61-year-olds dropped by 18.5 percent, but for 62-year-olds the rate slumped much more, by 27.6 percent.

Women so far show a different picture. To begin with, both their employment activity and participation rates show no discernible decrease (indeed, show an increase) over this 16-year period for certain single ages until age 62. But to return to a comparison with the data in the previous paragraphs about men, Table 21-4 provides the pertinent information.

PATHWAYS OF EARLY EXIT

Dealing coherently and simply with the U.S. retirement "system" is not an easy task, at least when attempting comparisons with other modern, industrialized nations. It has about 800,000 private-sector employer pension plans, not to mention 6,500 state and local government plans, the federal civil service retirement program (including some small special employee ones), and the military pension system, as well as the 16 million individual pension accounts (consisting mostly of employees' Individual Retire-

TABLE 21-4   Rate of Difference between the Employment Activity Rates of 61- and 62-year-olds in 1970, 1980, and 1986[a]

Year	Rate of Difference (%)	
	Men	Women
1970	−8.6	−6.7
1980	−18.6	−16.3
1986	−18.2	−15.9

[a]Rate of difference is calculated as follows: (employment rate for 61-year-olds minus rate for 62-year-olds)/(rate for 61-year-olds) × 100.

ment Accounts, and Keogh—self-employed—plans). Many labor force participants and retirees receive benefits from more than one of these retirement income sources.

The private-pension world, over the past 15 years or so, has been characterized by increases in plans with provisions providing for pre-62 "retirement" (but not necessarily labor force exit). It is difficult, however, to capture systematic information on the numbers of workers exiting with such pre-62 pensions. The pathways of early exit can nevertheless be clarified somewhat by examining the information on sources of men's non-Social Security pensions by age of recipients, as shown in Table 21-5. In Table 21-6, we exclude military pensions for men (because many young recipients are still in the labor force).

Male recipients as young as 50 to 54 (and 55 to 61) are disproportionately made up of persons receiving pensions from state and local governments, and the proportion receiving private pensions increases in parallel with the age of the recipient. But to repeat, these data only *suggest* the age at exit from the labor force. They do not tell us whether, for example, 55- to 61-year-old recipients of state or local government pensions are in or out of the labor force, or when they exited.

A significant finding cited in the GAO report concerns the accelerated downward trend of labor force participation by male pension recipients 55 to 61 years old, from 1974 to 1984. Starting in 1974 the rate was about 50 percent but decreased by 1984 to only 42 percent. The greatest drop occurred, however, in the first half of this period, 1974 to 1979; thereafter, it changed only slightly, from 43 percent to 42 percent. Dur-

TABLE 21-5   Non–Social Security Pension Sources, by Age and Sex of Recipient

Sex	Pension Source	% of Age Group Who Are Recipients			
		50–54	*55–61*	*62–64*	*65+*
M	Private	28.2	48.4	59.5	69.9
	Military	54.4	19.3	8.9	4.0
	Federal govt.	6.1	17.1	15.5	9.7
	State or local govt.	10.0	12.6	10.9	12.5
	Combinations of above	1.3	2.6	5.2	3.9
	Total	100.0	100.0	100.0	100.0
F	Private	54.3	59.2	55.0	56.2
	Military	6.5	2.2	2.9	1.6
	Federal govt.	24.5	17.0	14.9	10.7
	State or local govt.	14.7	18.3	23.8	28.1
	Combinations of above	0	3.3	3.3	3.4
	Total	100.0	100.0	100.0	100.0

SOURCE: General Accounting Office (1986:28–9), Tables 2.4 and 2.5.

TABLE 21-6   Pension Sources for Men by Age of Recipient

Pension Source	% of Age Group Who Are Recipients			
	50–54	*55–61*	*62–64*	*65+*
Private	61.8	60.0	63.3	72.8
Federal govt.	13.4	21.2	17.0	10.1
State or local govt.	21.9	15.6	12.0	13.0
Combinations of above	2.9	3.2	100.2	4.1
Total	100.0	100.0	100.0	100.0

ing the same period, it should be noted, the participation rate of nonrecipients declined at a far slower rate (from 88 percent to 83 percent).[8]

The Employer-Pension Pathway

The primary exit pathway in the United States, is, of course, through the retired-worker benefits program under Social Security. More than 95 percent of U.S. workers are covered by it. Actuarially reduced retirement benefits can be awarded as early as age 62. The 1982 New Beneficiary Survey found that during 1980–1, 37 percent of all such new beneficiaries, however, had left the labor force *before* that age; another 23 percent exited at age 62, and the remainder, 40 percent, exited when 63 or older (nearly all before age 65).

More than one-half of these retirees exiting before age 62 were married women, a finding that goes a long way toward explaining how such a large proportion of U.S. workers (37 percent) can leave the labor force before they are eligible to receive a retiree benefit under Social Security. In most cases, these wives are able to exit so early because their husbands still receive income, through either earnings or retirement benefits. Indeed, 70 percent of women who left the labor force before age 62 exited before their husbands did. Furthermore, women exiting before age 62 had the highest proportion of husbands receiving a private pension.

As for non-Social Security early-exit pathways, the Packard and Reno (1988) report using the New Beneficiary Survey shows that among all workers exiting before age 55, only 14 percent received any kind of employer pension (including private-sector, government, or military pension); for those exiting between 55 and 62, the proportion rises to 48 percent.[9] These proportions vary widely according to sex and marital status—for example, 44 percent of married men exiting before 55 received an employer pension compared with only 7 percent of married women. Among those exiting between 55 and 62, 64 percent of married men, but only 32 percent of married women, were pension recipients (Table 21-7).

In Table 21-8 we report our own analysis of the New Beneficiary Survey data concerning proportions of early exiters receiving private (i.e., exclusive of military, local government, and federal government) pensions. The overall generalization is that for

TABLE 21-7   Percent Receiving Private and Public Employer Pensions, by Age at Exit, Sex, and Marital Status

Exit Age	Men		Women		Total
	Married	Not Married	Married	Not Married	
Under 55	44	—a	7	20	14
55–61	64	45	32	48	48

aBased on fewer than 50 cases.

SOURCE: Table 9.5 of Packard and Reno (1988).

TABLE 21-8   Percent Receiving Private Pensions, by Early-Exit Age, Gender, and Marital Status

Exit Age	Men		Women		Total
	Married	Not Married	Married	Not Married	
Under 55	12	NA	4	13	6
55–61	39	27	18	29	29
Total under 62	36	21	12	24	22

SOURCE: Analysis of New Beneficiary data prepared for this chapter by John Henretta, University of Florida.

roughly one-fifth of all beneficiaries exiting before age 62, private-sector pensions were a pathway for their early exit.

State and local government pensions constituted the second significant non–Social Security pathway for early exit for the later beneficiaries of Social Security retired-worker benefits. Among all the New Beneficiary Survey respondents exiting before age 62, slightly more than 7 percent reported receipt of state and local government pensions, according to our preliminary analysis.

Early-Exit Incentive Programs

Because of economic difficulties, corporate mergers, "downsizing," and restructuring, along with product and technological changes, many private companies have introduced early-exit incentive programs, over and above traditional pension-plan liberalization aimed at encouraging older workers to leave.

A major characteristic of all such incentive programs is cited by Meier (1986): They "are in reality termination programs," not programs designed for workers in poor health or wanting more leisure. They are introduced as economy and profit-making measures.

Another important characteristic, one more relevant to the early-exit issue, is that they are typically targeted at relatively young employees, in their early or mid-50s. Accordingly, many early-exit incentive programs offering benefits without full actuarial reductions are quite expensive, at least in the short run.

Unfortunately, there is no systematic and comprehensive information about how many companies actually have introduced early-exit incentives or how many older employees have accepted them. Thus we have no way of knowing how many of the 22 percent reported as exiting before age 62 by the New Beneficiary Survey were participants in such programs.

What we do have are occasional surveys of selected corporations, by pension consultant firms, for example. From such surveys we find that some employers offer "carrots," such as the liberalization of exit benefits and temporary pension supplements; others offer "sticks," involving a deadline for acceptance of increased pensions after which pensions will be reduced (a "window") or the elimination of lump-sum payments (Mutschler, no date). Some of the special features of such plans include pension benefits without any actuarial reduction and salary continuity for limited periods (or until age 62 or eligibility for regular company retirement). Table 21-9 shows a comparison of 10 early-exit plans compiled by Shuman (1983) from data based on a survey by a prominent consultant company.

In a later study, Mutschler (1986) concentrates on the experience of a major corporation (in the Fortune 500) with more than 700 employees exiting in different years under different incentive plans or remaining in their jobs. She finds that, unlike the results of most previous research on factors in the exit decision, "in the absence of formal incentive plans, health status was not a major determinant . . . when incentives are offered." Instead, the financial attractions of the pension plans were dominant. It must be noted, however, that this study did not focus on age at exit, nor did it provide any information as to whether the employees left the labor force or merely left the employer covered in the study for another employer. Indeed, this is one of the major shortcomings of the research on this topic.

The Disability Pathway

A major government-based exit pathway for U.S. workers under the age of 62 is, of course, the Social Security program of disability benefits. (Unlike practices in some European countries, this program is not used deliberately to alleviate problems of older long-term unemployed workers or those in distressed industries.) From 1965 to 1987, the average age for awardees under this program declined from 53.0 to 49.0 for men and from 53.2 to 49.5 for women. The total awardee numbers are shown in Table 21-10.

The more rapid increase of women in this pathway is partly a result of the growth in the total numbers of women entering the labor force before and during this two-decade period. How do these statistics compare with those concerning the "normal" early retirement (at age 62 to 64) under the retired-worker program of the U.S. Social Security program? This question, in part, has to do with which of these programs has become the one more frequently used as an exit pathway.

The first thing to note is that over the 1965–87 period, total retired-worker awards increased by 40 percent, a lower rate of growth than total disability awards (62 per-

TABLE 21-9 Comparison of 10 Early-Retirement Incentive Programs[a]

Company	Eligible Employees	Percent Accepting	Pension Reduced	Cash Subsidy	How Paid	Continued Medical Coverage
Ameritrust Co., Cleveland, Ohio	176	72	No	$24,000	Over two years	Full
B. F. Goodrich, Akron, Ohio	768	22[b]	Yes	$52,500	Over three years	Full
Caterpillar Tractor, Peoria, Ill.	845	41	Yes	$19,200	Over four years	Full
Consumers Power, Jackson, Mich.	1,360	54	No	$17,300	Lump Sum	Full
Eaton Corp. Cleveland, Ohio	126	67	Yes	$20,000	Varies	Full
National-Standard Co., Niles, Mich.	108	52	No	Social Security– bridging pay	Varies	Reduced
Polaroid Corp., Cambridge, Mass.	6,328	14	Yes	$75,000	Varies	Full
Portland General Electric, Portland, Ore.	114	36	No	Social Security– bridging pay	Varies	Reduced
Public Service, Electric & Gas, Newark, N.J.	2,120	62	No	$42,000	Over seven years	Full
Sears, Chicago, Ill.	2,300	60	Yes	$45,000	Over three years	Full

[a]Assumes early retirement at age 58 with 30 years' company service and annual salary of $30,000.

[b]Maximum allowed.

SOURCE: Data based on a survey by the management consultant firm of Towers, Perin, Forster & Crosby and reported by Shuman (1983). Reproduced from Mutschler (no date).

cent). If we use this comparison, we would have to conclude that the early-exit pathway of disability pensions is moving in the direction of overtaking the overall retired-worker exit pathway. But further examination shows that the number of persons being awarded retired-worker benefits at age 62—the earliest age for such benefits in the U.S. Social Security program—has grown at a remarkably greater rate than the number receiving all disability awards and the total retired-worker awards (Table 21-11).

The comparison shown in Table 21-11 is but one way in which to highlight, once again, the accelerated pace of early, perhaps very early, exits from the U.S. labor force. Both pathways—disability and retirement at age 62—have tremendously outpaced the overall "regular" retired-worker benefit program. These two routes may indeed resemble the European pattern referred to previously, wherein "invalidity" pensions are partly an early-exit route.

Two of the major factors in this changing pattern have to do with (1) the growing availability of private pensions, especially at early ages, and (2) high unemployment levels at various times during this 20-year period.

It should be obvious by now that there is a need to single out the 62-year-olds and not to combine information about that single-year age category with data for those aged 63 and 64. The convention among gerontologists and labor force analysts—even this author—has been to use the "early-retirements" category of 62 to 64. One reason for the need to treat 62-year-olds separately is related to results of several research projects showing that some people "retiring" at 62 (or receiving retired-worker benefits for the first time at this age) had been unemployed or jobless prior to receiving such benefits, or had been receiving private and employer pensions before reaching age 62.

Disability is one pathway, then, that can be measured, at least in terms of the number of workers exiting before age 62. (Some disabled workers do exit, however, without receiving such disability benefits.) Joblessness is another pathway, but unlike several European countries, the United States has no formal government-sponsored program explicitly designed to provide early-exit pensions for unemployed older workers. When coupled with data on Social Security awards for disability and with our

TABLE 21-10   Disability Awards, 1965 and 1987

	1965	1987	% Increase
Both sexes	253,500	409,600	62
Men	186,800	265,900	42
Women	66,700	143,700	115

TABLE 21-11   Percent Increase in Social Security Awards for Disability, to All Retired Workers, and to Workers Retiring at Age 62, 1965–87

Type of Award	Total	Men	Women
Disability	62	42	116
All retired workers	40	31	55
Retired workers at age 62 only	252	323	195

insights into the separate and joint roles of unemployment and non-Social Security sources of early-exit income, the trends in awards at age 62 suggest that we may well be witnessing a substantial overlap of pathways of early exit from the labor force.

Job Loss

Whereas even in recent decades attention was focused on the sharp drops in the labor force participation rate of male workers 65 and older, or at best those 60 to 64, the declines among men as young as 55 to 59, and perhaps as young as 50 to 54, are impressive. In 1965 over 90 percent of men aged 55 to 59 were still in the labor force, but in a space of 20 years this proportion plummeted to less than 80 percent—a decline rate of nearly 12 percent. Nearly one-half of this decline took place in only one five-year period, from 1970 to 1975. This was a period in which U.S. unemployment was at one of its highest rates. As for the group aged 50 to 54, the labor force participation rate dropped from 95.0 percent in 1965 to only 88.6 percent in 1985—a rate of decline of 6.7 percent. Thus, about 12 out of every 100 men as young as 50 to 54 years old were not working in 1985, compared with only 5 out of every 100 in this age group 20 years earlier.

The 1982 New Beneficiary Survey of the Social Security Administration also deals with the issue of the influence of early unemployment experience. That study's data indicate that 36 percent of all the new retirees who were no longer working had stopped working before they were eligible for retired-worker benefits. (Not all stopped because of job loss, however.) This measure varies considerably by sex and marital status: 26 percent of married men and 33 percent of unmarried men stopped working before age $61\frac{1}{2}$, whereas 55 percent of married women and 30 percent of unmarried women did so. The pattern for married women who had stopped working before reaching the Social Security pension age is attributable to their leaving when their husbands did, or to the possibility that income from their husband's earnings (for those still working) reduced the incentive for the wife to continue working.

The more critical question here is to what extent joblessness is associated with age of exit. Data reported by Packard and Reno (1988) show that the issue is especially pertinent in early exits of men. As Table 21-12 indicates clearly, the younger the age at which men exit from the labor force, the greater the proportion citing joblessness as the reason—from only 8 percent of those exiting at 63 or older to nearly one-fourth of those exiting before the age of 55.[10]

Several sensitive and controversial policy issues are raised by Kingson (1981) in his report on early retirement for the U.S. House of Representatives' Select Committee on Aging:

Is early retirement primarily a cost problem for pension systems—including private and Social Security systems?

Will demographic developments increase these cost pressures?

Is the problem of early retirement essentially a matter of worker responses to "pension incentives"?

In contrast, what is the role of health problems and unemployment experience?

TABLE 21-12   Percent Exiting Because of Job Loss, by Age at Exit

	Total	Under 55	55–61.5	61.6–62	63 or older
Both sexes[a]	12	15	15	11	9
Men	11	24	13	11	8

[a]Separate data for women are not provided by Packard and Reno (1988).

"Exit" is defined here as leaving the labor force completely. It excludes part-time employment, or any work accompanied by earnings.

In regard to this last issue, it is Kingson's opinion that "pension incentives that encourage many able workers to retire early are, in large part, a symptom of an economy unable to provide employment for all who are willing and able to work" (p. 95). Whether early retirement is a matter of conscious and deliberate policy on the part of major actors in this domain, as was largely the case for the origins of the Social Security Act or, instead, the response of individual workers, there can be no question about the role of joblessness—especially prolonged joblessness—in the trend of very early exit from the labor force.

The Government Accounting Office report *Retirement Before Age 65* points to the increase in the proportion of all men 55 to 61 years old receiving a pension, from only 8 percent in 1973 to 17 percent 10 years later, in 1983. For women in the same age group, the corresponding proportions are 4 percent and 7 percent. These figures refer to the current age of these individuals, not the age at which they first started receiving such pensions, which makes the upward trend even more impressive.[11]

Findings of the New Beneficiary Survey

Much of the previous discussion and the empirical data presented have been based on all persons who were pension recipients, without regard to their age at complete exit from the labor force. The New Beneficiary Survey of the Social Security Administration, based on 1982 interviews with men and women first receiving their retired-worker benefits from mid-1980 to mid-1981, is unique in this regard and provides certain insights not possible through studies—whether longitudinal or cross-sectional—based on retirees regardless of when they first received their benefits.

The previously cited report on retirement based on the New Beneficiary Survey by Packard and Reno (1988) found that 35 percent of men exiting before age 55 were receiving an employer pension, compared with only 9 percent of women; for persons exiting at age 55 to 61.5 (before drawing retired-worker benefits), the corresponding proportions with employer pensions were 61 percent of men and 35 percent of women (Table 21-13).

Using the New Beneficiary Survey's data on the respondents' assertions as to the most important reason for their exiting—especially exiting before age 62—we may be able to gain a more detailed understanding of the major pathways through which American workers move completely out of the labor force.[12] This approach may be one of the few methods that can approximate the use of explicit, formal institutional pathways that better characterize the European situation.

TABLE 21-13   Percentage of New Beneficiaries Receiving an Employer Pension, by Age When They Left Their Last Job

			Age Left Last Job			
	Total	Under 55	55–61.5	61.5–62	63 or older	Still Working
Total	47	14	48	55	57	22
Men	58	35	61	61	59	28
Women	34	9	35	44	53	13

SOURCE: Adapted Packard and Reno (1988), Table 5.

TABLE 21-14   "Most Important" Reason for Retiring, by Age at Exit (in Percent)

	Under 62			62 or Later		
Reason	Total	Men Only	Women Only	Total	Men Only	Women Only
Bad health	24.8	30.5	21.4	23.6	22.7	24.4
Tired of working	20.5	28.2	15.9	40.0	43.0	33.5
Job loss	14.4	14.3	14.6	9.8	9.2	10.7
Mandatory retirement age	2.2	4.7		7.2	8.2	
Care for others			14.2			7.7
Spouse retired			6.2			4.8

Note: Columns include percentages only for the most frequently cited reasons and hence total less than 100 percent.

As stated earlier, in the United States the situation is much more complex and has much less of a coherent structure. The "formal" pathway for very early (under age 62) exit that does exist is the disability route under the Social Security system. It has already been pointed out that the number of persons exiting via this pathway has increased at a much greater rate than the "normal" retired-worker awards. Furthermore, the retired-worker awardees at age 62, it appears, experience job dislocations such as shutdowns and layoffs before that age, but cannot receive retired-worker benefits until they are 62. Many of these workers may have experienced disabling conditions as well. Others include working wives exiting before 62 but having to wait until that age for benefits.

Our analysis of the factors identified by the New Beneficiary Survey respondents exiting before age 62 as the most important reason for complete exit yielded a finding that reinforces the disability pathway, that is, "bad health" as a reason for exiting. Bad health ranked number one among early exiters in the list of their most important reasons for complete exit, regardless of sex. Among those exiting at 62 or older, its rank was second, way below the first-ranking "tired of working" (Table 21-14).

As discussed earlier, job loss is clearly another pathway for exiting followed more frequently by the early exiters than by the late ones. This is true of women as well as men in the New Beneficiary Survey. These two pathways (bad health and job loss), it needs to be emphasized, account for roughly two-fifths of all early exiters, compared with only one-third of those exiting at 62 or later. They are especially critical in the early exit of men. In accounting for the pattern among women, we cannot ignore their unique status in society as presently structured—not just in the labor market. As Table 21-14 shows, caring for others and/or the retirement of their husbands may also be conceptualized as special routes of early exit. More than one-fifth of the women exiting before age 62, but only one-eighth of those leaving after that age, left work primarily because of these factors.

These findings evoke another crucial question, the role of pensions (other than Social Security retired-worker benefits) in facilitating exit by the major pathways cited here, as well as the exits related to caring for others and spouse's retirement reported by women in the New Beneficiary Survey.

Pensions as Facilitators of "Very Early" Exit (Before Age 62)

Until recently, and even today, references to "early retirement" in the U.S. Social Security literature typically defined it as receipt of a retired-worker benefit from ages 62 to 64, that is, before age 65. But the New Beneficiary Survey findings point very definitely to large numbers and proportions leaving the labor force completely even before age 62: 37 percent at the time of the 1982 survey. For married women alone, the proportion was 60 percent! There is a widespread belief that age-at-exit decisions are heavily influenced by the availability of non-Social Security pensions (i.e., private and public employer pensions exclusive of Social Security retired-worker benefits). Is it possible that exit before age 62 is facilitated by a pension "opportunity"? More especially, how, if at all, does a pension facilitate exit before age 62 when the worker's primary reason for exiting from the labor force is taken into account? Finally, how does sex/marital status relate to these critical questions?

If we examine the New Beneficiary Survey sample as a whole, we would have to conclude that as far as exit before age 62 is concerned, pensions do not facilitate such behavior, at least not at the present time. Future developments in pension-age policy could change this for new generations of employees. But do pensions facilitate exit before 62 under selected conditions? We refer here to the reasons given by the New Beneficiary Survey respondents as the most important, or primary, reason for complete exit. Only job loss constitutes a distinct exception to the general conclusion that pensions do not facilitate exit before 62: Among workers exiting primarily through loss of employment, 51 percent of the ones with a pension, but only 43 percent of those without a pension, exited before age 62.

In addition to job loss, there is the possibility that spouse's retirement is another pathway for exit before age 62 facilitated by pension receipt: 53 percent of workers citing this factor as the primary exit reason and receiving a pension exited before 62, compared with only 47 percent of those without a pension (but leaving the labor force for the same reason).

To a very slight extent, bad health may be another pathway facilitated by pension receipt: Among workers citing bad health as their primary reason for exit, 39 percent of pension recipients and 37 percent of nonrecipients exited before age 62. But it ap-

TABLE 21-15   Percent Exiting Before 62, by Pension Receipt, Sex, and Marital Status

	Total Sample	Men		Women	
		Married	*Unmarried*	*Married*	*Unmarried*
With pension	36	31	35	59	23
Without pension	40	22	31	62	39

pears that with or without a pension, younger workers in poor health are forced to exit from the labor force.

These comparative statistics refer to primary reasons for exit and whether exit is facilitated by pension receipt. How do sex and marital status relate to the influence of pensions on "decisions" to exit before age 62? Analysis by sex/marital status shows that pensions do play a role in exit before 62, but only among men—regardless of marital status (Table 21-15). Pension influence is clearly at play in the case of the married men: 31 percent of them with a pension exited before age 62, compared with only 22 percent of those without a pension.

The more subtle (and precise) question, however, is how, if at all, pensions influence the "very early" exit phenomenon when we simultaneously take into account the primary exit reason and sex/marital status.

The basic source for our narrative here is the data in Table 21-16. It refers to proportions exiting before age 62, holding constant the following variables: (1) pension receipt, (2) sex, (3) marital status, and (4) selected (most frequently cited) "most important" reasons for exiting. The "most important" (or primary) exit reasons included in Table 21-16 are the five most frequently cited ones and encompass more than three-fourths of all the respondents.

Pension receipt facilitates exit before age 62 only for a few reasons and only for selected sex/marital status groups. The most crucial finding from this type of analysis is that for four or five primary exit reasons, pension receipt facilitates the exit of married men before age 62. For no other sex/marital status group are there so many primary reasons or conditions in which pensions facilitate "very early" exit. Pensions make a difference for married men who exit because of job loss, bad health, having to care for others, and being tired of work.

One paradox in this case lies in the fact that married men as a whole have the lowest "very early" exit rate: Only 26 percent exit before age 62.[13] In the event of job loss, bad health, and having to care for others, pension receipt facilitates "very early" exit for these married men at levels greater than their overall average rate.[14]

Myopia in Retirement Policy Research

It is pertinent at this point to comment on the general tendency in the economics of aging and related fields to draw major conclusions about retirement issues derived only from the study of men, and essentially to ignore the significance of women in the labor force and their own retirement patterns—or to assume that generalizations derived from analyses of data based on males apply, across the board, to women.

TABLE 21-16   Percent Exiting Before 62, with and without a Pension, by Primary Reason for Exiting, Sex, and Marital Status

Most Important Exit Reason and Sex/Marital Status	With Pension	No Pension
Job loss, total	51	43
Married men	42	29
Unmarried men	31	37
Married women	71	61
Unmarried women	34	45
Bad health, total	39	37
Married men	34	25
Unmarried men	37	32
Married women	58	58
Unmarried women	22	37
Care for others, total	55	66
Married men	39	17
Unmarried men	24	84
Married women	69	80
Unmarried women	43	58
Spouse retired, total	53	47
Married men	0	0
Unmarried men	0	0
Married women	57	53
Unmarried women	64	51
Tired of working, total	23	24
Married men	18	12
Unmarried men	33	6
Married women	39	48
Unmarried women	16	13

The "revolution" in sustained labor force participation of women (including wives) must be permanently recognized in policy research—including research directed at the retirement phenomenon. In addition, marital status is too often neglected or minimized. It should be clear from the approach used in our analysis of the New Beneficiary Survey data that both sex and marital status must be essential units of policy research scrutiny.

A dramatic and telling demonstration of this principle pertains to married women, judging from the New Beneficiary Survey data and our focus here on pensions as a potential facilitator of "very early" exit (exit before age 62), and taking into account primary reasons for exit. We stated earlier that pensions apparently do not facilitate "very early" exit among married women. Among those with a pension (including their own and their husband's), 59 percent exited before age 62. But this proportion is actually slightly less than the one for married women exiting without any pension—62 percent. These two percentages point once again to the conclusion that, generally speaking, in the case of married women pensions make no difference as far as exit before 62 is concerned. Attention to a more fundamental dimension is called for, however. That is the issue of *who* is the pension recipient, both husband and wife or wife only?[15]

If we isolate the married respondent herself as the only pension recipient, the results show—perhaps paradoxically—that only 43 percent of these wives exited before age 62—far lower than the 62 percent of wives reporting no pension at all (neither for themselves nor their husbands)! Even when we include cases in which both wife and husband are pension recipients, the proportion remains at 43 percent. Obviously, something other than pensions is at play among the factors and conditions influencing the exit of wives before age 62. More telling is the finding that when only the husband is the pension recipient, the proportion of wives exiting before age 62 is 73 percent—far higher than the 59 percent of all wives with access to a pension and the 61 percent of nonrecipients.

Returning to a principal topic of this section—the degree to which (if at all) pensions facilitate "very early" exit via such routes as job loss, bad health, and so forth—how does this interaction work itself out among married women? Without regard to *who* is the pension recipient, it is clear that pension receipt facilitates "very early" exit by wives. For example, among those giving job loss as the primary reason for exit, 71 percent of pensioners, but only 61 percent of nonpensioners, exited before age 62. The proportion is even greater (78 percent) if we focus on those cases in which *both* husband and wife receive pensions (Table 21-17). The more provocative finding, however, is that when the husband is the only pension recipient among wives citing bad health, job loss, or caring for others, the proportions of married women exiting before age 62 are substantially above that of wives without any pension whatsoever.

Even if there is *no* pension recipient, 80 percent of all wives exit before age 62 if having to care for others is their most important reason for doing so. Except when their husbands are the only pension recipient, nonrecipients among married women leaving

TABLE 21-17   Percentage of Wives Exiting Before Age 62, by Pension Recipient and Primary Reason for Retirement

| Primary Reason | Pension Recipients | | | | No Pension |
	Wife Only	Husband Only	Both	All Recipients	
Job loss	69	70	78	71	61
Bad health	45	71	39	58	58
Caring for others	27	94	52	69	80
Husband's retirement	59	56	56	57	53
Tired of working	32	52	33	39	48
Total, all reasons	43	73	43	59	62

for this crucial reason are more likely to exit before they reach age 62 than are recipients. This 80 percent among wives with no pension support exceeds by far the 69 percent of all other married women leaving before 62. Here again, the evidence suggests that pension receipt is not a crucial influence on wives who exit because they need to care for relatives or close friends. In this situation, wives leave the labor force before age 62 even if neither they nor their husbands are pension recipients. To be sure, some may have husbands who continue to work, thus making it possible for them to leave the labor force to provide the care.

THE POLITICS OF EARLY EXIT

The political issue that has succeeded the mandatory-age controversy relates to early exit. Some day there may even be debates over the need for a policy that discourages exit *below* a certain age. Current patterns and trends regarding incentives to exit (or disincentives to continue working) have moved to the foreground of the policy debate replacing compulsory retirement as an issue.

In explaining this change, we cannot rule out the role of political and other noneconomic incentives or that of sociocultural influences. Economic incentives (e.g., levels of anticipated retirement income, especially pension income) are not sui generis phenomena or "independent variables." Political pressures revolving, for instance, around the problem of youth unemployment have led to subtle and not-so-subtle techniques of removing "older" workers from the officially measured labor force.

But there are countercurrents in labor force developments. There is now a belated recognition by government and the private sector of a "labor gap" over the coming decades—a gap produced primarily as a result of declining fertility rates. These new demographic forces can move policy in an opposite direction (U.S. Department of Labor 1989). The "pool" of younger workers is shrinking, and when this is coupled with the current decline in the age at which older workers are exiting, a severely reduced rate of labor force growth (of about 1 percent per annum) is the result. That 1 percent growth rate in labor supply needs to be evaluated against a projected 2 to 3 percent growth rate in the economy. And all of these factors must, finally, be weighed against projections of an extremely poor productivity growth rate.

This impending labor shortage may result in a delayed "policy response" aimed at preventing the loss of qualified older workers to early exit caused by currently attractive exit incentives. The shortage may not be satisfactorily met through immigration and accelerated labor force participation by women under age 55—which may already be plateauing.

The history of retirement in the United States involves a scenario of seemingly opposite or conflicting policy directions resulting from the *government's* efforts to raise age at exit or to restrain the drift toward early exit and the *employer world's* efforts to expand on and accelerate the rate of early exit.

The U.S. government—concerned, for example, about a Social Security Trust Fund "crisis" (whether contrived or real) in the near future—started to face the problem as early as 1978, when President Jimmy Carter signed amendments to the 1967 Age Discrimination in Employment Act that would raise the allowable compulsory retirement age from 65 to 70; later, the Carter Commission on National Social Security Policy pondered the question more deeply. By 1983, as a result of President Ronald Reagan's bipartisan commission, Congress (to the astonishment of many observers) legislated several measures designed to restrain the early exit trend and thereby lighten the pressures on the trust fund. Social Security is no longer so sacrosanct as in the past. Measures to be implemented toward the end of this decade or later include:

1. An increase in the "penalty" for retiring before age 65
2. A gradual increase in the age for "full" benefit to age 67 (it is now age 65)
3. An increased "bonus" or incentive to defer retirement
4. A lower penalty for continuing to work on a reduced-income basis while in receipt of "retired"-worker benefits.

The taxation of part of a retiree's Social Security income can be another potential disincentive for early retirement; the 1988 Catastrophic Medicare Act required a surtax on the income taxes of *only* the 65-plus population, contrary to the "traditional" mechanism of a payroll tax on only the working population of all ages, to pay for the support of the older population. In this case, however, the pressure of the senior citizens' lobby was sufficient to get the Act repealed shortly after it was enacted.

Light (1985) reminds us that Social Security will always be a "hot political issue" and a part of the continuing conflict concerning "who gets what, when, where, and how." Despite the public opposition (reflected through opinion polls) to changing Social Security into a means-tested program, eliminating it altogether and replacing it with private retirement-income plans, or raising the full-benefit retirement age from 65, Congress in 1983 nevertheless did make the changes potentially affecting retirement age.

These changes were in response to the recommendations of the presumably bipartisan National Commission on Social Security Reform, the members of which were appointed by the Reagan White House and Congressional Democrats and Republicans. One of the options the commission discussed for resolving the potential crisis of the system's retired workers trust fund was an increase in the retirement age for full benefits from the then current 65 (with no increase from 62 for "early retirement" benefits but with further actuarial reductions to benefits at that exit age).

The debate over retirement age actually focused on two points. First, the commission proposed *incentives* to defer labor force exit by raising the Deferred Retirement Credit (DRC) for each year the worker postponed retirement after age 65 gradually from 3 percent to 8 percent (reaching the full 8 percent in 2009). Republicans, according to Merton C. Bernstein, one of the consultants to the commission, pushed this proposal, and Democrats went along with the recommendation despite their concerns about its increased cost (Bernstein and Bernstein 1988:56). Second, and most controversial, was the *disincentive* recommendation, which proposed gradually raising the age for full retirement benefits to 67. All but one Republican commission member backed it, but the Democrats criticized it as unfair, claiming that the existing provisions of the Social Security Act (e.g., the DRC) would achieve the same objective and that age 67 for full benefits would actually mean a benefit reduction for some workers.

Light (1985) lists labor, liberals, and the National Council of Senior Citizens (labor-backed) as among the groups opposing the increase in retirement age.

In the House of Representatives, the *only* commission recommendation that was debated was the increase in the retirement age. According to Bernstein and Bernstein (1988:5), "Congress decided to meet the one-third of the long-term projected deficit for which the commission did not make an agreed-upon recommendation by raising retirement age in two steps in the next century." (For a discussion of the arguments involved, see Chapter 8 of Bernstein and Bernstein in [1988], especially pp. 183–91.)

Another political thrust, in the United States at least, consists of a new form of "ageism" that may have certain implications for the issue of exit age. This new ageism contains two somewhat opposite images of the elderly: (1) as objects of resentment, because they are a "burden" on the "productive" population; and (2) as objects of envy because they have progressed more, economically, than young middle-aged and younger Americans. This is deemed unfair and inequitable. At times, this inequity is viewed as having been caused by the progress made by older persons in the United States.

This new ageism, as it makes further inroads among politicians, the media, and influential "public opinion" elements, could result in public policies aimed at keeping more older persons *out* of the retired population. In an effort to reduce the presumed burden of supporting older persons (and to meet the impending labor shortage), large segments of the "younger older" population may be encouraged to remain in the work force beyond current exit ages or may be discouraged from leaving it through the measures discussed earlier.

Some observers doubt that the recent changes in the Social Security provision will have much effect on the exit phenomenon (see Boaz 1987). This could be the case if early-exit "opportunities" in our private pension plans remain untouched. As long as employers sanction and prefer such possibilities, and as long as they, in so doing, benefit in the form of corporate tax savings and work-force size (or labor-cost) control, there is little chance of the legislative "reforms" of Social Security having much impact on that phenomenon.[16]

The future of the Social Security system continues to be under a cloud. In addition to proposals designed to reduce the costs of the system, there are even proposals to eliminate it altogether and rely instead on one or more forms of private-sector pensions and individual savings. Such proposals, it must be stressed, are unique to the United States. At the present time, they tend to be viewed as from the "radical-right fringe" and are not taken very seriously in the mainstreams of Republican and Democratic political circles or by their economic advisers. It should be noted, however, that at one time raising the retirement age for full Social Security benefits was considered outlandish. But while (in 1981) the vast majority of all Americans and those in the labor force aged 18 to 54 (85 percent of each sample) disapproved of reducing benefits for future retirees, only 58 percent rejected any gradual increase in the full-benefit retirement age under Social Security as a way of helping the Social Security system.[17]

Would it be outlandish to speculate on the implications of a draconian surgery on, or the actual elimination of, the retired-worker pension program under Social Security? In the event of that unlikely scenario, reliance on some form(s) of the private-pension approach, and on individual savings (made less attractive since incentives for Individual Retirement Accounts were virtually eliminated under recent tax law changes), might produce ideal retirement income resources, as the extremist advocates of such approaches would have us believe.

If the critics (see, for example, Stein 1986) of the extremists' proposals are correct in saying that the latter's schemes could not provide the level of retirement incentives under current schemes (including continued reliance on Social Security), or guarantee any protection from inexorable inflation, then we need not concern ourselves with any potential problems associated with continuing trends of early exit.

But we do not know just how entrenched the practice of early exit—especially before age 62—is in the United States. Ekerdt, Bosse, and Glynn (1985:405) of the Boston Veterans Administration's Normative Aging Study claim that retirement itself is "now firmly embedded in the life course. . . . Workers' intentions toward retirement may have a deep keel keeping them in a long-held structure of expectation about later life." The declining rate of labor force participation by persons as young as 55 to 59 points up the "institutionalization" of early exit. What is still not clear is just how strong these currents, or factors cited above, might be in their future potential for veering that deep keel from the structure of expectations.

The future of retirement-age policy will be affected by political and value dimensions, especially as we move past the early years of the next century. In 1979, Duke University's Richard Fox (in a paper prepared for a National Research Council conference on the Future of Aging) wrote:

> . . . given the upcoming conflict over the Social Security System and the moral and fiscal quandary brought on by a decreasing number of young workers supporting an expanding number of old retirees, I can foresee demands so great as to appear revolutionary (or a reaction to these demands so strong as to represent an economic and moral reordering of basic social institutions).

Fox leaves out of his admittedly speculative statement the possible scenario of a *change* in retirement-age policy as one response to the projected burden on "a decreasing number of young workers." The changes in Social Security since 1979 (especially those made in 1983) may be a portent of such a shift. Indeed, if we witness additional legislation resulting in new costs for the older population, they could be interpreted as turns in a new direction that make it more expensive than in the past to spend a given number of years in retirement. Pension coverage appears to be declining among the employed (Andrews 1985). It still is not clear, however, how much workers indulge in a sort of cost-effectiveness analysis when making a decision about when to exit voluntarily. Be that as it may, there remains the persistence of the pattern already discussed: a sort of schizophrenia characterized by conflicting, inconsistent policy directions regarding retirement-age policy.

There is also the issue of the "politicization" of the retiree population as some sort of relatively homogeneous voter bloc, especially on the issue of retirement-age policy. Apart from the critiques of the notion or belief that they do constitute such a bloc, there is the confusion over the degree to which an already-retired population cares about retirement-age policy and/or whether older workers are actually a self-conscious group with an identity separate from workers of younger ages. To be sure, age-related organizations such as the American Association of Retired Persons have programs for and about employment-related problems for mature men and women. But it is not clear to what extent there is any objective or felt intra-organizational conflict between striving to keep older persons in the labor force, on the one hand, and striving to maintain and/or improve the welfare of the already-retired population on the other.

As for the politics of inter-generational relations, we must bear in mind that this is not the same as tensions based on social class, sex, ethnic, or racial differences. As Heclo (1988) has put it, "we are dealing with a phenomenon that involves (a) *family* (which includes young and old)[and] (b) a *time* dimension, i.e., the young eventually become old."

NOTES

1. One might claim that Graebner's image of "New Deal liberals" is the opposite of the conventional image of them as soft-hearted sentimentalists not concerned about rationality and efficiency.

2. In 1984, according to the Bureau of Labor Statistics, more than three-fifths of all workers in companies with pension plans could retire before 65 with full pension benefits compared with only one-half in 1980; however for many of these employees years of service are a further requirement for such benefits. In a survey of roughly 350 companies in 1984–5, Rhine (1984) found that nearly 40 percent of them had early retirement ages as young as 55. Three-fifths of that group provided less than actuarially reduced pension—in other words, pension benefits higher than an actuarial formula would allow.

3. As a result of the influence of various church and private welfare groups, incidentally, the original Social Security Act did not cover their employees under any of its provisions (unemployment insurance, old-age insurance, etc.).

4. This caveat is applicable as long as lower proportions of women have long-term attachment to jobs, especially full-time jobs, and (2) lower proportions have pension coverage, and so forth. In a later section of this chapter, we concentrate in some detail on information that distinguishes men and women and also takes into consideration marital status.

5. See the section Job Loss for a detailed discussion of the role of job loss in early, and very early (before age 62), exit from the labor force.

6. This rate is calculated by using the Stouffer method for measuring rates of increase in proportions. See Table 21-1 for explanation.

7. This measure refers to the number actually employed as a percentage of the total number of persons in a given age category—not to be confused with the labor force participation rate, which includes in the numerator persons without employment but seeking it. Neither of these measures, incidentally, refers to work experience data.

8. It should also be noted that for women of the same age group (55 to 61) during the same period participation actually increased for nonrecipients, while it essentially declined for pension recipients.

9. For those exiting at 62 or later, the proportion is approximately 56 percent.

10. Other studies, such as the 1981 NCOA Survey (at about the same time as the New Beneficiary Survey) confirm the greater impact of joblessness on younger than on older retirees, regarding age at retirement and employment status. Sheppard's (1977) analysis of the 1966–73 data tapes for the National Longitudinal Survey also reveals a relationship between previous employment and early—or very early—withdrawal from the labor force.

11. The GAO suggests that the 1973–83 increase in pension receipts "may be due to eco-

nomic conditions." The 1983 unemployment rate was about double that in 1973. Workers laid off at these "young old" ages could then begin to take advantage of any pension opportunities.

12. This survey, conducted in 1982, included 9,100 retired-worker beneficiaries first receiving their benefits in 1980–1.

13. The comparable rates are 31 percent for unmarried women, 35 percent for unmarried men, and 60 percent for married women.

14. Another interesting sidelight is that while job tiredness is a factor *not* associated with early exit, pension receipt among married men citing this factor as a primary exit reason appears to make for "very early" exit: 18 percent of the pensioners citing work tiredness, but only 12 percent of nonpensioners exited before age 62. Pension receipt as a facilitator of "very early" exit among workers claiming work-tiredness as their most important exit reason is indeed confirmed for all of the New Beneficiary Survey respondents except married women (Table 21-16).

15. Among the retired workers in the New Beneficiary Survey, as reported elsewhere, married women have by far the greatest rate of exit before age 62 (60 percent). More than three-fifths of this subgroup (62 percent) had some kind of non-Social Security pension—their own or their husband's. More to the point, most of these pension recipients (two-thirds) actually had husbands who were the only pensioners in their marriage. That is, 41 percent of the husbands of the wives retiring before 62 were the only pension recipients. Wives who were the only pension recipient among this group amounted to a mere 15 percent.

16. The last time the U.S. government manipulated the Social Security system in order to cope with unemployment was in 1961, when there was a recession and unemployment was at 7 percent, a proportion deemed politically unacceptable at that time. Retirement under the system was lowered from 65 to 62, with reduced benefits, for men. Age-62 benefits had been available to women since 1956, but not as a measure to control unemployment.

17. Unpublished data from 1981 NCOA/Louis Harris survey.

REFERENCES

Andrews, Emily. 1985. *The Changing Profile of Pensions in America.* Washington, D.C.: Employee Benefit Research Institute.

Bernstein, Merton C., and Joan Brodshaug Bernstein. 1988. *Social Security: The System That Works.* New York: Basic Books, p. 56.

Boaz, Rachel Floersheim. 1987. "The 1983 Amendments to the Social Security Act: Will They Delay Retirement? A Summary of the Evidence." *The Gerontologist* 27:151–5.

Ekerdt, David J., Raymond Bosse, and Robert J. Glynn. 1985. "Period Effects on Planned Age for Retirement, 1975–1984." *Research on Aging* 7:395–407.

General Accounting Office. 1986. *Retirement Before Age 65: Trends, Costs, and National Issues.* Washington, D.C.: GAO.

Graebner, William. 1980. *A History of Retirement: The Meaning and Function of an American Institution, 1885–1978.* New Haven: Yale University Press.

Heclo, Hugh, 1988. "Generational Politics." In: John Palmer et al. (eds.), *The Vulnerable.* Washington, D.C.: Urban Institute, pp. 388–411.

Kingson, Eric. 1981. *The Early Retirement Myth: Why Men Retire Before Age 62.* Report by the Select Committee on Aging, U.S. House of Representatives, October.

Light, Paul. 1985. *Artful Work: The Politics of Social Security Reform.* New York: Random House.

Meier, Elizabeth L. 1986. *Early Retirement Incentive Programs: Trends and Implications.* Washington, D.C.: Public Policy Institute, American Association of Retired Persons.

Mutschler, Phyllis. No date. *Corporate Inducements to Retire and Subsequent Retiree Income Status.* Working paper 12, Policy Center of Aging, Florence Heller School, Brandeis University.

——— 1986. *Siren Song: The Effect of Financial Incentives on Workers' Retirement Decisions.* Working paper 13, Policy Center on Aging, Florence Heller School, Brandeis University.

Packard, Michael D., and Virginia P. Reno. 1988. "A Look at Very Early Retirees." In: Rita Ricardo-Campbell and Edward P. Lazear (eds.), *Issues in Contemporary Retirement.* Stanford: Hoover Institution Press, pp. 243–72.

Rhine, Shirley. 1984. *Managing Older Workers: Company Policies and Attitudes.* Research Report No. 860. The Conference Board.

Sheppard, Harold L. 1977. "Factors Associated with Early Withdrawal from the Labor Force." In: Seymour Wolfbein (ed.), *Men in the Pre-Retirement Years.* Philadelphia: Temple University Press.

Shuman, Eric. 1983. "The Golden Handshake." *Dynamic Years,* March/April, p. 15

Standing, Guy. 1986. "Labour Flexibility and Older Worker Marginalization: The need for a new strategy. *International Labour Review* 125:329–48.

Stein, Bruno. 1986. "Phasing Out Social Security: A Critique of Ferrera's Proposal." In: Charles W. Mayer (ed.), *Social Security: A Critique of Radical Reform Proposals.* Lexington: Lexington Books, Chapter 2.

U.S. Department of Labor. 1989. *Labor Market Shortage.* Washington, D.C.: Department of Labor.

IX

THE POLITICS OF AGE

Understanding the politics of age first requires knowledge of how "age" becomes an issue in political debate. Although people age in all societies, in Western countries our consideration of who is elderly is derived from a political decision. In the United States, when we speak of "the aged," we usually mean people over the age of 65—the age at which Americans become eligible for full Social Security benefits.

Entitlement to Social Security at age 65 makes age a politically important characteristic since pension systems are a direct result of political decisions about how surplus wealth will be redistributed. Government-administered pensions represent a portion of national wealth that has been removed from control of the market and placed under political control. They grant older workers "the right to cease work before wearing out" (Myles, 1989).

POLITICS AND STATE PENSION SYSTEMS

In Western Europe and North America, government pensions are the major source of income for the majority of older people. The first reading in this section underscores the inherently political nature of pensions. As John Myles points out, the capacity to ensure income security depends on a political process—the capacity to tax and redistribute wealth. He notes that, although these pensions have been both effective and efficient, current debates center on whether they can remain viable in the future. Myles concludes that as new technologies and a changing international marketplace force major adjustments in Western economies, political debate over income security for the elderly will remain controversial.

POLITICS OF AGE IN THE UNITED STATES

Although some research suggests that the elderly in the United States wield substantial political power (Callahan, 1986; Longman, 1987), most researchers argue that the interests of older people are diverse and fragmented along cultural, social, and economic lines (Binstock, 1984; Estes, 1986). Still, the notion that the elderly constitute a political force powerful enough to appropriate more than their "fair" share of limited social resources has become increasingly prominent. How did this debate about generational equity assume a dominant position in the rhetoric of age-based social programs in the United States?

In the second reading in this section, Jill Quadagno traces the generational equity debate back to its roots in the mid-1980s. She argues that one organization, Americans for Generational Equity (AGE), formalized the idea of current intergenerational competition and altered the framework of public debate. Despite AGE's efforts, public support for Social Security remains high, and AGE failed in its initial attempt to reduce public provision for the elderly. AGE's agenda remains a feature of current policy debate, however, and may have an effect in the future.

Although many social scientists discredit the underlying logic of the generational equity argument (Minkler, 1991; Morgan, 1993; Walker, 1993), the idea of conflict between the generations over a shrinking social welfare pie is very much alive in the United States, and Social Security and Medicare are still under intense political scrutiny (Jacobs, 1990; Street and Quadagno, 1993). The new message is that entitlement programs are fueling a growing budget deficit (Ball, 1994; Peterson, 1993). Debates over entitlement programs, the deficit, and health care reform seem likely to remain at center stage as we move toward the twenty-first century.

THE ELDERLY AS POLITICAL ACTORS

Older people are good citizens, for they vote in greater numbers than their younger counterparts. But there is simply no evidence to date that elderly people vote as a unified bloc (Jacobs, 1990). Nor does any evidence suggest that old-age political solidarity is increasing. According to analyses of national opinion surveys, on most issues (including aging policy issues) older Americans are nearly indistinguishable from younger adults (Binstock, 1992; Day, 1990). If elderly people are not politically powerful in terms of voting strength, how are they a political force in American politics?

To the extent that the elderly wield political power, most researchers conclude that it is not as individual actors, but rather through the collective actions of interest groups (Binstock, 1984; Pratt, 1993). The final reading in this section is Debra Street's case study of the politics surrounding the passage and repeal of the Medicare Catastrophic Care Act of 1988. Numerous old-age interest groups mobilized in response to the first political attempt to depart from the social insurance principles that undergird the Medicare program. Some observers contend that the role played by the old-age interest groups in the repeal of the legislation demonstrates their political clout, but this interpretation oversimplifies a more complex political process. As Street points out, age-based interest groups were divided in their support for or opposition to the legislation, and they exercised their political force only within a very limited context.

REFERENCES

Ball, Robert. "Social Security: Where Are We Going?" *Working Paper Series,* Pepper Institute on Aging and Public Policy, No. PI-94-27. Tallahassee, FL: Florida State University, 1994.

Binstock, Robert. "Reframing the Agenda of Policies on Aging." In Meredith Minkler and Carroll L. Estes (eds.), *Readings in the Political Economy of Aging.* Farmingdale, NY: Baywood Publishing Co., Inc., 1984.

Binstock, Robert H. "Older Voters and the 1992 Presidential Election." *The Gerontologist* 32, no. 5 (1992): 601–606.

Callahan, Daniel. "Health Care in the Aging Society: A Moral Dilemma." Pp. 319–339 in Alan Pifer and Lydia Bronte (eds.), *Our Aging Society: Paradox and Promises*. New York: W. W. Norton, 1986.

Day, Christine L. *What Older Americans Think: Interest Groups and Aging Policy*. Princeton, NJ: Princeton University Press, 1990.

Estes, Carroll. "The Politics of Ageing in America." *Ageing and Society* 6(1986):122–134.

Jacobs, Bruce. "Aging and Politics." Pp. 349–359 in Robert H. Binstock and Linda K. George (eds.), *Handbook of Aging and the Social Sciences*. 3rd ed. San Diego: Academic Press, 1990.

Longman, Phillip. *Born to Pay: The New Politics of Aging in America*. Boston: Houghton Mifflin Co., 1987.

Minkler, Meredith. "Generational Equity and the New Victim Blaming." Pp. 67–80 in Meredith Minkler and Carroll L. Estes (eds.), *Critical Perspectives on Aging: The Political and Moral Economy of Growing Old*. Amityville, NY: Baywood Publishing, 1991.

Morgan, Susan P. "Generational Equity and Measurement Bias: Who Is Really Poor?" *Journal of Aging Studies* 7, no. 4(1993): 453–464.

Myles, John. *Old Age in the Welfare State: The Political Economy of Public Pensions*. Revised ed. Lawrence: University of Kansas Press, 1989.

Peterson, Paul E. "Give Kids the Vote." *Harper's*, February 1993, pp. 23–26.

Pratt, Henry. *Gray Agendas: Interest Groups and Public Pensions in Canada, Britain and the United States*. Ann Arbor: University of Michigan Press, 1993.

Street, Debra, and Jill Quadagno. "The State, The Elderly, and the Intergenerational Contract: Toward a New Political Economy of Aging." Pp. 130–150 in K. Warner Schaie and W. Andrew Achenbaum (eds.), *Societal Impact on Aging: Historical Perspectives*. New York: Springer Publishing Co., 1993.

Walker, Alan. "Intergenerational Relations and Welfare Restructuring: The Social Construction of an Intergenerational Problem." Pp. 141–165 in Vern L. Bengtson and W. Andrew Achenbaum (eds.), *The Changing Contract across Generations*. New York: Aldine de Gruyter, 1993.

22

Social Security and
Support of the Elderly:
The Western Experience
JOHN MYLES

The Western experience with Social Security is a curious one. Despite enormous national differences in social structure and political ideology, the majority of old people in most Western democracies now depend on state-administered income security programs for most of their income. Myles first considers the reasons for this historical "bias" in favor of public over private solutions and then evaluates the effectiveness (product quality) and efficiency (relative cost) of both forms of provision. Myles concludes that only in societies that are economically and socially stagnant can private pensions ensure income security for the elderly. Government programs, by contrast, enhance economic development while maintaining the flexibility needed to adapt to changing economic conditions.

My purpose in this article is to examine the pros and cons of Social Security systems as a means for providing income support for the elderly. It is impossible to make such an assessment without reference to a particular historical and social context, and so my focus will be centered on the postwar capitalist democracies of Western Europe and North America. But even this is a very broad canvas to paint on and, by necessity, my discussion is pitched at a high level of generality, ignoring many national distinctions and peculiarities that may in fact be quite important at that level. It also means that the pros and cons I identify may be quite different when considered in the context of other political and economic systems.

Income security for the elderly has become the subject of considerable controversy during the past decade and a half. This is a major change from the 1950s and 1960s when these programs were expanding. Following World War II, the rapid growth of

"Social Security and Support of the Elderly: The Western Experience" by John Myles, from *Journal of Aging Studies*, 2 (1988): 321–337. Copyright © 1988 by JAI Press, Inc.

old age security entitlements was widely hailed as a necessary, indeed inevitable, consequence of industrialization and economic growth. Industrialization, it was thought, had simultaneously made the labor of older workers redundant and provided the wealth to make it unnecessary.

Although public old age security programs continue to enjoy great popularity among Western publics (Coughlin 1979), business and political elites have become less sanguine about the long-term viability of these programs. It is widely recognized that it is extremely difficult to provide income security to the elderly other than through state-organized social insurance programs. But it is no longer clear that such programs are compatible with sustained economic growth and the maintenance of social harmony. There is no clear consensus on these issues and no definitive evidence that would permit adjudication of the debates this lack of consensus has generated. But in comparison to the 1950s and 1960s when the neo-Keynesian consensus led many Western observers to talk about "the end of ideology," debates over the relative merits of Social Security have become very ideological indeed.

In the first part of this article I identify what is meant by Social Security by contrasting postwar income security programs with an earlier social assistance tradition. Second, I review some fairly conventional explanations of why real income security for the majority of workers requires centralized state administration. In the final sections I discuss the economic, social, and political trade-offs frequently imputed to such an arrangement.

SOCIAL ASSISTANCE, SOCIAL SECURITY, AND PRIVATE PENSIONS

Only in the United States is the term *Social Security* used almost exclusively to refer to income security programs for the elderly. Elsewhere, it is used in a much more generic sense to refer to the entire set of modern welfare state programs that protect workers against a wide range of labor market risks. This is not merely a peculiar semantic practice of Americans, however. In a very real way it captures a distinctive feature of the American welfare state. Quite rightly, Americans make a sharp distinction between social (or public) assistance and Social Security. The former refers to income maintenance programs directed exclusively or primarily at the "poor," those whose incomes are judged to be inadequate for subsistence. The latter refers to income maintenance programs intended not merely to prevent poverty but rather to allow individuals and families to maintain continuity of living standards in the event of labor markets exits through unemployment, illness, or retirement. The natural constituency of Social Security as opposed to social assistance programs is not the poor but rather the vast majority of wage earners. What distinguishes the American from the more typical European welfare state is the extent to which its core social programs continue to be directed at the poor. Old age security is the exception in the United States, an income maintenance program that incorporates a majority of wage earners.

American practice in this area, however, alerts us to the important distinction that must be made between these two forms of social provision. Prior to World War II, state initiatives in the area of income support for the elderly were generally in the so-cial assistance tradition (Perrin 1969). Benefits provided were low, often means-tested and were restricted to those groups in society (e.g., industrial workers) considered to be subject to a high risk of falling into poverty. Their purpose was not to induce or per-mit elderly workers to withdraw from economic activity but to provide a modest sup-plement to compensate for the declining incomes of aging workers.

After World War II, income programs for the elderly began to undergo a major transformation. Instead of providing subsistence benefits for those aged persons who fell into poverty, they gradually acquired the character of a "retirement wage," an in-come entitlement intended to replace market wages and allow the elderly worker to withdraw from economic activity. As Perrin (1969) documents, this involved the adop-tion of two rather novel principles of distribution. The first was the principle of univer-sality: coverage was extended to include all wage earners and, eventually, the self-employed. The second was the principle of wage replacement, providing benefits that would replace the market wage and allow workers to maintain a continuity of living standards after retirement. The result is that the adequacy of old age entitlement sys-tems in the West is now evaluated against two criteria. The first of these is the social as-sistance criterion—the extent to which old age entitlements protect the elderly against destitution or poverty; the second is the income security or income replacement crite-rion—the extent to which public entitlements replace market wages after retirement.

My concern in this article is with the income security component of contemporary social programs for the elderly because it is on this that the debates of the past decade have focused. This does not mean that debates over social assistance have been triv-ial but they have been of a fundamentally different order. In the case of social assis-tance, concern is typically directed at the adequacy of benefit levels. In the case of in-come security, there is a prior and even more fundamental problem to be solved: whether it should be provided by the state or through "private" insurance plans pur-chased in the market like any other commodity. In this respect, the debates about So-cial Security are similar to debates over the relative merits of any "nationalized" in-dustry. These include evaluations of the effectiveness ("product quality") and efficiency of public versus private sector alternatives as well as the economic and so-cial side-effects of "public ownership." I discuss these issues in the following section titled "pensions and income security." This discussion, however, is based on the as-sumption that we are simply comparing equivalent products: whether the state is able to offer a better product—income security in old age—at a lower price. Whereas de-bates over Social Security are often conducted in this fashion, this perspective over-looks the fact that the field of Social Security during the past hundred years, and es-pecially since World War II, has been terrain of a much more fundamental debate over social rights (Marshall 1964). I discuss these larger issues in the sequel titled "pen-sions and social rights." Throughout, one remarkable fact should be kept in mind: De-spite enormous national differences in social structure and political ideology, state-administered Social Security schemes are now the major source of income for the majority of elderly in all capitalist democracies. In part, then, our task is to determine why this is the case, on the one hand, and, on the other, to establish why this practice is now being questioned.

Pensions and Income Security

Liberal social thought (Rimlinger 1971) traditionally emphasized the importance of self-help and self-reliance with respect to old age. As a result, poverty in old age was often considered to be an indication of moral failure—the absence of thrift and self-denial during youth and middle age. In a low-wage economy, where current income was barely sufficient to meet immediate consumption requirements, such self-reliance was clearly an unrealistic expectation for the majority. But even in a high-wage economy, where some degree of personal saving might be considered normal, the principle of self-reliance poses difficulties, especially where "old age" represents an ever larger portion of the economic lifecycle. As Schulz points out (1985, p. 74), the typical worker would be required to save 20% of current income each and every year in order to provide income security in old age. And even if this was socially possible, the prudent individual is faced with the uncertainty of future events in planning for old age (Schulz 1985, pp. 71–72).

As a result, it has long been considered normal for prudent individuals to deal with this uncertainty by pooling risks in insurance programs. Private insurance is a means of providing collective income security to individuals in a commodity form; it can be bought and sold at market prices like any other good or service. Insurance does not violate notions of thrift and self-reliance because the security provided is proportional to the contributions made.

The insurance principle, however, does set in motion one of the elements that leads to the emergence of public old age security programs. This is the fact that the effective cost of income security is a function of the size of the insured group. The larger the group the less likely is an actuarial failure of the insurance program that may result from an imbalance between contributors and beneficiaries. Early efforts by workers to secure themselves against the risks of disability and old age through union-sponsored insurance schemes (e.g., the British friendly societies) often floundered during periods of high unemployment or as a result of technological changes that eroded the membership base. Plans organized at the level of the firm or industry encounter similar problems with the result that the income security system breaks down.

Even where it is able to solve the problems of individuals, however, voluntary insurance is unable to solve the social problem of providing for the vast majority who do not participate.[1] The result is that participation in pension plans—public or private—is now generally on a compulsory basis. This is for economic as well as social reasons. The actuarial soundness of a plan is difficult to establish if future participation rates are uncertain and subject to large variation. Despite the obvious violation of traditional liberal principles it represents, compulsory participation in both state-sponsored and employer-sponsored pension schemes is now rarely questioned. Rather debate has focused on the relative merits of centralized, state-administered pension schemes versus private employer-sponsored schemes.

Coverage

Historically, the main advantage of Social Security is quite simple: without it, there would be no income security for the majority of elderly. Since the turn of the century and especially since World War II there has been continued expansion of employer-sponsored schemes. But they have generally been both too selective and too unreliable to support the majority of the aged. In the absence of state intervention, private sector plans tend to stop far short of universal coverage of the work force. This problem has been particularly severe in Canada and the United States. Those not covered tend to be in small, labor-intensive enterprises in which wage costs represent a high proportion of total production costs and where the costs of marketing and administering pension plans are high. The result is that those not covered are often low-wage workers, especially women, who also face the greatest risk of poverty in old age.

The demand for governments to intervene in this situation is similar to other areas where governments respond to "market failure." Several options are open short of nationalization, however. The first is to provide incentives to the market. This has been done by making contributions to employer-sponsored pensions or individual retirement savings plans tax deductible. Both means have been widely used in Canada and the United States at enormous public cost (the result of foregone tax revenues). But because tax deductions disproportionately benefit high-income earners, it is among the better paid that growth has taken place. Well over half the work force in both countries remain uncovered by these subsidized private-sector alternatives.

The second alternative is state regulation: employers may be compelled to establish pension plans that meet criteria set by the state (mandated pensions). A version of this approach is practiced in the United Kingdom. There, employers may opt out of the public system so long as they provide an equivalent program. This solution, however, immediately raises two issues. The first is that of efficiency, the costs of administering a decentralized system. The second is that of effectiveness or "product quality." The British experience indicates that mandated systems are inferior on both counts and still require enormous public subsidies in order to function (O'Higgins 1985).

Efficiency

An obvious benefit of a centralized old age insurance program is the potential to realize economies of scale. In view of the routine nature of administering such a program, a large state monopoly will almost always be cheaper than a decentralized system organized on the basis of firms or industries.[2] The administrative costs of a decentralized system are especially onerous on small employers. Considerations of efficiency, moreover, are not limited to the immediate costs at the level of the firm because some system of coordination is still required to permit transfer of entitlements when workers lose or change jobs.

To realize these economies of scale, however, presumes the presence of a bureaucratic infrastructure capable of collecting revenues, and of calculating and disbursing benefits within a defined geographic area. It is no accident that the first state programs for the elderly began in Germany, a country with a highly developed state bureaucracy. Bureaucratic capacity was also an important factor determining the type of plan that could be adopted (Heclo 1974; Orloff 1985). Administration of a program in which benefits are linked to contributions, for example, requires greater bureaucratic capacity than the universal flat benefit programs adopted in many countries after World War II. And, indeed, bureaucratic capacity was sometimes a major reason for this practice.

Effectiveness

Historically, the preference of employees and labor unions for a national Social Security system can also be understood in terms of traditional differences in the quality of public pensions over private sector alternatives. Private pensions were often seen by employers as a form of labor control and used as a means to reduce labor turnover. As a result, private sector entitlements are typically not "vested" until the employee has met the stipulated number of years of service. This means that workers who change jobs frequently or experience an interrupted work history may have few or no benefits on retirement. Similarly, the absence of "portability" arrangements has meant that many employees are unable to transfer entitlements when they change employers. In contrast, national Social Security systems provide complete portability and immediate vesting.

A pension entitlement is essentially a "deferred wage," a promise by the employer or the state to provide a flow of income at some point in the future. A critical feature of any pension program, then, is the degree of certainty that what is promised will actually be forthcoming. A major factor that led to the expansion of state systems after World War II was the demonstrated incapacity of private sector plans to deal with the disruption and economic failure associated with war, depression, and massive inflation. Only the state, with its power to tax and reallocate costs and benefits, was capable of responding to such a situation.

This response to the experience of the Great Depression and World War II simply serves to highlight a more general principle: In the end, the capacity to ensure income security rests on the power to tax and redistribute. Throughout the postwar period this was demonstrated by the inability of private pensions to prevent the erosion of entitlements that resulted from inflation. Inflation essentially redistributes real wealth within the economy. Unless the individual enterprise is the beneficiary of this process, employer-sponsored plans will be unable to compensate plan members for the income lost in this fashion.[3] Only the state, with its power to tax, is able to recapture the wealth lost through inflation and redistribute it by indexing benefits. In Britain, for example, it is the state that provides insurance against inflation irrespective of whether the employer has opted in or out of the public-sector program.

Flexibility

The major weakness of a universal, centralized Social Security program is its lack of flexibility. Rules of participation, eligibility, and benefit levels tend to be standardized across large populations that may be quite heterogeneous. Workers in dangerous and physically demanding occupations (e.g., miners) as they age, tend to face different risks than workers in more sedentary occupations (e.g., office workers). The trade-off associated with pooling risks over large, heterogeneous populations comes from the fact that protection tends to be normed against the average risk. The result is that some groups receive less protection and others more than required by their situation. The trade-off, of course, is directly proportional to the heterogeneity of the population being served.

Standardization of costs and benefits across heterogeneous populations may also result in nonrandom forms of redistribution. It is inevitable in any pension program that there will be redistribution from those groups with shorter life expectancy to those with longer life expectancy. This may result, for example, in transfers from low-income groups with shorter life expectancies to high-income groups with longer life expectancies. It is possible for a public system to compensate for this by providing low-income groups with higher implicit rates of return on their contributions (and most do), but it is neither likely that all differences can be dealt with in this way, nor is it always socially desirable to do so. A case in point is gender differences in life expectancy. Other things being equal, women in most Western countries receive higher returns on contributions than men because of greater life expectancy and, in many countries, a lower age of eligibility for benefits. The private market has tended to reflect these differences by providing women with lower annual annuities than men under the assumptions they would be receiving them for a longer period of time. The result is less income security for elderly women.

The fact that it is difficult for a centralized state-administered program to provide the flexibility required to meet the needs of a heterogeneous population, explains the minor role that private plans continue to play even where the public-sector system is highly developed (e.g., Sweden). Nevertheless, it remains the case that the core of all income security systems in the West are centralized state programs. When one examines the history of income security there is no great mystery to this fact. Historically, private sector alternatives were slow to develop and, where they did, provided benefit provisions of inferior quality. I will return to this topic and consider some of the reasons for this in the conclusion.

The preceding discussion of income security suffers from two limitations. First, many of the debates on this subject have less to do with the actual income security provided to the elderly than with the economic and political side-effects or "externalities" of these programs. Second, we have been discussing different systems as though we were comparing equivalent products: The state, as it were, is simply able to provide a better product—income security in old age—at a lower price. While debates over Social Security are often conducted in this fashion, this perspective overlooks the fact that the field of Social Security during the past hundred years, and especially since World War II, has been the terrain of a much more fundamental debate over social rights (Marshall 1964). Once we scratch beneath the surface, we find that the issue is not merely one of comparing equivalent commodities but rather of two alternative forms of social organization.

PENSIONS AND SOCIAL RIGHTS

As Marshall (1964) pointed out in his seminal essay, the development of Social Security in the capitalist democracies has been inextricably linked to the development of citizenship—rights and entitlements that attach to persons by virtue of their membership in a national community rather than to their property, status, or market capacity.

In the twentieth century social rights of protection against economic security were added to civil rights (e.g., freedom of speech, equality before the courts), and political rights of voting and participation in the exercise of power. All three were formalized in the United Nations Declaration of Human Rights in 1948. Macpherson (1985, p. 23) observes that there are both historical and logical differences between the three types of rights. The struggle for political and civil rights dates back to the seventeenth and eighteenth centuries and were the main objectives of the English, American, and French revolutions of those centuries. Social rights are of much more recent origin. Logically, they differ as well.

The civil rights are chiefly rights against the state, that is, claims for individual freedoms that the state cannot invade. The political rights are rights to a voice in the control of the state. The economic and social rights are claims for benefits to be provided by the state, both by legislation and by positive provision of services and income supplements (Macpherson 1985, p. 23). Both the nature and importance of the emergence of social rights have to be understood against the backdrop of the emergent capitalist order in which they developed. As Marshall (and many others) observed, there is an inherent tension between a system of allocation based on market capacity and one based on principles of citizenship. The tensions are both economic and political. The economic tension is usually expressed in terms of the trade-off between efficiency and welfare: allocation on the basis of social and political criteria distorts market relationships and, it is argued, results in less wealth and a lower standard of living for all. The political tension emerges from the trade-off between welfare and equity: distribution based on social rights requires the redistribution of primary incomes generated by the market. As a result, some get more and some get less in benefits than what they have contributed to social programs. This in turn opens the door to social conflicts between those who win and those who lose in this process.

In the West, these trade-offs have a particular coloration because conceptions of efficiency and equity are given their content by the social relations of market capitalism. The principle of equity is violated in a capitalist society when owners are deprived of the full market rate of return on their capital in order to finance redistributive social programs. This is because they are not being rewarded in proportion to their contribution to the capitalist production process. More generally, redistribution of primary incomes or accumulated wealth of any sort violates the primary right that serves as the basis of capitalism—namely the property right.

But as Marx observed, the problem of redistribution does not disappear under socialism. In socialism, distribution would be based on the principle of "from each according to his abilities, to each according to his work." Only in communism would distribution be made on the basis of need. So long as societies are organized around the maximization of production, the tension between social rights and considerations of equity and efficiency remains.

THE TRADE-OFF BETWEEN WELFARE AND EQUITY

The language of "social rights" and "social citizenship" is most closely associated with postwar reforms in Britain and the principles of Lord Beveridge. Prior to the war benefits for the elderly were in the social assistance tradition. Subject to a means-test, they identified the beneficiary as being among the "poor," stigmatized and set apart from the rest of civil society. The major thrust of postwar reforms in Britain, Canada, and other countries in this tradition was to abolish the means-test and make benefits a right of citizenship. The intent was to remove invidious distinctions among the poor and nonpoor and to build social solidarity. The state, as it were, would refuse to acknowledge distinctions of class and status created by the market. This had the seemingly anomalous effect of providing state benefits of equal value to the wealthy as well as to the poor, and was justified in terms of a system of taxation and financing that made such programs redistributive: All received equal benefits but those with higher incomes paid a higher proportion of the total costs. The result, however, was that social assistance to the elderly poor was integrated into a system of income security for the nonpoor. The principle of universality meant that all citizens now acquired income entitlements that were independent of market capacity.

Benefits provided in this way, however, were typically at subsistence levels. For the average worker, withdrawal from the labor market still meant a sharp drop in living standards. As a result most programs that began with the flat-benefit system added a second tier of earnings-related benefits that did mirror market inequalities. This was also necessary to maintain solidarity among workers. Where public-sector benefits failed to meet the needs of better-paid workers, their support for the system tended to erode. The consequence was a hybrid system of citizen entitlements and "earned" benefits.

A similar result was reached in countries such as the United States that began with earnings-related social insurance programs. Financing and benefit formulas made such programs generally redistributive between income groups. Adjustments were also made to take account of individual needs such as the presence of dependents. Over time there was progressive erosion of the link between contributions and entitlements (Derthick 1979). Although the amount of redistribution between income groups varies enormously among countries, all systems violate traditional notions of market equity ("to each according to his contributions") to satisfy principles of income adequacy and need.[4]

Historically, all Social Security systems have also required redistribution between generations. This occurred for several reasons. In the start-up phase, most systems began to pay benefits long before individuals had time to make the contributions the market would recognize as necessary to finance these benefits. Second, as programs matured, ad-hoc improvements were applied to current beneficiaries as well as to those still in the labor force. Finally, because most systems are financed on a "pay-as-you-go" basis (benefits paid out of current revenues), there is a tendency for transfers to be made from small age cohorts to large age cohorts.

An important point, however, is that it is extremely difficult to determine the net effect of these transfers. The redistributive effects of Social Security may be negated by other programs that redistribute in favor of the rich (e.g., tax deductions on retirement savings programs and contributions to private plans). Intergenerational transfers between small and large age cohorts may take place within the program itself, but at the level of the economy as a whole small age cohorts will be net beneficiaries of the intergenerational transfer system (Easterlin 1980). Nonetheless, in terms of usual market-based accounting practices these programs do produce transfers between income groups and generations that violate market conceptions of equity. This in turn has generated concern over the political viability of such programs and their effects on social solidarity.

In recent years, conservative critics of Social Security have given enormous attention to the long-term effects of social solidarity that may result from intergenerational transfers. They decry the "windfall profits" received by the first generation of beneficiaries as being unfair. More important, however, has been their concern over the disruptive effects of intergenerational transfers that might occur in the future as a result of population aging. As the populations of the Western countries age, contribution rates will rise significantly, and it is thought this will lead to resistance and revolt by the young. Some have gone so far as to predict an "intergenerational class struggle" (Davis and Van Den Oever 1981). My own view is that these claims are at best highly exaggerated. The empirical evidence from countries that are already quite old by demographic standards (Austria, Sweden) gives no support to such claims. There are good reasons, both economic and social, for solidarity between generations, not the least of which is the greater economic capacity of small cohorts to finance benefits for the elderly.

Ironically, the chief concern of Social Democrats and left-wing reformers who have been in the forefront of Social Security development is over the effects of transfers between groups. For Social Democratic and Labor parties redistribution through Social Security was important as a means of enhancing solidarity among workers. The intent was to strengthen the economic position of the weakest workers who are otherwise likely to underbid wages, serve as strikebreakers, and otherwise create divisions and rivalries within the working class. Social Security also provided a means of bypassing the market to achieve wage demands. To do this, however, required winning parliamentary power through the electoral process, and this in turn required cross-class alliances to achieve parliamentary majorities. The most advanced welfare states (e.g., the Nordic countries) were built upon broad cross-class alliances between the traditional working class and the emergent "middle classes" of postwar Europe. Enhanced Social Security was both an objective and a means of sustaining these alliances.

To sustain these alliances, however, requires a "luxurious," and hence costly, welfare state. Benefits and services must be of high quality to satisfy average and above-average wage earners and thereby retain their support. As [social theorist Richard] Titmuss noted in Britain, flat benefit pensions established at subsistence levels simply encouraged better-off workers to pursue private occupational plans that reinforced market inequalities at state expense. And once they had satisfied their needs through private means they were less likely to lend their support to political struggles designed to enhance public-sector entitlements.

But to finance improved benefits for all requires increasing contribution rates. This has two results. First, as contribution rates increase, redistribution declines. Even a system financed out of a progressive tax schedule reaches a limit beyond which redistribution becomes impossible. As marginal tax rates on middle-income earners increase, the taxation of high incomes reverts toward proportionality.[5] Second, as the tax burden on average earners begins to approach or exceed the benefits they receive, their support for social spending can potentially erode and, with it, the alliance on which support for Social Security depends. Thus, the equality-equity dilemma emerges in a different guise and once again threatens to erode social solidarity. Social Security, in other words, is a two-edge sword. It may provide the source of cohesion and solidarity among wage earners; it also has the potential to generate status and equity conflicts that divide workers (Esping-Andersen 1985).

But here too fears of a tax-welfare revolt among the middle classes appear to have exceeded the reality. The tax-welfare revolts of the 1970s were generally limited to a few countries and directed against welfare state regimes in which high taxes (that were also highly visible) were combined with the provision of inferior benefits and services. And nowhere was this hostility directed at old age security programs. These have remained universally popular in the Western countries (Coughlin 1979), and Western politicians have learned that to attack them is to court electoral defeat.

The reason welfare-equity trade-offs have not generated more conflict is that at the level of the economy as a whole neither old age security nor the welfare state in general has greatly altered the final distribution of income. Countries with more developed welfare states have more equal income distributions, but this is because welfare state expansion is easier to achieve where inequality is low. The main function of social policy in the postwar capitalist democracies has been to provide income security. And income security only requires a great deal of redistribution when there is a great deal of inequality in the distribution of primary incomes.

The fact that Social Security has failed to substantially alter the final distribution of income when examined over time, however, does not imply that nothing has been accomplished. What Social Security does achieve is to stabilize income flows over the lifecycle—to mitigate the effects of unemployment, illness, and old age.[6] And the marginal utility of this stabilization is obviously greater for low-wage earners. Every dollar lost through unemployment, illness, or retirement has a more serious impact on low-wage earners than on high-wage earners. In the past, retirement from productive activity in advance of physiological decline was a privilege of wealth; today it is the normal condition of the elderly.

Moreover, making income security universally available has radically altered the nature of market capitalism. The corollary of the preceding discussion is that although total lifetime incomes of most workers remain closely tied to their market capacity, this is not the case at any given point in time. Income security means that the pattern of income flows over the lifecycle are made partially independent of market forces. In Marxian terms, labor power is decommodified (Esping-Andersen 1985; Offe 1984, 1985). From this fact emerge the debates over the trade-offs between welfare and efficiency.

POLITICS AGAINST MARKETS: WELFARE AND EFFICIENCY

Irrespective of whether Social Security provides better security at lower cost, the end result of the expansion of Social Security is the same—the expansion of state control over distribution. Just how this is regarded depends on one's view of the state. In classical liberal thought, the only economic function of the state was to protect property rights. In the neoliberal consensus that emerged after World War II, the state was given a much broader mandate to manage aggregate demand and this included programs that might reorganize the distribution of primary incomes in order to achieve full employment and sustained economic growth. Similar shifts in thought were evident within the political parties and unions representing the working class. Bismarck's reforms in nineteenth-century Germany were condemned by Socialists as a mechanism of the bourgeois state to co-opt the working class. In the decades after World War II many Socialists and Labor leaders came to view the state as a means of bypassing the market and its matrix of power structured around property relations. For a time, classical debates over the trade-off between welfare and efficiency gave way to a new consensus about welfare-enhanced market efficiency. Private ownership of the means of production could be combined with increasing socialization of consumption to the mutual advantage of both.

With the apparent failure of Keynesian demand-management strategies in the mid-1970s, analysts of both left and right began to rediscover the inherent strains between welfare and efficiency. Moreover, there was considerable agreement between them over the symptoms if not over the causes and solutions to the problem. I shall not attempt here to review all of these issues or to adjudicate among contending points of view. Rather, I shall merely highlight some of the major claims advanced with respect to the incompatibilities between a universal system of income security and market efficiency.

Income Security Restricts and Distorts Capital Markets

Many claims have been advanced about the effects of Social Security on the rate of savings, the incentive to invest, and the structure of investment. During the past decade, for example, there has been a heated, if inconclusive, debate in the United States over the effect of Social Security on the rate of savings (see Aaron 1982). It was argued that because U.S. Social Security is financed on a pay-as-you-go basis, it provides a form of pseudosavings that depresses the savings rate. Although the results of this debate were inconclusive, it is doubtlessly the case that the savings rate in pay-as-you-go systems is lower than it would be if the plan were funded as in Sweden and Canada. Funded Social Security systems, however, lead to a transfer of economic power from the private sector to the state. For conservative critics this compounds the problem of state control because there is no assurance the state will allocate this capital in ways that enhance market efficiency: Funds may be invested for social and political reasons rather than return and risk considerations (Economic Council of Canada 1979, pp. 61–63).

At a more general level, it is argued that the institutionalization of income security rights has resulted in what conservative analysts refer to as "democratic overload" and left analysts describe as a "crisis of legitimation." By this they mean that the establishment of income entitlements as social rights imposes an enormous fiscal constraint on the state budget and the economy as a whole. Social Security programs enjoy enormous popular support, and once established they are very difficult to dismantle or alter.

As the costs of these programs expand, they may put increasing pressure on capital markets and drive up interest rates. In effect, once they are established as rights, income security programs impose a new constraint on the future allocation of the social surplus.

Private sector alternatives pose other difficulties, however. Private pension funds have become a major vehicle of capital formation in countries such as Britain, Canada, and the United States. Two fears have been expressed about this fact. First, concern is expressed about the concentration of economic power in the hands of a few, large pension investment institutions. Second, because of the income security objectives of these funds, there is a tendency for them to be invested in conservative portfolios starving the market of needed venture capital.

Income Security Restricts and Distorts Labor Markets

By definition, income security is intended to allow individuals to exit from the labor market without a drastic reduction in their standard of living. In effect, the welfare state provides a means of control over the labor supply that is not given in nature. Unlike other commodities whose supply is determined by their expected salability, the supply of labor power "is determined by non-strategic demographic processes and the institutional rules of human reproductive activity" (Offe 1985, p. 16). Institutionalized systems of income security change all this. Whoever controls the rules of exit from the labor market and entry into the income security net also controls the size and composition of the labor force. And because of the relation between supply and price, control over the income security system may also provide indirect control over wage rates.

This capacity to control the labor supply may be used to enhance market efficiency by providing a means to absorb redundant workers or surplus labor (O'Connor 1973). Lowering the age of eligibility for old age security has frequently been used as a means for dealing with rising unemployment and clearing the market of older, less efficient workers (Graebner 1980). But because of the institutional separation between state and economy in the West, these same powers may be used in ways that are independent of market considerations or to deliberately alter the balance of power between market actors.

Conservative critics prefer to talk about these consequences in terms of "work disincentives"; the left speaks of altering the balance of class power between capital and labor and of reducing the compulsion for workers to sell their labor to any employer at any price. But irrespective of their linguistic and political differences, both have implicated Social Security in the serious economic problems faced by the developed capitalist democracies in the past decade. Income security, it is argued, produces a wage pressure-profit squeeze reflected in rising inflation, declining productivity, an erosion of investment incentives, the transfer of production to low-wage countries, and growing structural deficits inside the state. To conservatives, the implication of this is to reduce the role of the state and restore "market discipline." For the left, it indicates the necessity of extending democratic control to the spheres of investment and production.

Needless to say, cause-effect relations on these matters are difficult to establish. But whereas welfare-equity trade-offs have so far had limited effect, debates over welfare-efficiency trade-offs have been at the core of political debates and political struggles during the past decade. The reasons for this are not difficult to fathom in my view. Despite the uncertainty about the actual effects of Social Security on macroeconomic performance, it is clear that the expansion of Social Security entitlements has greatly expanded the role of the state not only in the distribution of wealth but also in its production. Decisions about old age security are also decisions about wage rates, capital markets, and investment. And because of the institutional separation of power between state and economy in the West, it is always possible (although never necessary) that decisions taken by politicians and state managers will be incompatible with those taken by the owners and managers of private capital. And even when this is not the case, there is a long-standing tradition among the Western business class to assign the blame for their own failures to the activities of the state. It is hardly surprising that this antipathy toward state involvement has been exacerbated as a result of a very difficult decade in the history of Western capitalism. It is useful, however, to put the antipathy toward income security in some perspective.

The main function of Social Security is to stabilize the flow of income to workers over the economic lifecycle. The Keynesian justification for this practice was that it would also help to stabilize the flow of profits for corporations over the business cycle. In sum, income security for workers was part of a larger package of economic stabilization for the economy as a whole, a social compromise between labor and capital that would benefit both (Piore and Sabel 1984). The failure of Keynesian demand–management strategies in the 1970s and 1980s, however, suggested the bargain was skewed in favor of labor. With indexed pensions and other entitlements guaranteed by the state, the future incomes of today's workers were assured, but the future of corporate profits was not. The result has been a widespread effort to restore "market discipline" by dismantling or cutting back on social entitlements. In the area of old age security this means encouraging the expansion of private sector pensions and retirement savings plans. This ties the future incomes of today's workers to the performance of the market rather than to their status as citizens.

Classical capitalism as described by Marx is a system of production in which those who control wealth must be induced to contribute to the production process by the promise of riches, and those who contribute labor by the threat of poverty. The difference between capital and labor is that those who hold capital can subsist even when they fail to contribute to production (i.e., invest), whereas labor cannot subsist when it withholds labor power. The welfare state, including Social Security, changes this by allowing people to withdraw from productive activity. As the welfare state expands, labor, like capital, must increasingly be induced to participate by the carrot of riches rather than the stick of poverty. Whether this "modified capitalism" is a viable form of economic organization in the long term is now the subject of heated debate and political confrontation in the West. As Marshall anticipated, it may well be that postwar "welfare capitalism" was but a temporary respite in the ongoing war between citizenship and social class. He warned: "This phase will not continue indefinitely. It may be that some of the conflicts within our social system are becoming too sharp to achieve its purpose much longer" (Marshall 1964, p. 134).

CONCLUSION

I have tried to show how debates over the pros and cons of Social Security in the West have developed at several levels of analysis. The first is the administrative-technical level: Assuming that we wish to ensure an adequate standard of living for nonworking elderly, how can this objective be achieved with the greatest efficiency and effectiveness? At this level, I have suggested that the Western preference for centralized state-administered old age security schemes is quite simple: without such provision, income security for the elderly on a mass scale would not have become available.

It is not clear that there is any logical necessity to this fact. It is possible to imagine an economy—even a market economy—in which a decentralized insurance scheme organized either by workers or employers could provide equal security at a low cost. But this imagined society would be one that was socially and economically static; one where there was little change in the structure of the economy over time, limited labor mobility and a stable demographic profile. The reason for this is that providing income security essentially implies the removal of uncertainty about future events. This is relatively easy for firms and industries whose position in the economy as a whole changes relatively slowly and in a predictable fashion, where workers remain in the same industry or firm throughout their lifetimes, and where there are no sudden changes in the ratio of workers to retirees. In a changing economy that produces "winners" and "losers" among firms and industries and where labor mobility is high, it is extremely difficult to provide income security at this level of the social structure. Indeed, imposing responsibility for income security on individual enterprises or industries may impede economic adjustment and act as a fetter on social change.

In the West, we have also seen that Social Security poses a problem for sociopolitical reasons. Income security can potentially alter capital–labor relations and set up a conflict between citizenship rights and property rights. Where the property right has been totally or partially abandoned, we would not expect to observe identical conflicts, but similar tensions may emerge in a different guise. To provide income security on a mass scale imposes a constraint on the future allocation of the social surplus. The wealth allocated in this way is fixed in advance and is simply not available either for investments or incentives that might otherwise enhance productivity. This is but one expression of a general problem in any society undergoing change—namely, how to allocate the costs associated with the dislocation that results from any major social transformation.

The creation of social rights may be seen as one device for ensuring that the costs of change are not borne disproportionately by the weak and the powerless, or that the benefits of development are not appropriated exclusively by the privileged and the powerful. The cost of social solidarity may impose short-term constraints on the development process, but it is also the case that the erosion of solidarity may impose an equal or greater cost. This is simply because it is irrational for workers to participate willingly in a process of economic modernization and rationalization that destroys their traditional way of life and generates economic insecurity. The history of Western capitalism provides ample evidence of the "costs" that result from popular resistance to the social dislocation produced by economic development. The alternative to the "costs" of income security is either the cost of the coercion and repression required to contain this resistance or economic stagnation. This is as true today as it was in the last century. New technologies and a changing international marketplace are forcing major adjustments on Western economies. Quite correctly, Western workers are greatly disturbed about the consequences of these changes for their jobs and incomes and those of their children. The result is resistance to technological innovation and political struggles to insulate national economies from the international marketplace. In effect it is insecurity, not security, that acts as a fetter on economic transformation.

NOTES

1. An early example is the Canadian Annuities Act of 1908. The intent of the act was to make available a voluntary insurance scheme for old age that did not suffer from the deficiencies of plans then available in the market. Payments neither had to be made on a regular basis nor were contracts cancelled during periods of nonpayment. However, a survey in 1915 indicated that participants were largely from among the lower professions (teachers, clergy), skilled craftsmen, and small businessmen. Laborers accounted for only 4% of sales (Guest 1985, p. 36).

2. I can illustrate this with the employer-sponsored plan at my university. In addition to the university staff required to administer the plan, the university retains an accounting firm, a bank, and two consulting companies to advise and manage the funds accumulated in the plan. By contrast, contributions to the centralized state program by university employees are managed with virtually no overhead costs.

3. Even when the firm is able to do so there is no guarantee that it will. Many firms in Canada and the United States simply retain inflation-generated wealth in order to reduce their liabilities and enhance profits.

4. Public subsidies of private pensions and retirement savings have the opposite effect, redistributing from low- to high-income earners.

5. Realization of this fact has led traditional Social Democrats to recognize the limits of the welfare state as a means to achieve a more egalitarian distribution of income.

6. It should also be apparent that such stabilization may require considerable redistribution at any given point in time—from the employed to the unemployed, from the healthy to the sick, from the young to the old. This is why cross-sectional studies of income distribution inevitably show that the final distribution of income (i.e., after transfers and taxes) is more equally distributed than the distribution of primary incomes generated by the market.

REFERENCES

Aaron, H. J. 1982. *Economic Effects of Social Security.* Washington, DC: The Brookings Institution.

Bryden, K. 1974. *Old Age Pensions and Policy-Making in Canada.* Montreal: McGill–Queen's University Press.

Coughlin, R. 1979. "Social Policy and Ideology: Public Opinion in Eight Rich Nations." *Comparative Social Research* 2: 1–40.

Davis, K., and P. Van Den Oever. 1981. "Age Relations and Public Policy in Advanced Industrial Societies. *Population and Development Review* 7(March): 1–18.

Derthick, M. 1979. *Policy-Making from Social Security.* Washington, DC: The Brookings Institution.

Easterlin, R. 1980. *Birth and Fortune.* New York: Basic Books.

Economic Council of Canada. 1979. *One in Three. Pensions for Canadians to 2030.* Ottawa: Ministry of Supply and Services.

Esping-Andersen, G. 1985. *Politics Against Markets: The Social Democratic Road to Power.* Princeton, NJ: Princeton University Press.

Graebner, W. 1980. *A History of Retirement*. New Haven, CT: Yale University Press.

Guest, D. 1985. *The Emergence of Social Security in Canada*. (2d ed.). Vancouver: University of British Columbia Press.

Heclo, H. 1974. *Modern Social Politics in Britain and Sweden: From Relief to Income Maintenance*. New Haven, CT: Yale University Press.

Macpherson, C. B. 1985. *The Rise and Fall of Economic Justice and Other Papers*. Oxford: Oxford University Press.

Marshall, T. H. 1964. *Class, Citizenship and Social Development*. Chicago: University of Chicago Press.

O'Connor, J. 1973. *The Fiscal Crisis of the State*. New York: St. Martin's Press.

Offe, C. 1984. *Contradictions of the Welfare State*. London: Hutchinson.

———. 1985. *Disorganized Capitalism*. Cambridge, MA: MIT Press.

O'Higgins, M. 1985. "Public-Private Interactions and Pensions Provision." *The Public-Private Interplay in Social Welfare,* edited by L. Rainwater and M. Rein. Armonk, NY: M. E. Sharpe.

Orloff, A. 1985. "The Politics of Pensions: A Comparative Analysis of the Origins of Pensions and Old Age Insurance in Canada, Great Britain and the United States." Unpublished doctoral dissertation. Princeton, NJ: Princeton University.

Perrin, G. 1969. "Reflections on Fifty Years of Social Security." *International Labour Review* 99(3): 249–290.

Piore, M., and C. Sabel. 1984. *The Second Industrial Divide*. New York: Basic Books.

Polanyi, K. 1944. *The Great Transformation*. Boston, MA: Beacon Press.

Rimlinger, G. 1971. *Welfare Policy and Industrialization in Europe, America and Russia*. Toronto: John Wiley.

Schulz, J. 1985. *The Economics of Aging*. (3d ed.). Belmont, CA: Wadsworth.

23

Generational Equity
and the Politics of
the Welfare State
JILL QUADAGNO

Themes of generational equity have framed recent debates about the future of
the U.S. welfare state. Jill Quadagno details the role one organization, Americans for Generational Equity (AGE), played in promoting the idea that the
problem of inadequate societal resources for children was the product of excessive benefits for the aged. Despite a well-funded and sophisticated campaign by AGE aimed at eventually turning Social Security and Medicare into
means-tested poverty programs, public support for Social Security remained
high, and politicians were not persuaded to cut Social Security. Still, as
Quadagno points out, AGE did succeed by becoming a source for media information on Social Security, and the generational equity idea became an acceptable framework for policy discussions. If future social policy changes
erode middle-class support for entitlement programs, AGE's agenda may become more politically viable.

On June 12, 1988, the U.S. House of Representatives defeated Representative Claude
Pepper's (D-Fla.) long-term home health bill. Although the bill would have extended
home health benefits to the disabled regardless of age, an article in *The New York
Times* noted that "the vote reflected a consensus that the elderly and their supporters
were being greedy" and that the defeat indicated "growing resentment of increasing
federal benefits for the elderly."[1] Further, according to *The New York Times*, "On
Capitol Hill there are increasing complaints that the elderly are casting too large a
shadow over the Congress, and receiving more than their fair share of Federal benefits
at the expense of the middle-aged and young."[2]

The significance of *The New York Times* article lies not so much in the defeat of the
bill—Congress has not created a new welfare program in a decade—but in the lan-

---

"Generational Equity and the Politics of the Welfare State" by Jill Quadagno, from *Politics and Society,* 17
(1989): 353–376. Copyright © 1989 by Sage Publications.

guage in which the defeat was portrayed. *Greedy elders. Generational conflict.* How can such terms accurately reflect public opinion when a recent Harris poll indicated that 80 percent of people in the United States supported a bill to provide home health care and that among those ages 19 to 29 support was even higher?

The concept that intergenerational inequity exists in the distribution of public benefits is not limited to this particular instance—it has become part of the public vernacular. A recent conference held at the University of Denver was entitled "Children at Risk: Who Will Support Our Aging Society?" In a similar vein, a poll sponsored by the Harvard Community Health Plan asked whether it was more important "to cover a treatment that would cure 50 very sick children" or one "that would save the lives of 1,000 people 75 years old and give them each three years of life."[3] What is disturbing here is not the response (of course 81 percent favored saving 50 sick children), but the fact that the question was posed in such a format.

What all the examples cited above reflect is the success of a single organization, Americans for Generational Equity (AGE), in shaping the parameters of public policy debates concerning social benefits for the elderly. Although *The New York Times* article cited above suggested that "the issue of conflicting interests among generations has been taken up by a nonprofit organization, Americans for Generational Equity," it was AGE, in fact, that *created* the notion that the problem of inadequate societal resources for children was a product of excessive benefits for the aged.

Who does AGE represent, what is the organization's public policy agenda, and how has AGE managed to achieve such success in structuring debates about Social Security? This article traces the development of the organization, examines its tactics, and analyzes the underlying policy agenda of the generational equity message. Understanding the tactics taken by AGE also requires some analysis of the historical developments in Social Security that explain the dynamics of public support for the program.

PUBLIC OPINION AND SOCIAL SECURITY EXPANSION

The Social Security bill that Congress approved in July 1935 provided national contributory old age (OAI) insurance for all industrial-wage workers. Although some old-age pension proponents advocated funding based on general revenues, President Franklin D. Roosevelt insisted on payroll taxes as the financing mechanism. His decision was based on the belief that U.S. citizens would readily approve of giving benefits to those who had *earned* them through contributions into the system.[4]

Although Social Security was defined as an insurance program with workers paying *premiums* for their old age, OAI was never truly designed as insurance with an actuarily sound relationship between contributions and benefits. The original act provided a greater return to poorer, recent contributors than to richer, long-term contributors. Further, in 1939 wives and widows were granted benefits, a measure that favored married workers over single workers with the same earnings record.[5]

In the long run the insurance model generated public support for Social Security, but in the 1930s public sentiment favored a flat pension for all older people, not a wage-based insurance system. Initially, workers feared that employers might keep their wages low to make up for their share of the payroll tax while reformers believed that the costs of the program would be passed on to consumers in the form of higher prices for manufactured goods. Thus while the public was pleased that Congress had passed pension legislation, public support was not strong at first, and workers had to be convinced that social insurance would benefit them.[6]

Beginning with the addition of dependents' benefits in 1939, Congress gradually expanded Social Security to include a larger proportion of the labor force and to include disability and medical benefits. By the mid-1960s the one remaining gap was in securing inflation-proof benefits. Because benefit increases were under the control of Congress, they occurred sporadically, usually right before an election. As Myles explains, "Benefits did not keep pace with the general rise in the standard of living or replace the labor market income being lost through a rising retirement rate. The combination of low benefits and a rising number of retirees was progressively pauperizing the American elderly."[7]

In 1971 the Advisory Council on Social Security reported that the program was greatly overfinanced and would produce cumulative reserves approaching $1 trillion by 2025. Projections of Social Security revenues had always been calculated on the assumption that average taxable wages would remain stable. When the council projected on the more realistic assumption of rising wage levels, they anticipated growing surpluses.

Included in the council's recommendations were automatic benefit adjustments to keep pace with price increases, liberalization of the income limit on earnings for Social Security recipients, and improved disability protection. In that same year the White House Conference on Aging had focused on the inadequate income of older people, calling for increased benefits and services.[8] Competition in an election year tempted both parties to vie for the old-age vote, and in 1972 Congress legislated the most substantive structural change in the program since 1935. It increased benefits by 20 percent, indexed benefits to inflation (COLAs) and maximum taxable wages to future wage movements, and abandoned the level-wage assumption.[9] The 1972 amendments represented a turning point for Social Security, a watershed for U.S. welfare-state development. The automatic cost-of-living increases removed benefits from politics and ensured older people that inflation would not erode the value of those benefits.

By the mid-1970s more than 80 percent of those over age 65 were receiving some income from Social Security.[10] Social Security also helped widows and widowers with dependent children and provided income security for the disabled. Social Security was one of the few government programs where people received something tangible for their taxes, and as a result public support for Social Security was high. Virtually every public opinion poll between 1977 and 1983 indicated that U.S. citizens supported Social Security.[11] The 1972 amendments had solidly incorporated the middle class into the welfare state.

THE REAGAN REVOLUTION

The Realignment of Welfare-State Politics

When Ronald Reagan was elected president in 1980, he initiated a series of public cuts directed at every social program. In 1981 Congress enacted the Omnibus Budget Reconciliation Act, which eliminated the entire public service jobs program and removed 400,000 individuals from the food stamp program.[12] Cuts directed at Social Security focused on the politically vulnerable: the elimination of the minimum benefit for low-income earners, an end to the modest death benefits for most recipients, and a phasing out of benefits for older children of deceased workers.[13] Congress legislated these cuts in mid-1981 with only minimum objections.

A more sweeping proposal aimed at Social Security that Reagan unveiled at the same time the welfare cuts slid through Congress touched off a storm of controversy. Its main recommendations were a 10 percent cut in future benefits, a 31 percent cut in early retirement benefits, and a further narrowing of eligibility for disability.[14] This second set of cuts attacked middle-class entitlements and reprisals were swift and harsh. Save Our Security, an organization formed in 1979 to fight President Carter's Social Security package, expanded its membership from less than 25 elderly groups to over 100. Days after Reagan's proposal appeared his public approval rating dropped 16 points.[15] In two congressional elections held after the Reagan proposals, Ohio Republican Michael Oxley barely held onto a seat that Republicans had occupied since the 1930s and a secure Mississippi Republican seat went to the Democrats.[16]

Although Social Security's appeal to middle-class voters made the program appear invincible, concern over a deteriorating economy and accelerating inflation also created middle-class resentment over a growing tax burden.[17] The very issues that welded the Republican party and the middle-class voter to the promarket agenda that had won the Republicans the election fractured the Democrats. The two-tiered structure of social programs in the United States—means-tested welfare versus universal entitlements—divided the poor from working-class Democrats, who came to resent the welfare burden when their earning power was eroding.[18] Economic stagnation had undermined the fragile consensus behind Democratic spending programs.

By contrast, the Republicans were able to capitalize on the dissatisfaction of both working and middle-class voters, focusing on discontent over government tax and spending policies. Supply-side economists attacked the state spending and tax system that discouraged the production of goods and services, arguing that a tax cut would encourage savings, investment, and work. With additional supplies of labor, inflation could be controlled and sustained growth continued.[19] The resultant tax cut reduced taxes for corporations and upper-income groups while leaving middle-class entitlements intact.[20]

The 1983 Amendments to the Social Security Act

Supply-side economic policy quickly lost its appeal as it illustrated its ineffectiveness in resolving the nation's economic woes. Budget deficits expanded after the 1981 tax cuts and economic growth came to a halt as the Federal Reserve Board tightened the money supply to control inflation.[21] Rather than resolving the problem of declining U.S. competitiveness, supply-side economics only exacerbated it. Instead of blaming supply-side economics, however, business attributed the skyrocketing deficit to federal entitlement programs. According to *Business Week*:

Entitlements . . . have been indexed to the cost of living. But the cost of such protection is proving to be a burden that the rest of the nation can no longer carry. No lasting solution to the deficit crisis is possible without tempering the explosive growth of Social Security and Medicare.[22]

Social Security reached its low point on November 5, 1982, when it was forced to borrow $581 million from its companion funds to pay benefit checks on time, a measure that was repeated twice in the next 13 months. If some resolution was not achieved by July 3, 1983, benefit checks would be delayed for the first time in the program's history.[23] The drain on the Social Security trust fund resulted from the deeper economic woes of the nation, but the justification for program cuts reframed the parameters of the debate. Rather than portraying Social Security as the victim of a failing economy, it now became the source of the budget deficit.

Even before the Reagan economic package of budget cuts, tax cuts, and defense increases was passed by Congress, Budget Director David Stockman's computer estimates indicated that the results of these measures would create a huge deficit that would grow even larger in the future. Further, drastic cuts in social programs would make only minimal reductions in the anticipated deficit, and since Reagan refused to consider reductions in defense spending, Social Security appeared to be the only answer.[24]

Stockman's attempt to cut Social Security by blaming it for the federal deficit failed, and in the 1982 elections the Democrats capitalized on public anger over Reagan's proposed Social Security cuts. In such a highly politicized atmosphere, all Social Security debate came to a halt, preventing Congress from reaching an agreement on how to restore the trust fund to solvency. With Congress stalemated, the only hope for reform lay with the bipartisan National Commission on Social Security Reform, appointed by Reagan the previous year. The commission held its first meeting in February 1982. Conservative members (who represented the interests of a number of business organizations) advocated benefit cuts, while liberals (taking the stance favored by organized labor and senior citizen organizations) pressed for tax increases. After a lengthy negotiation period during which a few of the commission members held secret meetings in hopes of reaching a compromise, a proposal was put before Congress. The package included a six-month COLA delay, increased tax rates, the inclusion of federal workers, and the taxation of benefits for upper-income retirees.[25] The 1983 amendments also included four measures designed to curb early retirement:

1. A greater penalty for retiring before age 65 (from 80 percent of benefits to 75 percent by 2005 and to 70 percent by 2022),
2. A gradual increase in the age for full benefits from 65 to 67,
3. An increased bonus to defer retirement, and
4. A lower penalty for continuing to work on a reduced basis while in receipt of retired worker benefits.[26]

Thus the 1983 amendments represented a compromise of benefit cuts and tax increases, not only directed toward stabilizing the trust fund but also likely to impact the future labor supply and unemployment rates.

Until the 1980s perceptions of Social Security originated primarily within the confines of the state bureaucracy, as Social Security administrators promulgated the view that the program was analogous to private insurance. Public understanding of Social Security was premised on the insurance metaphor. As Derthick notes: "Taxes became 'premiums' or 'contributions.' Workers had 'old age insurance accounts' in Baltimore. They were paying for their insurance for their old age."[27]

In the years prior to 1983 the insurance model came to haunt Social Security. Because the insurance model was designed to protect the program by guaranteeing public support during a period when people were suspicious of benefits that were not *earned*, the lack of public knowledge of how Social Security really operated became a weapon against it. If most contributors believed that each had an account in Baltimore, then the notion that their accounts were nearly drained was bound to cause uncertainty. In fact the term *actuarily unsound* simply means that projected expenditures exceed projected revenues "to a degree that would be unacceptable in the marketplace."[28] The soundness of the system depends solely on the state's ability to collect taxes, not on some actuarial criterion. By 1982, however, opinion polls indicated that only 8 percent of the public had "complete confidence" that Social Security would have the money to pay their benefits.[29] Given this basic misunderstanding of how Social Security actually operates, it is no wonder that public confidence could be so easily undermined by an apparently depleted trust fund.

By 1987 Social Security taxes not only covered current benefits but also added $67 billion to the reserve fund.[30] The growth of the trust fund, estimated to reach $6.9 trillion by 2015, eliminated the crisis rhetoric as a source of vulnerability but opened the program to attack on another front. The trust fund *crisis* of the early 1980s had not only unmasked the false insurance metaphor but had also generated uncertainty about its value as a source of protection for the program.

The undoing of the insurance metaphor created an opening for other groups, aside from program bureaucrats, to shape public perceptions of Social Security. Reconstructing Social Security as an intergenerational tax rather than an insurance program became the goal for program opponents, and under the guise of *generational equity*, a new attack was launched. The generational equity theme as an attack on Social Security originated in the business community, whose message was spread through an organization, Americans for Generational Equity (AGE), under the jurisdiction of a few representatives. Thus generational equity moved from the private sector to the state.

THE ISSUE OF GENERATIONAL EQUITY

Defining the Parameters of the Debate

The attack on Social Security based on generational conflict had begun in the early 1970s as part of the business community's response to the 1972 tax hike and benefit increases. A 1972 analysis of the Social Security system published by the Federal Reserve Bank of New York described it as a "huge Ponzi scheme" that depended on the power of the tax collector to extract increasing taxes from already overtaxed workers.[31] The funding problems the system faced in the late 1970s and early 1980s honed the argument. Bendix Corporation chairman William Agee direly predicted that:

Procrastinating until the burden forces the breaching of the promises will only make the problem worse. Young and old will be pitted against one another in a fearful battle over the remains of a shrinking economy.[32]

By 1982 *Fortune* magazine warned its readers: "It is part of the sorrowful lot of the baby boom generation that it will have to finance both its parents' retirement and a substantial portion of its own."[33]

Although such statements may have reduced confidence in Social Security, they were ineffectual in lessening support for the program, because most of the public did not understand the basic premise of the generational equity theme—that the taxes of today's workers were supporting today's retirees. They still believed that they were paying contributions into an insured account. Convincing the public that the baby boomers' future was in jeopardy thus first required demythologizing the insurance metaphor. In 1982 *Forbes* magazine informed its readers that "the Social Security taxes that are deducted from your pay are not insurance premiums—they are taxes."[34] That same year former Nixon cabinet member Peter G. Peterson reiterated the message, declaring "This view—probably the most damaging myth of all—bears no relation to reality."[35] Even clearer was a statement in *The New Republic*:

We have been banging home the point that Social Security *is* primarily a redistribution scheme, rather than an insurance program, in order to get liberals to evaluate it on its merits, not on the myths. Perhaps it is true that the myths are essential to Social Security's support or, to put it more crudely, that we must bribe the middle class in order to preserve a program that also benefits the poor.[36]

Demythologizing the insurance metaphor was then coupled with a new critique of Social Security. Under the banner of generational equity the message was simple: the generosity of entitlements to the old created poverty among children. "The old," Phillip Longman wrote, "have come to insist that the young not only hold them harmless for their past profligacy, but sacrifice their own prosperity to pay for it."[37] Because of entitlements, older people, only 7 percent of whom were in poverty in 1982 according to Longman's calculations, were taking resources from the young and were squandering the nation's limited wealth rather than investing in future economic growth. In contrast, by 1982 23 percent of children were in poverty, and funding for programs that supported children had been subject to budget cuts as expenditures for the aged increased. Responsibility for the expanding national debt, in Longman's view, also fell on the shoulders of the old who now held political power. Thus the old had seized political power and expanded the national debt "to satisfy the appetites of the present at the expense of the young and of future generations."[38]

The attack on entitlements became formalized in 1984 when Senator Dave Durenberger (R-Minn.), one of the three leading recipients of corporate PAC money in the 1982 elections, founded Americans for Generational Equity (AGE).[39] Durenberger's management intern, Paul Hewitt, became president and executive director and Phillip Longman was brought on board as research director.[40] In its first year in operation, AGE had attracted 600 members and had a budget of $88,000. By 1987 AGE revenues had increased to $367,316, with most of the funding coming from Social Security and Medicare's prime private-sector competitors: banks, insurance companies, defense contractors, and health care corporations, a total of 85 organizations and businesses.[41] And what is AGE's goal?

> To promote the concept of generational equity among America's political, intellectual and financial leaders. . . . The more America's leaders talk about and think in terms of generational equity, the more effective AGE will be in its education program, and the better chance we will have of making the difference on crucial legislative issues.[42]

AGE's aim is simple: to reframe the parameters of the Social Security debate and ultimately alter social policy.

In his keynote address at a conference held at the University of Minnesota on January 13, 1987, Senator Durenberger espoused the AGE theme: "We have entered an era in which the date of one's birth has become the prime determinate of one's prospects for realizing the American dream. Younger Americans—regardless of their class or ethnic origin—are in the grip of what seems like a permanent and compounding downward spiral."[43] Included among AGE's topics of concern were Medicare reform, educational priorities, savings and investment policy, deficit reduction options, and "a national strategy for the Baby Boom generation's retirement."

Representative Jim Moody (D-Wisc.), AGE co-chairman, who hails from a district that has reelected him on the argument that money belongs in the hands of the disadvantaged, also found a constituency in the AGE campaign. At a speech to the Allied Council of Senior Citizens in Milwaukee, Moody claimed that "many people receiving Social Security benefits are better off than those taxed to pay them. The federal deficit is out of control, and the young are too heavily taxed; everyone must sacrifice; Social Security must be curbed."[44]

In its *Generational Journal* AGE also published articles appealing to antipoverty liberals. One such article focused on the problems of inner-city schools espousing "quality education for all children by the year 2000." Another article in the same issue addressed the problem of health insurance for the poor.[45] Thus the theme of AGE publications suggested that the poor were the victims of misappropriated societal funds, which went disproportionately to the aged.

AGE was able to expound a thesis that crossed party lines by capitalizing on the fractured class interests that had split the Democratic party and turned working-class Democrats into Republicans. By focusing on middle-class discontent over the growing tax burden, the AGE theme had appeal for young, educated Republicans. At the same time the emphasis on the penalty poor children were paying aroused the resentment of low-income groups in traditional Democratic strongholds over the loss of welfare benefits. To maintain their constituency's support, Democrats from poor districts found the attack on entitlements enticing. This combination of a conservative ideology, attached to legitimate concerns of antipoverty liberals, gave AGE the political capital to build a broader coalition than one based solely on a narrow right-wing agenda dedicated to attacking entitlements.

The Strategy of AGE

Initially perceived as an organization dedicated to abolishing Social Security or, worse, "a new kind of yuppie lobby," AGE worked at changing its image to an organization "pursuing a constructive, responsible program."[46] By 1987 AGE president James Jones was able to reassure organization members:

> (Our) third year represented a coming of age for this small public education group. Our programs had awakened literally millions of Americans to the political and social implications of the aging of America. . . . It took a while, but in 1987 AGE found that it had begun to make supporters out of those who had previously been critics.[47]

So successful was AGE in its strategy that in the two weeks after the stock market crash of October 1988, AGE was contacted for interviews or background information by NBC, CBS, PBS, *The New York Times, The Wall Street Journal, Newsweek, Time, U.S. News and World Report, Fortune, Forbes,* the *Chicago Tribune,* and the *Des Moines Register.*[48]

How did AGE manage to accomplish this image change? The organization's strategy included a number of tactics designed to enhance its credibility and provide a public forum. First AGE expanded its boundaries beyond the narrow "yuppie" fringe of staff, adding a board of directors and an advisory board consisting of representatives from such right-wing think tanks as the Hoover Institution, the Heritage Foundation, and the American Enterprise Institute; it also added more moderate conservatives, officers from banks, life insurance companies and health care corporations, and a few academics from prestigious institutions, including Donald Kennedy and Michael Boskin of Stanford University, Samuel Preston of the University of Pennsylvania, and others. AGE also expanded its political base by establishing a bipartisan congressional advisory council.[49] By 1987 AGE could proclaim among its advisors former chief actuary of the Social Security Administration, Robert Myers.[50]

A second AGE strategy was to sponsor a series of conferences, which brought in a wider array of mainstream intellectuals. The first, held in 1986, on the "Baby Boom Generation's Retirement," was followed by three in 1987 and three more in 1988 on such topics as growth and productivity, Medicare reform, deficits and demographics, and downward mobility in America.[51] AGE's Autumn 1987 conference, "Ties That Bind: Debts, Deficits, and Demographics," specifically addressed the impact of Social Security on the private savings rate, a topic of concern to banks and savings and loan institutions.[52] The conferences enhanced the credibility of the organization, while providing a public forum for AGE.

As AGE moved into the mainstream political agenda, it sponsored more covert tactics. On January 18, 1988, AGE members received a letter from Tom Rodman, marketing vice-president with Smith Barney in New York, warning that "our children's future is going to explode," because of the huge budget deficit. Budget-cutting efforts have failed, according to Rodman, because of continued growth in entitlement programs: "Our children should burn their Social Security cards today." Rodman suggested that each AGE member find five friends who would "send one snapshot of a child—any child—to their five elected officials" along with a letter asking to "put entitlement spending reform back on the table."[53] The Rodman letter was accompanied by a memo from Paul Hewitt encouraging AGE members to respond.[54]

Finally, AGE sought to get its message out through a series of books, articles, and op-ed pieces. A 1985 *Atlantic Monthly* article by Phillip Longman expanded the AGE message to incorporate several new themes. First it revived the *crisis* scenario under a new guise. Although the Social Security trust fund was no longer insolvent and was, in fact, accumulating reserves, the system was still in trouble, because Congress was likely to adopt interfund borrowing to reduce the anticipated deficit in the Medicare trust fund.[55] Depending on how quickly Medicare exhausted its reserves, the trust fund could go broke anyway. Second, Americans were warned that future benefits would be less generous, with the result that most baby boomers would pay more into the system than they would collect.[56] And third, since recent poverty statistics indicated that the elderly as a group had a higher standard of living than the working population, there was no need to subsidize them so generously.[57]

The increased budget deficit and reports of a declining relative level of economic growth in the United States in the mid-1980s provided further fuel for attacks on Social Security, and AGE arguments focused more on economic issues. The month prior to the stock market crash, Peter G. Peterson, now research director for AGE, published an article in *Atlantic Monthly* coupling the generational equity message with broader economic issues. Peterson warned that as a result of feeble productivity growth, we have "witnessed a widening split between the elderly, among whom poverty is still declining, and children and young families, among whom poverty rates have exploded—a development with dire implications for our future productivity."[58] Although the public, according to Peterson, endorsed smaller and leaner government, federal spending increased significantly between 1979 and 1986, with most of the growth concentrated in middle-class entitlements, which had grown from 5.4 percent in 1965 to 11.5 percent of GNP.[59] By contrast, federal spending for America's public infrastructure, for research and development in industry (R&D), education, job skills, and remedial social services has been cut.[60]

From a list of suggestions for rectifying the sorry state of the U.S. economy, Peterson gave highest priority to slowing the growth of nonmeans-tested entitlements by cutting the cost-of-living adjustment in Social Security to 60 percent of the consumer price index, further raising the retirement age, lowering initial benefits to the affluent, and taxing benefits in excess of contributions.[61]

Less than two months after the publication of the Peterson article, A. Haeworth Robertson, former chief actuary of the Social Security Administration and AGE advisory board member, published a widely circulated op-ed piece, lauding 1988 presidential candidates Pete DuPont and Pat Robertson (both of whom were not long for the race despite AGE's endorsement) as the only announced candidates "courageous enough . . . to warn the public that all is not well with Social Security."[62] DuPont argued for allowing individuals to voluntarily receive tax-credit-funded investments in trade for proportionate reductions in Social Security benefits; Pat Robertson argued for privatizing the system.[63] "There is no reason," concluded Haeworth Robertson, "for this country to continue with a social insurance system that is controversial, constantly on the verge of financial collapse and out of phase with the times."[64]

The Impact of AGE

Has AGE had a discernible impact on Social Security? In terms of the social insurance program, AGE has had no impact. Congress has legislated no policy changes since 1983, and Social Security benefits are not likely to become a part of the budget-cutting agenda. However, Senator Durenberger has used his influence as chairman of the Health Subcommittee of the Senate Finance Committee to ensure that under the Medicare Catastrophic Coverage Act of 1988, the financing of the new benefits would be borne totally by persons eligible for Medicare. As Durenberger proclaimed, "For the first time, we are income testing part of the social insurance program. . . . Medicare insurance costs will be paid for by those who receive the benefits. In other words, this law will not penalize one generation for the sake of another."[65] The significance of this policy change—implemented with a generational equity message—can hardly be overstated. The new Medicare legislation represents the first successful attempt to desocialize an entitlement program.

In the long run, however, the more significant impact of AGE than this single piece of legislation may be its influence in reshaping the parameters of the debate so that all future policy choices will have to take generational equity into account. In addition to the articles cited above, AGE directors and staff have published articles in the *Washington Post*, *The New York Times*, *USA Today*, and *Newsday*. Its message has clearly spread, for as AGE has gained credibility, other politicians have cautiously echoed the AGE message. Senator Jack Danforth (R-Mo.) told an audience of trustees from children's hospitals that 35 percent of the federal budget goes for programs directed at the elderly while only 2 percent is spent on education. "The decision we've made as a country," declared Danforth, "is that our children come last."[66] Similarly, Representative Anthony Beilenson (D-Calif.) declared that Social Security should be included in deficit-reduction negotiations because "retired persons as a class are not worse off than other groups of Americans."[67]

That this message is being taken seriously is indicated by its influence on the media. A July 5, 1987, article in the *Washington Post* entitled "Fooling Around" claimed that "not only are today's young workers facing an insecure retirement, but they are being asked to fund more than their share of government."[68] In a similar vein *The Wall Street Journal* approvingly cited the Robertson article, concluding that "major reforms of Social Security cannot be ducked indefinitely. . . . Either policymakers will have to slash benefits or raise payroll taxes to undreamed of levels."[69]

It was not only business that was perpetuating the AGE message, however, for by 1987 the liberal magazine *The New Republic* launched a series of articles echoing the AGE philosophy. As the critique of Social Security gained credibility, the rhetoric became more heated.[70] By 1988 the attack had shifted from entitlement programs to older people. As Henry Fairlie proclaimed, "Something is wrong with a society that is willing to drain itself to foster such an unproductive section of its population, one that does not even promise (as children do) one day to be productive."[71]

Despite the proliferation of the generational equity theme, public support for entitlements remains high. A 1987 survey conducted for the American Association of Retired Persons concludes that there are "no signs of waning support for programs targeted for the elderly." Even among young adults (aged 21 to 29), 77 percent believe the government should spend more money on Medicare, 74 percent favor higher Social Security benefits, and 76 percent say the government is "not doing enough for older people."[72]

AGE's goal, however, has not been to undermine public support for Social Security so much as it has been aimed at providing a forum for attacks on entitlements within a particular framework of how production and distribution operates. Portrayed as a struggle between generations over scarce societal resources, what AGE actually espouses is a promarket policy, which would have the impact of reconstituting the labor market.

THE GENERATIONAL EQUITY WELFARE STATE

To understand the impact of the generational equity welfare state on the economy, we must reanalyze the arguments being put forth. Essentially, the AGE message revolves around the idea that Social Security is bad for the economy, because it removes capital from the marketplace where it could be used to stimulate economic growth. This argument implies that welfare policies are external or supplementary to the economy rather than constitutive of it. If we begin with a different assumption, namely that welfare policies create labor markets, then the meaning of the generational equity proposals changes significantly. Instead of representing pro-child policies, they may be analyzed by their potential labor market impact.

The idea that welfare policy helps shape labor markets was most clearly articulated by Polanyi, who described how the English Speenhamland Act of 1795, which provided relief to supplement wages, had the effect of lowering wages and productivity and discouraging migration to urban areas. By eliminating such wage subsidies, the poor law reform of 1834 reduced impediments to labor mobility, obliged the poor to work, and thus allowed industrial capitalism to flourish.[73]

Prior to 1935 the United States had what might best be termed a *social assistance* welfare state, that is, a welfare state for the poor "designed to allow individuals to subsist when the main breadwinner fell out of the labor market through unemployment, sickness, disability or old age."[74] The meager relief available to the aged poor was administered through local poor law authorities, who relied on means tests and drew heavily on the distinction between the *deserving* and *undeserving* poor.[75]

With the passage of the Social Security Act of 1935, the United States began the transition to a *social security* welfare state, "not an anti-poverty welfare state but rather (one) designed to ensure continuity of living standards over the ups and downs of the economic life cycle."[76] Instead of providing subsistence to the poor, it provides wage stabilization to the working and middle class. A social security welfare state accomplishes this through two novel principles: universality and wage replacement. Under the universality principle benefits become entitlements or earned benefits that cannot be reduced or eliminated at the discretion of local authorities. The principle of wage replacement means not merely that benefits are linked to past earnings but rather that benefit levels are guaranteed to be sufficient to allow individuals to maintain continuity of living standards.

The type of labor markets constituted under a social security welfare state differ from those of a social assistance welfare state. Rather than maintaining a manipulable labor force of low-wage workers, wage security guarantees are constituted around the needs of a mass-production economy to maintain steady rates of consumption. By smoothing out the flow of income over the economic lifecycle of individuals and families, a social security welfare state ensures high and stable levels of mass consumption.[77] Thus it is consonant with Keynesian economic policy.

For older people the transition to a *social security* welfare state was accomplished in stages. The first to gain full benefits were mass-production workers in the core sector of the economy, who negotiated supplementary private pension benefits in the post-World War II era while public pensions remained low.[78] After 1972 all Social Security beneficiaries were granted a measure of income security when Congress legislated significant benefit increases and guaranteed cost-of-living adjustments in benefits.

Despite these improvements, a core of old-age poverty remained. Unevenly distributed through the older population, the aged poor consisted primarily of older women, particularly single heads of households, and minorities. By 1987 the central feature distinguishing the aged poor from the more affluent was access to a second pension; and the key factor that reduced the availability of second pensions to most women and minority workers was employment in the service sector of the economy. While 50 to 60 percent of workers in manufacturing were covered by second pensions, in the trade and service sectors, where women are concentrated, only about 20 to 40 percent of workers had pension coverage.[79] For these citizens, the welfare state remained a social assistance welfare state of the prewar era.

The generational equity plan would not eliminate Social Security but rather would return the entire program to the social assistance model. A start toward this goal could be accomplished by either reducing or eliminating COLAs,[80] raising the retirement age, and encouraging private insurance through tax policy so that "Social Security and Medicare might be replaced gradually. . . ."[81] Universal rights to benefits would be replaced by means testing, which would require returning eligibility decisions to local authorities.[82] What would be left would be "generous public provision for the elderly poor" over age 70.[83] Reagan's so-called safety net would be the only remnant of the Social Security program.

AGE, quite simply, is advocating a return to a poor law welfare state. The universal Social Security program, legislated in 1935 by President Franklin Delano Roosevelt and expanded in subsequent years to incorporate more people and cover more needs, would be gone. In its place would be a social assistance type of Social Security, providing only subsistence benefits.

What are the implications of such an agenda? The most certain impact of a return to a social assistance model for old-age security would be to increase the labor-force participation rates of older people. With fewer of the aged guaranteed benefits at adequate wage replacement levels, there would be no option for many but to work. Although increased labor-force participation by older people is not necessarily a negative impact, the real issue is *who* would have to work and what kind of jobs would be available for them. In recent decades the basic shift in the U.S. economy has been from mass production to services. While the economy has grown, nearly all the growth has come in the service sector with no expansion in goods production. Among the many new jobs generated in the 1980s, most were in service-sector jobs paying less than the median wage while the number of high stratum jobs declined. As a result mean earnings and real hourly wages also declined.[84]

Although middle-aged workers have been relatively protected from these trends, it is the new entrants to the labor market, young men and women, who have ended up in the low-wage jobs.[85] The focus on young people, however, ignores a second transition that is also occurring—the reentry of formerly retired workers into the labor force. Since 1972 there has been a significant trend toward labor force reentry for both men and women after age 55, with those in secondary occupations (that is, low-wage, unskilled, low-status jobs) most likely to experience reentry. All older labor force reentrants, regardless of previous labor force location, however, are likely to spend their post-retirement second careers in secondary jobs.[86]

Because workers in the core manufacturing sector of the economy already retire even before reaching the minimum benefit age of 62, the impact on this diminishing segment of the U.S. economy would be relatively less than it would be on others. Further mass-production workers in unionized core industries would work to negotiate increases in private-pension agreements to make up the difference in Social Security reductions. Most vulnerable would be present service-sector workers, primarily women, those presently without private-pension coverage and already heavily represented in that sector of the economy where a labor shortage is developing.[87]

Although AGE arguments about the changing demographic structure of the United States are focused on the unfairness of the present Social Security structure to the *third generation*, the more persistent message is that the labor supply of the future will be inadequate to support the economic benefits guaranteed to the aged. Reducing benefits to the aged would only shift the burden from government to families unless other changes occurred as well. By eliminating universality and reducing wage replacements, the AGE Social Security system would induce greater participation by older people in the labor market. The argument suggests that with reduced benefits available at later ages only to those who qualified through means tests, the subsistence wages in low-wage service industries would become a more attractive income supplement than they are presently.

AGE proponents encapsulate advocacy for increasing the labor force participation of older people within a rejection of Keynesianism. According to Longman, age-based entitlements were enacted under the premise that paying the elderly to consume "would stimulate the economy and provide more jobs for younger workers." Such a goal was justifiable "in an era of massive unemployment and surplus capacity." But in an aging society with a declining industrial base,

It makes no sense to promote consumption or to encourage idleness. . . . Today the United States needs the talent and experience of its older citizens. As the baby boom generation ages and the pool of younger workers shrinks we will need the contributions of the elderly still more. . . . We cannot afford to promise today's elderly or our future selves, that for the last 20–25 percent of adult life we will all be automatically entitled to subsidized consumption and be free from labor.[88]

Keynesian economic theory provided the ideological justification for the development of the welfare state. Thus it is not surprising to find anti-Keynesianism as a source of attack for molding public opinion against Social Security.

EVALUATING THE AGE MESSAGE

The AGE message also contains serious internal flaws ranging from such narrow but significant issues as the erroneous reporting of spending patterns to skewed predictions about future population growth. Let us first examine the relationship between federal revenues and expenditures in the 1980s.

Between 1981 and 1984 total federal revenues fell marginally in real dollars while outlays rose by 14 percent. This imbalance was reflected in the near doubling of the federal deficit in those years. The increase in federal spending was accompanied by a shift in the composition of expenditures. AGE advocates are correct in arguing that relatively less has been spent on human resources, but the greatest increase has been in defense and on interest on the federal debt, not on middle-class entitlements. If federal outlays are broken down into their specific program components, the relative costs are quite apparent. Between 1981 and 1985 the percent of federal outlays for Social Security (OASDI) declined from 21 to 19.7, while in those same years the percent for defense spending increased from 24.2 to 26.7 and on net interest from 10 to 13.8 percent. Further, the Congressional Budget Office projected the percent of federal spending for Social Security to decline during the rest of the decade.[89] The only entitlement program to increase was Medicare; between 1981 and 1985 the proportion of federal outlays for Medicare and Medicaid combined increased from 8.6 to 9.8 percent. By contrast, outlays for means-tested programs—which include AFDC, the only source of public support for poor children—declined from 5.8 to 4.6 percent.[90]

AGE advocates also claim that R&D has suffered because entitlement programs have consumed what little growth increment remains in the 1980s. This argument ignores the fact that since World War II, 80 percent of R&D funds in the United States have gone into defense. Further, in nondefense industries corporations have used capital expenditures to expand acquisitions of existing facilities in diverse product and service lines rather than spending for R&D. The result has been the creation of huge conglomerates of unrelated products and services. In 1979 alone U.S. corporations made acquisitions totalling $40 billion, more than the total spent on R&D by all private firms in the country.[91] When U.S. corporations have made technological advances in domestic R&D, they have sold massive amounts of advanced technology abroad.[92] If the competitive position of the United States is declining relative to other nations in technological advances due to a lack of R&D, Social Security is hardly to blame.

AGE proponents also err in using the ratio of those over 65 to the total population rather than including the proportion of children under 18 in their calculations. This measure ignores the fact that the ratio of young/old to total population was less favorable in the 1960s and 1970s than projections for that ratio throughout the next 50 years. AGE concerns about an inadequate labor force to fund Social Security in the twenty-first century are based on projections that presume static or declining labor-force participation rates by women and older people and that ignore the increase in the labor supply likely to result from increased immigration rates.[93]

To what extent is the demographic panic fostered by AGE justified? As demographer Samuel Preston points out, between 1960 and 1982 lower fertility and a decline in old-age mortality reduced the proportion of the population under age 15 by 28 percent compared to a 28.4 percent increase in the over-65 population in the same period.[94] Certainly population change alone is no cause for alarm, but Preston notes certain consequences, which he attributes to demographic change. First, between 1970 and 1982 the incidence of poverty among the elderly declined substantially, while the incidence of poverty among children increased to more than 25 percent. Second, in that same period expenditures for the aged grew rapidly, whereas the share of public funding for children declined. According to Preston, these trends are partially due to the political impact of a powerful constituency supporting the expansion of programs for the elderly and the lack of a constituency supporting programs for children, particularly educational programs.[95]

Certainly, the above statistics are factually accurate, and there is no doubt that the incorporation of the middle class into a generous benefit program that has significantly improved the economic security of the aged is a source of both support for and expansion of Social Security. It is highly misleading, however, to presume any causal relationship between the improved status of the aged and the declining economic security of children. The same pattern exists in Sweden, where the level of poverty is very low both absolutely and relative to other countries, and where public sentiment supports a wide array of welfare programs for all ages. Between 1976 and 1980 the rates of poverty among children declined only slightly from 7.5 percent to 6.8 percent in Sweden whereas poverty among the elderly was reduced from 8.9 percent to 1.5 percent.[96] The reason poverty rates have declined for older people but not for children in both nations is that the incomes of families with children depend on wages to a much larger extent than do the households of the aged. The large increase in poverty among children in the United States is a result of the increase in female-headed households during the 1970s, and the inability of women in these households to support their families adequately. The low earning power of women, in turn, is a consequence of a sex-segregated labor force, in which more than half of the traditionally female jobs pay wages below poverty level.[97] The problem is not a function of demography but of the failure of U.S. public policy to support families, particularly families headed by women.

Compared to most European nations, the aged in the United States still represent a relatively small proportion of the population, yet no other country has raised the issue of generation equity. Why has this theme appeared only in the United States? The answer lies in the very lack of public programs for children to which Preston points. Other nations have an array of social policies that support families across the entire life course, including state-subsidized maternity leave, family allowances, state-subsidized day care, national health insurance, and training and job-placement programs for single mothers. Such programs reduce poverty over the lifecycle for all age groups and improve the earning capacity of women. The only family policies in the United States are Social Security and AFDC.[98] Little wonder that Social Security stands out so distinctly in the national budget, a highly visible target for conservative attacks.

Like other welfare programs, Social Security represents a share of the national wage bill that has been removed from the market and brought under the democratic political process. Although the program reflects market principles in the sense that benefits are tied to past contributions, it also redistributes income from high to low wage earners and makes allowances for need in the form of supplements for dependents. As such it is a form of state intervention that reduces the power of capital, for democratic control over wage and capital formation is the antithesis of capitalist control over wage and capital formation. As Myles notes, "The principal beneficiary of this shift is labor; the principal losers are the owners and managers of capital. The result is not an intergenerational *class struggle* but simply an expression of the traditional struggle between capital and labor."[99] If AGE were to succeed in restructuring Social Security into a poverty program, it would mean a significant reduction in the social wage, a victory for capital over citizen control of a portion of the national wage bill.

CONCLUSION

AGE has been markedly unsuccessful in undermining public support for Social Security or in having politicians take seriously the idea of reducing entitlement benefits, because Social Security has provided real benefits, not only for the poor, but for the middle class. AGE has succeeded in several arenas, however: it has become a media source for information on Social Security, the thesis of generational equity has forced senior citizen advocates to respond in kind, and the generational equity idea has become an acceptable framework for policy discussions. Equally significant, the sole piece of welfare legislation added to the public agenda since AGE was organized desocialized a major entitlement program by taxing only the elderly to pay for the benefits. Public support for Social Security presently remains high. Yet both the 1983 amendments, which taxed benefits of higher-income retirees and raised the future retirement age, and the Medicare Catastrophic Coverage Act of 1988, which laid the tax burden on the high-income aged, may lessen the sense of middle-class entitlement and possibly erode middle-class support. Should this scenario occur, then the AGE agenda represents a possible alternative should program changes become politically possible.

Although AGE purports to be an organization dedicated to improving the lot of poor children, it proposes no policies to reach this goal. Children are poor because they live in households headed by women whose earning capacity is limited. The lack of social provisions for women exacerbates the problem of low-wage work. Social Security is the only benefit program that has succeeded in significantly reducing poverty among one segment of the population. As such, it should serve as a model in creating other programs offering support throughout the lifecycle, programs that would attract a solid political base because they would offer real benefits to resolve the problems of families in poverty.

Senator Durenberger has asserted that "the assumption that each working generation will take care of the one that preceded it is finished."[100] Yet the concept of children caring for their aging parents has been an enduring facet of both western and eastern cultures for centuries. What AGE is attempting to undo is the socialization of the costs of such care across the generations and return it to the private sphere. Its success thus far can be attributed to its ability to obscure this right-wing agenda by building a broader coalition that speaks to the legitimate unmet needs of the poor.

NOTES

1. "Aid to Elderly Divides Young, Old, and Politicians," *The New York Times* (June 23, 1988):1a.

2. Ibid.

3. "Children Are Priority, Health Survey Shows," *The Philadelphia Inquirer* (February 7, 1988): 3a.

4. Martha Derthick, *Policymaking for Social Security* (Washington, D.C.: Brookings Institution, 1979), p. 230.

5. Edward Berkowitz, "The First Advisory Council and the 1939 Amendments," in *Social Security After Fifty, Success and Failure*, ed. Edward Berkowitz (Westport, Conn.: Greenwood Press, 1987), p. 58.

6. Jill Quadagno, *The Transformation of Old Age Security, Class and Politics in the American Welfare State* (Chicago: University of Chicago Press, 1988), p. 119.

7. John Myles, "Postwar Capitalism and the Extension of Social Security into a Retirement Wage," in *The Politics of Social Policy in the United States*, eds. Margaret Weir, Ann Shola Orloff, and Theda Skocpol (Princeton, N.J.: Princeton University Press, 1988), p. 273.

8. Andrew Achenbaum, *Social Security, Visions and Revisions* (Cambridge, Eng.: Cambridge University Press, 1985), p. 58; Myles, "Postwar Capitalism," p. 274.

9. Derthick, *Policymaking for Social Security*, p. 259.

10. Although the replacement rate in Social Security is higher return to low-income earners, basing benefits on past earning still penalizes women and minorities, whose average benefits are lower than those of white males and who are more likely to have incomes below poverty level (Quadagno, *Transformation of Old Age Security*, p. 2).

11. Paul Light, *Artful Work, The Politics of Social Security Reform* (New York: Random House, 1985), p. 59.

12. Thomas Byrne Edsall, *The New Politics of Inequality* (New York: W.W. Norton, 1984), p. 17.

13. Wilbur J. Cohen, "The Bipartisan Solution, Securing Social Security," *The New Leader* (February 7, 1983): 5.

14. Ibid.

15. Light, *Artful Work*, p. 124.

16. "The Battle Over Repairing Social Security," *Business Week* (September 28, 1981): 116.

17. Robert Kuttner, *The Revolt of the Haves, Tax Rebellions and Hard Times* (New York: Simon & Schuster, 1980).

18. Edsall, *New Politics of Inequality*, p. 39. Proposals for these cuts had appeared a few months earlier in a *Fortune* magazine article. See A.F. Ehrbar, "How to Save Social Security," *Fortune* (August 25, 1980): 37.

19. David Obey and Paul Sarbannes, *The Changing American Economy* (Oxford, Eng.: Basil Blackwell, 1986), p. 4.

20. William Greider, *The Education of David Stockman and Other Americans* (New York: E.P. Dutton, 1982), p. 49.

21. Obey and Sarbannes, *Changing American Economy*, p. 4.

22. "How to Cut the Deficit," *Business Week* (March 26, 1984): 52, 58.

23. Light, *Artful Work*, p. 33.

24. Ibid., p. 119.

25. Mildred and Claude Pepper Library, RG 309B, Box 87, File 20: "The Green Sheet." For a complete recounting of the history of the 1983 amendments, see Light, *Artful Work*.

26. The federal government began efforts to restrain the drift toward early retirement in the 1970s. In 1978 Congress passed amendments to the 1967 Age Discrimination in Employment Act, raising the allowable retirement age from 65 to 70. See Harold Sheppard, "The Early Retirement Age Issue in the United States," for the Committee on U.S.-Europe Early Exit Project, Tampa, Florida, November 12–14, 1987, p. 6; Rachel Florsheim Boaz, "The 1983 Amendments to the Social Security Act: Will They Delay Retirement? Summary of the Evidence," *The Gerontologist* 27 (1987): 151.

27. Derthick, *Policymaking for Social Security*, p. 199.

28. John Myles, "Trillion Dollar Misunderstanding," *Working Papers* (July/August 1981): 24.

29. Light, *Artful Work*, p. 66.

30. Quote from Dorcas Hardy, Commissioner of the Social Security Administration, *Kansas City Times* (May 18, 1987): 17.

31. Quoted in Peter G. Peterson, "The Salvation of Social Security," *The New York Review* (December 16, 1982): 50; "Social Security: The Real Cost of those Rising Benefits," *Fortune* (December 1973): 80. Ironically, economist Paul Samuelson had used the same terms in his 1967 description praising Social Security as the most successful program developed by any modern welfare state. Quoted in Achenbaum, *Social Security*, p. 54.

32. Ehrbar, "How to Save Social Security," p. 36.

33. Ehrbar, "The Wrong Solution," *Fortune* (August 17, 1980): 118. The proportion of GNP in the U.S. that is spent on old-age pensions is the lowest of all western, capitalist democracies and the quality of public pensions is comparatively low. See John Myles, *Old Age in the Welfare State* (Boston: Little, Brown, 1984), p. 71. Further, the tax increases in the 1983 amendments to the Social Security Act guaranteed the economic stability of the trust fund at least through the first quarter of the twenty-first century.

34. Ashby Bladen, "The Truth About Social Security," *Forbes* (December 6, 1982): 242.

35. Peter G. Peterson, "The Salvation of Social Security," *The New York Review* 35 (December 6, 1982): 52.

36. "An Exchange on Social Security," *The New Republic* (May 18, 1987): 23; see also A. Haeworth Robertson, "Is the Current Social Security Program (of OASI, DI, HI and SMI benefits) Financially Feasible in the Long Run?" *Journal of American Society of CLU and CHFC* (November 1986): 55.

37. Phillip Longman, "Taking America to the Cleaners," *Washington Monthly* (November 1982): 24.

38. Ibid., pp. 26, 30.

39. Edsall, *New Politics of Inequality*, p. 88.

40. American Association of Retired Persons, "Yankelovich Survey Finds Conflict Among Generations Mostly Fiction," *AARP News Bulletin* (April 1987): 2; see also AARP, "Poll Finds Little Friction Between Young and Old," *Highlights* 5 (July 1987): 13.

41. Americans for Generational Equity, Second Annual Report (1986–87).

42. Letter from Dave Durenberger to AGE Directors and Members (December 1, 1986): 2.

43. Remarks by Senator Dave Durenberger to the Conference on "An Agenda for the Aging Society," Minneapolis, Minnesota, January 13, 1987, p. 9.

44. Paula Schwed, "A Dirty Little Secret," *Campus Voice* (August/September 1986).

45. Ernest L. Boyer, "An Imperiled Generation," *The Generational Journal* 1 (April 15, 1988): 37; Uwe E. Reinhardt, "U.S. Health Policy: Errors of Youth," *The Generational Journal* 1 (April 15, 1988): 45.

46. James Jones, "Letter from the President," *Of Age* (Fall 1987): 8.

47. Ibid.

48. Ibid.

49. AGE Second Annual Report (1986–87), p. 7.

50. "AGE Adds Four Policy Experts to Board," *Of Age* (Fall 1987): 7.

51. Letter from Dave Durenberger to AGE Directors and Members (December 1, 1986): 1; Americans for Generational Equity, *Fiscal 1988 Plan of Operation*, pp. 2–3.

52. "Age Conference Looks at the Economics of an Aging Society," *Of Age* (Fall 1987): 3.

53. Letter from Thomas Rodman to Fellow Baby Boomers (January 18, 1988).

54. Memo to AGE Members from Paul Hewitt (February 4, 1988).

55. Phillip Longman, "Justice Between Generations," *Atlantic Monthly* (June 1985): 74; see also Lee Smith, "The War Between the Generations," *Fortune* (July 20, 1987): 78.

56. Ibid., p. 75.

57. Ibid., pp. 78–79.

58. Peter G. Peterson, "The Morning After," *Atlantic Monthly* (October 1987): 44.

59. Ibid., pp. 44, 60.

60. Ibid., p. 60.

61. Ibid., p. 69.

62. A. Haeworth Robertson, "Promises Social Security Won't Be Able to Keep," *Chicago Tribune* (December 1, 1987, Section 1): 19.

63. Governor Pete DuPont, "Creating Opportunities for the Next Generation of Americans," remarks to the Magazine Publishers Association, Orlando, Florida, November 10, 1986, p. 8.

64. Robertson, "Promises," p. 19.

65. "Catastrophic Health Insurance Debuts in New AGE Report Series," *Of Age* (Fall 1987): 2; "Medicare Catastrophic Coverage to Start in 1989," *A Portfolio of Articles about Americans for Generational Equity* (July 1988).

66. "Senator Pessimistic on Health Care," *Kansas City Star* (May 3, 1987): 6.

67. Anthony Beilenson, "Let's Put Social Security Back on Deficit-Negotiations Table," *Tallahassee Democrat* (November 11, 1988): 13a.

68. "Washington Post Changes Editorial Stance on Social Security," *Of Age* (Fall 1987): 7.

69. Ibid.; for other examples see "The Dawning of the Age of Emeritus," *Kansas City Star* (April 5, 1987): 1a, 12a; the cartoon "The Reading of the Will," *Kansas City Times* (April 27, 1987): 11a; James Kilpatrick, "For Blacks, the System Is a Ripoff," *Kansas City Star* (July 12, 1987); "Social Security's Ticking Time Bomb," *Tallahassee Democrat* (March 6, 1988): 3a.

70. Mickey Kaus, "The Right's Free Lunch," *The New Republic* (March 9, 1987): 14; "Tradeamok," *The New Republic* (April 27, 1987): 7–9; "An Exchange on Social Security," *The New Republic* (May 18, 1987): 20–23; "Reagan's Correction," *The New Republic* (November 16, 1987): 7–9; "You Call This Austerity," *The New Republic* (December 7, 1987): 4, 41.

71. Henry Fairlie, "Talkin' Bout My Generation," *The New Republic* (March 28, 1988): 19. See also John Tierney, "Old Money, New Power," *The New York Times Magazine* (October 23, 1988): 52.

72. *AARP News Bulletin* (April 1987).

73. Karl Polanyi, *The Great Transformation* (Boston: Beacon Press, 1957), pp. 63–67.

74. John Myles, "Decline or Impasse? The Current State of the Welfare State," *Studies in Political Economy* 26 (Summer 1988): 86.

75. Quadagno, *Transformation of Old Age Security*, p. 24.

76. Myles, "Decline or Impasse," p. 87.

77. Ibid.

78. Quadagno, *Transformation of Old Age Security*, Chap. 7.

79. Jill Quadagno, "Women's Access to Pensions and the Structure of Eligibility Rules: Systems of Production and Reproduction," *The Sociological Quarterly* 28 (Winter 1988): 541–558; Angela O'Rand and John C. Henretta, "Delayed Career Entry, Industrial Pension Structure, and Early Retirement in a Cohort of Unmarried Women," *American Sociological Review* 47 (June 1982): 366.

80. Schwed, "Dirty Little Secret," p. 74; Peterson, "Morning After," p. 69.

81. Longman, "Justice Between Generations," p. 81.

82. Phillip Longman, *Born to Pay, the New Politics of Aging in America* (Boston: Houghton Mifflin, 1987), p. 249.

83. Ibid.; Smith, "War Between Generations," p. 80; "Social Security: Will You Get Yours," *Readers Digest* (June 1988): 145.

84. Barry Bluestone and Bennett Harrison, "The Great American Jobs Machine: The Proliferation of Low-Wage Employment in the U.S. Economy," study prepared for the Joint Economic Committee, 1987, pp. 5, 21.

85. Ibid., p. 31.

86. Mark D. Hayward, William R. Grady, and Steven D. McLaughlin, "Changes in the Retirement Process Among Older Men in the United States: 1972–1980," *Demography*, in press; Mark D. Hayward, William R. Grady, and Steven D. McLaughlin, "The Retirement Process Among Older Women in the U.S.: Changes in the 1970s," *Research on Aging*, in press.

87. William J. Serow, "The Effects of an Aging Population on Immigration Policy," *Journal of Applied Gerontology* 1 (1982): 27.

88. Longman, *Born to Pay*, p. 247.

89. Patricia Ruggles and Michael O'Higgins, "Retrenchment and the New Right: A Comparative Analysis," in *Stagnation and Renewal*, eds. Martin Rein, Gosta Esping-Anderson, and Lee Rainwater (Armonk, N.Y.: M.E. Sharpe, 1987), p. 178.

90. Ibid., p. 177.

91. Barry Bluestone and Bennett Harrison, *The Deindustrialization of America* (New York: Basic Books, 1982), p. 41.

92. Paul Blumberg, *Inequality in an Age of Decline* (New York: Oxford University Press, 1980), p. 146.

93. Merton C. Bernstein and Joan Brodshaug Bernstein, *Social Security, the System That Works* (New York: Basic Books, 1988), pp. 64–73.

94. Samuel Preston, "Children and the Elderly: Divergent Paths for America's Dependents," *Demography* 21 (November 1984): 435.

95. Ibid., pp. 436–437, 446.

96. Robert Erikson and Johan Fritzell, "The Effects of the Social Welfare System in Sweden on the Well-Being of Children and the Elderly" (Swedish Institute for Social Research: University of Stockholm, Reprint Series No. 222, 1988), p. 314.

97. Isabel Sawhill, "Discrimination and Poverty Among Women Who Head Families," in *Women and the Workplace, The Implications of Occupational Segregation*, eds. Martha Blaxall and Barbara Reagan (Chicago: University of Chicago Press, 1976), p. 209.

98. For descriptions of such programs, see Helga Marie Hernes, *Welfare State and Woman Power, Essays in State Feminism* (Oslo: Norwegian University Press, 1987); Jennifer G. Schirmer, *The Limits of Reform: Women, Capital and Welfare* (Cambridge, Mass.: Schenkman, 1982); Mary Ruggie, *The State and Working Women: A Comparative Study of Britain and Sweden* (Princeton, N.J.: Princeton University Press, 1984).

99. John Myles, "Citizenship at the Crossroads: The Future of Old Age Security," in *Old Age in a Bureaucratic Society*, eds. David Van Tassel and Peter Stearns (Westport, Conn.: Greenwood Press, 1986), p. 206.

100. Dave Durenberger, "Action Needed Now for Future Long-Term Health Care Needs," *Generational Journal* (April 15, 1988): 7.

24

Maintaining the Status Quo: The Impact of Old-Age Interest Groups on the Medicare Catastrophic Care Act of 1988

DEBRA STREET

The Medicare Catastrophic Care Act (MCCA) of 1988 was the first major expansion of Medicare since its inception in 1965. Just after the MCCA legislation passed, controversy erupted, leading to the eventual repeal of most parts of the act. Street uses two levels of analysis, a structural elite model and a pluralist politics model, to demonstrate how, contrary to dominant health policy formation theories, old-age interest groups influence the policymaking process surrounding MCCA. The importance of the transformative capacity of policy structures is emphasized in her argument that the only structural change embodied in the legislation—a departure from the social insurance model of Medicare financing—was the catalyst for mobilizing financial interests among some old-age interest groups. This mobilization resulted in a cleavage between various old-age interests and led to the eventual repeal of the legislation.

When President Reagan signed the Medicare Catastrophic Care Act (MCCA) into law on 1 July 1988, no one predicted its "short life and painful death" (Holstein and Minkler 1991:189). Legislators on Capitol Hill congratulated each other over their successful bipartisan effort to pass the act (P.L.100-360), the biggest expansion of Medicare since its implementation in 1965. As the first major social welfare legislation in a decade, MCCA seemed like an idea whose time had come. To representatives and

"Maintaining the Status Quo: The Impact of Old Age Interest Groups on the Medicare Catastrophic Care Act of 1988" by Debra Street, from *Social Problems*, 40 (1993): 431–444. Copyright © 1993 by the University of California Press Journals.

senators, the Reagan administration, a variety of health and nonhealth interest groups, and to a number of old-age lobby groups and advocates, MCCA represented a mutually satisfactory compromise addressing some of the urgent health needs of elderly people.

On the surface, the changes embodied in MCCA appeared to offer something for everyone. The expansion of benefits increased opportunities for doctors and hospitals, drug manufacturers, and the business community to serve their material interests. More complete coverage of acute health care and prescription drug expenses represented a considerable augmentation of many older citizens' benefits. This expansion, championed by a number of old-age interest groups, could be viewed as a triumph for the older health care consumer.

But problems soon arose as implementation of MCCA became a reality. These problems did not result from the new benefits offered under MCCA. Rather, they resulted from what was *not* offered—and who would pay the bill. Under the provisions of the legislation, Medicare premiums were increased and a new income tax surcharge on the elderly was instituted. This constituted a substantial departure from the social insurance principle that had prevailed in earlier Medicare funding. Medicare beneficiaries bore the entire burden of paying for the expansion of services, with higher income elderly people footing a disproportionate share of the bill. Under mounting pressure from certain old-age interest groups, most parts of MCCA were repealed in 1989.

Using alternative theoretical models of policy formation and implementation, I address key questions about this case. Why was the Medicare Catastrophic Care Act, presumed to have such broad-based support, repealed less than 18 months after its passage? In a policymaking arena traditionally dominated by elite groups, how were old-age interest groups able to influence first the passage, then repeal, of the legislation? Much health policy research focuses only on political activities leading up to passage of legislation. I extend the analysis beyond prior research and show how policies both transform interests and create systems of stratification (Esping-Andersen 1990). This approach takes into account the processes resulting from policy implementation and the consequent transformations in actors' positions. Thus, this study aims at broadening theoretical models of policy formation to include implementation and its effects.

First, I use pluralist and structural elite theoretical frameworks to account for the political activities and interests of various groups during the policymaking process leading to passage of MCCA. Next, I extend the analysis to examine how the effects of implementation transformed various actors' positions. I argue that only one structural change to the health care system was embodied in the legislation. This single modification was responsible for the ensuing transformations in actors' positions, and served as a catalyst for the mobilization of class interests among the elderly. Finally, I show how this mobilization of class interests resulted in a cleavage between various old-age interests, and its contribution to repeal of the Medicare Catastrophic Care Act.

THEORETICAL BACKGROUND

U.S. health policy formation theories are dominated by models that emphasize power relationships among the structural interests that govern the field of health care policy

(Alford 1975; Starr 1982). Physicians' interests dominated health policy until the 1960s (Starr 1982). However, in recent years, other elite entities such as hospitals (Alford 1975; Starr 1982; Stevens 1989), government agencies (Marmor, Mashaw and Harvey 1990), insurance companies (Alford 1975), and corporate purchasers of health care benefits (Bergthold 1990) have also become instrumental in forming health policy.

This paper focuses on the interplay between elite and nonelite actors in health policy formation. Organizations and individuals representing the interests of "hands-on" health care providers—physicians and hospitals—constitute the "health elites." "Nonhealth elites" refer to individuals and organizations representing the health policy interests of other powerful groups, including politicians, the insurance industry, pharmaceutical manufacturers, and the business community. Finally, "nonelites" constitute the individuals and groups purporting to represent health care consumers.[1] These elite and nonelite actors took differing positions throughout the formation of MCCA.

Alford postulates a health policy formation model featuring dominant, challenging, and repressed interests. Within his model, a network of political, legal, and economic institutions guarantee "that certain dominant interests will be served and come to be taken for granted as legitimate, as the only possible way in which health services can be provided" (1975:17). Consequently, in Alford's model, health policy is formed through arrangements concluded between dominant and challenging elite interests. The health care consumer is categorized as a repressed interest, typically excluded from policymaking.

An elite model implies that power resides in structural arrangements which are the domain of an alliance of elites controlling key institutional positions (Mills 1956). An implicit alliance exists between interested health and nonhealth elites (Imershein, Rond, and Mathis 1992; Starr 1982); these elites' structural locations provide them sufficient power to arrange and maintain health policy to serve their interests. Repressed interests (the nonelite health care consumers) are peripheral to the decision-making domain, and, therefore, can do little to change the structure of health care.

"Crises" in health care arrangements in the United States are usually addressed symbolically by dominant and challenging elite interests so that the structural arrangements underlying health policy remain intact (Alford 1975). To the extent that "crises" in health policy occur, they are usually the creation of specific elite groups seeking to make political capital out of situations that have existed for many years. These crises tend to serve the needs of all or most of the elite interests; crises may incidentally have positive outcomes for repressed interests as well (Alford 1975). Various elites' interests include not only financial gain, but also expanded control over policy decisions and institutional resources.

A structural elite model entails several shortcomings. One is its limitations in handling forms of process and change. Another is its assumption of health care consumers' limited capacity to act. The repressed interests of nonelite actors are served only as a byproduct of policy formation, which results from structural arrangements negotiated and controlled by an alliance of elites. As I show, old-age interest groups (nonelite health care consumers) were major actors in both the passage and repeal of MCCA; therefore, a structural elite model alone is insufficient to explain the events surrounding this legislation.

An alternative approach to examining the MCCA legislation is the pluralist politics model. This model assumes that various interest groups compete within the state's democratic arrangements, achieving a political consensus which results in policy and legislation (Dahl 1967). A pluralist analysis of the passage and repeal of MCCA revolves around a wide range of political actors' capacities to influence political outcomes (Dahl 1961).

However, the pluralist model assumes open access to the political arena for all groups (Gamson 1990). It fails to take into account differences in groups' power to act and command policy agendas which are related to their structural locations. Since this model presumes that all interest groups—elite and nonelite—compete on a relatively equal footing, consensus is achieved through a series of compromises. So, while a pluralist model explains situational politics, underlying structural arrangements are not addressed (Alford and Friedland 1985).

Taken together, elite and pluralist models represent different levels of power within a given social system (Alford and Friedland 1985). While both elite and pluralist models provide insights into the dynamics of policy formation, each has limitations for historical analysis of the Medicare Catastrophic Care Act. The elite perspective presumes various actors' interests are relatively static over time, and that nonelites are not part of the policymaking process. Pluralist models presume interest groups (or alliances and coalitions of interests) of equal power that favor neither elites nor nonelites. Finally, both elite and pluralist theories take group and state interests as given. Thus, neither model alone, nor both taken together, can adequately explain historical transformations in interests resulting from policy implementation.

As a process, the formation of health policy does not end with the enactment of legislation. Rather, policy implementation and its effects must also be considered. When the sociological implications of health policy decisions have been considered, the focus has usually been upon static outcomes; for instance, inventories of how many more procedures or patients result when policy changes increase (or decrease) access to health care (Alford 1975). The interrelationship between the various actors and the structure of health care delivery resulting from policy implementation is usually overlooked.

Recent research in other social policy domains has focused on the impact of policy structures both in shaping actors' interests and the political contexts of policy formation (Burstein 1991). Korpi (1983) argues that whether social policy formation takes place within "marginal" systems that seek to limit assistance to the poor, or within "institutional" systems that emphasize universality is important for understanding both distributional processes and interest constituencies. Once implemented, social policies "change public agendas and the patterns of group conflict through which subsequent policy changes occur" (Skocpol and Amenta 1986:149). Policy legacies shape both the actions and interests of collectivities involved in the political processes of policy formation and implementation (Myles and Quadagno 1991; Skocpol and Amenta 1986).

Taking the implementation process into account demonstrates that policy structures can create cleavages in interests among categories of individuals. An example is the dualistic liberal welfare state model (of which the United States is a prototype), which divides benefits into those that are universal and those that are needs-based, and therefore stigmatizes recipients (Esping-Andersen 1990). Such stratification typically undermines societywide support for needs-based benefits while universal benefits, on the other hand, are widely supported and viewed as social rights (Esping-Andersen 1990; Quadagno 1990).

Although this dualistic liberal welfare state policy structure results in a stratified distribution of benefits, their costs are universally shared through social insurance. Medicare (nationwide health insurance for segments of the U.S. population) is such a program. Medicare is universally available to U.S. residents over the age of 65, disabled people, and children who qualify for Social Security survivor's benefits. Because its benefits are distributed as a right, and not a means-tested privilege, Medicare enjoys broad-based political support, characterized by power resource theorists as "middle class incorporation" (Quadagno 1990). Because there is no stigma attached to receiving Medicare benefits, Medicare coverage is considered an appropriate sharing of the burden of health care costs for a universally deserving segment of the U.S. population.

The transformative legacy of policy structures and their contribution to interest cleavages can be demonstrated by analyzing how implementation of the MCCA offered universalized benefits, yet stratified elderly U.S. citizens into payer and nonpayer groups. This stratification was sufficient to undermine support for MCCA by creating a conflict of interest between rich and poor elderly people; it catalyzed the transformation of the interests of groups affected by it. Thus, by using a payer-stratification framework to explain nonelite interest groups' mobilization, I complement and extend the analysis of interest groups' political activities by showing how the MCCA policy legacy transformed nonelite interests.

MEDICARE BEFORE MCCA

By 1987, Medicare provided uniform benefits meeting the acute health care needs of over 32 million aged and disabled persons. It did not, however, provide long-term care for chronic illness and placed no upper limit on acute care out-of-pocket expenses paid by beneficiaries. Thus, the Medicare program contained no "catastrophic" coverage provisions.

Part A, the hospital insurance program of Medicare, covered inpatient hospital services, posthospitalization skilled nursing facility services, home health services, and hospice care. The law specified limits on the amount of coverage available under each benefit category and imposed cost-sharing charges for the use of covered services (U.S. Senate 1987a). Part A of Medicare was financed through payroll taxes.

Beneficiaries who enrolled in Part B paid a monthly premium ($17.90 per month in 1987) which covered physicians' services and a range of other medical services such as outpatient hospital services, lab and x-ray, and physical therapy. After a deductible of $75 was met, 80 percent of the "reasonable" charge for services was covered by Part B, with the beneficiary responsible for the remaining 20 percent. The beneficiary was also responsible for paying the difference between Medicare's "reasonable" charge and the physician's actual charge (U.S. Senate 1987a). The combination of cost-sharing for covered Medicare services and high out-of-pocket expenses for uncovered services stratified Medicare beneficiaries into two groups—elderly people who could afford to purchase private "medigap" insurance policies, which supplement inadequate Medicare benefits, and low income elderly who could not.

Medicare's acute care benefits covered short-term hospital stays and significant portions of physicians' services. The focus on acute care reflects the impact of hospitals and physicians in shaping the original Medicare policy to serve their material and institutional interests (Marmor and Mashaw 1988; Starr 1982). Because Medicare reimbursed only treatment for acute care, many health expenses of elderly people were not covered, including dental care, eyeglasses, prescription drugs, and long-term care.

By 1984, Medicare covered only 48.8 percent of the health costs of elderly people (U.S. Senate 1987a). Furthermore, from the early 1970s on, Medicare payments failed to keep pace with rising medical expenses. Escalating health care costs and the lack of long-term care coverage under Medicare meant that many older people in the United States had to "spend down" to poverty in order to become eligible for governmental assistance through the stigmatizing need-based Medicaid program (Pepper 1989).

LEGISLATIVE ACTION

In 1987, President Reagan surprised both liberals and conservatives, by supporting the recommendation of Otis Bowen, Health and Human Services Secretary, to expand Medicare in response to the "crisis" resulting from the impoverishment of elderly people due to catastrophic illness (Newsweek 1987). MCCA, as it was enacted, appeared to represent a consensus among usually conflicting interests about the health care needs of the elderly. However, MCCA did not depart significantly from the path demanded by the pluralistically financed, private delivery system dominated by powerful health and nonhealth elites. MCCA represented an opportunity for different elite groups to serve both their own interests and, as they saw it, the greater public good.

After nearly two years of political wrangling on Capitol Hill, MCCA was passed in June of 1988. Supporters claimed the new law would go "a long way toward protecting people age 65 and over and the disabled against the ruinous costs of catastrophic illness" (Findlay 1988). MCCA was intended to reduce the potential for financial ruin in the event of a "catastrophic" illness for an individual on Medicare. This was to be accomplished through a number of programmatic changes—the maximum number of allowable service days in hospital, hospice, and skilled nursing care were increased; annual coinsurance and deductible expenses were capped; and new services such as mammography and prescription drug insurance were instituted. Further, the legislation protected individuals against spousal impoverishment and expanded Medicaid funds to pay Medicare premiums, deductibles, and coinsurance for the elderly and disabled whose incomes fell below the federal poverty level. It would have freed approximately 2.5 million Medicare beneficiaries from the cost-sharing requirements of catastrophic illness benefits (Inglehart 1989).

The augmentation of benefits offered under MCCA also increased opportunities for health elites. Most health and nonhealth elites (with the exception of the proprietary pharmaceutical manufacturing industry) supported MCCA. Superficially, at least, the legislation appeared to offer a considerable expansion of benefits for the elderly (nonelites) in terms of reduced out-of-pocket expenses and newly covered services.

But MCCA was fatally flawed. Not only were the new benefits insufficient to address many of the catastrophic medical costs of the elderly, but the funding mechanism represented a radical departure from the social sharing of costs that undergirds all other U.S. social policy legislation (Holstein and Minkler 1991).

SUPPORT FOR MCCA—SERVING THE INTERESTS OF HEALTH ELITES

Hospitals

Expanding the number of days of hospital coverage under Medicare Part A increased the potential for hospitals to fill empty beds and generate revenues. More patients and increased billings would increase revenues and fortify the hospital industry's power base and its strong role in health policy formation. The American Hospital Association had no vigorous objections to MCCA. Its representatives supported passage of MCCA, so long as reimbursement was sufficient to cover hospital expenses (U.S. Senate 1987b).

Physicians

Similarly, the cap on out-of-pocket expenses for doctor's visits meant that financial disincentives for Medicare beneficiaries seeking direct physician care no longer existed. At the same time, nothing in the legislation challenged physicians' professional autonomy. Alternatives to traditional fee-for-service care were not even discussed.

Although the American Medical Association vigorously opposed the 1965 Medicare legislation, perceiving it as a threat to the medical profession's autonomy (Marmor and Mashaw 1988), by 1987 the AMA supported its expansion to include catastrophic coverage. In testimony before the U.S. Senate Finance Committee, representatives of the AMA said catastrophic coverage should be "aggressively pursued." However, the organization's members preferred that coverage be provided in the private sector and "be limited to *acute* health care costs and should provide some form of means-testing" (U.S. Senate 1987b:126). As long as MCCA did not encroach on physicians' professional autonomy or alter the structure of private fee-for-service medical practice, the AMA supported the program.

SERVING THE INTERESTS OF NONHEALTH ELITES

Politicians

Politicians from both parties were sure that passage of the MCCA would generate political currency in terms of support from older voters and general popularity. Ronald Reagan, who had presided over an unprecedented dismantling of the U.S. welfare state during his tenure as president (Block et al. 1987; Fendrich and St. Angelo 1981), shocked many with an apparent about-face in declaring his support for catastrophic health insurance.

With Republican support on the table, and the 1988 election campaign approaching, the Democrats had to take advantage of the momentum and push for health care reform in the form of "legislative incrementalism" impossible only a few months earlier (Borger 1987). In the face of huge (and growing) budget deficits, both parties agreed that the funding mechanism for MCCA had to be revenue neutral—in other words, the costs of catastrophic coverage could not add to the federal deficit (Torres-Gil 1989). In fact, the funding compromise was more than revenue neutral. The surtax and increased Medicare Part B premiums in the early years would actually generate a short-term surplus to help mask the size of the federal deficit (Dentzer 1989a). And, since expansions to the plan were funded solely by beneficiaries, there was no need to shift resources from other programs—a favorable outcome for both political parties.

Insurance Industry

The insurance industry did not strongly oppose the catastrophic care proposals. While some commercial insurers stood to lose part of their lucrative medigap insurance market, most insurance industry organizations did not lobby strenuously against passage of MCCA (Inglehart 1989). Despite expansion of Medicare benefits under MCCA, beneficiaries by no means had total coverage against financial risk. Although insurers would have to revise medigap policies to avoid overlapping expanded Medicare coverage, there were still coinsurances and deductibles to insure against and profit from (Findlay 1988). As Benno Isaacs, spokesman for the Health Insurance Association of America put it, "We aren't worried about losing the Medigap market" (quoted in Murphy 1987:29).

There are two other possibilities for the insurance industry's lukewarm support for—or lack of spirited resistance to—MCCA. First, the industry hoped to capitalize on other health care problems not addressed by MCCA, specifically chronic long-term care (Findlay 1988). The insurance industry may have moderated its lobbying efforts against MCCA in hopes of generating sufficient legislative goodwill to avoid much government regulation in that area. A second consideration vital to private health insurance interests was avoiding national health insurance; an expansion of Medicare was not nearly so threatening. Consequently, they did not generate much vocal opposition to the "lesser of two evils."

Pharmaceutical Industry

The proprietary pharmaceutical manufacturing industry opposed MCCA from the outset, and launched a $3 million lobbying campaign against the legislation (Torres-Gil 1989). The phased-in drug benefits included in MCCA meant that the government would pay for prescription drugs. The Pharmaceutical Manufacturers Association opposed that provision, fearing that the government as purchaser would inevitably move to exercise cost control over drugs (Inglehart 1989; Longman 1989; Torres-Gil 1989), jeopardizing future profits.

Not all pharmaceutical interests were united in opposition to MCCA, however. The American Pharmaceutical Association (a national association of pharmacists), the National Association of Retail Druggists, the National Association of Chain Drug Stores Inc., and the Generic Pharmaceutical Industry Association all supported inclusion of the phased-in prescription drug benefit proviso of MCCA (U.S. House of Representatives 1987). Fragmentation of pharmaceutical industry interests undermined the Pharmaceutical Manufacturers Association's objections to the drug benefit, and it was maintained as a feature of the final MCCA legislation.

Business and Manufacturing Community

Robert W. Hungate, representing the National Association of Manufacturers (NAM), testified that his organization supported MCCA as long as employers did not have to "assume increased responsibilities when they are already struggling to maintain their position in global markets" which would be an "inappropriate shift in responsibility" producing "unintended consequences" (U.S. Senate 1987c:106). While Hungate acknowledged the need for long-term nonacute custodial care, he said NAM's position was that the federal government should not "use limited resources for this purpose at the expense of providing basic acute care protection" and recommended that nonacute care services be maintained through private insurance systems (U.S. Senate 1987c:109).

Representatives of business organizations generally supported the legislation that finally passed the House and Senate. Since the expansion was funded entirely by beneficiaries, business had no reason to fear increased taxes. In addition, during the 1980s the business community became increasingly aware of the rapidly escalating and underfunded financial obligations for providing Medicare supplementary health insurance to their retirees (Nielson 1987). Expanding benefits under MCCA could potentially relieve business of part of the burden of this provision. Retired workers (at least the wealthier ones) would pay from their own pockets for benefits previously paid for by employers (Farnham 1989). The business community supported a program limited to acute care services, provided that fiscal responsibility was not shifted to employers and that the private insurance market would be encouraged to continue providing supplemental protection (U.S. Senate 1987c). MCCA in its final form was much to the business community's liking.

SERVING THE INTEREST OF NONELITES

By expanding the number of hospital days covered by Medicare, capping annual out-of-pocket expenses for doctor's visits, and covering prescription drug costs, the Medicare Catastrophic Coverage Act appeared to address many of the needs of elderly citizens. Capping the annual out-of-pocket expenses for doctor's visits meant that Medicare beneficiaries no longer had to limit their visits because of an inability to pay. The legislation held the promise of protection from financial ruin in the event of an acute catastrophic illness or an accident requiring prolonged hospitalization. In sum, MCCA put a lid on spiraling individual health care costs by placing a ceiling on out-of-pocket expenses for acute care. Similarly, the phased-in prescription drug benefit offered relief to seniors who paid more than $600 annually for prescriptions—a substantial benefit for those requiring expensive medication for chronic conditions.

MCCA received substantial lobbying support from several prominent age-based interest groups, such as the American Association of Retired Persons (AARP) and the National Council of Senior Citizens (NCSC). AARP and NCSC were frequently publicly cited by congressional supporters as important private sector backers of the bill (Day 1990). AARP and NCSC officials and lobbyists helped supporters of the bill in Congress by researching the health care needs of older people, devising compromise positions, and testifying before committees.

NONELITE MOBILIZATION

Although some age-based interest groups such as AARP and NCSC advocated passage of MCCA from the outset, other age-based lobbying groups claimed MCCA was fundamentally flawed. The Gray Panthers, for instance, opposed MCCA from the beginning because it did not provide real structural reform of health care financing. Maggie Kuhn, founder of the Gray Panthers, testified before the Senate Committee on Finance that her organization could only support legislation that provided a national health insurance program for U.S. citizens of all ages (U.S. Senate 1987b).

The Gray Panthers were not alone. The National Association of Retired Public Employees opposed the bill because its members already had health insurance and would be paying twice for catastrophic care (Torres-Gil 1990). The National Committee to Preserve Social Security and Medicare (NCPSSM) lobbied against the MCCA from its introduction because it represented a radical departure from the intergenerational cost sharing of the Medicare program (U.S. Senate 1987b). NCPSSM did not object to MCCA's new provisions so much as its funding mechanisms. Once MCCA was passed, NCPSSM lobbied even more aggressively for the law's repeal.

The AARP opposed repeal of MCCA after enactment despite its reservations about the surtax; on the other hand, NCSC reversed its original position of support because of the uproar over funding. Its initial support reflected a pragmatic attitude toward the possibilities of health care reform, although both organizations preferred funding based upon social insurance principles. Initially, both AARP and NCSC were willing to compromise on the self-funded MCCA, believing that the advantages of expanded acute care outweighed the disadvantages of an altered funding mechanism. Both organizations saw MCCA as an incremental step toward their longer term goals—national health insurance and insurance for long-term chronic care for the elderly. AARP and NCSC were both influential in supporting the initial legislation. In the end, however, NCSC backtracked and withdrew its support. Grass-roots mobilization of many senior citizens and the stepped-up efforts of organizations such as NCPSSM turned the tide of support away from MCCA and towards its repeal.

The catalyst behind the repeal drive was the new surtax that represented 15 percent of seniors' tax liability and was capped at $800 per person (Dentzer 1989b). Although only the top 5 percent of upper income elderly would have to pay the full surtax amount (Garland 1989), many middle income elderly believed that they, too, would be responsible for the full $800 surtax. The complexity of the program and lack of information about the surtax's sliding scale led to many misunderstandings, and fueled the controversy over MCCA funding (Weisberg 1989). Some affluent seniors reacted by seeking investment advice to help them avoid paying the Medicare surtax (Weberman 1989). For others, the impending surtax was a call to political action.

Senior citizens across the country mobilized to oppose payment for Medicare coverage based on individual incomes. After an address in his home district at the South Chicago Polka Club, Chairman of the House Ways and Means Committee Dan Rostenkowski (D. Ill.) was accosted by nearly 50 angry seniors who surrounded his car and beat on it with picket signs (Miller 1989). It was not only individuals, however, who advocated repeal of the law.

The National Committee to Preserve Social Security and Medicare had made scare tactics directed at its senior citizen members a stock in trade in earlier forays at fundraising (Dwyer 1989). It continued in this vein in its opposition of MCCA; NCPSSM again organized a direct mail campaign to seniors, calculated to play on fears of a "seniors-only surtax" (Clift 1989). A mailing to its 4.5 million members stated "1989 income taxes for millions of seniors will increase by up to $1600 ($800 for singles)—it's a tax on seniors-only and it must be stopped!" (Weisberg 1989:11). More than two million members of the NCPSSM sent postcards to Capitol Hill urging legislators to repeal MCCA (Miller 1989). Although legislators disliked NCPSSM's tactics, they could not ignore the mail flooding their offices demanding repeal. Representatives of the Seniors Coalition Against Catastrophic Act, a grass-roots coalition of more than 50 seniors' organizations that sprang up after passage of MCCA, testified in vehement opposition to the law before the Senate Committee on Finance (U.S. Senate 1989).

The old-age organizations represented the interests of primarily white, middle and upper middle income seniors. Because MCCA's funding mechanisms stratified older citizens into payer and nonpayer categories, upper income elderly people had little to gain, and much to lose financially should MCCA be fully implemented. Their financial interests were threatened sufficiently to mobilize the "payer" group to sustained action calling for repeal of MCCA. Despite misgivings about the financing mechanism, AARP maintained its support for MCCA (U.S. Senate 1989). In the end, however, it was other old-age interest groups and mobilized individuals who prevailed. MCCA was rescinded, for the most part, by a 360 to 66 vote in the House in October of 1989—nearly the same margin of votes that had passed MCCA into law only 16 months earlier.

WHY MCCA FAILED

There were a number of factors underlying the repeal of MCCA in 1989. First, the changes represented by MCCA were in large measure symbolic. The legislation diffused the perception of a rising health cost "crisis" for Medicare beneficiaries without tampering with the fundamental structure of either health care delivery or financing conducive to elite interests. There was no change in the system of reimbursement through third-party intermediaries—private insurance companies—which contributed to high Medicare administrative costs. MCCA addressed none of the structural causes contributing to the rapid escalation of health care costs. It is ironic that legislation intended to address skyrocketing individual health care costs had no provisions for cost containment. In fact, MCCA was potentially inflationary, since it increased access without significant cost containment provisions, and could have ultimately contributed to the problem it was intended to address.

Second, MCCA did not address many of the real gaps between the health care needs of the elderly and the provisions of previous Medicare policy. In terms of acute cata-strophic care, only a small portion of elderly people (less than 4 percent annually) ex-ceeded the Medicare maximum number of hospital days (Gergen 1989). Few individu-als would have benefited from the expansion in eligible hospital service days under Medicare Part A. The phased-in prescription drug coverage in Plan B was estimated to benefit only 16.8 percent of senior citizens, and then only after a $600 deductible was paid (Gergen 1989). Although there was a cap on maximum annual acute medical ex-penses, the costs of coinsurance, deductibles, and health related services such as eye and dental care still fell to the consumer. No relief was provided in terms of chronic, long-term care expenses.

Third, the *only* fundamental structural change under MCCA was program financ-ing—and this change affected nonelites exclusively. Given the power of the health and nonhealth elites, that this was the sole structural change under MCCA is not surprising. Elite support for MCCA came precisely because the legislation largely maintained the status quo.

What is surprising, however, is that the elite interests, having reached the compro-mises necessary to conclude new health policy, were thrown a curve from the "re-pressed," or nonelite interests. One structural change had the power to inspire and mo-bilize particular segments of the elderly population to successfully oppose the implementation of MCCA.

MCCA fell short of meeting the catastrophic needs of elderly people in terms of acute versus chronic long-term care (nursing home, home health services). More im-portantly, however, its funding mechanism departed from the social insurance princi-ples that made universal programs like Social Security and Medicare popular suc-cesses. In other words, the "beneficiaries" of the MCCA were solely responsible for increases in premiums charged for Medicare Part B, and for a surtax on individuals with higher incomes. The result was that the wealthy elderly would subsidize the poor elderly; a public uprising by middle and upper income elderly ensued.

Under the original MCCA legislation, 40 percent of elderly people would have paid a progressive income tax surcharge (up to $800 per person) levied "solely on the afflu-ent elderly to help fund the program" (Gorey 1989). Because this surcharge required high income older people to pay approximately twice what medigap policies cost on the open market, and because the program was not specifically designed to meet this group's needs, the principles of social insurance and middle-class incorporation were undermined (Quadagno 1990). For the first time, the cost of Medicare coverage was based on a person's income. This was intolerable to a segment of the elderly popula-tion—precisely that segment whose resources and backgrounds were conducive to po-litical mobilization and who would have to pay. This was the catalyst for their opposi-tion of MCCA.

DISCUSSION

While elite and pluralist theories each offer insights into policy formation, neither model is comprehensive enough to encompass a full understanding of the dynamics of MCCA. Elite structural models treat nonelites' activities as peripheral, and pluralistic models ignore the structural arrangements favoring elite actors. An alternative approach uses both pluralist and elite perspectives to take into account the differences in resources and power available to groups acting within the policy arena, as well as the dynamics of situational politics. Analysis must include all groups as actors, while recognizing the structural constraints of power relations that typically advantage elites. Further, transformations in actors' interests must be accounted for. Focusing on policy implementation and formation serves as a bridge to understanding the transformation of interests and mobilization of different groups at different times in the formation/implementation process.

Thus, repeal of MCCA can be understood on several levels. In the first instance—from the perspective of pluralistic politics—old-age lobby groups successfully organized opposition and rolled back the legislation within the democratic arena of consensus building. At this level of analysis, the repeal of MCCA is the political system's response to the desires of the majority, or in this case, the desires of relevant interest groups.

The elite model offers another level of analysis of the Medicare Catastrophic Coverage Act's repeal. Health and nonhealth elites' interests were, to a large extent, unaffected by MCCA's initial passage and, consequently, unaffected by its repeal. Under MCCA, physicians and hospitals stood to gain financially: expanding the number of hospital days and removing financial disincentives to beneficiaries seeking doctors' services benefited both groups. On the other hand, neither group of health elites had a large stake in lobbying against the repeal of MCCA. The structural arrangements that made health elites dominant players in health policy remained essentially undisturbed with or without MCCA; neither implementation nor repeal disturbed the status quo.

Among nonhealth elites, politicians who initially hoped to capitalize on their election year responsiveness to elderly constituents' desires by passing MCCA could appear equally responsive by voting for its repeal in the wake of the implementation controversy. Likewise, business interests whose health insurance obligations to retirees might have been reduced under MCCA, could find solace in a traditional position opposing government intrusion and turning to the "market" to fulfill health care needs. Private health insurers could avoid revising policies to reflect major changes in Medicare, and still pursue the long-term chronic care insurance market. The proprietary pharmaceutical industry, which had opposed MCCA from the outset, was the unintended beneficiary of the actions of the elderly who opposed MCCA. Thus, none of the elites had any compelling reason to lobby against repeal of MCCA. They won either way.

The repeal of MCCA was not simply the product of traditional power relationships within the structural interests dominating the field of health policy. It was, rather, the result of the interplay between structural interests, pluralist politics, and policy implementation that stratified older U.S. citizens into payer and nonpayer groups. The resulting cleavage of the elderly mobilized the payer group to oppose MCCA through interest groups and individual participation in the political process.

That "third party" nonelite interests could have such an effect on health policy legislation acceptable to elite players underscores how insubstantial the MCCA's changes were for the various elites. Old-age groups, usually peripheral players in health policy politics, triumphed only because the outcome of the contest was a matter of indifference to the elites—the health policy changes either way were primarily symbolic, not substantial.

Although some groups within the old-age lobby were decisive actors in the repeal of MCCA, their political power was exercised within a very limited context. Old-age interest groups demonstrated apparent power in shaping health policy related to the Medicare Catastrophic Coverage Act, yet this power could be exercised only to the extent that the nonelite agenda coincided, or at least failed to conflict, with that of elite interests. Segments of the old-age lobby rallying against the MCCA funding mechanism exercised veto power over legislation they opposed. It is apparent that the old-age lobby's interests are neither homogeneous nor static over time. It is far less clear, however, despite popular perceptions of the political power of the elderly, whether age-based interest groups can exercise real power by setting a political agenda that coincides with their interests. As current debates over national health policy and "entitlement" programs are played out, a vision of a much less powerful old-age lobby may emerge.

NOTES

1. The health care consumer was not the only nonelite entity concerned with passage of MCCA. Nurses and hospice representatives, for instance, were nonelite actors interested in the policy decisions surrounding the legislation. So, too, were organizations concerned with catastrophic care legislation for segments of the population other than those over 65. However, since the focus of this paper is how old-age interest groups were able to affect the legislative process, the activities of other nonelite actors are not addressed in this study.

REFERENCES

Alford, Robert
  1975   Health Care Politics: Ideological and Interest Group Barriers to Reform. Chicago: The University of Chicago Press.
Alford, Robert R., and Roger Friedland
  1985   Powers of Theory. Cambridge, U.K.: Cambridge University Press.
Bergthold, Linda
  1990   Purchasing Power in Health. New Brunswick, N.J.: Rutgers University Press.
Block, Fred, Richard A. Cloward, Barbara Ehrenreich, and Frances Fox Piven
  1987   The Mean Season: The Attack on the Welfare State. New York: Pantheon Books.
Borger, Gloria
  1987   "Health care bandwagon gets rolling." U.S. News & World Report March 2:22–23.
Burstein, Paul
  1991   "Policy domains: Organization, culture, and policy outcomes." Annual Review of Sociology 17:327–50.
Clift, Eleanor, and Mary Hager
  1989   "A victory for the haves?" Newsweek 16 Oct.:38.
Dahl, Robert A.
  1961   Who Governs? Democracy and Power in an American City. New Haven, Conn.: Yale University Press.
  1967   Pluralist Democracy in the United States: Conflict and Consent. Chicago: Rand-McNally.

Day, Christine L.
1990   What Older Americans Think: Interest Groups and Aging Policy. Princeton, N.J.:
        Princeton University Press.
Dentzer, Susan
1989a   "The calamity of catastrophic coverage." U.S. News & World Report 8 May:36.
1989b   "A health care debacle." U.S. News & World Report 9 Oct.:16–20.
Dwyer, Paula
1989   "The torpedo that slammed into catastrophic care." Business Week 23 Oct.:70.
Esping-Andersen, Gosta
1990   The Three Worlds of Welfare Capitalism. Cambridge, U.K.: Polity Press.
Farnham, Alan
1989   "No more health care on the house." Fortune 27 Feb.:71–72.
Fendrich, James Max, and Douglas St. Angelo
1981   "The Reagan election and mandate: Their fiscal policy implications for the welfare
        state." Journal of Sociology and Social Welfare 8:553–586.
Findlay, Steven
1988   "Finally, a health cost cap." U.S. News & World Report 13 June:63–64.
Gamson, William A.
1990   The Strategy of Social Protest, 2nd ed. Belmont, Calif.: Wadsworth Publishing Com-
        pany.
Garland, Susan
1989   "A senior citizen rebellion has Congress retreating in disarray." Business Week 11
        Sept.:43.
Gergen, David R.
1989   "Repeal a bad health bill." U.S. News & World Report 15 Sept.:76.
Gorey, Hays
1989   "Invitation to catastrophe." Time 16 Oct.:33.
Holstein, Martha, and Meredith Minkler
1991   "The short life and painful death of the Medicare Catastrophic Coverage Act." In
        Critical Perspectives on Aging: The Political and Moral Economy of Growing Old,
        ed. Meredith Minkler and Carroll L. Estes, 189–206. Amityville, N.Y.: Baywood
        Publishing Inc.
Imershein, Allen W., Phillip C. Rond III, and Mary P. Mathis
1992   "Restructuring patterns of elite dominance and the formation of state policy in health
        care." American Journal of Sociology 97:970–93.
Inglehart, John K.
1989   "Medicare's new benefits: 'Catastrophic' health insurance." The New England Jour-
        nal of Medicine 320:329–335.
Korpi, Walter
1983   The Democratic Class Struggle. London: Routledge & Kegan Paul.
Longman, Phillip
1989   "Catastrophic follies." The New Republic 21 Aug.:17.
Marmor, Theodore R., and Jerry L. Mashaw
1988   Social Security: Beyond the Rhetoric of Crisis. Princeton, N.J.: Princeton University
        Press.
Marmor, Theodore R., Jerry L. Mashaw, and Philip L. Harvey
1990   America's Misunderstood Welfare State. New York: Basic Books.
Miller, Annetta
1989   "The elderly duke it out." Newsweek 11 Sept.:42–43.
Mills, C. Wright
1956   The Power Elite. New York: Oxford University Press.
Murphy, Caryle
1987   "Congress wakes up to Medicare reform." 50 Plus April:26–29.

Myles, John, and Jill Quadagno
  1991   "The politics of income security for the elderly in Canada and the United States: Explaining the difference." Paper presented at the conference on A North American Look at Economic Security for the Elderly, Yale University, May.
Newsweek
  1987   "Beyond Medicare." 5 Jan.:3.
Nielson, John
  1987   "Sick retirees could kill your company." Fortune 2 March:98–99.
Pepper, Claude
  1989   "Long-term care insurance: The first step toward comprehensive health insurance." Journal of Aging & Social Policy 1:9–15.
Quadagno, Jill
  1990   "Interest groups politics and the future of U.S. Social Security." In States, Labor Markets and the Future of Old Age Policy, ed. John Myles and Jill Quadagno, 36–58. Philadelphia: Temple University Press.
Skocpol, Theda, and Edwin Amenta
  1986   "States and social policies." Annual Review of Sociology 12:131–57.
Starr, Paul
  1982   The Social Transformation of American Medicine. New York: Basic Books.
Stevens, Rosemary
  1989   In Sickness and in Wealth: American Hospitals in the Twentieth Century. New York: Basic Books.
Torres-Gil, Fernando
  1989   "The politics of catastrophic and long term care coverage." Journal of Aging & Social Policy 2:61–86.
  1990   "Seniors react to the Medicare Catastrophic bill: Equity or selfishness?" Journal of Aging & Social Policy 2:1–8.
United States House of Representatives
  1987   Hearings before the Subcommittee on Health and the Environment of the Committee on Energy and Commerce, "Medicare and Medicaid Catastrophic Protection," Serial No. 100–74. 21, 27, 28 May and 2 June 1987.
United States Senate
  1987a   Hearing before the Committee on Finance, "Catastrophic Health Insurance," S. Hrg. 100–169, Part 1, 28 January 1987.
  1987b   Hearing before the Committee on Finance, "Catastrophic Health Insurance," S. Hrg. 100–169, Part 2, 19 March 1987.
  1987c   Hearing before the Committee on Finance, "Catastrophic Health Insurance," S. Hrg. 100–169, Part 3, 26 March 1987.
  1989   Hearing before the Committee on Finance, "Catastrophic Care: Excess Revenues," S. Hrg. 101–519, 1 June 1989.
Weberman, Ben
  1989   "Medicare tax." Forbes 20 Mar.:213.
Weisberg, Jacob
  1989   "Cat scam." The New Republic 30 Oct.:11–12.

X

THE ECONOMICS OF AGING

For much of American history, the economic security of the elderly has been linked to their families. In the eighteenth and nineteenth centuries, family-based economic systems of agricultural societies placed financial resources in the hands of the older generations. Census data for the mid-nineteenth century confirm the positive association between age and wealth.

While overall wealth increased with age, large differences in economic status existed within the elderly population. In the middle of the nineteenth century, at least one-third of older men had less than $100 in assets and nearly 70 percent had less than $800. Widowed women were also vulnerable to falling into poverty. Although some retained the wealth of their husbands, many more endured economic hardships in old age. As for the freed slaves, old age represented a period of indigence (Haber and Gratton, 1994).

The economic insecurity of the elderly was reduced somewhat during the Depression when Congress enacted the Social Security Act of 1935. Still, by 1960 one-third of older men and 40 percent of older women had incomes below poverty level. Between 1969 and 1972, Congress improved the Social Security system considerably by raising benefits three times and indexing them to inflation (Derthick, 1979). As a result, by 1979 the average income of the elderly had increased to nearly three times the poverty level. Put another way, Hurd (1990) estimates that median incomes in elderly households were 128 percent of the median incomes of nonelderly households in 1979.

Older people continued to gain ground during the 1980s. Between 1970 and 1986, the purchasing power of people age 65 and over increased by nearly 30 percent (Smeeding, 1990). Smeeding, Torrey, and Rainwater (1993) show that in 1990 the median disposable incomes of elderly couples in the United States were 109 percent of the median incomes for all families. And by 1993 poverty rates among the elderly had dropped to less than 12.3 percent.

Yet it would be misleading to imply that the elderly are a privileged group. Even among the more affluent elderly, the tax laws are such that older people return a considerable portion of their income to the government. In 1993 the maximum taxable income was 28 percent for all wage earners. However, middle-income elderly were subject to considerably higher tax rates because of two policies: the taxation of Social Security benefits and the earnings test. The 1983 amendments to the Social Security Act treated Social Security benefits as taxable income for the first time. Single persons with incomes above \$25,000 and couples with incomes above \$32,000 were now subject to taxes of 50 percent on benefits. In the 1993 federal budget, the tax rate on Social Security was increased to 85 percent. Under the earnings test, Social Security recipients under age 70 lost one dollar for every three dollars earned above \$10,000 a year. These taxes made the effective tax rate for older people potentially as high as 80 percent (Phillips, 1993). The first reading in this section, by Greg J. Duncan and Ken R. Smith, analyzes the factors that have contributed to improvements in the economic well-being of the elderly as well as the forces that continue to make them vulnerable to economic insecurity.

VARIATIONS IN THE ECONOMIC SECURITY OF THE AGED

Despite the improvement in the general well-being of the elderly, there are considerable variations within subpopulations. In 1990 the poverty rates for all persons was 13.1 percent of the population. Among blacks and Hispanics, however, the rates were 45.5 percent and 33.5 percent, respectively (Kassner, 1992).

The risk of impoverishment in later life is greater for women who are single, and it is compounded for single women who are members of minority groups. Changes in the structure of the family have increased this risk of impoverishment in old age for women. Over the past thirty years, both white and black families have witnessed higher divorce rates, increases in female-headed households, and a higher proportion of births to unmarried mothers. Among black women the proportion who will ever marry has declined from 94 to about 70 percent. By 1990, a total of 21.4 percent of single women over 65 had incomes below poverty level. The trends toward greater numbers of single women, especially among black women, indicate an aging population increasingly at risk for impoverishment in old age (Jackson, Chatters, and Taylor, 1993). And while the risk of poverty is great for women living alone, it increases even further if they have dependent children. The selection by Madonna Harrington Meyer addresses this issue by revealing how the operations of public and private pension systems position older women to be at greater risk of falling into poverty.

INEQUALITY AND GENERATIONAL EQUITY

Americans grow old in much the same way as they mature. Throughout the life course, there are sharp divisions between affluence and poverty in the United States, and these divisions persist into old age. There are large numbers of affluent and poor elders in the United States because there are large numbers of affluent and poor Americans in all age groups. Poverty in the United States is associated with being female, with having children, and with being a member of a minority group. Inequality and poverty are a generic feature of the American distribution of income, not a generational phenomenon.

REFERENCES

Derthick, Martha. *Policymaking for Social Security.* Washington, DC: Brookings Institution, 1979.

Haber, Carole, and Brian Gratton. *Old Age and the Search for Security.* Bloomington: Indiana University Press, 1994.

Hurd, Michael. "Research on the Elderly: Economic Status, Retirement, and Consumption and Saving." *Journal of Economic Literature,* 28 (June 1990): 565–637.

Jackson, James; Linda Chatters; and Robert Joseph Taylor. "Status and Functioning of Future Cohorts of African-American Elderly." In James Jackson, Linda Chatters, and Robert Taylor (eds.), *Aging in Black America.* Beverly Hills, CA: Sage, 1993.

Kassner, Enid. *Falling Through the Safety Net: Missed Opportunities for America's Elderly Poor.* Washington, DC: American Association of Retired Persons, 1992.

Phillips, Kevin. *Boiling Point: Democrats, Republicans, and the Decline of Middle-Class Prosperity.* New York: Random House, 1993.

Smeeding, Timothy. "Economic Status of the Elderly." Pp. 362–381 in Robert H. Binstock and Linda K. George (eds.), *Handbook of Aging and the Social Sciences.* New York: Academic Press, 1990.

Smeeding, Timothy; Barbara Torrey; and Lee Rainwater. "Going to Extremes: An International Perspective on the Economic Status of the U.S. Aged." LIS Working Paper, #87, May 1993.

25

The Rising Affluence of the Elderly: How Far, How Fair, and How Frail?

GREG J. DUNCAN
KEN R. SMITH

Improvements in the living standards of the elderly over the past twenty-five years have been dramatic. The rising affluence of the elderly has prompted a debate over what constitutes an equitable distribution of resources between generations. In this selection Duncan and Smith review the evidence on the changing well-being of the elderly in the United States. While successive cohorts of the elderly have attained higher levels of economic well-being, Duncan and Smith's review of the longitudinal evidence also shows that some elderly individuals, especially women and the chronically ill, remain economically vulnerable as they age. The central role played by health concerns in assessing the well-being of the elderly leads them to review evidence on two important health issues: recent trends in the physical frailty of the elderly, and the likely burdens, both to the elderly themselves and to society at large, of providing medical care for future cohorts of elderly.

INTRODUCTION

In the early 1960s, when one in three elderly men and two in five elderly women were poor, Gunnar Myrdal wrote of the "terrifying extent to which old people are left in poverty and destitution" in the United States. He thought that "it cannot possibly be the considered opinion of the majority of Americans that so many . . . (elderly) should be

---

"The Rising Affluence of the Elderly: How Far, How Fair, and How Frail?" by Greg Duncan and Ken Smith, from *Annual Review of Sociology*, 15 (1989): 261–289. Copyright © 1989 by Annual Review Inc.

left in misery, squalor and often forbidding loneliness, unattended though they are in need of care" (1963, as quoted in Schultz 1988, p. 17).

Improvements in the living standards of the elderly over the next quarter century could hardly have been more dramatic. By the mid-1980s, the incidence of poverty among the elderly had fallen to one in eight, broad medical care was being provided through the Medicare system, and earlier retirement meant that the elderly had more leisure time in which to enjoy their higher incomes.

The rising affluence of the elderly has prompted a debate over what constitutes an equitable distribution of resources between generations. Great publicity has been accorded the unprecedented situation in which the living standard of the typical elderly person—improved in large part by more generous Social Security retirement and medical benefits—is now higher than that of the typical child, for whom transfers have become less generous (Preston 1984, Binstock 1983).

Two kinds of health concerns darken the otherwise bright picture of the well-being of the elderly. First, have medical advances actually increased the frailty of the typical elderly person by prolonging the lives of disabled persons who would otherwise have died? A second, economic, concern is to what extent costs of long-term care for disabled elderly, currently not covered by public health insurance programs, threaten the economic well-being of the elderly and their children.

The purpose of this essay is to review the evidence on the changing well-being of the elderly. We begin with a review of cross-sectional data showing strong economic gains for the elderly, relative to other groups in the population, especially in the last two decades. Rising Social Security benefits and, to a lesser extent, income from assets account for much of the increase; these have more than offset falling earned income due to earlier retirement. But while successive cohorts of elderly have attained higher levels of economic well-being, a review of longitudinal evidence also shows that some elderly individuals, especially women, remain economically vulnerable as they age.

Few would deny the elderly their income earned from savings, private pensions, or work. But whether Social Security and other public expenditures that benefit the elderly are equitable is a key issue in the debate over whether the economic position of the elderly is "fair." We present two frameworks within which equity issues surrounding Social Security expenditures can be discussed.

The central role played by health concerns in assessing the well-being of the elderly leads us also to review evidence on the two important health issues: recent trends in the frailty of the elderly person, and the likely burdens, both to the elderly themselves and to society at large, of providing medical care for future cohorts of elderly.

PATTERNS OF CHANGE IN THE ECONOMIC STATUS OF THE ELDERLY

Ross et al. (1987) track the relative economic position of elderly and nonelderly men and women using data from the 1950 to 1980 Decennial Censuses (Figure 25-1). Their measure of economic status—the income-to-needs ratio—adjusts for family size differences by dividing each adult's total household income by the poverty threshold rele-

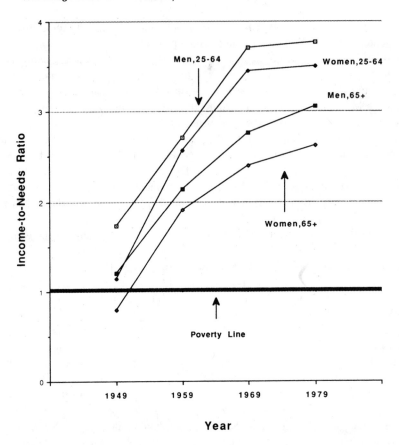

FIGURE 25-1 Average living standards of elderly and nonelderly individuals, by sex, 1949–1979. *(Source: Ross et al. 1987, Table 1)*

vant for his or her household's composition and then adjusts for changes in the cost of living. (The poverty lines for households of one and four persons in 1988 were about $6,000 and $12,000, respectively.) A ratio of 1.0 would mean that the average person in the group had a family income that was equal to the poverty line.

Figure 25-1 shows a striking improvement for all groups. Income for the average elderly household during the post-war period was near or below the poverty line but by 1979 it had increased to nearly three times the poverty level. The absolute improvement in the living standards of the elderly over the three decades—roughly 2.0 income-to-needs units—was matched by nonelderly men and women; in relative terms, however, elderly men and women fared much better than did younger people. The differential improvement was particularly striking between 1969 and 1979, when the average living standard improved significantly for the elderly but barely kept up with inflation for nonelderly men and women. If anything, the elderly have continued to gain relative to the nonelderly during the 1980s.[1]

Despite the differential improvement, the comparisons of income-to-needs positions in Figure 25-1 still show that the economic status of the average elderly person was below that of the average nonelderly adult in 1979. There are several reasons to suspect that additional adjustment to the income measure would eliminate or even reverse these differences. Danziger et al. (1984) find that adjustments for the consumption benefits of owning homes and tax advantages have a measurable positive effect on the relative economic status of the elderly; further adjustments for the monetary value of medical and other in-kind benefits (Smeeding 1982), the apparent underreporting of income by the elderly (Radner 1982), and the value of their greater leisure time would only add to the relative position of the elderly. Important adjustments that might reduce the relative status of the elderly are for ill health, the dimensions of which are explored in a subsequent section of this chapter, and fringe benefits to the working-age population. On balance, however, there appears to be little doubt that the economic status of the typical elderly person, when measured in a fairly comprehensive way, probably meets or exceeds that of the typical nonelderly individual in the 1980s.

Statements about the "typical" individual within a group often conceal important aspects of the distribution of experiences, especially among the least well-off members (Quinn 1985). Evidence on time trends shows that, if anything, the economic status of low-income elderly has improved faster than that of the average elderly person over the past several decades.[2] The incidence of poverty among elderly men fell from 59.4% in 1949 to 8.5% in 1986 and among elderly women over the same period from 75.7% to 15.2%.[3] Placing a value on in-kind medical benefits and some of the other factors mentioned above would almost certainly accentuate these favorable trends (Smeeding 1986).

But while the overall incidence of poverty among the elderly has fallen to unprecedented levels, there are several reasons to view the economic situation of some elderly as a serious social problem. First, poverty among widows and members of minority groups is still quite prevalent: In 1986, poverty rates for individuals aged 65 and older by sex and ethnic group were as follows: white men, 6.9%; white women, 13.3%; black men, 24.2%; black women, 35.5%; Hispanic men, 18.8%; Hispanic women, 25.2%. Second, there appears to be a substantial concentration of elderly in the income range just above the official poverty line who do not appear in the usual poverty statistics (Quinn 1985). Third, the distribution of cash and in-kind benefits appears to leave the near-poor elderly especially vulnerable to economic or health problems (Smeeding 1986). And fourth, fluctuations in income and the possibility of costly medical expenses, described below, also place substantial numbers of nonpoor elderly at risk of economic hardship.

In order to understand the issues surrounding the economic status of the elderly, it is important to distinguish between the experiences of different cohorts of elderly people and the experiences of a particular cohort as its members age. A tempting, but erroneous, interpretation of the rising affluence of the elderly depicted in Figure 25-1 is that the economic environment of old age is quite favorable, with the household income of a typical elderly person rising with advancing old age. The problem, of course, is that comparisons of same-aged elderly groups a decade apart confuse the experiences of the same individuals present at both times with the situations of a newly entering cohort of elderly and a departing cohort of elderly who did not survive the decade.

Depicted in Figure 25-2 are the experiences of four five-year cohorts of individuals, as revealed by census data and reported in Ross et al. (1987, Table 3). For most cohorts, average household incomes rise with age from their early 50s to mid-60s *and then incomes fall* as these cohorts enter their 70s. Thus, the economic environment of old age is not as favorable as one might infer from Figure 25-1. Also striking, though, is the greater affluence of the newer cohorts at every age: although somewhat reduced, the relative economic advantages enjoyed by more recent cohorts of elderly merely reflect the advantages they enjoyed prior to retirement. Clearly it is important to distinguish between aging and cohort factors. We do this first by reviewing what has been

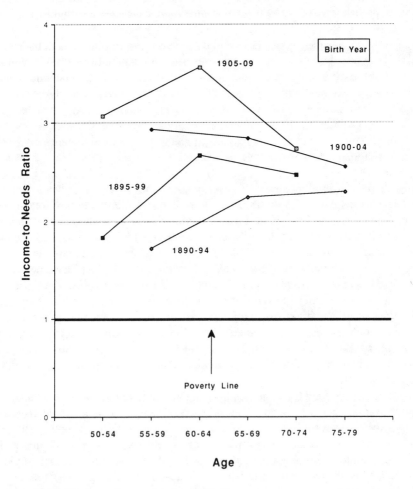

FIGURE 25-2 Average living standards for four cohorts of men and women. *(Source: Ross et al. 1987, Table 3)*

learned from longitudinal data on the dynamics of well-being in old age and then by examining cohort differences in economic status.

DYNAMICS OF WELL-BEING IN OLD AGE

Tracking cohorts of elderly across time, based on census data as in Figure 25-2, is problematic. Not only may the selective nature of mortality lead to erroneous inferences about the income path of the typical individual, but also such tracking does not show the diversity of individual experiences. A still limited, but burgeoning, body of literature using several national longitudinal survey data sources has shown that the economic environment of old age is rather turbulent, much more threatening to women than men, and often reflecting a continuation of economic conditions prior to old age.

Burkhauser & Duncan (1989) follow individuals who were aged 66 to 74 in 1969 over the decade between 1969 and 1979, using data from the Panel Study of Income Dynamics. They find that while the *average* income-to-needs ratio of both the men and women in this group fell only modestly, a substantial minority (27%) within each group experienced at least one very substantial drop (i.e. of 50 percent or more) in economic status. One fifth of the men and more than one third of the women were poor at least once in the decade, while about one tenth of each group were poor more than half the time. They find that large changes in asset income, the death of a spouse, and other family composition changes involving grown children or other relatives figured prominently in producing the income fluctuations.

Coe (1988) uses data from the Panel Study of Income Dynamics to compare the dynamics of poverty spells for elderly persons with those of the general population, as presented in Bane & Ellwood's (1986) path-breaking article. He finds that the chances an elderly person will exit from poverty in the first, second, or third year of a spell are just as high as for the nonelderly, but that the exit probabilities fall substantially after the third year, producing an average poverty spell length for the elderly (5.3 years) that is considerably longer than for the nonelderly (4.2 years). That nearly two thirds of the elderly escape poverty spells within three years is a surprising and little-understood aspect of the economic well-being of old age.

Burkhauser et al. (1988) take a careful look at the economic consequences of retirement, the death of a spouse, and pension choice, using data from the Retirement History Survey (RHS) and family income-to-needs as a measure of economic status.[4] Their longitudinal data clearly show that the average economic position of both intact couples and eventual widows declines with time, from about 80% of preretirement income-to-needs immediately following retirement to about 50% seven to eight years later. Not surprisingly, both the decline in average living standards and the risk of poverty were greater for widows than for intact couples. More than one fifth of the eventual widows were poor at least once in the eight-year period following retirement, as compared with less than one tenth of the intact couples.

A somewhat more controversial issue addressed by Burkhauser et al. (1988) is the role played by the husband's decision for or against a pension that provides spousal benefits after his death.[5] They find that pension choice has a substantial effect on the economic status of widows, although subsequent calculations using the same data by Holden & Burkhauser (1988) show that many of the economic advantages enjoyed by widows who receive spousal benefits were present prior to the death of their husbands.

COHORT IMPROVEMENTS IN ECONOMIC WELL-BEING

There is little doubt that recent cohorts of elderly are much better off financially than are older cohorts. A useful starting point for our discussion of the reasons for improvement is to examine the income packages of elderly families at various points in time. Figure 25-3 uses income data from the *Current Population Surveys* covering 1967, 1979, and 1984 to decompose incomes of family units headed by an elderly individual into four categories: earnings, Social Security, property, and all other income.[6]

The average income of elderly family units rose by 55% between 1967 and 1984, despite a large drop in the average amount of earned income. Although pay rates older workers can command in the labor market have risen substantially over the past several decades, falling retirement ages have more than offset the higher earnings, producing the falling amount—and share—of earnings in the total family income package appar-

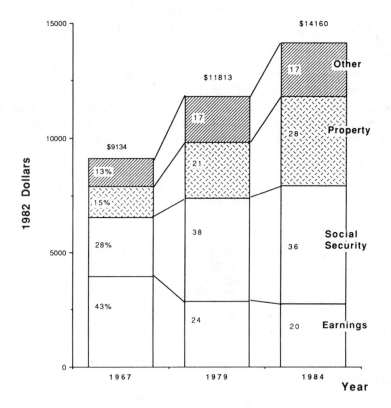

FIGURE 25-3   Composition of income packages of family units headed by an elderly individual, 1967, 1979, and 1984. *(Source: Ross et al., Table 3)*

ent in Figure 25-3. In 1967 earned income accounted for 43% of average total income of elderly family units; by 1984 its share had fallen to 20%.

In contrast, Social Security benefits have gained in importance, doubling in average amount between 1967 and 1984 and increasing as an average share from 28% to 36%. By the late 1970s, Social Security benefits had become the dominant source in the income packages of the elderly.

The wealth of the elderly grew in other ways as well, leading to a tripling of the average amount of rent, dividend, and interest income between 1967 and 1984, and a doubling of the share of income coming from those sources. By 1984, property income had become more important than earned income in the income packages of the elderly. Asset income from pensions other than Social Security (included in the "Other" category in Figure 25-3) was considerably less important than property income in 1984, although its share increased between 1967 and 1987.

In sum, recent cohorts of elderly are much better off economically than are older cohorts. The improvement is due largely to rising Social Security benefits, combined with greater amounts of income from financial assets and private pensions. Increases in these sources have more than offset falling earnings, to produce a sharp improvement in the average economic position of the elderly.

IS THE INCREASING AFFLUENCE OF THE ELDERLY FAIR?

The improved economic status of the elderly contrasts sharply with the economic fortunes of other groups in the population, especially children. Between the late 1960s and mid-1980s the poverty rate for the elderly fell by half, to about 13%, while the rate for children rose by half, to about 20% (Smolensky et al. 1988). The debate over the fairness of this turnabout in the well-being of America's two largest dependent groups has raged throughout the 1980s, and it shows no sign of abating.

A comprehensive review of both positive and normative issues in the debate over what constitutes an "equitable" distribution of income between generations is beyond the scope of this review article (see Palmer et al. 1988 and Kingson et al. 1986 for a more complete discussion). We can, however, summarize some of the central facts and insights in the argument, and we devote considerable attention to equity aspects of Social Security—the largest and by far most important program that redistributes wealth between generations.

Smolensky et al. (1988) review evidence from Decennial Censuses since 1940 and show that the divergent economic paths of children and the elderly are a recent and brief anomaly in the longer-run trend of similar and substantial gains for both groups. The divergence in the fortunes of the elderly and children first emerged in the early 1970s and has accelerated during the 1980s. However, crucial changes in the nature of the economic dependence of both groups may mean that the recent past is indeed to a large extent predictive of the future.

Smolensky et al. (1988) observe that, until recently, the economic status of both children and the elderly was determined almost exclusively by the income of the working men and women with whom they resided. The explosion in the number of female-headed families and the growth of transfer programs such as Aid to Families with Dependent Children have shifted the burden of supporting some children from the labor market to transfer programs. For the elderly, an increasing propensity to live independently, apart from grown children, combined with earlier retirement and more generous Social Security benefits have almost completely severed their dependence on current earnings.

The discrepancy in the economic situations of children and the elderly since the early 1970s can be accounted for, in large part, by the differential success of the labor market vs. income transfers such as AFDC and Social Security benefits in keeping family incomes growing faster than inflation. The differences are dramatic, with earnings and AFDC benefits falling in real terms, while Social Security benefits more than kept up with inflation. By 1980, the average Social Security benefit paid to retired workers and their wives amounted to 55% of median male earnings, 30% higher than the official poverty line for an elderly couple and nearly twice as high as the average AFDC benefit paid to a three-person family (Smolensky et al. 1988, Table 3.5). All of these figures are sharply higher than a decade before. Although some levelling off can be observed, similar trends are likely to persist. The key role played by the Social Security system in producing this divergence and the complications involved in assessing the system's "equity" lead us to focus considerable attention on it.

Equity Aspects of Social Security Benefits

Begun in the midst of the Great Depression as an old age retirement benefit program, the Social Security system has since expanded to include life and disability insurance coverage for nonelderly workers and, in 1965, the comprehensive elderly health program, Medicare (Davis & Rowland 1986). The retirement program makes up the largest part of Social Security and is the focus of our discussion.[7] In 1974, benefits began to increase automatically with inflation—a key development, since the decade that followed saw unprecedented inflation that led prices to rise faster than wages.

By 1988 the System's expenditures totaled nearly $300 billion, most of which are financed by a flat rate tax on the annual earnings of workers up to a maximum level (currently around $40,000). Half of the tax is deducted from employee paychecks; the other half is paid, at least initially, by employers, but may well be borne in the long run by employees in the form of lower earnings (Brittain 1971). In 1990 the combined tax rate is scheduled to be 12.4% of earnings, up from the 10.8% rate that prevailed in the early 1980s. Social Security retirement benefits are, for the most part, not treated as taxable income. Benefit levels are geared to career earnings although, as we shall see, they replace a much higher fraction of the career earnings of low-wage than high-wage workers.

Pay-As-You-Go

The Social Security system is currently financed on a "pay-as-you-go" basis, with payroll taxes collected each year paying the bulk of the expenditures incurred in that same year. Some analysts (e.g., Pechman et al. 1968) have argued that pay-as-you-go has a compelling theoretical justification analogous to that of a multitude of other current-period tax and transfer programs. In this view, revenue burdens on current workers ought to be evaluated according to standard criteria such as ability to pay; benefits ought to be allocated according to society's judgments of need; and there need not be any linkages between the taxes paid by an individual during his working life and the benefits he receives in retirement. Thus, the pay-as-you-go system is a kind of social insurance in which each generation contributes to the care of the currently retired in return for a promise that the next generation of workers will do the same. Rather than explicitly linking past contributions and current benefits, pay-as-you-go decisions about benefit levels and payroll tax rates are based more on political than actuarial considerations.

In a steady-state world in which all workers contribute taxes throughout their working lives, pay-as-you-go does produce a direct linkage between a given worker's tax contributions and his retirement benefits, with each cohort receiving a return on their payroll tax "investment" equal to the sum of the population growth rate and the rate of growth of real wages (Aaron 1966). The real world is not as cooperative, since differential rates of inflation and real wage growth, different cohort sizes, and shorter-than-full-lifetime tax contributions cause large imbalances between system expenditures and costs. A short-run "crisis" in Social Security financing in the early 1980s was created by the combination of stagnant wages (and therefore payroll tax contributions) and inflation-indexed retirement benefits. A longer-run "crisis" was projected to loom in the twenty-first century when baby-boom retirees would threaten to drop the ratio of workers to beneficiaries from 3.3 in 1980 to 2.1 in 2030, causing the system to run large deficits.[8]

Important changes in the Social Security system were implemented in 1983 and are instructive in the application of pay-as-you-go principles. Rather than turning outside the system to other revenue sources (such as the personal or corporate income tax), the commission recommended and Congress legislated a political compromise in which current beneficiaries bear some costs, primarily with a delay in cost-of-living adjustments and income taxation of the benefits of high-income beneficiaries. Current workers bear the bulk of the costs in the form of higher payroll tax rates and an expansion of earnings subject to taxation. Longer-run imbalances were "solved" in large part with an increase from 65 to 67 in the retirement age at which full benefits could be received, an increase to begin early in the twenty-first century. "Equity" in this compromise appeared to consist of spreading around the costs among current beneficiaries and current workers (who are, of course, future beneficiaries), with due regard to the political power held by each group.

The Pension Model

An alternative way to view Social Security retirement benefits is as a public analogue to a private pension system. In order to make the issues clear, it is first helpful to describe the salient features of private pensions and then to examine Social Security in their light.

In a private pension system, workers contribute (either explicitly or implicitly, in the form of lower earnings) to a company pension fund, which, in turn, is invested in stocks, bonds, and other financial instruments which accumulate dividends, capital gains, and interest. At the point of retirement, workers receive pension benefits either geared explicitly to their contributions plus accrued interest (as in a defined contribution plan) or as some fraction of their earnings in the years just prior to retirement (as in a defined benefit plan).

In either case, but most clearly with defined contribution plans, an important feature of benefits is that the bulk of them constitute accrued interest rather than worker contributions. A person making contributions for 40 working years and then receiving benefits over a 15-year retirement period will receive between one and six dollars in interest for every dollar in contribution, depending on the interest rate.[9] Thus, in a private pension system, workers "deserve" benefits that are much higher than their contributions.

Although President Roosevelt originally proposed the establishment of a fully funded pension fund for the retirement portion of the Social Security system, Congress initially legislated a system with only partial funding. Furthermore, when actuarial projections showed that the fund would accumulate large reserves, Congress spent much of the reserves by expanding the set of beneficiaries to include individuals who would never make substantial contributions to the system but would otherwise have needed public transfers from income-tested programs that have some stigma attached to them. A fully funded system would in any case be utterly impractical under the current program, as it would lead to government ownership of trillions of dollars of American business stock, which is unnecessary given the power of the US government to tax to make good on its obligations. But while there is no Social Security pension fund analogous to private sector funds, one can still evaluate aspects of the Social Security system within the context of a pension model.

The Pension Model's Equity Rule

Under the pension model of Social Security, workers contribute through payroll taxes during their working years, and then they and their spouses receive benefits throughout their retirement years. The equity principle for judging optimal benefits is straightforward: *Each generation of beneficiaries is entitled to benefits that represent its payroll tax contribution plus accrued interest,* where the interest accrual is similar to what would have been earned during the same period of accumulation by a private pension fund. Benefits in excess of what a private pension would pay constitute a transfer to the beneficiaries.

There are several important qualifications and implications of the pension model's equity rule. First, it applies to each generation of beneficiaries *taken as a whole,* and not necessarily to individual beneficiaries. As with private pensions (or any other insurance for that matter), there can be redistribution *within* generations of beneficiaries without violating the equity rule. Individuals who die early in retirement receive a much lower level of benefits than long-lived individuals—an insurance-based redistribution from the unlucky to the lucky.

Somewhat more controversial is redistribution within generations of Social Security beneficiaries owing to the much higher career benefits-to-earnings ratios for low- than high-wage workers and for married couples and single female earners than for single male earners.[10] Some analysts argue for a Social Security model that includes such redistribution; others view Social Security as pure insurance and feel that there should be no such redistribution.[11]

Rates of Return

The pension model views the relationship between payroll contributions and benefits as a crucial criterion in evaluating the system's equity. As with private pensions, calculations that show that the typical worker gets much more out of the system than he puts in are irrelevant; workers are entitled to the large amount of interest earned—explicitly in private plans and implicitly in the Social Security system—on their contributions.

More relevant are so-called "rate of return" calculations, which show the implicit interest rate that equates inflation-adjusted benefits with contributions. A 3% inflation-adjusted rate of return is often taken to be a useful dividing line between above- and below-market rates of return. Rates that differ by as little as one percentage point may seem similar, but in fact make a significant difference in the size of total benefits and costs.

Boskin et al. (1987) calculate rates of return for various cohorts of single-earner couples incorporating all of the changes introduced in 1983 and reasonable assumptions about life expectancy and other parameters that determine benefits and costs. Shown in Figure 25-4 are their rate-of-return figures for high, medium, and low wage workers.[12] Cohorts with rates of return in excess of 3% can be thought of as receiving both pension benefits and transfers. One can consequently use a 3% rate to discount tax contributions and benefits in order to allocate benefits into a portion that represents a pension payment and a portion representing a transfer to the beneficiary. Figure 25-4 also shows the resulting ratio of transfers to total benefits.

Figure 25-4 shows both the dramatic decline—to below market levels—in rates of return for recent cohorts and the substantial redistribution from high- to low-wage workers within cohorts. Cohorts born in 1915, who turned 65 in 1980, receive very high returns, with about half of their benefits representing a transfer. High- and medium-wage workers in cohorts born in 1930 will receive essentially no transfers and thus earn rates of return close to the 3% rate, while medium- and high-wage workers in cohorts born in 1960 and beyond are scheduled to receive far less than would be warranted by a 3% return on their payroll contributions. Thus, the pension model would view current beneficiaries (i.e. the 1915 cohort) as receiving rather large transfers, with current workers facing the prospect of earning below-market rates of return on their payroll tax contributions.

Balancing Revenues and Expenditures

In contrast to the emphasis of the pay-as-you-go model on balancing current-period expenditures and revenues, there need not be any relationship in the pension model between expenditures and costs at any given point. The relative sizes of the population of current retirees and workers have no bearing on the level of retiree benefits, and the pension model views each generation of retirees as entitled only to a market return on

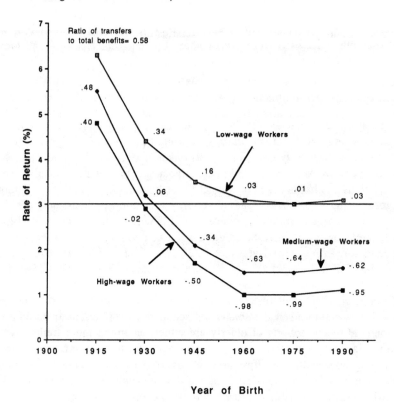

FIGURE 25-4   Social Security rates of return and ratio of transfer to total benefits for various cohorts of workers. *(Source: Boskin et al. 1987, Table 1A)*

its contributions. Implementation of a pension-based benefit formula in a world of different cohort sizes may at times require the use of revenue sources outside the system, while at other times revenues will exceed expenditures and could either accumulate or, if prudent fiscal policy dictates, be spent for other purposes.

The pension model offers a different view of the changes implemented in the 1983 reforms. Rather than helping to equalize the disparate rates of return between current and future generations of retirees, these changes will have the opposite effect. Changes such as delayed cost-of-living increases that affect current retirees lower the rather high rate of return enjoyed by current beneficiaries. But the most significant changes— in particular the jump in the payroll tax rate and the increase in the retirement age from 65 to 67—lower still further the rate of return to current generations of workers.

Are Social Security Benefits Fair?

Whether Social Security costs and benefits are equitably distributed, then, depends on the model under which one chooses to view them. The pension model views current beneficiaries as receiving rates of return that are considerably higher than what the private market would pay, while future beneficiaries are likely to receive below-market rates. Recent "reforms," constrained by the level of pay-as-you-go payroll tax revenues, increased rather than decreased the disparities.

The pay-as-you-go model views all benefits to current beneficiaries as a kind of transfer, while the pension model views only the higher-than-market-return portion of returns to current beneficiaries as representing transfers. Such transfers may be perfectly appropriate if so judged by society, but, according to advocates of pay-as-you-go, they ought to be evaluated in the context of the whole set of possible societal transfer and tax decisions (Kingson et al. 1986). Given the extremely broad-based support accorded to Social Security expenditures, it is quite possible that current transfers to the elderly—even as defined by the pension model—do indeed reflect a societal consensus.[13]

HEALTH STATUS AND THE ECONOMIC WELL-BEING OF THE ELDERLY

The rising prosperity of the elderly has been accompanied by two important developments that may affect their financial standing: increasing longevity with possibly increasing frailty and mounting out-of-pocket health care expenses, particularly for nursing homes. If recent cohorts of elderly are either becoming more frail or incurring more medical costs, then measures of economic well-being based on income may overstate the true financial status of the elderly. To further determine whether or not the aged are indeed becoming better off, we examine recent evidence on the relationship between their longevity, morbidity, and health expenditures.

Increasing Longevity and the Elderly

There has been a dramatic increase in life expectancy at birth during this century for both men and women (Chapman et al. 1986). While these gains are partly the result of a decline in infant and childhood mortality, significant improvements in longevity have also been observed at all ages in adulthood. Perhaps most remarkable has been the significant and unexpected decline in mortality among the elderly. For example, in 1935, when the Social Security system was established, white men and women aged sixty could expect to live approximately fifteen more years (National Center for Health Statistics 1987). This figure had grown to eighteen years for white men and twenty-three years for white women by 1984. A consequence of increasing longevity has been a steady rise in the proportion of elderly in the population. Only 4.1% of the population was over age 65 in 1900, increasing to 11.6% in 1982; that proportion is expected to rise to 13% by 2000 (Spencer 1984). More important in terms of health, those over age 75 comprise a growing proportion of the elderly—by 2000 half of those over 65 will be older than 75, up from 30% just 50 years earlier.

Models of Health Status When Life Expectancy Increases

Predicting changes in average health status among the elderly during a period of increasing longevity is difficult because of the complex relationship between mortality, morbidity, and disability. It is crucial to examine the dynamics between the onset of fatal and nonfatal illnesses, on the one hand, and the expected duration of the disability produced by these diseases.

As the average life span increases among the aged, to what extent will their additional years be free of disease, and to what extent will the increase be due to a rise in the number of frail elderly, who otherwise would have died in the absence of life-saving advances in medical technology and whose lives will be lengthened, but marked by poor health? Fries & Crapo (1981) and Manton & Soldo (1985) provide a useful framework for understanding the debate over these two questions. They propose two "survival" curves, one representing the current mortality patterns and the other showing the time of the first significant chronic disease. The area between these two curves represents the cumulative morbidity years lived by the population between the onset of a chronic illness and death.

What happens to cumulative morbidity years when life expectancy increases—i.e. when the survival curve for mortality becomes more "rectangularized"? Gruenberg (1977) argues that the age at onset of morbidity will not change because the health care system focuses not on prevention, but on the management of disease. This model predicts an extension of life marked by additional years of poor health. In other words, the healthy elderly go on to live more healthy years and they benefit least from the medical and lifestyle changes that have produced declines in elderly mortality. The frail elderly, on the other hand, may now live longer because of these changes, but they do so in poorer health. This position predicts that an increase in life expectancy translates into an increase in cumulative morbidity years. That is, the survival curve for mortality becomes more rectangular, but the curve representing the first significant morbidity event remains unchanged, resulting in an increase in person-years of morbidity.

Fries (1980, 1983) has proposed an alternative prediction based on a theory of the compression of morbidity. He contends that the elderly may experience a postponement of the age at which chronic disease symptoms first appear and suggests that the age at which the first significant onset of disability occurs will rise more quickly than will life expectancy. He argues for the existence of a "natural death" without disease, because all major organs decline in functioning from birth to death simply as a result of senescence, even without any specific pathology. This means that as life expectancy increases, a person's age at the time of the first significant chronic illness increases at an even greater rate and cumulative morbidity years decline. Thus, morbidity should become increasingly concentrated in the years just before death.

Manton (1982) suggests that a type of "dynamic equilibrium" exists which affects the duration of morbidity associated with chronic illnesses. He theorizes that the average duration of a chronic disease may increase in one of two ways. First, the rate of progression of the disease may be slowed, which would increase longevity and the prevalence of disability but reduce the severity of the disease. Alternatively, the rate of progression of the disease may remain unaltered but the lethal complications of the disease (e.g. pneumonia), are eliminated. Manton feels that a large share of the gains in life expectancy have resulted from the first mechanism, but it is difficult to predict what effects these changes will have on the societal costs of caring for the elderly. He suggests that medical costs will rise in order to reduce the severity of the chronic diseases and, accordingly, to lower the mortality rate. Costs might also increase because the prevalence rate of many chronic conditions will naturally rise. However, these health care expenditures may be offset by gains in the economic productivity of the elderly and increases in the length of their working lives.

Empirical Evidence on the Relationship Between Longer Life and Health Status Among the Elderly

The problem with assessing the changing patterns of morbidity during periods of increasing life span is that no systematic data are available that adequately measure the timing of the onset of chronic illnesses relative to the timing of death. The issue is whether the elderly are becoming more or less healthy, on average. Manton & Soldo (1985) question the idea that survival curves are becoming more rectangularized because of reduced mortality at older ages. If the elderly live longer while enjoying proportionately fewer years with chronic illnesses, then one would expect the average age at death to rise, but also the distribution of ages at death to decline over time. In other words, as the elderly approach the natural limits of the life span, there should be an increasing concentration of the timing of death. However, Myers & Manton (1984) and Manton & Soldo (1985) report that while male and female elderly have enjoyed longer lives between 1960 and 1980, this change has not been accompanied by a greater concentration of ages at death.

In order to assess the changing living standards among the elderly and their sensitivity to changes in health conditions, we concentrate on the consequences of changing morbidity patterns rather than on specific diseases. The National Health Interview Survey (NHIS) provides valuable information for tracking the changing health status of the elderly. The NHIS is based on interviews with a national sample of households among the noninstitutionalized population and has been conducted continuously since 1957.

Figure 25-5 shows changes in health status for men and women over age 65 during the past two decades. Two different health status measures are shown: annual restricted activity days due to acute conditions, and annual bed days resulting from acute conditions. Again, these figures are based on the noninstitutionalized elderly population.

Restricted activity days are the most inclusive measure of disability because they include days spent in bed, missed days from work or school, and days when a person limits the things he or she usually does (i.e. cut-down days). There is no clear trend in restricted activity days for either men or women, although the younger noninstitutionalized elderly (ages 65–74) did experience a rise during the 1970s. Bed disability days better represent more severe short-term disability than do work-loss, school-loss, or cut-down days. Figure 25-5 shows again that there are no clear improvements nor deteriorations in health among the elderly.

Trends are also stable as regards limitations in major activity (e.g. work, school, housework) due to chronic conditions, and they do not correspond to declines in mortality rates during this time period. For men, no clear trend can be detected with the possible exception of a decline in limitations during the 1980s (following significant

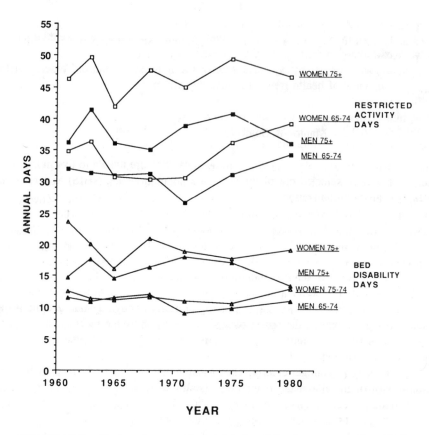

FIGURE 25-5   Changes in annual restricted activity days among the elderly, 1961–1980. *(Source: Adapted from Poterba & Summers 1987, Table 9)*

changes in the structure of the NHIS questionnaire in 1982). For elderly women, the pattern is one of relatively modest increases coupled with decreases in disability, with no apparent trend except, again, for a modest decline during the 1980s.

Verbrugge (1984) also used the NHIS to track the health status of middle-aged and older individuals; however, she had no data available to her from the 1980s and did not distinguish between younger and older elderly. She concluded that there has been some decline in health during the 1970s, and that restricted activity days for all conditions have increased gradually for those over 65. This occurred most significantly during the 1970s, the same period that witnessed declining heart disease mortality. Trends shown in Figure 25-5 indicate that total restricted activity days are gradually rising only for the younger elderly. Verbrugge's conclusion that there is increasing disability among the elderly may therefore apply only to this subgroup. The percentages of those limited in their major or secondary activities (either in the labor market or the home) have also slightly increased for all elderly (65 years or older). However, Baily (1987) finds that the percentage of elderly men and women who were unable to perform their major activity (a more stringent measure of disability than "any" limitations in major activity) between 1960 and 1980 was relatively constant; any increases were largely attributable to changes in the design of the NHIS survey.

An examination of disability rates among the noninstitutionalized elderly yields only a partial view of health trends because those in poorest health are not surveyed (Brody et al. 1987). Using the 1982 National Long-Term Care Survey (NLTCS) of noninstitutionalized persons over age 65 conducted by the Health Care Financing Administration (HCFA), Manton & Soldo (1985) find that disability rates among the elderly remain relatively stable as one moves from one age category to the next. This is largely because the most severely disabled persons, who are unable to live in the community, have been selected out of the surveyed population (i.e. NHIS) as a result of mortality or institutionalization.

It is not yet clear whether more recent cohorts of elderly, with their higher rates of survival, will show higher rates of disability among the noninstitutionalized (i.e. they will survive in greater numbers to become disabled but remain healthy enough to avoid institutionalization) or will have higher rates of institutionalization (i.e. they will survive in greater numbers only to succumb to serious disabilities later in life). Figure 25-6 shows that since 1963 a small rise has occurred in the annual percentage of younger elderly (ages 75–84) living in nursing homes, although a small decline is observed in 1982. However, the oldest old (85 or older) show the most substantial and sustained decline in the percentage living in nursing homes since the early 1970s. Poterba & Summers (1987) argue that this may indicate the improving health of the oldest old relative to younger elderly. They assume that non-health factors, such as the availability of financial assistance and home health care, operate equally among all elderly who are in need of nursing home care. Therefore, they argue that the recent drop in nursing home residency rates among the oldest old is likely to be the result of improving health status.

Soldo and Manton (1985) and Doty (1986) expect institutionalization rates for the elderly to increase because of reduced opportunities for alternative home care. For example, elderly parents may receive less care from their adult children since those children, elderly themselves, have health concerns of their own to contend with.

According to Poterba & Summers (1987), the relatively stable measures of morbidity over the past 20 years indicate that general improvements in morbidity are offset by higher rates of morbidity among "marginal survivors" who are living longer lives. While they conclude that longer life does not necessarily mean worsening health, they imply that current and possibly future cohorts of elderly will endure the same rates of morbidity but for more years. They adopt a position somewhere between that of Fries (1983) and Gruenberg (1977): on average, the elderly are living longer, but their patterns of disability remain the same.

Overall, it appears that the elderly have not benefitted from the improvement in health predicted by Fries (1983). Instead, the noninstitutionalized elderly are experiencing steady rates of morbidity and disability. Disability among the elderly in the community has remained relatively constant, both when rates of institutionalization were increasing and now when they are decreasing.

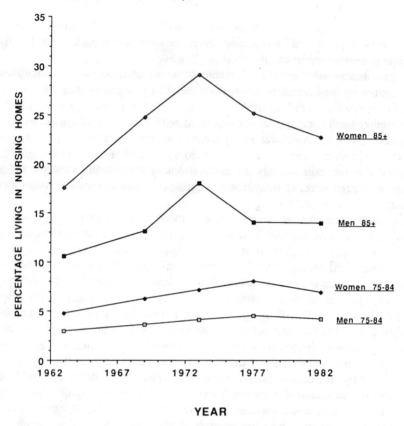

FIGURE 25-6   Proportion of elderly living in nursing homes, 1963–1982. *(Source: Adapted from Poterba & Summers 1987, Table 7)*

Changes in Morbidity and the Economic Status of the Elderly

Medical costs associated with care of the elderly pose a threat to recent economic gains made by this group. Before we discuss the expenses incurred directly by the elderly, it is important to describe briefly the primary sources of funding for medical care for the elderly: Medicare and Medicaid (see Davis & Rowland 1986 and Gornick et al. 1985 for a full discussion of these programs). Medicare went into effect during July 1966 and was designed to reduce financial burdens and therefore increase access to medical care for the elderly, the age group with the highest rates of illness and the lowest income. Medicare has two components: hospital insurance (Part A) and supplementary medical insurance (Part B). Part A covers the majority of hospital costs associated with acute inpatient hospital care as well as a fixed number of days in skilled nursing facilities. In general, the beneficiary must pay a small out-of-pocket inpatient hospital deductible, which rose from $40 in 1967 to $400 in 1985. To avoid further deductibles and coinsurance stipulations, many elderly purchase so-called Medigap health policies to cover additional expenses (Rice 1987). The Part A trust fund relies on revenues generated from a payroll tax of current workers. Part B is designed to provide payments for physician expenses and physician-ordered services and supplies. The individual must pay a monthly premium ($3 in 1967, $15.50 in 1985) as well as a yearly premium. For each accepted claim for payment for physician services—and not all claims are granted—the Medicare beneficiary must pay 20% of the allowed expenses. Part B is funded by enrollee premiums as well as general tax revenues.

Medicaid covers many medical expenses incurred by the poor and near-poor elderly that are not covered by Medicare. Perhaps one of its most important functions is to provide coverage for nursing home expenses. In order to become eligible, individuals must "spend down" their savings and assets to satisfy the program's income and asset restrictions (i.e. in 1988, an individual is eligible if he has less than $1900 in income and assets).

While both Medicare and Medicaid will continue to undergo changes that will directly affect the economic status of the elderly (e.g. greater contributions by the elderly; see Davis & Rowland, 1986), there is no question that this group will continue to show the highest health care utilization rates and, correspondingly, health care costs. Recent trends indicate that the differential in this respect between the elderly and younger cohorts is growing (Lubitz & Deacon 1982). This is in keeping with the higher rates of self-reported disability among the elderly, relative to the rest of the adult population. Davis & Rowland (1986) note that the rate of hospitalizations is growing faster for those over 65 than those under 65.[14]

Are the elderly seriously threatened by the potentially catastrophic costs of health care, or are they protected by public and private medical insurance programs? Gornick et al. (1985) and Waldo & Lazenby (1984) show that the percentage of all medical costs paid out-of-pocket declined among the elderly from 53.2% in 1966 to 29.3% in 1977, then to 25.2% in 1984. Correspondingly, the portion of medical expenses paid by Medicare rose from zero to 44.1 to 48.8%.

Out-of-pocket medical expenses among the elderly have continued to be a small portion of their personal income. The US Senate's Special Committee on Aging (cited in Gornick et al. 1985) estimated that the elderly spent approximately 15% of their personal income on out-of-pocket medical expenses prior to Medicare. While this figure dropped to 12% in 1977, it was back to 15% in 1984. However, because of accelerating inflation in medical care costs, the proportion of out-of-pocket health care expenditures paid by the elderly is expected to rise to 18% in 1989 (Rabin & Stockton 1987).[15]

Impoverishment and Nursing Home Costs

There is little doubt that many medical expenses incurred by the elderly for acute conditions have been covered by Medicare. In spite of these benefits, many disabled elderly remain economically vulnerable to the high costs of nursing home care, most of which are paid by the elderly themselves and their families. What are the financial implications for an elderly person and his family when he enters a nursing home?

Medicaid coverage has reduced the institutionalization costs borne by the individual from their pre-Medicaid levels. For example, two years prior to the initiation of Medicaid, nearly two thirds of all nursing home care expenditures were covered by private payments (Rabin & Stockton 1987). This percentage dropped to roughly 50% in 1967, the year after the Medicaid program began, and remained at that level throughout the 1970s. By 1984, Waldo & Lazenby (1984) find that only 3% of hospital expenses and 25% of physician costs were paid out-of-pocket; in sharp contrast, half of nursing home expenses were paid directly by the elderly.

A recent Congressional report found that nearly half of the elderly whose nursing home expenses were covered by Medicaid became eligible by spending down their income and assets after they entered the nursing home (US House of Representatives 1987). The same report estimated that in the 1980s, "after only 13 weeks in a nursing home, 7 in ten elderly persons living alone find their income spent down to the federal poverty level" (p. 6). Nearly half of elderly couples living alone are impoverished by the end of one year in a nursing home. Given that large portions of nursing home care are paid out-of-pocket, and 40% of those 65–69 will enter a nursing home at some time during their lifetime (US House of Representatives 1987), there will be a significant financial impact resulting from institutionalization among the growing ranks of the elderly.

Comparable statistics are not available for earlier pre- and post-Medicaid years, but Davis & Rowland (1986) report figures that point to worsening financial consequences of institutionalization. They find that between 1972 and 1981, the number of elderly Medicaid beneficiaries increased slightly from 3.3 million in 1972 to 3.7 million in 1974, falling slowly to 3.5 million by 1981. However, the annual expenditure per beneficiary increased from $580 in 1972 to nearly $2800 in 1981. The trends in the number of beneficiaries reflect the fact that there are proportionately fewer elderly poor who are eligible for Medicaid coverage, although the number of elderly is growing. But for those who enter nursing homes, the financial burden to both the Medicaid system and the elderly themselves has risen dramatically. Recall that the Medicaid expenditures for the elderly represent costs incurred to the system after the elderly have spent down their savings and assets.

Unfortunately, no long-term individual-level cohort data exist to shed light on how it happens that elderly living in the community become institutionalized, or how they cover the associated expenses. However, Rivlin & Wiener (1988) report simulated financial consequences of institutionalization based on current and projected utilization and expenditure patterns among the elderly. Given current levels of public support for nursing home care and prevailing medical and demographic trends, Rivlin & Wiener project that the risk of impoverishment will rise in the coming decades for the institutionalized elderly. Out-of-pocket nursing home costs for those 65 and older will average (in constant 1987 dollars) nearly $30,000 for the entire stay in 2016–2020, with 17% of nursing home residents paying over $50,000. They estimate that of all nursing home expenses, the proportion paid out-of-pocket will nearly double between 1988 and 2020. Total Medicaid expenditures for nursing homes are expected to more than double during the same period.

SUMMARY

In purely economic terms, the typical elderly person today enjoys a standard of living that is much higher than at any time in the past, and perhaps higher than that of the average nonelderly person. While part of the improvement stems from a greater accumulation of wealth in the form of owned homes, financial assets, and private pensions, much of it is due to more generous Social Security benefits. When viewed as a pension, Social Security payments to current retirees provide a much higher rate of return on past payroll contributions than private pensions would generally have paid. Soon, however, this situation will be reversed: under current rules, the typical worker retiring after the year 2000 will receive benefits that reflect a lower-than-market rate of return, and the rate of return will continue to drop for new retirees throughout the first quarter of the twenty-first century.

Whether or not one concludes that current retirees are unfairly advantaged and future retirees unfairly disadvantaged by the structure of Social Security depends on the model used to assess system equity. Within the context of a pension model, high benefits to current retirees represent a huge income transfer from current workers to current retirees. Given the overwhelming support accorded Social Security expenditures by both elderly and nonelderly, the transfer may well reflect a societal consensus that the elderly constitute the group most deserving of higher transfers, perhaps in part because Social Security benefits substitute for the more problematic transfers from adult children to elderly parents that would otherwise have to be made. However, the pension model also views the higher payroll taxes on current workers used to finance the transfer as increasing society's obligation for future benefits when current workers retire. Current projections indicate that these obligations will not be met.

Although the status of the average elderly person appears to be quite comfortable, many subgroups of elderly enjoy little economic security. Poverty rates are quite high among female and minority elderly, and the surprising turnover witnessed among the elderly poor means that larger numbers are at risk of at least occasional poverty than single-year figures would suggest. Economic status typically falls substantially after retirement, following a dynamic that is not well understood.

Fortunately, the elderly in the United States are enjoying longer lives without an apparent decline in health. For those elderly requiring medical care, access to hospital and physician care has been enhanced by the advent of Medicare and Medicaid. These programs have allowed many elderly to avoid large out-of-pocket expenses for acute care. However, as the population continues to age, the elderly may be required to pay more of their medical expenses directly, a change that currently is the subject of heated debate. Part of this change is driven by a decline in the view that children should be financially responsible for their elderly parents (Crystal 1982). The more immediate factor that places the elderly in increased economic jeopardy is the risk of institutionalization. Many elderly live in the community free of disabling health conditions, but those who must enter nursing homes run a substantial risk of losing any gains they may have made during their later years.

NOTES

1. Radner's analysis (1987, Table 7) of income changes between 1967 and 1984 using data from the *Current Population Surveys* showed that between 1979 and 1984 the average annual percentage change in real income for family units headed by an elderly person was 3.4 percent, while it was minus .4 percent for family units headed by a nonelderly person.

2. Radner (1987, Table 9) found that income inequality for family units headed by elderly individuals fell substantially between 1967 and 1979, and then rose slightly between 1979 and 1984. The share of family income received by the bottom quintile of family units headed by elderly individuals rose from 4.6% in 1967 to 5.6% in 1984; comparable shares for the bottom quintile of nonelderly family units fell from 5.2 to 3.9%.

3. The 1949 rates are reported in Ross et al. (1987). The 1986 poverty rates and those presented below are based on *Current Population Survey* estimates as reported in *US Special Committee on Aging* (1987–1988), Table 2–7.

4. The Retirement History Survey interviewed households headed by a person aged 58 to 63 in 1969 and repeated the interviews at two-year intervals over the following ten-year period. Burkhauser et al. (1988) restrict their analysis to couples who were nonpoor and intact at the time of retirement.

5. Myers et al. (1987) find that the majority of widows in the Retirement History Survey (RHS) lost all pension income when their husbands died. RHS data cover the period from 1969 to 1979. The Retirement Equity Act of 1984 required workers, beginning in 1986, to obtain their spouse's signature if they opted for a single-life pension. This legislation may well increase the prevalence of pensions with spousal benefits; it does nothing for widows whose spouses had no pension and is therefore likely to have a rather limited effect on the poverty rates of older women (Myers et al. 1987).

6. Data used in Figure 25-3 come from Radner (1987, Tables 12 and 16) and are expressed in 1982 dollars. Income amounts are adjusted for family size using the poverty threshold adult equivalent scales and are normalized on one-person family units. For example, income amounts for units consisting of a single elderly individual are divided by .943; the division factor for units with two elderly persons is 1.190. Unrelated individuals are treated as one-person family units. The "Property" income category includes interest, dividends, rent and income from estates and trusts. The "Other" category includes public transfers such as Supplemental Security Income as well as public (non-Social Security) and private pensions and several other miscellaneous income sources.

7. Equity aspects of financing Medicare medical benefits are considerably more complicated and not addressed here.

8. These ratios come from the "Intermediate (B) Projections" in the 1983 Trustees' Report as reported in Thompson (1983) and are generally regarded as the most reasonable.

9. At a 3% interest rate, interest constitutes 58% of total benefits; at a 6% rate the comparable fraction is 83%. Unfortunately, using market interest rates in these calculations is misleading, because most of the resulting accumulation reflects inflation rather than inflation-adjusted real increases in purchasing power. It is safer to use interest rates of 2%–3% in these calculations because they represent the historical difference between nominal interest rates and the rate of inflation.

10. Thompson (1983, Table 1) reports calculations from the Social Security Administration of benefit-to-earnings ratios for workers with uninsured spouses retiring at age 65 in 1983. Workers who worked half-time at minimum wage jobs throughout their careers would receive benefits equal to 1.35 times their earnings just prior to retirement. Comparable rates for full-time minimum wage workers, full-time workers with average earnings and workers at the maximum taxable earnings are .95, .69 and .39, respectively.

11. Thompson's (1983) review article gives a full set of references to the so-called "annuity-welfare" model, which has an explicit role for redistribution within generations, and the "insurance" model, which does not.

12. High, medium and low wage levels are defined as $50,000, $30,000 and $10,000, respectively, in 1985 dollars. These figures were chosen to correspond roughly to the earnings levels of well-paid professionals, median workers and poverty-line workers.

13. For example, the 1986 General Social Survey, taken after the 1983 reforms, showed that a majority (56%) of respondents thought that the country was spending "too little" on Social Security. If anything, younger respondents were *more* supportive of increased spending, which suggests that organizations lobbying on behalf of increased spending for the elderly are tapping

a deep reservoir of support for transfers to the elderly among voters of all ages (Ponza et al. 1988).

It may seem that support for Social Security among the nonelderly runs contrary to self-interest. Of course, many of the nonelderly have elderly parents or other relatives who are current beneficiaries, and Social Security benefits may be a much smoother way of transferring money from adult children to their elderly parents. But it is also in the financial self-interest of many current workers to support the system. For example, the below-market rates of return shown for median earners in the 1945 birth cohort reflect calculations based on likely benefits and *total* payroll contributions. Boskin et al. (1987) show that if one compares likely benefits with *future* payroll contributions, then the rate of return jumps from 2.1% to 4.5%. Thus, workers who consider past contributions to be "sunk costs" should view continuing the system as very much in their self-interest.

14. In 1967, those under 65 had fewer than 130 admissions per 1000 population and this figure increased to only 135 admissions per 1000 by 1979. The comparable figures for those over age 65 are 260 and 350 in 1967 and 1979, respectively.

15. Gornick et al. (1985) report that the growth in costs for hospital inpatient care between 1973 & 1983 can be accounted for by five factors: overall inflation, 51%; increase in the size of the covered population, 7%; excess inflation in hospital input prices, 15%; higher admissions per capita, 4%; and more services used per hospital admission, 23%.

LITERATURE CITED

Aaron, H. J. 1966. The social insurance paradox. *Can. J. Econ. Polit. Sci.* 32:371–74

Baily, M. N. 1987. Aging and the ability to work: policy issues and recent trends. See Burtless 1987, pp. 59–97

Bane, M. J., Ellwood, D. T. 1986. Slipping into and out of poverty: the dynamics of spells. *J. Hum. Resour.* 21:1–23

Binstock, R. H. 1983. The aged as scapegoat. *Gerontologist* 23:136–43

Boskin, M. J., Kotlikoff, L. J., Puffert, D. J., Shoven, J. B. 1987. Social security: a financial appraisal across and within generations. *Nat. Tax J.* 11:19–34

Brittain, J. A. 1971. The incidence of Social Security payroll taxes. *Am. Econ. Rev.* 61: 110–25

Brody, J. A., Brock, D. B., Williams, T. F. 1987. Trends in the health of the elderly population. *Annu. Rev. Publ. Health* 8:11–34

Burkhauser, R. V., Duncan, G. J. 1989. Economic risks of gender roles: income loss and life events over the life course. *Soc. Sci. Q.*

Burkhauser, R. V., Duncan, G. J. 1988. Life events, public policy, and the economic vulnerability of children and the elderly. In *The Vulnerable,* ed. J. Palmer, T. Smeeding, B. Torrey. Washington, DC: Urban Inst.

Burkhauser, R. V., Holden, K. C., Feaster, D. 1988. Incidence, timing, and events associated with poverty: a dynamic view of poverty in retirement. *J. Gerontol. Soc. Sci.* 43:S46–52

Burkhauser, R. V., Warlick, J. L. 1981. Disentangling the annuity from the redistribution aspects of social security in the United States. *Rev. Income Wealth.* 27:401–21

Burtless, G. 1987. *Work, Health, and Income among the Elderly.* Washington, DC: Brookings Inst.

Chapman, S. H., LaPlante, M. P., Wilensky, G. 1986. Life expectancy and health status of the aged. *Soc. Secur. Bull.* 49:24–48

Coe, R. C. 1988. A longitudinal examination of poverty in the elderly years. *Gerontologist* 28:540–44

Crystal, S. 1982. *America's Old Age Crisis.* New York: Basic

Danziger, S., van der Gaag, J., Smolensky, E., Taussig, M. K. 1984. Implications of the relative economic status of the elderly for transfer policy. In *Retirement and Economic Behavior,* ed. H. J. Aaron, G. Burtless. Washington, DC: Brookings Inst.

Davis, K., Rowland, D. 1986. *Medicare Policy.* Baltimore: Johns Hopkins Univ. Press

Doty, P. 1986. Family care of the elderly: the role of public policy. *Milbank Mem. Fund Q./Health Soc.* 64:34–75

Fries, J. F. 1980. Aging, natural death, and the compression of morbidity. *New Engl. J. Med.* 303:130–35

Fries, J. F. 1983. The compression of morbidity. *Milbank Mem. Fund Q./Health Soc.* 61:397–419

Fries, J. F., L. M., Crapo. 1981. *Vitality and Aging: Implications of the Rectangular Curve.* San Francisco: Freeman

Gornick, M., Greenberg, J. N., Eggers, P. W., Dobson, A. 1985. Twenty years of medicare and medicaid. *Health Care Finan. Rev.* (Suppl):13–59

Gruenberg, E. M. 1977. The failures of success. *Milbank Mem. Fund Q./Health Soc.* 55:3–24

Holden, K. C., Burkhauser, R. V. 1988. From riches to rags: the economic consequences of widowhood. Mimeo

Kingson, E. R., Hirshorn, B. A., Cornman, J. M. 1986. *Ties That Bind: The Interdependence of Generations.* Washington, DC: Seven Locks

Lubitz, J., Deacon, R. 1982. The rise in incidence of hospitalizations among the aged, 1967 to 1979. *Health Care Finan. Rev.* 3:21–40

Manton, K. G. 1982. Changing concepts of morbidity and mortality in the elderly population. *Milbank Mem. Fund Q./Health Soc.* 60:183–244

Manton, K. G., Soldo, B. J. 1985. Dynamics of health changes in the oldest old: new perspectives and evidence. *Milbank Mem. Fund Q./Health Soc.* 63:206–85

Morgan, J. N. 1977. An economic theory of the social security system and its relation to fiscal policy. In *Income Support Policies for the Aged,* ed. G. Tolley, R. Burkhauser, pp. 107–126. Cambridge, Mass: Ballinger

Myers, D. A., Burkhauser, R. V., Holden, K. C. 1987. The transition from wife to widow: the importance of survivor benefits to widows. *J. Risk Insur.* 54:752–759

Myers, G. C., Manton, K. G. 1984. The compression of morbidity: myth or reality? *Gerontologist* 24:346–53

Myers, R. J. 1985. *Social Security.* Homewood, Ill: Irwin 3rd ed.

Myrdal, G. 1963. *Challenge to Affluence.* New York: Pantheon

National Center for Health Statistics. 1987. *Vital Statistics of the United States, 1984,* Vol. II, Sec. 6, *Life Tables.* DHHS Pub. No. (PHS) 87-1104. Washington, DC: USGPO

Palmer, J. L., Smeeding, T., Torrey, B. B. eds. 1988. *The Vulnerable.* Washington, DC: Urban Inst.

Pechman, J. A., Aaron, H. A., Taussig, M. K. 1968. *Social Security: Perspective for Reform.* Washington, DC: Brookings Inst.

Ponza, M., Duncan, G. J., Corcoran, M. C., Grosskind, F. 1988. The guns of autumn: age differences in the support of transfers to the younger and old. *Publ. Opin. Q.* 52:441–66

Poterba, J. M., Summers, L. H. 1987. Public policy implications of declining old-age mortality. See Burtless 1987, pp. 19–58

Preston, S. 1984. Children and the elderly: Divergent paths for America's dependents. *Demography* 21:435–58

Quinn, J. F. 1985. The economic status of the elderly: beware of the mean. *Rev. Income Wealth* 33:63–83

Rabin, D. L., Stockton, P. 1987. *Long Term Care for the Elderly.* New York: Oxford Univ. Press

Radner, D. B. 1982. Distribution of family income: improved estimates. *Soc. Secur. Bull.* 45:13–21

Radner, D. B. 1987. Money incomes of aged and nonaged family units, 1967–84. *Soc. Secur. Bull.* 50:9–28

Rice, D. P., Feldman, J. J. 1983. Living longer in the United States: demographic changes and health needs of the elderly. *Milbank Mem. Fund Q./Health Soc.* 61:362–96

Rice, T. 1987. An economic assessment of health care coverage for the elderly. *Milbank Mem. Fund Q./Health Soc.* 65:488–520

Rivlin, A. M., Wiener, J. M. 1988. *Caring for the Disabled Elderly: Who Will Pay?* Washington, DC: Brookings Inst.

Ross, C. M., Danziger, S., Smolensky, E. 1987. Interpreting changes in the economic status of the elderly, 1949–1979. *Contemp. Policy Iss.* 5:98–112

Schultz, J. H. 1988. *The Economics of Aging.* Dover, Mass: Auburn House. 4th ed.

Smeeding, T. M. 1982. Alternative methods for valuing selected in-kind transfer benefits and measuring their effects on poverty. *Technical Paper 50.* Washington, DC: US Bur. Census

Smeeding, T. M. 1986. Nonmoney income and the elderly: the case of the 'tweeners. *J. Policy Anal. Mgmt.* 5:707–24

Smolensky, E., Danziger, S., Gottschalk, P. 1988. The declining significance of age: trends in the well-being of children and the elderly since 1939. In *The Vulnerable,* J. L. Palmer, T. Smeeding, B. B. Torrey, Washington, DC: Urban Inst. Press

Soldo, B. J., Manton, K. G. 1985. Changes in the health status and service needs of the oldest old: Current patterns and future trends. *Milbank Mem. Fund/Health Soc.* 63:286–319

Spencer, G. 1984. Projections of the population in the United States, by age, sex, and race: 1980 to 2080. *Curr. Popul. Rep. Ser. P-25, No. 952.* Washington, DC: US Bur. Census

Thompson, L. H. 1983. The social security reform debate. *J. Econ. Lit.* 21:1425–67

US House of Representatives, Select Committee on Aging. 1987. *Long term care and personal impoverishment: seven in ten elderly living alone are at risk. Comm. Pub. No. 100–631.* Washington, DC: USGPO

US Special Committee on Aging. 1987–88. *Aging America: Trends and Projections,* Washington, DC: US Dep. Health Hum. Serv.

Verbrugge, L. M. 1984. Longer life but worsening health? Trends in health and mortality of middle-aged and older persons. *Milbank Mem. Fund Q./Health Soc.* 62:475–519

Waldo, D. R. Lazenby, H. C. 1984. Demographic characteristics and health care use and expenditures by the aged in the United States: 1977–1984. *Health Care Finan. Rev.* 6:1–29

26

Family Status and Poverty among Older Women: The Gendered Distribution of Retirement Income in the United States

MADONNA HARRINGTON MEYER

Although the elderly in general enjoy improved economic status, older women continue to face disproportional impoverishment. In fact, nearly three-fourths of the elderly poor in the United States are women. Harrington Meyer suggests that old-age income schemes are gendered in three key ways: (1) retirement income is linked to waged labor, which is itself gendered; (2) nonwaged reproductive labor, performed predominantly by women, is not recognized as labor; and (3) family status is conceptualized as permanent rather than transient. Her examination of supposedly gender-neutral eligibility and benefit structures in Social Security, private pensions, and personal pensions such as Individual Retirement Accounts demonstrates how they produce a gendered distribution of old-age income.

While the elderly in the United States have made remarkable economic gains in recent decades (U.S. Bureau of Census 1989:9), these gains have not been enjoyed evenly. Certain groups—women, blacks, and the oldest old—still suffer high rates of poverty (Pearce 1989). Among these groups, older women are among the most disadvantaged. Women comprise 59 percent of the aged population and 71 percent of the aged poor population (U.S. Bureau of Census 1989:58).

Marriage generally serves to protect the elderly from poverty; household income data reveal that just six percent of married older men and women are poor (U.S. Bureau of Census 1989:32). Poverty rates for all other categories of marital status are sig-

"Family Status and Poverty among Older Women: The Gendered Distribution of Retirement Income in the United States" by Madonna Harrington Meyer, from *Social Problems*, 37 (1990): 551–563. Copyright © 1990 by the University of California Press Journals.

nificantly higher. For example, Table 26-1 shows that 20 percent of widowed and 24 percent of divorced older women are impoverished. Unmarried older people are more likely to be poor than their married counterparts. The greater incidence of poverty among older women is directly linked to their greater likelihood of being unmarried; 25 percent of older men and 60 percent of older women are unmarried (U.S. Bureau of Census 1989:58).

Reports of household income hide latent poverty among married women (U.S. Congress: Senate 1990:32, 29). In 1988 the median income for married older women—considered separately from their husbands' incomes—was just $5,485, only 43 percent of that received by married older men. With such relatively low incomes, many married women are at risk of impoverishment should their spouses die, divorce, or enter a nursing home. The cessation of marriage in old age raises the risk of poverty for all older citizens, but the consequences for older women, following a lifetime of economic subordination, can be devastating (Older Women's League 1988). Phrases like "the aged poor" or "the impoverished elderly" obscure the fact that these people primarily are women (Pascall 1986:6).

To understand the mechanisms that reproduce gender inequality, I critically examine the supposedly gender-neutral arrangements of old-age income programs. I begin with a review of feminist arguments on how retirement income is structured around gender, examine the benefit and eligibility structures of three major sources of retirement income—Social Security, private pensions, and individual retirement accounts —and discuss various policy proposals in terms of their effects on older women.

WAGED LABOR, REPRODUCTIVE LABOR, AND FAMILY STATUS IN OLD AGE

Recent research suggests that we could expect retirement income to be significantly gendered in that it reflects: (1) the influence of the waged labor force; (2) a gendered conception of work; and (3) a view of marriage and family life as permanent.

Gender and the Waged Labor Force

On the basis of two cohort studies of women born in the 1910s and 1920s, O'Rand and Henretta (1982) and Herz (1988) argue that women's working and retirement income is low because of the competing demands of child care, homemaking, and waged labor. Old-age income schemes currently favor those with higher working wages and lengthy and continuous waged labor force participation. Men tend to be relieved of domestic work and are available for the more stable, higher waged, and better protected market positions (Sokoloff 1980:201). Responsibility for child care and domestic labor delays and interrupts women's waged labor force participation, causing them to be segregated into secondary sectors of the labor market, and into part-time work in particular. As a result, they typically receive low working wages, low public pensions, and little or no private pensions. After breaks in their work careers, women are often treated as new employees (Land 1978). Over time they often exchange some flexibility in working hours for lower pay and prospects. Women are less likely than men to be employed in core industries where pension coverage is high (Quadagno 1988). They are less likely to receive benefits even when they work in industries with high coverage because eligibility requirements favor lengthy and continuous service. When women do receive benefits, the amount is considerably lower than men's because retirement wages are based on working wages. This gender gap in working wages is replicated in retirement wages; women's working and retirement wages are on average just 60 percent of men's (Reskin and Hartmann 1986:1). Women's pattern of labor force participation fails to approximate men's; thus they are denied access to maximum old-age benefits.

Some are optimistic that the picture will improve for later cohorts of women because younger women today are less inclined to interrupt full-time work for childbearing or other reproductive labor (Herz 1988; O'Rand and Henretta 1982). Labor force participation rates of never-married and married women ages 25–34 differed in 1957 by 50 percent, but by 1987 the gap had narrowed to only 15 percent (Herz 1988). Although today's cohort of older women often delayed, interrupted, or eliminated waged labor force participation to perform reproductive labor, current cohorts of women in their reproductive years show no drop in overall labor force participation. With time, then, women will be fully integrated into the waged labor force and will compete on an equal footing with men for old age income.

Others are less optimistic, arguing that women's increased participation in the labor force has not significantly lessened the effect of reproductive labor on women's waged labor (Ferree 1987; Reskin and Hartmann 1986). Moreover, Reskin (1988) points out that sex segregation in the labor force has remained remarkably stable. Ferree (1987) demonstrates that where women have increased their numbers in traditionally male jobs, the rewards and opportunities attached to these jobs have typically diminished. Finally, Reskin argues that the segregation of women into secondary labor markets is but one of many ways that men retain their economic advantage. Because the structure of retirement income reflects men's interests more than women's (Quadagno 1988), the integration of women into the labor force alone will not significantly diminish women's economic dependency.

Excluding Reproductive Labor from the Definition of Work

Retirement income is based on a gendered conceptualization of work. Women's old-age poverty is directly linked to a sexual division of labor that relegates the reproduc-

TABLE 26-1   Poverty Rates by Race, Sex, and Marital Status, Age 65 and Over, 1987

	Male			Female		
	Total	White	Black	Total	White	Black
Single	17.7	15.9	—	23.3	22.3	33.5
Married, spouse present	5.9	4.9	17.3	5.7	4.7	19.5
Married, spouse absent	17.1	11.3	34.8	35.2	26.9	—
Widowed	14.6	11.6	36.7	20.0	16.9	48.0
Divorced	19.1	15.5	—	23.9	20.4	50.5

SOURCE: Calculated from U.S. Bureau of Census, 1989, Table 8:32–37.

tive labor performed almost exclusively by women to the non-waged or private sector of society (Hartmann 1981; Young 1981; Acker 1988). For much of the work women do, they earn neither working wages nor retirement wages (Ferree 1987:338; Stone and Minkler 1984:232). Women are almost exclusively responsible for non-waged reproductive labor including the provision of food, clothing, and shelter and care for children, the disabled, and the elderly (Laslett and Brenner 1989:384). Despite increasing participation in the paid labor force, women have retained almost complete responsibility for unpaid domestic work and childrearing (Ferree 1987:325; Reskin and Hartmann 1986:16). Pascall (1986) argues paid work lessens women's identification with housework but fails to substantially shift the burden.

With age, women often exchange mothering for other family caregiving responsibilities (Stone and Minkler 1984:233; Brody 1981:471; Pascall 1986; McIntosh 1979; Land 1983; Lewis 1983). In 1982, 72 percent of the unpaid caregivers for the frail elderly in the United States were women (U.S. Congress: Senate, 1988:19). Unpaid responsibilities often interfere with or prohibit women's participation in the paid labor force. Caring for an ailing parent causes thousands of working daughters to rearrange their work schedules, take time off from work without pay, and reduce their working hours (Stone 1989:27). In one national sample of married persons working shift hours, 12.3 percent of the women (and 2.5 percent of the men) said they did shift work so they could care for an adult family member (Presser 1990). This labor, which consumes so much of women's time and energy, is not paid and not regarded as work.

Some seek to liberate women from their work in the domestic sphere while others celebrate reproductive labor, demanding that it be reasonably compensated. Brenner (1987) and Bergmann (1982), for example, argue that women must be relieved of the burden of reproductive work, which should be regarded as a societal rather than a woman's responsibility. Bergmann suggests that the disadvantages of being a housewife are so great that the role should be avoided on even a temporary basis. She opposes policies that would increase the economic security of traditional homemakers in old age because they reinforce the traditional division of labor. O'Brien (1981) and Pascall (1986), alternately, argue that the answer cannot lie in devaluing reproductive labor; to deny women's reproductive work is to deny the labor that has in part historically defined women. Quadagno (1988) asks why the rules are structured to penalize women for their reproductive work rather than rewarding them for the work they do in the domestic sphere. The objective is to rewrite the rules so that women are rewarded, both in terms of working and retirement wages, for their reproductive labor.

The Transiency of Family Status in Old Age

Rule structures of old age pension schemes are grounded in a conceptualization of family status as permanent despite insurmountable evidence that it is transient. Retirement wage programs are based on a traditional family model with a male breadwinner and a dependent female caregiver. But the model does not describe contemporary social structure (Pascall 1986:47). Most people are only in nuclear families for brief portions of their lives. A lifetime of unpaid or underpaid labor leaves many older women ill-prepared for economic security without a spouse (Glasse 1988:2; Stone and Minkler

1984:230), yet with age women are increasingly likely to become single. U.S. old age income schemes are maximally beneficial only to men and women who manage to sustain a traditional marriage. While men and women alike are penalized for their failure to do so by the increased likelihood of poverty, women, because they are more likely to be dependent within marriage, and less likely to sustain a traditional marriage into old age, suffer the greater risk of impoverishment under existing policies. By ignoring that marriage ends for a large proportion of older women, pension plan and individual retirement account rule structures systematically penalize women as a group.

THE GENDERED STRUCTURE OF RETIREMENT INCOME IN THE UNITED STATES

Social Security

Social Security is the primary source of retirement income for most elderly people and the only source for many elderly women (Older Women's League 1988). Table 26-2 shows that nearly 40 percent of all elderly income comes from Social Security. Table 26-3 shows that 70 percent of all income received by the poor elderly comes from Social Security. For the nonpoor elderly, Social Security accounts for just 40 percent of total income. Because Social Security benefits are based on working wages, women's mean monthly benefits are significantly lower than men's. Average monthly benefits in 1987 for men were $576 compared to $403 for women; women's benefits were just 70 percent of men's (Social Security Bulletin 1988:2). The gender gap in Social Security benefits is less severe than the gap in working wages because Social Security benefit formulas are purposely designed to redistribute money from higher waged to lower waged earners; thus the variation of wages by gender is truncated.

Eligibility for Social Security is based on 40 quarters or 10 years in the waged labor force (Greenberg 1978). The quarter years need not be continuous; thus women's eligibility is not penalized for interrupting waged work with reproductive labor. Initially, under the 1935 Social Security Act, one-half of all workers were excluded from coverage by their occupation (Quadagno 1984). Increasingly Social Security coverage approaches universality (Quadagno 1988), but coverage is limited to formal wage relationships. Workers in informal wage relationships are not covered by Social Security. No statistics are available on how many people are excluded, but there is evidence of underreporting of both migrant work and private household work. For example, domestic workers, who are almost exclusively women, have been covered by Social Security since 1951. However, "employers and domestics both avoid paying the 5.85 percent of domestic's wages that would be their share of the tax" (Rollins 1985:56). After a lifetime of marginal earnings, most domestic workers face old age with no regular source of retirement income.

Social Security benefits are based on earnings averaged over 35 years (or the number of years between age 21 and age 62, excluding the five lowest years of earnings; Burkhauser and Holden 1982; Greenberg 1978:38). Because the denominator in this calculation includes all years between ages 21 and 62, employees with the longest and most continuous work records earn the highest benefits (Olson 1982:67). The five lowest years, dropout years, are removed so that "persons who did not have an opportunity

TABLE 26-2   Sources of Total Aged Income, 1986

Social Security	38%
Assets	26
Earnings	17
Pensions	16
Other	3
TOTAL	100%

SOURCE: U.S. Congress: Senate, 1990:43.

TABLE 26-3   Total Aged Unit Income from Various Sources, in Percent

	Poor	Non-Poor	Total
Earnings	1.0	11.4	10.9
S.S. and Railroad	70.3	40.8	42.2
Pensions	2.0	17.7	16.9
AFDC, SSI, Gen. Asst.	10.8	.4	.9
Interest/Dividends	3.7	27.7	26.6
Other	12.2	2.0	2.5
TOTAL	100%	100%	100%

SOURCE: U.S. Congress: Senate, 1990:47.

to work under the [Social Security] program would not be disadvantaged by a lower benefit amount" (Greenberg 1978:38). Limiting the number of dropout years to five has the consequence of not penalizing workers for temporary absences from the labor market (Greenberg 1978) and severely penalizing those with extended absences. A substantial length of time without earnings, whether due to part-time employment or unemployment, illness, or family responsibilities, reduces benefits considerably. Occasionally, the federal government grants workers wage credits for wages not received. During the Second World War, for example, members of the armed forces and interned Japanese-Americans received "gratuitous" wage credits (Greenberg 1978:54). No such provisions have ever been enacted for women who temporarily leave the waged labor force for reproductive labor. Workers with long absences are further penalized because each year's earnings are indexed according to current wage structures before they are averaged in the benefits calculations (Greenberg 1978). Years with zero earnings cannot be indexed and are entered into the equation as zeros.

Social Security has a dual eligibility structure that entitles beneficiaries based on either their own earnings record or their spouse's. Spousal Social Security benefits are based on marriages of at least 10 years and are equal to one-half of the worker's benefit. Nearly all men receive benefits based on their earnings record, but the majority of women receive spousal benefits; 99 percent of all spousal beneficiaries are women (Social Security Bulletin 1988:2). Of the new women beneficiaries in 1982, 60 percent received benefits based on their family status rather than their life's work. Though spousal benefits are just half of the wage-earner benefit, many dually entitled women do better to claim spousal benefits. Holden (1982) reports in one study that 84 percent of dually entitled women who had any zero-earnings quarters were eligible for spousal benefits higher than their own worker benefits. The Social Security Administration describes women who are dually entitled but taking spousal benefits as receiving a "combined benefit" in which "their retired worker benefit is supplemented by a partial wife's benefit" (Social Security Bulletin 1985:9). This is misleading, however, because they would be entitled to the exact amount they are currently receiving had they never participated in the labor force.

Some might argue that by providing spousal benefits, Social Security recognizes women's unwaged domestic labor, childrearing, and caregiving as work. However, women do not earn spousal benefits by performing reproductive labor but by maintaining a marital relationship. Spousal benefits cannot be considered an earned, delayed wage on several grounds: married women who hire domestic workers to do household labor still receive a spousal benefit; women who perform reproductive labor outside marriage do not earn a spousal benefit; and married women who perform reproductive labor within a marriage for nine (but not 10) years do not receive a spousal benefit. Benefits based on family status rather than reproductive labor are not earned and always subject to change pending any change in family status.

Social Security benefits are most advantageous to women if the marriage ends in death rather than divorce. Table 26-4 shows that when one spouse dies, the surviving spouse, whether male or female, receives two-thirds of the couple's combined Social Security benefit. After a divorce, each spouse retains his or her portion of the combined Social Security benefit; the wife typically receives one-third of the couple's combined benefit while the husband receives two-thirds. Divorced or widowed women who are remarried at the time of application forfeit earlier spousal benefits (Olson 1982). If one spouse enters a nursing home, Social Security income is divided as under divorce. Since the spouse remaining in the community is most often the woman possessing only a spousal benefit, community spouses are often left impoverished (Kasper 1988; U.S. Congress: Senate, 1988).

The dual structure of the Social Security system is thus a mixed blessing for women. To a certain extent, it ameliorates the effects on retirement income of a lifetime of low or no wages by providing women with spousal benefits more generous than benefits they could earn in their own name. Indeed the persistence of the wage gap complicates debates about the spousal benefit because for many older women it is a necessary source of income (Burkhauser and Holden 1982). But it also "reveals the underlying assumptions about a form of the family predicated on the economic dependence of women" (Acker 1988:492). The spousal benefit option means that one-earner families actually can receive higher benefits than two-earner families with identical household incomes; couples are rewarded for maintaining a traditional family structure (Burkhauser and Holden 1982).

Despite the gender-neutral language of Social Security benefit criteria, the primarily male worker benefits are based on a male pattern of work, while the primarily female spousal benefits are based on the notion of a stable nuclear family. As more women remain in the labor force throughout their childbearing years, the spousal benefit grows increasingly controversial. Some regard it as a working wife's penalty because a waged woman who contributes to the system but receives the spousal benefit because it is greater, pays a redundant tax, and is not rewarded with higher benefits for her efforts (Lampman and MacDonald 1982).

Private Pensions

Private pensions are offered by employers, including state and local governments, to certain groups of full-time employees. Increasingly, access to private pension income differentiates the poor from the non-poor aged (Quadagno 1988:541; Kammerman and Kahn 1987:49). Because so many older women do not receive private pensions, relying instead on Social Security as their sole source of income, they are much more likely than men to be impoverished. Like Social Security, private pension plans are based on a gendered waged labor force, but the mechanisms by which private pensions gender the distribution of retirement income are somewhat different. Private pension access and coverage vary widely, but across all sectors of employment women are much less likely than men to be covered (O'Rand and Henretta 1982:366). Pension coverage is tied to industries and specific jobs within industries, length of service, and continuity of service. Private pensions are more likely to be offered by large, unionized firms where women are underrepresented, and less likely to be offered by smaller, non-unionized firms where women are significantly overrepresented (*Nation's Business* 1986:11; Stone 1989). One-fourth of all working women work in retail and service industries, which have the lowest pension coverage (Reskin and Hartmann 1986:13).

Of full-time employees, 40 percent of women and 55 percent of men are covered by private pensions (Reskin and Hartmann 1986:13). Among those aged 65 and older, only 10 percent of women, compared with 27 percent of men, actually receive any monthly private pension income. When women do receive private pension benefits, their benefits are just half of men's; men's average benefits are $442 per month compared with $221 for women (Meier 1986:14).

Because private pension plans favor lengthy and continuous employment (Quadagno 1988:542), women are considerably less likely than men to actually receive benefits. Passage of the Employee Retirement Income Security Act (ERISA) in 1974 increased standardization of vesting and portability requirements, eliminating requirements for extremely lengthy service and continuity of service, yet considerable variability remains (O'Rand and MacLean 1986:227).

In calculating benefits, many private pension plans practice *pension integration* by

TABLE 26-4   Proportion of Couple's Social Security Benefit Received by Each Spouse under Different Family Statuses, for Women Taking Spousal Benefits, 1989

	Marital Status			
	Married	Widowed	Divorced	Spouse Institutionalized
Husband	2/3	2/3	2/3	2/3
Wife	1/3	2/3	1/3	1/3

taking into account the amount of Social Security benefits a worker will receive (Borzi 1985:2). Pension payments are offset by deducting a percentage of the worker's Social Security benefit from the private pension benefit. For example, a woman who had earned a monthly private pension benefit of $120 and a Social Security benefit of $300 would expect her combined retirement income to be $420. But if her pension plan calculates private pensions by subtracting one-third of the Social Security benefit from the private benefit, she will be left with a private pension of just $20, and a combined monthly benefit of only $320. Pension integration penalizes women more severely than men because women's private pensions are typically half of men's, but their Social Security incomes are significantly more than half of men's. Therefore, when a proportion of the Social Security payment is subtracted from the private pension payment, women are much more likely than men to have their private pensions all but disappear. Social Security's benefit formula is currently weighted to provide lower- rather than higher-income workers with a higher wage replacement. However, pension integration schemes "are designed to help close such replacement rate gaps" (Employee Benefit Research Institute 1987:75), thus neutralizing Social Security's weighted formula (Olson 1982:85).

Finally, like Social Security, private pensions are based on a gendered view of work and a misperception of marriage as permanent. Women do not receive private pensions for performing unwaged labor such as domestic work, childrearing, and caregiving. Although few older women receive private pensions based on their own life's work, many have access to private pension income through marriage. But their claim to that pension income upon dissolution of a marriage is, at best, tentative (U.S. Congress: Senate 1988:39). Although private pension plans do not pay spousal benefits in the sense that Social Security does, some pay a half benefit to the spouse after the death of the wage earner. After the death of her husband, a widowed woman receives at most one-half of the couple's private pension benefit. The distribution of private pensions following divorce or institutionalization of a spouse varies by state. In most states, the pension is regarded as the sole property of the worker. The spouse receives none of the pension following divorce or institutionalization and the worker receives the full private pension (U.S. Congress: Senate 1988:39). In California and other states with community property laws, however, the private pension is more likely to be regarded as marital property and divided evenly upon divorce or institutionalization of one spouse.

Individual Retirement Accounts

Due in part to criticisms of private pension plan eligibility schemes, new personal pension plans have been developed that are more portable and often require no vesting. But these plans vary sharply from private pension plans in that often only the worker makes a contribution. Individual Retirement Accounts (IRA) and Keogh plans were designed to encourage pension savings among those not already covered by a private pension scheme. Keogh accounts, which permit earners to save either $30,000 or 20 percent of their income, apply primarily to self-employed, high-waged entrepreneurs.

IRAs, though much smaller in scale, apply to all workers but often exclude women because they are secondary wage-earners or traditional homemakers.

Since 1974, the federal government has encouraged Americans to create individual retirement accounts to supplement Social Security and private pension income during retirement (Olson 1982:94). Prior to the 1987 tax code revisions, each worker could save up to $2,000 per year tax-free, whether covered by a private pension plan or not. The response was immediate: IRAs became a popular tax shelter. However, when the 1987 tax reform law was passed, restrictions on the tax-free status of IRAs greatly diminished use of this mechanism for saving private money for old age (*Wall Street Journal,* January 10, 1989).

Currently, people not covered by private pensions through work may invest up to $2,000 a year tax-free in an IRA. Those covered by private pensions may invest in an IRA but the extent to which investment is tax-free depends on annual income. Single-earner families retain complete tax-free status up to $25,000, and partial tax-free status up to $35,000 a year. Two-earner families retain tax-free status up to $40,000, and partial tax-free status up to $50,000 a year in combined annual income (Internal Revenue Service 1989).

However, if only one member of a dual-earner couple is covered by a private pension plan, the other member loses his or her right to tax-free status if their combined income exceeds the limit. Because men are more likely to receive private pension coverage, and because women are more likely to receive lower wages, the following scenario often arises: a woman without private pension coverage, married to a man with private pension coverage, loses her right to invest in a tax-free IRA because of her current marital status.

For the most part, only earnings can be invested in an IRA. A traditional homemaker is permitted to invest tax-free in an IRA if her husband's earnings do not exceed $35,000. However, the couple is only permitted to exceed the current $2,000 limit by $250. They may divide the $2,250 in half or however else they see fit, so long as neither IRA exceeds $2,000. If his income were regarded as a family wage that both owned equally, they could each invest $2,000 a year. Instead, in a single worker family—because the family wage is regarded as his property alone—a traditional homemaker loses her right to a tax-free IRA if her husband receives a pension and his income exceeds $35,000. Like Social Security and private pensions, IRAs do not regard reproductive work as labor, and they assign ownership of the family wage to the breadwinner.

IRAs are most relevant for people in marginal or secondary labor market segments—primarily women and other low paid workers. They differ from Social Security and private pension plans in that they are merely tax-free savings programs. Thus, the people least able to forego current wages are encouraged to forego them to provide a source of retirement income (Olson 1982:95). Working women, though covered by Social Security, are seldom covered by private pensions, yet they are often deemed ineligible for IRAs because of their marital status. Traditional homemakers are not covered by Social Security or private pensions, yet their failure to earn wages also prevents them from being eligible for IRAs. Recent IRA rule changes clearly turn on the conceptualization of family status as permanent. A reconceptualization of family status as temporary would undermine the logic of the new rule structures. Many women are denied tax-free IRA status based on their current husband's income or pension coverage only to find later they are without either husband or IRA.

DISCUSSION

Because analyses of gender inequality in the United States are typically tied closely to labor force participation and child care, relatively little attention has been given to the economic circumstances of women after retirement. For example, the economic costs to women of providing long-term care to a frail relative are well-documented in research on aging but rarely alluded to by researchers discussing women's reproductive work. This and other caregiving are a vital component of women's reproductive labor that is often all but ignored. In addition, while the gender gap in working wages is well-documented, the gender disparities in retirement income from Social Security, private pension plans, and individual retirement accounts—also often ignored—serve to further widen the gender gap (Kammerman and Kahn 1987). Finally, while the importance of marital status for the economic security of women in the childbearing years is widely recognized, there is little attention given to the fate of unmarried older women.

Given the gendered status of working and retirement wages, women of all ages tend to be dependent on the family wage (Pascall 1986). But the family wage, supposedly designed to provide economic security to dependent wives, has historically served to increase men's status in both the labor market and within the family (May 1985; Acker 1988). The family wage is not necessarily distributed to dependent wives and it does not, in the eyes of the state, belong to them upon the dissolution of marriage (Pascall 1986; McIntosh 1979). The same is true of the Social Security spousal benefit. Married older women fare relatively well, but upon dissolution of marriage many find they own precious few of the family resources. If she was not married to her spouse for ten years she receives no spousal benefit at all. If she remarries, she forfeits any right to a spousal benefit based on his earnings. If he fails to enroll for his benefit she may not be able to attain her half benefit. If he works and his income exceeds set limits, her benefit is reduced proportionately with his. Her claim to the spousal benefit is as tentative as her claim to the family wage; for many women, economic security is linked to marital status throughout the life-cycle. Similarly, her claim to a share of his private pension is debatable, despite her life-long contributions in reproductive and waged labor. Finally, her ability to invest in an IRA is dependent on her family status, whether she is a traditional homemaker or a paid worker.

Current wage and retirement policies have contradictory effects for women and cannot be understood in one dimension. According to Pascall (1986), the great paradox for women is to either live without a male wage and risk impoverishment, or to live with a male wage and risk dependency. Policies that deny the realities of women's lives by assuming or forcing economic independence ignore the economic dependency associated with reproductive labor under the current system. Yet policies that recognize women's economic dependency also sustain that dependency.

Some policy analysts have proposed the institution of childcare credits or homemaker credits for public pensions (Burkhauser and Holden 1982). Few feminists would support this proposal, despite its capacity to reward reproductive labor and alleviate economic dependency, because it reinforces a traditional division of labor (Land 1983; Lewis 1983). Lewis (1983) argues, for instance, that policies based on women's reality as economic dependents only serve in the long run to reinforce the role. Fierst (1982:71) takes a very different approach, arguing that like the current dual entitlement system, childcare credits give preference to the traditional homemaker without alleviating the pressures on working mothers: "Fair play requires that the woman who works and pays taxes should get more for her efforts." Holden (1982) points out that while homemakers would earn credit for childcare, they would not be compensated for subsequent lower earnings related to the interruptions of reproductive work.

Only one policy proposal currently under debate seems to balance the need to alleviate the realities of women's economic dependency without further tying them to reproductive roles: earnings sharing (Burkhauser 1982). This proposal applies only to Social Security—but it is particularly significant for older women since Social Security makes up a substantial share of their old-age income. Earnings sharing is regarded as an easy to institute, relatively inexpensive incremental change to existing old-age policy that will at once recognize women's reproductive labor and increase women's economic independence in old age (Burkhauser 1982).

Earnings sharing calls for the elimination of dual entitlement, or spousal benefits, and the institution of equal credit for both marital partners. Whatever the total household income, regardless of length of marriage or imbalance in individual earnings, both spouses would earn direct credit for Social Security based on half of the household income. In a study of projected costs under earnings sharing, Burkhauser (1982) found that there would be little decrease in Social Security benefits to traditional one-earner families and little increase in benefits to most two-earner families. The principal losers would be high income one-earner families. Burkhauser and Holden (1982) argue that earnings sharing assumes that labor force withdrawal is a joint decision and that both spouses should share in the burden of the decision. The working spouse shares the cost of the decision through lower benefits, while the at-home spouse's contributions are explicitly acknowledged. Homemakers earn credit under their own names; thus the link between marital status and old-age poverty is weakened. With divorce, death, or institutionalization of her spouse, a wife need not lose her economic security (Bergmann 1982).

Earnings sharing would not increase women's claim to the family wage, it would not alter the gender gap in wages, and it would not reconceptualize work to include reproductive labor. But it would distribute the long term costs of reproductive labor in terms of Social Security to both men and women, offset the gender gap in retirement wages for married women, and give all married older women incontestable claim to half of the Social Security portion of the retired family wage. Neither a husband's failure to enroll in the program or level of earnings in retirement, nor a wife's marital status or length of marriage would be relevant. Men, too, might experience greater old age income stability under earnings sharing since they are also more likely to face impoverishment under the existing rules if not married.

Of course earnings sharing alone will not erase old-age poverty. For many older

Americans, and for blacks particularly, even marriage in old age does not prevent impoverishment. A substantial increase in the minimum benefit would be required to off-set the effects of a lifetime of economic subordination. Provision of an adequate living wage to all people throughout their lives, regardless of age, race, sex, marital status, or type of labor would require major transformations of the existing social structure. At bare minimum, women must no longer be forced to bear the burden of reproductive labor without compensation. The gendered structure of waged labor, the gendered definition of work, and the conceptualization of family status as permanent rather than transient all intersect to impoverish older women. Until policies that reward women for their life's work, rather than fostering dependency and poverty in old age, are put into place, present improvements in economic conditions for the elderly in the United States will not be shared by all.

REFERENCES

Acker, Joan
    1988   "Class, gender, and the relations of distribution." Signs 13:473–97.
Bergmann, Barbara R.
    1982   "The housewife and Social Security reform: a feminist perspective." In A Challenge to Social Security: the Changing Roles of Women and Men in American Society, ed. Richard Burkhauser and Karen Holden, 229–233. New York: Academic Press.
Borzi, Phyllis
    1985   "Pension integration may mean income disintegration for women." In The OWL Observer Special Edition: Women and Pensions, November:2. Washington D.C.: The Older Women's League.
Brenner, Johanna
    1987   "Feminist political discourses: radical vs. liberal approaches to the feminization of poverty and comparable worth." Gender and Society 1:447–65.
Brody, Elaine
    1981   "'Women in the middle' and family help to older people." The Gerontologist 21:471–80.
Burkhauser, Richard
    1982   "Earnings Sharing: Incremental and fundamental reform." In A Challenge to Social Security: the Changing Roles of Women and Men in American Society, ed. Richard Burkhauser and Karen Holden, 73–99. New York: Academic Press.
Burkhauser, Richard, and Karen Holden, eds.
    1982   A Challenge to Social Security: the Changing Roles of Women and Men in American Society, 1–18. New York: Academic Press.
Employee Benefit Research Institute
    1987   Fundamentals of Employee Benefit Programs. Washington, D.C.: Employee Benefit Research Institute.
Ferree, Myra Marx
    1987   "She works hard for a living: gender and class on the job." In Analyzing Gender, ed. Beth Hess and Myra Marx Ferree, 322–47. Newbury Park, Calif.: Sage.
Fierst, Edith
    1982   "Discussion." In A Challenge to Social Security, ed. Karen Holden and Richard Burkhauser, 66–72. New York: Academic Press.
Glasse, Lou
    1988   "A message from Lou Glasse, president of the Older Women's League." In The Road to Poverty: A Report on the Economic Status of Midlife and Older Women in America, Mother's Day Report. Washington, D.C.: Older Women's League.

Greenberg, Joel
    1978   "The Old Age Survivors and Disability Insurance (OASDI) system: a general overview of the social problem." HS 7094 U.S. Report No. 78-200 EPW. Washington, D.C.: Health Care Financing Administration.
Hartmann, Heidi
    1981   "The unhappy marriage of Marxism and feminism: toward a more progressive union." In Women and Revolution, ed. Lydia Sargent, 1–41. Boston: South End Press.
Herz, Diane
    1988   "Employment characteristics of older women, 1987." Monthly Labor Review 3:3–12.
Holden, Karen
    1982   "Supplemental OASI benefits to homemakers through current spouse benefits, a homemaker credit and child-care drop-out years." In A Challenge to Social Security: The Changing Roles of Women and Men in American Society, ed. Richard Burkhauser and Karen Holden, 41–72. New York: Academic Press.
Internal Revenue Service
    1989   Individual Retirement Accounts. Publication No. 590. Washington, D.C.: Internal Revenue Service.
Kammerman, Sheila, and Alfred Kahn
    1987   The Responsive Workplace: Employers and a Changing Labor Force. New York: Columbia University Press.
Kasper, Judith
    1988   Aging Alone, Profiles and Projections. Washington, D.C.: Commonwealth Fund Commission on Elderly People Living Alone.
Lampman, Robert, and Maurice MacDonald
    1982   "Concepts underlying the current controversy about women's social security benefits." In A Challenge to Social Security: The Changing Roles of Women and Men in American Society, ed. Richard Burkhauser and Karen Holden, 21–39. New York: Academic Press.
Land, Hilary
    1978   "Who cares for the family?" Journal of Social Policy 7:257–84.
    1983   "Who still cares for the family?" In Women's Welfare, Women's Rights, ed. Jane Lewis, 64–85. London: Croom Helm.
Laslett, Barbara, and Johanna Brenner
    1989   "Gender and social reproduction: historical perspectives." Annual Review of Sociology 15:381–404.
Lewis, Jane
    1983   "Dealing with dependency: state practices and social realities, 1870–1945." In Women's Welfare, Women's Rights, ed. Jane Lewis, 17–37. London: Croom Helm.
May, Martha
    1985   "Bread before roses: American working men, labor unions and the family wage." In Women, Work and Protest, ed. Ruth Milkman, 1–21. London: Routledge and Kegan Paul.
McIntosh, Mary
    1979   "The welfare state and the needs of the dependent family." In Fit for Work, ed. Sandra Burman, 153–71. London: Croom Helm.
Meier, Elizabeth
    1986   Employment Experience and Income of Older Women. American Association of Retired Persons. Bulletin No. 8608. December. Washington, D.C.: American Association of Retired Persons.
Nation's Business
    1986   "Pension gender gap: no narrowing." February:11.

O'Brien, Mary
    1981   The Politics of Reproduction. Boston: Routledge and Kegan Paul.
Older Women's League
    1988   The Road to Poverty: A Report on the Economic Status of Midlife and Older
             Women in America, Mother's Day Report. Washington, D.C.: Older Women's
             League.
Olson, Laura Katz
    1982   The Political Economy of Aging. New York: Columbia University Press.
O'Rand, Angela, and John Henretta
    1982   "Delayed career entry, industrial pension structure and early retirement in a co-
             hort of unmarried women." American Sociological Review 47:365–73.
O'Rand, Angela, and Vicki MacLean
    1986   "Labor market, pension rule structure and retirement benefit promise for long
             term employees." Social Forces 65:224–40.
Pascall, Gillian
    1986   Social Policy. A Feminist Critique. London: Tavistock.
Pearce, Diana
    1989   "The feminization of poverty: a second look." Presented at the Annual Meetings
             of The American Sociological Association, San Francisco.
Presser, Harriet
    1990   "The complex work schedules of dual-earner couples in the United States: choice
             or necessity." Presented at Annual Meetings of The American Sociological Asso-
             ciation, Washington, D.C.
Quadagno, Jill
    1984   "Welfare capitalism and the Social Security Act of 1935." American Sociological
             Review 49:632–47.
    1988   "Women's access to pensions and the structure of eligibility rules: systems of
             production and reproduction." The Sociological Quarterly 29:541–58.
Reskin, Barbara
    1988   "Bringing the men back in: sex differentiation and the devaluation of women's
             work." Gender and Society 2:58–81.
Reskin, Barbara, and Heidi Hartmann
    1986   Women's Work and Men's Work: Sex Segregation on the Job. Washington,
             D.C.: National Academy of Sciences Press.
Rollins, Judith
    1985   Between Women: Domestics and Their Employers. Philadelphia: Temple Uni-
             versity Press.
Social Security Bulletin
    1985   "1982 new beneficiary survey: women and Social Security." Vol 48:17–26.
             Washington, D.C.: U.S. Department of Health and Human Services.
    1988   "Annual statistical supplement." Washington, D.C.: U.S. Department of Health
             and Human Services.
Sokoloff, Natalie
    1980   Between Money and Love. The Dialectics of Women's Home and Market Work.
             New York: Praeger.
Stone, Robyn
    1989   "The feminization of poverty among the elderly." Women's Studies Quarterly
             17:20–34.
Stone, Robyn, and Meredith Minkler
    1984   "The sociopolitical context of women's retirement." In Readings in the Political
             Economy of Aging, ed. Meredith Minkler and Carroll Estes, 225–38. Farming-
             dale, N.Y.: Baywood Publishing Co.
U.S. Bureau of Census
    1989   Poverty in the United States, 1987. Current Population Reports, Series P-60, No.
             163. Washington, D.C.: U.S. Government Printing Office.

U.S. Congress: Senate
  1988   Developments in Aging: The Long Term Care Challenge. Special Committee on Aging. Vol. 3, S. Res. 80, Sec. 19. Washington, D.C.: U.S. Government Printing Office.
  1990   Aging America: Trends and Projections. Special Committee on Aging. Serial No. 101-5. Washington, D.C.: U.S. Government Printing Office.
Wall Street Journal
  1989   "Labor letter" January 10.
Young, Iris
  1981   "Beyond the unhappy marriage: a critique of the dual systems theory." In Women and Revolution, ed. Lydia Sargent, 43–70. Boston: South End Press.

XI

HEALTH CARE AND INSTITUTIONALIZATION

Health care in the United States differs in substantial ways from health care in other countries. All other Western industrialized nations provide some form of national health insurance for citizens of all ages, regardless of age or income level. In contrast, the United States restricts access to government-insured health care to individuals who are either elderly, poverty-stricken, or both. These conditions of age and income eligibility give the U.S. system for old age health care provision its unique character.

MEDICARE AND MEDICAID

Medicare and Medicaid provide insurance against some of the costs of medical care for older people. Medicare has two programs. Medicare Part A is compulsory hospital insurance, which covers 90 percent of the cost of a specified number of days in hospitals or extended-care nursing facilities, once the individual pays a substantial deductible (nearly $700 in 1994). Part B is a voluntary program (the beneficiary pays a monthly premium) and covers a number of outpatient hospital services, doctors' services, minimal home health benefits, and some medical supplies.

Before Medicare was enacted in 1965, the elderly spent, on average, 15 percent of their income on health care. By 1990 this amount had risen to more than 19 percent. So despite the real benefits that Medicare provides for older people, they currently spend a higher proportion of their income on health care than they did before Medicare was put in place (Meyer and Moon, 1988).

The high cost of medical care is not the only challenge facing the elderly. Medicare does not cover routine physical examinations, foot care, eye or hearing examinations, eyeglasses, or false teeth, all of which are vital to the health of older people (Hickey, 1980). And because of the acute care focus of the Medicare program, only 3.5 percent of the Medicare budget in 1986 was spent on long-term care—an urgent health need of many elderly people (U.S. Social Security Administration, 1988).

HEALTH CARE POLICY AND THE AGED

The shortcomings and inadequacies outlined above regarding the Medicare and Medicaid programs are not the only problems facing policymakers concerned with health care policy for the elderly. The very structure of the medical care system virtually guarantees that the health needs of elderly Americans are not fully met. The first reading in this section, by Steven P. Wallace and Carroll L. Estes, traces the problems for health care provision in old age to the underlying structure of the medical-industrial complex, the commodification and medicalization of health care, and the reification of the marketplace as the appropriate arena for health care delivery. Improving elderly Americans' chances of obtaining affordable, quality health care will require substantial reform of the existing system.

INSTITUTIONALIZATION

Although fewer than 5 percent of elderly Americans reside in nursing homes at any one time, the risk of being institutionalized increases with age. Among individuals 85 and over, over 40 percent will spend some time in a nursing home. Overall, single women represent the largest segment of nursing home populations.

Medicare and Medicaid spurred the growth of the nursing home industry in the United States. Medicare reimburses costs for individuals admitted to skilled nursing facilities for up to 100 days; Medicaid pays the entire cost of nursing home residence for medically indigent elderly people who are unable to care for themselves. In 1988, 47 percent of Medicaid payments went to the nursing home industry (Lamphere-Thorpe and Blandon, 1991).

Few Medicare or Medicaid benefits are available to pay for in-home nursing assistance or to help with the activities of daily living. Consequently, both programs create a bias toward institutionalization of the frail elderly. Even so, there is no guarantee that disabled older people will receive the care they need. Some individuals who are poor and require nursing home care fall into the "Medicaid Gap"—that is, their incomes are barely over Medicaid cutoff limits, and so they are totally excluded from assistance with nursing home costs under the Medicaid program (Quadagno, Harrington Meyer, and Turner, 1991).

The last reading in this section provides a window into what sociologist Erving Goffman characterized as a *total institution*—a place where independence is surrendered, and life is ordered and controlled by a series of institutional imperatives. Timothy Diamond's reading, based on his participant observation research as a nursing home aide, demonstrates how total the effects of institutionalization are—both for residents and for workers. Although it is surely true that many nursing home residents are safer and receive better care than they could provide for themselves, Diamond's reading raises the question, Can't we do better than this for our elderly citizens?

REFERENCES

Hickey, Tom. *Health and Aging.* Monterey, CA: Brooks/Cole, 1980.
Lamphere-Thorpe, Jo-Ann, and Robert Blandon. *Years Gained and Opportunities Lost: Women and Health Care in an Aging America.* Southport, CT: Southport Institute for Policy Analysis, 1991.
Meyer, Jack A., and Marilyn Moon. "Health Care Spending on Children and the Elderly." Pp. 171–200 in John L. Palmer, Timothy Smeeding, and Barbara Boyl Torrey (eds.), *The Vulnerable.* Washington, DC: Urban Institute Press, 1988.

Quadagno, Jill; Madonna Harrington Meyer; and Blake Turner. "Falling Through the Medicaid Gap: The Hidden Long Term Care Dilemma." *The Gerontologist* 31 (1991): 521–526.

U.S. Social Security Administration. *Annual Statistical Supplement, Social Security Bulletin.* 1988.

27

Health Policy for the Elderly

STEVEN P. WALLACE
CARROLL L. ESTES

Population aging has raised concern among policymakers because of the high costs of providing health care to older people. Wallace and Estes argue that it is not just demographic and health trends that affect health policy; political and economic conditions frame these trends as well. The authors show that health care for the elderly has been placed at risk by the predominance of the biomedical model of care, the changing ideology of the "New Federalism" with its emphasis on market solutions, the fiscal crises of the 1980s, and the growth of the medical-industrial complex. Changes during the 1980s set limits to the directions health policy could take in coming years. Wallace and Estes are nonetheless hopeful about the future, although they do not suggest that the necessary reforms will be easy. Coalition building between the elderly and others, combined with restructuring the medical care system through federal leadership (and a federal role) in developing a system of universal, quality care, can ensure adequate health care for elderly Americans.

When Ronald Reagan assumed the presidency, both conservative and liberal analysts predicted revolutionary changes in the health and welfare system of the country. When Reagan left office eight years later, major programs affecting the elderly that had been targeted for radical modification or elimination still existed. Medicare continues as a federal program that pays half of the medical bills of the elderly. Medicaid remains a joint federal-state program that pays the medical bills of a large number of elderly poor. Social Security offers federally administered income support, while other programs provide federal funds for social services, food, and other needs.

While the Reagan years did not revolutionize health policy for the elderly, significant structural trends were initiated and/or reinforced. These trends could have long-lasting consequences for the elderly. As the number of elderly grows dramatically over the next fifty years, the federal health policy for the aged will reflect the heritage of New Federalism, fiscal crisis and austerity, and deregulation.

"Health Policy for the Elderly" by Steven P. Wallace and Carroll L. Estes, from *Society*, (Sept/Oct 1989): 66–75. Copyright © 1989 by Transaction Books.

THE DEMOGRAPHIC "IMPERATIVE"

Two factors cause policymakers to worry about the future of health policy for the elderly: the growing number of the elderly and their health status. It is possible to reliably estimate the health-care demands of the elderly at the turn of the century because of two factors. All of those who will be elderly have already been born, and the health of the elderly as a group changes gradually.

The number of elderly in the United States will grow rapidly over the next forty years. In 1980 there were 25.5 million persons age sixty-five and over, accounting for 11.3 percent of the population. That number will double by the early part of the next century; those age sixty-five and over will number 51.4 million by the year 2020. During this time the "oldest old," those age eighty-five and over, will increase threefold, from 2.2 million to 7.1 million.

Because the elderly are more likely to suffer from chronic illnesses than younger people, the growth in the number of elderly raises concerns. Table 27-1 shows that the elderly are much more likely to suffer from chronic conditions than the general population, even though they are less susceptible to common acute conditions.

Chronic conditions often lead to limitations in the activities of daily living among the elderly, such as dressing, bathing, or walking. Of the younger elderly (those between sixty-five and seventy-four), 37 percent are limited in some way in their activities. For the oldest old, almost 60 percent have limitations. About one-third of the oldest old with limitations are totally unable to carry out one or more activity.

Most of the elderly who have activity limitations remain in their communities. Only about 5 percent of those sixty-five and over reside in nursing homes, although this percentage rises sharply to almost 22 percent of those eighty-five and over. Studies have estimated that about 80 percent of all caretaking needs of the elderly are provided by their families.

Chronic activity limitations require long-term care for some, while acute episodes of underlying diseases generate hospital costs. For 1987, U.S. expenditures for health care are projected to total almost $500 billion for the entire population, exceeding 11

TABLE 27-1   Acute and Chronic Illness Rates for the Elderly, 1983

	Total Population	65 Years and Over
Acute conditions (rate/1000 population)		
infective and parasitic	20.3	7.3
upper respiratory	40.6	18.1
digestive system	7.6	7.2
Chronic conditions (rate/1000 population)		
heart conditions	82.8	303.0
hypertension	121.3	387.9
arthritis and rheumatism	131.3	471.6

SOURCE: U.S. Bureau of the Census, 1986.

percent of the GNP. Over half of the total will be spent on hospital and nursing home care. While the elderly comprise 12 percent of the population, they account for 31 percent of those expenditures. Actually, a small proportion of the elderly are responsible for the lion's share of health-care expenses. The last year of life is typically the sickest—only about 6 percent of the elderly die in a given year but they account for 28 percent of all Medicare expenses.

Demographic and health trends are not independent forces on federal health policy for the elderly. Political and economic conditions that frame these trends shape the policy response. The central structural constraints on future health policy for the elderly include the health care system, the changing shape of federalism, the fiscal crisis of the state, and deregulation.

THE BIOMEDICAL MODEL

While chronic illness has become the nation's primary health problem, the medical care system remains biased towards acute care. The biomedical model is oriented towards treating individuals who have short-term conditions that can be fully reversed. Chronic illnesses, on the other hand, are usually long-term conditions that require supportive and palliative care, and environmental modifications. Federal health policy virtually ignores these needs as it spends the majority of its health funds on institutional and acute care.

Some of the most significant health problems of the elderly are sensitive to social and environmental interventions. The reduction in mortality due to heart disease can be attributed to changes in diet and smoking patterns. The large increase in lung-cancer deaths is attributable almost entirely to the increased percentage of smokers in the aging population. Functionally impaired elderly frequently use low-tech equipment to adapt to their illnesses, such as special grab bars or raised toilet seats.

The medical care system individualizes living problems. Illness and functional disability are typically addressed with little attention to the family, community, or social context. Medical research and treatment for the problems of the elderly focuses on the human organism, even though social forces such as poverty, widowhood, or housing conditions may be equally significant.

CHANGING SHAPE OF FEDERALISM

Federalism denotes the relationships among different levels of government. Since the Great Depression and the New Deal, the federal government has taken an increasingly large responsibility for the health and welfare of the population. The federal government has assumed full responsibility for some programs that address needs of the elderly, such as Social Security for income and Medicare for acute medical care. For other programs, such as Medicaid, which provides health care for the poor, the federal government has developed cooperative relationships with states and localities.

In the 1970s President Nixon initiated policies that increased state and local discretion and responsibilities; President Reagan has vigorously followed this lead by limiting the federal role in health and welfare through block grants, program cuts, and increased state responsibility. Clark C. Havighurst, in *Deregulating the Health Care*

Industry, Planning for Competition, reflects New Federalism's ideology that the individual in an open market should be unaffected by government. He states that, "the competitive process, precisely because it is based on choice, validates the outcomes whatever it may turn out to be. . . . [A]n intensely personal matter as what to do about disease should be kept within the realm of private choice." This ideology resulted in proposals to eliminate direct federal involvement in most major health and welfare programs, including Medicare, Social Security, and even the National Institute of Health. In its most basic form, New Federalism challenges the idea that there is any societal responsibility for meeting basic human needs in health, income, housing, or welfare.

New Federalism's goals have been more far-reaching than its achievements. While the Reagan administration has proposed various program changes that would have sharply limited the federal role in the health and welfare of the population, actual changes have followed a historically incremental course. Proposed dramatic changes, such as placing Medicare recipients in the market for private health insurance, have not been successful in Congress. Concurrent policy changes, however, are significantly restructuring the health care system for the elderly.

The *ideology* of the proper federal role has shifted dramatically. The federal government was viewed as the key agent for solving the nation's problems under Johnson's Great Society. Under Reagan's New Federalism, it is seen as a source of the nation's problems. The ideological shift away from a strong federal role provides a powerful constraint on future policy initiatives. This will be significant for the elderly because of their dependence, along with the poor, on federal programs for their health and welfare. While the ideology of New Federalism is to reduce the involvement of the federal government in the lives of citizens, demographic changes in society will increase the pressure on the federal government to take a larger role in the health and welfare of the elderly.

The reliance of the elderly on federal programs is most evident in the importance of Social Security and Medicare to the elderly. If Social Security were eliminated, the poverty rate among the elderly would soar from 12.4 percent to 47.6 percent. Many of those helped out of poverty by Social Security are not far from falling into poverty. Congressional Budget Office analyses of a proposed cost-of-living-adjustment freeze in 1985 estimated that a one-year freeze would have dropped 420,000–470,000 elderly into poverty. The dependence of the elderly poor and near poor on Social Security is shown in Table 27-2. Low-income couples depend on Social Security for 82 percent of their income, while high-income couples have assets as their primary source of income.

The elderly's dependence on Medicare and Medicaid is similarly large. Medicare paid almost half the medical expenses of the aged in 1984; Medicaid paid an additional 13 percent. Despite these programs, each elderly person had an average of $1,059 in out-of-pocket health expenses, not including insurance premiums. This is a substantial sum, particularly for those living in or near poverty. When the elderly need long-term care for a chronic illness they are particularly vulnerable because Medicare pays for limited nursing home or home health care. The only way for the elderly to get assistance with prolonged long-term-care bills is to spend themselves into poverty and qual-

TABLE 27-2   Comparisons of Sources of Income between High- and Low-Income Elderly, 1984

| | Percent of Total Income | | | |
| | Couples | | Individuals | |
Source	Income Less than $10,100	Income Greater than $30,100	Income Less than $4,200	Income Greater than $13,700
Social Security	82	18	75	22
Pension	5	17	1	16
Income from assets	6	38	3	49
Earnings	2	26	1	12
Means-tested cash transfer	3	0	18	0
Other	2	1	2	1
Total	100	100	100	100

SOURCE: U.S. General Accounting Office, 1986.

ify for Medicaid. This threatens the independence of the elderly since few have resources to remain out of poverty after paying for as little as 13 weeks of nursing care.

As a result of their reliance on federal programs for income and health care, the elderly are particularly vulnerable to changes in federal policy that affect the health and welfare of the nation. The needs of the growing number of elderly persons conflict with the antigovernment ideology of New Federalism. While it is unlikely that the federal government will repudiate all responsibility for the health care of the elderly, the legitimation of New Federalism may limit federal government growth to a level below what is necessary to keep up with needs of the growing number of elderly.

FISCAL CRISIS

There are two ways to define a condition of fiscal crisis. One is the objective deficit between revenues and expenditures. This is particularly critical for state governments, since they must normally have balanced budgets. There is also a subjective element to fiscal crises, since "crisis" implies that there are no easy solutions to the fiscal imbalance. The level of taxation that a jurisdiction can support and the level of program reduction that citizens are willing to suffer are political issues. For a condition to be a crisis, therefore, policymakers and the public must perceive a lack of politically legitimate options.

The objective aspects of a fiscal crisis have been observed in local, state, and federal budgets since the late 1970s. The crises have been brought to a head by taxpayer revolts, federal tax cuts, and economic recession. Just as economic crisis provided the context for government expansion during the New Deal, the fiscal crisis of the 1980s is a driving force of New Federalism's attack on government. At the federal level, declining revenues have been caused by massive tax cuts enacted in 1981 and the largest peacetime military buildup ever. This reordering of budget priorities has also led to national debt levels of historic size, both in dollar amounts and as a percent of the GNP.

The subjective component of fiscal crisis is present in the belief that federal spending on the elderly and poor is a major cause of U.S. economic problems. This belief legitimates proposals to decrease the federal deficit by reducing programs for the elderly and poor, even though over half of the current deficit can be traced directly to the 1981 tax cuts. While the tax burden in the United States is lower than in almost all other industrialized nations, austerity is presented as the only possible response to declining revenues. As a result, Social Security and Medicare expenditures, which are funded by a special tax and trust fund, have been used in a political maneuver to reduce the size of the general revenue deficit. In fiscal year 1988, Social Security alone is projected to have a *surplus* of up to $38 billion, with the accumulated surplus growing to an estimated $12 trillion by 2020 when baby boomers will begin to draw it down. Medicare's surplus for 1988 is projected to be approximately $20 billion. On paper this reduces the federal deficit, even though Social Security and Medicare funds can be used only for those programs. The fiscal crisis has entrenched austerity in the public debate, as evidenced by austerity (versus equity) becoming the driving ideology behind health and social policy for the elderly.

Austerity hits the elderly particularly hard because it focuses on governmental finances rather than on total social support for dependents. Attention to the total social support notes that the number of dependents in society (children under eighteen and the aged) has been *decreasing* since the mid-1960s. Children, however, are largely supported by their parents and local programs while the elderly are most dependent on federal programs for their health and welfare. As the aged segment of society grows, and the under-eighteen segment declines, an increasing proportion of society's support for dependent populations will be channeled through the government rather than through the family economy. The dependence on family caused by 65.7 children per 100 adults in 1965 shifted towards dependence on government by 1985, as the *total* dependency ratio (aged and children) fell to 62.1 dependent persons per 100 adults. As the total dependency ratio falls through the end of this century, the proportion of dependents who rely on the federal government will continue to rise.

The elderly are also frequently blamed for the increasing costs of the medical system. Recent data, however, show that factors other than the increasing number of elderly are much more important. A study of 1985 health expenditures and spending projections to the year 2000 indicate that health care costs are rising primarily because of rising prices in the medical care system itself (e.g., rising hospital and physician charges, 55.6 percent of increase), and secondarily to increased intensity of care (higher technology services, 22.9 percent of increase). Increased utilization of services and the much-heralded demographic changes have contributed far less to rising health expenditures. Population growth has contributed less than 8 percent to the rising cost of care, and changes in utilization have no effect. Blaming the elderly for contributing to the fiscal crisis questions the deservedness of those receiving the medical care (the aged) rather than the deservedness of those receiving payments and making profits from providing medical services to the aged.

The politics of fiscal austerity define health and welfare expenditures for the elderly as involved in a zero-sum competition with other sectors of the economy. The argument assumes that if the country is in a fiscal crisis someone *has* to lose out. An alternate way of conceptualizing expenditures on the elderly is to include those expenditures as part of a "citizens' wage." This approach views payment to the elderly as part of delayed wages, rewarding the recipient for previous work. During the post–World War II period, increased health and pension benefits were given to workers as part of wage compensation to promote labor peace and productivity. The broad social benefits of delayed compensation are reconceptualized as burdens on business and society by the politics of austerity. As long as fiscal crisis is the focus of public policy, this dynamic of austerity will continue to define the parameters of the possible.

DEREGULATION

Deregulation is a hallmark of New Federalism. Minimizing government influence on markets is a key goal of New Federalism since competition and other market forces are seen as maximizing socially valued ends. This approach incorporates the view of people as primarily economic beings. In health care, this approach assumes that health can be treated as a commodity, with the consumer making fully informed rational decisions about the costs and benefits of treatments to prevent pain, illness, and death. A deregulated health market would have little incentive to address the social and environmental bases of many illnesses.

An important example of the impact of deregulation in health care is the eradication of federal restrictions that precluded the entry of for-profit firms in government-financed programs. We are witnessing a federal health policy shift from a concern with benevolence to a concern with economics. With U.S. personal health care expenditures exceeding $400 billion per year (29 percent spent for the elderly), corporate attraction to for-profit markets in medical care for the elderly is obvious. Four proprietary hospital chains already own or manage 12 percent of U.S. hospitals, and some experts predict that in a competitive environment ten giant national firms will capture 50 percent of the medical market in the next ten years.

Deregulation is also giving increased discretion to states in federal-state programs. In 1981, for example, federal funds given to the states for social services (Title 20) were reorganized into a block grant, eliminating most targeting and reporting requirements. Federal regulations have also been relaxed in state-run programs that affect the elderly, such as Medicaid and other health programs.

Deregulation is supposed to foster efficiency in the marketing of services, and give states discretion to shape programs to local needs. The increasing concentration of power in the medical care industry, however, may simply shift the power from the government to corporate boardrooms. While some states have a history of providing adequate benefits to their citizens, states' commitments to and abilities to fund health and welfare programs vary widely and are increasingly disparate.

The structure of the health care system, the ideology of New Federalism, the fiscal crisis of the state, and deregulation are all influences on health policy that have developed or been shaped during the Reagan years. In the years ahead we suggest that these forces will result in future changes in the medical system and health policy, including medicalization, the commodification of health, and the continued growth of the medical-industrial complex.

MEDICALIZATION

Medicalization involves the expansion of medical power over social problems. The cost-containment strategies under New Federalism have created conditions that further the medicalization of health services for the elderly. As noted earlier, the major health problem of the elderly is chronic illness that creates needs for supportive care and social services. Families currently provide the majority of the assistance needed by the chronically ill, resorting to institutions only when they are unable to provide the needed care at home. For those without families, services similar to nonmedical family care are necessary to maintain the elderly in the community.

In contrast, cost containment has focused on limiting the use of costly medical services and reducing services for the least disabled. One of the most significant cost-containment actions has been changing Medicare hospital reimbursement to payment of fixed rates based on diagnosis. By fixing reimbursements by diagnosis, hospitals now have an incentive to discharge elderly patients as early as possible, resulting in a decrease in the average length of a hospital stay for the elderly by two days. The release of sicker people into the community has increased the demand for higher technology and skilled services in the community. This increased demand is accompanied by a narrow interpretation of Medicare's home health benefit in an attempt to keep those costs under control. The result is that the skilled nursing paid for by Medicare is being directed towards only the sickest in the community.

The reductions in federal funding for social services (down 42 percent between 1982 and 1988) have forced agencies to reorient their services to be able to obtain reimbursement from other sources, such as Medicare and Medicaid. By shifting their services from social programs to medical support, the agencies reduce their commitment to a "continuum of care" that can offer services at the least restrictive (and least medical) level needed.

COMMODIFICATION

The biomedical model defines the needs of the aged around a medical-services strategy: as individual medical problems rather than as a result of societal treatment of the elderly, inadequate income, or other social problems. Similarly, the government's response to the needs of the elderly as primarily medical rather than social (e.g., housing, social services, and family care allowances) reinforces the mistaken view that rising health care costs are attributable to the elderly. Contemporary health policies attempt to "solve" the health care cost crisis by addressing only symptoms through medically based management strategies.

There does not appear to be any movement away from the trend of treating the problems of the elderly as primarily medical in nature. Because of the politics of austerity, the expansion of nonmedical community services can only be legitimated if it costs no more than the current medically oriented system. A recent review of demonstration projects that provide community care concludes that programs designed to reduce nursing home use fail to save government money. Noninstitutional care does improve the quality of life of the recipients, but advocating community care based on reducing costs does not appear viable. As long as fiscal crisis defines policy options, it will be difficult to include quality of life as a cost or benefit. Thus, the fiscal crisis, New Federalism, deregulation, and the health care system each support the continuation of health policy that emphasizes an acute medical model in its treatment of the chronic illness and support needs of the elderly.

Rather than treating the health of the aged as a public good that is provided and enjoyed collectively, health is increasingly marketed like other goods and services. Providers of health care to the aged are being forced to abandon charitable goals in the face of the economic "realities" of the market.

Shifting health care into a competitive market is a central aspect of New Federalism. The federal government now allows states to award contracts based on competitive bids to providers of medical care for the poor, with California and Arizona taking the lead in implementing this approach. Other states are using competitive bidding to select providers of community care services for the elderly and social services under Title 20. Entry into the market is typically justified as a cost-containment measure, and is made possible by loosening public program regulations.

As health is treated more as a commodity, health providers come to operate increasingly as do other businesses. We shift from "outreach" programs designed to bring needed services to the community, to "marketing" strategies designed to attract paying customers. This is apparent even in the nonprofit sector, as strategic planning and other business practices become necessary for the economic survival of health care providers. Concern has been raised about what will happen to those unable to pay for their care, an important issue since only one-third of noninstitutionalized poor elderly are covered by Medicaid.

As a commodity, health care relies on the market where access and distribution are based on the ability to pay. As commodification increases, hospitals are shifting their goals from providing services for those in need to offering services to customers. Rather than satisfying a need, medical providers are increasingly in the position of trying to attract profitable patients while avoiding others who may be needy. The structure of medicine as a commodity puts physicians in a particular dilemma since they must balance their role as patient advocates with their role as fiscal agents of hospitals and other health care organizations. As social good (health) becomes a commodity that is valued for its ability to create profit, many of the conditions that maximized the well-being of the elderly are weakened. The growing reliance on the market has intensified a perennial and profound health care question: should health care be provided as a "market good" that is purchased as a commodity by those who can afford to pay, or should it be provided as a "merit good" that is available as a right, regardless of ability to pay? The ideology of New Federalism, politics of austerity, and deregulation are all fostering a situation where health care is increasingly treated as a commodity.

MEDICAL-INDUSTRIAL COMPLEX

The medical-industrial complex consists of the growing concentration of private for-profit hospitals, nursing homes, and other medical care organizations, along with businesses related to medical goods and services. By 1980 the growth of the medical-industrial complex had become a significant enough force in American medicine to cause Arnold S. Relman, the editor of the *New England Journal of Medicine*, to warn of its impact on the shape of American medicine. In his Pulitzer Prize-winning book, *The Social Transformation of American Medicine*, Paul Starr notes that medicine is losing its basis in voluntarism and local control as a result of the growth of the complex. Not only are an increasing number of hospital beds and other medical services becoming profit-oriented, but even nonprofit hospitals are often establishing for-profit subsidiaries to help generate revenues. Both proprietary and nonprofit hospitals are also integrating both horizontally, into multihospital chains across the country, and vertically, establishing a host of lab, supply, home health, and other services so the patient's medical dollars stay entirely within one company.

The medical-industrial complex has been able to grow because medical care programs for the elderly and poor have bought into the existing medical system rather than establishing a national health service. Since Medicare and Medicaid were designed to provide equal access to "mainstream medicine," government clinics were established only in areas that were unattractive to private providers (via community health centers, Indian Health Service, etc.). While the government philosophy of Johnson's Great Society was expansionist, new programs worked to help the elderly participate in the medical market rather than to change or eliminate the market to meet the needs of the elderly. Publicly funded medical assistance thus greatly enlarged the market for medical providers. The increased number of paying customers for services, and guaranteed profits in some sectors, fueled the expansion and consolidation of medical services.

The medical-industrial complex is best organized to survive and even thrive during a period of austerity. Proprietary facilities are organized around costs, while public and religious facilities are traditionally organized to provide care to needy populations. Profit-oriented providers are therefore more able to respond quickly to cost-cutting policies, as well as to expand into the most lucrative new areas.

New Federalism's emphasis on the market gives the medical-industrial complex an advantage since proprietary hospital chains are the best-positioned to take advantage of a market-oriented system. Hospital chains are moving to "multi-clustering" where a hospital serves as the core of a regional health care network owned by one corporation. These networks can include skilled nursing facilities, home health agencies, durable-medical-equipment centers, and psychiatric, substance-abuse, and rehabilitation units. One large chain, National Medical Enterprises (NME), is already establishing such "multis" in Tampa-St. Petersburg, Miami, St. Louis, New Orleans, Dallas, San Diego, and Long Beach. American Medical International, Inc. (AMI) and Hospital Corporation of America (HCA) have targeted fifteen other cities for their multis. Private nonprofits are also moving in this direction, but they have neither the capital nor the institutional size to create comparable networks nationwide.

With the aging population and a concern with costs, there is an increasing move towards home care services. There are strong incentives for profit-making companies to expand in this area. In 1985, nine profit-making companies, including giants like Upjohn Health Care Services, operated over a thousand full-service home health care offices across the country. Some of these companies, like American Hospital Supply, have integrated their services vertically so that they not only manufacture supplies for hospitals but also deliver those same supplies in individuals' homes.

The linkage that will give proprietaries the largest advantage is their merging with or starting insurance divisions. AMI already has its own group health plan, AMI-CARE, that offers integrated services at its own facilities, and NME is preparing to enter the insurance arena. With insurance companies already among the largest sources of capital in the United States, proprietary chains will be able to further strengthen their market position by accessing the capital made available through their insurance subsidiaries. In contrast, nonprofits face possibly worsening problems in obtaining capital for maintaining their facilities and modernizing care. In addition, Humana and other chains are promoting "brand name medicine" by putting their corporate names on all of the facilities they own. To the extent that health care is deregulated and commodified, providers will do the best by marketing brand name medicine and insurance rather than by emphasizing intangibles like public service.

One of the hazards of a large medical-industrial complex is that the power concentrated within such an industry can shape the direction of health policy to the benefit of the industry, which does not necessarily coincide with the needs of the elderly. A recent example of this is the attempt by the drug industry to defeat the inclusion of drug coverage in the Medicare expansion to cover catastrophic illnesses. Since Medicare has not covered outpatient drug costs, they have been a major burden on the resources of the elderly. Drug companies worried that the inclusion of drugs as a Medicare benefit would lead to a limiting of the costs of drugs, pinching profits.

It should be noted that the growth of the medical-industrial complex is not unique. During the Reagan years, a deregulatory approach to mergers facilitated increased concentration of ownership in a variety of sectors, from transportation to industrials. It is important to keep in mind that many of the structural conditions discussed here extend beyond medicine to affect other sectors of the economy as well.

HOSPITAL REIMBURSEMENT FOR THE ELDERLY

Federal changes in hospital reimbursement for the elderly under Medicare demonstrates how New Federalism, fiscal crisis, and deregulation result in increased medicalization and commodification, and the growth of the medical-industrial complex. When Medicare began in 1966 it paid hospitals retrospectively, i.e., hospitals were paid after providing care for all "reasonable" expenses incurred in treating a patient (including construction costs and profits). In 1983 the federal government began to set limits on the amount Medicare would pay per hospital admission for illness groupings, called diagnosis related groups (DRGs). Establishing payment rates per diagnosis before services are provided creates significant incentives for hospitals to reduce inpatient days by discharging patients "sicker and quicker." Introduced as an austerity measure to reduce federal Medicare costs, DRGs have indirectly raised new discussion about quality of care and access to medical care, both of which were major issues during the 1960s.

The shifting concept of federalism is reflected in the early discharge of ill Medicare patients, shifting care into the community where Medicare pays a smaller proportion of the costs and state and local governments and individuals pay a larger share. Increasing copayments and deductibles for individuals have accompanied DRG-based reimbursement. Out-of-pocket health care costs for the elderly averaged 15 percent of their median income in 1984, while elderly blacks paid 23 percent of their income for health care expenditures in 1981. States and localities also shoulder increased responsibility for expenses not covered by Medicare incurred by the elderly poor.

Although the DRGs regulate payment by diagnosis, decisions about how to cut costs are left entirely to providers, reflecting their deregulatory aspect. Tax laws and deregulation have also encouraged the increased entry of for-profit corporations into medical markets (including both hospital and home health care).

The medical-industrial complex is uniquely positioned to take advantage of DRG-based reimbursements. Proprietary hospital chains, linked to supply companies and post-hospital care services, benefit from economies of scale, mass marketing, and the ability to shift costs. Proprietary chains have pioneered new services to maximize profits, such as freestanding emergency rooms, sports-medicine clinics, and drug/alcohol-abuse programs which are well reimbursed or which draw the middle class who can pay the fees. Hospitals have reacted swiftly to the new system, *increasing* their profits after the introduction of DRG-based payment. Investor-owned hospitals made the highest returns on their investments. At the same time, some public hospitals are being closed or bought by investors.

By focusing on the issue of hospital costs, the major component of Medicare expenditures, DRGs perpetuate Medicare's bias towards medically oriented institutional care of the acutely ill. Federal interest in developing an integrated long-term care system that adequately addresses the chronic-illness problems of the elderly remains low since ensuring a continuum of care is not likely to reduce costs or federal responsibilities, nor will it result from deregulation.

THE FUTURE OF AUSTERITY AND COST CONTAINMENT

A recent survey of the nation's health system leaders found that those most influential in health care and health policy are divided as to whether cost containment or quality of care will be the most important issue at the turn of the century. These leaders primarily wanted to improve service delivery and financing within the current health system. One in five, however, felt more fundamental changes are needed, including the creation of a national health service or an insurance plan involving federal resource allocation.

Continuing efforts to balance the federal budget indicate that cost containment will remain the central feature of health policy in the near future. Continuing austerity at the federal level was institutionalized by the Gramm-Rudman-Hollings Balanced Budget Act, passed in 1985 and revised in 1987. This act required that the federal budget be balanced by decreasing the deficit each year. If Congress does not make budget changes that reduce the deficit by a predetermined amount, automatic expenditure cuts occur. In contrast to tax surcharges that were used in the 1960s to compensate for a growing deficit, this bill embodies an austerity approach to the budget by addressing only spending. The automatic cuts are across-the-board, with the dollar reduction split between military and nonmilitary spending. Program changes are not mandated, only spending levels. This budget-led planning typifies the politics of austerity that is driving health policy.

There are a set of "protected" programs exempt from the cuts, including basic entitlement programs. Inflation and/or increased needs would still create de facto cuts in these programs. Medicare and other health programs were semiprotected by a ceiling on the amount they could be cut automatically. In 1987, Congress avoided the automatic cuts by passing spending and revenue bills that lowered the deficit. The package included increased premiums and deductibles for Medicare recipients, further increasing the out-of-pocket medical expenses of the elderly without modifying the system that generates rising medical costs.

The continued viability of a budget centered around the issue of the deficit ensures that federalism, austerity, and deregulation will remain at the forefront of the policy agenda. Policy concern over medicalization, commodification, and the growth of the medical-industrial complex must wait until the focus of policy concerns returns to the health care system and the health of the elderly and others.

Just as the focus of health policy shifted from access in the 1960s to cost containment in the 1970s, the economics of austerity is leading health and aging policy into retrenchment for the 1980s and 1990s. Retrenchment fits into the ideology of New Federalism, where the federal government is considered primarily responsible only for the national defense. Forcing cutbacks in social programs to help balance the budget would further move the burden of aiding the elderly and disadvantaged citizens to states and localities. The nonprofit health sector will also continue to face increased demand. While about 35 percent of free health care is provided in public institutions, almost all of the balance is provided in nonprofit institutions.

Program changes can only be justified if they save money under the politics of austerity. Unmet needs or inequitable distribution, key arguments for program changes before New Federalism, will continue to be insufficient rationales. Within the last ten years attention has shifted from a proactive discussion of the government's role in ensuring the nation's health via national health insurance to a reactive debate about whether the government should stop regulating health care and let the market control decisions. This debate directs attention away from an adequate assessment of the needs of the elderly and others.

The next significant step likely to be taken in providing health care for the elderly within the framework of New Federalism's limits, the politics of austerity, and deregulation is the further contracting out of services and programs that the government currently provides. Medicare is a likely candidate for contracting out since private companies already play a significant role in administering the program by acting as fiscal intermediaries. Demonstration projects can be implemented under current law to give contracts to insurers like Blue Cross making them responsible for all Medicare recipients in defined geographic areas. These contracts could either be competitively bid (as California did with MediCal—i.e., Medicaid—hospital contracts) or they could be offered at a fixed sum (as current Medicare expenditures are). While the private insurer would have to offer recipients the option of keeping the same Medicare benefits, the private insurer could also offer cost-saving options. Options might include offering recipients reduced copayments if they agreed to go only to specified providers. Contracting out gives private insurers the responsibility of designing options, assuming some underwriting risks, and negotiating with and regulating medical providers. This can be seen as a step towards deregulation since the insurers would be given discretion over program options. The prospect of keeping some or all of any savings (profits) would provide an incentive for the insurers to focus their efforts on costs. A smaller-scale effort in this direction is occurring with the federal interest in increasing the use of health maintenance organizations (HMOs) and other prepaid group practice.

One of the consequences of contracting out is that it removes the program from the political process. This can be seen either as a benefit because it weakens the hands of special interests, or as a disadvantage because it makes the program less sensitive to those affected by it. In the case of a contracted out Medicare, politicians could depoliticize increases in deductibles and copayments by blaming them on insurers' decisions, while the insurers could blame increasing costs on their contracts. The end result would be to defuse the ability of the elderly and other advocates to shape the costs and benefits of Medicare.

Deregulation assumes that the marketplace is the most efficient and effective distributor in society. This implies, a priori, that there is no need to discuss what policies could be enacted to foster the health of the elderly, nor is there a need to carefully evaluate the consequences of deregulation. Thus, to the degree that deregulation is embodied in public policy, it obviates the need for program data or debate about public policy for the elderly.

Another challenge will come from the special health needs of elderly women and minorities in the next century, many of whom will be among those least able to pay for it. The feminization of poverty, coupled with the longer life spans of women, results in older women comprising a higher share of those needing health care while having fewer resources. Similarly, blacks, Hispanics, and other disadvantaged minorities have poorer health, more chronic illnesses, and lower incomes than whites, as well as inferior access to health care. The proportion of minority communities that are elderly, historically small in number, is increasing faster than the proportion of whites who are elderly. Minority elderly will need expanded, culturally relevant, low-cost health care.

If the nation continues to be influenced by New Federalism, austerity, and deregulation, health policies will continue to contribute to the medicalization, commodification, and corporatization of health care. Who will pay for the costs of these "unprofitable" patients is likely to be a growing question. Relegating health care distribution to the market assumes that consumers will be sufficiently informed to make the best choices. Fostering public knowledge of costs, quality, and optimal treatments is problematic.

Unless precautions are instituted, severe fragmentation of health care will occur as companies are drawn to the most profitable sectors of care and unbundled services for the elderly, neglecting unprofitable treatments and populations. This growing fragmentation will decrease the possibility for policies that rationalize the system along criteria of need. Fragmentation of less-powerful interest groups is possible as they are pitted against each other for shrinking government resources. Finally, with federal reimbursements to the elderly made primarily in medical services and with the reduced social service expenditures, broadly conceived "health" care will be a low priority.

SCENARIOS FOR CHANGE

The two competing approaches to health policy challenges for the elderly have been based on models of market competition and government regulation. While New Federalism emphasizes market-oriented policies, a return to more regulatory approaches would not necessarily change the trends of the Reagan years. The growth of the medical-industrial complex, for example, may have given it sufficiently concentrated power that it could effectively control local attempts at health planning and regulation. Rather than reforming the present system at the margins through regulation or competition, a substantial restructuring of the health system is needed to best confront the basic problems that affect the health of the elderly.

Because of the power of the medical profession and the medical-industrial complex, restructuring health care for the elderly will require forming coalitions that transcend age and unite groups with common interests (e.g., the elderly and the disabled). These groups could advocate redefining health care away from a strict medical model toward the organization, financing, and delivery of health care along a continuum. This continuum would range from respite care for relieving families who already provide most of the nation's caretaking, to adequate incomes, to acute medical services. In place of austerity and New Federalism, health policy will have to treat health care as part of the Constitution's federal mandate to "promote the general welfare" rather than as a private commodity.

It should be noted that children and the poor do not compete with the elderly in the challenges of health policy, but share these concerns. The medicalization of health care deflects concern with health issues of inner city children such as lead poisoning, nutrition, and mother-and-child health promotion. The commodification of health threatens to widen the gap between the care available to those who can pay and those who cannot, regardless of age. Comparisons between the economic status of the elderly and children are typically made to assert that the elderly have too much, implying that poverty among the elderly should be as shamefully common as it is among children. On the other hand, since the government has been successful in reducing poverty among the elderly, it could be argued that the government should now do the same for children, whether through guaranteed jobs for parents, increased minimum wages, or other income-enhancement policies. If adequate and appropriate health care and an adequate income become federal policy priorities, citizens of all ages would benefit.

In sum, the Reagan years have redirected the course of health policy for the elderly. This change in course has not been the sharp turn hoped for by advocates of the Reagan agenda, but the changes have set up limits to the directions that health policy can take in the coming years. As currently structured, health care for the aged will become increasingly medicalized, commodified, and provided by corporations. Coalition building is needed between the elderly and others concerned with the direction that health policy is taking us if the medical care system is to be reoriented by public policy.

Health policy debate and action for the elderly in the future needs to be indivisible from struggles to:

- redress restrictions to access to health care that have grown markedly in the 1980s as a result of funding cuts and an increased uninsured and underinsured population. The uninsured population of 30–35 million includes 3 million persons aged fifty-five to sixty-four and almost 400,000 persons over sixty-five. Rising out-of-pocket costs to the elderly will further contribute to access problems as health care increasingly moves out of the hospital, since 60 percent of the elderly's physician charges, for example, are paid out-of-pocket. These statistics challenge the concept that the elderly can bear increased cost shifting and continue to have any reasonable access.
- develop workable alternatives in providing long-term care services and in preventing the need for institutionalization. The challenge is to strengthen ambulatory care, the continuum of community-based services (e.g., adult day care, congregate meals) and in-home services, and to find mechanisms to bolster the role (acknowledging the limits and personal costs) of family caretaking and other vital sources of personal and social support.
- refocus attempts at health-care cost containment from the ill to the structure of the medical care system itself. It will be difficult and expensive to target appropriate health services to those most in need as long as health care is increasingly commodified and medicalized. The government needs to reshape the medical care system rather than simply buying into the medical-industrial complex.

Given the scope and costs involved, long-term care and acute care can no longer continue to be financed and developed separately. Piecemeal development of policies based on either market reforms or regulatory cost-containment strategies that leave the basic health care financing system and medical system intact are inadequate. Developing a system that provides universal, quality care at an affordable cost will require concerted federal leadership and a federal role.

28
Making Gray Gold
TIMOTHY DIAMOND

In these excerpts from his book *Making Gray Gold,* Timothy Diamond explains how he became interested in studying residents and workers in nursing homes. He takes us inside the nursing homes where he worked for a year, alternating his own experiences and observations with the voices of his fellow workers and nursing home residents. The circumscribed world described in Diamond's chapter "Why Can't I Get a Little Rest around Here?" demonstrates one of the imperatives of nursing home life—schedules dictated by the institutional demands of caring for large numbers of people with limited staff. As a result of hectic schedules, staff pay scant attention to the needs and tempo of the lives of individual nursing home residents. What shines through in Diamond's account, however, are the survival strategies and tactics nursing home residents undertake to preserve their sense of self in an organizational setting that relegates them, for the most part, to the occupancy of a numbered bed.

It was 9:30 on a Sunday morning in the winter of 1981 when I first heard nursing assistants talk about their jobs. Ina Williams and Aileen Crawford worked in a nursing home across the street from a coffee shop where I spent leisurely weekend mornings. We had seen each other several times in Donna's Café and now were about to have the first of many conversations. While I was enjoying my coffee and newspaper, I joked to Donna that because of some part-time tutoring of students, I was forced to be up and on the move at this early hour.

"It's tough to have to set the alarm on Sundays," I griped.

"Tough?" Donna whipped back, hands on her hips. "Why don't you try getting up at 6:30 to open this place?"

"Tough?" interrupted Aileen from a corner booth, as she and Ina shared a laugh. "Why don't you both try 4:30 like we do six days a week?"

At the time, I looked at them with some skepticism, sure that they were exaggerating. As the months passed, however, and as Ina, Aileen, and I talked at length about our work, it became clear that they were not joking about their early rising. They were two African-American women who had to travel a long way on public transportation before reporting to work at 7:00 A.M. Though they were not kidding about rising at 4:30, they did joke about many things related to the nursing home and their work. As they did, I became curious and asked them to tell me more.

"Nursing assistant," said Ina, "is a new name for nurses' aides, even though we still say 'aides' a lot. In nursing homes we do most of the work—I mean we're the ones with the people." At this point she stroked one hand over the other, suggesting the hands-on nature of her job.

They were curious about my work as well, and they found it odd that I knew so little about theirs.

"You're supposed to know what we do," they teased. "You're the professor."

They were teasing a sociologist, one who had studied health care organizations for almost ten years. When we were getting to know each other I was teaching a course in medical sociology at a nearby university. Statistics indicate that nursing assistants are the largest single category of health care workers and one of the fastest growing occupations in general. What the work actually involves, however, is mentioned in only a handful of books and articles. I had carried an image of these workers, almost all of whom are women, doggedly performing simple, menial tasks.

But when Ina and Aileen came to the coffee shop on those morning breaks, they expressed strong feelings about their work. One day Aileen sat quietly gazing out the window with a sad expression. Eventually she shared her sorrow with us. "One of my ladies died during the night," she said. "I was with her for almost two years. I'm gonna miss that old goat." Another day Ina made a biting quip about the low wage scale: "For what we get, it ain't hardly worth our time to come out here."

Often they got Donna and me laughing over some of the antics in the home, like the couple who ran away and got married at eighty-two, or the ninety-six-year-old woman who wore black and gray wigs on different days to confuse the new staff. Almost every time we talked they contradicted my image of their work as dull, unskilled labor.

These conversations turned out to be only an introduction to the study reported in this book. We went on talking and laughing during their breaks for several months, and I even asked them if I could start taking notes on their stories. The notion of looking more closely at the nature of their work was dawning on me as a research opportunity. At first I thought of doing some interviews with them and some of their co-workers. Ina and Aileen thought this a bit strange, but they also liked the idea. Then one day they abruptly stopped coming to the coffee shop. It was weeks before Donna and I learned that staff at the nursing home would no longer be allowed to leave the building during breaks or lunch. Since Ina and Aileen lived too far away for them to drop in at the shop before or after work, we seldom met. Still, partly as a result of this forced breach in our developing friendship, my curiosity about their work and nursing home life increased.

From previous studies of health care organizations, I had come to the same conclusion as Robert Butler, then director of the National Institute on Aging, who said in an interview, "We know precious little about what goes on inside nursing homes." That seemed to be true of the professional literature, yet almost everyone I knew had some personal story to tell about nursing homes, and I began to wonder what they looked like from the inside. Ina and Aileen were no longer available to tell me.

Over the next several months, while I was deciding to undertake research and figuring out what method to pursue, I formulated the basic theoretical questions that fed this developing interest. There were nursing homes scattered throughout the United States, growing rapidly as health care institutions. Most had pleasant-sounding names referring to a valley or a view, a rest or a happy mood, like Sunset Manor or Pine View Hills or Merry Rest. What was Ina and Aileen's work like that it could give rise to such strong positive and negative reactions? What kind of rules operated there so that our conversations could now be canceled so abruptly? What was life like inside, day in and day out? Who lived in nursing homes, and what did they do there?

These questions crystallized under one overarching research issue, which provides the title of the book. One of my students brought to my attention an article about nursing homes that had appeared in a financial journal. Strongly recommending investment in this growing industry, the author concluded that "the graying of America . . . is a guaranteed opportunity for someone. How the nursing home industry can exploit it is the real question." The title of the article was "Gray Gold."

The author of the article assumed that nursing homes constitute an industry and went on to discuss how they could prosper as such. But nursing homes, like hospitals and other health care organizations, have not always been considered businesses, nor are they now in many societies outside the United States. A sociological approach which does not assume that care for older, frail people is naturally a business might ask how nursing homes have become an industry and how it is that their current expansion comes to be defined in those terms. The terms of exchange that make up an industry—productivity, efficiency, labor, management, ownership, stocks, profits, products—have not always characterized caretaking; they are relatively recent, historically. Moreover, caretaking does not seem to be much like building a car or selling merchandise, nor does it easily conform to the logic of commodity production.

So I began to wonder how nursing homes operate as industrial enterprises. How does the work of caretaking become defined and get reproduced day in and day out as a business? What is the process by which goods and services are bought and sold in this context? How, in other words, does the everyday world of Ina and Aileen and their co-workers, and that of the people they tend, get turned into a system in which gray can be written about in financial journals as producing gold, a classic metaphor for money? What is the process of making gray gold?

If this substantive issue explains the title, the subtitle refers to the method I pursued in answering these questions. I wanted to collect stories and to experience situations like those Ina and Aileen had begun to describe. I decided that if they could not come outside to talk about their work, I would go inside to experience the work myself. I became a nursing assistant.

First I went to school for six months in 1982, two evenings a week and all day Saturdays, to obtain the certificate the state required. Then, after weeks of searching for jobs, I worked in three different nursing homes in Chicago for periods of three to four months each. These homes were situated in widely different neighborhoods of the city. In one of them residents paid for their own care, often with initial help from Medicare.

In the other two, most of the residents were supported by Medicaid. Between jobs and for several years thereafter, I assembled and analyzed field notes, read the relevant literature, and wrote this book. In the course of writing, I visited many homes across the United States to validate my observations and to update them in instances where regulatory changes had been instituted.

In part, this book is a collective story told by the residents and the nursing assistants I came to know. It is also an analysis of administrative language as contained in formal documents. I weave the two threads together and intersperse my own interpretation of how they are connected. These, then, are my narratives from inside nursing homes.

"WHY CAN'T I GET A LITTLE REST AROUND HERE?"

By 7:00 in the morning the work day was under way for the nurses, the nursing assistants, the cooks, and the housekeepers, and it was time for those who lived in the homes to begin their day as well. The four waiting nursing assistants learned our assignments this way: "Today you have beds 201 to 216, you have 217 to 232, you have . . ." and so on until all of the residents had been assigned. Despite the words, this did not refer to the beds we had to make but to the people who occupied them. The first task was to wake residents, help them up if they were scheduled to get out of bed, and prepare them for breakfast and medications.

This early morning regimen was the hardest part of the day for many nursing assistants, a source of continual jokes and complaints. It was difficult, too, for some of the residents, and they frequently fought against it. The first moments of the day, therefore, were often spent in conflict.

"Bed 201" was Irene O'Brien. "Morning, Irene, rise and shine. Let's go," was a typical reveille on the firing line.

"Oh . . . no . . . ," Irene mumbled, pulling the blankets over her face. "Work all my life waiting for retirement, and now I can't even sleep in mornings."

I fumbled for an explanation. This was like a hospital, I told her, or at least she and I had to follow the early morning regimen of a hospital. At 7:15 in the morning this made little sense to her or to me, so we always started the day in tension.

It started that way with Helen Donahue as well. "Oh . . . I don't feel like getting up today," she moaned forlornly after I nudged her two or three times. "Why can't I get a little rest around here?"

For Irene and Helen, neither of whom was bedridden, to stay in bed was simply not an option, and if I had let them it would have been failing at the job and cause for reprimand. As I quickly learned from the other nursing assistants, the trick was to engage each person in some kind of conversation, something personal if possible, to execute the task and minimize the conflict. With Helen Donahue this soon turned into a series of delightful episodes.

Helen was nearing ninety and visually impaired, so it was a long, slow walk down the corridor to the day room. Since there was plenty of time for conversation, I often asked her to tell a story about some earlier time in her life, in part to get her animated so that she would walk down the hall to the day room without a fuss. She laughed and paused to think of some tale. Frequently, when we got to the third room down the hall, she interrupted her train of thought to yell into the room, "Mary Helen, Mary Helen, let's go, time to get up now, time for school." Mary Helen was the daughter that she had had to rouse out of bed for many years. There seemed little sense in demanding that Helen come back to reality. It made for a much smoother exchange when I leaned into the room and chimed in with her, "C'mon, Mary Helen, if you don't get up, you'll be late." I was stepping outside of the present reality for a moment but, after all, I had just chided Mary Helen's mother with a similar warning—that if she did not get up she too would be late—and we were both still trying to make sense of that.

As the long walks continued down the hall, Helen sometimes came up with rich stories of the first years of the century. My favorite was from 1915, when an excursion steamer, *The Eastland,* sank after catching fire in the Chicago River. She recaptured in vivid images the screams of the people, the chaos of the makeshift fire engines, the heroics of the volunteers, each of which was part of a different story on a different morning, each recaptured with the excitement of a teenager who had watched the whole thing, remembered by an elderly woman now nearly blind. On those walks, my sense of what was real and what was mental confusion was already being disrupted, and it was not yet 7:30 A.M.

The hour before breakfast went by quickly for staff, if not for residents. Each of the four nursing assistants on the floor was charged with waking and preparing fifteen to twenty people, each with her or his distinct circumstances, moods, stories, and needs. Grace DeLong was difficult to work with because when getting into her wheelchair, she always insisted on packing up virtually all her possessions to take with her into the day room. Bankbook, purse, small radio, wool sweater, an expired membership card from the American Association of Retired Persons, a greeting card from her nephew, an extra pair of socks—they all had to go with her in what she called her little mobile home. The difficulty arose from the pressure of time. On the other hand, Grace was invaluable in getting the work accomplished, for she would prompt her two roommates to get up and sometimes was more successful than the nursing assistants.

When all of the people had finally been awakened, dressed, and, if possible, helped into the day room to await breakfast there was, if the morning had been without unintended incident, a brief lull before the 8:00 A.M. breakfast trays arrived. It was then that I would look out to a roomful of forty to fifty people sitting in their assigned spots and notice, for the first of several times in the day, two characteristics of the group that continued as puzzling issues all my stay in the nursing homes. The first was to be seen, the second heard.

The first was the gender character of the group. The terms I had read and used to describe the people who lived in this setting had not accounted for what I saw. Residents, patients, people—all these collective categories are genderless. Yet in the day room those mornings, as in most homes throughout the industrialized world, the vast majority of those who sat there were women. This fundamental social fact could not be ignored.

The second mystery was something heard or, to be precise, not heard. The room was filled with quiet. Forty women and ten or twelve men sat assembled together, not talking. In the few moments before breakfast that was easily understandable, with people still half-asleep in their morning daze. Yet frequently the same overarching quiet could be noted as breakfast went on, and after breakfast as well. It was present during the lull between breakfast and activities, and before and during lunch, and sometimes all day long. It was an intriguing sound of silence, what seemed like an absence where one might expect the presence of conversation, during mealtime for instance. It took several months of experiencing it at more than one home before I was able to piece together some ideas about this mystery.

There was little time for speculation on the issue before the trays arrived for those forty or so who did not go to the main dining room for meals. Indeed, it was a rare morning when waking people and the time for serving breakfast trays did not overlap. Accidents of incontinence or other unplanned episodes of sickness needed attention, one or two who refused to come to the day room had to be coaxed or forced, an argument between residents had to be adjudicated, a new admission had to be given orientation—any or all of these could make eight o'clock come too early for the nurses and nursing assistants.

By contrast, it never seemed to come too early for residents. From the way they stared at the elevator door waiting for the trays to appear there could be no doubt that their overriding concern at that moment was hunger. In the language and records of the authorities who directed food production, there was little room to question its validity: three meals and two snacks were served each day, all scientifically designed for adequate nutrition. From the standpoint of living out this scheduled and documented design, the result was often hunger.

This morning hunger was expressed pointedly in the Australian film *Captives of Care*, a film about living in a hospital for handicapped persons, in which actual residents have the major speaking parts. One resident explained it clearly, "They give us our three meals all right, but they don't understand that it's fourteen or fifteen hours between the close of dinner and the beginning of breakfast. By the time breakfast comes around, we're weak with hunger." This explanation made the silence during these moments slightly less mysterious. Most were waiting and watching for the first sign of the elevator doors to open so they could break their fourteen-hour fast.

After breakfast, vital signs were taken—blood pressure, pulse, temperature, and respiration. They were taken frequently during the day, so it was easier over time to understand why the proper procedure had been drilled so repetitively in school. "Vitals" is a word drawn directly from the Latin word for "life." In medical settings, bodily functions are defined as vital, and they are measured and recorded as life signs.

Many people had identical vital signs day in and day out for the years of their residency, as their charts indicated. When residents lined up for the procedure, it was often a time for levity, for over the months and years many had built up repertoires of jokes that mocked the process and set it off more as a ritual than a requirement of health care. It was a rare morning that I did not head for the charts to record the day's vitals with an inner smile, reflecting on, for example, Irene O'Brien's feigned excitement— "I went up a whole point today, wow!"—or Jack Connelly's favorite crack as he rolled up his sleeve, "I guess you got to make sure I'm alive again today, huh?" "Vital" might have come to mean many things, like emotional state, personal biography, or social environment. Here, because everyday life was molded into a hospital environment, vital meant the physical survival of bodies.

After the vitals were taken, they were recorded. This task was a welcome relief for nursing assistants, for it was the first chance to sit down after several hours of standing and bending and running around. It was also an opportunity to become acquainted with the residents through their formal documentation. Vitals were recorded in the formal record of residents' existence in the home—the chart. This set of documents began at the first moment of one's residency and was continually updated all through the day, week, and month by various health care personnel. The specific sections of the charts varied slightly in the homes where I worked, but they always contained at least the following eight sections: diagnosis, drug regimens, consultations with medical specialists, bath and bowel record, restraint and position sheet, social and medical history, vital sign record, and nursing notes. In one home the head nurse urged the nursing assistants, "Get to know the patients better by reading their charts as much as possible." To get to know them better through the charts was to get to know them primarily through their sicknesses and medical care.

Interspersed in these records were bits of information about personal histories that served as jumping-off points for conversations while the assigned tasks proceeded. This information was especially helpful during the intimate contact that was next on the agenda: showers or bed baths.

A midmorning walk into the day room where most of the residents had been kept since breakfast was again a walk into a notable absence of conversation, even as thirty or forty sat in their assigned places, some with heads slumped over in sleep. By now it was not silence, however, since one of the staff had turned on the television, and the game shows or soap operas were blaring away, with some residents watching them. When a particular person was notified that it was her or his time for a shower, one-to-one relations began. The collective non-talk so characteristic of the day room gave way to conversation, and an initial element of the puzzling quiet began to unfold. While it may have been a silent collectivity, in one-to-one encounters these women and men had a lot to say.

Sometimes the conversations that followed were not pleasant. "I've taken baths all my life, and I gave them to all my children," Marian Gregg used to retort. "Why do I have to be told when to do it now?"

When Marjorie McCabe was told that it was time for her regularly scheduled shower, she got up with reluctance. "You keep washing me this often and pretty soon there's not going to be anything left of me."

"Three times a goddam week. Three times a goddam week!" Margy Anderson began, before her convulsive emphysemic cough overtook her in this moment of agitation. "Soon I'm not going to have any skin left!"

Trying to change the subject I once asked Mrs. Anderson, "Do you prefer to be called 'Mrs.' or 'Miss?'"

"'Mrs.,' my boy," she chuckled. "I've never been missed!" And it was off to the shower to begin the cleaning and to converse about her twenty-two years as a furniture saleswoman.

"I Gotta Get Going"

As time went on, such conversations challenged another image I carried into the research—that what was being lived in nursing homes were lives of passivity. I had thought of residents as on the receiving end of human activity, acted upon rather than acting. The training had reinforced such an image, with its focus on what we as care-givers were to do for them, the patients. The charts reinforced the same image. Mrs. Gregg's records had only a fleeting reference to the fact that she had mothered for twenty-five years, and Mrs. Anderson's had no mention at all of the saleswork that characterized her entire working life. Instead, their charts, the formal record of their membership in this organization, named them in terms of sicknesses and diagnostic categories. Everything that followed from this first page was about what health-care goods and services were rendered to them, about what was done to them, not about what they themselves did in the home or what they had done before arriving there.

It can easily appear as a passive existence to outside observers, as it had to me in the early days of the work. A quick visit to most day rooms will yield a snapshot image of people just sitting and is likely to convey the sound of silence. Getting to know the residents, however, dissolved that notion. From the conversations, even from the whis-pers, grunts, and babbles of those who seemed less coherent, my image of passivity gradually transformed into one of some activity. My research questions soon turned away from issues like "What can 'we' do for 'them?'" That very question contains within it the seeds of reinventing passivity, with its "we" as the active ones and "them" as the objects of action. I began to wonder "What is it that they are doing?" then "By what criteria does it come to be viewed as doing nothing or just sitting?" Ultimately, these questions came to center on one issue: "What kind of human activity does it take to live in a nursing home?"

Hazel Morris was one of the people who did not spend her days just sitting. Hazel was the first person I helped into the shower on certain days. In her tennis shoes she roamed all over the floor, from her room to the day room and up and down the halls, sometimes quite rapidly. "I gotta get going," she said when I caught up with her. With her full head of black hair and robust energy, I took her age to be about sixty-five—until the second time I assisted her to the shower. On that occasion her wig fell off; she was bald. An African-American woman with three children, the oldest of whom was herself sixty-five, Mrs. Morris was in her early nineties.

The chart labeled her a wanderer, which meant that her roaming was to be seen as a manifestation of her disease, Alzheimer's. She shared her room with three other people and did not like staying there, nor was she content sitting in the day room, so around and around she walked. To judge from her specific direction and comments, where she wanted to wander was out of the place. She headed for the door at every opportunity.

While the chart noted this wandering tendency in more than one place, it did not note that the shower was assisted by a man. Yet this gender difference permeated our interaction. As I blushingly proceeded to help Mrs. Morris, she seemed to sense my embarrassment and attended to it gracefully with questions like "You're new here, aren't you? How do you like the place? Don't worry, you'll get used to it."

It is not as though it was planned that a man should give women showers. What was so shocking during the first weeks, however, was that it was not planned that a man should *not* give them. It was as though, given the age differences, the available labor, and the dictates of the shower schedule, gender did not matter. It did matter, as several residents observed. Sometimes they would make sexual remarks, tell a joke, even venture an overture, if not a serious one.

"How ya doin' in there?" I asked Mrs. Ryan as she showered.

"There's only one thing I want from you, baby," this eighty-eight-year-old fired back, with a twist of voice that left no doubt about the innuendo.

Maggie Kuhn, founder of the Gray Panthers, said in a public address just before her eightieth birthday that as far as she could determine, "Sexual desire doesn't stop until sometime after rigor mortis sets in." Shower time confirmed this observation more than once, though never in an overtly tense way, and almost always in a way that mitigated the embarrassment with humor, as Hazel Morris had done with poise in the face of this institutional insult. Nevertheless, the entire interaction was made asexual when the encounters were entered into the records. Shower given. Check. The documentation procedures, which drove us into those delicate encounters in the first place, now rendered them invisible.

Not surprisingly, many men residents expressed relief when a man was assigned to tend to them. They had had to become accustomed to being tended by women, since almost all nursing assistants were women. Generally, though, men seemed to appreciate men, at least in domains like shaving. Resident Lito Esparza thought there should be many more men around. "They won't let me shave myself because they're afraid I'll cut my face. But look at it!" he muttered, while scratching various cuts on his cheek. "Women don't know how to shave a man."

There was not much time to pursue conversation in any given cleaning encounter, since eight or ten people were on the morning schedule. Between showers there were others in the day room waiting to be assisted to the toilet. Many needed help not only because of their own lack of mobility but because they were unable to move from the chairs in which they had been placed after breakfast. They had been secured in the chairs by restraint vests. In effect, these functioned as the opposite of a vest, which is by definition a piece of clothing that opens at the front and gives freedom to the arms. These garments were tied behind the chairs and made escape virtually impossible, even though many residents spent much of their day in that effort. Anyone who tried and failed to get out of the restraint was, by the time a nursing assistant arrived for the trip to the toilet, in a state of disarray, with the vest wrapped around shoulders and neck, half in, half out of the chair. Sometimes the disarray was total: chair, vest, and person all tipped over.

Nursing assistants had to snatch time when they could to take people to the toilet, and the time did not always coincide with residents' bodily needs. Often an accident happened, and a nursing assistant arrived after the fact. Yet this was not considered an organizational disruption, nor did it mean that messes would be on the floor, for most people were secured with a diaper first thing in the morning. The toilet trip included replacing the diaper, returning the resident to her or his chair, and making the restraint vest secure.

"Nurse, Nurse—are you my nurse today?" Bernice Calhoun beckoned, "Hurry, I've got to go!"

One of us would yell back from across the room, "No, Bernice, Laina is assigned to your section today. You'll have to ask her to take you." Bernice already knew that, but she had developed a timing and a way of asking that at least half the time one of us yielded to: "Well, all right, here I'll take you, but let's be quick about it."

"No problem, you don't have to worry about me," she smiled wryly, proceeding to strike up a conversation, which had been at least part of what she wanted in the first place.

Though we did not have to worry about Bernice, by now, about 10:30, we did have to worry about filling in the Restraint and Position sheets in the charts. It was a Board of Health directive that for each person these had to be completed and signed every two hours of the twenty-four hour day. For the bedridden this involved the crucial gesture of turning them to one of three rotating positions so as to make at least a formal attempt at circumventing bedsores. For about half of the people on the floor it meant noting that they were "up with restraints." "Up" meant out of bed, but the only real up was there on the records; in actual practice it meant down, that is, secured into the chair. In writing this into the records down became up, just as tied from behind became vest and the person a bed. It was difficult at first to learn these administrative terms, when the meanings seemed so firmly rooted in their opposites.

Active Range of Motion, known by its acronym AROM, was a program of exercises conducted in the late morning. It was mandatory for every resident who was up to participate. Conducted most often by the activities director, substituted occasionally by a nursing assistant, it involved a set of hand, arm, and neck exercises usually timed to music. The leader was likely to elicit only varying degrees of participation. Some residents were asleep in chairs; a few were absorbed in TV, a book, or a crossword puzzle, and they resented the interruption. A few were frustrated that their infirmities allowed them only limited engagement in the exercises, and some were insulted by the whole procedure. "I don't know why they make me do this foolishness," Mrs. Karlaski griped. "It's not my arms that need therapy, it's my legs." Despite these reactions, AROM was conducted twice daily, once in the morning, once in the evening, six days a week. It was over by about 11:20, forty minutes before lunch.

For residents there was a lot of time for which activities were not planned. At first it seemed that they spent such time just lying in their beds or sitting in the chairs. As I got to know them, however, their everyday lives became more complex than this image of passivity might indicate.

Grace DeLong sat in her little mobile home attending to painfully arthritic hands. When there was time during the late morning a nursing assistant cleaned the brace that kept her fingers from clenching inward and wiped the perspiration that had accumulated. Grace seemed continually engaged in a relationship with her hands—one of struggle, quite unlike those who take their painless, working hands for granted. She tried to make light of her shooting pain, in part to instruct the staff how to deal with each hand. The pain was so much a part of her existence that her hands took on a life of their own. "Watch the baby, watch the baby!" she admonished when we got near her left and more troublesome hand. "You know she doesn't like to be disturbed at this time of day."

Robbie Brennan, 46, liked rolling his wheelchair around, but sometimes his paralyzed foot fell to the floor, immobilizing him, and he would spend a lot of time trying to lift it. He insisted on going to the toilet by himself, an activity that could take up to an hour while he struggled to position his body in and out the chair. He understood the workings of his body and had to correct the staff when they did not.

David Forsythe wandered around, glancing into the ashtrays for leftover cigarette butts, then turned to a staff member to plead, "Hey, give me a cigarette, will you please?" Often his monthly allowance had run out, so his nicotine dependency was compounded by his financial dependency. He spent a lot of time in economic activity, in his case carrying on with the work of being penniless.

Elizabeth Stern, ninety, diagnosed with Alzheimer's disease, sat tapping her fingers on the table, sometimes raising them to wipe her face, for she cried a lot while sitting there. It became evident eventually that her crying had a focus.

"What's wrong, Elizabeth?" a staff person might ask.

She looked up and asked from some distant sphere of thought, "Are we going to the funeral?" Then she stood up as though en route. "He was a very good man, you know." Elizabeth was still actively grieving for her husband.

"No, no, he's gone now, Elizabeth. Lunch will come soon."

She was confused about time and place, but she knew something about grieving: "I'm still in mourning, you know. You think it's going to get easier as time goes on, but for some it gets harder. I'm one of those. I miss him more than ever."

These residents were active in their own way, like most others, with their physical, economic, and emotional wants and needs. While there were some people who seemed completely out of consciousness, for many more than I ever imagined, living in the home began to appear less and less like sitting doing nothing.

Next door to Elizabeth Stern, Mrs. Herman, nearly blind, sat at the side of her bed, waiting for someone to orient her, as with "How are you today, Mrs. Herman?"

"Not bad. Is it day or night?"

"Day."

"Oh good." With that she stood up and reached for the washcloth and towel that she always kept neatly folded within reach. She taught the staff something about how to ask "How are you today?" At first I said it too loudly. She snapped back, "I'm blind, you fool, not deaf!" Later she instructed, "It's not that I can't hear you, it's that I can't understand you. You don't speak slow enough. Most people around here talk too loud to the blind."

Many mid-mornings Mrs. Herman reached out her hand, palm down. At first it seemed that she was reaching for support. But when I put my hand under hers, change dropped out. "Here, get me a cup of coffee on your break, will you?"

"Sure, but there's sixty-five cents here, Mrs. Herman, and coffee is only fifty."

"I know. The rest is a little tip."

Her gesture presented a dilemma. It was against the institutional rules to accept money from the residents, but it was an insult to her not to do so. I accepted, more gladly all the time, for it became increasingly clear that the rule was part of a larger organizational ethos many struggled against: that the people who lived in this institution were not there to give; they were there only to receive.

Photographs that feature old, frail people in nursing homes frequently portray caregiving through pictures of hands. Typically, the hands of the caregiver are on top of those of the resident. In day-to-day operations, both parties sometimes had their hands on top; both gave as well as received.

Many were involved first and foremost in their own caretaking. Grace DeLong taught us how to situate her in the wheelchair, how to get the sand out of her eyes, how to adjust the hand braces, how to place the bedpan. In her jovial yet commanding manner, she was an active participant in her care. And she was fond, as well, of getting us out of her way. "I'm fine now that I'm in the chair. You go tend to the other girls. I can take care of my-self." Moreover, she tended to her somewhat confused roommate, especially in waking her, talking her through getting dressed, and guiding her down the hall.

In fact, many took care of fellow residents. "Rose," yelled the charge nurse from across the room, "take care of Georgia, will you?" That meant getting Georgia Doyle's shoes off the table, a habit she had picked up in the course of her senility. Rose Carpenter tended to Georgia, coaxing her slowly, knowing well her capacities, often able to deal with her better than the staff could. This involvement in caretaking was a logical extension of the earlier lives of these women. Grace and Rose had raised children and taken care of husbands, one of whom was in a deathbed for nearly two years. Mrs. Herman liked to remind everyone that she had been a field nurse for many years as well as a wife and homemaker. Their orientation and skills at caretaking work did not abruptly change in the last part of their lives, even if the institutional definitions of them had.

This orientation extended into observing and caring for staff as well. Part of the activities of surviving in this environment seemed to involve studying the staff. "Tomorrow's your day off, isn't it, Tim?" asked Bernice Calhoun.

"Yes, how did you know?"

"Oh, I know everybody's day off," she chuckled.

"How's your mother?" Irene O'Brien once asked, "I heard she was sick." It was true, although I had not told her.

"You're new here, aren't you?" asked a resident from another floor, who made it her business to know every staff person.

Many could account precisely for the staff who came and went. On my last day of clinical training a man who often sat in the hallway pulled me up short. As I brushed by him I tossed off the cliché, "Hey, Roger, see you later." But this was where he lived, and he knew I was just passing through. "No you won't," he retorted coldly. "Don't tell me you will."

When residents got to know staff, they often expressed interest in and concern for them. Rose and Irene both worried aloud about nursing assistants' overwork and high blood pressure, and they urged one of the cleaning women to find other work, knowing that the constant exposure to disinfectants was making her sick. At the end of a day as I slumped in a chair, Fern Sagrello put her hand on my shoulder and advised, "You know, you're too skinny. You should eat more." Hazel Morris, diagnosed with Alzheimer's disease, had not lost her capacity to evaluate nursing care. "You see that one," she observed, pointing to one of the nursing assistants, "she's too rough on these girls." Pointing to another, she said, "But look at her. She's kind. I can tell by the way she washes their faces."

In addition to involvement in caretaking, part of the efforts of residency involved clinging to some benchmarks of time and place, not an easy task amid such repetitive monotony. "Is this Wednesday?" Laura Blumberg asked as she sat waiting for lunch. Volunteers often came in on Wednesday to offer a bake sale. Notwithstanding the large calendar at the entrance to the floor where activities and birthdays were posted, the days folded into one another, so that special strategies of concentration were needed to keep track of them. For Mrs. Blumberg Wednesday meant the bake sale, and the bake sale meant it was Wednesday. Questions about what day of the week it was were voiced by staff, too. It seemed a particularly odd measure of reality orientation when a psychologist or social worker tested residents by asking them what day of the week it was. Nursing assistants used to joke about how lucky we were that they never asked us the same question.

XII

DEATH AND DYING

According to Elisabeth Kübler-Ross (1970), the fear of death is universal, and all cultures develop rituals to allay these fears. The ancient Hebrews regarded the body of a dead person as unclean; the early Native Americans shot arrows into the air to drive away evil spirits; the Managalese of New Guinea continue to exchange relationships with the ghosts of the dead. There is even evidence that the tradition of placing a tombstone on the grave stemmed from a desire to keep bad spirits in the ground. Every society develops its own cultural forms to deal with the deaths of its members.

TRANSFORMATION OF THE EXPERIENCE OF DYING

While death has always been present, the attributes of those most likely to die have changed considerably. In preindustrial societies both birth and death rates are high, while life expectancy is low. Death is concentrated at the beginning of the life cycle, among infants and young children, and results mostly from infectious disease.

Modernization brings greater knowledge of public sanitation and improvements in personal hygiene. As a result, infant mortality rates decline and life expectancy increases. The long-term result is the shifting of death from youth to old age.

Some statistics illustrate these transformations. Among children born in 1910 who survived to their fifteenth birthday, more than half experienced the death of a parent or sibling. Today the death of a parent isn't likely to occur until the child reaches middle age.

Until recently, most grandparents did not live long enough to know their grandchildren well. Now grandparents aren't likely to die until their grandchildren reach early adulthood, and for many young adults the loss of a grandparent is their first encounter with death (Hagestad, 1986).

The first reading in this section, by Nancy S. Jecker and Lawrence J. Schneiderman, examines why people experience the death of a child as a greater injustice than the death of an old person and discusses the ethical consequences of those differences.

Death does not occur in the abstract, however, for the death of each person reconfigures the family and alters the family members' awareness of their own mortality. Most of the research on the impact of the death of a family member on survivors has concentrated on how young children react to the death of a parent (Stillion and Wass, 1984). However, the more common experience is to lose a parent when the survivor is in middle age. The selection by Debra Umberson and Meichu D. Chen examines the response of adult children to the death of a parent.

When dying becomes the province of the old, a nation has experienced population aging. In the United States, for example, between 1950 and 1985 the number of persons 65 and over more than doubled and the number of people over age 85 more than quadrupled (Siegel, 1993). The population explosion among those older people most likely to require extended care and the ability of science to prolong life have raised new issues about the right to die.

THE RIGHT TO DIE

In Western industrialized nations, advances in modern medicine have lengthened life but have also prolonged the process of death (Glick, 1991). Life-sustaining technologies can keep people alive long past the time they would otherwise have died, but this achievement raises new questions and ethical issues. How long should life be maintained? Is *passive euthanasia,* permitting a patient to die naturally, morally more acceptable than *active euthanasia*, deliberately terminating the life of a terminally ill or nonfunctional patient (Aiken, 1985)?

Several prominent cases have brought public attention to the use of these technologies. One prominent case was that of Nancy Cruzan, a 32-year-old woman who was a victim of an automobile accident. Cruzan lay in a vegetative state for seven years while her parents and physician sought permission to disconnect her feeding tube. In 1990 the Supreme Court ruled against their request. Months after this decision, Congress passed the Federal Patient Self-Determination Act, requiring hospitals to ask patients if they have a "living will." By affirming the right of a patient to refuse treatment, the courts have confirmed the legality of voluntary, passive euthanasia. The reading by Henry Glick discusses the legal issues surrounding the controversy over the right to die.

REFERENCES

Aiken, Lewis. *Dying, Death and Bereavement.* Boston: Allyn & Bacon, 1985.
Glick, Henry. "The Right to Die: State Policymaking and the Elderly." *The Gerontologist* 5(1991): 283–307.
Hagestad, Gunhild. "The Family: Women and Grandparents as Kin-Keepers." Pp. 141–160 in Alan Pifer and Lydia Bronte (eds.), *Our Aging Society.* New York: W. W. Norton, 1986.
Kübler-Ross, Elisabeth. *On Death and Dying.* New York: Macmillan, 1970.
Siegel, Jacob. *A Generation of Change: A Profile of America's Older Population.* New York: Russell Sage, 1993.
Stillion, Judith, and Hannelore Wass. "Children and Death." Pp. 225–249 in E. S. Schneiderman (ed.), *Death: Current Perspectives.* Mountain View, CA: Mayfield, 1984.

29

Is Dying Young Worse Than Dying Old?
NANCY S. JECKER
LAWRENCE J. SCHNEIDERMAN

In contemporary Western society, the feelings people have about death depend on the age of the deceased. The death of an older person may bring a
sense of loss but is rarely viewed as a great tragedy. Dying in old age is a natural part of the life cycle. The death of a child, however, elicits stronger feelings—of despair and outrage. It is considered unfair for a young child to die.
Jecker and Schneiderman examine these responses critically to determine
whether they are backed by ethical considerations that can be reasonably dis-
cerned and defended. They contrast contemporary attitudes with those of ancient Greece and show the relevance that different attitudes toward death
have for health care decision making.

Often we experience the death of a very young person differently than the death of an
older individual. We may be disposed to feel not only greater sorrow, anger, despair or
bitterness, but also a greater sense of injustice when death strikes a very young child. Is
there any ethical justification for these divergent feelings? Or are such tendencies
prompted by false stereotypes that should be shed? Furthermore, what practical difference might our responses to death make? If we are warranted in feeling comparatively
worse in response to the death of a very young person, does this mean that we are also
warranted in recognizing a greater duty to avert such a death? For example, should we
measure the call upon medicine to preserve the life of people in different age groups as
different? Should scarce medical resources be used first to save the life of younger patients even when this entails letting elderly patients die? Should health professionals
exert a greater effort to defeat the odds and apply futile treatments when the patient is
very young, while avoiding "heroics" on behalf of older patients?

GIVING FEELINGS THEIR DUE

To begin to answer these questions, we first consider the weight that ethical argument
should give to ordinary moral feelings. Ethical argument is more than a description of
moral feelings or beliefs, but instead involves reflecting critically on competing moral
claims in order to clarify their nature and underlying basis of support. Thus we ask: Is
there anything that is uniquely of *ethical* importance about responding differently to
different deaths? One line of thinking is that our feelings surrounding death are more

---

amenable to psychological, than to ethical or philosophical, justification. According to some views, reasoners should not assign special weight to ordinary moral sentiments, but should strive to be wholly impartial. Feelings cloud judgment, it is said, and render ethical reasoning suspect if not spurious.

Should we then resist the pull of emotion and sentiment? Does ethical reasoning demand this? Against this approach we note that the different psychological reactions to death we observe often present themselves not simply as feelings, but as *normative* truths. That is, we not only feel sharper regret when a small child dies, but feel that sharper regret is *merited* because such a death constitutes a greater injustice. Likewise, we sometimes sense that a lesser injustice takes place when an older person dies and so feel that a lesser degree of anger or bitterness is appropriate. Understood in this light, our different reactions to death may prove helpful to ethical reasoning because they may point to underlying ethical reasons.

Yet some might challenge the assumption that having certain moral feelings automatically shows that those feelings are backed by valid ethical norms. Perhaps our moral feelings are instead instincts that we are innately programmed to feel. Or perhaps they are the product of crude indoctrination by our parents and teachers. These suggestions await empirical analyses, and are more properly the domain of the social sciences (psychology) than the humanities (philosophy). However, ethical reasoning might take as its starting point what the philosopher Thomas Nagel (1986; see also Gibbard, 1990) has described as a middle ground view. Rather than either automatically debunking common moral sentiments as coarse and unfounded, or trusting them blindly and uncritically, Nagel suggests that we place enough faith in moral feelings to inquire what more precisely they involve and whether or not they are ethically justified. In support of this approach it can be said that ethical inquiry is not infrequently rewarded by tentatively trusting moral sentiments and letting them navigate inquiry in the direction of underlying norms. For instance, when moral feelings and critical ethical analysis are at odds, letting feelings guide reason may induce us "to continue looking beyond the proposed arguments, to keep searching and broaden the review. Later we may . . . feel profoundly grateful that we were not carried away by abstractions" (Callahan, 1988, p. 12).

Let us consider our response to death's timing in light of Nagel's model. We will attempt to clarify the content of our response, lay bare the underlying reasons that might support it, and explore alternative responses. Throughout, our inquiry will be limited to specific Western attitudes toward death and to current and ancient time frames; a more complete analysis of attitudes toward death must address a fuller range of cultural and historical perspectives.

OUR RESPONSE TO DEATH'S TIMING

In characterizing our response to death's timing, Daniel Callahan (1987, 1993) has written that when we view people's deaths in distant retrospect, we tend to regard the deaths of very young persons with sharp regret, while seeing the deaths of older individuals as sad, but relatively acceptable, events. For example, recalling the death of a young child who could not raise the money needed to pay for a bone marrow transplant may still arouse in us bitter disappointment and the feeling that death was cruel and unnecessary. But we may feel comparatively less regret upon learning of the death of a 70-year-old who failed to obtain kidney dialysis due to age-based rationing of this technology. Extending this point, we may also find that the *anticipation* that death is imminent, and that there is nothing medicine can do to forestall it, is frequently met with deeper resistance in those treating small children as opposed to those treating elderly patients. Thus, a medical team may be more inclined to press for aggressive interventions, despite low odds of success, when the dying one is a child, rather than someone age 80. Extending this point still further, we may discover that many people find the actual *event* of death harder to witness in patients whose lives have barely begun to unfold than in those with many years behind them. Death in an elderly patient may be deemed "peaceful," implying "free from strife or commotion," "undisturbed, untroubled, calm, tranquil, quiet" (*Compact Oxford English Dictionary,* 1971). By contrast, a child's death may be called "senseless," which indicates it is "without sense or meaning . . . purposeless".(*Compact Oxford English Dictionary,* 1971).

Suppose, for the purpose of this article, that such observations are roughly true. That is, suppose that we as a matter of fact feel worse when we recall, anticipate, or witness the deaths of very young persons than when we recall, anticipate, or witness the deaths of elderly persons. (Actually validating this assumption would require collecting empirical evidence which we do not attempt, although others have done so [Reynolds, 1979]). These divergent feelings and attitudes toward death would not yet suffice to show that dying at a very young age is genuinely worse than dying late in life. After all, our psychological responses may be underlaid by illusions and false stereotypes about old age and youth. Or they may be backed by nothing more than an arbitrary cultural bias of Western industrialized societies that favors youthfulness and disparages old age. Should the death of a very young person truly merit the deeper resistance we apparently feel, we should be able to produce the reasons that support our feelings and attitudes.

One consideration that lends credence to the view that death is more acceptable when it occurs in old age is that "the elderly have lived a full life, have done what they could, and thus are not victims of the malevolence of the forces either of divinity or of nature" (Callahan, 1987, p. 72). By contrast, the death of a very young person may strike us as evidence that cruel forces govern the universe, and that responsible adults have failed to shield defenseless children against these forces.

Yet even when we assign no one responsibility for a person's death, we may still undergo more profound or bitter regret when the dying person is quite young. For example, the fact that the instrument of a small child's death is seen as an accident or fluke, rather than the product of divine will, does not necessarily make it seem less senseless or cruel. Even when God and nature are exculpated, we may continue to hold that death occurring early in the life-span is particularly unfair.

A different justification for thinking death worse when it befalls a young child is simply that such a person has more potential years ahead to lose. What's more, when many future years are forgone, the individual is likely to miss major stages of life in their entirety. Thus, unlike the 65-year-old, the 5-year-old will never grow up to become an adult, or experience the events typically associated with this, such as falling in love, becoming a parent, developing and fulfilling life ambitions, and sustaining and deepening close relationships over time.

A related point holds that losing very young persons is a greater blow because younger persons have more potential contributions to make to society. Older persons, by contrast, have fewer years remaining to contribute. Moreover, beyond a certain age, older persons as a group may have contributed most of what they will contribute in areas such as economically productive labor, science and technology, or art and culture.

A further reason why the loss of a very young person may be harder to bear is that to lose such a person is tantamount to losing the future. Not infrequently, we refer to children as "our country's future." In contemporary American society the ideal of perpetual progress for each new generation continues to inspire us. This inclines us to invest special meaning in the welfare of our children: children stand for the improved life toward which our present labors are leading. By contrast, our nation's elderly may symbolize a past that will inevitably be improved upon and surpassed.

On a more personal level, the death of one's own child may convey what psychiatrist Irvin Yalom (1989, p. 132), has called "project loss": the loss of "what one lives for, how one projects oneself into the future, how one may hope to transcend death." By contrast, the death of an aging parent is not the loss of a life project but of an "object" or figure who has played an instrumental role in the constitution of one's personal past. Thus, with the loss of a parent one's personal future remains viable, even enlivened. Robert Jay Lifton and Eric Olson (1974) convey a similar thought, noting that offspring can represent a kind of "symbolic immortality" for parents. Lifton and Olson describe "symbolic immortality" as a psychological process of creating meaningful concepts, imagery, and symbols that fulfill the human need for a sense of historical connection beyond the individual life. Offspring afford parents symbolic immortality not only through continuing their physical/genetic material, but also by virtue of showing the imprint of parents' values and attitudes in the way they lead their lives. Parents may feel that their influence on children connects them to humankind as it enters "into a general human flow beyond the self" (Lifton & Olson, 1974, p. 77).

Finally, our attitudes toward death's timing may reflect our underlying attitudes toward time and temporal passage (Mellor, 1981). Although an individual's personal past grows more distant with the death of those (i.e., the elderly) who store its memory, the loss of the past may already be perceived as inevitable. Thus, the forward march of time makes the past appear increasingly temporally distant, further and further away from present reality. By contrast, we perceive the future as perpetually approaching, rather than slipping away. Parents fully expect their children to be represented in the future, even if they themselves are not. Thus, when death befalls children, parents feel deprived of something they did not expect to lose. The future that they imagined, and that seemed to be moving closer and closer to fruition, is now gone forever.

AN ALTERNATIVE RESPONSE

Are the above considerations compelling? Are our different responses to death in children and the elderly indeed warranted? It is instructive to juxtapose the response to death elaborated above with an alternative response. This approach features the aging process from youth to maturity as *adding* to the individual's capacity to appreciate life, and so *heightening* one's capacity to experience loss and deprivation of tragic dimension.

The response that treats the death of a mature adult as a greater hardship is particularly salient in the philosophy and literature of ancient Greece. Greek tragedies, for example, often take as their subject great men brought low. A great man's fall aroused compassion by leading the audience to put themselves in his place and feel empathy for his tremendous suffering. Thus, Sophocles takes Oedipus, a good man and king, as his subject and depicts Oedipus' downfall; the audience is drawn into Oedipus' despair and led to feel his upheaval and horror upon learning that he has killed his father and slept with his mother. Similarly, Aeschylus tells the tale of an eminent and morally blameless man, Orestes, who is ordered by Apollo to kill his mother. The audience is made to experience Orestes' torment as the Eumenides (which symbolically represent the fury of Orestes' mother) pursue him relentlessly.

Whereas Greek playwrights expected the losses of great men to excite compassion, they did not consider compassion equally applicable when similar harms were visited upon children. In contrast to our contemporary ethos, the ancient Greeks apparently regarded the death of small children as beneath tragic dimensions. This was perhaps because the infant or very small child lacks the adult's capacity to appreciate what is happening. An infant whose death is imminent may coo and wiggle; a toddler, not comprehending the import of a terminal diagnosis, may appear bored or listless. When Greek literature portrayed a child's death, the implications that the child's death carried for others received greatest emphasis. Thus, in *Medea*, Jason's wife seeks revenge against Jason by maliciously killing the children she bore him. Euripides treats the tragedy as befalling King Jason, rather than his murdered children, and makes the climactic moment the moment when Jason's fury erupts in the aftermath of his children's murders:

> [T]hou hast broken me! . . . Thou wife in every age abhorred . . . who didst kill my sons, and make me as the dead . . . Out from my road . . . And let me weep alone the bitter tide that sweepeth Jason's days, no gentle bride to speak with more, no child to look upon whom once I reared. All, all forever gone! (Euripides, 1943, pp. 491–492).

The point of view described here places our contemporary perspective in sharper focus. To begin with, whereas our forebears regarded maturing as heightening tragic potential, our contemporary ethos treats maturing as limiting tragic possibility. Contemporary attitudes tend to regard the death of young children as representing a greater injustice because the younger one is, the more innocent and blameless one is thought to be. According to contemporary thinking, maturing spoils purity and innocence, so it inevitably lessens the tragedy of death by inviting the possibility that one is somehow responsible for one's own downfall. The mature man is considered "worldly" and accountable, in contrast to the babe in arms who is considered naive and good.

A second contrast concerns the distinct emotions that ancient and modern attitudes call forth. Whereas the ancients underscored the adult's travails to summon empathic concern, contemporary views highlight the child's defenselessness and vulnerability to awaken a sense of *responsibility* that triggers protective impulses. We view a mature man as strong and self-reliant in the face of danger, but feel disposed to nurture and protect an imperiled child from harm.

Finally, our modern thinking envisions aging as *consuming* and *reducing* a person's entitlement to a finite resource, namely, the lifespan. The older people become the more they have "had their share" and depleted their entitlement to further existence. Whereas a newborn possesses the greatest entitlement to life, an aged person, like a gentle but lame horse, has already "drunk from the trough," and now it is time for her to let the next horse drink. Switching metaphors, some invoke a "fair innings" concept to convey that early in life people have not yet played the game, but once they have had their turn at bat playing further innings is no longer a strict entitlement (Somerville, 1986).

Notwithstanding these differences, certain affinities exist between ourselves and ancient Greeks. Thus, both we and our predecessors may anticipate with excitement the birth of a healthy baby, take special care in choosing names, feel pride in our children's development, and enjoy nursing and caring for our young. Despite notable differences then, the Greeks' intuitions are not exactly in counterpoint to our own. For all that is said here, the Greeks may well *support* the claims of children over very old persons, even if they subordinated the claims of both to the mature man. Or they may regard the death of a mature person of base character as less significant than the loss of a very young child from a good family who promises well.

Yet why should we even take Greek views about children seriously? Perhaps the Greeks simply became inured to child death because the survival of children was so precarious. Rates of childhood mortality were high, and in contrast to our society the survival of infants and small children was unpredictable. What's more, for all their vaunted tragedies, the Greeks had less than admirable views about women and non-native Greeks. Why should we expect their attitudes toward children to be any better? The answer here, as before, is that even if Greek views about children turn out to be unfounded, we cannot dismiss them outright. Instead, we ought to examine their views critically, and learn whether or not they are supported by ethical considerations that reason can come to discern and defend.

The response that treats the death of a small child as a more catastrophic event might gain an initial foothold from the observation that as one becomes a mature adult, the greater becomes one's capacity to comprehend the nature and import of catastrophe and so to experience and feel wounded by misfortune. Recognizing this, onlookers rightly perceive a mature adult's death as more potently tragic than the death of a young child.

In reply, however, it can be said that we recognize misfortunes as befalling persons who do not experience suffering and who are even wholly unaware of their condition. Thus, we count betrayal and deception as evils even when those betrayed or deceived remain ignorant of their situation. And we consider a disease process that results in gross mental deterioration as a tragic misfortune to its victim, even when the victim does not understand or mind the condition (Nagel, 1979). These reflections seem to indicate that tragedy can also befall an infant or small child who cannot comprehend tragedy's dimensions.

Yet the viewpoint that takes death as worse when it befalls a mature adult might spring from an alternative set of premises. A mature adult's death may be thought more tragic because mature persons are in the prime of life: they are at the height of their physical strength, and many of the life goals they have set may, for the first time, appear within reach. Hence, there is more reason to shake one's fist at the world when death takes a mature adult, since it brings to an end a more fully realized perfection.

The conviction that death qualifies as a greater evil for the mature person also may be accounted for on the ground that the death of an adult cancels the realization of goals and projects already underway. As the philosopher Ronald Dworkin observes, the frustration of desires and aspirations that death produces "is greater if it takes place after rather than before the person has made a significant personal investment in his own life . . ." (1993, p. 88). Thus the mature adult, unlike the infant or small child, has dreams for the future and death deprives such a person of the chance to realize hoped-for possibilities.

A further reason for regarding the death of a mature person as worse than the death of an infant or small child is that by maturity a person has entered into more relationships with others, and these relationships have grown more meaningful over time. For example, the Akamba people of Kenya treat the death of a mature person as worse for this reason. According to their view, "the more personally interwoven a person becomes with others through time, the greater the damage done to the social fabric when that person is torn away by death" (Kilner, 1990, p. 88).

Finally, persons may feel greater aversion to the death of mature adults because more than children, mature persons have earned our respect and honor. As a group, they merit respect merely by virtue of having lived through life. According to Jonsen, "Living a life is an achievement. Some persons do it with great vigor and style; others barely make it; yet everyone who survives accomplishes it. The accomplishment deserves acknowledgement" (1991, p. 346).

IMPLICATIONS FOR HEALTH CARE DECISION MAKING

So far we have provided some basis for questioning our contemporary response to death by setting it alongside an alternative view gleaned from our own historical past. To summarize what has been said, the contemporary conception that a youthful death is a more tragic event may stem from a variety of sources. When a very young person dies we may feel that that individual has not yet lived a full lifespan or has not yet had an opportunity to make lasting contributions to society. Further, contemporary observers may find the loss of a young child less acceptable because the young stand for the future and seem to afford us the opportunity for progress and for exerting an enduring influence on humankind.

An alternative response toward death's timing is provided by the ancient Greeks, who portrayed tragedy in terms of a mature man brought low through death or personal devastation. Unlike the child, the mature individual understood his predicament and experienced the anguish it occasioned. He felt the loss of a hoped-for future as he found his plans and desires disappointed. To the extent that ancient Greeks considered a mature man to be an exemplar of the human species, the mature man's death or ruin was a greater loss than the death or devastation of a small child.

With this background, we now proceed to show that even if we continue to find contemporary attitudes compelling, their scope of practical application is limited. It might at first glance be thought that how we regard death carries immediate practical implications in many areas, including health care. Thus, ancient Greek attitudes toward death are apparently reflected in that society's treatment of newborns. The Greeks routinely "exposed" infants to the threat of death by abandoning them when they were born with deformities or were healthy but unwanted. Reflecting the ethos of ancient Greek society, caring for sick or defective newborns "was not a medical concern in classical antiquity"; moreover, no laws existed to prohibit either the killing of defective newborns or the exposing of healthy ones (Amundsen, 1987, p. 15). Philosophers, including both Plato and Aristotle, generally accepted the morality of exposing infants for the purposes of selective breeding or on purely economic grounds (Rist, 1982). Nor does Greek civilization stand alone in permitting the active or passive killing of infants. According to Post, "the Netsiliks, an Eskimo society that placed importance on having enough sons as hunters to ensure food for its members, practiced female infanticide because suckling a female infant for several years would prevent the mother from having a son" (Post, 1988, pp. 14–17). Other societies, including the !Kung of the Kalahari and the Tikopia of Polynesia, apparently practiced infanticide due to the difficulty of providing food for children.

If contemporary responses to death are justified, does it follow that our society should take an opposite tack? Should we, for example, devote great resources in medicine to saving the lives of children while investing comparatively few resources to saving the lives of older persons? Should we engage in heroic efforts to beat the odds on behalf of the tiniest babies, while refraining from exerting extraordinary efforts to benefit older patients? To address such questions we explore several possible claims one might be led to make on the basis of the view that death is worse when it happens to a very young person. Although we continue to focus on attitudes toward death at different ages, it is important to note that age is but one of several factors that inform our contemporary conception of "valuable-person-we-want-to-keep-alive." A more complete analysis would place attitudes toward age in the broader context of attitudes toward race and ethnicity, gender, economic status, and other factors.

Resource Allocation. —In considering possible ramifications of contemporary attitudes toward death, one set of issues relates to how we should distribute finite lifesaving resources among different age groups in society. It might be assumed that if the death of very young persons is worse than the death of very old persons, for example, then the young merit comparatively more lifesaving resources than the old. Callahan has argued for rationing publicly financed lifesaving resources on the basis of old age (as well as other criteria). He claims that by old age, people have passed the marker of a natural life span and their death may then be viewed as a sad, but relatively tolerable event (Callahan, 1987).

However, even assuming that our attitudes concerning death in old age are warranted, there are other reasons that tell against old-age-based rationing. First, it might be argued that the young and old alike deserve equal access to basic health care because unequal access signals unequal respect for persons. Persons treated with lesser respect doubt their own value as persons and find their sense of self-worth and self-respect undermined (Gutmann, 1983).

Second, old-age-based limits on medical care might be opposed because they violate the moral thrust of Judaic and Christian religions. Both traditions emphasize the equal worth and dignity of human beings. Both regard human dignity as age-transcendent rather than age-influenced (Post, 1991).

Special duties to the old might also follow from the fact that older persons as a group have made substantial contributions to society. Society therefore owes the elderly a debt of gratitude, and this debt cannot be paid unless the elderly have access to basic forms of medical care, including lifesaving care. Old-age-based rationing represents, in this view, an ungrateful response to all that the elderly have given us.

Finally, old-age-based rationing may be challenged on the ground that it affects women disproportionately. Women live longer than men, and so would be affected by ageist policies in greater numbers. Moreover, the deprivation of life-saving medical care in old age would be a greater deprivation for women because they have on average more years ahead to live (Jecker, 1991).

In light of these remarks, we conclude that it is wrong to suppose that old-age-based rationing is justified just because death in old age is less tragic than death early in life. Even assuming it is correct to feel that an older person's death is relatively acceptable, it does not follow that the old can be ethically deprived of scarce life-saving medical resources so that such resources may be distributed to young age groups. Instead, a host of other considerations emerge as relevant.

Medical Futility. —A different set of issues is at stake when the tragedy associated with the loss of a small child disposes health care providers to pursue medical interventions against all odds in order to rescue a small child from death. Whereas rationing has to do with treating different groups fairly in the allocation of scarce resources, futility concerns the likelihood and quality of benefit that medical treatment affords for a single individual (Jecker & Schneiderman, 1992). By calling a life-saving treatment futile, we mean that the likelihood that it will in fact prolong life is exceedingly low or the quality of life thereby gained would be exceedingly poor (Schneiderman, Jecker, & Jonsen, 1990). Under such circumstances, some may insist that even when the chance of a successful outcome is slim, health professionals have a stronger duty to attempt beating the odds on behalf of very young patients. The reasoning here may be that the death of a small child is a more terrible thing, and so more effort must be expended to prevent it from occurring.

Yet this reasoning breaks down once the odds of success approach a very low threshold. When the odds of success become exceedingly slim, attempting to defy them is not in the patient's best interest, but instead functions as a means for health professionals, patients, and family to evade hard choices and flirt with fantasies of omnipotence. Clinging relentlessly to the life of a very small child by pursuing aggressive medical treatments may even add to the patient's or parents' misery by creating an emotional roller coaster of raised, then dashed, hopes. In addition, efforts to beat the odds through medical means may only increase suffering by prolonging the dying process; entailing the use of painful and invasive methods; and leading the medical team to dwell on pointless therapies rather than focusing their attention on truly beneficial measures, such as palliative and comfort treatments (Jecker & Schneiderman, 1993). In light of this, we urge health professionals who care for very young patients to move beyond the relentless pursuit of futile technologies to an ethic of care (Schneiderman, Faber-Langdeon, Jecker, 1994).

There is a slightly different objection one might raise in defense of making a greater effort to forestall death in the young. It might be claimed that even if health professionals have no ordinary duty to provide an intervention that is very unlikely to succeed, they should be more inclined to make an exception on behalf of the very young patient on the basis of compassion. In other words, empathizing with the very small child should prompt health professionals to exceed their ordinary duty and do everything possible to ward off death.

Yet this reasoning does not withstand careful scrutiny. Compassion involves an attempt to "be in" the patient's persona and experience the suffering the patient does. As suggested already, a very small child may feel immediate pain or fear, yet lacks the deeper understanding and capacity for suffering we attribute to an adult. Thus, when the physician "steps into" a very young patient's shoes, the physician is unlikely to find there a stronger basis for compassion. When compassion is stirred in response to some harm that befalls a small child, it is often more properly directed toward the child's parents than the child. For example, when a small child's life is in peril, the child's parents are more likely to grasp the moment's finality and recognize an incalculable loss. The life that is lost may even be perceived as *theirs* (the parents'), as much as the child's. The parents, like the protagonist in Euripides' *Medea*, may sense that they have been "broken" and are "as the dead."

CONCLUSION

We submit that the response of deeper anger, despair and bitterness in the face of a youthful death is not universal. Following Nagel's model, we have placed enough faith in these sentiments to inquire what more precisely they involve, and the reasons that can be advanced to support them. The juxtaposition of ancient and contemporary attitudes has made evident that the various norms that underlie contemporary attitudes are subject to alternative interpretations. Thus, the impending death of an infant or very small child will seem less cruel when it is emphasized that the infant or child does not comprehend the magnitude of the situation. On the other hand, the imminent death of a mature adult will appear more tragic when the mature adult is portrayed as innocent of wrongdoing, e.g., when death is attributed to the malign acts of others, or to genetic causes beyond the person's power to control or influence.

Finally, even assuming that contemporary responses to death's timing are justified, it does not immediately follow that the ethical obligations of physicians toward very young patients are more stringent. Nor does it follow that a tendency to "write off" elderly patients more readily, or feel absolved sooner of responsibility toward them, is warranted. Instead, justice standards are far too complex to reduce to a single rationing criterion, such as age. With regard to medical futility, it is clear that the boundaries of medicine apply to young and old alike, and even death's specter cannot undo medicine's ineluctable limits.

REFERENCES

Amundsen, D. (1987). Medicine and the birth of defective children: approaches of the ancient world. In R. McMillan, H. T. Engelhardt, & S. F. Spicker (Eds.), *Euthanasia and the newborn* (pp. 3–22). Dordrecht: D. Reidel.
Callahan, D. (1987). *Setting limits.* New York: Simon and Schuster.
Callahan, D. (1993). *The troubled dream of life: Living with mortality.* New York: Simon and Schuster.
Callahan, S. (1988). The role of emotions in ethical decision making. *Hastings Center Report, 18,* 9–14.
Compact edition of the Oxford English dictionary. (1971). New York: Oxford University Press.
Dworkin, R. (1993). *Life's dominion.* New York: Alfred A. Knopf.
Euripides (1943). *The Medea.* In L. Cooper (Ed.), *Fifteen Greek Plays* (pp. 447–494). New York: Oxford University Press.
Gibbard, A. (1990). *Wise choices, apt feelings.* Cambridge, MA: Harvard University Press.
Gutmann, A. (1983). For and against equal access to health care. In President's Commission for the Study of Ethical Problems in Medicine and Biomedical and Behavioral Research, *Securing access to health care, vol. 2* (pp. 51–66). Washington, DC: U.S. Government Printing Office.
Jecker, N. S. (1991). Age-based rationing and women. *Journal of the American Medical Association, 266,* 3012–3015.
Jecker, N. S., & Schneiderman, L. J. (1992). Futility and rationing. *American Journal of Medicine, 92,* 189–196.
Jecker, N. S., & Schneiderman, L. J. (1993). Medical futility: the duty not to treat. *Cambridge Quarterly of Healthcare Ethics, 2,* 149–157.
Jonsen, A. R. (1991). Resentment and the rights of the elderly. In N.S. Jecker (Ed.), *Aging and ethics* (pp. 341–352). Clifton, NJ: Humana Press.
Kilner, J. (1990). *Who lives? Who dies?* New Haven, CT: Yale University Press.
Lifton, R. J., & Olson, E. (1974). *Living and dying.* New York: Praeger Publishers.
Mellor, D. H. (1981). *Real time.* New York: Cambridge University Press.
Nagel, T. (1979). Death. In T. Nagel, *Mortal questions* (pp. 1–10). New York: Cambridge University Press.
Nagel, T. (1986). *The view from nowhere.* New York: Oxford University Press.
Post, S. G. (1988). History, infanticide and imperiled newborns. *Hastings Center Report, 18,* 14–17.
Post, S. G. (1991). Justice for elderly people in Jewish and Christian thought. In R. H. Binstock & S. G. Post (Eds.), *Too old for health care?* (pp. 120–137). Baltimore: Johns Hopkins University Press.
Reynolds, F. (1979). Natural death: A history of religious perspectives. In R. M. Veatch (Ed.), *Life span: Values and life-extending technologies.* San Francisco: Harper and Row.
Rist, J. M. (1982). *Human value: A study in ancient philosophical ethics.* Leiden, The Netherlands: E. J. Brill.
Schneiderman, L. J., Faber-Langdeon, K., & Jecker, N. S. (1994). Beyond futility to an ethic of care. *American Journal of Medicine.*
Schneiderman, L. J., Jecker, N. S., & Jonsen, A. R. (1990). Medical futility: Its meaning and ethical implications. *Annals of Internal Medicine, 112,* 949–954.
Sommerville, M. A. (1986). "Should the grandparents die?": Allocation of medical resources with an aging population. *Law, Medicine and Health Care, 14,* 158–163.
Yalom, I. D. (1989). *Love's executioner and other tales of psychotherapy.* New York: Harper Collins.

30

Effects of a Parent's Death on Adult Children: Relationship Salience and Reaction to Loss

DEBRA UMBERSON
MEICHU D. CHEN

Umberson and Chen assess the impact of a parent's death on adult children's physical and psychological functioning. Individuals from 24 to 96 years of age were interviewed in 1986 ($N = 3, 617$) and again in 1989 ($N = 2, 867$). In the intervening three years, 207 respondents experienced the death of a biological parent. Their results indicate that when compared to adult children who are not bereaved, bereaved adult children experience a significant increase in psychological distress and alcohol consumption and a decline in physical health status. Umberson and Chen also developed a theoretical framework to guide an analysis of group differences in adult children's reactions to a parent's death. Their analysis shows that some groups experience a substantially greater decline in functioning than others following a parent's death, whereas other groups actually experience improved functioning following a parent's death. Depending on the type of outcome assessed, several factors are associated with children's reactions to a parent's death: age and marital status of the child, gender of the child and the deceased parent, the quality of previous adult interactions with the deceased parent, and childhood memories of the deceased parent.

Most research on the effects of a parent's death has been concerned with effects on minor children. This research overwhelmingly has indicated that negative effects on younger children are substantial (Stillion and Wass 1984). However, the death of a parent is much more likely to occur when children are middle-aged than when they are minors. Only 1 in 10 children has lost a parent by age 25 but by age 54, 50 percent of children have lost both parents, and by age 62, 75 percent have lost both parents (Winsborough, Bumpass, and Aquilino 1991). While the death of a parent is a common life event of adulthood (Winsborough et al. 1991), there has been little research on how the death of a parent affects adult children. Our study addresses this issue using a prospective study design and a national sample.

FAMILIES OF LATER LIFE: WHY A PARENT'S DEATH MATTERS

Relationships with parents have unique symbolic importance for adult children (Atkinson 1989; Rossi and Rossi 1990). This symbolic importance derives, in part, from special aspects of the parent-child relationship that set it apart from other types of relationships. For example, initially a child is fully dependent on the parent for survival; parents socialize the child and help shape the child's definition of self (Rosenberg 1979). As the thriving practices of psychotherapists suggest, this parental influence continues to be important throughout adulthood, even in the absence of physical proximity and perhaps beyond the death of the parent (Atkinson 1989; Rossi and Rossi 1990). Social norms encourage continued relationships and mutual identification of parents and children throughout life (Atkinson 1989). The symbolic importance of intergenerational relationships may be even greater now than in the past because the duration of the parent-child relationship is longer than at any previous time—the life spans of parents and children now commonly overlap by 50 years or more.

Social interaction patterns also suggest that relationships with parents remain central to adult children's lives. Parents and adult children typically remain in frequent contact with one another (Rossi and Rossi 1990), share many values and attitudes (Glass, Bengtson, and Dunham 1986), engage in mutual exchanges of support and services (Mancini and Blieszner 1989), and feel high levels of positive sentiment toward one another (Bengtson, Mangen, and Landry 1984).

Finally, empirical evidence indicates that relationships with parents are important to an adult child's psychological well-being. Studies that focus on adult children's provision of care to old and infirm parents show that providing care can have detrimental effects on children's well-being (Mancini and Blieszner 1989). More commonly, however, parents provide assistance and support to adult children, and this may enhance the children's well-being. For example, Bankoff (1983) found that parents were the most helpful source of emotional support to recently widowed daughters. Adult children are more likely to characterize their parents as emotionally supportive than as critical or demanding, and socioemotional support from parents is inversely associated with psychological distress among adult children (Umberson 1992a).

RELATIONSHIP SALIENCE AND REACTIONS TO PARENTAL LOSS

Although many people experience psychological and physical symptoms following the death of a significant person, particularly of a spouse or child, some individuals appear to react to such losses more strongly than others (Stroebe and Stroebe 1987). In part, this is because particular social roles and role identities are more *salient* to some individuals than to others—with salience indicating the degree of centrality or importance that the role has for the individual. When life events disrupt role identities, the degree of disruption and distress that follows the life event is linked to the salience of the role or roles affected (Burke 1991; Mutran and Reitzes 1984; Thoits 1991). This suggests that individuals for whom relationships with parents (and, by definition, identities as children) are more salient will respond more strongly to the death of a parent.

However, response to parental loss is further complicated because highly salient relationships may be either positive or negative in quality. The quality of relationships with parents may further influence the symbolic meaning and value of the relationship and the child's subsequent reaction to a parent's death. For example, Wheaton's (1990) work on role histories suggests that loss of a strained relationship results in less distress than loss of a neutral or positive relationship. We hypothesize that loss of highly salient and salient-positive relationships will result in greater distress than will loss of low salience or salient-negative relationships.

A substantial literature on later-life families suggests three sociological factors that are associated with the degree and quality of filial relationship salience: sociodemographic characteristics of the child, gender of the parent, and previous social interactions between parent and adult child.

Child's Sociodemographic Characteristics

Individuals in different sociodemographic positions face different constraints, demands, and opportunities in their daily lives. These life experiences shape the meaning and importance of relationships with parents for adult children (Umberson 1992a). For example, social structural features encourage females to place more emphasis than males on relationships—and on family relationships in particular (Antonucci 1990). Previous research suggests that filial roles are generally more salient and more positive for daughters; adult daughters are in more frequent contact with parents (Umberson 1992a) and report greater affective closeness (Rossi and Rossi 1990) with parents than do adult sons. These findings suggest that daughters would be more adversely affected by the death of a parent than would sons.

The salience of relationships with parents may also depend on the marital status of the child. Unmarried children are more likely to receive instrumental or financial assistance from parents (Rossi and Rossi 1990) and to return home at times to live with parents (Ward and Spitze 1992). While there is little specific information about never-married children, several studies identify unique features of relationships between parents and widowed or divorced children. Widowed children visit with parents more often and report higher levels of emotional support from parents than do married children (Bankoff 1983; Umberson 1992a). This suggests that widowed children would be more adversely affected by a parent's death than married children. Divorced adult children have more contact and receive more assistance from parents than do married children (Huber and Spitze 1988). On the other hand, divorced adult children report greater strain in relationships with parents (Umberson 1992a). Taken together, previous research does not yield a clear hypothesis about differences between married and divorced children in responses to a parent's death.

Income (Treas and Bengtson 1987) and education (Rossi and Rossi 1990) of adult children are inversely related to children's involvement with parents, perhaps because of greater structural need and interdependence in lower socioeconomic families. This involvement appears to be generally positive for parents and children (Treas and Bengtson 1987) and suggests that parental death would result in stronger adverse effects on individuals with low levels of income and education than on those with high income and education.

Several authors have argued that intergenerational ties are closer in black families than in white families (Sussman 1985; see a review by Chatters and Taylor 1993). However, racial differences in family closeness may be due to other factors, such as socioeconomic status (Antonucci 1990; Mutran 1985). In black families, children are more likely to identify their mothers than their fathers as a source of assistance (Chatters and Taylor 1993), and, compared to nonblack adult children, black adult children report that their mothers are more emotionally supportive (Umberson 1992a). Although the literature does not suggest a clear hypothesis about racial differences in responses to parental death, it does suggest that relationships with mothers may be more salient to black adult children than to white adult children; therefore, black adult children may be more adversely affected than white children by a mother's death.

Older adult children seem to have more intimate (Rossi and Rossi 1990) and more positive relationships (Umberson 1992a) with parents than younger adult children. On the other hand, younger adult children see their parents more often (Rossi and Rossi 1990) and receive more support of various types from their parents (Cooney and Uhlenberg 1992). Furthermore, research on the timing of life course events (McLanahan and Sørensen 1985) suggests that the death of a parent would have less impact on older adult children because parental death is normative late in life. So, even though the gerontological literature suggests that older adult children experience greater positive relationship salience, it suggests they might be less affected by a parent's death than younger children.

Gender of the Deceased Parent

A parent's gender may be the most important social characteristic in determining intergenerational relationship salience. Throughout the life course, social-structural contingencies associated with gender foster greater closeness between children and their mothers than between children and their fathers. Rossi and Rossi (1990) reported that adult children's relationships with mothers are more likely to be characterized by shared values and views, greater affective closeness, and greater stability than are relationships with fathers. These findings suggest that a mother's death would be more distressing to adult children than a father's death.

Past Social Interactions with the Deceased Parent

The significance and meaning of a parent's death may also depend on the quality of previous social interactions between the parent and child. These interactions help to form the child's own definition of self (Rosenberg 1979; Gecas and Schwalbe 1983; Atkinson 1989) and to shape the symbolic meaning of the relationship for the child.

Research and theory on parent-child relations have suggested that both childhood and adult interactions with parents are associated with the well-being of adult children (Rossi and Rossi 1990; Umberson 1992a). We hypothesize that adult children who assess childhood memories of the deceased parent as more problematic will be less adversely affected by the death than will children without such memories since the latter group is presumably losing a more salient-positive relationship.

Similarly, adult social interactions with parents vary in intensity and quality. We hypothesize that the loss of a parent with whom the adult child was more closely and positively involved prior to the death will be more upsetting than the loss of a parent with whom the adult child had little contact or had more strained interactions. Many adult children witness the slow decline of a parent's health and sometimes provide care to the parent prior to death. Providing such care can be stressful for the child (Mancini and Blieszner 1989) and affect the quality of the intergenerational relationship. We hypothesize that a parent's death will have less impact on the adult child if the parent was mentally or physically impaired prior to the death.

PREVIOUS RESEARCH ON FILIAL BEREAVEMENT

Only a few studies have directly addressed how the death of a parent affects adult children. Most of these studies were conducted by clinicians who observed that a parent's death precipitated severe distress in patients (e.g., Birtchnell 1975; Horowitz et al. 1981; Kaltreider and Mendelson 1985). Qualitative research (Moss and Moss 1983) and at least one survey of recently bereaved adult children (Scharlach 1991) also suggest that filial bereavement adversely affects adult children. Scharlach's (1991) survey of 220 bereaved adult children concluded that 25 percent of the respondents experienced impaired social and emotional functioning for from one to five years following the loss. However, all of these studies share some methodological problems. First, all lacked control groups—the psychological status of bereaved children could not be compared to nonbereaved children. Seemingly high levels of distress among the bereaved may have been no higher than distress in a comparable sample of nonbereaved adult children. Second, since the data were cross-sectional and collected after the parent's death, *post*-bereavement functioning could not be compared to *pre*-bereavement functioning. Retrospective reports about relationships with parents are highly subject to bias—children may idealize their deceased parent or distress may color memories of past relationships with parents.

While there has been increasing attention to filial bereavement in adulthood, at this time there is no empirical verification that bereaved adult children are significantly more distressed than their nonbereaved counterparts, and no studies have addressed how filial relationship salience affects reactions to the death of a parent. The prospective data used in this study have provided a unique opportunity to analyze how the death of a parent affects adult children in the general population: Our data allowed us (1) to compare over time the physical and psychological functioning of adult children who have experienced the death of a parent with adult children who have not had this experience and (2) to test the filial salience hypothesis.

METHODOLOGY

Data

The data for this study are from a national two-wave panel survey of individuals, ages 24 to 96 in 1986 in the contiguous United States (House 1986).[1] This survey was designed to assess issues of health, productivity, and social relationships over the life course. Face-to-face interviews lasting approximately 90 minutes each were conducted with individuals in 1986 (N = 3,617) and again in 1989 (N = 2,867).[2] Between 1986 and 1989, 207 adults in the sample experienced the death of a biological parent. We compared this group of individuals to individuals who had at least one living biological parent and had not experienced a parental death between 1986 and 1989. All individuals in both groups were interviewed in 1986 and 1989. Individuals who did not meet the criteria for inclusion in one of the two groups were excluded from the analyses. This reduced the sample size for analysis to 1,417: 1,407 respondents were excluded because both parents died prior to 1986, 30 were excluded because they experienced the death of a *step*parent, and 13 were excluded because of missing data on the parent's status.[3]

Measures

Possible modifying variables. Three general types of modifying variables were considered: (1) sociodemographic characteristics of children, (2) adult relationships with parents, and (3) childhood memories of parents. *Sociodemographic characteristics* of respondents included gender (1 = female, 0 = male), race (1 = black, 0 = other), marital status (married, divorced or separated, widowed, and never-married; married constituted the omitted category in regression analyses), age, family income, and years of education. Information on gender, marital status, age, and income was obtained from the 1989 interview.[4] Means and standard deviations of sociodemographic variables are reported in Table 30-1.

Adult relationships with parents were assessed by asking respondents several questions about the current nature of their relationships with living mothers and fathers in 1986. (1) *Emotional support* assessed the positive content of prior relationships. This standardized measure was comprised of two questions: "How much does your (mother/father) make you feel loved and cared for?" and "How much is your (mother/father) willing to listen when you need to talk about your worries or problems?" (mother α = .71, father α = .74). (2) *Relationship strain* assessed the negative content of prior relationships with parents. This standardized measure was comprised of two questions: "How much do you feel your (mother/father) makes too many demands on you?" and "How much is your (mother/father) critical of you or what you do?" (mother α = .65, father α = .74). There were five response categories to the strain and support questions: "a great deal, quite a bit, some, a little, or not at all." (3) *Functional status* gauged the parent's impairment prior to death. Respondents were asked whether their (mother/father) was "mentally and physically capable of giving advice or help if you need it?" (1 = no, 0 = yes). (4) *Frequency of contact* indicated how often children visited with their parents: "During the past 12 months, how often did you have

TABLE 30-1 Death of a Parent. Means and Standard Deviations of Variables: Total Sample, U.S. Adults Ages 24 to 96 in 1986

Variable	Mean	Number of Cases
Death of a Parent Between 1986 and 1989		
Nonbereaved	.854 (.353)	1,417
Mother died	.084 (.277)	1,417
Father died	.067 (.250)	1,417
Modifying Variables		
Sociodemographic Variables		
Gender (0 = male)	.596 (.491)	1,417
Race (0 = nonblack)	.301 (.459)	1,417
Married	.609 (.488)	1,417
Divorced, separated	.205 (.404)	1,417
Widowed	.052 (.223)	1,417
Never-married	.134 (.341)	1,417
Age	42.925 (11.853)	1,417
Family income	35.095 (27.077)	1,417
Years of education	12.757 (2.795)	1,417

Variable	Mean	Number of Cases
Adult Relationships with Parents, 1986		
Emotional support from mother	-.047 (1.049)	981
Emotional support from father	-.102 (1.099)	689
Relationship strain with mother	.080 (1.021)	981
Relationship strain with father	.059 (1.037)	689
Functional status of mother	.093 (.290)	1,081
Functional status of father	.093 (.291)	760
Frequency of contact with mother	4.081 (1.179)	981
Frequency of contact with father	3.707 (1.441)	689
Childhood Memories of Parents, 1986		
Alcohol problem, mother	.028 (.166)	1,417
Alcohol problem, father	.128 (.334)	1,417
Mental health problem, mother	.030 (.172)	1,417
Mental health problem, father	.019 (.137)	1,417
Violent behavior, mother	.022 (.146)	1,417

Variable	Mean	Number of Cases
Childhood Memories of Parents, 1986 (Continued)		
Violent behavior, father	.073 (.260)	1,417
Marital problem between parents	.205 (.404)	1,417
Adult Child Functioning		
Psychological distress, 1986	.119 (1.070)	1,417
Psychological distress, 1989	.010 (1.028)	1,417
Physical health, 1986	3.821 (1.014)	1,417
Physical health, 1989	3.603 (.999)	1,417
Alcohol consumption, 1986	15.409 (32.435)	1,417
Alcohol consumption, 1989	12.485 (32.242)	1,417

Note: Numbers in parentheses are standard deviations.

contact with your (mother/father)—either in person, by phone, or by mail? Would you say more than once a week, once a week, 2 or 3 times a month, about once a month, less than once a month or never?" (coded 0 to 5, with 5 indicating more frequent contact).

Childhood memories of parents were assessed with four questions: (1) "While you were growing up, did anyone in your home have a *serious drinking problem?* (2) What about a *mental health problem?* (3) Was anyone *violent?* (4) Did your parents have serious *marital problems?"* Respondents were asked to indicate if it was the mother or father who exhibited each of these problems (yes = 1, no = 0 for each question). Marital problems between parents were coded as present (= 1) or absent (= 0) for both mothers and fathers.

Death of a parent. In 1989, respondents were asked whether a biological mother or father had died since the time of the first interview. Between 1986 and 1989, 112 adult children experienced the death of a mother, 88 experienced the death of a father, and 7 had lost both parents. The bereavement variables include a dummy variable for mother's death (1 = mother died, 0 = otherwise) and father's death (1 = father died, 0 = otherwise).

Dependent variables measuring adult child functioning. Psychological distress was measured with an 11-item version of the Center for Epidemiological Studies Depression Scale (CES-D). The CES-D has demonstrated high reliability and validity in community surveys and is widely accepted among epidemiologists as a measure of psychological distress in general populations (Radloff 1977). Respondents were asked how often they experienced each of the following in the past week: "I felt depressed"; "I felt lonely"; "people were unfriendly"; "I enjoyed life"; "I did not feel like eating, my appetite was poor"; "I felt sad"; "I felt that people disliked me"; "I could not get going"; "I felt that everything I did was an effort"; "my sleep was restless"; and "I was happy." CES-D item responses were coded so that higher scores indicated greater distress; item scores were summed and standardized to a mean of zero and a standard deviation of one for the full sample (1986 $\alpha = .89$; 1989 $\alpha = .82$).

Sociologists sometimes speak of "functional equivalents" to psychological distress to describe alternative ways of expressing distress. The most commonly discussed functional equivalent is alcohol consumption, which may be a common expression of distress in certain sociodemographic groups, particularly among men as compared to women (Horwitz and White 1991). A standard approach to measuring alcohol consumption involves assessing both the frequency and volume of consumption (Berkman and Breslow 1983). In our study, *alcohol consumption* was measured by multiplying the number of days per month that respondents drank by the number of drinks that respondents typically consumed on those days. Scores ranged from 0 to 600.

Some individuals experience physical symptoms and/or impaired physical health in response to stress (Stroebe and Stroebe 1987). There is evidence that self-reports of health are valid measures of physical health status. Idler and Angel (1990) found that self-reported health is a stronger predictor of subsequent mortality than are physician assessments of health. Self-reports of *physical health status* were obtained from respondents by asking, "How would you rate your health at the present time? Would you say it is excellent, very good, good, fair, or poor?" (coded 1 to 5, with 5 indicating excellent health).

RESULTS

Effects of a Parent's Death

We first compared the physical and psychological functioning of adult children who experienced the death of a parent between 1986 and 1989 with the functioning of adult children who did not have this experience. This analysis assessed whether there are measurable effects of filial bereavement on adult children in a general population. We regressed the 1989 values for the dependent variables on the bereavement variables (i.e., mother died, father died), the sociodemographic variables, and the 1986 value of the dependent variable. Controlling for the 1986 value on the dependent variable allowed us to assess the amount of change in the dependent variable over time.

The results in Table 30-2 indicate that the impact of filial bereavement depends on both the type of dependent variable considered and on which parent died. Compared to nonbereaved adult children, adult children who recently experienced the death of a mother exhibited a significant increase in psychological distress and a decline in self-reported physical health. Adult children who recently experienced the death of a father exhibited a significant increase in alcohol consumption and a decline in self-reported physical health.

One of our hypotheses was that the death of a mother would have more impact on children than the death of a father. The results suggest that this might be true for the outcome of psychological distress. However, a father's death had more impact on children's alcohol consumption, and there was about the same impact on physical health. We conducted t-tests for the difference between the estimates for the impact of a mother's death versus the impact of a father's death on the dependent variables. Although the results show some difference in the magnitude of the estimates for maternal death versus paternal death, the difference was significant only when predicting changes in alcohol consumption—a father's death had substantially greater impact than a mother's death on adult children's alcohol consumption.

Factors That Modify Reactions to a Parent's Death

The remainder of our analysis assessed factors that may modify an adult child's reaction to a parent's death. Possible modifying factors included sociodemographic characteristics of children and the nature of prior relationships with parents (see Table 30-1). We tested a series of intermediate models to derive the final models. First, a separate equation was estimated for each two-way interaction between bereavement and a possible modifying variable (interactions were assessed between possible modifiers and a mother's death and between possible modifiers and a father's death). This involved regressing the 1989 value of the dependent variable on the bereavement variables, a modifying variable, an interaction term between bereavement and a modifying variable, the sociodemographic variables, and the 1986 value of the dependent variable. Missing data were handled by including control variables to indicate the availability of data on specific variables. Where more than one interaction significantly ($p < .05$) predicted a dependent variable, additional equations were estimated which included all significant interactions to determine if a particular interaction predominated as the source of the effect.

TABLE 30-2   Unstandardized OLS Coefficients for the Effects of a Parent's Death and Sociodemographic Characteristics on Adult Children's Functioning in 1989: U.S. Adults Ages 24 to 96 in 1986

Independent Variable	Dependent Variable		
	Psychological Distress	Alcohol Consumption	Physical Health
Death of a Parent (0 = no death)			
Mother died	.183[a]	1.020	−.235[b]
	(.085)	(2.748)	(.080)
Father died	.018	9.781[c]	−.209[a]
	(.090)	(2.909)	(.085)
Sociodemographic Characteristics			
Gender (0 = male)	−.018	−5.348[c]	−.039
	(.047)	(1.569)	(.044)
Race (0 = nonblack)	.129[a]	.438	−.025
	(.052)	(1.672)	(.049)
Marital status (0 = married)			
Divorced, separated	.134[a]	6.952[c]	−.087
	(.062)	(1.999)	(.058)
Widowed	.116	2.011	−.001
	(.111)	(3.571)	(.104)
Never-married	.095	1.208	.081
	(.073)	(2.357)	(.069)
Age	−.004	−.017	−.001
	(.002)	(.070)	(.002)
Family income	−.003[b]	.001	.003[c]
	(.001)	(.033)	(.001)
Years of education	−.025[b]	−.177	.013
	(.009)	(.299)	(.009)
1986 value of dependent variable	.474[c]	.501[c]	.542[c]
	(.022)	(.023)	(.022)
Intercept	.445[b]	8.313	1.365[c]
	(.165)	(5.304)	(.175)
R^2	.327	.288	.366
Number of cases	1,417	1,417	1,417

[a]$p < .05$ [b]$p < .01$ [c]$p < .001$ (two-tailed tests)

Note: Numbers in parentheses are standard errors.

Next, since there are theoretical reasons to believe that the nature of relationships with parents differs for sons and daughters, we tested three-way interactions involving bereavement, measures of prior relationships with parents, and child's gender to consider whether the modifying effects of prior relationships with parents operate the same way for sons and daughters. We used the basic model resulting from the procedures described above as the baseline model. We then applied the same estimation procedures we used to assess two-way interactions to test possible three-way interactions to derive the most parsimonious final models. The final models included all significant interaction terms, controls for their component variables and lower-order interactions, the basic set of sociodemographic variables, and the 1986 value on the dependent variable.[5] The significant three-way interactions are presented graphically to illustrate the pattern of the interactions. The values plotted in Figures 30-1 through 30-5 were obtained by estimating predicted values on the dependent variables, net of the 1986 value, for bereaved and nonbereaved respondents in relevant subgroups.

Modifying effects and psychological distress. The final model predicting psychological distress in response to a parent's death is presented in the first column of Table 30-3. Of all the possible modifying variables that could affect the impact of a mother's death on psychological distress, only the three-way interaction involving a mother's death, mother's 1986 functional status, and child's gender is statistically significant. There are two significant interactions involving a father's death. The effect of a father's death significantly interacted with (1) childhood memories of a father's drinking problem and (2) memories of a father's mental health problems and child's gender. The regression coefficient for death of a mother was not significant once the additional control variables and interaction terms were included in the equation. These findings suggest that our initial analysis overstated the effect of a mother's death on psychological distress for some groups. Furthermore, the significant effect of a father's death on psychological distress for some groups was concealed in the basic model.

The interaction involving a mother's death, 1986 mother's functional status, and child's gender is illustrated in Figure 30-1, which shows the predicted values on distress for the subgroups of men and women who did and did not report their mother as functionally impaired in 1986. Figure 30-1 shows little variation among the nonbereaved groups in predicted distress levels. However, among the bereaved, 1986 functional status of mother was associated with psychological distress, and this association was very different for sons and daughters. Women who had an unimpaired mother seemed to experience more distress following the mother's death, supporting the salience hypothesis. In contrast, sons seemed to be more upset by a mother's death if the mother was functionally impaired prior to the death.

The significant two-way interaction of a father's death with childhood memories of a father's drinking problem suggests that the death of a father has a much greater effect on the psychological distress levels of adult children who recall that their father had a drinking problem during the respondent's childhood—however, this effect is in the direction of *reduced* distress.

The three-way interaction of a father's death with child's gender and childhood memories of a father with mental health problems is illustrated in Figure 30-2. This figure shows that, among the nonbereaved respondents, there was little variation in predicted distress scores on the basis of gender and fathers' mental health problems. However, both sons and daughters seem to be more affected by a father's death if they had childhood memories of a father with mental health problems. Sons who recalled that their fathers had a mental health problem during the son's childhood exhibited

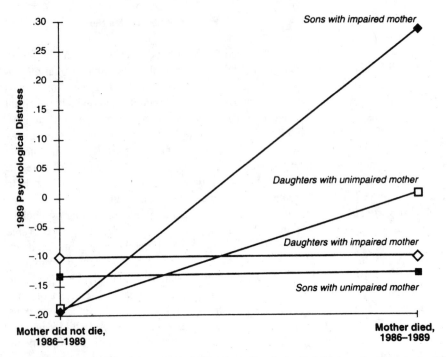

FIGURE 30-1   Effect of a Mother's Death on Psychological Distress by Respondents' Gender and 1986 Functional Status of Mother.

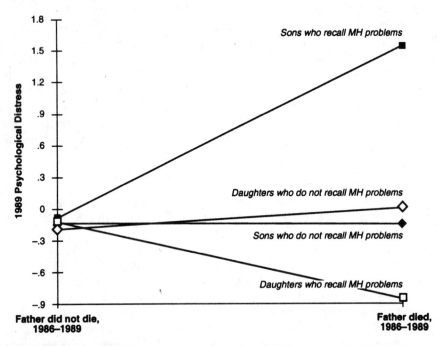

FIGURE 30-2   Effect of a Father's Death on Psychological Distress by Respondents' Gender and Childhood Memories of a Father's Mental Health (MH) Problem.

much higher distress scores than bereaved sons who did not have this childhood memory. In contrast, daughters who recalled a father's mental health problem exhibited *lower* distress scores following the father's death.

Modifying effects and alcohol consumption. The final model predicting alcohol consumption is presented in the second column of Table 30-3. Even though the main effect of a mother's death on alcohol consumption was nonsignificant in the final model, there was a significant three-way interaction regarding a mother's death. This interaction indicates that there was a group of people whose alcohol consumption was significantly affected by a mother's death but that the effect was confounded in the basic model. The main effect of a father's death remains statistically significant in predicting alcohol consumption; however, the effect was in the opposite direction to that reported in the basic model of Table 30-2. Important interaction effects appear to influence the estimated effect of a father's death on alcohol consumption for different groups in different directions. Once we controlled for the modifying influences, a father's death was associated with a *reduction* in alcohol consumption. As we show below, this occurred because some groups seemed to decrease alcohol consumption following a father's death, while others increased their consumption levels.

The significant three-way interaction regarding a mother's death involves gender of the child and having childhood memories of a violent mother. This interaction is illustrated in Figure 30-3. This figure suggests that women who have childhood memories of a violent mother consume more alcohol in response to a mother's death than do other bereaved children. Sons who recall having violent mother in childhood also have high predicted values on alcohol consumption—but this is true whether or not sons had lost a mother.

Statistically significant two-way interactions indicate that adult children's reactions to the death of a father depend on age of the child, marital status of the child, and prior levels of emotional support from the father. The positive interaction with age suggests that older children are more likely to drink in response to a father's death. Older children actually drank less than younger children among the nonbereaved, while the opposite was true among the bereaved. The effect of a father's death on alcohol consumption was negative for persons less than 47 years old and positive for persons age 47 or older.

The interaction of a father's death with marital status in predicting alcohol consumption suggests that the effect of a father's death is strongest for married children and weakest for widowed children. Married, never-married, and divorced children reduced their alcohol consumption following a father's death (about 34, 19, and 15 drinks per month respectively), while widowed children basically did not change the amount they drink.[6]

The positive interaction between a father's death and 1986 levels of emotional support from fathers indicates that children who received more emotional support from their fathers drink more following a father's death. Previous levels of emotional support from fathers were not associated with alcohol consumption among the nonbereaved. However, once an adult child's father died, prior levels of emotional support from the father were positively associated with alcohol consumption (15 drinks more per month for each increment increase in 1986 emotional support from fathers).

TABLE 30-3 Unstandardized OLS Coefficients for the Effects of a Parent's Death and Modifying Variables on Adult Children's Functioning in 1989: U.S. Adults Ages 24 to 96 in 1986

Independent Variable	Dependent Variable — Psychological Distress	Dependent Variable — Alcohol Consumption
Death of a Parent (0 = no death)		
Mother died	.004 (.185)	1.295 (3.797)
Father died	-.012 (.145)	-33.707[a] (15.268)
Sociodemographic Variables		
Gender (0 = male)	-.057 (.058)	-2.852 (2.170)
Race (0 = nonblack)	.133[a] (.053)	.217 (1.586)
Marital status (0 = married)		
Divorced	.134[a] (.063)	5.105[b] (1.943)
Widowed	.089 (.111)	-2.135 (3.554)
Never-married	.090 (.073)	.973 (2.266)
Age	-.004 (.002)	-.058 (.071)
Family income	-.003[b] (.001)	.005 (.031)
Years of education	-.025[b] (.009)	-.151 (.284)
1986 value of dependent variable	.471[c] (.023)	.497[c] (.022)

Independent Variable	Dependent Variable — Psychological Distress	Dependent Variable — Alcohol Consumption
Interactions Involving a Mother's Death (Continued)		
Mother died × violent behavior × gender	—	70.786[c] (19.256)
Interactions Involving a Father's Death		
Father's drinking problem	.184[b] (.071)	-6.563 (3.535)
Father died × father's drinking problem	-.578[a] (.250)	128.746[c] (13.250)
Father's mental health problem	.051 (.379)	—
Father's mental health problem × gender	.020 (.428)	—
Father died × gender	.209 (.187)	-19.876[a] (8.259)
Father died × father's mental health problem	1.641 (.937)	—
Father died × father's mental health problem × gender	-2.575[a] (1.132)	—
Father died × divorced child	—	19.183[b] (7.312)
Father died × widowed child	—	33.187[b] (10.594)
Father died × never-married child	—	15.040 (9.774)
Father died × age of child	—	.781[b] (.268)

INTERACTION EFFECTS AND RELEVANT MODIFYING VARIABLES

Interactions Involving a Mother's Death		
Mother's functional status	-.063 (.123)	—
Data presence indicator, mother's functional status	.035 (.105)	—
Functional status × gender	.151 (.111)	—
Mother died × gender	.192 (.245)	-.611 (5.042)
Mother died × functional status	.476 (.252)	—
Mother died × functional status × gender	-.671[a] (.333)	—
Mother's violent behavior	—	48.976[c] (9.248)
Mother's violent behavior × gender	—	-53.139[c] (10.847)
Mother died × mother's violent behavior	—	—
Emotional support from father	—	.700 (.982)
Data presence indicator	—	-1.979 (3.104)
Father died × emotional support	—	14.953[c] (4.225)
Father's drinking problem × gender	—	3.350 (4.427)
Father died × father's drinking problem × gender	—	-123.963[c] (16.094)
Frequency of contact with father	—	.559 (.856)
Frequency of contact × gender	—	-.662 (.697)
Father died × frequency of contact	—	-5.789[a] (2.262)
Father died × frequency of contact × gender	—	11.804[c] (2.755)
Intercept	.410[a] (.193)	9.814 (5.326)
R^2	.332	.377
Number of cases	1,417	1,417

[a] $p < .05$ [b] $p < .01$ [c] $p < .001$ (two-tailed tests)

[d] Parameter cannot be estimated in this model.

[e] Only one indicator is needed because "frequency of contact with father" and "emotional support from father" use the same set of cases.

Note: Numbers in parentheses are standard errors.

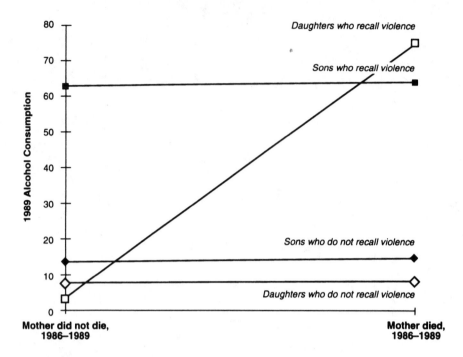

FIGURE 30-3   Effect of a Mother's Death on Alcohol Consumption by Respondents' Gender and Childhood Memories of a Violent Mother.

Table 30-3 also reports significant three-way interactions concerning a father's death and child's gender with two measures of previous relationships with fathers. These effects are illustrated in Figures 30-4 and 30-5 with plots of the predicted values on alcohol consumption for the relevant subgroups.

Figure 30-4 suggests that the effect of a father's death on alcohol consumption was much greater for sons with childhood memories of a father's drinking problem (an increase of about 100 drinks more per month following the father's death). Such memories seem to have had less influence on daughters' drinking behavior following the death of a father (an increase of about 15 drinks per month). On the other hand, sons who did not have childhood memories of a father with alcohol problems actually reduced their alcohol consumption by about 29 drinks per month following the father's death, while daughters increased their drinking by about 10 drinks per month.

Figure 30-5 shows little variance among nonbereaved groups in the association of 1986 frequency of contact with fathers and alcohol consumption. However, previous frequency of contact with fathers did influence the drinking patterns of children who had experienced a father's death. Supporting the salience hypothesis, daughters who were in more frequent contact with their fathers prior to the death exhibited much higher levels of alcohol consumption following the father's death than did daughters who were not in frequent contact with their fathers. Women who were not in contact

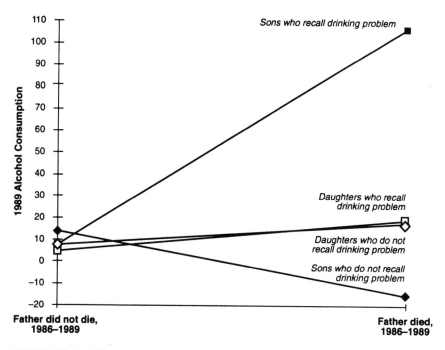

FIGURE 30-4   Effect of a Father's Death on Alcohol Consumption by Respondents' Gender and Childhood Memories of a Father's Drinking Problem.

with their fathers prior to the death appear to have reduced their alcohol consumption more than nonbereaved women. In contrast, sons who were in frequent contact with their fathers prior to the death exhibited lower levels of alcohol consumption than did their nonbereaved counterparts. Sons who did not see their fathers prior to the father's death did not differ from nonbereaved sons on alcohol consumption.

Modifying effects and physical health. The estimated effects of bereavement on physical health status were not modified by any of the child's sociodemographic characteristics or by any of the variables indicating the quality of previous relationships with parents. This suggests that reactions to a parent's death, as expressed in physical health status, do not differ on the basis of sociodemographic characteristics of children or the nature of prior relationships with the parent.

DISCUSSION

The death of a parent appears to be a stressful life event that adversely affects the physical and psychological well-being of adult children in the general population. However, these general effects of parental death provide an incomplete picture. Some groups of adult children were more adversely affected than others by the death of a parent, while some groups actually exhibited improved functioning following a parent's death. The nature of these effects depended on which parent died, the sociodemographic characteristics of the adult children, and the particular dependent variable considered.

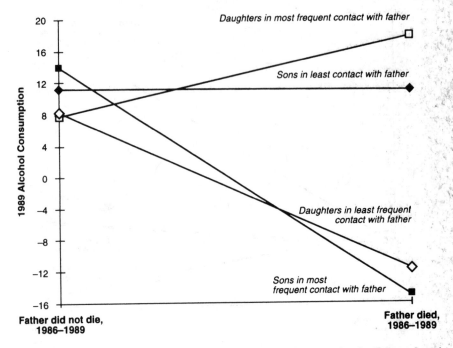

**FIGURE 30-5   Effect of a Father's Death on Alcohol Consumption by Respondents'
Gender and 1986 Frequency of Contact with Father.**

Positive Salience and Reactions to Loss

Our theoretical framework suggests that individuals for whom relationships with parents were more salient and positive prior to the parent's death would be more adversely affected by the parent's death. Many of our results support this hypothesis. For example, having a more emotionally supportive father in adulthood is associated with stronger bereavement reactions as expressed by increased alcohol consumption following the death of a father.

We sometimes found that negative childhood memories of a parent were associated with stronger reactions to the death of a parent as expressed in the amount of change in the dependent variables over time. Notably, this reaction was often expressed in *reduced* levels of distress, suggesting that the loss of a parental relationship characterized by negative-salience sometimes leads to improvement in an adult child's well-being. These findings fit with Wheaton's (1990) work on role histories by suggesting that the death of a parent may come as a relief to the child who has a more difficult family history; these findings also support the filial salience hypothesis—children who did not have negative childhood memories seemed to be more upset by the loss.

Possible Positive Effects of a Parent's Death

The results for alcohol consumption suggest that a parent's death may sometimes result in positive changes in health behavior. For example, while older adult children increased alcohol consumption in response to a father's death, adult children under age 47 actually reduced their alcohol consumption following a father's death. It may be that younger children reduce their alcohol consumption following a father's death because they are concerned about the implications of the death for their own mortality. On average, young children have young parents, and the experience of premature death of a parent may have a deterrent effect on alcohol consumption (and possibly other negative health behaviors as well) that could affect the child's own health status.

The possible deterrent effect of a father's death on alcohol consumption is also seen in the findings for marital status: Married children reduced their alcohol consumption following a father's death much more so than did other children. This may have occurred because of the relationship between marital status and health behaviors generally. There is evidence that married adults drink less than unmarried adults, in part because they have a spouse available to monitor and regulate their drinking habits (Umberson 1992b). Spouses are particularly likely to serve this role if they perceive that the individual is vulnerable to a specific health risk (for example, if there is a history of heart disease in the spouse's family). Following the death of a parent, the spouses of bereaved adult children may become more concerned about the health of the bereaved child and serve an even stronger regulatory role.

Gender of Parent and Child

Sons and daughters often react to a parent's death in different ways. This is not surprising in light of the substantial literature on gender differences in the dynamics and quality of relationships between adult children and parents (Chodorow 1978; Rossi and Rossi 1990; Umberson 1992a).

Gendered patterns of reactivity following the loss of a relationship may reflect differences in sons' and daughters' previous relationships with mothers and fathers. Sons may respond to a father's death in a way that parallels how their fathers dealt with stress. This sort of modeling effect is suggested by two findings. First, sons with childhood memories of a father with mental health problems experienced more psychological distress that other children in response to a father's death. Second, sons whose fathers exhibited alcohol problems were more likely to increase their own alcohol consumption following the father's death. Daughters identify less than sons with fathers (Chodorow 1978), and as a result, daughters may be less likely to respond to the father's death in a way that mirrors the father's previous problems.

In contrast to sons, daughters with negative childhood memories of fathers (e.g., memories of a father's mental health or alcohol problems) exhibited either no change or improved functioning following the father's death. Daughters may have been less upset than sons when a troubled father died because the death has a very different symbolic value for daughters. Daughters may have been more likely than sons to perceive fathers with mental health or alcohol problems as threatening. Daughters are also more likely than sons to assume caregiving responsibility for impaired parents (Mancini and Blieszner 1989) and to feel responsible for the well-being and problems of others (Baines, Evans, and Neysmith 1991). This sense of threat or responsibility may be burdensome, and consequently, daughters may feel more relief than sons when a troubled father dies. On the other hand, we found that childhood memories of a violent mother resulted in stronger negative reactions from daughters than sons following the mother's death. Freud argued that the loss of ambivalent and conflicted relationships is more difficult for individuals to resolve than the loss of stable relationships; however, other theoretical perspectives and empirical studies (including our own) generally have reached the opposite conclusion (see Stroebe and Stroebe 1987). It may be that extremely troubled relationships between mothers and daughters juxtaposed with the unique closeness of mother-daughter ties (see Chodorow 1978; Rossi and Rossi 1990) are particularly likely to undermine the well-being of daughters following the mother's death.

Adult relationships with parents also modify the bereavement reaction differently for sons and daughters. For example, daughters appeared to drink more alcohol following a father's death if they were in more frequent contact with fathers prior to the death, supporting the salience hypothesis. Among sons, however, more frequent contact was associated with a reduction in alcohol consumption. Perhaps sons make positive health behavior changes whereas daughters do not partly because sons identify more with fathers and consequently with the possibility that the father's mortality foreshadows the son's own mortality. Furthermore, frequency of contact with fathers may be positively associated with the degree to which sons identify with fathers, explaining why more frequent contact with fathers in 1986 was associated with greater reductions in sons' alcohol consumption following a father's death. We also found that sons' psychological functioning in 1989 was more adversely affected than daughters' by the loss of a mother who was functionally impaired in 1986. This may have occurred because sons were less likely than daughters to care for impaired mothers and thus felt some sense of failed responsibility or guilt following the loss.

Unsupported Hypotheses

We generated a number of specific hypotheses indicating which groups would be more adversely affected by a parent's death. Yet a number of factors that we expected to influence children's reactions to a parent's death appeared to have no influence in this regard (e.g., the socioeconomic status and race of the child and the degree of strain in prior adult relations with parents). There are three plausible explanations for these unsupported hypotheses. First, group differences in relationship salience may not always be reflected in degree of response to the loss of relationships—thus, challenging the salience hypothesis and theoretical framework. Second, certain variables may be invalid as proxies for salience. Finally, the overall impact of losing a parent may be great enough to override minor group differences in the salience of relationships with parents.

A Theory of Group Differences in Reactions to Stressful Life Events

The factors we have identified as reflecting relationship salience (e.g., sociodemographic characteristics, and frequency and quality of prior relationships with parents) are not perfect proxies. Nonetheless, our findings suggest a link between these proxies for relationship salience and reactions to relationship loss. While our findings provide some support for the theoretical framework of group differences in reactions to bereavement, they raise additional theoretical concerns. First, they highlight the importance of better conceptualizing and operationalizing relationship salience. The specific hypotheses in this study are limited because they are based on the assumption that we know which groups of individuals experience relationships with parents as more salient. Previous research provides evidence about group differences in quality of relationships and frequency of contact with parents, but frequency and quality of relationships may not translate directly into salience. For example, the relationship with a mother may be highly salient to an adult child even if the child rarely sees the mother. Theory and research, both qualitative and quantitative, should include a direct analysis of the salience and symbolic meaning of relationships with parents for adult children.

Our findings further suggest that reactions to the death of a parent depend not only on group differences in relationship salience, but also on differences in the ways that social groups express distress. For example, sons and daughters may experience different levels of relationship salience with parents, but they may also respond to the loss of an equally salient relationship in different ways, perhaps with psychological distress as compared to alcohol consumption or with a decrease rather than an increase in the particular outcome of distress. Health behaviors may be particularly important outcomes following the death of a biological parent because adult children begin to think seriously about their own mortality for the first time (see Donnelly 1987). In response, some children may make positive health behavior changes, even while they are upset by the loss. This highlights the importance of examining a range of expressions of distress when considering group differences in reactions to a stressful life event. Moreover, there may be different *time lines* of reactivity depending on how a particular group expresses distress. For example, changes in psychological distress and alcohol consumption may be apparent in the first few months following a death, but physical health effects may not be apparent until much later.[7] If different groups express distress in ways that are time dependent, data collected at one point in time may not reveal distress in a particular group since it may have already dissipated or not yet appeared. A more complete and predictive theoretical model of socially patterned reactions to stressful life events must incorporate propositions regarding group differences in expressions of reactivity and the timing of those reactions, as well as group differences in relationship salience.

NOTES

1. Data from Wave 2 of the Americans' Changing Lives Survey were obtained through the Survey Research Center, Institute for Social Research, University of Michigan, Ann Arbor, MI.

2. The attrition rate between the 1986 and 1989 interviews was 21 percent (N = 750). Twenty-two percent of that attrition (N = 166) was due to mortality of respondents; the remaining attrition (N = 584) was due to nonresponse. Excluding deceased respondents, nonrespondents were more likely to be black, male, never-married, of low socioeconomic status, and to exhibit higher scores on psychological distress and alcohol consumption. Individuals who were more likely to be distressed by a parent's death may have been more likely to drop out of the study; this could result in *underestimation* of the impact of filial bereavement for some groups. Differences in the dependent variables were less important because we were assessing *change* in the dependent variable over time. We had no information on whether respondents who lost a

parent after 1986 were more or less likely to drop out of the survey. Nonrespondents did not differ from respondents on any of the measures of relationships with parents in 1986.

3. Children whose stepparent died were excluded because the status of adult-child–stepparent relationships is ambiguous. Many of these relationships are established after children become adults.

4. We used information from 1989 because, theoretically, one's "current" sociodemographic position should be more strongly linked to one's current well-being. Preliminary analyses which included a control variable for marital status change between 1986 and 1989, suggested that marital status change would not affect the results of this study.

5. Results from tests of intermediate models are available from the authors.

6. These values were obtained from Table 30-3, where the change in the predicted number of drinks per month for married children is -33.7 (coefficient for father died). The values for the other marital status groups can be obtained by adding the value for the interaction term to -33.7 for each relevant group.

7. An additional analysis of our data suggests that psychological distress is most apparent in the first few months following a parent's death, but that physical health effects are not apparent until much later. However, since the main effects of most categories of time (using a 4-category variable) were not statistically significant and the coefficient for any particular time category was difficult to interpret, these findings should be considered with caution.

REFERENCES

Antonucci, Toni. 1990. "Social Supports and Social Relationships." Pp. 205–27 in *Handbook of Aging and the Social Sciences*, 2d ed., edited by R. Binstock and L. George. San Diego, CA: Academic Press.

Atkinson, Maxine P. 1989. "Conceptualizations of the Parent-Child Relationship: Attachments, Crescive Bonds, and Identity Salience." Pp. 81–98 in *Aging Parents and Adult Children*, edited by J. A. Mancini. Lexington, MA: D. C. Heath.

Baines, Carol, Patricia Evans, and Sheila Neysmith. 1991. "Caring: Its Impact on the Lives of Women." Pp. 11–35 in *Women's Caring: Feminist Perspectives*, edited by C. Baines, P. Evans, and S. Neysmith. Toronto, Ontario: McClelland and Stewart, Inc.

Bankoff, Elizabeth A. 1983. "Aged Parents and Their Widowed Daughters: A Support Relationship." *Journal of Gerontology* 38:226–30.

Bengtson, Vern L., David J. Mangen, and Pierre H. Landry, Jr. 1984. "The Multigeneration Family: Concepts and Findings." Pp. 63–73 in *Intergenerational Relations*, edited by V. Garms-Homolova, E. Hoering, and D. Schaeffer. New York: Hagrefe.

Berkman, Lisa F., and Lester Breslow. 1983. *Health and Ways of Living: The Alameda County Study*. New York: Oxford University Press.

Birtchnell, John. 1975. "Psychiatric Breakdown Following Recent Parent Death." *British Journal of Medical Psychology* 48:379–90.

Burke, Peter J. 1991. "Identity Processes and Social Stress." *American Sociological Review* 56: 836–49.

Chatters, Linda M. and Robert J. Taylor. 1993. "Intergenerational Support: The Provision of Assistance to Parents by Adult Children." Pp. 69–83 in *Aging in Black America*, edited by J. S. Jackson, L. M. Chatters, and R. J. Taylor. Newbury Park, CA: Sage.

Chodorow, Nancy. 1978. *The Reproduction of Mothering: Psychoanalysis and the Sociology of Gender*. Berkeley, CA: University of California.

Cooney, Teresa M. and Peter Uhlenberg. 1992. "Support from Parents over the Life Course: The Adult Child's Perspective." *Social Forces* 71:63–84.

Donnelly, Katherine Fair. 1987. *Recovering from the Loss of a Parent*. New York: Dodd, Mead.

Gecas, Victor and Michael L. Schwalbe. 1983. "Beyond the Looking-Glass Self: Social Structure and Efficacy-Based Self-Esteem. *Social Psychology Quarterly* 46:77–88.

Glass, Jennifer, Vern L. Bengtson, and Charlotte C. Dunham. 1986. "Attitude Similarity. in

Three-Generation Families: Socialization, Status Inheritance, or Reciprocal Influence." *American Sociological Review* 51:685–98.

Horowitz, Mardi J., Janice Krupnick, Nancy Kaltreider, Nancy Wilner, Anthony Leong, and Charles Marmar. 1981. "Initial Psychological Response to Parental Death." *Archives of General Psychiatry* 38:316–23.

Horwitz, Allan V. and Helene R. White. 1991. "Becoming Married, Depression, and Alcohol Problems Among Young Adults." *Journal of Health and Social Behavior* 32:221–37.

House, James S. 1986. "Americans' Changing Lives: Wave I" [MRDF]. Ann Arbor, MI: Survey Research Center [producer], 1989. Ann Arbor, MI: Inter-University Consortium for Political and Social Research [distributor], 1990.

Huber, Joan and Glenna Spitze. 1988. "Trends in Family Sociology." Pp. 425–48 in *Handbook of Sociology,* edited by N. J. Smelser. Newbury Park, CA: Sage.

Idler, Ellen L. and Ronald J. Angel. 1990. "Self-Rated Health and Mortality in the NHANES-I Epidemiologic Follow-Up Study." *American Journal of Public Health* 80:446–52.

Kaltreider, Nancy and Sherry Mendelson. 1985. "Clinical Evaluation of Grief After Parental Death." *Psychotherapy* 22:224–30.

Mancini, Jay A. and Rosemary Blieszner. 1989. "Aging Parents and Adult Children: Research Themes in Intergenerational Relations." *Journal of Marriage and the Family* 51:275–90.

McLanahan, Sara S. and Aage B. Sørensen. 1985. "Life Events and Psychological Well-Being over the Life-Course." Pp. 217–38 in *Life Course Dynamics: Trajectories and Transitions, 1968–1980,* edited by G. H. Elder, Jr. Ithaca, NY: Cornell University.

Moss, Miriam S. and Sydney Z. Moss. 1983–1984. "The Impact of Parental Death on Middle Aged Children." *Omega* 14:65–75.

Mutran, Elizabeth. 1985. "Intergenerational Family Support Among Blacks and Whites: Response to Culture or to Socioeconomic Differences." *Journal of Gerontology* 40:382–89.

Mutran, Elizabeth and Donald C. Reitzes. 1984. "Intergenerational Support Activities and Well-Being Among the Elderly: A Convergence of Exchange and Symbolic Interaction Perspectives." *American Sociological Review* 49:117–30.

Radloff, Lenore S. 1977. "The CES-D Scale: A Self-Report Depression Scale for Research in the General Population." *Applied Psychological Measurement* 1:385–401.

Rosenberg, Morris. 1979. *Conceiving the Self.* New York: Basic Books.

Rossi, Alice S. and Peter H. Rossi. 1990. *Of Human Bonding: Parent-Child Relations Across the Life Course.* New York: Aldine de Gruyter.

Scharlach, Andrew E. 1991. "Factors Associated with Filial Grief Following the Death of an Elderly Patient." *American Journal of Orthopsychiatry* 61:307–13.

Stillion, Judith and Hannelore Wass. 1984. "Children and Death." Pp. 225–49 in *Death: Current Perspectives,* 3d ed., edited by E. S. Schneidman. Mountain View, CA: Mayfield Publishing.

Stroebe, Wolfgang and Margaret S. Stroebe. 1987. *Bereavement and Health: The Psychological and Physical Consequences of Partner Loss.* New York: Cambridge University.

Sussman, Marvin B. 1985. "The Family Life of Old People." Pp. 415–49 in *Handbook of Aging and the Social Sciences,* 2d ed., edited by R. Binstock and L. George. San Diego, CA: Academic Press.

Thoits, Peggy A. 1991. "On Merging Identity Theory and Stress Research." *Social Psychology Quarterly* 54:101–12.

Treas, Judith and Vern L. Bengtson. 1987. "The Family in Later Years." Pp. 624–48 in *Handbook of Marriage and the Family,* edited by M. B. Sussman and S. K. Steinmetz. New York: Plenum.

Umberson, Debra. 1992a. "Relationships Between Adult Children and Their Parents: Psychological Consequences for Both Generations." *Journal of Marriage and the Family* 54:664–74.

———. 1992b. "Gender, Marital Status and the Social Control of Health Behavior." *Social Science and Medicine* 34:907–17.

Ward, Russell A. and Glenna Spitze. 1992. "Consequences of Parent-Adult Child Coresidence: A Review and Research Agenda." *Journal of Family Issues* 13:553–72.

Wheaton, Blair. 1990. "Life Transitions, Role Histories, and Mental Health." *American Sociological Review* 55:209–23.

Winsborough, Halliman H., Larry L. Bumpass and William S. Aquilino. 1991. "The Death of Parents and the Transition to Old Age" (Working Paper 39). Center for Demography and Ecology, University of Wisconsin, Madison, WI.

31

Death, Technology, and Politics

HENRY GLICK

Before the 1950s, the right to die was of little concern because medical science was not able to extend the lives of terminally ill patients. Since then, advances in medical technology, treatment, and drugs have created a specter of lingering death for the terminally ill. This reading surveys the political, moral, and technological aspects of the right-to-die debate. It discusses the various meanings of the term *right to die,* including passive euthanasia and assisted suicide, describes the opponents and supporters of right-to-die legislation, and examines the costs associated with prolonging the lives of the terminally ill.

Nancy Cruzan, an attractive and vivacious twenty-five-year-old, probably fell asleep while driving home from work at the cheese factory near her home in Carterville, Missouri. She lost control of her 1963 Nash Rambler on lonely Elm Road and was thrown out of the car as it crashed. Nancy lay face down in a roadside ditch for about fifteen minutes without breathing or having a heartbeat before a state highway patrolman and paramedics discovered her and began resuscitation. Her lungs and heart began to work again, but since permanent brain damage begins after about six minutes without oxygen, Nancy was in a coma and soon descended into a permanent unconscious vegetative state. Not brain dead, her body performed respiration, circulation, and digestion without medical devices, but she would never regain consciousness or become aware of her surroundings.

Shortly after the crash, which occurred in January 1983, her then husband, hoping that she might awaken and recover, agreed to have a feeding tube implanted in Nancy's stomach. Later her parents, Lester "Joe" and Joyce Cruzan, brought her home from the Missouri Rehabilitation Center forty miles east at Mt. Vernon, hoping that familiar surroundings would stimulate her, but nothing worked. Years passed, and Nancy lay in a tightly contracted fetal position with her muscles and tendons irreversibly damaged, spinal fluid gradually replacing destroyed brain tissue. There was no hope whatever that Nancy Cruzan would change for the better, although with food and water administered artificially through the stomach feeding tube, she could have lived for several decades. Her care cost $130,000 per year, paid by the state of Missouri. Social Security contributions for medical care had long been exhausted.

Four years after her accident and with no change in her condition, Nancy's parents tried to reverse the early approval of the artificial feeding tube so that Nancy could be, in her father's words, "turned loose" and allowed to die. Medical personnel refused, however, and the Cruzans asked the Missouri chapter of the American Civil Liberties Union for help. In turn, the ACLU obtained the free services of a young and vigorous attorney from a large, prestigious Kansas City law firm. Again, the rehabilitation center refused, and the only remaining path was a lawsuit to persuade a local judge to order the feeding tube removed.

A trial began in March 1988 with the Cruzan's lawyer presenting medical testimony from several neurologists, who confirmed that Nancy was in a persistent vegetative state, and from her family and friends, who testified that Nancy had clearly told them that she would not want to be kept alive in her condition. The state rehabilitation center, represented by an assistant state attorney general, countered with doctors and nurses who said Nancy sometimes exhibited awakelike reactions, such as crying, grimaces, and eye movements, that seemed to indicate awareness. Nurses also testified that they did not want to see Nancy's treatment stopped. But the doctors admitted that Nancy's reactions, including tearing, were common in a vegetative state and did not indicate that Nancy was interacting with her environment. A few months after the trial began, Judge Charles Teel, Jr., ruled that a patient has a state and federal constitutional right to refuse medical treatment and that Joe and Joyce Cruzan, acting as Nancy's guardians, had the right to act in her best interests and to order the withdrawal of treatment, including the artificial feeding and hydration.

But the dispute did not end. The state appealed to the Missouri Supreme Court, and Nancy Cruzan's plight quickly changed from a personal tragedy to a state and national issue. Seven medical, right to die, and right to life organizations and advocates for the retarded and disabled filed friend of the court (amicus curiae) briefs on both sides of the issue.

In November 1988, in a 4–3 split decision, the court reversed the trial judge (*Cruzan v. Harmon*). It concluded that there is no right to privacy that allows a person to refuse medical treatment in all circumstances and that removal of the feeding tube would result in death by starvation; it found that Nancy's wishes expressed to a friend were unreliable and denied that Nancy's parents had the power to act on her behalf. The court also ruled that, although Nancy had not executed a living will and was not terminally ill, Missouri's living will statute indicated the legislature's intended policy in such cases; the statute has a prolife preamble, and the law prohibits the withdrawal of food and hydration from terminally ill patients. Also, to the court majority, Nancy was alive and the treatment was not a burden to her. Therefore, the state had a legitimate interest in preserving her life.

The Cruzans' lawyers quickly filed a petition for certiorari with the U.S. Supreme Court. In the past the Court had declined to hear right to die cases, but this time it granted the request. The Bush administration filed an amicus brief in support of Missouri's appeal. On June 25, 1990, the U.S. Supreme Court upheld Missouri in a 5–4 decision (*Cruzan v. Director, Missouri Department of Health*). Writing for the majority, Chief Justice William Rehnquist agreed that Missouri had the right to require clear and convincing evidence of Nancy's wishes not to be kept alive if she were in a vegetative state, and that the state may guard against potential abuses by a patient's surrogate or guardian.

The majority also indicated that oral agreements and instructions were generally suspect in legal transactions but that written instructions concerning medical treatment left by a competent patient would be binding. But, unlike Missouri, the Court did not distinguish between food and hydration and other medical treatment, indicating that both could be withdrawn if a patient had requested. In a concurring opinion, Justice Sandra Day O'Connor urged adults to use living wills or the durable power of attorney to convey in writing their advance wishes concerning final medical care. The dissenters argued that the Cruzans should be permitted to order the withdrawal of Nancy's artificial feeding.[1]

Nancy Cruzan's case continued. Her court-appointed guardian and her lawyer returned in November to the Missouri trial court where the case had begun with three newly discovered former friends who testified that Nancy Cruzan had told them she would not wish to be kept alive if she were in a vegetative state. This time the state of Missouri did not contest the renewed request to disconnect the feeding tube, and within a few weeks Judge Teel ordered its removal so that Nancy could die.

The Society for the Right to Die praised the Cruzans and the decision while right to life protesters denounced what they termed the frenzy to kill Nancy Cruzan. Right to life organizations filed several unsuccessful petitions in state and federal courts to overturn Judge Teel's ruling, and twenty-five protesters were blocked and arrested as they tried to get to Nancy Cruzan's hospital room to force the reconnection of the feeding tube. The day after Christmas 1990—twelve days after the feeding tube had been withdrawn, nearly seven years after her automobile accident, and almost three years after the first court hearing—Nancy Cruzan died.

In January the Missouri legislature considered a bill allowing individuals to designate another person to make health care decisions in the case of incapacitation. However, since the governor has vowed to veto any right to die legislation, bill sponsors have planned to place the issue on the November 1992 ballot (*New York Times,* 23 January 1991:A12).

INTRODUCTION

The Cruzan case is only a recent part of the right to die story. The campaign for a government-sanctioned right to die did not begin with Nancy Cruzan in 1988 but started much earlier in other states. However, identifying particular earlier events also oversimplifies the origin of the issue, and it is impossible to find a single starting point.

The issue became most visible in the United States in 1976 with the first appellate court case involving Karen Quinlan, another young woman in a vegetative state whose parents sued to have life support systems removed. It also began independently in California that same year with the first living will law in which competent adults were empowered to indicate their wishes in writing concerning final medical treatment. But it began earlier than 1976 as well, since right to die proposals had been placed before the Florida and California legislatures in earlier sessions, and the issue gradually had been penetrating the consciousness of Americans at least since the 1950s. New awareness reflects major changes in modern medical technology and social beliefs concerning appropriate medical treatment and the quality and sanctity of life.

Just as the right to die has no single starting point, it has not ended with the Supreme Court's decision in the Nancy Cruzan case. First, the impact of the Supreme Court's decision is mixed and uncertain. The Supreme Court ruled that conscious, competent adults have the right to refuse unwanted medical treatment, including the artificial administration of food and hydration. However, a person's desires need to be clearly expressed while competent and conscious. Ideally, they need to be written down so that an unconscious or incompetent patient's wishes can be honored later.

But the Court also accepted widely quoted evidence that only 15 percent of Americans have living wills directing their final medical treatment, and that perhaps ten thousand people currently are being maintained on life support equipment. Therefore, from one perspective the Court's decision is a victory for those who argue for a right to die and who stress the importance of living wills and other written instructions, but the decision leaves the Nancy Cruzans in medical limbo—forever unable to express their wishes concerning medical treatment but sustained indefinitely by medical technology. It also leaves vulnerable the vast majority of Americans who have no living wills or other written medical instructions.

Equally important the Supreme Court has imposed no particular policy requirements on the states: in the absence of a written living will, the states may require various standards of evidence concerning a patient's prior wishes. The states also may develop their own rules regarding the form and implementation of living wills and other advance medical directives. Policy-making on the right to die will continue.

Politics and the Right to Die

Much has already been written about the right to die in mass circulation magazines and newspapers, in religious, legal, and medical journals, and in book-length treatments. In most of this literature, clergy, journalists, ethicists, lawyers, and doctors grapple with the moral issues involved in the right to die, the conditions when life-saving equipment should be withdrawn, and who should decide for patients who are unable to indicate their own wishes. Examining particular court cases, legal writers explain the logic of judges, describe differences among closely related decisions, and provide guidance for doctors, nurses, and others making treatment decisions. Still others examine differences in the details of state statutes. Much of the writing is prescriptive and is designed to influence policymakers and practitioners.[2]

There is little political analysis of the right to die, and most of that examines public opinion about new health policies. Surveys typically measure support for limiting the use of technology to preserve life in hopeless situations, and numerous social characteristics, such as age, religion, and region, have been related to differences in opinion.

My examination of the right to die takes a different approach. It is not designed primarily to add to the debate over the pros and cons of the right to die but to analyze how policy originated and evolved in state politics and how state governments responded to it. It is principally about the right to die rather than a prescription for making policy or decisions in individual cases. The theme is that the right to die became an issue on state social and political agendas long before state courts and legislatures confronted the problem. Later, over a fifteen-year period, the states produced different innovative policies for dealing with it.

Although there are many similarities among state laws and court cases, they are not identical, and there is no single right to die policy accepted throughout the nation. Instead, the states have produced distinctive policies with important consequences for its citizens. Additionally, innovation in right to die policies has not been the preserve of one branch of government but has involved important and sometimes intense political conflict between courts, legislatures, and the executive branch. To understand the content of right to die policy and, equally important, how it came to be, it is necessary to consider the political roles of all three institutions. Finally, a complex web of political influences accounts for state right to die policies. National political and social trends combined with state political environments, the power of state interest groups, and the power of individual politicians tells us much about how the right to die emerged and the forms it takes in the various states.

DEFINITIONS

Before beginning the story of the right to die, it is important to discuss what the right to die means, the controversies that constantly swirl around it, and its origins.[3] There is no complete agreement on the meaning of the right to die. Terms such as *the right to die with dignity, death with dignity, a natural death, passive euthanasia,* and *abating treatment* are all used to convey a similar but often unclear notion of an ideal environment for and form of final treatment.

Figure 31-1 portrays right to die policies and proposals as a continuum from the least to the most active measures, according to the current levels of public support for each one. It is provided as a guide to the definitions and discussion that follow. Most contemporary policy proposals and law in support of the right to die concentrate on the withdrawal or withholding (abating) of treatment. They generally do not include more active ways of ending life, such as assisted suicide or active euthanasia. However, assisted suicide in particular is fast becoming a new item on the social agenda.

Withdrawing and Withholding Treatment

Withdrawing and withholding treatment is the least active and most widely accepted policy. It is legal and is practiced widely as part of ordinary medical procedure where

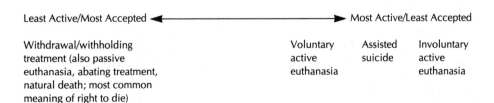

FIGURE 31-1   Continuum of Right to Die Policies and Proposals.

doctors use their professional judgment in making appropriate treatment decisions. In hopeless cases, many doctors routinely stop treatment and withdraw life-sustaining measures. However, the large number of court cases involving disputes over the withdrawal and withholding of treatment also makes it clear that some doctors and health care institutions are uncertain and unwilling to end treatment without explicit legal protection.

State living will laws and court cases generally include two related processes in defining and implementing this definition of the right to die. First, a patient's wishes concerning final medical care in the case of terminal illness and, in a few states, permanent vegetative state, are to be honored by attending physicians, other medical personnel and medical institutions. Second, presuming the patient does not wish to have his or her life extended through aggressive medical treatment, the right to die requires the withdrawal and withholding of treatment that only postpones the process of dying. However, as discussed below, getting agreement on the definition of a terminal illness and exactly what constitutes life-sustaining treatment and when it should be withdrawn or withheld is elusive and at the center of political conflict over the right to die.

For patients who have become permanently unconscious, their recorded prior wishes are to be honored, but if their wishes are unknown, their situation is uncertain. In a dozen states, appellate courts have allowed designated surrogates or court-appointed guardians to make medical treatment decisions on their behalf and in the best interests of the patient. Some state living will laws have similar provisions. But a few courts, such as in Missouri, have required absolutely clear, written proof of a patient's prior intent before treatment may be ended. In addition, most states have recently enacted durable power of attorney or health care proxy statutes that permit individuals to designate another person to make medical treatment decisions on their behalf, but several of these do not cover life-sustaining treatment or do not address the withdrawal of treatment.

As applied to ending treatment, the right to die is synonymous with passive euthanasia; however, that term generally is not used by supporters of the right to die because euthanasia is an emotionally and politically charged word that often is confused with active euthanasia, or is presented by opponents as just one step down the "slippery slope" to active euthanasia. Organizations, such as the early Euthanasia Society of America, have changed their names to more innocuous ones, such as Concern for Dying and Society for the Right to Die (recently recombined as Choice in Dying), to avoid the charged connotations associated with the word *euthanasia*.

Active Euthanasia

Active euthanasia occurs when doctors or others act directly to end a patient's suffering before a natural end to life. Active euthanasia is divided into two categories: voluntary active euthanasia and involuntary active euthanasia. In the former, a patient and/or the family asks another person, most likely a doctor, to terminate the patient's life. In the latter, others take it upon themselves to kill the suffering patient. Active euthanasia differs from the withdrawal or withholding of treatment in which the disease or injury is allowed to take its course, with only "comfort care" provided by hospital or hospice staff. Both forms of active euthanasia are mercy killing and criminal, possibly murder, although convictions for manslaughter with suspended sentences or probation are typical (Humphry and Wickett 1986).

While active euthanasia refers to ending the suffering of the dying, it sometimes is seen as the modern forerunner or even synonymous with Nazi-like "euthanasia" programs in which millions of the medically and mentally handicapped, homosexuals, Jews, Gypsies, and other "undesirables" were murdered through explicit and planned government policy.

Although active euthanasia is criminal because it hastens death, many doctors and a growing majority of Americans believe that voluntary active euthanasia should be legal. Support for passive euthanasia has been high and increasing since the 1950s (Adams, Bueche, and Schvaneveldt 1978; Crane 1978; Haug 1978; Singh 1979; Duff and Campbell 1980; Ward 1980; Perlin 1989; *Washington Post National Weekly Edition*, 1 April 1985:n.p.).

Assisted Suicide

The usual meaning of the right to die has not included assisted suicide, in which others, probably doctors, are enlisted by patients to help end their lives. It usually entails providing the means of death, such as a prescription for sleeping pills or other device. Assisting a suicide is illegal in many but not all states.

Assisted suicide is a quiet but accepted practice in the Netherlands, and it is receiving more attention in the United States (*New York Times*, 31 October 1986:6). The Oregon based Hemlock Society (formerly located in California) has sought, unsuccessfully so far, to place a citizen's initiative on the California ballot legalizing assisted suicide. However, a similar effort was successful in Washington state, although the measure was defeated (*New York Times*, 6 July 1990:A7, 7 November 1991:A10).

Increased professional and public interest in assisted suicide is also underscored by the recent cases involving Dr. Jack Kevorkian's "suicide machines" of lethal drugs and carbon monoxide, which were used in the planned death of Alzheimer's sufferer Janet Adkins in Michigan and later in the deaths of two other women, and Dr. Timothy E. Quill in Rochester, who described in the *New England Journal of Medicine* his decision to provide a prescription of barbiturates knowing that a leukemia patient he had been treating would use them to kill herself. Dr. Quill wrote the article because he believed it important for doctors to begin to explicitly discuss their duties and obligations to terminally ill and suffering patients (*New York Times*, 6 and 7 June, 1990:1; Altman, *New York Times*, 12 March 1991:B6; *New York Times*, 3 July 1991:1, 25 October 1991:1).

Locating voluntary active euthanasia as less "active" than assisted suicide in Figure 31-1 may seem incorrect or arbitrary, and individuals might change the order to fit their own views of proper policy. However, the public supports voluntary active euthanasia more than assisted suicide, possibly because voluntary active euthanasia has been a social issue for many decades.

There also is disagreement in society concerning how "active" each of these measures is. Some individuals and organizations consider all measures, possibly other than the withdrawal or withholding of treatment, to be extreme and unacceptable ones. But others argue that helping a patient to commit suicide requires less action by others than either form of active euthanasia, and that assisted suicide places more responsibility on the patient who wishes to die than on a doctor or others who might help. Still others view voluntary active euthanasia as a logical extension of medical care. If doctors are able to sustain life through modern medical technology, they ought to be able to painlessly end life in hopeless situations as well, so long as patients and/or their families request it.

Finally, both assisted suicide and voluntary active euthanasia are often discussed together in the news media as equally controversial policy proposals. However, practically no support exists for involuntary active euthanasia, which is mercy death administered by doctors or others without patient consent or request. Most would agree that it is the most extreme and least acceptable measure.

ORIGINS AND IMPACT

The right to die has been a social concern for eons. The term *euthanasia* is derived from the Greek meaning good or easy death, a process that the Greeks and Romans wrote about and practiced. In the sixteenth century Catholic theologians distinguished between a patient's obligation to undergo "ordinary" medical treatment to sustain life and the right to forego "extraordinary" procedures (Weir 1989:216–17). Euthanasia also was an issue in Great Britain and the United States in the early 1900s, but the concept of euthanasia was blackened as a result of Nazi policy, and the word is still not used often or openly in Germany (*New York Times,* 6 December 1986:6). However, euthanasia has received increasing attention since the 1950s with the fading of World War II, and in 1957 Pope Pius XII formally addressed the differences between ordinary and extraordinary care.

Modern Medicine

Before the 1950s, the right to die was not of great concern because medical science was unable to appreciably extend the lives of terminal patients. Those in a permanent unconscious state died quickly from additional illnesses and complications or because they were unable to eat and drink. Before the widespread use of antibiotics and the control of communicable diseases, people also died quickly when they contracted pneumonia, tuberculosis, and influenza—the common illnesses of the early 1900s. Those with cancer and heart disease or victims of debilitating accidents frequently contracted pneumonia and died before their otherwise terminal illness took its toll. Until midcentury most people also died at home without extraordinary medical equipment or treatment. Today, however, probably less than 20 percent of the population die outside hospitals or nursing homes.

With victory over most common communicable diseases now possible and lengthening life spans, the nature of illness has changed, and modern medicine is able to treat today's common degenerative diseases such as cancer and heart disease. In the 1950s surgical techniques improved, and cancer patients, for example, could undergo surgery that might not cure but could postpone the ravages of illness. Developments during this period included intravenous feeding, new drugs to fight infection, and cardiopulmonary bypass machines and coronary angiography for open heart surgery and for studying coronary circulation. In the 1960s ventilators, cardiac resuscitation, kidney dialysis, organ transplants, artificial heart valves, and more antibiotics were added to the medical arsenal. Computer axial tomography (CAT scanners) and nuclear magnetic resonance imaging, which were superior to x-rays, appeared in the 1970s and 1980s. New drugs for fighting the progression of AIDS and other diseases are on the way, and organ transplant and artificial skin technology is improving. There is no end to medical innovation and the power of doctors and new machines to prolong life.

Advances in technology and knowledge and the cost of new medical treatment also have led to increasing medical specialization and large, centralized, and impersonal medical centers and hospitals. Increasing urbanization and population mobility inevitably produce growing impersonality in many business and professional relationships, and traditionally close doctor-patient bonds that last a lifetime have given way to constantly changing faces and institutions. With any condition out of the ordinary, family practice physicians quickly refer patients to one of perhaps several specialists who have not had any prior relationship with the patient and cannot know the patient's concerns and desires. Inevitably, busy doctors in impersonal settings focus on treating particular physical problems rather than learning about a patient's outlook on illness, treatment, and the quality of life.

Changes in the technology and practice of medicine, coupled with traditional medical training and ethics that champion conquering disease and preserving life, and doctors' fears of liability for discontinuing treatment have all created a specter of a lingering death for many terminally ill or comatose patients and the growing elderly population. Modern medical tools are valued lifesavers for accident victims and those suffering from reversible serious illness or undergoing surgery, but the new technology can also be a threat to the elderly and the hopelessly ill who inevitably will die, but not quickly or easily because the same machines that preserve life can exacerbate inevitable death.

Individuals have had the legal right to refuse unwanted medical treatment for many decades, but this was before the advent of powerful and modern medical technology. Now, there is heightened social and political concern with the right to control the use of medical technology and to establish the rights of individuals to determine the course of their own treatment.

Karen Quinlan and Beyond

Social concern with the right to die is evidenced by articles in newspapers and popular magazines and legal and medical journals which appeared sporadically since the 1950s, but the galvanizing event which stimulated a rapidly rising chorus of concern is the 1976 Karen Quinlan case (*In the Matter of Karen Quinlan*). Then, a young woman in a coma, but not brain dead, was placed on a respirator in "an altered state of consciousness" with no hope of recovery. Her parents pressed attending physicians to remove the respirator so that she could die, but were refused. The New Jersey Supreme Court, relying on an expansive interpretation of the constitutional right to privacy and the right of parents to act as guardians, finally ordered the respirator removed. Although the respirator was withdrawn, Karen Quinlan was fed artificially and lived for another ten years. The case inaugurated new policy for allowing patients and/or their families to make decisions concerning the use of life prolonging medical treatment.

When this case first entered the New Jersey trial courts in 1975, and continuing through 1976, newspaper, magazine, and journal coverage of the right to die zoomed. The total number of articles published in 1975 and 1976 equaled or exceeded all articles published in the previous decade. From 1976 until the end of 1990, dozens of appellate court cases were decided in 17 states affecting the use of life-support systems and other treatment for the terminally ill and those in a permanent vegetative state. Generally, the states have endorsed the policy produced in the Quinlan decision, but other courts have produced distinctive policies. In 1976, California enacted the nation's first living will law, followed in 1977 by similar laws in seven additional states. Nearly all states had living will bills before the state legislature in 1977 (Society for the Right to Die 1988). By the end of 1990, forty-one states and the District of Columbia had enacted living will legislation.

As indicated earlier, living will laws allow individuals to specify their wishes in advance of a terminal illness concerning the administration of life-saving treatment. In contrast, the court cases generally deal with terminally ill or permanently comatose patients who have not executed living wills and where there is doubt concerning a patient's wishes or doctors require a court order to disconnect equipment. However, certain court cases have interpreted legislation and on occasion have sanctioned the validity of living wills in the absence of legislation.

DILEMMAS AND AMBIGUITIES

Despite the quantity of state law produced in the past fifteen years, the right to die is not a settled issue. There are numerous dilemmas and ambiguities and associated political conflicts that continually crop up and keep the right to die a frequent if not permanent issue on state political agendas. Disagreement over the meaning and availability of the right to die is reflected in wide variation in state law. Some states have generally permissive or facilitative laws while others have imposed serious limitations on patient control. Most state courts permit the withdrawal of treatment in most hopeless cases and generously interpret the meaning of terminal illness, but others require absolutely clear evidence of patients' wishes, have narrowly interpreted the meaning of terminal illness, and have restricted the types of treatment that may be withdrawn.

As indicated earlier, a complete examination of the legal, medical, and ethical issues involved in the right to die is beyond the scope of this study. But as background to the politics of the right to die, it is important to recognize that many of the concepts and practices involved in treating terminally ill or comatose patients are unclear and unsettled. Some have been the focus of many political battles in the states while others have been addressed by courts but not by legislatures.

The Continuum of Care

Aggressive medical care and passive and active euthanasia are three elusive points on a treatment dimension that is even broader than the right to die proposals depicted in

Figure 31-1. At one extreme end of the continuum, a minority of doctors object to any withdrawal or withholding of treatment and would continue to sustain any patient who is not brain dead. At the other end, a few doctors publicly—and probably more, privately—condone ending the life of a patient who is suffering and cannot be restored to any reasonable level of health. Most others are in the middle. They would refuse to kill a patient out of mercy, termed an act of commission, knowing that such action clearly is illegal. Most also resist enlarging the role of medicine to include assisted suicide since doctors are pictured as healers, not killers or abettors of death. Involving doctors in mercy killing or suicide confuses the traditional medical role and suggests to some that medicine could become an agent of state policy permitting or encouraging active euthanasia.

But most physicians also recognize that there is a time for ending futile treatment which can only postpone the inevitability of death. However, doctors and medical institutions sometimes fear medical malpractice suits or even criminal liability for withdrawing treatment, which occurs through omission, i.e., not doing everything possible to sustain life.

Medical fears of liability for not doing everything possible to preserve life are the basis of most lawsuits concerning requests by patients and families to withdraw medical treatment. However, occasionally disputes arise when family members disagree over whether treatment should be stopped and doctors refuse to end treatment without the legal protection of a court order. Living wills are designed to prevent such conflicts, but even with living wills, doctors sometimes are satisfied only with an explicit court order which absolves them of criminal or civil liability for ending treatment.

There apparently have been only two disputes with the roles reversed—in which the families of patients on artificial life support objected to its removal, and doctors and the hospital have gone to court to get permission to end what, in their view, was futile and inhumane treatment. In a case in Minneapolis, the patient's husband stood by strong religious beliefs which require preserving life, whatever its condition. In Atlanta, the parents of a thirteen-year-old girl disagreed about her treatment, and the father insisted he was waiting for a miracle. Trial judges in both cases ruled that families were in the best position to decide for the patient. The hospital in the Minneapolis case said it would not appeal, and the patient died a few days later (*New York Times,* 10 January 1991:1; 2 July 1991:A3; 6 July 1991:8).

Ending life-sustaining medical treatment also may seem easy to specify, but there is disagreement and confusion concerning the particular treatments that patients should and should not receive and what constitutes ordinary and extraordinary care. Artificial respiration and heart resuscitation are the "extraordinary" life-sustaining treatments that are withdrawn most frequently, but other routine or ordinary medical procedures, such as the use of antibiotics to fight pneumonia and other infections, also postpone inevitable death from the underlying terminal illness or injury. Should they be used because they can fight a treatable illness or employed as "comfort care" because they keep a patient comfortable while they die? In contrast, pain killers used as comfort care procedures also can hasten death by depressing breathing and circulation, and further blur the distinction between passive and active euthanasia. These details of treatment generally are not addressed by legislatures, and ambiguities surrounding day-to-day medical decision making increasingly are seen as shortcomings and problems in living will laws.

Withholding and Withdrawing Treatment

Disagreements also flare over the ethical difference between withholding and withdrawing life-sustaining procedures. Some doctors feel more comfortable not beginning a life-prolonging treatment than withdrawing it, which fits within broader concerns over the difference between acts of commission and omission. To omit a treatment is justified as passive euthanasia since a doctor stands aside while illness takes its toll, but removing a device or stopping a treatment requires action and possibly seems closer to the commission of active euthanasia. Clearly, the result to the patient is the same, and many commentators and ethicists no longer see a difference between withholding and withdrawing or between a decision not to act (i.e., not starting treatment) and a decision to act (i.e., withdrawing treatment). The courts also generally have taken this view, but the conflict still plagues daily clinical decision making.

Food and Hydration

Political battles have raged most recently in state legislatures and courts over the artificial administration of food and hydration. Patients who are unable to take food and liquids by mouth often are routinely given them through intravenous, nasogastric, or implanted stomach tubes. Artificial feeding frequently is considered part of regular patient maintenance and comfort care that all patients—regardless of their condition—should receive. Many patients, such as Nancy Cruzan and other young people in a permanent vegetative state, could be kept alive for years or decades through such procedures.

Since the mid-1980s many states (but by no means all) and the U.S. Supreme Court have concluded that there is no meaningful distinction between ordinary and extraordinary care, and that the artificial administration of food and hydration is a medical procedure that can be withdrawn or withheld like any other. But to opponents, the withdrawal of sustenance, however administered, is enforced starvation and active euthanasia. Political battles between state courts and legislatures and interest groups continue to be fought on allowing or curtailing the right to end artificially administered food and hydration.

Diagnosis

A related political issue concerns the diagnosis of terminal illness. Most state living will laws specify that in order for medical treatment to be withheld and a patient allowed to die, he or she must be diagnosed by two or more physicians as terminally ill and judged that death is imminent. However, the term *terminal illness* is not very precise, and since doctors are trained and medically socialized to treat illness, not to give in to death, they sometimes are unwilling to diagnose a patient as terminally ill until death is very close and the patient already has undergone various life-sustaining procedures.

In turn, and paradoxically, treatment that preserves various organ functions may make the patient technically not terminal. Consequently, dilemmas concerning the timing of a diagnosis of terminal illness and the willingness to end life-sustaining treatment is even more basic than differences over passive and active euthanasia and the medical procedures which may be withdrawn. If doctors are reluctant to term the patient terminal or in a permanent unconscious state, various life-sustaining treatments will be administered, at least for a time, regardless of a patient's wishes.

Moral Conflicts

Finally, but certainly not least, there are fundamental religious and moral conflicts over the right to die, which have been channeled into state politics. While not condoning incessant suffering, opponents of living will laws and court decisions which permit the withdrawal or withholding of treatment see the right to die as an infringement on the power of God to control life. It also involves government in matters that ought to be managed privately by patients and their families and doctors. In this view, although man has increased the power to extend life, he should not take steps which actively seek its end. Government-sanctioned passive euthanasia also is seen by opponents as a step toward mercy killing, assisted suicide, and probably involuntary Nazi-like euthanasia. In this view, the frail and poor elderly and the medically and mentally handicapped are most vulnerable, although unnamed others could be threatened in the future.

POLITICAL COMBATANTS

Supporters

Until very recently there has been little organized political support at the state level for the right to die. National groups, especially Concern for Dying and the Society for the Right to Die, provide information and support to sponsors of legislation and aid individuals and families involved in litigation, but few in-state interest groups have actively campaigned for the right to die or supported legislators who put the issue on legislative agendas. In most states, the issue has been too controversial and divisive for organizations to take a stand. In addition, the right to die does not affect a particular group of citizens more than another, which leads no group to champion it as a legislative issue. Even the elderly, a group that is disproportionately affected by the right to die, have been divided and largely silent on this issue. Other groups that often are sympathetic to the right to die, such as state nurses' associations, have many other items on their agendas more central to their interests, so they do not devote time or resources to lobbying directly on this issue.

In the early 1970s, except for the occasional legislative testimony of individual doctors and nurses—often associated with universities—and citizens with personal tragedies to tell about the protracted death of a loved one, legislators sponsoring living will bills frequently found themselves working alone for legislation. Today, as the issue has permeated the social and political agendas, supporters include the American Medical Association and various state medical societies, bar associations, hospital associations, various Protestant and Jewish denominations, the American Association of Retired Persons and their state affiliates, other groups of the elderly, and many others. However, while these groups are supporters, they rarely lobby hard for living will laws and other legislation.

Opponents

In sharp contrast to the sporadic support among those who are sympathetic, the right to die always has had very powerful and active opponents. The most well-organized and influential opposition comes from the Catholic church through state Catholic conferences, which are the lobbying arms of the Catholic dioceses. However, the Catholic church recently has modified its position in recognition of increased public support of the right to die. It has not endorsed living will laws, but actively tries to influence their content in order to insure that Church interests are included. Additionally, various state and local right to life organizations also oppose living will laws and permissive court decisions, and they take the most extreme positions against the right to die, linking it to Nazi euthanasia and other totalitarian measures. These groups also generally refuse to compromise on living will legislation. Finally, state and national organizations representing the disabled and retarded also have opposed living will laws and permissive judicial policies, seeing them as a likely first step to ridding society of the dependent and unwanted.

Representatives of state Catholic conferences frequently claim they have no bonds with right to life groups and that they do not coordinate political activities with them, but the two have been closely linked in the past. The National Right to Life Committee and its state and local affiliates were created as separate organizations by the U.S. Catholic Conference in order to avoid jeopardizing the Church's tax-exempt status as a result of its active political promotion of prolife causes. But the right to life committees were and continue to be heavily dominated by Catholic lay persons, and various researchers and journalists maintain that the Catholic church continues to channel funds to these groups (Tribe 1990; Paige 1983; Tatalovich and Daynes 1981; Steinhoff and Diamond 1977).

The rise of conservative Protestant evangelical groups in the Republican Party in the 1980s has attached conservative Protestants to this formerly mostly Catholic movement. State Catholic conferences and state right to life committees separately manage their own political activities, but on abortion and the right to die, they have parallel political goals, and often there is a tacit but sometimes uneasy alliance between them. The Catholic church and right to life groups are not always in harmony for two main reasons. Right to life organizations often take conservative positions on a wide range of social issues on which the Catholic church is more liberal, and the right to life groups often use extreme tactics, such as sit-ins, demonstrations, searing language, and graphic advertising and other visual displays against supporters of the right to die. State Catholic conferences often officially distance themselves from these strategies while pursuing the same political objectives.

In each of the states, Catholic conferences have been much more prominent than right to life organizations or evangelical Protestants in opposing the right to die and they lobby in much more conventional ways, which gives them greater access to state legislators. However, in the past few years, the National Right to Life Committee, its state affiliates, and new right to life groups, such as the International Anti-Euthanasia Task Force, have linked the right to die to abortion in an effort to mobilize broader political opposition to the withdrawal of treatment, particularly artificially administered food and hydration (*New York Times,* 31 July 1990:1).

CONVERGING POLICIES

The right to die is one element of a much larger set of medical, health care, and social issues that appeared at a similar time and evolved in response to the transformation of modern medicine. While it is not possible to thoroughly explore these other issues here, it is important to emphasize that the right to die has not emerged separate and apart from other problems and developments. The appearance of other related issues also underscores that policy innovation is much more complex than the emergence and evolution of a single policy.

Brain Death

Not only have advances in medical technology made it possible to extend life, they have made it much more difficult to pronounce death. Before the availability of brain scan technology and medical devices which can prolong breathing and circulation, death was defined as the cessation of voluntary breathing and heartbeat. However, with increased use of respirators and resuscitators, doctors have begun to rely on newer definitions which include brain death as an additional basis for the pronouncement of death.

Like withdrawing medical treatment, determining brain death may seem simple at first, but there are at least seven different definitions of death, which include a brain death component, that have been developed since 1968 (Blumberg and Wharton-Hagan 1988). All state laws require that the entire brain—the cerebellum and the brain stem—cease functioning in order for a person to be declared brain dead. Persons in a permanent vegetative state have suffered complete loss of cerebral function, but the brain stem continues to operate and these people are not considered brain dead.

Recently, critics have argued that definitions of brain death should be changed to include only the cerebellum and higher brain functions so that those in a vegetative state could be declared brain dead, which would permit the withdrawal of treatment (Meisel 1989:134–35). The Catholic church and other opponents maintain that so long as part of the brain continues to function, life exists. Brain death policies also are crucial for organ transplant policies since minimal lifelike functions can be preserved through artificial respiration and circulation which permits organ transplants from those who are brain dead.

Of the states that have adopted living will laws, nearly 70 percent previously had enacted one or another brain death statute, indicating that most of the states previously had dealt with an issue closely related to the right to die. Although brain death and the right to die are not the same thing, the adoption of one creates psychological and political linkage to the other. Previous adoption of a brain death statute "softens up" the political environment and probably makes a living will law more acceptable.

Medical Costs

Doctors and medical researchers are not the only ones in our society who have come to expect continued advances in treatment and aggressive battles against disease. Nearly everyone strives for better health and longer life and expects medical salvation for every illness. Medicine is expected to conquer the next health challenge and extend its frontiers; there is no end to our preoccupation with medical miracles. But all of the medical innovations cost enormous amounts of money and critics are beginning to argue that it is impossible to provide expensive and innovative treatments and procedures to everyone for every illness. Many people no longer can afford health insurance and those covered on the job face rising premiums and reductions in benefits. Government programs to aid the poor and the elderly cost more every year. Some limits or rationing—done either by government or through market forces—must occur, it is argued, or there will be continuing economic and social crises in providing health care.

Daniel Callahan has argued for a revolution in the way we think about health care (1987; 1990). We need to set limits of all sorts, guaranteeing a certain level of health care for everyone, but eliminating the exotic cures that save or extend few lives at great cost and which spur even more innovation and social expectations about the next generation of medical miracles. Although such a revolution in medicine has not and probably will not take place soon, discussion and debate about a national health care crisis is occurring at the same time the states have adopted right to die policies. Indeed, a few politicians and political commentators make a clear and direct link between the two, although these arguments rarely have been raised in state legislatures.

A drive to extend life through sophisticated diagnostic procedures, treatments, and life-sustaining measures means that those on the verge of death, or in a permanent vegetative state, and the infirm elderly increasingly receive huge amounts of health care resources. If society reexamines the meaning of life and death and the role of health care, our conception of appropriate treatment must come under greater scrutiny.

There is no evidence that medical costs and treatment have been reduced by living will laws or court decisions. On the contrary, some recent research and events suggest that profit motives are related to decisions to use life-prolonging technology. In 1989, a New York intermediate appellate court ruled that the family of a nursing home resident, who was in a permanent vegetative state, would not be required to pay $100,000 in nursing home fees for treatment which the family repeatedly insisted the resident did not want. The nursing home continually pressed for payment but had repeatedly refused to honor requests for the removal of a stomach feeding tube and the end to antibiotic treatment as contrary to the policies and philosophy of the nursing home (*Elbaum v. Grace Plaza of Great Neck*).

A recent survey of the use of artificial nutrition and hydration in nursing homes found that state living laws had no effect on nursing home policy regarding the use of artificial feeding. However, artificial feeding was more likely to be used in private nursing homes owned by large corporate chains. A large proportion of residents supported by private and public assistance also leads to greater use of feeding tubes. Other research has shown that highly debilitated nursing home residents are less costly to maintain than mobile and active clients, which reinforces the possibility that nursing homes may be motivated by profit to keep the very elderly and disabled alive through life-prolonging technology (Almgren 1990; Danis 1991). The Associated Press also reported recently that some privately owned hospitals in various cities lure doctors with cash payments, low cost loans, gifts of equipment and guaranteed supplemental incomes to admit more patients to fill empty hospital beds (*Tallahassee Democrat,* 17 October 1990:1). Once the patient is there, perhaps private hospitals are reluctant to cease unwanted or perhaps unnecessary treatments.

THE INCREASING ELDERLY

Occurring with changes in medical technology is a huge demographic shift in the age of the American population, with enormous implications for all types of public and private policies from advertising and marketing to health care, housing, and transportation. The proportion of the elderly is fast increasing, and the biggest jumps are yet to come. In 1900 those over age sixty were little more than 6 percent of the total population. This doubled by 1950 and increased to nearly 17 percent in 1990. The level is likely to remain fairly constant to the end of the century, but will increase again to 25 percent between 2000 and 2025 and 30 percent by 2080. While the total U.S. population tripled between 1900 and 1980, from 76 million to 227 million, those over age sixty increased sevenfold, from 5 million to 36 million. The oldest old is the fastest-growing group. The percentage of all elderly under the age of seventy is declining while the percentage of those over age seventy and especially over age eighty-five is increasing. In 1900, those age eighty-five and older were 1 percent of the total population; in 1980 they had increased to 6 percent. The meaning of "old age" is changing with the statistics.

The implications for health care are clear. Between 1965 and 1981 the nation's health care expenditures for the elderly increased from 23 to 33 percent of the total. In 1973 the number of nursing home residents age sixty-five and older was 961,500. By 1980 the number had increased 37 percent to 1,315,800. Those age eighty and above constituted nearly 65 percent of all residents. Nearly half of all nursing home care is paid by Medicaid and other government funds (Serow, Sly, and Wrigley 1990; *New York Times,* 27 March 1990:A10). In any particular year, Medicare spends six times the amount for health care for elderly who die as opposed to those who do not die. The largest increases (over 45 percent) occur within the last sixty days of life (Weir 1989:21–22).

Political debate about health care costs and the allocation of medical resources and the concerns of medical institutions are bound to focus heavily on treatment for the elderly, and the concerns will heighten as the size of the elderly population—especially the oldest old—increases. The elderly are also disproportionately involved in and affected by right to die policies. Half of all deaths in the United States each year occur among the elderly, although those over age sixty-five constitute only 11 percent of the population. Half of all the right to die appellate cases in the states also have concerned persons over age sixty-five. Again, the right to die is not the same issue as the cost and allocation of health care, but connections between the two are being made and are bound to become more compelling in the future. Policies in one area implicate policies in others.

Legislators and judges rarely link these converging policies or produce solutions to new problems according to a large, encompassing plan. But the right to die is part of a larger process of agenda setting and innovation, and related policies have implications for each other. The simplest connections occur when the adoption of a certain policy at an earlier point in time eases the way for the adoption of related policies in the future. But some policies emerge more or less simultaneously and motivate divergent groups to support them as solutions to different problems that they have identified as important to their own constituency.

NOTES

1. Information on the Cruzan case is derived from *Cruzan v. Harmon; Cruzan v. Director; New York Times,* 25 July 1989:1; 27 November 1989:11; 7 December 1989:1; 26 June 1990:A7; and 27 June 1990:A10; *Kansas City (Missouri) Times,* 7 December 1989:n.p.; *Los Angeles Times,* 29 July 1990:1; *Time,* 19 March 1990:62.

2. For extensive discussion of these and related issues see Weir 1989; Meisel 1989; and Horan and Mall, eds., 1980.

3. The following discussion partly relies on *Deciding to Forego Life-sustaining Treatment* 1983; Humphry and Wickett 1986; Callahan 1987, 1990; Meisel 1989; Weir 1989; and Society for the Right to Die 1988. For much earlier writing on these subjects, see the extensive notes and bibliography in Weir 1989, especially chapter 6.

CASE REFERENCES

Cruzan v. Harmon. 1988. 760 S.W.2d 408 (Missouri).
Cruzan v. Director, Missouri Department of Health. 1990. 110 S.Ct 2841.
Elbaum v. Grace Plaza of Great Neck. 1989. 140 A.D.2d 244. (New York).
Quinlan. 1976. 355 A.2d 647 (New Jersey).

GENERAL REFERENCES

Adams, Gerald R., Nancy Bueche, and Jay D. Schvaneveldt. 1978. "Contemporary Views of Euthanasia: A Regional Assessment." *Social Biology* 25:62–68.
Almgren, Gunnar. [1991]. "Bedside Decisions Pertaining to Artificial Nutrition and Hydration: Influences of Public Policy Versus Nursing Home Industry Structure." Unpublished paper, Ogburn-Stouffer Center for the Study of Population and Social Organization. Chicago: University of Chicago.
Blumberg, Melanie J. and Michele Wharton-Hagan. 1988. "How Dead Is Dead? Policy-making on Questions of Morality at the State Level." Presented at the annual meeting of the American Political Science Association, Chicago.
Callahan, Daniel. 1987. *Setting Limits.* New York: Simon and Schuster.
———. 1990. *What Kind of Life.* New York: Simon and Schuster.
Crane, Diana. 1978. "Consensus and Controversy in Medical Practice: The Dilemma of the Critically Ill Patient." *Annals* 437:99–110.
Danis, M. et al. 1991. "A Prospective Study of Advance Directives for Life-sustaining Care." *New England Journal of Medicine* 324:828–88.
Deciding to Forego Life-sustaining Treatment: A Report on the Ethical, Medical, and Legal Issues in Treatment Decisions. 1983. Washington: President's Commission for the Study of Ethical Problems in Medicine and Biomedical and Behavioral Research.
Duff, Raymond and A. G. M. Campbell. 1980. "Moral and Ethical Dilemmas: Seven Years into the Debate about Human Ambiguity." *Annals* 447:19–28.

book

euthanasia

3rd ed.

Henry Glick

Henry Glick

Henry Glick

0022-1422

567

Haug, Marie. 1978. "Aging and the Right to Terminate Medical Treatment." *Journal of Gerontology* 33:586–91.

Horan, Dennis J. and David Mall, eds. 1980. *Death, Dying and Euthanasia.* Frederick, Md.: University Publications of America.

Humphry, Derek and Ann Wickett. 1986. *The Right to Die: Understanding Euthanasia.* New York: Harper & Row.

Meisel, Alan. 1989. *The Right to Die.* New York: John Wiley.

Paige, Connie. 1983. *The Right to Lifers.* New York: Summit Books.

Perlin, Terry M. "On the Physician's Role in Hastening Death." *The Aging Connection,* August-September, 1989.

Serow, William J., David F. Sly, and J. Michael Wrigley. 1990. *Population Aging in the United States.* New York: Greenwood Press.

Singh, B. K. 1979. "Correlates of Attitudes Toward Euthanasia." *Social Biology* 26:247–54.

Society for the Right to Die. 1988. *The First Fifty Years: 1938–1988.* New York: Society for the Right to Die.

Steinhoff, Patricia G. and Milton Diamond. 1977. *Abortion Politics: The Hawaii Experience.* Honolulu: The University Press of Hawaii.

Tatalovich, Raymond and Byron W. Daynes. 1981. *The Politics of Abortion.* New York: Praeger.

Tribe, Laurence H. 1990. *Abortion: The Clash of Absolutes.* New York: Norton.

Ward, Russel A. 1980. "Age and Acceptance of Euthanasia." *Journal of Gerontology* 35:421–31.

Weir, Robert F. 1989. *Abating Treatment with Critically Ill Patients.* New York: Oxford University Press.

ABOUT THE AUTHORS

Jill Quadagno (Ph.D., University of Kansas) is professor of sociology and Mildred and Claude Pepper Eminent Scholar in Social Gerontology at Florida State University. In 1994 she served as senior policy analyst on the President's Bipartisan Commission on Entitlement and Tax Reform. She has received the Distinguished Scholar Award from the American Sociological Association's Section on Aging. Her recent books include *The Color of Welfare* (Oxford University Press, 1994) and *The Transformation of Old Age Security* (University of Chicago Press, 1988).

Debra Street (Ph.D. candidate, Florida State University) is a doctoral student studying with Professor Quadagno. She is the recipient of a National Science Foundation grant for her dissertation research, a comparative study of the politics of aging in Canada, England, and the United States. Her work has been published in the journal *Social Problems.*